ANOTHER KIND OF WAR

JOHN A. LYNN II

Another Kind of War

THE NATURE AND HISTORY OF TERRORISM

Yale UNIVERSITY PRESS   NEW HAVEN AND LONDON

Copyright © 2019 by John A. Lynn II.
All rights reserved.
This book may not be reproduced, in whole or in part, including illustrations, in any form (beyond that copying permitted by Sections 107 and 108 of the U.S. Copyright Law and except by reviewers for the public press), without written permission from the publishers.

Yale University Press books may be purchased in quantity for educational, business, or promotional use. For information, please e-mail sales.press@yale.edu (U.S. office) or sales@yaleup.co.uk (U.K. office).

Set in Scala and Scala Sans type by Integrated Publishing Solutions, Grand Rapids, Michigan.
Printed in the United States of America.

Library of Congress Control Number: 2018962999
ISBN 978-0-300-18881-3 (hardcover : alk. paper)

A catalogue record for this book is available from the British Library.

This paper meets the requirements of ANSI/NISO Z39.48-1992 (Permanence of Paper).

10 9 8 7 6 5 4 3 2 1

For my grandchildren, with hope for a more peaceful and just world

Helena Grace Lynn
John (Jack) A. Lynn III

CONTENTS

A Brief Note to the Reader ix

1 On Terrorism 1

2 Rule by Fear: State-Regime Terrorism 31

3 War on Civilians: Military Terrorism 51

4 White Knights: Social Terrorism in America, 1865–1965 76

5 Propaganda of the Deed: The First Wave of Radical Terrorism, 1848–1920 105

6 Second-Wave Ethno-Nationalist Terrorism: The FLN and the PIRA 151

7 Tales of Two Tragedies: Palestinians and Israelis, 1881–1985 183

8 Urban Guerrillas: Marxist Terrorism during the 1960s and 1970s 205

9 Islamist Terrorism: Ideology and Radicalization in the Third Wave 235

10 Regional Jihad: Hezbollah and Hamas 267

11 Global Jihad: Al-Qaeda and the Islamic State 289

12 Radical Right-Wing Violence in the United States 332

13 Narcoterrorism 359

14 Homeland Security 389

15 Confronting Terrorism 416

Appendix: A Descriptive Model of Four Strategies of Terrorism 433
Notes 437
Suggested Further Reading 479
Index 489

A BRIEF NOTE TO THE READER

This book grew out of my response to the catastrophic events of 11 September 2001 (which I will refer to, in common parlance, as 9/11). In search of a way to contribute something, I decided to create an undergraduate-level course on the history of terrorism. That course was first offered in 2003 and has been taught in a constantly evolving form to this day, in the classroom and online. With this experience, the next step was to write this book. It well may be that experts within the academic, national security, and military communities will find something of value in its pages. I certainly hope they do. However, *Another Kind of War* is tailored for readers new to the subject; it is an effort in civic education and, in a sense, civil defense.

Radical terrorism is warfare, but it is another kind of war, unlike other American conflicts fought since 1900. In those struggles, only those in the war zone were on the front lines. However, terrorism puts us *all* at the front and in the enemy's crosshairs. We really have no choice. In attacking relatively few victims, radical terrorism seeks to exert psychological impact on a far larger target audience. Terrorism aims to manipulate us by inflicting fear and inciting outrage, dominating our consciousness and turning us into unwitting agents of our own defeat.

Therefore, in our part of the fight, we need to recognize the terrorists' goals and thwart them by refusing to react in ways that work to the terrorists' advantage. The citizens' task is different from those at the tip of the spear facing terrorists in the field—those in the intelligence community, law enforcement, and the military. The citizens' battle must be engaged, above all, through knowledge, understanding, and judgment.

Another Kind of War is offered as an aid in developing these capabilities. It is an introduction to the subject that makes few assumptions about prior knowledge. It begins by considering the nature of terrorism, suggesting a conceptual foundation, complete with considerations of traits, levels, strategies, and chronologies of terrorism. These are not offered as rules, as rigid classifications that must be accepted and applied without question or interpretation. But we need a base that allows us to recognize patterns and to appreciate similarities and differences. The approach is inclusive, encompassing forms of terrorism ranging from that committed by powerful repressive states against their own citizens to that perpetrated by isolated individuals, lone wolves, in the name of some grand political cause. We need to learn something about the variety of political violence referred to as "terrorist" or "terrorism," if only to be able to judge between apples and oranges.

Once equipped with some guides, we can explore the history of terrorism to test conception against reality, which is never as neat. Ultimately it is the facts that must test the ideas, not the ideas that should be imposed on the facts. When discussing state, military, and social terrorism, we will consider millennia of historical experience, but when considering the modern radical terrorism of sub-state groups, including violent Islamist extremists, we will focus on the last two centuries. Historical examples will be explained, rather than simply referenced in a rush to reach conclusions. Conclusions matter, but it is essential to trace how we got there.

It is clear that when considered on a global stage, modern radical terrorism is a serious threat, particularly when terrorist groups evolve into larger forces. Nonetheless, when dealing with terrorists within our own borders, American citizens ought to maintain a sense of perspective and proportion. Sub-state radical groups are by nature weak relative to those they attack; this is even more the case with lone wolves, typical of recent terrorism in United States inspired by the so-called Islamic State (IS). The real damage they inflict is characteristically small, even if the human tragedy suffered by the immediate victims is profound. Overreacting to terrorist acts can make the terrorists look stronger than they really are, increasing their impact and even winning them converts and recruits. In dealing with terrorism, wisdom consists of knowing what *not* to do, as well as what should be done. Exaggerating the real threat of terrorism poses another danger as well: it may drive us to sacrifice our principles or constitutional rights and protections in the hope of shoring up our security. And there is the additional possibility that misguided political leaders may play the terrorism card to increase their own popularity and power.

In order to keep this volume within a manageable page limit, while expanding what I can offer, we have coordinated a website with *Another Kind of War* at www.yalebooks.com/lynn. The website and its offerings are keyed to this book and to my courses, but it is available to all who care to visit it. There are three subdivisions on the website: Gallery, Bibliography, and Supplements. While this book includes twenty-two key images, the Gallery of the website presents about 400 images and also links users to other images, videos, and even music. In addition, although readers of this book will find some modest suggestions for further reading associated with each chapter, the website presents a much more detailed Bibliography of works relating to terrorism. Since the Bibliography is on the web, it can be periodically revised with ease. The Supplements include a short statement of the book's theses and approaches designed for those would like to understand the website without tackling the book. Moreover, the visitor will find some segments of the original manuscript that were cut in the interest of limiting the final book's length, but that still might add to the discussions. For example, I include these in my classes. Last, in a rapidly moving world, we plan to post discussions of terrorist activities and groups to keep the book/website duo up to date.

This work has been a collaborative effort, in the sense that it builds upon an extensive range of published scholarship. Whether I have ever met the authors or not, they have taught me. You will find their works listed in both the print and the online bibliographies. There are too many to mention here, but I am deeply indebted to them all. I have also benefited from the comments of those who have heard my work in classes, seminars, and conferences. Above all I would like to thank Conrad Crane and Peter Mansoor for their careful reading of my manuscript and their extremely helpful comments and suggestions. Thanks too to Zachary

Cleary, who gave me a student's view of each chapter. Thanks as well to Kenneth Cuno, Mark Steinberg, and Poshek Fu for translating passages in Arabic, Russian, and Cantonese. Many thanks to my son, Daniel Morgan Lynn, for repeatedly using his considerable IT skills to rescue me from hardware and software crises. And of course, I want to also thank Yale University Press and my editor there, Sarah Miller, her assistant, Ash Lago, and my copy editor, Harry Haskell.

And of course, I must express my gratitude to my wife, Andrea E. Lynn, an author in her own right. Not only did she endure my single-minded perseveration with terrorism for years, but she also devoted a great deal of time to correcting the proofs of this volume in order to protect me from myself.

CHAPTER ONE

On Terrorism

FIGURE 1.1. The towers of the World Trade Center are ablaze shortly before collapse on the morning of 9/11. dpa picture alliance/Alamy Stock Photo.

THE ATTACKS on the World Trade Center towers in New York on 11 September 2001 projected a vision of hell: massive explosions, unquenchable fires, clouds of smoke, doomed figures leaping to their deaths rather than perish from the searing heat and choking fumes (Fig. 1.1). When the towers collapsed, they pulverized into a suffocating gray surge that caught and engulfed survivors, turning them into ghostlike beings. Such fearful images cannot and must not be forgotten. On that day, al-Qaeda suicide terrorists piloting four Boeing airliners killed 2,977 people, by far the highest number of fatalities inflicted by any single modern act of terrorism. The toll of death that day surpassed even that suffered by Americans at Pearl Harbor on 7 December 1941 or on the Normandy beaches on 6 June 1944.

The tragedy of 9/11 was not typical of terrorist attacks; it was *unique* in its malevolent magnitude. No previous attack by radical terrorists comes close, and hopefully none will in the future. Osama bin Laden and his lieutenants brought down an inferno on New York, and the United States soon responded by raining destruction on the Taliban in Afghanistan and, before long, by obliterating Saddam Hussein's regime and forces in Iraq. It is not surprising that thoughtful observers have claimed that 9/11 changed everything.

Bin Laden pursued this catastrophic attack to advance his radical Islamist vision. We will have much to say about radical Islamism in later chapters of this volume, but let it suffice here to say that Islamism is an extreme fundamentalist form of Islam, a form embraced by a minority of Muslims. Theologically and politically, Islamism believes in the subordination of government to religion and in the imposition by the state of penalties and punishments that date back to the seventh and eighth centuries. *Radical* Islamists advocate and practice enforcing these principles and practices by violence. Conflating Islamists with Muslims is unfair, inaccurate, and dangerous. Today, when people talk about terrorism, they generally are talking about radical Islamist terrorism, and we will explore it at length in later chapters. Of course, through its history, radical terrorism has taken many other forms, and we must consider them as well.

Bin Laden sought his justification in the Quran and his reading of Muslim tradition, and this led him to declare jihad, or holy war, against the West, particularly the United States. America's allies were in the crosshairs as well. On 11 March 2004, terrorists set off bombs on four Madrid commuter trains during the morning rush hour, killing 192 and wounding about 2,000. Spain had never suffered radical terrorism on this level before. The perpetrators of the Madrid attacks, though not formally linked to al-Qaeda, were al-Qaeda–inspired. Spanish authorities later tried twenty-nine individuals suspected of being involved in the attack, and twenty-one were convicted of a variety of offenses. So a network carried out this deadly series of bombings. Actually, it can be argued that this terrorist attack succeeded. The terrorists struck three days before national elections, and whatever the terrorists' goals, the electorate voted in a government that withdrew the Spanish contingent of troops fighting alongside Americans in the Iraq War.

The next year, on 7 July 2005, suicide bombers killed fifty-two and injured 700 in London. This was the work of a cell composed of four suicide bombers and a few others. As in Madrid, the terrorists hit the transport system during a high traffic period in the morning, attacking three Underground trains and a double-decker bus. Again, al-Qaeda did not direct the London bombing, but inspired it. A tape made by Mohammad Sidique Khan, one of the London suicide bombers, and broadcast on Al Jazeera, praised al-Qaeda, its leaders, and cadres.[1]

These three terrorist attacks were perpetrated in the name of the same extreme Islamist ideology and were all associated with al-Qaeda, but they differed in scale, organization, setting, and tactics. An understanding of modern radical terrorism must encompass a range from 9/11 to solitary attacks by committed lone wolves. It must confront political actors from the dedicated European nationalists of the 1850s to the radical Islamists of the Middle East today. The task is daunting but doable, and it is hoped that this volume may provide a useful first step for those intent on taking on the important challenge.

In this chapter we will attend to some of the basics. We will consider the traits, levels, and waves of terrorism. I will advance my argument that radical terrorism should be considered a form of warfare with identifiable categories of strategy. Along the way we will also point out the particular role of morality in terrorism and learn that terrorists cannot be explained away as sociopaths, but must be taken seriously as rational actors. What we cover in this chapter provides a point of departure and a structure for the rest of the volume.

But I must offer a caveat from the start. Even as we consider typologies, continuums, and analyses, we need to bear in mind that the neatness of intellectual conception should not be allowed to impose order on the disorder of hard-world reality. Be wary of sweeping generalizations about terrorism that are more likely to mislead than to enlighten. Understanding can begin by drawing distinctions, but wisdom requires knowing how those distinctions can blur. The careful scholar John Horgan warns, "Pick any debate on any aspect of terrorism. You can be guaranteed that whatever you choose will be shrouded in controversy, inaccuracies and so much polemic that Louise Richardson confidently announced that the only certainty about terrorism is the pejorative nature in which the word is used."[2] What is stated here is part of the controversy, a controversy that does not result from ignorance but from the fact that the subject matter is of such importance that it draws the attention of commentators with different values, focuses, and purposes.

Let me alert the reader that while this is far from being the longest chapter in the book, it is necessarily the most dense, because it constructs a framework of analysis for the rest of the volume. The later, more narrative chapters are easier going, but we need to start with a bit of a steep climb.

TRAITS THAT CHARACTERIZE TERRORISM

Let me begin by being clear about what I mean by "terrorism." This explanation is usually phrased as a definition, but constructing a dictionary definition of terrorism poses a special set of problems. One of the most renowned scholars of the field, Walter Laqueur, despaired of the possibility of drafting a universal definition of terrorism: "The disputes about a detailed, comprehensive definition of terrorism will continue for a long time, they will not result in a consensus and they will make no notable contribution towards the understanding of terrorism."[3] One solution is to say as little as possible, as does Jessica Stern when she offers her sparse definition: "an act or threat of violence against noncombatants with the objective of exacting revenge, intimidating, or otherwise influencing an audience."[4] Understandably, those drafting laws, legislation, and international agreements must hone their language to stipulate the specific forms of terrorism that concern them, but their sharp distinctions and legal language are more about labeling than understanding.

We will sidestep the question of constructing a precise definition of terrorism by *describing* it rather than *defining* it. We can identify traits that characterize terrorism and allow us analytical flexibility. Terrorism characteristically:

- employs violence or the threat of violence;
- attacks people and property;
- strikes defenseless victims, often described as civilians or noncombatants;
- strives to inflict fear and/or incite outrage in a much larger target audience;
- uses violence and its psychological impact to advance political, social, and cultural goals.

To these I would add a sixth trait: terrorists propagate public knowledge of their acts in order to reach their intended target audience(s). Today, this usually means the media—the twenty-four-hour news cycle—but it can also be by something as basic as word of mouth.

Terrorism deals in violence, from beatings to bombings, but the greatest power of the violence is, with rare exceptions, not in its immediate actual harm, but in its implicit threat of further violence against the target community. That threat influences perception and behavior. Certainly people can suffer harm from abuse short of overt violence, such as verbal condemnation, cultural prejudice, economic disadvantage, and repressive laws, but terrorism as considered in these pages must involve the resort to physical force or the threat of it. In considering violence it is important to recognize not only its physical effect, but also the way it demeans and dishonors the victim.

To speak of attacks on property in the same vein as attacks on people's bodies and spirits may seem a mismatch; however, the destruction of houses, farms, livestock, or other possessions can jeopardize people's livelihoods and even survival. Destroying a community's property may be a more convenient and effective tactic than striking out at individuals, because people can flee, but buildings cannot. Terrorist groups can also choose to attack symbolic property, such as government or commercial offices. Other attractive targets for terrorists include public utilities and infrastructure, such as electric power grids and water supply systems. In some cases, attacks on property can also be less culturally costly to terrorists, since by not directly attacking people they may avoid alienating supporters who would not condone murder. This was part of the calculation made by the Weathermen, as described in Chapter 8.

Focusing violence against the defenseless, people unable or unprepared to defend themselves, is the very essence of terrorism. By doing so terrorists gain three advantages: 1) they can attack readily available "soft targets"; 2) they magnify the moral shock they inflict by their actions; and 3) they spread a sense of vulnerability among the larger target audience, beyond those who are actually assaulted. The immediate victims of terrorist violence are most commonly described as "civilians" or "the innocent," a term freighted with moral condemnation of the attackers. However, my emphasis on the "defenseless" is intended to make clear that terrorist violence is distinct from self-defense—kill or be killed—

which is morally acceptable violence in war. Some commentators, such as Stern, use the term *noncombatants*. This would include those who might be in uniform but are not in the fight, as well as military personnel struck at times when they have no ability to defend themselves, as were the 241 U.S. Marines killed in their Beirut barracks in October 1983.[5]

Common definitions of terrorism almost always stress instilling fear as the goal of the terrorists. In *Understanding Terrorism*, James M. Poland echoes the common emphasis: "Terrorism is the premeditated, deliberate, systematic murder, mayhem, and threatening of the innocent to create fear and intimidation in order to gain a political or tactical advantage, usually to influence an audience."[6] Official definitions repeat this formula; the *Department of Defense Dictionary of Military and Associated Terms*, as amended to 15 February 2012, defines terrorism as "the unlawful use of violence or threat of violence to instill fear and coerce governments or societies."[7]

There is no doubt that generating fear is a basic effect of terrorism; however, it is dangerous to neglect the impact of outrage, because it is as likely, or more likely, to generate reactions on the part of the target community. In fact, within the context of modern radical terrorism, outrage can be the more important consequence of terrorist acts, as we shall see. Doubtless, there is a relationship between fear and outrage; the same action can lead to both reactions, and fear can be an element in stimulating outrage. Yet at this point, it is valuable to consider them as differing points along a continuum of response. Put simply, fear has more to do with paralysis than with assertion, and the measures it promotes are mainly protective and defensive. In contrast, outrage inspires retaliation, and, importantly, that retaliation is seen as righteous. Outrage demands that the victim strike back, and such retribution heated by fury runs the strong risk of being the kind of ill-considered reaction that works to the terrorists' advantage. In stressing fear and outrage, we recognize that terrorism is psychological warfare that weaponizes the target community's emotions.

To achieve maximum psychological force, terrorists require that their actions become known, at least among the community they wish to affect. The al-Qaeda and al-Qaeda-inspired terrorism with which this book begins were meant to capture the twenty-four-hour news cycle around the globe. However, in times past, word of mouth could be effective enough. Indeed, some terrorists might well prefer that their actions only be known by a specific target community. For example, it attracted the wrong kind of attention if lynchings by the Ku Klux Klan in the American South received national publicity; it was enough that the locals understood what happened to those who did not "know their place" and behave as required. From the onset of first-wave radical terrorism, many terrorists have stressed propaganda of the deed—the deed becomes the ultimate propaganda. However, for the deed to have the full effect news of it must be spread by the word.

And the intent of terrorism is to accomplish a political goal—that is absolutely basic. I employ the term *political* broadly; it can run the gamut from strictly political to deeply cultural, including matters of identity and religion. Terrorism is not linked to any one cause; it is violent political resistance employed in the name of many different rationales. The point is that terrorism aims at larger goals than simply immediate personal or material interest. Terrorist actions are by their very nature crimes, but what separates a terrorist act from sheer criminality is the greater motivation, the intention, of the act.

Beyond the traits listed above, some authorities would add that to qualify as terrorism, an act must be indiscriminate, rather than purposely directed against specific individuals. Thus, Shlomo Ben-Ami, an Israeli foreign minister who negotiated with the Palestine Liberation Organization, declared in a debate, "Terrorism, in my view, is an indiscriminate attack against civilian population."[8] Even some terrorists themselves have held that indiscriminate attacks on random victims are more vile than striking particular individuals chosen for attacks because they have deserved such violence, at least according to their attackers. On the other hand, some commentators, such as Randall Law, view assassination as *by definition* an act of terror.[9] In this volume we will take a middle course, judging killing by its intent. If the goal of the assassin is not simply to eliminate one individual, but to undermine or overthrow an institution, often by instilling fear and inciting outrage in a wider community, such a killing can be considered terrorism.

SIX LEVELS OF TERRORISM

A broad spectrum of violence meets the criteria of terrorism, as set out above. My approach is inclusive, encompassing everything from the actions of states and regimes against their own populations to violence committed by sub-state groups, and even individuals, against those very states and regimes. There are good reasons for such an inclusive approach, including the ability for sub-state terrorist groups to evolve into states, or statelike entities, themselves. Several have done exactly this, including Hezbollah of Lebanon, the Liberation Tigers of Tamil Elam of Sri Lanka, Hamas of Palestine, and, most obviously, the Islamic State.

However, some authorities on the subject argue that too inclusive a view of terrorism becomes useless. They fear that dealing with anything other than radical terrorist groups confuses the issue and diverts attention from the most pressing threat. Thus, Bruce Hoffman, perhaps the most-read terrorist expert in the United States, specifies terrorism as violence "perpetuated by a subnational group or nonstate entity."[10] Such a tightly focused, closeup perspective has its value, particularly when the ultimate aim is to offer solutions for immediate problems of counterterrorism. However, a historical study such as this requires a wide-angle lens. When Walter Laqueur rejected the effort to craft a detailed definition of terrorism, he did so because he insisted, "Any attempt to be more specific is bound to fail, for the simple reason that there is not one but many different terrorisms."[11] Like "cancer," "terrorism" is an umbrella term for a number of similar but still quite distinct maladies. It is important to recognize its variety.

While no simple list can ever capture the complexity of terrorism, we will categorize terrorism into six levels determined by the perpetrators of the terrorist acts. The typology here sets up the major forms of terrorism based on the capacity of the terrorists, from the strongest to the weakest. These six levels include:

- terrorism by state regimes to impose their wills on their own populations;
- terrorism by military forces to achieve victory in war;
- terrorism by social groups to dominate or drive off other groups;
- terrorism by criminal groups to achieve political ends;
- radical terrorism by sub-state activist groups for a variety of purposes —political, social, economic, religious, ethnic, and so on;
- radical terrorism by individuals.

My use of the term *capacity* for matters of strength and weakness derives from Wayne E. Lee's deceptively simple but analytically useful trilogy of "capacity, calculation, and culture" in understanding the history of war. Here, "capacity" encompasses those assets that a terrorist entity can translate into power. "Calculation" entails, among other conscious matters of decision and organization, the formulation of strategy. "Culture" includes the beliefs, values, and sensitivities that both demand and limit the use of violence in war. We will have more to say about calculation and culture in this chapter, but in identifying the levels of terrorism, capacity is foremost.

The chapter organization of this volume follows the descending order of levels of capacity from strong to weak. Because the different levels listed in this schema will be discussed at length in succeeding chapters, comments at this time will simply indicate their historical variety.

State-regime terrorism includes actions and campaigns committed by rulers and regimes, with the full strength of their political entities, with the goal of terrorizing their own subjects or citizens into obedience. Such state-regime terrorism, along with military and social terrorism, extends back millennia in human history. Examples can be found in ancient chronicles and in today's newspapers. Chapter 2 considers cases from the earliest Chinese dynasty to Mao Zedong's Cultural Revolution (1966–1976), along with cases from the French Revolution (1789–1799) and Stalin's Soviet Union of the 1930s. Note that the state terrorism discussed in this book is terrorism by the state itself, within its own boundaries, not support that a state might supply to a sub-state terrorist group acting in another country. Such state support will be discussed when relevant to radical terrorism by sub-state groups.

Armies fighting in the name of peoples, princes, or polities have long used tactics that qualify as terrorist in their attempts to break the will of enemy populations. Chapter 3 discusses this use of terrorist tactics by military forces since ancient times. The fact that this violence has occurred during wartime does not excuse attacks on the defenseless from the charge of being acts of terrorism.

Social terrorism, which is that used by a stronger ethnic or racial group against a weaker one, has had two major faces in the last two centuries. One is the use of terror by one group to subjugate another, rendering it subservient and compliant. The most serious damage ever inflicted by terrorism on the United States of America was not the horror of 9/11, but the violence and intimidation perpetrated by White supremacists on the African-American community. The high point of positive change came as a result of the civil rights movement, the story of which is the centerpiece of Chapter 4. The other most obvious face of social terror is ethnic cleansing. Both subjugation and ethnic cleansing can combine the actions of members of one social/ethnic group with that of the state, sometimes enforced by the state's military. In fact, the most apparent modern examples of ethnic cleansing have involved such combinations of repression in one form or another.

In this typology of terrorism based on the capacity, or power, of those who commit acts of terror, the next avatar of such violence is criminal terrorism, most often associated with the drug trade as narcoterrorism. We have offset criminal terrorism in Figure 1.2 below because it is something of a special case. We have described terrorism as something other than criminal activity for personal material gain; however, such gain is at the very heart of criminal groups, such as drug cartels. Yet their actions need to be considered under the rubric of terrorism when, for their own reasons, criminal groups enter the political sphere, as did the Medellín cartel in Colombia under Pablo Escobar. Chapter 13 will explore these and other characteristics particular to narcoterrorism.

Chapters 5–12, the majority of this book, specifically address radical terrorism by sub-state activist groups. Radical terrorism serves many masters in different political and cultural contexts, so there is considerable variety in radical terrorist groups and their campaigns of terrorism. But there are important similarities, which can be summarized as *mindset, means,* and *methods*. The "mindset," always important, will be explored in greater depth in Chapters 5, 8, and 9. Elements of the mindset include notions of absolute right and wrong, apocalyptic fixation on destruction as necessary for reconstruction, belief that the only recourse for achieving positive change is violence, and a maudlin fixation on the need for sacrifice and martyrdom. This mindset is characteristic of secular as well as religious terrorists, from Marxists to jihadis.

"Means" is a simpler matter: it is capacity in Lee's terms. Because radical terrorist groups generally have limited numbers of members, or cadres, and limited resources, they are characteristically weak. They must do things on the cheap. And meager means restrict the range of "methods." These must be calculated to maximize the psychological impacts of relatively small-scale attacks. Raymond Aron, the French philosopher and political scientist, wrote: "An action of violence is labeled 'terrorist'

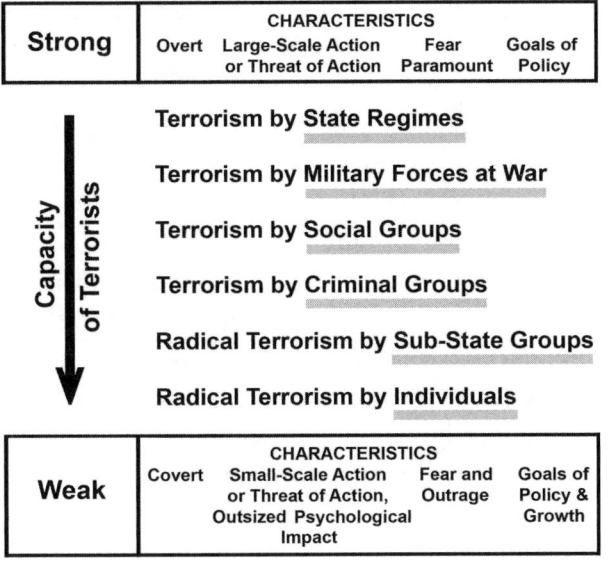

FIGURE 1.2. Six Levels of Terrorism. This graphic differentiates levels of terrorism in descending order of capacity, or strength, while stressing contrasts between the characteristics of strong-capacity and weak-capacity terrorism. Much of the discussion in this volume will be structured around these levels.

when its psychological effects are out of proportion to its purely physical results."[12] This explains attacking civilians who can do little to defend themselves and resorting to particularly culturally shocking forms of public violence. Radical terrorist groups can be parsed into central organizations, networks, and cells, and we will do so when relevant to our arguments, but for now we will simply distinguish terrorist groups from terrorist individuals.

Radical terrorism by individuals comes at the bottom of the strong-to-weak scale in Figure 1.2. Such a lone wolf terrorist can answer to a terrorist group, or, more commonly, he or she can simply be influenced or inspired by the group or its message. In either case, I would argue that the existence of a lone wolf implies that there is a "wolf pack," a group, somewhere. Terrorism carried out by a single actor or by two or three similarly minded individuals, as in the cases of the attack on *Charlie Hebdo* in Paris and the massacres in San Bernardino, California, and Orlando, Florida—all committed between January 2015 and January

2016—have captured the news media and increased the sense of vulnerability in Europe and America. The lone wolf is not a recent addition to terrorism, but individual radical terrorists were a factor from the start, particularly prominent among the anarchists of the late nineteenth and early twentieth centuries discussed in Chapter 5.

At the other end of the scale, strong terrorist entities can act overtly and undertake large-scale operations, like those of the Soviet state under Stalin during the purges of the late 1930s. Because of their relative weakness, revolutionary terrorist groups need to be covert and are, with rare exceptions, limited to small-scale violent actions designed with the intent of maximizing their psychological impact. Strong terrorist actors, such as states and militaries, rely on fear above all, since their policy goals toward those terrorized are simply to enforce compliance and stifle dissent. However, small and weak revolutionary terrorist groups may be as adamant to grow in numbers and strength as they are to achieve their immediate policy goals. And one way for terrorist groups to grow is to incite outrage in their adversaries with the intention of provoking them into committing ill-considered reprisals. Such reprisals may so alienate a population that it provides the terrorists with new recruits and resources. So while fear can be exploited by radical terrorists, outrage also provides key leverage.

Certainly, the study of terrorism should not degenerate into splitting hairs over matters of definition or typology. The value of stressing characteristics and categories in a book such as this is not to create sealed compartments into which we can force different terrorist groups, but to point out important tendencies and aspects of a complicated reality. We present this material at the start, but you should judge the validity of the generalizations by the details of the specific examples we will present in the chapters to come. It is not enough that you remember the conclusions, you must master enough facts to support them, or to challenge them. My problem with other general historical treatments of terrorism is that they do not provide enough of the actual history; I will try to do more here.

Still, there remains real value in establishing commonalities and contrasts within the diversity displayed in the historical record. For example, understanding the differences between types of violence helps shield against being misled by the ambiguity implicit in a blanket condemnation of "terrorism." Case in point: confusion between Osama bin

Laden as a radical jihadi terrorist and Saddam Hussein as a state terrorist enabled the George W. Bush administration to gin up war fever in 2003 to invade Iraq; after all, they were both terrorists! On the other hand, in light of the Islamic State, it is important to recognize that terrorist groups can ascend our hierarchy of levels. At its inception, what would eventually evolve into IS was a small activist group, but it morphed into a state, guilty of state terrorism, while at the same continuing as a radical terrorist group—including networks, cells, and individuals—in areas that IS had not absorbed into its caliphate

THREE WAVES OF RADICAL TERRORISM BY SUB-STATE GROUPS

Just as I propose six characteristic traits and six levels of terrorism, I also contend that modern revolutionary terrorism occurred in three waves. The treatment of radical terrorism in this volume advances chronologically through these waves: from after the Revolutions of 1848 to around 1920; from roughly 1945 through 1980; and from 1980 to the present.

Others, before this book, have identified waves of radical terrorism, most notably the political scientist David C. Rapoport, who writes of four waves. I am basically in accord with his criteria for a wave: "a cycle of activity at a given time period," with a "crucial feature" being "its international character . . . driven by a common predominant energy that shapes the participating groups' characteristics and mutual relationships."[13] I would simply say that rather than a wave being defined by a single "predominant energy" or cause, we need to realize that a wave can be typified by more than one ideology. However, I strongly contest the way Rapoport breaks down his phases. For one thing, he only begins his first wave around 1880, whereas I argue that the first wave arose as a result of the failure of the Revolutions of 1848, three decades before.

Marc Sageman, who also takes issue with Rapoport, argues in a recent volume that we should see the origins of terrorism much earlier, in the French Revolution of 1789–1799.[14] He specifically condemns the notion that terrorism began with the Russian attacks that Rapoport and others regard as the starting point of modern terrorism. Here I share more with Sageman than with Rapoport. I am less convinced when Sageman insists that what he defines as "political violence" increased markedly during the revolution and that from this emerged terrorism. He points out a number of violent attacks, particularly assassination attempts, from 1793 through the 1830s that either prefigure terrorism or could be called terrorist. Sageman makes a good point about the recurrence of political violence, running from acts by individuals to mass crowd events, following the French Revolution. However this violence ran the gamut from acts committed by a few individuals to that associated with armed crowds in the streets. The predominance of radical terrorism as a mode of violent political resistance only came when mass crowd events, usually buttressed with urban barricades, clearly failed during the Revolutions of 1848. This will be discussed at length in Chapter 5. Let it suffice to say here that dating the onset of radical terrorism is a matter of contention.

Both Rapoport and I would end the first wave about 1920. But we differ strongly on dating and categorizing terrorism from 1920 to 1980. While he characterizes those decades as having two distinct waves (1920 to 1960 and 1960 to around 1980, or into the 1990s), I see a decline in the extent and intensity of radical terrorism from 1920 through World War II. We will note terrorist actions in Ireland during the 1920s and in Palestine through the 1940s, and there were certainly terrorist elements in the Chinese Civil War before World War II. However, these were essentially self-contained, lacking the international or transnational interrelationships characteristic of a "wave." The second wave, as identified in this volume, extended from the end of World War II until the onset of radical Islamist terrorism about 1980. This wave was a period of intertwining complexities that Rapoport fails to recognize and elaborate. Both Rapoport and I date the current, Islamist wave as extending from 1980 to the present, but he considers this a fourth wave, while it is the third in my schema.

Yet within contention discussed above, there is agreement. We three agree that modern terrorism emerges during the nineteenth century. Yes, Sageman pushes its "origins" back to the last decade of the eighteenth, but he argues for an evolution that becomes recognizable as terrorism only with time. None of us tries to see the roots of radical terrorism in earlier ages.

Ultimately, for me, radical terrorism does not really qualify as an "ism" before the middle of the nineteenth century. By an "ism" I mean not a particular political ideology but a belief that terrorist attacks are a legitimate, even necessary, form of political resistance that can be adopted to advance very different causes. There were acts of violence, even limited campaigns of such attacks, before, but they failed to establish continuous, enduring, and widely adopted patterns of terrorism that spanned barriers of time and space as did radical terrorism in Europe after the failure of the Revolutions of 1848. The literature, the theory, of terrorism followed soon after those debacles. Karl Heinzen published his "Murder and Liberty" in 1850, Sergey Nechayev penned his "Catechism of a Revolutionary" in 1869. To my mind an "ism" requires a literature, among other things, so I am willing to see the first wave beginning with such works. We will examine this logic at greater length in Chapter 5.

RADICAL TERRORISM AS ENTRY-LEVEL WAR

This volume argues that radical terrorism by sub-state groups can be usefully considered as a form of warfare, albeit on the entry level. This is not an unprecedented assertion, but it is controversial. As a witness to defend my position, I call upon the most noted theoretician of war, Carl von Clausewitz. Following the Napoleonic Wars, this great Prussian soldier-philosopher wrote his classic study *On War*, which remains the most referenced work on war even today. The most quoted statement from that work, "War is merely the continuation of policy by other means," can be boiled down to an assertion that war is violence in the service of politics. I believe that violence committed by sub-state terrorist groups in the name of political goals, "radical terrorism," qualifies. True, Clausewitz was thinking of war as an affair of states, but the reality we face 180 years after the publication of *On War* is hardly limited to this kind of conflict.

Granted, there is no consensus as to whether terrorism is warfare. The noted Israeli expert Ariel Merari has stated, "Political terrorism is a mode of warfare."[15] However, the impressive Bruce Hoffman asserts that war and terrorism are separated by "a fundamental qualitative difference."[16] He offers two lines of argument to support this strong claim. First, in contrast to conventional armies or even guerrilla insurgents, terrorists lack the numbers and resources to hold territory or exercise "control and governance over a population." Second, and far more important, terrorists do not abide by the laws of war as do the forces engaged in what he would consider to be war.

In regard to the control of territory and population, small sub-state radical terrorist groups characteristically lack these, but that does not mean their violence is without political purpose, or cannot be discussed as war. In fact, modern military literature distinguishes between "symmetrical" and "asymmetrical" warfare. This generally centers on whether the warring parties are armed similarly, symmetrically—tanks and planes versus tanks and planes—or on strikingly differently levels, asymmetrically—tanks and planes versus AK-47s and booby traps. Asymmetrical warfare usually references the warfare of states versus sub-states—for example, regular armies fighting guerrilla insurgencies. If we are comfortable considering sub-state insurgencies as being at war, I see no good reason why we cannot see terrorism as warfare, albeit on a lower level of capacity and intensity.

Moreover, terrorists can accumulate resources and power, growing in capacity and power, and achieving some control over territory and population. Consider the histories of the Palestine Liberation Organization (PLO), the Liberation Tigers of Tamil Elam, or Tamil Tigers (LTTE), Hezbollah, Hamas, and the Islamic State, all of which began as sub-state groups and evolved to field large forces and rule over territory. If it was always the terrorists' hope or plan to grow, does their campaign of violent political resistance only become war at a certain threshold, or was it always a war, even when on a very small scale? The lower end of a continuum still belongs on the continuum. As Merari quipped, "One might say that all terrorist groups want to be guerrillas when they grow up."[17]

When we see terrorism as entry-level warfare, it is all the more disturbing to realize how few resources it takes to commit a major terrorist act. Consider the bombing of the Murrah Federal Office Building in Oklahoma City on 19 April 1995 by Timothy McVeigh, as dealt with in Chapter 12. This attack killed 168 and wounded 680, making it the most deadly terrorist attack on U.S. soil before 9/11. McVeigh received the direct help of only two, less-than-wholly-committed coconspirators. For a delivery system, he rented a Ryder truck that he then loaded with explosives, primarily barrels of fertilizer mixed with racing fuel and fuel oil. The fertilizer and fuel were legally purchased for a few thousand dollars. After lighting the fuses, he parked the truck in front of the building. The result was catastrophic. Terrorism can be cheap.

If any generalization applies to terrorists as a whole, it is that they have come to the conclusion that only through recourse to violence can they bring about essential change. It is a small step from that conclusion to terrorism. In a sense, terrorism has democratized war.

Hoffman makes a seemingly more formidable case against considering terrorism as war when he claims that military forces engaged in war are guided by the laws of war but that terrorists flout them. He charges that terrorists specifically kill noncombatants, murder prisoners, take and abuse hostages, refuse to respect ambassadors, and so forth. Such failures to abide by the "proper" conduct of war, it is claimed, deny terrorists any right to the honorable category of soldiers at war. This contrast might well apply to U.S. forces and the terrorists they are fighting in Afghanistan and Iraq. However, for millennia the military forces of large political entities have been quite willing to commit the kind of brutality that is currently considered outside the laws of war. And it is not simply the "bad guys" who have engaged in terrorist violence in modern warfare; for example, the British carpet bombing of German cities in World War II clearly meets our criteria for terrorism, a case we will make in Chapter 3. Even in the twenty-first century, the soldiers of some armies show little respect for the Geneva Conventions of 1949 that defined war crimes. Trying to draw a sharp line between war and terrorism by asserting that the former respects the law of war while the latter does not is more than questionable.

As to transgressing against the laws of war, terrorists have historically argued that it is not moral depravity, but their own limited capacity that must shape their calculations. In his "Murder and Liberty," Heinzen argued that revolutionaries had to resort to assassination because they lacked the strength to face contemporary armies in the field. With heavy sarcasm, he challenged the forces of order and repression to "lend us your army . . . or their weapons, . . . and we will no longer require 'assassination,' for then we will murder openly in battle; whether according to 'martial law' or the 'law of war,' however you wish."[18] This kind of argument surfaces repeatedly in terrorists' declarations. In 2005, a senior Hamas chief similarly explained his organization's calculation to deploy suicide bombers: "I will answer in one way: we don't have jets, we don't have tanks. So we made the decision. It is one of the ways we resist."[19]

The degree to which terrorists defy the laws of war also results from a kind of culture-based calculation. On one hand, in order to instill fear and incite outrage among their adversaries, inherently weak radical terrorists often commit extremely savage acts, what will call "ostentatious atrocities." Such atrocities are chosen because they lie so far outside what is culturally tolerable to the target community that that they will shock and unbalance that population. Terrorists can see their acts as brutal necessities, not simply as bloody mindedness. In this sense, to conform to the laws of war would disarm the terrorists in their kind of war. On the other hand, should terrorists' actions be judged as contemptible by the very community the terrorists need to win over—should terrorists transgress against their potential supporters' cultural tolerance for violence—their barbarity may undermine their own legitimacy. Terrorism requires calculations based on readings of the cultures of adversaries and of allies.

THE CENTRALITY OF MORALITY IN CONSIDERING TERRORISM

This brings us to considering the cultural issues inherent in terrorism. While radical terrorism can usefully be considered as entry-level war, there is an aspect of it that conflicts with the classical consideration of war by Carl von Clausewitz. This difference arises from the centrality of morality in radical terrorism.

Clausewitz says next nothing about the morality of war in terms of ethics, of humane conduct. When he uses the term *moral* it is in the sense of morale, not ethics. Chapter 4 of Book 3 of *On War* is entitled "The Principal Moral Elements." Its first sentence reads: "They are: the skill of the commander, the experience and courage of the troops, and their patriotic spirit."[20] Obviously, this is not a discussion of right and wrong but of mettle. Clausewitz is not blind to the brutality of war: "War itself is anything but humane."[21] Nonetheless, he dismisses morality and law: "Attached to force are certain self-imposed, imperceptible limitations hardly worth mentioning, known as international law and custom, but they scarcely weaken it."[22]

Cold reasoning does not serve well in explaining the nature of radical terrorism. Dedicated extremists generally define the world in absolutes and seeing themselves on the side of righteousness and regarding those who oppose them as partisans of evil. Everything that advances the righteous cause is good, even when it goes counter to conventional morality. In 1869, the Russian radical Nechayev described the true revolutionary:

"For him, morality is everything which contributes to the triumph of the revolution. Immoral and criminal is everything that stands in its way."[23] Terrorist manifestos echo this justification of violence by appeals to high purpose.

Acts that advance the cause are "moral," even when they paradoxically run counter to normally accepted concepts of morality. Moreover, terrorists are keenly aware that their actions gain force by transgressing against conventional codes. Generating moral shock magnifies the fear they inflict and the outrage they incite on a target audience. In weaponizing emotions, terrorists weaponize morality, turning cultural principles of humane conduct into psychological liabilities through which they can manipulate their adversaries.

Since those threatened by terrorism view it as evidence of moral depravity, they must damn it with the language of evil. Israeli prime minister Benjamin Netanyahu wrote, "I cannot agree that a terrorist can ever be an idealist, or that the objects sought can ever justify terrorism. The impact of terrorism, not merely on individual nations, but on humanity as a whole, is intrinsically evil, necessarily evil and wholly evil."[24] President George W. Bush's habitual use of the word *evil* to describe 9/11 is also exemplary: "Osama bin Laden is an *evil* man. His heart has been so corrupted that he's willing to take innocent life. And we are fighting *evil*, and we will continue to fight *evil*, and we will not stop until we defeat *evil*."[25] But the language of evil can be dangerous. It blinds the opponents of terrorism to the rational intent of the terrorists. And it can justify ill-considered retaliation that can work to the terrorists' advantage.

In addition, what is condemned as evil cannot be dignified by including it in what is popularly considered as a setting for bravery and admirable sacrifice—war as conducted by soldiers. Obviously, even though religious tenets may forbid killing another human being, the taking of human life in self-defense is virtually always considered justified. This notion of self-defense against a capable foe who is willing to do harm puts killing during war on a very different moral plane than murder. The soldier is honored. However, to kill or maim those who pose no immediate danger is seen as immoral, and should the victims have no intention or capacity of engaging in violence—"innocent" in a full sense—an attack is particularly heinous. This, I believe, lies at the heart of refusing to categorize terrorism as war and to valorize terrorists as soldiers.

It would be tone deaf to discuss terrorism without emphasizing terrorists' intentions to exploit moral shock. And that shock also magnifies the sense of vulnerability essential to terrorism's impact. Indiscriminate attacks on the innocent rivets the attention of those who imagine that they too could become the immediate victims of terrorist violence. As Horgan observes, Alex P. Schmid "describes a core feature of terrorism that gives it potency: a calculated exploitation of people's emotional reactions due to the 'causing of extreme anxiety of becoming a victim of [what appears to be] arbitrary violence.'"[26]

TERRORISTS AS PSYCHOLOGICALLY "NORMAL," BUT INHABITING A DIFFERENT MORAL UNIVERSE

The tendency to condemn terrorists as morally depraved, as evil, often rises to the level of condemning them as sociopaths, as crazy. In *Blood and Rage: A Cultural History of Terrorism*, Michael Burleigh declares, "As endless studies of terrorist psychology reveal, they are morally insane, without being clinically psychotic."[27] His words reflect a common opinion that the "barbarity" of terrorists demonstrates that they are psychologically deficient or deviant. Burleigh phrases his condemnation carefully, to be sure, but it still carries the judgment that they are fundamentally aberrant, as shown by "endless studies." However, if read with reasonable care, the most important works in the field say very much the opposite. Recognizing that radical terrorists are "normal" and rational is essential to understanding and intelligently responding to the phenomenon of terrorism.

One of the most senior scholars in the field of terrorism, the political scientist Martha Crenshaw, has consistently maintained that data "suggest that the outstanding common characteristic of terrorists is their normality."[28] In probably the most important recent work on the subject, *The Psychology of Terrorism*, John Horgan argues, "Despite the attractiveness of the theme, terrorist movements should therefore not be seen as organizations of necessarily psychopathic individuals because of the brutality of behavior involved, nor should terrorist groups be seen in the main as likely to recruit people with psychopathic tendencies."[29] In fact, an al-Qaeda manual found in Manchester, England, specifically prescribes that a member "should have a calm personality that allows him to endure psychological traumas."[30] Jerrold M. Post, another much-cited scholar, insists in *The Mind of the Terrorist*, "Those of us who have studied terrorist psychology have concluded that most terrorists are 'normal' in the sense of not suffering from psychotic disorders."[31]

However, to declare that most terrorists are clinically normal is not to deny that they are unusual or extreme in their views and values, as we have previously noted. Scholars Ami Pedhazur and Arie Perliger describe terrorists as driven by "totalist ideologies," which these analysts characterize as "based on an absolute division of humanity into dual categories such as saved versus damned, godly versus demonic, and dark forces versus light forces."[32] In his intriguing study *Anatomy of the Red Brigades: The Religious Mind-Set of Modern Terrorists*, Alessandro Orsini draws parallels between religious extremists and the Italian Marxists of the Red Brigades in the 1970s. His list of shared characteristics also includes a dualist concept of the world as sharply divided between good and evil and an apocalyptic obsession with bringing perfection by destroying a corrupt world.[33] Even the earliest radical terrorists embraced an ideology that was heavily laced with religious concepts, including martyrdom, although these revolutionaries were violently opposed to the church. These are elements of the terrorist mindset.

When individuals join radical activist groups, they tend to leave their previous daily existences behind and adopt new lifestyles among like-minded companions. Their decisions to join can be motivated by personal issues at the start, including their social networks. But it is still likely that they already share some or most of the terrorists' vision of reality. Once immersed in the group, they characteristically become further radicalized, fully accepting the group's narrative that defines virtue, evil, and history. They enter a different "moral universe."

Red Brigades terrorist Adriana Faranda explained that the group became a world unto itself. "The isolation from reality is total," she said, and it focused on "the hideousness of things as they are" as justification for radical violence.[34] People and ideas that do not conform are excluded from the terrorist community. Radicalism feeds on radicalism. Repetition of ideology and the narrative produces a kind of *ideological echo chamber*, in which members hear their own convictions bounced back to them by their comrades.

Describing terrorists as inhabiting a different moral universe reinforced by an ideological echo chamber says much more than condemning them as "morally insane." In a sense, it would be comforting to see terrorists as insane, incomplete in their humanity, drawn from a fringe of the truly aberrant. It is far more disturbing to see them as normal people with radically different conceptions of reality and morality. As the film director, actor, and screenwriter Jean Renoir once famously observed: "The truly awful thing in this world is that everyone has their reasons."[35]

TERRORISTS AS RATIONAL ACTORS

When we accept that radical terrorists are "normal," we open the door to seeing them as rational actors, as defined by rational choice theory. This approach does not describe rational as "reasonable," but as intelligently systematic. Rational actors set goals, consider alternative means to achieving those ends, evaluate success or failure, and revise practices on the basis of those evaluations, all with the purpose of maximizing effect for the effort made. The history of terrorism provides abundant examples of such rational, even if terrifying, choices. The attacks of 9/11 are a case in point.

Taking into consideration our six levels of terrorism, it is not difficult to consider state or military leaders who adopt terrorist violence as rational actors, even if their goals may be repugnant. Popular opinion finds it more difficult to accept radical terrorists as rational, since they lack the legitimacy of high office, are driven by strong passions, and commit actions that are characteristically savage. But Clausewitz himself pointed out that "primordial violence, hatred, and enmity, which are to be regarded as a blind natural force," are intrinsic to war, which he still argued ought to be conducted as a rational act of policy.[36] We need to accept that the terrorist mindset, for all its fervor, does not exclude rational choice in war.

GOALS, STRATEGIES, OPERATIONS, TACTICS, AND STRATAGEMS

Rational actors at war establish goals, calculate strategies, support them by operations, and execute them with tactics and stratagems. To the extent that we accept radical terrorism as a form of warfare, these terms of war apply and can be employed to analyze and describe terrorist campaigns. Goals are ultimate objectives—for example, overthrowing the czarist regime in nineteenth-century Russia, establishing a communist society and government in post–World War II Italy, or precipitating an

Islamist revolution in the twenty-first-century Middle East. The following chapters present a great variety of terrorists' goals. The term *strategy* encompasses the design for the war as a whole. We will emphasize four strategies of terrorism in this volume: intimidation, initiation, attrition, and evolution. Terrorist operations—what terrorists do to support their campaigns—could be said to include recruitment, training, financing, travel, and such miscellany as maintaining safe houses and providing false identification documents. As opposed to strategies, which encompass entire wars, "tactics" are about engaging in particular battles. They involve more immediate military choices on a lower level than strategy. Examples of terrorists' tactical choices include directing assaults against specific individuals versus indiscriminate attacks, kidnapping hostages for ransom or for political impact, or relying on car bombs using timers to detonate charges versus resorting to suicide bombers. The menu of tactical alternatives is the easiest element for one terrorist group to borrow from another. The dictionary defines a stratagem as "any artifice, ruse, or trick devised or used to attain a goal or to gain an advantage over an adversary or competitor."[37] These could be seen simply as tactics; however, they are so integral to radical terrorism that they deserve a category of their own. We will briefly consider three primary stratagems: provocation, outbidding, and spoiling.

Strategies of Intimidation, Initiation, Attrition, and Evolution
Intimidation, the most basic strategy, is the very essence of terrorism as practiced by the strong: state, military, and social. The strong rely on intimidation to eliminate opposition and impose obedience though fear. The use of terror by state regimes to stifle dissent, by military forces to cow enemy noncombatants, and by social/cultural groups to dominate those deemed as inferior, or to expel those reviled as pariahs, all qualify as intimidation. So too does politically driven terror by criminal groups meant to scare people into docility. Since so much public discussion of terrorism revolves around the role of fear, there is little surprising in the strategy of intimidation. However, inciting outrage does not directly serve intimidation, since outrage fuels resistance rather than compelling acquiescence.

Intimidation is also a factor in radical terrorism in two senses. First, it can be part of the effort to panic or wear down a target population through fear and chaos: intimidation of the enemy audience. Second, intimidation may be directed within the group to deter or punish slackers, deserters, or informers. It can also be directed against another radical group seen as a rival. Martha Crenshaw, in her pathbreaking study of the Algerian National Liberation Front (FLN), called this second aspect of intimidation "compliance terrorism."[38]

Although we must recognize the roles of intimidation in radical terrorism, we need to stress the fact that radical terrorism primarily employs three other strategies consistent with the radical terrorists' characteristically weak position. Terrorists relying on initiation believe that the ills and evils of a society or government are so damning that the oppressed need little encouragement to tear down the existing regimes. The discontented masses will rebel if their eyes are fully opened and they are given hope that their resistance can usher in a better future. Radical terrorists can initiate an uprising by exposing the wickedness and weakness of the current regime. Terrorists need not have the force to overcome the status quo themselves, they need only leverage the great boulder of discontent enough so that it can roll down the slope of history, gain momentum, and destroy all in its path. Initiation has special appeal to small ideological groups such as Narodnaya Volya, since it holds out the hope that a few dedicated members might exert an immense impact. Yet the mix of limited resources and great expectations, made all the more fatal by overestimating the degree to which the people support the terrorists, has historically doomed initiation to failure.

A terrorist strategy of attrition relies on wearing down and outlasting adversaries by imposing a cost on them that they ultimately will not be able to continue paying. Such a strategy generally requires that terrorists command more resources than do radical groups pursuing initiation, but at the same time, those who adopt attrition commonly recognize that they lack the strength sufficient to succeed on the level of conventional warfare. For example, by 1977 the Provisional Irish Republican Army (PIRA) adopted the "long war" strategy designed to exhaust the British will to remain in Northern Ireland. Attrition may also work by buying time for the radical group to garner support in the domestic and/or international political arena. But while attrition has a logic to it, it can wear down the terrorists as well as their adversaries; it can become a game of who breaks first.

A strategy of *evolution* entails climbing from a lower level of warfare to a higher, advancing from a group employing terrorist methods toward a larger political entity with the attributes of a state, capable even of conventional warfare. It seeks to increase its means to maximize its impact. Historically, a group can pursue evolution as a predetermined plan, the result of unexpected circumstance and opportunity, or a combination of both. The evolution of the Islamic State from its origins as a small group in 1999 to its proclamation of a caliphate in 2014 provides the most impressive example of the strategy of evolution.

As a consciously developed theory, evolution can be traced back at least to the Chinese Communist champion Mao Zedong, who authored classics on revolutionary warfare as early as the 1930s. He argued that after preparing the ground with political education and propaganda, revolutionaries began the armed struggle as a guerrilla insurgency and then advanced step by step until they could form large military units and engage in conventional warfare. Mao's theory of evolving revolutionary warfare influenced other combatants in wars of liberation, as in Vietnam. Because terrorism as a form of violence required even less preparation and resources than guerrilla warfare, terrorists in the 1960s believed that through radical terrorism they could enter a revolutionary armed struggle and begin the Maoist evolution faster than they could if they strictly followed Mao's original ideas. This fast track was advocated by the urban guerrilla terrorists of the 1960s and 1970s, discussed in Chapter 8.

A successful evolution in size, resources, and power has its advantages, but it also means that groups with a history of terrorism and guerrilla warfare would have to fight toe to toe with enemies better armed and prepared for conventional warfare. The terrorist group ISIS (Islamic State of Iraq and Syria), which became the Islamic State and seized the cities of Mosul in Iraq and Raqqa in Syria, eventually lost both because it was ultimately overmatched by the conventional military forces marshaled against it.

Stipulating four strategies does not imply that these categories are exclusive; for example, all levels of terrorism rely on intimidation to one degree or another, and to the extent that a particular terrorist group makes efforts to increase its size and power, it could be said to be pursuing evolution, whatever else it was doing. It might be more accurate to speak of "strategic tendencies" to do justice to the malleability of terrorist groups and their goals.

The Appendix at the end of this volume, "A Descriptive Model of Four Strategies of Terrorism," offers a graphic representation of the strategies introduced here. However, because Figure A.1 depends on detail and analysis presented in Chapters 5–11, it seemed best to present it later, separated from the main text.

Stratagems

Stratagems are often confused with strategies, but the importance of stratagems in terrorism requires that we consider them with some specificity here. Andrew Kydd and Barbara Walter have contributed a valuable essay, "The Strategies of Terrorism," which presents five "strategies": intimidation, attrition, outbidding, spoiling, and provocation. However, this list in my opinion confuses "stratagems" with "strategies," and it is worth unscrambling them. The first two—intimidation and attrition—mirror our discussion of strategies, but the other three—outbidding, spoiling, and provocation—fit better as stratagems.

Terrorist groups *outbid* rival radical groups by committing actions and attacks meant to display their greater resolve and effectiveness, undercutting their rivals. So Hamas in Gaza has carried out operations against the Israelis precisely to advertise its superiority over the PLO and thus improve its status among the Palestinian community. Similarly, a more radically militant group might launch terrorist attacks to undermine efforts at accommodation and compromise by another less militant group; this is *spoiling*. Again, Hamas provides examples of spoiling in attacks intended to scuttle the Oslo peace process and thus ruin plans for a compromise between Palestinians and the state of Israel.

Provocation

Provocation is such an important stratagem that it deserves our close attention. In 1975, long before terrorism became such a preoccupation of U.S. foreign and military policy, Daniel Fromkin wrote what is probably the most important article on terrorists' resort to the stratagem of provocation. He pointed out that terrorists seek to provoke their adversaries into committing ill-considered responses that weaken those adversaries or make the terrorists stronger. He pointed out that the FLN committed ostentatious atrocities against European settlers in Algeria with the goal of provoking outrage among the far stronger French, who then retaliated with disproportionate violence. As expected, extreme French reprisals so aroused and alienated the Muslim Algerian population that it further embraced and reinforced the FLN. Fromkin called this "a sort of jujitsu" in which terrorists exploit the strength and the momentum of their opponents to throw them off their feet. We will often refer to this terrorist jujitsu in the chapters to come.

One of my rationales in writing this book is to warn Americans against responding to terrorism in ways that simply make the terrorists stronger. In the psychological warfare that is terrorism, we must beware of giving outrage full sway, because provocation and terrorist jujitsu are so fundamental to successful radical terrorism. Note in Figure 1.2 that for weak radical terrorist groups, the goal of growing and strengthening the group can be at least as important in the short run as achieving a particular policy objective. Do not become the terrorists' prime recruiter.

VICTIMS, AUDIENCES, AND POLITICAL THEATER

There are a few more important terms and concepts we need to nail down before moving on. Referring back to Raymond Aron's wisdom about how relatively small-scale violence by radical terrorists generates outsized psychological effects, we should distinguish between immediate victims of terrorism and the much larger target audience that the terrorists hope to affect. I will try to restrict the term "victims" to individuals who are killed, wounded, or otherwise immediately harmed by a terrorist attack. Thus the "victims" of the 2005 suicide bombings in London include the fifty-two killed and the 700 injured. However, those terrorists intended to impact a far, far larger "target audience" across the British Isles and beyond.

Moreover, terrorists can undertake to affect multiple audiences when staging one particular terrorist attack. An important contribution of the Kydd and Walter article is that they point out that the same terrorist act or campaign can be directed both at the terrorists' adversaries and at the terrorists' supporters. They simplify this point in terms of an "enemy audience" and an "audience of [the terrorists'] own population." The bombers in London, for example, intended to alarm the general British population and drive it to pressure its government to abandon any commitment to the United States in Iraq and Afghanistan. At the same time, the terrorists also hoped to convince British Muslims of their own alienation and the need for them to oppose British policy.

It is commonplace to describe radical terrorism as political theater. It entails a public performance meant to be witnessed by many, even though few players are on stage. Novelist and playwright Don DeLillo has a key character in his *Mao II* declare that terrorism, killing the innocent, is "the language of being noticed."[39] To mesmerize their audiences, terrorists tend to push violence to extremes, what Mark Juergensmeyer, an authority on religious terrorism, calls "acts of deliberately exaggerated violence" and that I label "ostentatious atrocities."[40]

The stage upon which the terrorists act can be small, but the audiences can stretch to the horizon and beyond. We will need to consider local, national, regional, and global audiences, both adversaries and allies of the terrorists.

One of the first questions to ask about a terrorist act is, "To whom are the terrorists playing?" The answer to that question was never more complicated than during the Algerian War of Independence (1954–1962), to be discussed in Chapter 6. The FLN conducted a campaign of terrorist attacks, guerrilla operations, and political actions designed to impact several target audiences: the indigenous Arab and Berber populations of Algeria, the Algerian immigrant population in France, the European colonial population in Algeria, the French government and military authorities in Algeria and in France, the general population in France, and an international audience.

Bear in mind that different audiences perceive the same acts in very different ways. To study terrorism is not simply to study a reality; it must be a study of the perception of that reality. Perception is reality viewed through a cultural lens—a matter not only of what actually happens but of what we expect, want, or dread. This is true of target audiences, and of the terrorists themselves.

By now it should be clear that terrorism is a direct assault on the will of the target audiences. Here, too, terrorism aligns with Clausewitz's characterization of war: "War is thus an act of force to compel our enemy to do our will."[41] Yet in dealing with conventional conflicts, Clausewitz stressed the major physical violence that ultimately affects the will. Radical terrorism is more immediately focused on the psychological impact that results from relatively minor attacks.

We must become students of this kind of war. Terrorists are. They write about their goals, strategies, operations, tactics, and stratagems. Moreover, they learn not only from other terrorists, but from the classics of revolutionary and military literature. To my mind, the attention that radical Islamists and other terrorists pay to military literature further illustrates that terrorism is war. For example, as Chapter 11 will argue, the military theory that informs the IS, in particular *The Management of Savagery* by Abu Bakr Naji, can be traced back to Clausewitz, Mao Zedong, and other military and political thinkers. As argued above, terrorists, particularly their leaders, are rational actors and can be very well informed, as well as highly ideological.

Some who discuss terrorism point out that it has had a poor record of success in the past. Statistical studies demonstrate that the great majority of radical terrorist groups have had short lives and ended in failure. Radical terrorist groups begin with few members and limited means, so their lack of success is not surprising. But the ability to begin with so little also means that new groups can form and launch new campaigns with relative ease. Moreover, particular terrorist groups have conducted long and costly campaigns of attrition, as did the PIRA, while others have evolved into far more powerful entities, most notably the Islamic State. And even lone wolves, whose terrorist actions can be measured only in days, not years, can undermine our sense of well-being. Remember, we do not know what will arise in the future. Who foresaw the destruction of 9/11 in 2001 or the proclamation of the Islamic State in 2014? So we must learn to deal with terrorism in the present and the foreseeable future.

Because terrorism is primarily psychological warfare, it can be confronted with knowledge and understanding that blunt its moral shock and limit its ability to infuse a target audience with a sense of vulnerability. Each chapter of this volume begins by recounting the brutal nature and the human cost of terrorism in a single example, a reminder of the tragedy that underlies the history. This chapter opened with 9/11. No single act of terrorism on American soil or anywhere else inflicted a greater toll than did 9/11; none has even approached it. It was so devastating that the destruction of the World Trade Center towers has become the iconic image of terrorism in American eyes. Yet as real as that attack was, and as great as is the need to remember the suffering and sacrifice of that day, its memory should not be allowed to magnify the actual threat posed by terrorism here and abroad. We must maintain a sense of proportion and perspective if we are to deal with terrorism effectively. It is hoped that the history of terrorist groups and attacks presented in the following chapters will provide the basis for valuable context, comparison, and conception.

CHAPTER TWO

Rule by Fear

STATE-REGIME TERRORISM

FIGURE 2.1. This target of Red Guard violence during the Chinese Cultural Revolution is being "struggled," or publicly abused, in the "airplane position." The placard hung from his neck reads "Anti-Party Revisionist Huang." This much-reproduced image, certainly a Red Guard photograph, is presented here under fair use as displayed in the February 2012 issue of the *Well-Tempered Ear* (https://welltempered.files.wordpress.com/2012/02/cultural-rev olution.jpg).

SIMA QIAN (145–86 BCE), a grand historiographer of the Han Dynasty, wrote in his *Historical Records* how the first Qin emperor, Qin Shi Huang (r. 221–210 BCE), ordered a mass burning of books in 213 BCE. Sima Qian served the Han, enemies of and successors to the Qin, so it is not surprising that he disparaged Qin tyranny, but we still know Qin Shi

Huang mainly through Sima Qian's writing. He condemned the first emperor as "a man of scant mercy who has the heart of a wolf."[1] Qin Shi Huang's excesses are legend; it was he who conscripted 700,000 workers to build his fabled tomb, guarded by an army of thousands of terracotta soldiers, rediscovered during the 1970s, and it was he who marshaled still more to labor on the Great Wall, projects that caused the deaths of hundreds of thousands.

The Qin burning of the books had political reasons and cultural repercussions. Qin Shi Huang's chief minister, Li Si, advised him that although the emperor had brought unity and performed great works, scholars still spoke of earlier, better times. "Those who have studied privately collaborate with each other to reject the laws and teachings, and when people hear ordinances promulgated everyone criticizes them in accordance with his own studies," Li Si argued. "If such things are not prohibited, then above the sovereign's power will decline, and below factions will form. To prohibit this would be expedient. Your servant requests that the records of the historians apart from those of Qin should all be burnt."[2] The emperor allowed practical books to survive and permitted certain official scholars to retain copies of condemned volumes; however, all other records of earlier rulers' accomplishments were to be burnt. Those who disobeyed risked severe punishment. When he learned of scholars who defied his regulations and retained forbidden books, the Qin emperor became furious, and "although they tried to exonerate themselves, more than 460 who had infringed the prohibitions were all buried alive at Xianyang, and the whole Empire was made to know about this to serve as a warning for the future."[3]

The first casualties of Qin Shi Huang's project were books and those who preserved them, but his real target was dissent and dissenters. The emperor's acts in pursuit of regime control meet all our criteria for terrorism, including publicizing his repression to intimidate other potential resistance.

Qin Shi Huang was remembered for two millennia mainly for his excesses, but a later Chinese "emperor" did not shy away from comparing himself to him. At the Eighth Party Congress held in May 1958, Mao Zedong boasted in his first address to those assembled: "He only buried alive 460 scholars, while we buried 46,000. In our suppression of the counter-revolutionaries, did we not kill some counter-revolutionary intellectuals? I once debated with the democratic people: You accuse us of acting like Qin Shi Huang, but you are wrong; we surpass him 100 times. You berate us for imitating Qin Shi Huangin enforcing dictatorship. We admit them all."[4] A decade later Mao carried out his own Great Proletarian Cultural Revolution in which political dissidents would again perish and cultural monuments be destroyed. The first violence would be associated with the young Red Guards, as exemplified by the public humiliation of Mr. Huang shown in Figure 2.1. But public punishment could be followed by much worse. The Cultural Revolution took as many as two million lives. We do not know the fate of Mr. Huang.

During all epochs and across the globe, regimes have terrorized their own populations in order to silence dissent, punish resistance, and maintain power; thus, they have employed their considerable capacity to carry out campaigns of terror within a strategy of intimidation. Certainly, the number of those who have suffered abuse, torture, and death as a result of state-regime terrorism beggars the tally inflicted by radical terrorism. The use of terrorism by rulers and regimes has been so common that this chapter could exemplify it by any of a great number of cases across the globe involving governments of the left and the right. Just considering the past century, the list of ruthless authoritarian regimes who have employed terrorist tactics would include those of Benito Mussolini (Italy), Adolf Hitler (Germany), Francisco Franco (Spain), François Duvalier (Haiti), Augusto Pinochet (Chile), Jorge Rafael Videla (Argentina), Idi Amin Dada (Uganda), Charles Taylor (Liberia), Mobutu Sese Seko (Democratic Republic of Congo), Muammar Gadhafi (Libya), Saddam Hussein (Iraq), Bashir al-Assad (Syria), Pol Pot (Cambodia), Islam Karimov (Uzbekistan), and Kim Il-sung, his son, and grandson (North Korea).

As apparent as it normally is, identifying something as state-regime terrorism remains a matter of degree. It is important to bear in mind that even in liberal states, laws prescribe penalties for those who transgress them. Moreover, the fate of those convicted and punished is supposed to deter others from disobedience, and to accomplish this political purpose, the act of punishment must be made public knowledge. Legal punishments from other times and places can strike us as barbaric, such as in the practice of drawing and quartering in medieval and early modern Europe. The renowned political theorist Niccolò Machiavelli (1469–1527) wrote in *The Prince* that fear was the most reliable lever in public affairs: "fear preserves you by a dread of punishment which never fails."[5] Discriminating between reasonable use of punishment and terrorism demands that we take into account the standards of the times, how legitimate a regime's use of violence was considered, and how many fell victim to it.

This chapter discusses three cases in which the character, magnitude, and purpose of violence inflicted by regimes upon their own citizens warrant being categorized as state-regime terrorism. The examples developed in the following pages—the French Reign of Terror (1793–1794), Stalin's Great Purge (1936–1938), and the Red Guard phase of the Chinese Cultural Revolution (1966–1968)—displayed links, commonalities, and contrasts that make them particularly interesting for the history of terrorism. Each regime was personified by a particular individual who employed terrorist tactics in order to deal with perceived internal political threats and to advance the cause of revolution. Each terror campaign was overtly defended as legitimate and necessary; it was proud terrorism, making it all the more shocking. And each campaign, its agents, and its ideology became an example for other rulers, revolutionaries, and terrorists who will be discussed in this volume. In a sense these instances of *state terrorism* ultimately supplied precedents and principles for *radical terrorism*.

THE FRENCH REIGN OF TERROR

It is obligatory in discussions of terrorism to note that the terminology of this political violence—"terror," "terrorist," and "terrorism"—all entered the political lexicon in reference to the Reign of Terror during the French Revolution at its peak, 1793–1794. However, the terrorism of the radical French government was *state* terrorism, not *radical* terrorism. As mentioned in Chapter 1, Marc Sageman makes much of the rise in *political violence* during the French Revolution, but the violence inflicted by the revolutionary regime was an instrument of state repression, not of political resistance. Certainly we ought not to confuse levels of terrorism. However, while the terminology originally arose to describe the policy and practice of a ruling authoritarian regime, it later became attached to the concept of violent revolution and through that to radical terrorism.

In any case, the French Revolution was a hopeful but tortured era.

This revolution resulted from a perfect storm, the confluence of fundamental social tensions, looming government fiscal collapse, and suffering caused by major famine. France was a land of privilege and inequality that greatly favored the aristocracy and the church, a social reality that became less and less tolerable over the course of the eighteenth century. Threatened by bankruptcy from wars and mismanagement, the monarchy could only save itself by paring down the tax advantages and exemptions enjoyed by the nobles and the church, but they balked at granting concessions. Their reluctance infuriated those outside the bastions of preferment. Particularly hard hit were the working classes and the peasantry, driven to starvation in 1788–1789 by the worst famine to strike France since 1709. This famine itself was not caused by human action, but the poor blamed the monarchy for not providing greater relief. Tradition dates the start of the French Revolution to the storming of the Bastille by a revolutionary crowd on 14 July 1789.

Once revolution was in motion it moved further and further to the left. Leaders rose and fell, and others took their places. A new constitution adopted in September 1791 transformed France into a limited monarchy, with the king ruling in conjunction with a Legislative Assembly, but this formula was short-lived. War between revolutionary France and its conservative neighbors broke out in the spring of 1792, and rebellious crowds attacked the monarchs' Parisian palace and seized King Louis XVI and his queen, Marie Antoinette, on 10 August 1792. Now a republic stood on the ruins of the old the monarchy. In 1793 tensions grew worse as the war went badly for the French and violent counterrevolution shook France, as major towns such as Bordeaux, Lyons, and Toulon took up arms against Paris. An even greater internal threat arose from outright counterrevolutionary insurgency in the Vendée in western France. This cavalcade of crises, military and political, called for an emergency government, elements of which appeared in the spring of 1793 but which hardened into the Reign of Terror in the fall and lasted into late July 1794.

The institutions of the Terror were largely ad hoc, because France lacked a new republican constitution to replace the one voided by the end of the monarchy. A series of committees wielded executive power, and the most powerful of these was the Committee of Public Safety, composed of twelve members. Among its coequal members, Maximilien Robespierre stood with the more radical individuals and served as the committee's preeminent spokesman. He belonged to a staunchly republican political club that styled itself "Friends of Liberty and Equality," but is best known as the Jacobins. The Jacobins functioned much as a political party in support of the Terror

Robespierre was the theorist and the apologist of the Terror. His revolutionary language reflects the political philosophy of Charles de Secondat, baron de Montesquieu. In describing the three forms of government in *Spirit of the Laws* (1748), Montesquieu attributed a "spirit" to each: fear to despotism, honor to monarchy, and virtue to republican government. He equated virtue with a sense of public responsibility and sacrifice to accomplish the public good. Without this, a republic could not survive. The enthusiasts of the Terror believed they must engender a new public spirit and spoke of the need to create, to "regenerate," a Republic of Virtue.

Even when the French wrote a new constitution, they immediately suspended it because of the pressing military and political crisis. Until peace returned, the French relied on terror—the extreme of fear—to suppress those who opposed the revolution. On 5 September, the president of the interim legislature, the Convention, proclaimed to great applause, "It is time to horrify all the [counterrevolutionary] conspirators. So legislators, place Terror on the order of the day!"[6]

While Robespierre believed passionately in republican virtue, he argued for relying on despotic terror to achieve his goals. In a famous address, "Report on the Principles of Public Morality," given on 5 February 1794, he explicitly recognized the apparent contraction involved in his stand: "If the mainspring of popular government in peacetime is virtue, amid revolution it is at once *virtue* and *terror*: virtue, without which terror is fatal; terror, without which virtue is impotent. . . . It has been said that terror was the mainspring of despotic government. Does your government, then, resemble a despotism? Yes, [but only] as the sword which glitters in the hands of liberty's heroes resembles the one with which tyranny's lackeys are armed. . . . Subdue liberty's enemies by terror, and you will be right, as founders of the Republic."[7]

Robespierre's insistence that political emergency requires curtailing liberties is old and enduring, and it will impose itself on us again and again in this volume. We will discuss this in a modern context in Chapter 14.

To achieve their goals, Robespierre and the Jacobins willingly sacrificed colleagues who did not share their vision, even if those victims had contributed to the progress of the revolution. The record of the Terror was bloody, but it did not come close to twentieth-century tallies of death compiled by state terrorism. In state trials, the Revolutionary Tribunal in Paris sentenced about 2,600 people to be executed by the guillotine, that bloody symbol of the new state. In all, about 40,000 were condemned to die at the hands of revolutionary justice across France.

This figure does not include the costly campaigns against the counterrevolutionary rebels of the Vendée. Partisans still dispute the nature and cost of war in the Vendée, with some on the extreme right seeing it as genocide launched against a people who refused to accept the Revolution. The hyperbole of revolutionary rhetoric seems to support their case. In October 1793, the Convention urged the army: "Soldiers of liberty, the brigands of the Vendée must be exterminated."[8] Horror stories abound on both sides, and some estimate the toll of the dead as high as 500,000, but this number seems far too large; 250,000 fatalities, of whom 100,000 were Republicans, seems closer to the truth.

Eventually, the French turned against Jacobin terrorism, and Robspierre and some of his colleagues were themselves condemned to the guillotine in July 1794. Crowds cheered at his execution, just as they had when Louis XVI was beheaded eighteen months before.

To reference the Reign of Terror during the French Revolution is not simply to cite the origins of our lexicon of terrorism; it is to discover one of the most direct theoretical defenses of state terrorism. Robespierre's words represent an enduring mindset that links terrorism with the necessary defense of the good, of revolution. His sincerity encourages us to take the rhetoric of terrorists seriously, although wisdom also cautions us to be wary of idealistic phrases employed as camouflage in a battle for power.

STALIN'S GREAT PURGE, 1936–1938

The Bolshevik leadership that managed the October Revolution in 1917 and mastered the Soviet state that emerged from it was well aware of the French Jacobins. The central figure of the October Revolution, Vladimir Ilyich Lenin, wrote in praise of them: "The class-conscious workers and working people generally put their trust in the transfer of power to the revolutionary, oppressed class for that is the essence of Jacobinism, the only way out of the present crisis, and the only remedy for economic dislocation and the war."[9]

A primary legacy of the French Revolution was the idea of revolution itself. The Jacobins demonstrated a new political alternative for those who lost faith in things as they were and dedicated themselves to creating what should be. Some who looked back on the French revolutionary precedent were nationalists, some liberals, some anarchists, and others socialists. Among the last, Karl Marx believed he had discovered laws of history revealing class struggle as the engine of progress, and the French Revolution was his greatest case in point.

Both Lenin and Leon Trotsky, another preeminent revolutionary theorist and practitioner, looked to the use of terror during the French Revolution. During the Russian Revolution of 1905, Lenin quoted his former colleague Georgi Plekhanov, "The terrorism of the great French Revolution . . . began on July 14, 1789, with the storming of the Bastille. . . . The history of that terrorism is exceedingly instructive for the Russian revolutionary." Lenin immediately affirmed, "Yes, a thousand times yes! The history of that terrorism is instructive in the extreme."[10] In 1920, at the height of the Red Terror that followed Bolshevik dominance, Trotsky declared the French Revolution as far and away "the greatest event in modern history" and concluded approvingly, "To this classical revolution there was a corresponding classical terrorism."[11]

The Russian Revolution of 1917 was followed by civil war and the Red Terror, 1918–1922. The new Soviet state security force, the Cheka, spearheaded the Red Terror against those charged with counterrevolution. In an interview, the director of the Cheka declared: "We stand for organized terror—this should be frankly admitted. Terror is an absolute necessity during times of revolution. Our aim is to fight against the enemies of the Soviet Government and of the new order of life. We judge quickly. In most cases only a day passes between the apprehension of the criminal and his sentence."[12] Perhaps the most infamous statement concerning the state terrorism of the Red Terror came from N. V. Krylenko, chairman of the Revolutionary Tribunal of the All-Russian Central Committee in 1918: "We must execute not only the guilty. Execution of the innocent will impress the masses even more."[13]

Lenin died in January 1924, but before he passed from the scene he had secured the appointment of Joseph Stalin as general secretary of the Communist Party in 1922. In the power struggle that followed Lenin's death, Stalin emerged triumphant. His rival Trotsky was first ejected from the Party in 1927 and then exiled from Russia in 1929. Eventually, on Stalin's orders, Trotsky was assassinated while living in Mexico in 1940.

Once in power, Stalin proved himself brutally willing to rely on state terrorism. Historians debate the degree to which Stalin's violence expressed profound paranoia or reflected the great challenges and hard times implicit in establishing a revolutionary regime. In any case, he piteously crushed real and imagined threats. In the process he erected about himself a cult of personality.

Stalin instituted his most extensive state terror campaign with the Great Purge of 1936–1938. This climaxed a decade typified by suffering and fear, beginning with the First Five-Year Plan in 1928–1932. While this attempt at economic transformation benefited industry, it brought on famine in 1932, as peasants resisted forced agricultural collectivization. Grain production fell by 32 percent, even though state demands on what was harvested increased. As did Lenin before him, Stalin regarded the better-off peasants, the kulaks, as an obstructive, hated class that had to be destroyed. "In order to oust the kulaks as a class, the resistance of this class must be smashed in open battle and it must be deprived of the productive sources of its existence and development."[14] The Ukraine was particularly hard hit, and millions died of starvation.

Believing himself threatened in the mid-1930s, Stalin buttressed his political position by turning the state apparatus against perceived opponents. As a pretext, he exploited the assassination of a prominent and charismatic leader, Sergei Kirov, in December 1934. In Moscow, the Central Committee rallied to support a purge: "The Central Committee must be pitiless—the Party must be purged . . . the record of every member must be scrutinized."[15] This was the beginning, but only the beginning. The Great Purge—or, as historian Robert Conquest calls it, the Great Terror—began in August 1936 with the first of three major show trials in Moscow, bringing sixteen prominent defendants to the bar. Prisoners were accused of plotting against Stalin and being allied with the archdevil Trotsky. Jailors tortured their prisoners to extract confessions, and all sixteen were convicted and executed. Two later show trials, in January 1937 and March 1938, brought other lists of political figures to "justice." Of the seven members of the Politburo who directed the October Revolution in 1917, Stalin was the only one left alive in Russia by 1939.

Eliminating major political rivals may have been the most spectacular aspect of the Great Purge, but it was far from accounting for most of the victims. Party members great and small suffered in extraordinary numbers. Local Party officials demonstrated their own loyalty by sacrificing those below them. It was not simply those charged with being "enemies of the people" who were in danger, but their families as well. The NKVD, which had become the primary state security organization in 1934, issued its Order No. 00486 on 1 August 1936, stating, "On receipt of this order, proceed to the repression of the wives of traitors of the motherland."[16] Special camps were set up for theses wives. Children were turned against their parents and encouraged to denounce them. One official commented in 1938, "You know they are putting people in prison for nothing now."[17] People lived in fear of footsteps on the stairs and a knock on the door at 2 or 3 a.m., a preferred time for arrests.

Even as war clouds darkened the horizon, the Great Purge also struck at the army. Three of its five highest-ranking commanders were arrested, tried in a secret court martial held during June 1937, and shot or perished in prison. The most notable of the three, Marshal Mikhail Tuchachevsky, a rising star in the army, was executed by a bullet in the back of his head. His wife and brothers were also eventually shot; his young daughter, once she grew to adulthood, was arrested and condemned to a forced-labor camp. The Purge eliminated a great deal of the upper echelons of the officer corps, including 154 of 186 division commanders.[18]

Stalin's fear of rivals, and power struggles within the Communist Party at the central and on the local levels, brought on the Great Purge, but the suspicion-driven terrorism loosed by the Purge went beyond the political elites. NKVD Order No. 00447 of July 30, 1937 was entitled "About Repression of Former Kulaks, Criminals, and Other Anti-Soviet Elements."[19] Once more the hated kulaks, ex-kulaks, and their families came under fire. They were to be rounded up, quotas of arrests were set, and those inevitably convicted were to be shot or removed to labor camps. Other "anti-Soviet elements" included clerics, certain ethnic minorities, including Poles, and the intelligentsia, of whom thousands were arrested.

Scholars debate the numbers who died during the Great Purge. The noted scholar Nicolas Werth states that during the Great Purge 1,575,000 were arrested, 1,345,000 sentenced, and 681,692 executed.[20] Conquest tallied those executed at about one million.[21]

There is some atom of justice in the fact that the two men who led the NKVD during the Great Purge, Genrikh Yagoda and Nikolai Yezhov, both fell from power, suffered, and were put to death in 1937 and 1940, respectively. This execution of the executioners follows the precedent of the French Revolution. Then, both Martial Herman, head of the Revolutionary Tribunal, and Antoine Fouquier de Tinville, its public prosecutor, who together ushered many to the guillotine, including Marie Antoinette, were themselves decapitated on 7 May 1795. But they were small-time merchants of death compared to Yagoda and Yezhov.

CHINA'S CULTURAL REVOLUTION AND THE RED TERROR OF THE RED GUARDS

The Twentieth Congress of the Communist Party of the Soviet Union completed its formal public sessions on 24 February 1956, but the delegates were informed that they were to return for a special closed session that night. Shortly after midnight, Nikita Khrushchev shocked those attending with his "secret talk" denouncing Stalin's tyranny and his cult of personality as displayed in the Great Purge: "Whoever opposed these concepts or tried to prove his [own] viewpoint and the correctness of his [own] position was doomed to removal from the leadership collective and to subsequent moral and physical annihilation. This was especially true during the period following the 17th Party Congress, when many prominent Party leaders and rank-and-file Party workers, honest and dedicated to the cause of Communism, fell victim to Stalin's despotism."[22]

When it leaked to the major Western press, the talk caused turmoil in Communist Parties across the world. Disillusionment with the past was further highlighted by revolt in the present. Polish workers protested in Poznan on 28–30 June 1956, attacking the offices of the local Communist Party. Officials repressed the demonstrations with troops and tanks, leaving 50–100 dead. Full-scale anti-Soviet insurrection broke out in Hungary on 23 October and continued for over two weeks, only to be crushed by Soviet armed intervention.

The revelations and rebellions disillusioned many Communists and alarmed others. No one was more agitated than Mao Zedong, who revered Stalin. To Chairman Mao, Khrushchev personified not the dream of a better day but the nightmare of revisionism, revolutionary back-sliding. Mao's Cultural Revolution of 1966–1976 would be his way to fight against it.

Because Stalin and Mao were both hardline Communist leaders, determined to maintain their dominance ruthlessly, there may be a tendency to see them as virtually identical, but they, and the purges they conducted, differed greatly. The flags of both the now-defunct Soviet Union and the Chinese Communist Party both display a yellow hammer and sickle on a red background; but Stalin was more hammer and Mao more sickle. Stalin's power came down like a blunt instrument, while Mao's had a sharper, shrewder edge. The U.S.S.R. was more centralized than was China, Stalin called into play great national instruments of repression, but Mao was willing to let loose local forces that he could exploit. He was expert at playing one faction against another to neutralize both, and he adroitly changed horses to win the race when necessary. Stalin imposed order; Mao was willing to set free chaos if he thought it would do his work for him. In Soviet terms, Mao was China's Lenin *and* Stalin, the author of "Mao Zedong Thought" and its enforcer, the focus of a more multifaceted cult of personality than was Stalin.

Chinese repression was more confessional and more theatrical. Built into Chinese Communist practice was the formal process of self-criticism. On the one hand, this was supposed to encourage improved revolutionary values and conduct by acknowledging mistakes and weaknesses. Mao could require oral and written self-criticism even from the highest officials. Although officially intended for the self-improvement of the offender, these critiques still left the author open to public censure and could be employed to attack shirkers or undermine those in power. Mao exploited them to weaken or to destroy some. But he also put them in play to control others by granting them a kind of absolution that made it clear to whom the confessed party owed his or her continued security and authority. Mao might seem magnanimous when he was, in fact, being manipulative.

Theatricality surrounded the ritual of self-criticism and the condemnation of those found unforgivably lacking. Individuals would be paraded about wearing placards announcing their failings and forced into the "airplane position," bent over at the waist with arms thrust back and hands held at a higher level than the head, which would often be pulled up by the hair—a combination of humiliation and torture. The photograph of the "revisionist" Huang at the beginning of this chapter portrays such punishment during the Cultural Revolution. The most common penalty inflicted on those who were important enough to be publicly shamed was imprisonment and forced labor, although others were immediately put to death.

Two campaigns that preceded the Cultural Revolution suggest difference and similarity between China and the Soviet Union. The first was the Hundred Flowers Campaign, in which Mao encouraged open criticism: "Let a hundred flowers bloom; let a hundred schools of thought contend." This began as a concept late in 1956 and reached its most intense level during the spring of the following year. Mao naively expected that freedom of speech would lead to some criticisms of officials, but would also express great praise for his ideas and actions. However, articles not only criticized individual policies, but also attacked the Communist Party and, most shockingly, Mao himself. Mao's private physician reported: "Mao had grossly miscalculated. . . . He was furious."[23] By mid-May, he changed course, planning to use his miscalculation to his advantage, telling his doctor, "We want to coax the snakes out of their holes. . . . Then we will strike. My strategy is to let the poisonous weeds grow first and then destroy them one by one. Let them become fertilizer." He confided that Khrushchev's secret talk and the Hungarian Revolution had initiated an anticommunism that Mao resolved to stem in China, and in July 1957 he halted the Hundred Flowers Campaign. By then, those who were critical of the regime had risen high enough into the light that they were ready to be cut down. The Anti-Rightist Movement of 1957–1959 followed, and 300,000–600,000 "revisionists" were persecuted, with intellectuals being particular targets.

The Great Leap Forward (1958–1962) that came next repeated in a more exaggerated form the agricultural disasters of Stalin's First Five-Year Plan. Like it, the Great Leap was intended to advance industry, particularly steel production, and complete the collectivization of the countryside. State demand for agricultural production increased to feed the rapidly growing cities and also to supply the grain that Mao slated for export to the U.S.S.R. as payment for loans. However, production on the farms decreased drastically because of badly conceived agricultural innovations and the misappropriation of resources and manpower, all complicated by the imposition of more extreme forms of collectivization and by bad weather. The result was a horrific famine during the "Three Bitter Years" (1959–1961) that, according to historian Frank Dikötter, caused a minimum of forty-five million deaths.[24] Authorities responded to crises with terrorism. In 1959, the government set an annual quota for executions related to the Great Leap at 4,500, along with 213,000 people arrested and 677,000 publicly humiliated.[25]

Mao drew criticism for the failures of the Great Leap Forward as early as the plenum of the Central Committee held in July 1959. Important dissident voices were silenced, and according to historians Roderick MacFarquhar and Michael Schoenhals: "From this point on, loyalty to his *person* rather than to his *policies* became the touchstone for the Chairman."[26]

Mao supported the Socialist Education Movement (1963–1966), which sought to remove reactionaries and revisionists. But the Great Proletarian Cultural Revolution would go much further. Mao intended it to reinvigorate revolutionary sentiment, halt revisionist back-sliding, and preserve his vision of the revolution. To that end he exploited the spontaneous enthusiasm of Chinese youth. Much like Robespierre, Mao believed that a socialist China required abandoning old cultural norms, that a new world required a new people.

But trying to encapsulate the Cultural Revolution in any brief description necessarily oversimplifies it. The first years of this movement (1966–1968) were dominated by the actions of the young, self-proclaimed Red Guards, followed by the army's reassertion of order; the second period witnessed the dominance of the army under Lin Piao and ended with a failed coup and his death in December 1971. During the last years (1972–1976), Mao, now in declining health, tried to solidify his power and was largely successful. However, his death in September 1976 brought the Cultural Revolution to an end. In 1977 a leader whom Mao had twice disgraced but not eliminated, Deng Xiaoping, skillfully regained leadership and led China in a more moderate, and more capitalist, direction. While the Cultural Revolution consumed a decade, the discussion here will emphasize the first period as the most dramatic, and intriguing, phase of the kaleidoscope of targets, tactics, and terror that made up the movement.

Mao set the Great Proletarian Cultural Revolution in motion with a circular from the Central Committee of the Communist Party on 16 May 1966. It declared the need to purge the "bunch of counter-revolutionary revisionists" who had infiltrated "the government, the army, and various cultural circles" and associated these dangerous people with Khrushchev.²⁷ China's secondary school and university students and young professors quickly reacted to the proclamation. On 25 May, Nie Yuanzi, a lecturer at Peking University, posted a "big-character poster" supporting a purge of revisionists, and within half a day 1,500 big-character posters for and against her position appeared on campus. Mao ordered Nie's poster published; it appeared in newspapers and was read on radio across the country on 2 June.

The student movement swelled with astounding rapidity. Posters appearing within hours after the national publication of Nie's were signed as being by the "Red Guard," a title generated by students themselves. One such poster proclaimed the virtual credo of their Cultural Revolution: "Beat to a pulp any and all persons who go against Mao Zedong Thought—no matter who they are, what banner they fly, or how exalted their positions may be."²⁸ On 13 June the Chinese Communist Party and State Council "suspended" classes at schools and universities, freeing thirteen million secondary school students and half a million university students to take to the streets.²⁹ This great mass of youthful men and women coalesced into diverse Red Guard groups. On 18 June students "struggled"—that is, publicly abused—forty "monsters and freaks" whom the students considered to be counterrevolutionaries, or members of the "black band." On 5 August Mao authored his own big-character poster, entitled "Bombard the Headquarters," urging attacks against revisionists at all levels.

Red Guard terrorism operated from the bottom up, rather than from the top down. When the Central Committee tried to supervise and constrain the students, Mao sided with the Red Guard: "We should not . . . issue directives and give orders. . . . Let the teachers and students themselves continue by themselves; that's the only good way to do it."³⁰ Mao inspired the Red Guards, but he didn't need to control them; as long as they revered him and targeted his enemies, he was not much concerned about their methods. These young acolytes were guided by the bible of Mao Zedong Thought: the pocket-sized, ubiquitous *Quotations from Chairman Mao Tse-Tung*, published in over a billion copies between 1964 and 1976. Mao strengthened his relationship with the Red Guards by bringing them to meet him in a series of eight mass rallies between 18 August and 26 November 1966. About twelve million Red Guards gloried in his presence.³¹

Red Guards campaigned to destroy the "Four Olds": "old ideas, old culture, old customs, and old habits of the exploiting classes."[32] Destruction was already a theme in Mao's work; point 6 of his 16 May circular stated: "Chairman Mao often says that there is no construction without destruction. . . . Put destruction first, and in the process you have construction."[33] The Red Guards served as Mao's revolutionary wrecking ball. August and September witnessed the height of the demolition. In Beijing alone 33,695 families' homes were looted. Throughout China, nearly 400,000 city-dwellers were expelled from cities and driven back to their ancestral villages. Worse still, thousands were tortured, killed, or chose suicide. Red Guards set up their own detention centers. At one they wrote on the wall "Long Live the Red Terror," some said with the blood of their victims.[34]

Cultural monuments tumbled. Among the most notable casualties was the temple of Confucius in Qufu. There, Red Guards desecrated the grave of Confucius and destroyed 6,618 registered cultural artifacts, although they did not burn down the temple itself.[35] Over the course of the entire Cultural Revolution, Beijing suffered the loss of 4,922 of 6,843 "places of cultural or historical interest," most of them destroyed in August and September 1966.[36]

This period of inspired destruction brought an undeniable sense of exhilaration. Later in life, a woman who was sixteen in the summer of 1966 wrote: "Starting in late August 1966, Red Guards were beginning to travel to all parts of China free of charge. Our task was to spread the idea of the Cultural Revolution. We were seeds of fire. Chairman Mao was the spring wind. . . . *From now on, we no longer need envy our parents for their heroic deeds in revolutionary wars and feel sorry because we were born too late.*"[37] To the extent that Mao wanted to revolutionize the youth, he was succeeding, at least in the short run.

The revolutionary tide did not simply carry off the little fish, it also drowned grander creatures. When they got their hands on important revisionists, the Red Guards subjected them to denunciation, humiliation, and abuse in front of large crowds. Above all, Mao punished those who had been critical or disloyal. Peng Dehuai, a former defense minister who had criticized the Great Leap Forward, was arrested in December 1966. After 130 brutal interrogations, he was denounced and humiliated in a stadium packed by tens of thousands in August 1967. After this, he was imprisoned until his death in 1974. His wife was also arrested and sent to a labor camp.

The rampage of the Red Guards in late 1966 took some aback, but these youths were not put under control. Violence increased and turned inward as rival Red Guard units began fighting each other. At his birthday celebration on 26 December 1966, Mao offered a toast: "To the unfolding of nationwide all-round civil war!"[38] He got that war in Shanghai during the winter of 1966–1967, when local Red Guards did battle over the city with the Scarlet Guards organized by the Shanghai Party Committee, with victory going to the Red Guards. Contending groups moved up the scale of weaponry from clubs to machine guns. The army even handed over weapons to the leftist Guards. The summer of 1967 turned China into hundreds of battle zones.

Finally, the Central Committee took steps to rein in the chaos. Localities were to form new revolutionary committees composed of members of the People's Liberation Army (the state military, or PLA), cadres, and "revolutionary masses." As it turned out, officers from the PLA supplied the great majority of the 48,000 revolutionary committee members.[39] Lin Biao, chosen to head the army because of his great loyalty to Mao, was in fact militarizing the revolution. In late July 1968, Mao summoned Red Guard leaders to the Great Hall of the People in Beijing. Mao told the Red Guards that enough was enough. Where needed, PLA units occupied campuses, and plans were laid to send Red Guards to the countryside, where they were to learn from common folk "up to the mountains and down to the villages." The great days of the Red Guards were over.

However, contests over power continued at the center, and China paid a dreadful price in lives twisted and lost. Mao played faction against faction with skill. When a coup plot threatened to put Lin Biao in charge, it collapsed, with Lin, his wife, and son dying in a plane crash during Lin's attempted escape. Mao backed different jockeys to ride his legacy to victory, even granting power to Deng Xiaoping in 1975, only to take it back and give to other hands. By the time of Mao's death, the old power of the Red Guards was long past, but a Party member's position concerning them and their work comprised an aspect of that individual's political definition. Mao died on 9 September 1976, and history overcame his legacy. Within a month, Mao's widow, Jiang Qing, and three of her associates, the so-called Gang of Four, were arrested. In the political maneuvering that followed, Deng Xiaoping emerged victorious in July 1977 and repudiated the Cultural Revolution.

Limited access to records and the unavoidably incomplete scholarship based upon them have not produced what are regarded as definitive figures for the cost in human life and suffering associated with the Cultural Revolution. However, this does not deny all progress on the question of losses. It is now impossible to claim, as had been before, that the purges took their toll primarily among the elites of the Communist Party, that the Cultural Revolution was almost exclusively urban in character, or that the killing abated sharply after 1968. It seems reasonable to propose a figure of two to three million killed and tens of millions more arrested, "struggled," or imprisoned.[40] This figure probably reached well over fifty million out of a population of some 800 million.

THE THREE CASES COMPARED

The three examples of state-regime terrorism are linked and yet quite distinct. The French Revolution really pioneered the concept and practice of revolution, creating a revolutionary tradition, including terrorism, that would inspire the Bolsheviks who created the Soviet Union. Stalin came to rule that state and fought off real and perceived threats to his authority with the terrorism of the Purges. Mao revered Stalin's strength and ruthless pursuit of revolution, and feared the kind of revisionism personified in Khrushchev. To defeat that threat, he launched, manipulated, and later directed the Cultural Revolution. All three regimes conceived of themselves as revolutionary and believed in creating a new society, inhabited by a new kind of man and woman, and all pursued this transformation through state terrorism.

However, each of the three examples was unique. The French Reign of Terror was state terrorism by committee, not by an individual. Robespierre was its most obvious proponent, but its leadership was diverse, and that diversity left open the possibility of the citizenry to turn against the sacrifices of the Terror once the dangers posed by war and counterrevolution declined. If one dates the Terror as lasting from September 1793 to July 1794, it was brief. Stalin ruled ruthlessly from at least the late 1920s until his death in 1953. He was a totalitarian dictator who began and directed the Purges; his power was overt, dictatorial, and unrepentant. He sent old comrades and new challengers to their deaths to insure his rule.

Mao was wilier. He wanted to rid Communist China of revisionists and declared the necessity of doing so. But when this sparked a spontaneous radical movement among Chinese youth, he was willing to ride that wave without utterly controlling it. He let the tsunami do its destructive work, clearing the path for him. In a sense, he decentralized state terrorism under the Red Guards; only in 1968 did he take firm control of the reins.

While the Bolsheviks looked to the French Revolution for inspiration, and Mao viewed Stalin as an archetypical revolutionary strong man, the Marxist revolutionaries of the second wave of radical terrorism were likely to idealize the Red Guards—certainly that was the case with the Weather Underground in the United States, as we shall see in Chapter 8. And the radical Islamists of the third wave learned from Mao's revolutionary career and writings, as we shall see in Chapter 11. All three of the examples of state terrorism presented here had legs.

Historically minded commentators are fond of citing Machiavelli's *The Prince* as a revealing work on tyranny, and reference his questioning "whether it be better to be loved than feared or feared than loved." He responded to his own query: "It may be answered that one should wish to be both, but, because it is difficult to unite them in one person, it is much safer to be feared than loved."[41] But it is also important to recognize Machiavelli's advice that "a prince ought to inspire fear in such a way that, if he does not win love, he avoids hatred." Going further, it should be noted that in a mass culture, fear and love may be closer than Machiavelli supposed, and the agent of both can be the cult of personality. Robespierre certainly enjoyed a powerful following, at least for a time. Stalin and Mao both fashioned cults of personality around themselves.

Robespierre, Stalin, and Mao all defended the state terrorism they pursued as essential to bring about a necessary transformation of society and culture, and to defend that transformation against counterrevolutionaries. Stalin is most likely to be charged with a paranoid obsession with threats to his own power, but there is no question that his regime propelled and compelled the Soviet Union into a new era. In all three cases, we see similar language concerning revolutionary righteousness and fear that evil forces were at work to undermine it.

Virtually inventing the office of emperor in a united China, Qin Shi Huang focused the power of the state on consolidating his military and political power, accomplishing grand construction projects, and attempting to shape culture within his realm. He was hardly averse to using force and fear, exacting horrific punishments if need be to compel obedience. He mastered and manipulated through acts of state terrorism, including his burning of books and executions of scholars.

Mao Zedong, with far greater resources and capacity, pursued analogous goals. Both he and Qin Shi Huang behaved as if they could defy the normal bounds of individual human life and influence. The emperor hoped to retain power and glory beyond life; he sought immortality, built a magnificent tomb to house his body and sustain his spirit, and fashioned an army of terracotta troops to defend him in death. His earthly prominence and eternal presence constituted a cult of personality suitable to his times. Mao's cult was less gilded but directly affected a greater range and expanse of humanity. Certainly, both influenced their times and posterity, but neither was able to perpetuate his regime past his death. The Qin Empire only outlasted its founder by a bit over three years. Mao sought to reinforce his concept of revolution and the reverence awarded him, but the Party soon repudiated his Cultural Revolution.

The formal "Resolution on Certain Questions in the History of Our Party," adopted in 1981, concluded: "The 'cultural revolution,' which lasted from May 1966 to October 1976, was responsible for the most severe setback and the heaviest losses suffered by the Party, the state and the people since the founding of the People's Republic. It was initiated and led by Comrade Mao Zedong. . . . The history of the 'cultural revolution' has proved that Comrade Mao Zedong's principal theses for initiating this revolution conformed neither to Marxism, Leninism nor to Chinese reality. They represent an entirely erroneous appraisal of the prevailing class relations and political situation in the Party and state."[42] The path taken by the People's Republic of China would not be the one that Chairman Mao would have chosen for it. Although the Chinese regime and people continued to respect Mao for his contributions to the revolutionary struggle and for the "correct" aspects of his Mao Zedong Thought, China abandoned his desire for permanent revolution.

CHAPTER THREE

War on Civilians

MILITARY TERRORISM

FIGURE 3.1. A pleasant view of Dresden's Baroque old city in peaceful times, ca. 1900 (*above*), contrasts with the photograph of the city's buildings reduced to shells by the firebombing of 1945 (*left*). The latter view, from the tower of the city hall, is all the more poignant because the statue in the foreground, seeming to look down, is the Allegory of Goodness, sculpted by August Schreitmüller. *Above:* Library of Congress. *Left:* Deutsche Fototek, Wikimedia Commons, CC BY 3.0.

BETWEEN 10:13 AND 10:28 on the night of 13 February 1945, 244 British Lancaster heavy bombers of the Royal Air Force dropped 880 tons of bombs, 43 percent of them incendiaries, on the heart of the old city of Dresden, igniting a firestorm of demonic intensity. Three hours later, when many people had left shelters and firefighters battled the flames, a second wave of 524 Lancasters struck. From 1:21 to 1:45 a.m. they disgorged another 1,758 tons of bombs, of which 45 percent by weight were incendiaries, to feed and extend the fires. A large force of 316 American B17s was sent to attack the city the next morning with 782 tons of bombs. In a final raid on 15 February, a force of 211 B17s that cloud cover prohibited from attacking their primary target, a synthetic oil plant near Leipzig, scattered their 465-ton bomb load on Dresden in an ill-directed manner. The firebombing of Dresden consumed 25,000 lives, the vast majority of them civilians, in what Americans have come to call the "Good War" (Fig. 3.1, bottom).

No recitation of the facts conveys the horror of 13–15 February 1945 as powerfully as do the stories of its victims. Lothar Metzger was anxious to celebrate his upcoming tenth birthday when the air raid alarm sounded at 9:30 p.m. to warn of the approach of the first wave of bombers. Lothar, his thirteen-year-old sister, and their mother retreated to the cellar; his mother carried his five-month-old twin sisters in a basket. Soon fire and smoke drove them out of their building to another. But they had to flee this cellar as well because of the spreading flames:

> It was beyond belief, worse than the blackest nightmare. So many people were horribly burnt and injured. It became more and more difficult to breathe. . . . Dead and dying people were trampled upon. . . . The basket with our twins covered with wet cloths was snatched up out of my mother's hands and we were pushed upstairs by the people behind us. We saw the burning street, the falling ruins and the terrible firestorm. . . . We saw terrible things: cremated adults shrunk to the size of small children, pieces of arms and legs, dead people, whole families burnt to death, burning people ran to and fro . . . and all the time the hot wind of the firestorm threw people back into the burning houses they were trying to escape. . . . The basket with the twins had disappeared and then suddenly my older sister

vanished too. . . . The last hours of this night we found shelter in the cellar of a hospital nearby surrounded by crying and dying people.[1]

Why did Dresden suffer this fate? The intersection of rail lines there, and the city's proximity to the front, gave Dresden value as a transportation target, and it contributed somewhat to war production. But this misses the point. The British had long advocated area bombing as a way to crack German morale, and they pressured the Americans to participate in this kind of war. Dresden was the seventh largest city in Germany, with a pre-war population of 650,000, which had swelled significantly as refugees fled the approaching Russians. Whatever else the Royal Air Force attack on center of Dresden was, it rates as an exercise in terrorism.

No less a figure than Winston Churchill labeled British bombing strategy "terror." On 28 March, six weeks after Dresden and with the end of the European war nearing, he wrote General Hastings Ismay, a key military advisor and Churchill's link to the British Chiefs of Staff: "It seems to me that the moment has come when the question of bombing of German cities simply for the sake of increasing the terror . . . should be reviewed. . . . The destruction of Dresden remains a serious query against the conduct of Allied bombing. . . . I feel the need for more precise concentration upon military objectives, such as oil and communications behind the immediate battle-zone, rather than on mere acts of terror and wanton destruction, however impressive."[2]

This chapter pursues two goals by examining several case studies that span millennia of history. The first of these goals is relatively simple: to establish that regular armed forces have historically used tactics that exhibit the six traits of terrorism laid out in Chapter 1. Clearly, definitive statements that terrorism is only perpetrated by nonstate or sub-state entities is too narrow a perspective for this historical study. The second goal is more challenging: to sharpen our sense of what is and what is not terrorism and to reveal more of the complexities implicit in terror tactics and strategies.

Along the way, we must consider evolving cultural standards toward the practice of war. This requires some familiarity with the evolving law of war and the modern-day legal concepts of war crimes and crimes against humanity. We will note that as odious as certain actions in war are, as much as they qualify as crimes against humanity, they might not meet the criteria of terrorism proposed in this volume. Callous disregard of human life in itself does not qualify as terrorism. Terrorism is not simply a matter of dreadful things happening to civilian populations. Acts must be judged by their intended design to affect public attitudes and behavior.

TERROR TACTICS, MILITARY TERRORISM, AND RADICAL TERRORISM AS WAR

Before going further with this consideration of military terrorism we should differentiate between 1) terror tactics on the battlefield, 2) resort to terrorism by conventional forces and insurgents in warfare, and 3) radical terrorism as a form of war itself. This may seem a technical matter of semantics, but it gets to the heart of the way we think about terrorism and the way we talk about it.

Because war is a test of wills, battlefield tactics commonly have the double goal of overcoming the enemy physically and undermining him psychologically, draining his courage, confidence, and will. Hannibal used elephants against the Romans as agents of fear. In the age of cold steel, the bayonet charge was meant to induce panic as much as to inflict casualties. It is no accident that the 2003 campaign against Iraq was called Shock and Awe, defined in U.S. military doctrine as operations "based on affecting the adversary's will, perception, and knowledge through imposing sufficient Shock and Awe to overcome resistance, allowing us to achieve our aims."[3] However, even when they stun foes, such tactics are not terrorism in our sense, since they are directed at *combatants* rather than noncombatants.

To go further, we need to distinguish between tactics and strategies. Recall that tactics are about fighting battles, and strategies are about conducting wars.

Military forces at war employ terrorism when they attack *noncombatants* with a terrorist's intent to use physical violence to exert a psychological effect on a target audience. This chapter will explore a variety of cases of such military terrorism. When military forces, from regular armies to insurgent guerrillas, have the capacity to employ a range of different violent options, from conventional to terrorist, their decision to resort to terrorism is a tactical choice. We can accurately describe terrorist violence employed by armies as a matter of *tactics*.

Some commentators argue that terrorism is *always* a tactic; however, I disagree. Sub-state radical terrorists are characteristically too weak in capacity to have the option of anything but terrorist methods. When terrorism is not a choice but the sole available option it defines not only tactics but *strategy*—it defines the conduct of the war as a whole, not simply one attack. When terrorism is the only route to success, it is the essence of the fight; it is the *strategy* of radical terrorists in their entry-level form of warfare.

We will discuss radical terrorist strategies in Chapters 5–12; in this chapter we are talking of powerful military forces, conventional and insurgent, that make the choice to employ terrorism in support of a larger war effort to achieve goals and execute strategies.

THE SACK OF BESIEGED CITIES FROM ANCIENT TIMES TO THE EIGHTEENTH CENTURY

We can demonstrate the Western practice of military terrorism from biblical times through the mid-seventeenth century by concentrating on the extreme violence inflicted on civilian populations of towns and fortresses that were sacked by besieging armies. Ancient, medieval, and early modern cities had walls for good reasons, the most paramount of which was defense. If a besieged town refused to capitulate in a timely manner—thus forcing the attackers to storm the walls—the defenders could expect no quarter. In this circumstance, the assaulting troops were free to sack the town when it fell. This meant that they could pillage, rape, and kill the now-defenseless townspeople.

Several rationales justified this unfettered brutality; one was terrorist in character. Knowledge that such a fate awaited those who resisted too adamantly could dishearten defenders and encourage garrisons and populations to capitulate. Unlike the frenzy of battle, sieges went on for days, weeks, or months, so the town's military commander and civil authorities could ponder the wisdom of fighting on. Obviously, the defenders' anxieties weighed in these decisions, and it was inevitable their attackers played upon such fears to attain their goals. Seen in this way, sacking of one town gave an army psychological leverage over other towns and fortresses. It was terrorism in the service of victory.

Ancient conquerors advertised their victories, and their barbarities. Assyrians erected particularly cruel monuments. Palace bas reliefs depicted torture, death, and slavery in store for those foolish enough to resist. Among the gruesome visions, the reliefs included captives impaled in agony on poles. The conquering Ashurnasirpal II (r. 883–829 BCE) boasted of what he did to those he captured after taking a besieged city: "Of some I cut off the feet and hands; of others I cut off the ears noses and lips; of the young men's ears I made a heap; of the old men's heads I built a tower. . . . The male children and the female children I burned in the flames."[4]

In the Old Testament, Deuteronomy provides a law of siege warfare that not only served the ancient Israelites, but also remained as a guide to the law of war as late as the seventeenth century. Traditionally ascribed to Moses, the form of Deuteronomy read today was probably set down in the seventh century BCE. Deuteronomy 20:10–14 details how to deal with an enemy city:

> [10] When you draw near to a city to fight against it, offer terms of peace to it.
>
> [11] And if it responds to you peaceably and it opens to you, then all the people who are found in it shall do forced labor for you and shall serve you.
>
> [12] But if it makes no peace with you, but makes war against you, then you shall besiege it.
>
> [13] And when the Lord your God gives it into your hand, you shall put all its males to the sword,
>
> [14] but the women and the little ones, the livestock, and everything else in the city, all its spoil, you shall take as plunder for yourselves. And you shall enjoy the spoil of your enemies, which the Lord your God has given you.

The attackers negotiate, undoubtedly informing the besieged of what happens to those who fail to surrender. Prowess would be proclaimed and fear instilled. Carrying out the prescribed actions against the defeated fulfilled the will of God and also intimidated future foes. Put in secular terms, this rule of siege warfare appears as a means by which to break the will of potential enemies, and was interpreted in this manner by jurists as late as the seventeenth century.

Later, although the Romans succeeded most effectively through incorporating former rivals and enemies as allies, they could be murderously ruthless, particularly in repressing rebellion. Such harshness both punished resistance and advertised the fate of those who resisted. During the First Jewish-Roman War (66–73 CE), also known as the Great Revolt, the Roman commander Titus besieged Jerusalem for seven months, breached the city walls, and sacked the city. The contemporary historian Josephus described the slaughter: "[The legionaries] ran everyone through whom they met with, and obstructed the very lanes with their bodies, and made the whole city run down with blood."[5] The Second Temple was destroyed and many of its treasures taken away, an act memorialized on the Arch of Titus in Rome. The Romans were bent on eliminating the rebels in Jerusalem and breaking the will behind the rebellion as a whole. Eventually the Romans would drive the Jews out of the Holy Land.

Popular imagination today associates medieval warfare with practices of chivalry; however, those outside the privileged community to which the aristocratic codes of chivalrous behavior applied were subject to horrendous abuses. When the English under Edward III took the city of Caen by storm in July 1346, they killed about half the population in a sacking that lasted five days. Shakespeare imagined the threat of violence to another city the English besieged during the Hundred Years' War: Harfleur, attacked by Henry V in 1415. The great author penned *Henry V* some 185 years after the fact, yet these kinds of threats remained just as alive in the late sixteenth century as they had been in the early fifteenth. In the play, Henry menaced the governor of Harfleur with the unimaginable catastrophe awaiting the town should it continue to resist:

> I will not leave the half-achieved Harfleur
> Till in her ashes she lie buried.
> The gates of mercy shall be all shut up,
> And the flesh'd soldier, rough and hard of heart,
> In liberty of bloody hand shall range
> With conscience wide as hell, mowing like grass
> Your fresh-fair virgins and your flowering infants. . . .
> What is't to me, when you yourselves are cause,
> If your pure maidens fall into the hand
> Of hot and forcing violation?[6]

The early modern period of European military history, roughly 1500–1789, was dominated by siege warfare, particularly in those areas in which fortresses lay thick on the ground, such as the Netherlands, northern Italy, and the eastern and northern borders of France. The fortifications were adapted to withstand gunpowder artillery, but the issue of how to deal with civilians caught within besieged towns and fortresses remained. The potential for unlimited violence against combatants and noncombatants was all too often realized before 1650.[7] The brutality and rapacity of attackers were in direct proportion to the resistance put up by defenders; if the latter fought off the besiegers until they had to storm the town in a costly infantry assault, the garrison and inhabitants could pay heavily for their resolution. In such cases, it was still believed legitimate to deny any quarter to the garrison and to sack the town, subjecting its population to "all the rigors of war," as contemporaries called the mayhem of a sacking.

Military and civil authorities even used biblical texts, such as Deuteronomy, to justify excesses. But there were more immediate reasons to allow troops to do their worst. In his 1540 work on international law, the Spanish philosopher Francisco de Vitoria listed three rationales for violent extremes against besieged towns, fortresses, and their residents. These included overall strategy, boosting soldiers' morale by letting them plunder, and, most relevant to us here, terrorizing other cities into surrendering, rather than resisting an attack.[8] The bloody sack of one city could be justified as a way of speeding the surrender of another. For example, the deadly sack of Magdeburg in 1631 that claimed the lives of 25,000 of its 30,000 inhabitants seems to have induced other towns to capitulate quickly.

The classic jurists of eighteenth-century limited war, such as Emer de Vattel, frowned on attacks on civilians and believed that the "civilized" people of Europe had gotten beyond sacking cities, but conceded that it was not expressly forbidden by military law. By the late seventeenth century, military practice had evolved to allow fortress commanders to surrender honorably after the enemy had broken down part of the fortress wall and the garrison had beaten off one assault. This shift in military civil and military culture spared the civilians from sack. Although there were instances when European cities were stormed and sacked by besieging armies, notably by the French at Bergen-op-Zoom in 1747 and by the English and Portuguese under the Duke of Wellington at Badajoz in 1812, these were cases of troops going berserk, not of a conscious policy.

Military terrorism in the ancient, medieval, and early modern European wars was not limited to the sack of cities, but these orgies of pillage and murder were the most striking examples, integral to the practice of warfare among Europeans for centuries.

THE CONQUEST OF ALGERIA, 1830–1847

European imperial wars of the nineteenth century witnessed violent excesses and military terrorism; nowhere was this truer than in the French subjugation of Algeria. When imperial warfare pitted Westerners against indigenous peoples, a fundamental cultural discord between the warring adversaries tended to strip warfare down to its most brutal nature. Differing concepts of identity and loyalty, legitimate violence, religious values, and interpersonal relationships created gulfs of understanding and the dismissal of the other party as unreasonable and, perhaps, as only partially human. Wayne Lee argues in *Barbarians and Brothers* that "war is defined by *both* violence *and* restraint, consciously and unconsciously, materially and mentally."[9] Conscious restraint by calculation is less a matter of capacity than of culture; it is not what one *can* do but what one *should* do. When adversaries harbor contrasting concepts of prescribed violence and restraint, they are likely to see the enemy's actions as moral outrages. The result is what I called in my own *Battle: A History of Combat and Culture* (2004) an "extreme reality" of war, in which reprisals drive violence to extremes.

The French had a long history with their Mediterranean neighbor, the Ottoman Empire's province of Algeria, which lay about 450 miles due south of Marseilles. In 1830 the French sent a large expedition to Algeria ostensibly to deal with an insult to the French counsel in Algiers but in fact to shore up the prestige of the weak Bourbon monarchy. Once the French occupied the area around Algiers they expanded their rule in stages until they established the modern borders of Algeria. Meanwhile, in 1832 Emir Abdelkader ibn Muhieddine, a leader noted for his holiness, began an armed guerrilla resistance based in western Algeria. This resistance continued, with some breaks, until 1847, when he was forced to surrender.

The French suppression of the insurgency became increasingly brutal, particularly after the arrival of Thomas Robert Bugeaud as military commander and governor-general in 1840. Bugeaud believed he held the key to defeating Abdelkader. Bugeaud advocated a scorched earth policy of *razzias*, or raids, meant to destroy settlements, crops, camps, and herds. Bugeaud defended his policy by arguing that this was not a European war, and that the only thing of value was "the agricultural interest spread over the whole surface of the country."[10] In an essay on Algeria, written in 1841, the famous Alexis de Tocqueville, perhaps not fully grasping the worst implications of *razzias*, characterized them as "unfortunate necessities": "If we do not burn harvests in Europe, it is because in general we wage war on governments and not on peoples.... We shall never destroy Abdelkader's power unless we make the position of the tribes who support him so intolerable that they abandon him. This is an obvious truth. We must conform to it or give up the game. For myself, I think that all means of desolating these tribes must be employed."[11]

Actual accounts of *razzias* stress their devastation, their character as military terrorism. One officer wrote in 1841 describing a "perfect" *razzia*: "Once the tribe's location is known, we each charge, dispersing in all directions. We reach the tents, whose inhabitants, awoken by the soldiers' approach, emerge pell-mell with their animals, wives, and children; all these people flee in all directions; gunshots ring out from all sides at these miserable, defenseless, surprised people; men, women, children are pursued, quickly surrounded and assemble by the soldiers who gather them up. The stampeding cattle, sheep, goats, and horses are soon rounded up.... Then we set fire to everything we can't carry away, while the beasts and people are taken to the convoy."[12]

Razzias not only destroyed homes, crops, and stole livestock, but also imposed a heavy toll of death. Fleeing the French exposed whole communities to extremes of heat and cold; in Algeria one could perish from sun or snow. In February 1843, Armand-Jacques Leroy de Saint-Arnaud, who would eventually rise to the rank of marshal, described to his brother the macabre result of a winter *razzia*: "I began my journey the next morning and had hardly gone a few hundred meters, what a spectacle, brother, and how war appears hideous to me! Heaps of bodies pressed one against the other and frozen to death during the night! It was the unfortunate population of the Beni-Naâseur that was before me, those whose villages I had burned and whom I had hunted."[13]

Some French opposed Bugeaud's tactics, but he declared to the

French Chamber of Deputies, equivalent to the U.S. House of Representatives: "If you want the ends, you must accept the means."[14] And the means could be atrocious, including displaying the heads of slain Algerians, rewards for each pair of ears sliced from the Algerian foe, and punishments for actually capturing prisoners rather than killing them.

The worst of these atrocities occurred in 1844 and 1845, when French soldiers asphyxiated large numbers of Algerian rebels in caves. This was done either by *enfumades*—the French for "to smoke" is *fumer*—building fires at the cave openings to "smoke out" those sheltered within; or by *emmurades*—the French for "wall" is *mur*—sealing, walling up the mouth of a cave, making it an air-tight tomb. The precedent for *enfumades* came in 1844, when a French detachment under Cavignac pursued a band of Sbéahs and found them holed up in a cave. When the French tried to negotiate, the officer sent to parlay was shot dead. The French troops then piled wood at the cave entrance. The next day a few survivors of the band surrendered, but the rest of the men, women, and children were dead.

The next year, Bugeaud recommended this tactic when he dispatched the paradoxically named Aimable Pélissier to deal with the Ouled Riah tribe in the Dahra mountains. When Pélissier caught up with about 800 of the Ouled Riah, they had retreated into the caverns of Ghar el Frachich, a traditional place of refuge for them. When they refused to surrender, Pélissier ordered fires set at the openings of the caverns. After stoking the fires for two days, the French snuffed out the flames and entered the caves. One soldier testified that he counted 760 dead and only sixty survivors, of whom forty soon died. Ten were released to tell their story to their tribes. A French Algerian paper defended the *enfumade*: "To ask that the army behave in a distant country as with civilized enemies [was] an act of the most complete unreason."[15]

Military tactics of terrorism "pacified" Algeria, allowing an influx of European colonists, but memories survived. A century after the surrender of Abdelkader, Algeria would errupt in an insurgency that would drive the French out of Algeria, as we shall see in Chapter 6.

NINETEENTH-CENTURY PROGRESS IN THE LAWS OF WAR: THE LIEBER CODE

For all its imperial sins, the nineteenth century also witnessed important advances in the law of war, none greater than General Orders 100, better known as the Lieber Code, issued by the United States while in the grips of the Civil War in April 1863. The author, Francis Lieber, was a German immigrant who became an authority on the law of war. As a general principle, Article 16 stipulates, "Military necessity does not admit of cruelty—that is, the infliction of suffering for the sake of suffering or for revenge, nor of maiming or wounding except in fight, nor of torture to extort confessions." The code was one of the first, if not *the* first, to expressly forbid the sacking of a city or fortress (Article 44). Article 22 exempts civilians from the worst of war: "The principle has been more and more acknowledged that the unarmed citizen is to be spared in person, property, and honor as much as the exigencies of war will admit." Articles 37, 44, and 47 declare the sanctity of the persons of women and order the death penalty for rape as a *military* crime.

And yet in 1864, General William Tecumseh Sherman led Union troops in a march to the sea from Atlanta to Savannah, Georgia, an operation explicitly designed to savage the property and well-being of Southern civilians. Certainly, this did not even approach the brutality of the *razzias*, but the civilian population would suffer. Sherman defended this: "I attach more importance to these deep incisions into the enemy's country, because this war differs from European wars in this particular. We are not only fighting armies, but a hostile people, and must make old and young, rich and poor, feel the hard hand of war, as well as their organized armies."[16] In fact, Sherman's ultimate goals were psychological: to undermine the confidence and the will of the South. Therefore, Sherman's march could be considered as military terrorism.

Southern opinion reviled Sherman as guilty of barbarous acts. But he could justify his acts by the high-minded Lieber Code. Notably, it allowed for the destruction and pillaging of civilian property in Article 15: "War is not carried on by arms alone. It is lawful to starve the hostile belligerent, armed or unarmed, so that it leads to the speedier subjection of the enemy." In December 1863, Sherman had famously stated, "War is cruelty. There is no use trying to reform it. The crueler it is, the sooner it will be over."[17] Surprisingly, the Lieber Code prefigured this logic in Article 29: "The more vigorously wars are pursued the better it is for humanity. Sharp wars are brief."

And Articles 27 and 28 of the Lieber Code explicitly authorize "retributions," acts of punishment by military forces against "barbarous outrage." In fact, retributions include collective punishments, attacks on groups or communities for acts committed by members of that group or community. Collective punishment would not be formally condemned as a war crime until after World War II.

WORLD WAR II

World War II, the deadliest conflict in history, ended the era of twentieth-century great power wars and ushered in the atomic age. Belligerents suffered enormous casualties. Germany, as defined by its 1937 borders, lost from 5.5 to 6.9 million, or as much as 10 percent of its population, and its great nemesis, the Soviet Union, paid a terrible price for victory, 20 to 25 million, or 14 percent of its population. Japan suffered 2.6 to 3.1 million deaths, or as much as 4.4 percent of its people, while the death toll among the Chinese reached somewhere between 10 and 20 million, or as much as 4 percent of total population. The United Kingdom suffered 451,000 killed, or nearly 1 percent of total population. Compared to these catastrophic losses, those of the United States, at 420,000 killed, of which only 12,000 were civilians, seem modest—0.32 percent—although not to the families of the killed and wounded. We will need to keep the astronomical casualties suffered in Europe and Asia in mind when we put the price of post-war radical terrorism into the scale of things.

In such an environment of apocalyptic warfare, military forces perpetrated acts of terrorism targeting the will of noncombatants with fear —a strategy of intimidation. Yet not all that was utterly inhumane can be categorized as terrorism. The Nazi "final solution" was an attempt not to terrorize European Jews but to exterminate them. (See the discussion of this on our website in the Supplements section.)

German Army Collective Punishments in World War II
Retaliations exacted by German occupation forces in response to the actions by local partisan attacks constitute clear examples of Nazi military terrorist tactics. These occurred throughout Nazi-occupied Europe, but the examples of Greece and France will suffice to make the point here.

Hitler's plans for the invasion of Russia in 1941 depended on securing his right flank in the Balkans. Fascist Italy was supposed to conquer Greece; however, Mussolini's invasion in October 1940 turned into a fiasco, with the Italian advance reeling back into Albania. The Germans rescued the Italians in April 1941, conquering mainland Greece and taking Crete as well in May. But many Greeks did not accept the occupation, and partisans rose to resist the German troops and their Italian and Bulgarian allies.

German forces responded by killing innocent Greeks and razing their villages in reprisal for the actions of partisans; Nazi violence fell into the category of collective punishment. The Germans believed such savagery would make the partisans less willing to act or turn the local population against the partisans. The attacks on villages and towns encompassed all of Greece and spanned the three years of occupation. The list includes Kalokastro and Mesovouno in 1941, Kommeno and Viannos in 1943, and Distomo and Kedros in 1944. For example, after discovering in August 1943 that a party of resistance fighters was based in Kommeno, the Germans swept into the village and indiscriminately shot down 317 men, women, and children; seventy-four of the victims were younger than ten years of age. This was a punishment of a particular population, but it was also a warning to all.

The French resistance, more discrete than the Greek, held off its most concentrated attacks until the D-Day landings neared. Then the Nazis, true to form, did their worse. On 10 June 1944, when informed that a German prisoner was being held at Oradour-sur-Vayres, a force of confused Waffen-SS Panzergrenadiers brought down hell on a different village with a similar name, Oradour-sur-Glane. The vengeful grenadiers killed a total of 190 men, 247 women, and 205 children. The men were rounded up, shot, and their bodies incinerated; women and children were locked in the church, which was then set afire, and those who tried to escape were gunned down. As a reprisal for actions of the French resistance, German SS troops also massacred 124 villagers, of whom forty-eight were children, at Maillé on 25 August 1944.

Allied Area Bombing of Germany
It is easy to convince modern readers about the vile and vicious nature of the Hitlerian regime and the atrocities committed by it and its collaborators in Europe. Yet the Allied bombing campaigns also caused catastrophic civilian casualties that may be considered as terrorism on a grand scale. While the aerial war against enemy cities was intended to

cripple the war-making capacities of Germany and Japan, it was also directed against the morale of enemy populations and the resolve of their governments. To the extent that this second motive shaped Allied strategic and tactical choices, attacks on civilian populations in area bombings, as at Dresden, challenge us to see them as terrorism, even though they were carried out by states fighting what we accept as a just war.

World War I added aerial bombing to war's repertoire of destruction. England was attacked by dirigibles as early as January 1915 and by German heavy bombers in 1917 and 1918. After the war, the international community attempted to establish agreements limiting the use of this new form of warfare. Delegates from Great Britain, France, Italy, Japan, the Netherlands, and the United States gathered at The Hague from December 1922 through February 1923. Their final draft was not ratified, but was nonetheless important.[18] Article 22 read: "Aerial bombardment for the purpose of terrorizing civilian population, of destroying or damaging private property not of military character, or of injuring non-combatants is prohibited." In 1938, another meeting in Amsterdam produced the Draft Convention for the Protection of Civilian Populations against New Engines of War.[19] It mirrored the provisions proposed at The Hague. Article 4 stated, "Aerial bombardment for the purpose of terrorizing the civilian population is expressly prohibited." The same year the League of Nations unanimously declared the principle that "the intentional bombing of civilian populations is illegal."[20]

However, if international law of war gave signs of moving in the direction of forbidding or limiting attacks on civilians, some interwar military theory stressed the value of breaking enemy morale precisely by bombing civilians. The most obvious advocate of this was Giulio Douhet. Historians debate how influential this Italian theorist, who died in 1930, actually was, but he certainly expressed a point of view that eventually had advocates in power. Civilians, he argued would break under the strain of bombing, which he saw as a direct attack on morale: "At this point I want to stress one aspect of the problem—namely, that the effect of such aerial offensives upon the morale may well have more influence upon the conduct of the war than their material effects. . . . A complete breakdown of the social structure cannot but take place in a country subjected to this kind of merciless pounding from the air. The time would soon come when, to put an end to horror and suffering, the people themselves, driven by the instinct of self-preservation, would rise up and demand an end to the war."[21]

Douhet did not see any moral roadblock hindering the bludgeoning of civilian populations: "In the face of instructive self-interest, of national survival, every convention loses its value, every humanitarian sentiment loses its weight. The only principle to be considered is the necessity of killing to avoid being killed."[22] In fact, he seems to echo Clausewitz here.

During World War II, the head of British Bomber Command, Air Marshal Arthur "Bomber" Harris, "adopted a Douhetian strategy for mass night raids on German cities to break civilian morale," in the terse judgment of historian Conrad C. Crane.[23] The Royal Air Force was less bloody-minded at the beginning of the war, but daylight precision bombing proved impossible. Bad weather, imprecise aiming technology, and the vulnerability of bombers to fighter aircraft drove the British to adopt area bombing by night. Bomber Harris was brutally frank about his intentions in October 1943: "The destruction of German cities, the killing of German workers, and the disruption of civilized community life throughout Germany [is the goal]. . . . It should be emphasized that the destruction of houses, public utilities, transport and lives; the creation of a refugee problem on an unprecedented scale; and the breakdown of morale both at home and at the battle fronts by fear of extended and intensified bombing are accepted and intended aims of our bombing policy. They are not by-products of attempts to hit factories."[24]

In addition to formal policy, a moral drift eroded scruples against harming the "innocent." Freeman Dyson, the distinguished physicist, testifies to the moral compromise, even corruption, brought about by the bombing campaign against Germany. During the war he served in operations research for Bomber Command in the Royal Air Force. He observed that no one "had any feeling of responsibility. None of us ever saw the people we killed. None of us particularly cared. . . . Since the beginning of the war I had retreated step by step from one moral position to another, until at the end I had no moral position at all."[25] In a sense, it can be argued that the Allied bombing of German cities was regarded by the British as reprisals for the German bombings of British population centers. But such logic could amount to a British version of collective punishment.

Americans were more reluctant to bomb civilians in Europe, preferring to strike targets of military value, such as railroad marshaling yards. U.S. Army Air Force generals such as Carl Spaatz (commander of U.S. Strategic and Tactical Air Forces, USSTAF, in Europe), James "Jimmy" Doolittle (commander of the Eighth Air Force), Ira Eaker (commander of Mediterranean Allied Air Forces), and Charles Cabell (director of plans for USSTAF) opposed raids meant to break German morale by attacking civilians. This was particularly clear in the debates over targeting late in the war. In August 1944, the British pushed for Operation Thunderclap, which entailed area bombing of Berlin. Cabell objected to the plan as one more of the typical British "baby killing schemes."[26] Eaker objected, "We should never allow the history of this war to convict us of throwing strategic bombing at the man in the street."[27] At this time, Doolittle voiced a more sophisticated critique of terror bombing: "Terror is induced by the unknown. The chance of terrorizing into submission, by merely an increased concentration of bombing, a people who have been subjected to intense bombing for four years is extremely remote."[28]

It is important to note that not all U.S. Army Air Forces generals were as reluctant to hit civilian targets. Reacting to criticism of the Dresden bombing, the commander of U.S. Army Air Forces, General "Hap" Arnold, snapped: "We must not get soft. War must be destructive, and to a certain extent inhuman and ruthless."[29] And the morality of area bombing of civilians seemed not to bother Curtis LeMay, who cut his teeth in Europe before taking over XXI Bomber Command in the Pacific in January 1945.

American Incineration of Japanese Cities during the Pacific War
In contrast to the Allied air offensive over Germany, the bombing of Japan was an entirely American enterprise and began late in the war; it did not get into full gear until early 1945, with long-range B-29 bombers of XXI Bomber Command flying from bases on the Mariana Islands. Daytime, high-altitude precision bombing with high-explosive bombs did not prove very effective. But under the new leadership of Curtis LeMay, the American bombers operating against Japan changed tactics to low-level attacks carried out during nighttime. Coming in low saved gas, since the planes did not have to climb to altitude. Moreover, the weak Japanese night defenses also meant that LeMay could strip his bombers of their machine guns, gunners, and ammunition. Weight saved in fuel

and guns could be invested in an increased load of the new M-69 bomb, a cluster of small 6.2-pound napalm-filled packages that dispersed to ignite a large area.

Japanese cities were exceptionally vulnerable to fire raids. Before the Pacific war began, in mid-November 1941, George C. Marshall warned the Japanese, "We'll fight mercilessly. Flying Fortresses will be dispatched immediately to set the paper cities of Japan on fire."[30] LeMay inaugurated his devastating new tactics in a fire raid on Tokyo during the night of 9–10 March 1945, when 334 B-29s dropped 2,000 tons of incendiaries on the city. Fire devastated nearly sixteen square miles of Tokyo and killed 83,000 men, women, and children. In addition to Tokyo, over sixty other Japanese cities were burned with conventional incendiaries. Late in life, Robert McNamara testified, "LeMay said, 'If we'd lost the war, we'd all have been prosecuted as war criminals.' And I think he's right. He, and I'd say I, were behaving as war criminals."[31]

The American decision to employ the atomic bomb to drive Japan out of the war needs to be put in the context of the firebombing campaign already unleashed on Japan months before. The scholarly debate over the military necessity and the moral acceptability of dropping atomic weapons on Hiroshima and Nagasaki continues, still freighted with charges of racism and accusations of Machiavellian intentions to incinerate 100,000 at Hiroshima and 45,000 at Nagasaki as a warning to the Soviets. There is no question that racism in the Pacific affected ideas of fighting to the death, the taking and treatment of prisoners, and the abuse of wounded and the dead. However, it did not alter strategy.

What matters here is the extent to which the bombing offensive and its last two blinding paroxysms of death can be considered as military terrorism. A strong case can be made that they were. The primary victims were civilians, and the Japanese had demonstrated that they had little effective defense against the fleets of B-29s. With the Japanese government making no real move to surrender even after the Americans had almost exhausted their target list in the firebombing campaign, something even more shockingly powerful would be required to break the Japanese will to continue the war. A meeting chaired by Secretary of War Henry Stimson assembled at the end of May to consider the potential unleashing of the atomic bomb on Japan and concluded that it should be used to "make a great psychological impression" on the Japanese.[32] In any case, whether one accepts the label of terrorist tactics or not, the dropping of the bomb accomplished the goal of bringing the war to an end quickly, spared the Americans the tremendous loss of life an invasion would have entailed, and, incidentally, cost the Japanese fewer fatalities than such an invasion would have inflicted on them.

THE LAW OF WAR SINCE 1945

Assaults on and crimes against civilian populations reached unprecedented magnitudes during World War II; of course, not all of these fit our criteria of military terrorism. Given the brutality of the war, it is not surprising that the victors turned their attention to redefining the laws of war in the years immediately following the war's end. It is important to recognize the strides taken then and in the decades that followed.

Laws of war go back to the prescriptions of conduct, called articles of war, issued by individual commanders to their troops as far back as the late Middle Ages. During the seventeenth and eighteenth centuries philosophers and jurists discussed the evolving culture of restraint in the conduct of war, but this restraint was more cultural than legal, as there was no international body to enforce higher standards. The Lieber Code, essentially articles of war for the entire Federal army, marked a major advance, but these were not international standards. In 1864 some major powers agreed to a convention at Geneva dealing with the treatment of wounded and sick prisoners of war. Hague Conventions of 1889 and 1907 sought to set standards for the conduct of war itself, although their focus was not noncombatants. After World War I, the League of Nations established the International Court of Justice, usually called the World Court. It was later maintained by the United Nations. However, this court adjudicated cases between countries in an attempt to avoid armed conflict; it did not judge offenses against the laws of war. Tribunals to judge war crimes were only created after World War II, and then they were not permanent but only focused on punishing German and Japanese political and military figures.

Soon after the end of the war, the international community addressed the humanitarian law of war. In reaction to the Nazi attempt to eradicate the European Jewish population, the United Nations General Assembly condemned genocide in 1946 and passed the Convention on the Prevention and Punishment of the Crime of Genocide in 1948. In August

1949, international delegates formally agreed to the Geneva Convention Relative to the Protection of Civilian Persons in Time of War, one of four agreements collectively referred to as the Geneva Conventions.[33] Since then the Geneva Conventions have been ratified by nearly 200 countries, including all members of the United Nations. Article 3 forbids a range of abuses, including torture. Article 27 requires that noncombatants "shall at all times be humanely treated, and shall be protected especially against all acts of violence or threats thereof." Rape and "indecent assault" of women were explicitly forbidden in the original conventions, but they were not yet officially defined as war crimes; that would happen later. Article 33 outlaws collective punishments against "protected persons," essentially enemy noncombatants: "No protected person may be punished for an offence he or she has not personally committed. Collective penalties and likewise all measures of intimidation or of terrorism are prohibited." Article 49 prohibits a state from carrying out "individual or mass forcible transfers [of populations], as well as deportations of protected persons from occupied territory," and also forbids a state to "transfer parts of its own civilian population into the territory it occupies." All of these articles will bear on our discussion of military terrorism after World War II.

Further addenda to the Geneva Conventions followed. An additional protocol of 1977 forbids recruiting or compelling children below age fifteen to fight in armed forces or groups. The horrors of ethnic cleansing finally commanded the attention of the United Nations in the early 1990s. The UN defined this crime as "a purposeful policy designed by one ethnic or religious group to remove by violent and terror-inspiring means the civilian population of another ethnic or religious group from certain geographic areas."[34] Only in June 2008 did the UN Security Council declare rape in war zones to be a war crime.

As to enforcing military law and punishing breaches of it, after the close of the war crimes trials immediately after World War II (1946–1949), enforcement was essentially self-enforcement. There was no international court established for such cases. The 1990s witnessed the creation of special tribunals to try those who committed ethnic cleansing and genocide in Bosnia and Rwanda; however, only in 2002 was the International Criminal Court (ICC) established to try war crimes across the globe. As the court came into existence, the United States and Israel refused to join it, because they did not want their citizens subject to trial and judgment by the ICC. As of mid-2017 the ICC had convicted only nine individuals of genocide, war crimes, and crimes against humanity.[35]

In regard to international laws of war concerning the treatment of noncombatants, several points need to be noted. First, considering the long history of warfare, internationally recognized laws of war are a relatively recent phenomenon; those that most specifically apply to terrorism are largely post–World War II. Of course, terrorist actions have by nature always been illegal under national laws and punishable by national legal systems. Second, international mechanisms to punish breaches of the international law of war, while admirable in conception, have been sporadic in the past and, even with the creation of the ICC, meager in results. The international law of war functions primarily as a body of principles, and its greatest force is in the desire of individual countries to act in ways that will earn them respect as worthy members of the international community. There is no question that radical terrorism operates in contradiction to national and international law. But it is also clear that uniformed militaries have as well, both in particular instances and by broad policy. In a notably thoughtful but pessimistic piece, George Packer, who has written on warfare in Iraq, Sierra Leone, and elsewhere, offered a stark conclusion in 2015: "The laws of war hardly ever matter to the combatants."[36]

Breaches of the Law of War: Americans in Vietnam, 1965–1973
Many charges were leveled against the conduct of American troops in Vietnam. There, Americans faced both South Vietnamese insurgents known as Viet Cong and regular forces from the North Vietnamese Army, the NVA. There is no question that war crimes were committed on both sides, including the torture of prisoners and massacres. Two mass killings by American troops at My Lai and Son Thang were acknowledged and prosecuted. The South Korean armed forces, allied with the Americans, have been accused of several instances of mass shootings and killings in 1966, including the killing of 1,200 at Tay Vinh in February and March.

There is no reason to believe that the mass execution at My Lai was terrorist in nature; rather it was a horrific war crime attributable to the soldiers who committed it. It is hard to prove that U.S. massacres were common enough to be policy. More systematic, but also hard to classify as terrorism, was the U.S. military practice of using heavy concentrations of firepower to deal with the enemy. In places where civilians were present, this could mean large numbers of civilian casualties. Keven Buckley, writing in *Newsweek* magazine in 1972, charged that the Americans killed at least 5,000 noncombatants, out of 11,000 total fatalities inflicted during Operation Speedy Express from December 1968 through May 1969.[37] These casualties may well have been the result of callous indifference to the lives of civilians among a population believed to be pro–Viet Cong and pro-NVA, but unless the deaths were intended to warn others against continued support of the guerrillas, they cannot be considered as military terrorism per se. But that does not mean that they were any less horrific.

Breaches of the Law of War: Rape as Terrorism in Bosnia-Herzegovina, 1992–1995

There is no doubt, however, about the terrorist nature of tactics employed by Serbian soldiers and militiamen who fought in the three-sided civil war between Serbs, Croats, and Bosnian Muslims, or Bosniaks, in Bosnia-Herzegovina from 1992 to 1995. From the point of view of our analysis, the only confusion is one of level: should the terror be "state" because it was ordered or condoned by state authorities, "military" because it was conducted by soldiers at war, or "social" because it was directed by one ethnic group against another? All apply, as the Serbs waged a war of ethnic cleansing to drive the Muslim population away from areas that the Serbs wanted to repopulate with their own people.

This campaign involved beatings, torture, and massacres, but it also brought back as conscious policy a weapon that had not been used as such in Europe since the seventeenth century: rape. Certainly, rape by individual soldiers has been a common, although not universal, feature of modern war; it has ranged from an expected and tolerated form of violence by soldiers to a forbidden disciplinary infraction punishable by death. Judged by the number of victims, the worst mass rape in European history occurred when the Soviet Army crossed into Germany and smashed German resistance in 1945. Two million German women were reputedly raped, and the Soviet military authorities did nothing to stop this sexual revenge. This was a crime of violence and humiliation, but it was not committed for grand policy reasons. However, since World War II, and particularly during the last few decades, rape has become a terrorist tactic committed as part of ethnic cleansing, and sometimes as a prelude to genocide, and it would seem in the case of the Islamic State to serve as an incentive to its own cadres, as discussed in Chapter 11.

The exploitation of rape as a weapon of war struck the Western conscience with compelling force during the Bosnian War. The estimates of women raped range from the European Community's figure of 20,000 to the 50,000 claimed by the Bosnian Federal Ministry of the Interior.[38] And these attacks on women were not the result of disciplinary infractions or simple lack of concern by a callous high command; they were policy! The UN commission of experts declared, "In Bosnia-Herzegovina and Croatia, rape has been an instrument of 'ethnic cleansing.'"[39] Alexandra Stiglmayer, who conducted extensive interviews in Bosnia, became convinced: "Besides brutal terror, deliberate murders, mass execution, internment camps, deportations, and torture, one of the means [Serbian forces] are employing is rape. Rapes spread fear and induce flight of refugees; rapes humiliate, demoralize, and destroy not only the victim but also her family and community; and rapes stifle any wish to return."[40]

At Foca, the Serbs established "rape camps," where troops would rape imprisoned Bosniak women multiple times. Part of the humiliation was to impregnate women with the children of the rapists. One witness, Hatiza, reports that when she was being taken to a camp, the men transporting her announced, "We're bringing you to a concentration camp. The next time we meet, you'll have one of our kids in your belly."[41] After a few weeks, a number of women from the camp, including Hatiza and her daughter, were deported to a place where they could cross over into Muslim-controlled territory.

It is true that Muslim women were not the only victims of rape during the war in Bosnia-Herzegovina. Serbian women suffered from the rage and retaliation of Muslim men, and Croat women were not immune; however, it was the Muslim women who were targeted in a vicious campaign of sexual assault used as terrorism to achieve ethnic cleansing. When the radical Islamist narrative claims that there is a Western war against Islam, one of the cases used to prove the point is Bosnia-Herzegovina.

The use of rape as a form of ethnic terrorism has not been limited to Bosnia-Herzegovina. During the Guatemalan Civil War (1960–1996), 100,000 women were raped in a war estimated to have cost 200,000 dead; the rapes were focused on the Mayan population seen by the government to have been pro-rebel. During the 1994 massacre of Tutsi in Rwanda, a tragedy that cost 800,000 lives, the horrors visited upon the victims included the rape of over 350,000 women. This was encouraged by the government; Pauline Nyiramashuko, the Rwandan minister for family welfare and the advancement of women, is reputed to have told militia, "Before you kill the women, you need to rape them."[42] She is reviled as "the Minister of Rape." She was tried by the International Criminal Tribunal for Rwanda and given a life sentence for genocide and incitement to rape. Rape is also one of the forms of assault used by the Janjuweed militia in Sudan to attack the non-Arab population.

The events in Bosnia-Herzegovina have been emphasized in this chapter because there, the rapes were specifically the work of military forces under formal command.

This discussion of terrorism by military forces at war should lead us to question again if radical terrorism can be clearly differentiated from war by claims that military forces at war obey the laws of war and terrorists do not.

Just as in the case of state-terrorizing for regime control, military tactics of terrorism go back to the beginnings of human society. It is true that judging whether acts of war were intended *either* for their physical destruction *or* for their psychological impact can lead to disagreements and debates. I would suggest that military operations can have multiple rationales, and that "either-or" controversies can be resolved by a simple "and." Dresden is a case in point, since whatever else the British hoped to accomplish, commanders like Bomber Harris regarded the area bombing of civilians as a legitimate means toward the end of undermining German morale.

The consideration of military tactics of terror can also be confounded by ambiguity of another kind. The resort to rape by Serbian soldiers in Bosnia as a method of achieving ethnic cleansing poses the question of whether acts of terror should be characterized by their perpetrators— soldiers, and thus military terrorism—or their strategic goals—ethnic cleansing, and thus social terrorism. It is far better to accept the ambiguity rather than to try to resolve it. Ambiguity is very much a part of reality. Nonetheless, there is little ambiguity in the suffering imposed on victims tortured by Assyrians in the seventh century BCE or asphyxiated by Allied bombs in 1945.

CHAPTER FOUR

White Knights

SOCIAL TERRORISM IN AMERICA, 1865–1965

FIGURE 4.1. Two works by the editorial cartoonist Thomas Nast juxtapose hope and despair. The first (*above*), from 1865, contrasts the evils of slavery with the blessings of emancipation. The second (*left*), from 1874, reveals the oppression and suffering that resulted from the return of White supremacy. Library of Congress.

ON 5 AUGUST 1868 John Lawson, a young, illiterate African-American farm laborer, appeared before the Military Committee of the Tennessee General Assembly to testify about his brush with death at the hands of the Ku Klux Klan (KKK). He reported that he had asked Pat Harvey, a White farmer for whom he worked, to give him some of his back pay so he could go to Nashville and buy clothing. Harvey became insulting and charged the eighteen-year-old with wanting to go to town in order to join the Black militia, a creation of the Reconstruction era. Lawson denied this, and Harvey reluctantly paid him seven dollars. Harvey then left, and Lawson remained at a cabin on the farmer's land until evening. But Harvey later returned with two Klansmen, who broke down the cabin door and threatened to kill Lawson. Lawson ran off into the night, pursued by the Klansmen; they fired four shots at him, but he escaped unhurt. Lawson continued his testimony: "The next morning I started for Nashville, and within about one quarter of a mile from where I started, I found a man hanging up by his feet. He had been skinned. His skin was hanging over his neck, and his privates had been cut off and put in his mouth. . . . I came directly to Nashville, and am here for safety."[1]

Lawson had been fortunate to escape alive. Not so the African-American who hung at the side of the road, where his mutilated body warned travelers of the fate that awaited those Blacks who did not accept their subservient place. This ghoulish execution exemplified the Klan's design to intimidate Blacks and enforce submission to their White betters.

In 1865 the renowned New York–based editorial cartoonist Thomas Nast published a vision of emancipation (Fig. 4.1, top). It juxtaposed subjugation under slavery, on the left, with the promise of liberation and well-being after emancipation on the right. In the center Nast portrayed a warm vision of African-American family life, with mother, father, and children around a stove. That was the dream. In 1874 he drafted another image of the KKK and the White League joining hands to oppress the "freed" Black population, describing it as "WORSE THAN SLAVERY" (Fig. 4.1, bottom). The mother and father shown now are grieving over their slain child, as a schoolhouse burns in the background. Nast illustrated the betrayal of hope.

Following the American Civil War, the population of the South, though defeated on the battlefield, strove to reassert itself in a campaign of White supremacist social terrorism against the African-American community. Groups committing social terrorism define themselves in terms of identities based on race, ethnicity, culture, religion, or history and stress the differences between themselves and those they target. As defined in Chapter 1, social terrorism is a strong versus weak form of terrorism, a tool of stronger, dominant social groups. This dominance is a matter of power, not necessarily of numbers. Thus, the social terrorism of South Africa before 1994 was that of a powerful White minority against a disenfranchised Black majority. This chapter explores the history of White supremacist terrorism by a majority White community in the United States South until the passage of civil rights legislation in the 1960s. Of course, White supremacist hate groups exist to this day. However, they are small and comparatively weak groups. When they turn to violence in pursuit of their goals, they are best considered as racist-inspired *radical terrorist* groups. They will be considered in Chapter 12.

The emphasis on White supremacy here is not meant to distract the reader from other uses of social terrorism in the United States. If time permitted we could also consider other serious indictments of ethnic cleansing by the White community against others, most notably Native Americans. The story is long and varied. In the single largest relocation of Native Americans, Andrew Jackson advocated the Indian Removal Act of 1830 and then, against a decision by the Supreme Court favoring the Indians, forced tens of thousands of Choctaws, Cherokees, Chickasaws, Creeks, and Seminoles to move west across the Mississippi—the "Trail of Tears" along which many thousands died between 1831 and 1838.

Before going further, we need to point out that campaigns of violence directed at social groups fall into three categories: 1) *subjugation*—meant to impose or maintain the dominance of one group and the inferiority and subservience of the other; 2) *ethnic cleansing*—meant to drive off the target group from a territory claimed or desired by those resorting to cleansing; and 3) *genocide*—meant to exterminate a group in whole or in part. Violent subjugation and ethnic cleansing by dominant groups qualify as social terrorism because they aim to control or drive off a target population through the agency of fear. The White supremacist terrorism covered in this chapter is fundamentally about subjugation.

Genocide, though an ultimate horror, is not terrorism because it aims not at psychological control but at physical extermination. The last chapter discussed a campaign of ethnic cleansing carried out by Serbian military and paramilitary forces in Bosnia. It has been my experience that when introducing the subject of terrorism to a classroom of college students, they often propose the Holocaust, or Shoah, carried out by the Nazi regime as an example of terrorism. In fact, efforts to drive off the German Jewish population before 1939 do qualify as ethnic cleansing, but not the Nazi attempts to eradicate European Jews after World War II began. In that effort, terror could have been counterproductive after 1939, since the Nazi machinery of death worked best on a docile but doomed population, not one terrorized into hysteria or resistance. (See the book website for a discussion of ethnic cleansing and genocide by the German Nazi regime, 1933–1945.)

THREE REASONS TO CENTER ON WHITE SUPREMACY
My choice to focus on White supremacist social terrorism from the Civil War to the 1960s drives from three goals. First and foremost, it allows me to make the point that the most enduring, vicious, and harmful terrorism in the history of the United States has been White supremacist terrorism against our African-American population. One of the themes of this volume is that we need a sense of proportion in dealing with terrorism. Facing the power and brutality of homegrown racist terrorism puts the threat of foreign-generated terrorism in some perspective. Terrorist campaigns rarely exceed a decade or two, but White supremacist terrorism endured for the entire century under discussion here. We will need to divide this era into three periods: 1) 1865–1915, which in turn can be broken down into Reconstruction and Jim Crow; 2) 1915–1944, the era of the very strong and popular second Klan; and 3) 1945–1965, the surge of anti–civil rights groups, governmental entities, and policies, and their unraveling in the 1960s.

Second, the fate of White supremacist terrorism generates an important comment on the critical issue of how terrorist campaigns end. The much-read work on this subject, Audrey Kurth Cronin's *How Terrorism Ends*, posits six ending scenarios:

1. capture or killing of the terrorist group's leader
2. entry of the group into legitimate political processes

3. achievement of the group's aims
4. implosion of the group's public support
5. defeat and elimination of the group by brute force
6. transition of the group from terrorism to other forms of violence[2]

Obviously, the fate of terrorist campaigns and groups concern us greatly, and we will reference Cronin's analysis in the discussions of radical terrorism to follow in succeeding chapters. More immediately, considering social terrorism here, we see different circumstances and results in the three periods defined above. During Reconstruction, White supremacy was initially spearheaded by small clandestine groups, including the Ku Klux Klan. It should be remembered that after the Civil War the federal government engaged in a military occupation of the South, lasting from 1865 to 1877. Rationales for this included forestalling any resurgence of the Confederacy and establishing the new freedom, civil rights, and equality that were promised to African-Americans in the Thirteenth, Fourteenth, and Fifteenth Amendments. Essentially this period of Reconstruction was intended to build a new society in the South. However, White supremacism survived and eventually triumphed, and its principles were enshrined by Jim Crow state governments. This represents Cronin's endings 2 and 3. The emergence of a new Klan in 1915, its phenomenal growth during the early and mid-1920s, and its subsequent precipitous decline can be described as ending 4, since the public corruption of the Klan caused it to lose its membership and following.

However, the defeat of the post–World War II klans is not accounted for in Cronin's list. They fell because of the work of a protest movement opposed to White supremacy, because a corps of exceptional leaders raised and led a multitude of high-minded opponents against bigotry. So, a study of White supremacy may argue for the addition of another "end" to Cronin's list—terrorism can be overcome by a social movement directed against it.

This leads me to my third reason for dealing with White supremacy in the United States here, and this rationale is entirely personal. In a book so full of victims and villains, I wanted to talk about heroes for a while, and those who overcame the resistance of the post–World War II Klan were heroes to me.

THE VICTORY OF WHITE SUPREMACY DURING RECONSTRUCTION, 1865–1877

Acts of social terror against African-Americans began as soon as African prisoners were sold to toil in the North American colonies in the seventeenth century. According to the 1860 census, there were four million slaves in the slaveholding states on the eve of the Civil War. At that time the free population in those states stood at about eight million. Since Black slaves were essential to the economy, White supremacist terrorism was directed at subjugating, controlling, and monitoring Blacks. The Declaration of Independence may have claimed "that all men are created equal, that they are endowed by their Creator with certain unalienable Rights"; however, Black slaves were not considered as full human beings, as men. They were something less, making their White contemporaries something more. White supremacy told Whites, however poor they might be, that they were still above Blacks.

History books report that Robert E. Lee surrendered to Ulysses S. Grant at Appomattox in April 1865, and that the Union won the Civil War. But victory and defeat are not so easily judged. To the extent that forcing the Confederate states back into the Union and ending chattel slavery constituted Northern war aims, the armies in blue triumphed. But to the extent that the armies in gray fought to maintain a Southern society based on extreme concepts of White supremacy, the South was ultimately not defeated. Black slavery had been a social and economic reflection of a more basic belief in the innate inferiority of Blacks to Whites, and it is disturbing how quickly and how successfully southern Whites reasserted the principles of their dominance.

Social terrorism served as the primary weapon wielded to assert White dominance in the South. This terrorism burned hottest during Reconstruction, when its most obvious manifestation was the Ku Klux Klan, which emerged during the winter of 1865–1866. But the garishly clad Klansmen were only the visible flames of an indignant fervor, and suppressing the Klan through the 1871 federal anti-Klan legislation only served to redirect the fire, posing new dangers. After Reconstruction ended in 1877, the principles of White supremacy gained legitimacy in local regulations and state laws.

Deadly Urban Race Riots in 1866

It did not take long for armed resistance to emerge from behind the fragile facade of peace. Deadly turmoil struck Memphis during the first three days of May 1866, barely a year after Appomattox. This riot marshaled crowds of Whites, a great many of them Confederate veterans, against Blacks, of whom a substantial number were recently discharged Union soldiers. Forty-six Blacks died before the rioting subsided; while the victims were usually men, Black women and children were also targeted. The mob also burned ninety-one houses, four churches, and twelve schoolhouses. The *Chicago Tribune* called it "The Memphis Massacre."[3] Two Whites also perished, but they were the victims of White "friendly fire."

Tennessee suffered from particular turmoil. It had split during the Civil War, sending regiments to both the Confederate and the Union armies. Shortly after the riot, the Radical Republican governor, William Gannaway "Parson" Brownlow, forced through a law to enfranchise Blacks while denying the vote to those who had worked and fought for the Confederacy. The Memphis *Daily Avalanche* virulently condemned denying the vote to Confederates, finding it horrendous to "give a greasy, filthy, stinking negro the right to crowd them from the polls, to exercise those rights of franchise which belong not to Indians and negroes, but to White men."[4]

For all its deadly fury, the turmoil in Memphis was hardly an isolated affair. Another bloody riot broke out in New Orleans two months later. This violence directly resulted from demands to enfranchise Blacks and to overturn the enactments of the conservative Democratic legislature. On 30 July thirty-four African-Americans and four Whites died, and an additional 119 Blacks were injured, along with twenty-seven Whites. In his report to Grant on 2 August, General Philip Sheridan characterized what happened: "It was no riot. It was an absolute massacre by the police."[5]

The Ku Klux Klan

The Klan did not encompass all the White supremacist brutality of the time, but it was the most notorious organization dedicated to such racial violence. A band of six well-educated but bored Confederate veterans created the Klan as a kind of social amusement during the winter of 1865–1866 in Pulaski, Tennessee. But what began as an outlandish, almost buffoonish, diversion soon turned combative and then vicious. It grew first in Tennessee, but chapters, or klaverns, spread throughout the South. The different local organizations shared certain practices, such as secret membership and masked attire, but the Klan was loosely organized and never rigidly hierarchical. The Tennessee Klan's *Prescript* of 1868 was full of high-sounding ideals, declaring that "this is an institution of Chivalry, Humanity, Mercy, and Patriotism; embodying in its genius and its principles all that is chivalric in conduct, noble in sentiment, generous in manhood, and patriotic in purpose."[6] But practice sank to a much lower level than principle.

Klan membership was overwhelmingly composed of Confederate veterans, and it is not surprising that they looked to Rebel officers, particularly generals, for leadership. The ruthless, but highly successful, cavalry commander Nathan Bedford Forrest, played a role in the Klan. One oft-repeated story tells that when he was informed of the Klan, Forrest replied, "That's a good thing; that's a damn good thing. We can use it to keep the niggers in their place."[7] Considering Forrest's history as a slave dealer and his record at the massacre of Black Union troops at Fort Pillow in April 1864, these words were very much in character. Reputedly, in 1867, Forrest became the national head of the Klan, its Grand Wizard, but national office was more symbolic than effective.

Violence increased to such a level that that the Military Committee of the Reconstruction-era Tennessee General Assembly held hearings on the subject in August 1868. Certain brutal themes repeat themselves in the testimony: special violence directed against Black veterans, assaults on teachers and pastors devoted to raising the knowledge and spirits of Blacks, and the marshaling of threats, beatings, and killings to maintain power by destroying Black organizations and driving Blacks away from the polls.

Lewis Powell gave the Military Committee an account of the murder of his wife by the Klan's self-proclaimed champions of chivalry. Six of these men entered his house asking for food, and Powell's wife started to cook for them. But "they asked her her name, being told, they said to her: 'You are the head of the damned Union League,' and at once shot two balls through her. She died instantly."[8] He went on to explain how the Klan intended to ensure their political control: "The rebels say that on the day of the election they intend to buckle on their revolvers and go to the polls, and when the negro comes to vote, they intend to tell him to stand back, and if he does not do this they will shoot him at once."

Klan violence rose to such a level that even Grand Wizard Forrest found it too extreme. In General Order No. 1, issued on 20 October 1869, he charged: "The Order of the K.K.K. is in some localities being perverted from its original honorable and patriotic purposes" and has become "injurious instead of subservient to the public peace and public safety."[9] Yet Forrest's direct assault on Klan practice came down to little more than calling for the elimination of masks and robes, thus making membership public, and forbidding the kind of ostentatious violence that had become standard fare for the Klan.

Given the patchwork of local groups that was the Klan, Forrest's order had an uneven effect. Accounts of Klan violence after Forrest's order fill the thirteen volumes of testimony given before the U.S. Congress's Joint Select Committee to Inquire into the Condition of Affairs in the Late Insurrectionary States. A witness from Georgia, George Burnett, appeared before the committee on 11 July 1871 and gave exemplary testimony. Asked about the frequency of the killings of Blacks, Burnett replied: "These things occur frequently—so frequently that really I never pay much attention to them."[10]

The increasingly militant excesses of the night riders led Congress to answer requests from President Grant by passing the Enforcement Act of 1871. Enacted on 20 April, its official title was "An Act to Enforce the Provisions of the Fourteenth Amendment to the Constitution of the United States, and for Other Purposes," but it was often called simply the Enforcement Act, or the Ku Klux Klan Act of 1871. The bill forbade the Klan's particular actions and customs, outlawing the practice of going "in disguise upon the public highway or upon the premises of another for the purpose, either directly or indirectly, of depriving any person or any class of persons of the equal protection of the laws."[11] It criminalized interfering with African-Americans' right to vote. The language of the Ku Klux Klan Act is the language of war, for the violence of the Klan amounted to a kind of renewed civil war in the South. The act even suspended habeas corpus for those arrested for infractions defined by the act and put federal forces and federal courts in charge of enforcement.

The Battle of Colfax and the Rise of White Supremacist Paramilitaries
The 1871 legislation led to the dismemberment of the Klan over the following months. Yet White supremacist violence did not end, it simply emerged out from under the sheet and into the light of day, as new, overtly racist paramilitary organizations took the lead. In Louisiana, the paramilitaries would be known as the White Leagues; in Mississippi and the Carolinas they were the Red Shirts, while other groups elsewhere styled themselves as rifle clubs.

A pivotal event in this transformation took place in Louisiana in late March and April 1873: the Battle of Colfax, also reviled as the Massacre of Colfax.[12] On one side of this fight, units of Black militia, a creation of the Republican regimes that ran Southern states during Reconstruction, defended the Colfax courthouse. These militiamen were primarily composed of fellow veterans of the Union army. On the other side, White paramilitaries made up of Confederate veterans attacked. The issue at stake was who would rule in Grant Parish, the seat of which was Colfax. The disputed gubernatorial election in 1872 led to two rivals claiming victory. In March the Republican-appointed officials broke into the courthouse and claimed it as theirs. In early April, angry Whites moved to unseat the Republicans, and in the process, they murdered a Black man. In response, a company of Black militia mustered to defend the Black community and the Republican appointees. This move was countered by a White paramilitary force that outnumbered the Black militia and had the advantage of a small cannon. The dispute finally led to open battle on 13 April. The Blacks held for nearly two hours and then broke; many died in the fighting and at least thirty-seven surrendered. That night the victors executed their prisoners with shots to the head. Given the military character of the fight at Colfax, it might be considered military terrorism, but it was part of the pattern of social terrorism as well.

The Battle of Colfax served as a template for the creation of paramilitary White Leagues in Louisiana and other overt paramilitaries elsewhere across the South. By August 1874, 14,000 men had joined the White Leagues established in nearly half the parishes of Louisiana.

If White paramilitaries took on the work of the Klan in the countryside, in New Orleans they became prime players in political struggles. Organized, openly marshaled companies of the White Leagues, totaling

3,500 men, fought in the streets of the capital on 14 September 1874. They defeated an equal number of state forces, including Black militia units, in a furious but brief open battle that left thirty-eight dead and seventy-nine wounded. The White Leagues celebrated victory by installing their candidate for governor. But this victory turned to defeat in a matter of days, as Grant dispatched federal troops that reinstated the Republican governor.

Still, the White League in New Orleans achieved its victory in 1877. The elections of 1876 were contested in Louisiana and nationally. Both the Republican candidate for governor in Louisiana, Stephen Packard, and his Democratic opponent, Francis Nicholls, claimed to have won. But in January 1877, Nicholls employed 3,000 White Leaguers to force a bloodless coup against Packard, whose supporters continued to hold only the statehouse itself. Nicholls further gained from the national dispute as to who would succeed Grant in the White House. In order to secure his victory, the Republican Rutherford B. Hayes agreed to end Reconstruction, including the occupation of the South by federal troops. When Hayes ordered federal soldiers to stay in their barracks in New Orleans on 24 April 1877, Nicholls sent the White League paramilitaries into the statehouse and effectively seized the entire government.

By 1877 the Fourteenth Amendment (ratified 1868), guaranteeing full citizenship to Blacks, and the Fifteenth Amendment (ratified 1870), assuring them the vote, had already been greatly compromised in the South, although pushing them completely aside would take a bit more time. Still, the decisive battles had been won and White supremacy restored.

THE WORLD OF JIM CROW

During the forty years after Reconstruction, the culture of White supremacy was formalized into a racist system enshrined in law, maintained by state institutions, and buttressed by popular violence against Blacks. This did not happen overnight. Even as post-Reconstruction laws eroded the Black franchise, Blacks continued to vote and hold office after 1877. The U.S. Congress helped to preserve Black electoral participation by refusing to seat representatives whose elections were deemed to have been won by fraud. However, a generation of political maneuvering, gerrymandering, and intimidation reduced Blacks' ability to determine elections.

The 1890s and the first years of the twentieth century brought the triumph of Jim Crow laws throughout the South. (The label "Jim Crow" derived from a demeaning minstrel-show portrayal of Blacks popularized before the Civil War.) Jim Crow laws mandated segregation and denied Blacks the right to vote. Racial segregation in public spaces, accommodations, and schools was a self-fulfilling prophecy; it created, perpetuated, and demonstrated inequality. Jim Crow laws instituted penalties for not conforming to segregation and thus added the force of arrest and punishment to the principle of White supremacy. And in restricting voter registration, laws also excluded Blacks from juries, making Blacks subject to White men's judgment.

Old Confederate states amended their constitutions or adopted new ones that effectively excluded Blacks from the polls through the institution of poll taxes, literacy tests, or other barriers. Louisiana had 130,334 Black voters in 1896, about the same number as Whites. Then in 1898 it adopted its new basic law, about which Governor Murphy Foster immediately boasted, "The White supremacy for which we have so long struggled . . . is now crystallized into the constitution."[13] By 1900 the number of registered Black voters had fallen to 5,320. On the second day of 1901, the president of the Alabama convention charged with drafting a new constitution rose to define the task at hand: "And what is it that we want to do? Why, it is within the limits imposed by the Federal Constitution, to establish White supremacy in this State."[14] Before adopting its revised constitution, Alabama counted 181,471 Blacks registered to vote, but that total fell to only 3,000 with the new regime.

Even with considerable vote fraud and intimidation, the approval of Jim Crow constitutions and laws was not always easy. North Carolina's new constitution received only 58.6 percent of the vote in 1900, even with Blacks almost entirely excluded from the polls. Historians have established that Jim Crow voter restrictions hurt not only Blacks, but poor Whites as well, and that the system can be interpreted as a mechanism by which a Southern aristocracy exerted its control and safeguarded its power.

The victory of White supremacy in Alabama was challenged before the U.S. Supreme Court in a landmark case, *Giles v. Harris*, in 1903. Jackson Giles, a literate Black who had voted from 1871 to 1901, challenged his and other Blacks' exclusion from the roles of voters. The case reached the Supreme Court, but it supported a lower court decision that ruled against Giles. Justice Oliver Wendell Holmes wrote what seems an unusually tortured majority opinion. He recognized that the issue at stake was a "general scheme to disenfranchise" Blacks. However, he shied away from tackling this issue head on and decided that if Giles was correct, the only effective course would be for the court to do much more than Giles was asking. The Court was unwilling to undertake such an effort.

Soon after the *Giles v. Harris* decision, the House Committee on Elections refused to unseat a representative from South Carolina, who, it was charged, only won because Blacks were excluded from voting. Thus, the Elections Committee reversed thirty years of taking seriously the complaints of Blacks excluded from voting.

LYNCHING

Lynchings of Blacks stand out as the most overt manifestation of social terrorism directed at the African-American community in the century after Reconstruction. Such killings demonstrated the power of White mobs to arrest, judge, and execute those Blacks they considered to be offenders, with no need for the intervention of the state. A number of attempts have been made to tally the grim cost of lynching. Estimates almost certainly fall short of the real total of victims, since much data derives from newspaper accounts, and lynchings could take place without being registered in public media. In any case, this discussion will accept the widely available Tuskegee Institute tabulation of lynchings.

The Tuskegee study defined conditions that constituted lynching: "There must be legal evidence that a person was killed. That person must have met death illegally. A group of three or more persons must have participated in the killing. The group must have acted under the pretext of service to justice, race or tradition."[15] Although the popular imagination of lynching involved hanging, the Tuskegee definition could include deaths by beating, shooting, or other means. Most commonly the perpetrators were a crowd in which some committed the act and still more witnessed the results of this public performance.

The study covers the eighty-seven years between 1882 and 1968, during which, by its count, 3,445 Blacks were lynched. Some Blacks were lynched in other states, but fully 94 percent of those lynched died in the old Confederate states plus Kentucky and Missouri. Not coincidently, by far the heaviest frequency of lynchings occurred from 1889 to 1901, when 1,340 were killed during the era that forged the chains of the Jim Crow system. The toll of lynchings gives us one consistent barometer of anti-Black racial violence during the late nineteenth and twentieth centuries.

Lynchings, and the threat of them, constituted terrorism, but an important principle needs to be noted. Many experts argue that radical terrorism is by definition the action of a sub-state group, while others have accepted that terrorism can be the work of self-radicalized individuals. Typically, a lynch mob was neither. During the 1890s, when lynching was at its peak, neither the Ku Klux Klan nor other similar organized groups existed. Rather, lynch mobs contained a number of people acting in concert, but without belonging to a recognized organization; they were neither a sub-state group nor simply self-radicalized individuals. Lynch mobs were a collection of likeminded people acting according to the White community's cultural standard of appropriate violence. The most shocking photos of lynchings show children allowed or, worse, brought to see victims hanging from a tree, as if to demonstrate the propriety of such murder.

It is particularly revealing that, according to the meticulous research by E. M. Beck and Stewart E. Tolnay, the reported rationale for a third of lynchings included claimed sexual assault or other violations of sexual norms.[16] The fear that "Black fiends" raped White women haunted the Southern imagination. This speaks to the racist stereotype and social fear of Black male sexuality, and to the Whites' belief that they must contain Black lust.

After the peak period 1889–1901, when the annual average number of lynchings in the Tuskegee study stood at 113, the tally of lynchings steadily declined, although it was still a tragic toll. And even as it subsided, the specter of lynching continued to haunt the United States.

Contemplating a photo of the widely publicized lynching of two Black men, Thomas Shipp and Abram Smith, in Marion, Indiana, on 7 August 1930, New York teacher Abel Meeropol penned a poem, "Bitter Fruit," in 1937. Shipp and Smith had been arrested for robbing and killing a White man and raping his girlfriend. A mob broke into the jail, beat, and hanged the two in the last recorded lynching of Blacks in the

North. This poem was then set to music as the song "Strange Fruit" and recorded by Billie Holiday in 1939. This mournful dirge had only three verses, the first of which despaired of "strange fruit"—lynched Blacks—hanging from Southern poplar trees.[17] As disturbing as it was, Holiday's rendition sold a million copies and became her signature performance.

"Strange Fruit" reminded everyone of the terrorism, but it was also witness to growing concern over and condemnation of racial murder. There were repeated efforts to pass anti-lynching legislation in the American Congress, nearly 200 attempts by one tally.[18] The best-known were the Dyer Anti-Lynching Bill, first proposed in 1918, and the Castigan-Wagner Bill, put forward in 1934. Both had support in the House but failed in the Senate.

The success of White supremacist terrorism during Reconstruction fits Cronin's third scenario, "achievement of the group's aims." This in turn was further solidified by the supremacists' takeover of state governments before and, particularly, during the Jim Crow era—Cronin's second scenario, "entry of the group into legitimate political processes." The rise and fall of a new Ku Klux Klan followed a very different pattern.

REVIVAL: THE SECOND KLAN, 1915–1944

After being in abeyance for over forty years, the Ku Klux Klan reemerged in a new form in 1915. This second Klan claimed a membership in the millions across the United States during the 1920s under the banner of "100 percent Americanism." This new avatar of intolerance varied from state to state, but it was above all a political, social, and religious movement of White Protestant Americans. The final decades of the nineteenth century and the early decades of the twentieth intensified nativist sentiment—a perception by those native-born Americans of northern European and Protestant descent that "their" America was threatened by the immigration of eastern and southern Europeans, Jews, and Catholics. The new Klan directed its enmity against all these, while still demeaning and attacking African-Americans. So extensive was its membership that the new Klan put wealth and political power in the hands of its leadership, and this opened the door to corruption.

The second Klan, unlike the first was and the third would be, was not clandestine, but boldly open. In a sense it was a creation of the dark side of popular culture. Fittingly, while the social and racial antagonism that fueled the resurgence of the Klan was piled high and dangerously flammable, the spark that set it alight was surprisingly superficial: D. W. Griffith's movie *The Birth of a Nation*, released in February 1915. Technically, it ranks as a cinematic masterstroke, but socially it must be condemned as virulent.

Griffith based his plot on the Thomas Dixon novel *The Clansman* (1905), a racist work that includes the line: "For a thick-lipped, flat nosed, spindle-shanked Negro, exuding his nauseating animal odor, to shout in derision over the hearth and homes of White men and women is an atrocity too monstrous for belief."[19] The film portrayed a chivalrous Ku Klux Klan saving Whites in the South from the evils of Reconstruction and its Black henchmen. Its plot deals in stereotypes of ignorant and violent Blacks, driven by the desire for sexual dominance over White women. In the climactic scenes, a cavalcade of Klansmen ride to the rescue of a town whose White residents are under assault by "crazed negroes," including Black militiamen in Union uniforms.[20] Following the victory, the Blacks are disarmed and, at the next election, dissuaded at gunpoint from voting. "Virtue" triumphed. The novel's portrayal of the Klan established what would become Klan ritual, including the white robes and the burning cross. The latter was not part of the first Klan's ceremony, but a creation of Dixon's imagination.

Later in 1915, movie drama gave way to real-life tragedy with the lynching of Leo Frank, a Jewish factory manager in Marietta, Georgia, on 17 August. In 1913, Frank had been accused of murdering Mary Phagan, a thirteen-year-old employee at Frank's pencil factory. Frank was arrested, tried, and condemned to death in a flawed trial, as crowds outside the courthouse chanted, "Kill the Jew!" The governor of Georgia commuted the sentence to life imprisonment on 21 June 1915, because he thought the evidence had been badly mishandled. This infuriated a group that included prominent citizens. They organized an elaborate conspiracy to seize Frank from prison and hang him. The name they chose for themselves, "The Knights of Mary Phagan," was reminiscent of the Reconstruction-era Knights of the White Camelia. They carried out their plan on 16–17 August. The trial and lynching of Leo Frank shook the Jewish community in the United States. In response to Frank's conviction, the Anti-Defamation League was formed in Chicago with a mission to combat anti-Semitism.

The second Klan was the creation of William Joseph Simmons of Alabama, a failed Methodist preacher inspired by the Griffith film. While convalescing after being struck by an auto in 1915, he dreamed of resurrecting the Klan, but delayed action until the lynching of Leo Frank. The Knights of Mary Phagan celebrated their triumph on 16 October 1915 by gathering on Stone Mountain near Atlanta to burn a massive cross. Simmons recruited members of the Knights, sanctified his venture by the presence of two aged veterans of the original Klan, and repeated the climb to the summit of Stone Mountain on the night of Thanksgiving 1915. The group was attired like the Klansmen in the film and took their oath to the new organization from the grandson of Nathan Bedford Forrest. Once again, a cross was set ablaze in a ceremony that the *Atlanta Constitution* described as "impressive" and "most interesting."[21]

After a slow start, the second Klan boomed, demonstrating the wide appeal of racist fantasy and hatred. In 1920, Simmons contracted with the Southern Publicity Association, led by Edward Young Clarke and Mary Elizabeth Tyler, to propagate the new Klan as a money-making scheme that rewarded those who brought in new paying members in what had the marks of a pyramid scheme. Local chapters pursued their own programs. During the first fifteen months of the agreement with Clarke and Tyler, Simmons received $170,000 in commissions, a huge sum for the day. In a letter publicized by the *New York World* in an exposé of September 1921, a Klan recruiter, a Kleagle, resigned his position, condemning the Klan as "conceived in avarice, sired in ignorance, and damned in greed."[22]

Such rewards of power and money attracted a more ambitious leadership, including Hiram Wesley Evans, executive of the Texas Klan, and David Curtiss (D. C.) Stephenson, the leader of the Indiana Klan, largest of the state organizations. In 1922 Evans and Stephenson carried off a coup at the national level. Simmons was kicked upstairs into the symbolic position of Emperor, and Evans replaced him as the real head of the Klan, Imperial Wizard, a position he retained until 1939. The new leadership canceled the contract with Clarke and Tyler. Evans published a pamphlet, *Ideals of the Ku Klux Klan*, explaining the Klan's essence and program: "1. This is a White man's organization, exalting the Caucasian Race and teaching the doctrine of White Supremacy..., 2. This is a Gentile organization..., 3. It is an American organization, and we do restrict membership to native-born American citizens . . . , 4. It is a Protestant organization . . . our forefathers founded this as a Protestant country and . . . it is our purpose to re-establish and maintain it as such."[23] Evan's and the Klan's public visibility became so great that his picture appeared on the cover of *Time* magazine on 23 June 1924.[24]

However, scandal soon embroiled the second Klan, and it would never recover. The power-oriented D. C. Stephenson, head of the Klan in Indiana, split off from the national organization in 1923 and enjoyed wealth and influence within the state, even being close to the new governor, Edward L. Jackson, elected with Klan support in 1924. Although the Klan touted itself as a moral beacon, a staunch proponent of prohibition, and a defender of White womanhood, Stephenson was a hard-drinking womanizer with few scruples. On 27 March 1924 he kidnapped and brutally raped Madge Oberholtzer, a young woman he had lured to his mansion with the offer of a job. She would die from poison she took to escape Stephenson. Stephenson was arrested, tried, and finally, on November 1925, convicted of second degree murder and sentenced to life imprisonment.

While this national scandal was unfolding, Evans staged a mammoth Klan parade in Washington, D.C., on 8 August 1925. It was an impressive gathering, with 30,000–45,000 parading up Pennsylvania Avenue in oppressive heat. Evans could not have known, but this was the apogee of the Klan; membership and dues began dropping in 1926. Evans tried to shore up Klan support by another great Washington march on 13 September 1926, but it drew only half as many participants as had marched in 1925.

The moral decay of the Klan became more and more apparent. Since Stephenson believed that the governor and the mayor of Indianapolis owed their elections to him, he expected his sentence would be commuted. However, the governor refused, and Stephenson exacted his revenge by releasing a list of politicians who were or had been on the Klan payroll. This precipitated an investigation of the Klan and politics in Indiana that further discredited the Indiana Klan and shook confidence in the national organization. Concurrently, a lesser but still embarrassing scandal struck the Klan in Colorado, where the organization was also a great political force. The mayor of Denver, Benjamin F. Stapleton, was elected with Klan support in 1923, as was the governor, Clarence F. Morley. The head of the Colorado Klan, John Galen Locke, seemed unassailable, but in 1926 Mayor Stapleton denounced the Klan and its oppressive power. National membership in the Klan, which had reached four million in 1924, plummeted to 30,000 by 1930. The *Washington Post* dismissed the Klan: "Once the world's most high powered 'racket,' today a crumbling shell."[25] The second Klan sputtered on through the 1930s and into the 1940s, but was officially disbanded in 1944, when an IRS suit for the payment of back taxes caused the final collapse of the national organization.

How terrorist was the second Klan? There is no question that it spewed racist and nativist rhetoric that condemned Blacks, Jews, Catholics, and those immigrants that Klan members regarded as dangerous. Certainly, such talk reinforced and intensified prejudices. Moreover, it is also true that in some areas, particularly the South, the new Klan carried out an agenda, from tarring and feathering to torture, mutilation, and murder, meant to intimidate its racial enemies.

Yet according to the Tuskegee Institute database on Black lynchings, racial violence declined. The average annual toll of these murders stood at 62 during the period 1902–1915, the years immediately preceding the rise of the second Klan. The deadly tally fell dramatically during the 1920s, from an average of 54 in 1920–1922 to 17 in 1923–1929. In fact, Evans explicitly credited the Klan with the *decline* in lynchings, as bizarre as that might seem. The number of lynchings continued to fall during the 1930s to an average of 12, with the years 1937, 1938, and 1939 witnessing only 8, 6, and 2, respectively.

The zenith of the second Klan lasted only a few years during the 1920s, blustering but brief. The lurid history of the second KKK is more important for exposing the prevalence of racism and nativism in American culture than for what it did. It preserved the Jim Crow society of the South, but the Klan was not militant in extending it; the status quo was already based on White supremacy. The failure of the second Klan fits Cronin's fourth scenario, "implosion of the group's public support." The corruption of its leadership, most notably D. C. Stephenson, brought it down by revealing its hypocrisy. As it was, the second Klan fought no major battles, as did the first Klan in Reconstruction and the third in opposing the civil rights movement after World War II.

WHITE SUPREMACISTS AND THE THIRD KLAN, 1945–1965

The disappearance of the national organization of the second Ku Klux Klan did not mean there were no Klansmen left. Some local klaverns held on, and a new incarnation of the Klan emerged after World War II. It would direct its violence above all at the burgeoning civil rights movement. The third Klan shared much with the first: it was clandestine, decentralized, and extremely violent, and it focused on some of the old causes, including restricting the enfranchisement of Black voters in the South. Its Klansmen were more radical in their views than the second Klan, in part because the more "respectable" White supremacists had the alternative of joining the White Citizens' Council. This Council, created in 1954, quickly increased its open membership to 60,000 by 1955, and the next year it changed its formal title to the Council of Conservative Citizens. The more palatable Council used economic, political, and social pressure rather than cruder terrorist methods and was more likely to defend its actions in the name of states' rights than of racial superiority. The attraction of the Council left the Klan in the hands of those quite willing to appeal to a strategy of brutal intimidation.

Only two weeks after the surrender of Japan, a blazing cross illuminated the face of Stone Mountain once again, so as, in the words of one participant in the ceremony, "to let the niggers know the war is over and the Klan is back on the market."[26] When, in his 1963 "I Have a Dream" speech in Washington, Martin Luther King, Jr. proclaimed, "Let freedom ring from Stone Mountain Georgia," he referenced racism as well as geography.[27]

Assaults on Segregation: Federal Force at Play
The Klan had reason for concern; White supremacy was losing its institutional stranglehold. Racial equality made important strides in the decade after 1945 in government and in society. In December 1946 President Harry Truman formed an executive commission on civil rights and took its findings and suggestions seriously. In 1948 he issued executive orders desegregating the federal workforce and the armed forces. Southern segregation of higher education began to crack. By 1952 the universities of Kentucky (1949), Virginia (1950), Texas (1950), and Tennessee (1952) had admitted their first Black students in graduate or professional

programs. Virginia and North Carolina integrated their undergraduate student bodies as well in 1955, and Texas did so a year later.

More important, the United States Supreme Court struck down the longstanding ruling in *Plessy v. Ferguson* (1896) that legitimated segregated schools under the principle of separate but equal. The Court's unanimous finding in *Brown v. Board of Education*, declared in April 1954, ruled that "separate educational facilities are inherently unequal." In response, southern legislators in Congress issued the Southern Manifesto opposing racial integration in 1956. In 1957 Arkansas governor Orval Faubus tried to prevent Blacks from integrating Little Rock's Central High School. His defiance forced the hand of President Dwight D. Eisenhower, who ordered the 101st Airborne Division to Little Rock and federalized the Arkansas National Guard. This was the first real test of *Brown v. Board of Education*, and the nine Black students were admitted, although a court order the next year suspended the integration for two years.

Southern opposition stiffened, but the tide was turning. Integration of southern universities continued, and in 1962 the integration of Ole Miss came close to touching off civil war. James Meredith applied to the university, but was denied entry in 1961. His lawsuit went all the way to the U.S. Supreme Court, which ruled in Meredith's favor. Tensions mounted and Attorney General Robert Kennedy dispatched 500 federal marshals, who were supported by federalized Mississippi National Guardsmen. To oppose them, a great number of men, many of them armed Klansmen, flooded into Oxford, Mississippi. On 30 September and 1 October confrontation turned to riot, during which the marshals and guardsmen showed admirable restraint, although 160 marshals and forty guardsmen were injured. By next morning two people lay dead, killed by racist protesters, but the mob had lost, and Meredith registered for classes.

The next year, at 11 a.m. on 11 June 1963, Governor George Wallace blocked entry to Foster Auditorium at the University of Alabama, keeping two Black students from registering. However, the day was choreographed to avoid violence. President John F. Kennedy federalized the Alabama National Guard. Guardsmen arrived on campus at 3:15 p.m. and respectfully asked Wallace to leave. Within minutes after he left, the two Black students registered and attended classes the next day.

Violent Repression and Nonviolent Victories
The desegregation of education made it clear that the power of the federal government could be brought to bear to break Jim Crow. But the greatest effort was expended and the greatest cost endured by citizen-based civil rights organizations, not by Washington. Given the sheer force available to White supremacists and their willingness to use it, trying to match extralegal brutality blow for blow made no sense. Besides, civil rights activists commanded the high moral ground and resolved not to abandon it for short-term gain.

But victory came only after much struggle and much cost. The traditional recourse to public lynching virtually disappeared, since it was likely to draw unwanted attention and encourage opposition. Deadly violence became more surreptitious and anonymous, with assassination and bombing taking the lead. As strong as violence might seem, it eventually failed because it elicited a cultural and moral revulsion throughout most of the United States and roused federal intervention against the racist character of southern law and practice.

Not long after victory over Nazi racism in World War II, citizen-based civil rights organizations sought victory at home. Joining the National Association for the Advancement of Colored People (NAACP) in its battles for equality, the Congress of Racial Equality (CORE) sent eight White and eight Black men on a "Journey of Reconciliation" in 1947, to challenge segregation on interstate bus lines in the South; those on the journey suffered abuse and arrest, but they prefigured the Freedom Riders of the 1960s.

The first steps toward racial equality met vicious resistance by White supremacists. From the outset, the repertoire of repression included assassination of notable civil rights leaders. On the evening of Christmas Day 1951, Klansmen bombed the house of Harry Moore, the executive director of the Florida NAACP. Moore and his wife, Harriette, both died in the explosion. The killing was front-page news in the *New York Times* on 27 December. Moore was the first member of the NAACP to be assassinated because of his activism, but there were ten other bombings of activists in Florida that year.

Bullets also struck down those considered dangerous to Jim Crow. The Reverend George W. Lee, along with Gus Courts, established a local chapter of the NAACP in Belzoni, Mississippi, and worked for voter registration. On 7 May 1955 he was driving when a passenger in another car murdered him with a shotgun blast; the killer was never found. His death and funeral drew national attention. Courts was later shot in the arm, but survived. On 13 August 1955, Lamar Smith, a Black farmer who was also working for voter registration, was gunned down in broad daylight in front of the county courthouse at Brookhaven in southern Mississippi.

The killing of civil rights activists served a strategy of intimidation, with the added goals of retribution against troublesome Blacks and decapitation of the civil rights movement. Yet assassination failed to deter those determined to advance civil rights.

A milestone of the civil rights movement, the Montgomery Bus Boycott, began in December 1955, when Rosa Parks refused to give up her seat on a bus to a White passenger. The Black community showed originality in maintaining the boycott, resorting to car pools and even horse-drawn carts for transport. Martin Luther King, Jr. recalled in his "Letter from Birmingham Jail" that an old Black woman who participated in the boycott testified: "My feets is tired, but my soul is at rest."[28] Not only endurance, but also courage was required. King's role in the boycott would bring him to national prominence. Terrorists bombed his home on 30 January 1956, and that of his colleague in the Montgomery Bus Boycott, E. D. Nixon, was struck two days later. The boycott continued until December 1956, finally ending when the U.S. Supreme Court declared its support for a lower court that found the Alabama laws decreeing segregation in buses to be unconstitutional.

After success in Montgomery, prominent civil rights crusaders including King, the Reverend Fred Shuttlesworth, and Ralph Abernathy, men firmly committed to nonviolence, formed the Southern Christian Leadership Conference (SCLC) in mid-February 1957. Though the SCLC honored its pledge of nonviolence, its White supremacist opponents were anything but nonviolent. When Shuttlesworth tried to enroll his daughters in Birmingham's Phillips High School on 9 September that year, he was brutally beaten. White supremacists repeatedly targeted him for violence. On Christmas Day 1958, the seventh anniversary of the murder of Harry and Harriette Moore, bombers struck Shuttlesworth's parsonage residence. Somehow surviving the blast of twelve sticks of dynamite, he could only see it as a miracle. Birmingham suffered dozens of bombings between 1945 and 1963, earning the label "Bombingham."

The work of desegregation that made such strides with the Montgomery Bus Boycott continued with sit-ins, protests against segregation at lunch counters and other businesses. Protesters occupied seats in Whites-only sections, subjecting themselves to arrest and abuse. There were lesser-known sit-ins before 1960, but that year the most important took place at a F. W. Woolworth store in Greensboro, North Carolina. On 1 February, four Black college students sat at the Whites-only lunch counter; they were denied service but refused to leave. Within days, hundreds of protesters were involved in sit-ins in Greensboro. When their actions attracted national attention, the sit-in movement spread to other North Carolina towns and beyond the borders of the state. Eventually, 70,000 individuals took part in the protests. As a result, the F. W. Woolworth chain as a whole desegregated in July, as did many other business establishments.

Freedom Rides and Birmingham
Supreme Court decisions in *Irene Morgan v. Commonwealth of Virginia* (1946) and *Boynton v. Virginia* (1960) established the principle that interstate busses and bus stations could no longer be segregated. Nonetheless, segregation remained, so Freedom Rides, planned primarily by CORE and the Student Nonviolent Coordinating Committee (SNCC), were dispatched to bring attention to reveal the problem and force compliance with the law. The first left Washington, D.C., on 4 May 1961, on an itinerary intended to take the participants to New Orleans; however, the group was viciously assaulted in Alabama. These attacks were the work of the Mississippi White Knights, with the connivance of the Birmingham commissioner of public safety, Theophilus Eugene "Bull" Connor. With the Freedom Riders on their way, Connor agreed to give Klansmen fifteen minutes to do as they wished to the unwanted outsiders before police would intervene. When the first of two Freedom Rider busses reached Anniston, about seventy miles from Birmingham, on 14 May, Klansmen overturned the bus and set it ablaze, threatening to burn the passengers alive. Klansmen brutally beat Freedom Riders escaping the inferno. The second bus picked up the battered survivors and continued on to Birmingham, where they met a gang of twenty-five Klansmen from the Eastview Klavern, who maximized their infamous fifteen minutes by beating the riders with baseball bats, pipes, and chains. Freedom

Rider James Peck required fifty stitches on his head to staunch the bleeding. These beatings shocked the nation, but the protest continued, with dozens of Freedom Rides traversing the South from May to September.

The third Klan lacked an overarching national organization, but it came closest to it with the creation of the United Klans of America (UKA) in July 1961, as a response to the "invasion" by Freedom Riders. The new leader of the UKA was Robert Marvin "Bobby" Shelton, who had come out of the Georgia and Alabama Klans. Membership in this Klan organization peaked at 30,000 in 1965 from Alabama, Georgia, and the Carolinas. Even at its height, the UKA was rivaled by other Klans, most importantly the Mississippi White Knights.

The Birmingham Campaign, led during the spring of 1963 by Fred Shuttlesworth and Martin Luther King, Jr., aimed at desegregating the downtown of the harshly segregated city. The nonviolent protesters expected an over-the-top violent reaction by local authorities, including Bull Connor, who obliged, winning national sympathy for the demonstrators. Instead of using Klansmen as surrogates, Connor employed both his police and his firemen to punish protesters in May 1963. At first he arrested protesters, but after filling the Birmingham jails he changed tactics. On 3 May firemen directed high-pressure hoses on protesters; then Connor unleashed police and dogs.

King was nonviolent himself and insisted on nonviolence by those who participated in civil rights demonstrations. However, he understood that if peaceful protests could provoke violence from the likes of Bull Connor, that violence would discredit the oppressors. This strategy was akin to the "jujitsu" identified by Daniel Fromkin, but multiplied in its impact because the demonstrators were innocent of using violence themselves to precipitate the vicious reaction of their adversaries.[29] President Kennedy is reported to have said, "The civil rights movement should thank God for Bull Connor. He's helped it as much as Abraham Lincoln."[30]

The assassinations continued in the early 1960s. In 1961 Herbert Lee, a SNCC representative working for voter registration, was shot and killed by E. H. Hurst, a state legislator, who claimed self-defense and was found innocent by a White jury. On 12 June 1964, the director of the NAACP in Mississippi, Medgar Evers, was shot in the back at his home in Jackson by a sniper. Byron De La Beckwith, an ardent White supremacist, was arrested for the assassination, but hung juries refused to convict him. Only in 1994 was he finally convicted of the murder of Evers.

By June 1963, President Kennedy was pushing for a comprehensive civil rights act, but he also fell to an assassin's bullet in November, while the bill was bottled up in committee. President Lyndon Johnson used his considerable legislative skills to advance the bill as a tribute to the slain Kennedy, and it became law in July 1964.

Meanwhile, the most shocking of the southern bombings took the lives of four Black girls, ages eleven to fourteen, at Birmingham's 16th Street Baptist Church on 15 September 1963. Speaking with the wisdom brought by time, the dean of television journalists, Walter Cronkite, commented in 1997 that the "moment that that bomb went off and those four little girls were blasted and buried in the debris of the church, Americans understood the real nature of hate that was preventing integration. . . . This was the awakening."[31] The suspects in the 16th Street Baptist Church case, Robert "Dynamite Bob" Chambliss, Bobby Frank Cherry, Herman Frank Cash, and Thomas E. Blanton, Jr., belonged to the UKA. For lack of evidence, no federal charges were forthcoming during the 1960s. When the new Alabama attorney general, William Baxley, reopened the investigation in 1971, three were eventually tried, convicted, and sentenced to life, although this took years. Only Cash was not indicted; he died in 1994.

Freedom Summer and Selma
In June 1964, Freedom Summer brought civil rights workers to campaign for the still unfinished work of registering Black voters in Mississippi. Its leadership came primarily from the SNCC, but also involved a coalition with the NAACP, CORE, and the SCLC. White supremacist violence awaited the "outsiders" who braved the Mississippi heat. Many were arrested and abused; three were killed: Andrew Goodman and Michael Schwerner were young Jewish men from New York and members of CORE, while James Earl Chaney was a Black native of Mississippi and CORE activist. On 21 June, after investigating the burning of a church in Longdale, Mississippi, and the beatings of church members, the three were arrested on trumped-up traffic charges by Cecil Price, a Neshoba County deputy sheriff and Klansman of the Mississippi White Knights. He waited until ten other Klansmen were summoned and then released

the three CORE workers. Outside town, the Klansmen stopped, seized, chain-whipped, and finally shot them, burying their bodies in an earthen dam. Authorities found the remains of the three only on 4 August. Several individuals were arrested, but the state refused to try them for murder, so they were tried in federal court on civil rights charges. Seven were found guilty in 1967 and sentenced from three to ten years. In 2005, Edgar Ray Killen, who planned the murders, was finally convicted of manslaughter and sentenced to spend twenty years in prison. He died behind bars in 2018.

The fight for voter registration climaxed in the March 1965 with three marches from Selma, Alabama, to the state capital in Montgomery. These grew out of a voter registration campaign in Marion, Alabama. The arrest of a worker with the SCLC precipitated a peaceful protest by civil rights groups, but the local police reacted with force, beating participants as they fled the violence. In the mayhem, Jimmie Lee Jackson, an Army veteran, tried to protect his mother but was shot twice in the stomach by police; he died eight days later. His death mobilized the community, and organizers in nearby Selma called for aid from the SCLC and Martin Luther King. The first march, which took place on 7 March, became known as "Bloody Sunday," when the 600 demonstrators were attacked crossing the Edmund Pettus Bridge spanning the Alabama River in Selma. Sheriff's deputies with helmets and clubs attacked on signal and fired tear gas into the crowd of marchers; then others on horseback carried out a virtual cavalry charge. A great number of marchers were injured and seventeen hospitalized. It was only fitting that Edmund Pettus was a Confederate general, who, after the Civil War, became Grand Dragon of the Klan in Alabama.

The SCLC pursued a court order affirming the demonstrators' right to march and prohibiting the police from perpetrating further violence, but the process took some time. The second march, on 9 March, went down as "Turn-around Tuesday" because the demonstrators halted after crossing the Edmund Pettus Bridge, to comply with the judge's temporary restraining order. The march was peaceful, but not the day. That night the Reverend James Reeb, a White minister who had taken part in the march, was fatally beaten by four Klansmen.

After the court ruled in favor of the demonstrators, 8,000 people set out on the third march on 21 March. On the fifth day on the route, the marchers swelled to 25,000, entered Montgomery, heard King's "How Long, Not Long" speech, and delivered a petition to the governor's office. The day, however, would not be without cost, as that evening Klansmen gunned down Viola Liuzzo, a White mother of five from Detroit, who was driving marchers back from Montgomery to Selma.

On 15 March President Johnson presented a draft of the Voting Rights Act to a joint session of Congress, and it would become law on 6 August. Its official title was "An Act to Enforce the Fifteenth Amendment to the Constitution of the United States, and for Other Purposes." The Fifteenth Amendment, ratified in 1870 but subverted by southern legislatures after Reconstruction, would now be effectively applied. A hundred years after Appomattox, the White supremacist South would be forced to accept defeat. Yet the Confederate battle flag was not removed from the capitol grounds in Columbia, South Carolina, until 10 July 2015.

The accomplishments of the Johnson administration's first two years in office did not eliminate the Klan, but the Civil Rights Act of 1964 and the Voting Rights Act of 1965, enforced by an insistent federal government that was backed by the majority of the American people, undercut the White supremacist system that the Klan sought to enforce and defend. These acts would later be complemented by the Fair Housing Act of 1968. FBI Director J. Edgar Hoover estimated that Klan membership as a whole declined from 40,000 in 1965 to 14,000 in 1968. By the 1980s it had plummeted to fewer than 1,000.

In January 1966 the executive committee of the Democratic Party of Alabama removed explicit racist language from the logo that had symbolized the party for decades. The old symbol consisted of a white rooster surmounted by a banner that read "White Supremacy," with another at its feet "For the Right." Only by a close vote, thirty-nine to thirty-two, did the committee strike the words "White Supremacy" and replace them with "Democrats."[32]

Klan violence did not cease, but it was more and more the action of a dwindling rear guard. Martin Luther King, Jr. was assassinated in 1968 by James Earl Ray, an admitted racist without clear ties to the Klan or any other conspirators. In 1981, Klansmen were enraged by a mistrial in the prosecution of a Black accused of murdering a White policeman in Mobile, Alabama. (The individual was convicted in a later trial.) After a meeting that night, two Klansmen, aged 17 and 26, went looking for a Black victim, and by chance found nineteen-year-old Michael Donald, whom they beat, strangled, mutilated, and then hanged. His killers were arrested two years later and convicted in 1984. The chief culprit was eventually executed, the first White to be executed for a White-on-Black crime since 1913. In 1987, Morris Dees of the Southern Poverty Law Center brought a wrongful death suit against the UKA in the murder of Donald and won a $7 million judgment. The UKA was forced to liquidate its assets and dissolved. In 1994, Shelton, who had founded the UKA in 1961, told the Associated Press: "The Klan is my belief, my religion. But it won't work anymore. The Klan is gone. Forever."[33]

White supremacy was virulent and dominant in the post–World War II South, although it was not unchallenged. Despite its long history and deep roots, it was defeated. Yes, it still exists, but it has been greatly weakened in capacity. When we look at radical right-wing terrorism in Chapter 12, it will not be the terrorism of a dominant population, but of a minority that has spawned radical sub-state groups. Victory was won in the 1950s and 1960s by a social movement, one that marshaled national values against intense regional bigotry. The civil rights movement benefited from the intervention of the federal government, but it paid a heavy price in beatings, bombings, and bullets. It demonstrated that a social movement could undermine terrorist radicals; may we not forget that lesson. This goes beyond Cronin's useful list.

Ultimately, this chapter celebrates the civil rights heroes who achieved the words of the civil rights anthem "We Shall Overcome." The abolitionist Theodore Parker (1810–1860) expressed his faith in words later paraphrased by Martin Luther King, Jr. in his "How Long, Not Long" speech: "How long? Not long, because the arc of the moral universe is long, but it bends toward justice."

CHAPTER FIVE

Propaganda of the Deed

THE FIRST WAVE OF RADICAL TERRORISM, 1848–1920

FIGURE 5.1. In this illustration from a contemporary tabloid, the *Allgemeine illustrirte Zeitung*, Czar Alexander II lies mortally wounded by a bomb thrown by a Narodnaya Volya terrorist who was also killed by the explosion on 13 March 1881. Wikimedia Commons.

ON THE AFTERNOON of 13 March 1881, Czar Alexander II and his escort returned from his weekly Sunday visit to a military review in St. Petersburg. Four revolutionaries of Narodnaya Volya, People's Will, waited to assassinate him on his return to the Winter Palace. Once they determined which route he would take, the assassins deployed on the road along the Catherine Canal to attack him with hand-held bombs. They had agreed to employ bombs rather than revolvers, because, as a member testified, shooting the czar "would have been interpreted as an ordinary murder, and would not have expressed a new stage in the revolutionary movement."[1]

The evening before the attack, one of the bombers, Ignati Grinevitsky, a radical young aristocrat, prepared for his role by composing a dramatic will and testament: "Alexander II must die. His days are numbered. He will die and we, his enemies, his killers, will die with him.... History will show that the luxuriant tree of freedom demands human sacrifices.... Fate has doomed me to an early death, and I will not see victory, I will not live a single day, a single hour in the radiant time of triumph.... But I believe that with my death I will have done everything I had to do, and no one in the entire world can demand more of me."[2]

On the fatal day, Sophia Perovskaya led the party of four assassins and served as look-out to signal the route the czar's party would take. Nikolai Rysakov, Grinevitsky, and Ivan Emelyanov carried the bombs. The carriage carrying Alexander rolled by Rysakov first, and he tossed his bomb under it, but the bomb exploded only when the carriage had nearly passed over it. The blast killed a Cossack and a delivery boy, as well as wounding others, but it did not harm the intended target. Although warned by his guards not to exit his carriage, Alexander alighted to survey the scene and console the wounded. When he did, Grinevitsky achieved his fate by advancing and throwing his bomb to the pavement between him and the czar. Its blast mortally wounded both men; the czar's shattered legs bled profusely (Fig. 5.1).

One of the plotters, Vera Figner, reported her joy at the success of their attack: "I wept, and many of us wept; that heavy nightmare, which for ten years had strangled young Russia before our very eyes, had been brought to an end... the blood of our martyrs, all were atoned for by this blood of the czar, shed by our hands. A heavy burden was lifted from our shoulders; reaction must come to an end and give place to a new Russia. In this solemn moment, all our thoughts centered in the hope for a better future for our country."[3]

The assassination of Alexander II culminated a campaign by Narodnaya Volya to eliminate a ruler whom revolutionaries condemned for blocking Russia's regeneration. But Figner's hopes were dashed. The slain czar's son and successor, Alexander III, proved to be unrelentingly oppressive. Five of the conspirators were quickly tried and executed. Figner was arrested in 1883 and spent the next twenty years in prison, after which she lived in exile, returning to Russia only in 1915.

Many of the basic characteristics that mark radical terrorism to this day were already true of Narodnaya Volya. Networked in small, clandestine bands, these profoundly dedicated idealists abandoned traditional moral norms in the name of exalted goals. They were imbued with an intense spirit of self-sacrifice that embraced martyrdom.

We now turn to radical terrorism by sub-state groups in its first and most varied wave, from the onset of modern radical terrorism after the Revolutions of 1848 to shortly after World War I. This chapter will concentrate on the European manifestation of such terrorism, although the first wave was transnational in its reach. It was characterized primarily by strategies of initiation designed to precipitate the collapse or transformation of political and social regimes. Such terrorist campaigns might take some time, but they were not generally conceived of as long, grinding struggles of attrition to gradually wear down the regime; nor did terrorists emphasize expectations of evolving their fight to higher levels of warfare. As in the case of Narodnaya Volya, they expected that small-scale acts of violence could have grand consequences.

It is the contention of this book that the first wave of radical terrorism emerged only after the spontaneous mass revolutionary violence that had seemed so effective before was discredited by the ultimate failure of the Revolutions of 1848. To make this point, we will have to survey the history of violent political resistance in Europe before, during, and immediately after the French Revolution of 1789–1799. Only then can we turn to recounting the record of the first wave.

REPERTOIRES OF VIOLENT POLITICAL RESISTANCE

It is not an easy matter to identify the onset of modern sub-state radical terrorism. The argument I will present here is built around the concept of repertoires of violent political resistance and then identifying when radical terrorism appeared as a recognized and continuous alternative in modern repertoires.

Human beings are creatures of habit and imitation. They tend to do things because that is the way they have done them before or because they believe that other people have succeeded by doing them that way. As the social scientist Charles Tilly proposed, political contention followed certain patterns in times past. He termed the accepted alternatives for action "repertoires of contention." Over time such repertoires changed, but at any one point people chose within a given menu of possibilities. I will borrow this notion and focus it on repertoires of violent resistance, which vary from stone throwing to outright civil war. We need to ask when and why sub-state radical terrorism joined the repertoire of violent political resistance. To be part of the repertoire of political resistance, radical terrorism had to have a theory, a method, and a history. One-offs are not part of a repertoire by the very fact that they are one-offs and not part of a repeated pattern. When we talk of *waves* of terrorism, we are talking about patterns that typified a given time.

Assassination in Times Past and the History of Terrorism
If we are to date terrorism by its place in a repertoire of violent political resistance, we must ask what kinds of violence qualify as terrorist. And the most challenging questions concern assassination, which is often considered an act of terrorism. Obviously, the killing of one human being by another dates from time immemorial. And political murder has existed since the beginning of political institutions. Rivals for positions of power have killed their rivals; those believing themselves abused have killed their rulers. Palace murders that go no further than exchanging one monarch with another hardly qualify as terrorism. We have stressed that radical terrorism is not simply about personal aggrandizement and that it aims to create a psychological impact far greater than the physical attack. To qualify as terrorism, an assassination must be committed for some grand cause and intended to help bring about some major change, often through its impact on a much larger target audience. Beyond eliminating hated figures of authority and power, terrorist assassinations are designed to demonstrate the vulnerability of institutions, to undermine confidence among elites, to induce chaos and collapse, or to inspire greater resistance among the disaffected. In fact, determining the terrorist nature of an assassination often comes down to a judgment call.

We must immediately confront assassination because it figures so large in first-wave terrorism, as in the killing of Czar Alexander II. But it goes further than that, because those historians and social scientists who claim that radical terrorism is of ancient lineage are prone to use assassination as the critical marker. For some commentators, such as Randall Law, assassination is intrinsically an act of terror, and in his book on the history of terrorism he devotes entire chapters to "tyrannicide."[4] This goes too far.

It has also become something of a commonplace that histories of terrorism begin by discussing the Sicariis of ancient Judea and the Hashashins of the medieval Middle East. But these cases were too special and too isolated to become part of an established repertoire of political resistance. Sicariis were Jewish Zealots who wielded daggers (*sicae*) in Jerusalem and elsewhere to kill Roman occupiers and Jews who collaborated with them during the First Jewish-Roman War (66–73 CE). Here the question is not the character of the act but if the group actually drew from or established a tradition of terrorist assassination. The Sicariis did neither.

The Hashashins are a more complicated case. In the late eleventh century, their founder, Hassan-i Sabbah, gathered around him fellow Ismali Shia Muslims who were being persecuted by the Sunni Abbasid caliphate. With his followers he occupied the fortress of Alamut in northern Iran. They resorted to assassination as a political and military tool; in fact, the very word *assassin* derives from Hashashsin. There are several explanations of the term, one of which claims they were intoxicated by hashish. We are searching for the origins of radical terrorism by sub-state groups, and it is hard to consider the Hashashsins as a sub-state group, since they eventually controlled entire fortress cities and areas, from Iran to Syria. And while they had a long run, Alamut fell to the Mongols in 1256 and the Mamluks took control of their Syrian strongholds in 1273. Most important, the organized use of murder by the Hashashins was not systematically replicated by others, although some surviving Hashashins went on to become paid killers.

The phenomenon of assassination afflicted medieval and early modern Europe, but it was not part of a chain of terrorism. There was the occasional attack that meets our criterion for terrorist acts but does become part of an enduring, self-conscious pattern—a repertoire of political resistance. One of these was the Gunpowder Plot to assassinate English King James I by means of a massive black-powder bomb to be set off at the House of Lords in 1605. The plot was discovered and the conspirators, including Guy Fawkes, executed. Their goal was not simply to kill the king and cause the incidental deaths of many others, but to alter the monarchy's hostile treatment of Catholics. The cause was great, but the attempted demolition was not the start of a terrorist campaign.

Stressing the Sicarii and the Hashashins, or other harbingers, in overviews of the history of terrorism raises another problem in my mind. In pushing the history of radical terrorism back that far, we lose the sense of the modern manifestations of the kind of terrorism that concerns us. Radical terrorism as we know it arose in a time and space; its context was the growing power of modern states and militaries that limited more traditional forms of violent political resistance. Its context was also one of changes in economies, demographics, and political aspirations. Trying to push it back centuries does not deepen our understanding; it is more likely to confuse the issue.

The Genesis of Radical Terrorism as an "Ism"
To mark the emergence of modern radical terrorism we should determine when it became an "ism." We generally think of an "ism" as a body of thought, such as a political ideology. However, "ism" here refers not to a cause but to a practice: a way of doing something rather than a reason for doing it. In this case, it is the advocacy and adoption of a particular form of political violence as valid and effective.

My checkoff list for terrorism in this light includes four criteria. First, it should have a conscious theory, a literature, about its necessity, efficacy, and methods. Second, it should be practiced as a form of violent political resistance adaptable to different causes. Third, it should be transportable across political borders; it should be transnational. And fourth, we should be able to trace a line between a series of terrorist acts. They should follow in a continuous succession rather than being the occasional harbinger or one-off. This last criterion is another way of saying that terrorism should be a recognized and repeatable part of a repertoire of violence.

In dealing with the first wave of radical terrorism, this list produces different estimates of when it began. If one emphasizes the theory, it begins around 1850, immediately after the Revolutions of 1848. If it has to be recognized as applicable to different causes and transnational in nature, that is certainly there in the 1860s. If we need to mark the start of a succession of terrorist acts that referenced one to another, then that argues more for the late 1870s. But there is one more way to point to the emergence of modern radical terrorism, and that is to argue that we must see it rising to the fore when other alternatives in the repertoire of violent political resistance demonstrate themselves to be impotent. Here is a primary reason to see the failure of the Revolutions of 1848 as key. To make this argument, we must resort to the historical record.

VIOLENT POLITICAL RESISTANCE BEFORE THE FRENCH REVOLUTION

The medieval and early modern periods were hardly eras of placid compliance with authority. During the centuries before the emergence of radical terrorism, European populations had employed repertoires of violent resistance that fitted their times and circumstances. The most prominent forms of violent intrastate resistance in medieval and early modern France were overt: riots, uprisings, and rebellions. Mass violent resistance faced off against what can be called the forces of order, from ad hoc bands or militias marshaled by local elites to armed forces dispatched by the state.

It is surprising how well rebels could match up against the forces of order. Large-scale resistance could be aristocratic, led by the privileged and powerful, or popular, as in revolts of peasants and urban commoners. Even in the latter case, the rebels could muster numbers large enough and well enough armed to put up a credible fight, at least in certain circumstances. With the possibility of achieving rapid and decisive success, there was little reason for resisters or rebels to pursue their causes by adopting slower, more difficult terrorist tactics committed by small and inherently weak groups.

Popular revolts concern us most since the line between them and the rise of radical terrorism is most direct. Popular rebellions were hardly rare. Samuel Cohn in his study of medieval social rebellion in Europe as a whole puts together a sample of "1,112 revolts and social movements" between 1200 and 1425.[5] Yves Marie Bercé counts 450–500 peasant revolts that broke out in southwestern France *alone* from 1590 to 1715.[6]

The spirit of revolt in the countryside could also take hold in the towns, either as urban manifestations of peasant revolt or within the context of the towns themselves. Urban rebellions could result from complex causes, but high taxes were major grievances. Town environments, with their narrow streets walled in with buildings, rendered the arms and tactics of field warfare inapplicable, giving rebellious crowds parity with their better-armed opponents. Not surprisingly, Paris ranks as the most rebellious French city, with about 200 revolts in the period 1200–1425, according to Cohn.[7]

Violent urban resistance continued to play a dramatic role in French history during the sixteenth and seventeenth centuries, and Parisian crowds asserted themselves with innovative tactics to hold off better-armed and more experienced opponents. A key event in politics and memory occurred in May 1588, when Parisians resorted to barricades during a confrontation with the troops of King Henry III.[8] Parisians erected these improvised barriers of barrels, trees, paving stones, and so forth to block streets, turning neighborhoods into fortresses. The king deployed 6,000 royal troops, a sizable force for the time, into Paris, but instead of intimidating the townsfolk, the troops spurred crowds into armed resistance on 12 May, known as the Day of the Barricades. Henry extracted his troops and fled the city himself. This would be a forecast of things to come.

By the late seventeenth century the scope of rebellion shrank and the repertoire of violent resistance altered. These changes resulted from the concentration and effectiveness of state authority engineered by Louis XIV, who reigned from 1643 to 1715. The state's increasing power against domestic resistance is most dramatically demonstrated by the great expansion of the French Army under Louis. Peacetime troop levels multiplied from the 10,000 men maintained by Henry IV, around 1600, to the 150,000 troops that served his grandson, Louis XIV, by the 1670s. Wartime levels reached over 360,000 in the 1690s, when earlier monarchs had been fortunate to field 60,000–80,000 in times of conflict. Along with the growth in sheer numbers came improvements in weaponry, organization, and command.

A broad overview of violent resistance in France before the outbreak of the French Revolution reveals no absence of tensions and turmoil. Overt aristocratic and popular revolts and riots enjoyed enough success to be seen as reasonable means for asserting interests and redressing grievances against regimes of power. The last major uprisings in France prior to the French Revolution were the tax revolt of the Papier Timbré and Bonnets Rouges in Brittany, along the Atlantic coast, in 1675, and the more religiously based rebellion of the Camisards in the Cévennes region of southern France in 1702–1704.

THE TRIUMPH AND FAILURE OF MASS CROWD ACTION

Peasant revolts could no longer stand up to the forces of order in open field battle, and eighteenth-century France was not struck by the great tax revolts of earlier years. However, the tradition of violent group contention remained; most important, urban crowds still took to the streets in actions such as grain riots by hungry crowds. The most important grain riots before 1789 occurred during the so-called Flour War of 1775, when, according to the historian Cynthia Bouton, 300 distinct riots struck France.[9] In any case, the memory of mass crowd action was strong when the great trials of the French Revolution began.

In his new and challenging book *Turning to Political Violence: The Emergence of Terrorism*, Marc Sageman makes the case that the origins of what we are calling radical terrorism can be traced back to the French Revolution. He points to the increased levels of political violence during the revolution. It is key, I believe, that Sageman is specifically speaking of *political violence*, while my emphasis is on *violent political resistance*. By stressing political violence, he adds together individual, group, crowd, and state-directed violence—what we have described as state terrorism in Chapter 3. This understandably raises the total of political violence, which he sees as carrying into the nineteenth century, where it eventually took the form of radical terrorism. Since he is most concerned with the seed time of terrorism, he insists that we go back to the French Revolution. I am more concerned with the flowering than the seed. I agree that the revolution raised the level of public violence, but I hold that it would take more time for radical terrorism per se to take shape as a prominent form of violent political resistance. As I said above, depending on what you rate as most important, you can date the outset of radical terrorism differently.

Let us look more closely again at the French Revolution, which loomed over the century that followed the storming of the Bastille. It left an indelible concept of political/social revolution, adding full-scale revolution to the repertoire of violent resistance. This transformation was linked to several forms of political violence:

- grand demonstrations and actions by crowds of citizens, often armed
- state repression—the Reign of Terror, for example, and the civil war in the Vendée, which could be categorized as state and/or military terrorism
- plotting and planning by radical and counter-revolutionary clubs and cabals, some of which precipitated or directed crowd actions

- killing through formal executions of state leaders—Louis XVI most obviously, but thousands of others, including Maximilien Robespierre
- much rarer assassinations of prominent revolutionary figures by isolated individuals—above all, the assassination of Jean-Paul Marat by Charlotte Corday

Given the variety of levels and forms of violence associated with the revolution, to lump them together as a turn to political violence that later resolved into radical terrorism strikes me as being as confusing as it is enlightening.

Still, the French Revolution could be seen as setting the stage for the eventual rise of terrorism, as Sageman insists, although it also provided precedent and argument for very different forms of political violence. The next few generations of European radicals referenced the revolution as they sought the most effective way to achieve their goals through violent means. I see this evolution of and competition between revolutionary options finally resulting in the rise of radical terrorism soon after the failure of the Revolutions of 1848. This is the case because that failure discredited what had seemed the most promising means of compelling radical change: the large-scale, overt, armed crowd resistance, often employing urban barricades, that drove the revolution in its first year.

The Alternatives of Violent Political Resistance, 1789–1827
On 14 July 1789, as crowds stormed the Bastille, Parisians constructed barricades for the first time since 1652. The last appeal to barricades during the revolution came in 1795, and this effort was unsuccessful; however, the earlier triumphs of the revolutionary *sans-culottes* battling in the streets had already entered the popular memory.

French sub-state political resistance in the years 1789–1815 ran the gamut from assassinations to plots for insurrection. Assassins saw killing as a means of initiating radical change. It was not simply palace murder, but violence designed to not only decapitate but shock—the small action with a great consequence. Some assassins were driven by causes, others more by hate or revenge, but the ultimate effect in the nineteenth century was to make uneasy the heads that wore crowns and the elites who supported them. Before Napoleon came to dominate

France in 1799, the most notorious assassination by an individual was the work of the counterrevolutionary heroine Charlotte Corday, when she fatally stabbed the revolutionary firebrand Jean-Paul Marat on 13 July 1793. She hoped to alter the course of the revolution, but failed. At the other extreme, a radical cabal, led by Gracchus Babeuf, plotted a coup de main known to history as the Conspiracy of Equals. The conspirators wished to overthrow the ruling post-Terror government, the Directory, and replace it with a more egalitarian and socialist regime. But before they could carry out their unlikely plan, it was discovered in May 1796. Babeuf and another of the plotters were arrested, tried, and executed. One of his fellow conspirators who survived, the ardent Philippe Buonarroti, would later publish his *History of Babeuf's Conspiracy of Equals* in 1828, an account of Babeuf's work and his trial. The Russian anarchist Mikhail Bakunin (1814–1876) called Buonarroti "the greatest conspirator of his age."[10] Here you can see links between revolutionaries inspired by their predecessors and comrades.

After Napoleon seized power, plotters conspired to assassinate him in 1800. On 24 December royalists attempted to kill him with a large bomb. The ill-timed explosion left the emperor unscathed, but it did kill as many as ten and injure as many as sixty innocent bystanders.

When Napoleon met defeat and abdicated his throne, first in 1814 and finally after Waterloo in 1815, France reverted to a restored Bourbon monarchy ruled by the brothers of the slain Louis XVI: Louis XVIII (1814–1824) and Charles X (1824–1830). Louis XVIII made the best of a difficult situation, but both old revolutionaries and proponents of Bonaparte opposed his rule. Resistance to the new order was not long in coming. In 1820, a lone assassin killed the Duke de Berry, second in line for the Bourbon throne at the time. Of greater long-term significance, the opponents of the restored monarchy formed secret societies and hoped for a new world. Perhaps the most important secret society, the Carbonari, began in Italy, patterning itself after the Freemasons, advocating a liberal and nationalist program, and trying to win converts. The French produced their own reflection of the Carbonari in the Charbonnerie, whose loose agenda included freedom of the press and a more generous franchise.

Auguste Blanqui, a perpetual revolutionary inspired by Buonarroti, joined the Charbonnerie in 1824, before he was twenty. In this role he took part in the anti-monarchical uprising of 1827 in Paris, when crowds once again took to the barricades. Blanqui was seriously wounded in the street fighting, but this experience only fueled his revolutionary enthusiasm. In 1830 he joined a secret republican association that played a role in the revolution that struck in July of that year.

The Trois glorieuses on the Barricades of 1830

Parisian urban revolt triumphed in July 1830 by compelling Charles X to abdicate. He had succeeded his brother in 1824 and tacked to the right to preserve monarchical authority, but bad economic conditions in 1827–1830 made things worse. Facing growing criticism in the liberal press, Charles planned to transform the constitution by decree. Ordinances he issued on 25 July 1830 dissolved the Chamber of Deputies, restricted freedom of the press, redefined the franchise to include only the wealthy, and ordered elections to the Chamber on the basis of the new privileged electorate.

When Parisians learned of the king's actions, thousands took to the streets and raised as many as 4,000 barricades. Over the course of the Three Glorious Days (*Les trois glorieuses*), 27–29 July, Parisians overthrew not only the king but the Bourbon monarchy as well. Charles X sat out the fighting in his palace at Saint-Cloud, on the Seine just west of Paris. During the afternoon of the last day, the city hall of Paris, the Hôtel de Ville, fell to the rebels, and self-appointed politicians met there to form a provisional government. Charles formally abdicated, and the Charter of 1830 established a more liberal constitutional monarchy under Louis Philippe, the Duke of Orléans. His reign is known as the July Monarchy because of the month of its violent birth. The cost in lives of this Revolution of 1830 was about 500 among the revolutionaries and 150 among the king's defenders.

Several military factors had worked to the crowds' advantage. The population of Paris stood at 785,000 in 1830, but the royal garrison of the city numbered only 10,300–11,500 troops. It was not difficult for the populace to put its hands on weapons, and rebels could stand on the defensive, while the offensive burden was on the forces of order. Aiding those on the barricades, men and women at high windows and on rooftops hurled rocks and roof tiles at troops below.

Barricades benefited the crowds in more subtle ways. They became rallying points for resistance, at which those committed to revolt could meet and reinforce their resolve. Historian Mark Traugott, from whom much of this discussion of barricades is borrowed, argues that barricades also served as places of fraternization where rebels could try to win over troops, individually or as entire units.[11] And troops or their officers proved reluctant to fire on civilians. Some soldiers even joined the rebels or surrendered their weapons to them.

The Competition between Revolutionary Methods, 1830–1848
France had a new king, but he too soon showed an authoritarian streak, and subsequent repression stymied most activists. Among radicals, hope still gravitated to the crowd and the barricades. However, hope did not guarantee success. In June 1832, anti-monarchist radicals mounted the barricades in Paris, but unlike the crowds two years before, they were defeated by the king's forces. (This is the failed insurrection featured by Victor Hugo in *Les misérables*.) But if overt crowds failed, covert conspirators continued, with Louis Philippe being the target of *attentats* in 1835 and 1836. (*Attentat* literally translates as "attempt," but it took on the meaning of "attack.") The first *attentat* involved a bizarre, multibarreled weapon designed to sweep a broad area with bullets and buckshot. This device was the project of several conspirators, but it was Giuseppe Frieschi who fired it on 28 July 1835, as the king and other dignitaries reviewed the Parisian National Guard during the fifth anniversary celebration of the revolution that brought Louis Philippe to power. The king was slightly wounded, but eighteen were killed, including Édouard Mortier, a Napoleonic marshal then serving Louis Philippe as war minster and head of the council of ministers—essentially prime minister.

The reaction of radicals to the failure of 1832 and the dramatic *attentat* of 1836 demonstrates that at least some were thinking in terms of a menu of alternatives in a repertoire of violent political resistance. In an article titled "On Regicide," published in the underground journal *Le moniteur républicain* in May 1837, the author complained, "We will regret that in the heyday of popular societies we have not thought first of attacking Louis Philippe." The article defined "a law of progress": that "clubs, riots, insurrections having failed, it is the turn of the *attentat* to cut the Gordian knot of the future."[12] The author spoke too soon, as the February Revolution of 1848 in Paris would prove the efficacy of the barricades again. Most important, however, the article sets out a menu of failed political violence: clubs (people's societies, *sociétés populaires*), riots (overt protests), and insurrections (large-scale armed crowd actions, such as the Revolution of 1830). To these the author juxtaposes the potential success of assassinations. The author may not have accurately predicted the future, but he certainly described violent alternatives in an uncertain present—a repertoire of violent political resistance.

In 1839, the Society of the Seasons, with Blanqui as one of its founders and leaders, attempted another republican uprising in Paris, but his supporters melted away and the insurrection was an abysmal failure. The author of "On Regicide" must have felt vindicated. A member of the society tried to shoot down Louis Philippe on 15 October 1840, but the inept marksman overloaded his carbine, which blew up and severely wounded the would-be assassin, who was caught, tried, and executed. On 13 September 1841, another man tied to the society bungled an attempt to shoot the king's son, the Duke d'Aumale. One of his bullets struck a horse, but that was about it.

The Barricades of the February Revolution, 1848
Attentats drew attention to profound political dissatisfaction and thus ultimately encouraged protest, but their violence fell short of its goal to rid France of its monarch. However, the Revolution of 1830 had accomplished just that, and Parisian radicals tried that formula for change again in 1848. While a return to the barricades succeeded at first, its ultimate failure discredited the overt mass crowd action on the barricades, and this exclusion left violence by covert, small sub-state groups as the more promising means of political violence. Radical terrorism may have emerged not because of its success, but because of the failure of a revolutionary method that had seemed so promising and had won victories in the past. This is why I date the first wave of terrorism as beginning *after* the failure of the Revolutions of 1848, accepting that the precise timing remains a matter of discussion.

I have chosen to emphasize the French example in the discussion so far, but the French experience in 1848–1849 is part of a much broader European phenomenon. According to Traugott's accounting, an unprecedented series of fifty-two barricade events occurred across Europe from 12 January 1848 through 19 June 1849.

The February Revolution in France grew out of a contentious campaign for political reform during a time of economic recession and social tension. The monarch, tired of criticism and resistance, forbade a protest meeting planned for 22 February 1848. Outraged Parisians took to the streets that afternoon and again the next morning. On the evening of 23 February, demonstration turned into revolution when troops fired on protesters on the Boulevard des Capucines, killing fifty-two. During the night, rebels erected some 1,500 barricades, the largest of them rising to the height of a two-story building. The king and his counselors at the Tuileries Palace in the heart of Paris thrashed about for new options and personnel, appointing new civilian and military leadership, including Marshal Bugeaud, who had commanded in Algeria.

On 24 February things reached an impasse. The rebels adamantly refused to accept the king's concessions, while Louis Philippe, his ministers, and the military command sought to limit violence—a firm resistance confronted a hesitant force. Shortly before noon, Louis Philippe abdicated and departed Paris. The crowds had triumphed in about forty-eight hours of protest and barricades. Power passed to a provisional government that fashioned a republic to replace the July Monarchy. Another king had fallen to mass Parisian protest and the barricades in a matter of days. The fighting cost the lives of 290 insurgents and eighty among those defending the king.

The Barricades of the June Days, 1848
The February Revolution created the Second Republic in France, a regime with far greater public support and much more backbone than the July Monarchy. When threatened by hostile crowd action in June 1848, it responded not with royal diffidence but with republican determination.

Economic hard times contributed to the crises of 1848, and once installed in February, the new government quickly moved to alleviate unemployment by declaring it would "guarantee work for every citizen."[13] However, the policy of providing work through newly created National Workshops evolved into one of simply giving monetary subsidies to the unemployed. Eventually 117,000 Parisians drew wages from the government, exceeding the means of the republic. Thus, on 23 June, the moderate-to-conservative elected National Assembly voted to close the workshops, and Paris braced for a new revolt.

Having seen two regimes fail to meet the challenge of crowd action in 1830 and February 1848, the new government provided sterner security. In June, the government in Paris would be defended by 20,000 regular troops backed by 16,000 men of the Garde Mobile, a newly formed full-time security force. Behind these stood a National Guard militia of 237,000 men in the Parisian area. Some of the National Guard units were of questionable loyalty, but this would not stall the government's repression.

Armed resistance, known as the June Days, broke out on 23 June and continued over four bloody days. The National Assembly quickly granted General Louis-Eugène Cavaignac a virtual dictatorship to put down the rebellion. He prepared to suppress dissent, not to offer accommodation. French troops improved their tactics of street fighting and launched resolute assaults on the barricades. The rebels put up a stiff resistance, but on 26 June Cavaignac won a complete victory.

Casualty rates illustrate how the fighting had been more intense than in 1830 or the February Revolution. One thousand soldiers and guardsmen died. Although only 500 rebels perished on the barricades, Cavaignac's troops hunted down rebels after the main fighting was over, killing 3,000. About 12,000 more were arrested, and although the majority were released in short order, 4,500 were deported to Algeria.

The Anomaly of the Barricades of the Commune, 1871
The failure of the barricades during the June Days was later replicated in other European cities. As we shall see, the meaning of this failure was quickly noted by European radicals, who sought other means of violent political resistance. However, the story of radical barricades had one more chapter in Paris, with the rising of the Paris Commune in 1871. The circumstances there were very different, but to complete the story we need to tell the tale.

At the close of the Franco-Prussian War, disgruntled Parisian radicals asserted that their self-declared city government, the Paris Commune, was distinct from, and at odds with, the French Government of National Defense then in power. The Commune wanted to fight on against the Germans, but the Government of National Defense sought terms from the German political and military command. After concluding an agreement with the Germans, the French government turned on its own rebellious city, which prepared to resist. Part of that resistance involved constructing barricades, but contemporary photographs show that they were much more regular and militarized than those of 1830 and 1848. The best examples were more rational structures, with embrasures for Parisian artillery. In the photos, those mounting the defense wore the uniforms of the Commune. This was an outright civil war, with the new barricades as defensive works erected by a rebel government. The Commune hoped to match the technology and organization of a regular army. However, even the newer barricades of the Commune could not hold against a well-armed regular army, and the Commune and its forces were crushed during Bloody Week, 21–28 May. This debacle simply reinforced the realization that barricade defenses were no longer viable.

REQUIEM FOR THE BARRICADES

To return to the main point, the defeat of mass armed crowd actions, even buttressed by barricades, during the Revolutions of 1848, was read by many European radicals as discrediting this form of violent resistance. For them, it should be excluded from the revolutionary repertoire and new tactics found to take its place. We will soon explore in some depth how Karl Heinzen recognized the need for new alternatives in the days immediately following the debacle, but let us first survey other key revolutionaries who testified in a requiem for the barricades.

At the time and in retrospect, important radicals and revolutionaries saw the Revolutions of 1848 as a watershed. As early as November 1848, the father of communism, Karl Marx, reported in the *Neue rheinische Zeitung*: "The purposeless massacres perpetrated since the June (in Paris) and October (in Vienna) events . . . will convince the nations that there is only one way in which the murderous death agonies of the old society and the bloody birth throes of the new society can be shortened, simplified and concentrated, and that way is revolutionary terror."[14]

In his *Instruction pour une prise d'armes* (Manual for an Armed Insurrection), written twenty years after the June Days but before the Paris Commune, the old revolutionary warhorse Auguste Blanqui intoned the last rites for mass urban revolts and their barricades. He dismissed the triumph of the February Days in 1848: "However, it will be said, in 1848 the people triumphed using the methods of 1830. So be it. But let us not have any illusions! The victory of February was nothing but a stroke of luck. If Louis-Philippe had seriously defended himself, supremacy would have remained with the uniforms [the troops]."[15] He blamed the failure of the June Days on a naive faith in the uncoordinated enthusiasm of the people, and warned that similar appeals to the barricades would end in disaster: "When . . . the great Parisian revolt of [June] 1848 was shattered like glass by the most pitiful of governments, what catastrophe should we not fear if we begin again with the same stupidity, before a savage militarism, which now has in its service the recent conquests of science and technology: railways, the electric telegraph, rifled cannon, the breech-loading rifles?"[16]

Perhaps the most insightful critique came from the pen of Friedrich Engels, Marx's collaborator and an armed participant in the Revolution of 1848 in Germany. Engels declared in 1895, not long before his death: "Rebellion in the old style, street fighting with barricades, which decided the issue everywhere up to 1848, had become largely outdated."[17] Should the military forces be resolute and well led, the crowd was lost: "No wonder, then, that even the barricade fighting conducted with the greatest heroism—Paris, June 1848; Vienna, October 1848; Dresden, May 1849—ended in the defeat of the insurrection as soon as the leaders of the attack, unhampered by political considerations, acted according to purely military criteria, and their soldiers remained reliable." Further advances in military and transportation technology only made mass resistance less likely to achieve victory. Railroads made it possible for troops to concentrate rapidly against rebellious cities: "Garrisons can, in twenty-four hours, be more than doubled, and in forty-eight hours be increased to huge armies." Small arms had been greatly improved: troops once armed with the smooth-bore muzzle-loading musket were now armed with the "breech-loading magazine rifle, which shoots four times as far, ten times as accurately and ten times as fast as the former." Instead of firing iron balls, artillery now shot exploding shells "of which one is sufficient to demolish the best barricade." And there was more, but the case was made.

Radicals who lost faith in the barricades came to believe in the necessity and efficacy of terrorism, and none was more adamant than Karl Heinzen.

KARL HEINZEN AND A DOCTRINE OF TERRORISM

The scholar of terrorism Walter Laqueur identifies Karl Heinzen as "the first to provide a full-fledged doctrine of modern terrorism" and declares his "Der Mord," or "Murder," to be "the most important ideological statement of early terrorism."[18] We contend that for terrorism to be an "ism" it should have a self-conscious literature advocating its means and methods. "Murder" does that and more. Heinzen was known and read in his lifetime, but it can be argued that he only achieved his greatest audience after his death in 1880. The point here is what he saw, and when he saw it.

Heinzen was a fervent nationalist who hoped to create a unified and democratic Germany. He began his life in a prosaic enough way, but in 1840 his reformist principles gave way to radicalism. By 1847, Engels, who knew Heinzen, condemned him as a hothead spouting "bloodthirsty radicalism."[19] That year Heinzen left Europe for the United States, but he returned to Europe soon after learning that revolutions had broken out in France and Germany. A man of outsized ego, he seems to have felt that he could save the day. He involved himself in revolutionary action in Baden that took the form of full-on civil war. When its failure was final, he fled to Switzerland in 1849. That fall he traveled to London, and from there sailed back to the United States. He first set up in New York, then in Louisville, where he began publishing his radical German-language newspaper *Pionier*, and in 1859 he finally moved to Boston.

Heinzen's "Murder" first appeared in 1849 in *Die Evolution*, a radical journal published in Switzerland, where he was sheltering between forays into the revolutionary fighting in Baden. While Heinzen was in London in 1850 he began work on a much longer exposition of his thoughts, "Mord und Freiheit," or "Murder and Liberty," which he then published as a German-language pamphlet in New York during 1853.[20] We will draw from both.

Heinzen brazenly insisted: "Murder is the principal agent of historical progress."[21] State armies may call it something different, but they murder, so radical revolutionaries should own up to being murderers as well, though on a much smaller scale. "Let us call ourselves murderers as our enemies [call us], let us take the moral horror out of this great historical tool."[22] For Heinzen, justification of such an act depended only upon the ends it serves. "It is a tool, like a knife, and the only question of any relevance is whether it is used to this or that end and, further, whether it succeeds or fails in achieving it."[23] References to the French Revolution and Robespierre make it clear that Heinzen looked to the Reign of Terror for inspiration. "The path to humanity leads over the summit of barbarism."[24]

As mentioned in Chapter 1, Heinzen pointed out that radicals lacked the forces to fight openly against government troops. Sarcastically he pleaded, "Lend us your army." Recent events had proven that open confrontation with the forces of order was suicidal. Lacking sufficient capacity, radicals must employ violence condemned by common morality; they must resort to what we would call terrorism. It is not committed simply for physical effect, but for psychological impact as well: "The revolutionaries must try to bring about a situation where the barbarians are afraid for their lives every hour of the day or night."[25] In "Murder and Liberty" he praised employing "terrible weapons calculated to make single fighters frightful to organized masses [armies]" that served oppressors.[26]

Fortunately, Heinzen wrote, modern science provides the means by which a few can defeat many. "The aim of our study must be to eliminate the superiority of the barbarian party through the invention of new methods of killing, so as to nullify the numerical advantage of the organized masses by means of instruments of destruction which can be operated by a small number of people."[27] Dynamite would not become part of the terrorist arsenal for another twenty years, but new explosives, such as mercury fulminate, excited Heinzen with their possibilities. He posited that the "greatest benefactor of mankind will be he who makes it possible for a few men to wipe out thousands."[28] He threatened reactionaries: "Gentlemen, physics and chemistry can be more important for the revolution than your entire chivalry and science of war."[29]

Heinzen endorsed the assassination of rulers, but went much further: he preached the destruction of an entire system by attacks on *all* its agents. "It is folly and self-betrayal, if the revolution confines self-defense to the result of the moment. It must exterminate the reaction's representatives, its bearers, and its accomplices, because its enemies are ... irredeemable.... May the people carry out the verdict!"[30]

He held, "The revolution is nothing other than self-defense."[31] Against righteous radicals, the reaction deploys its forces, its "tools," but "the revolution alone has martyrs."[32] Terrorist "murderers" are the true heroes.

THE CONTEXT OF EMERGING RADICAL TERRORISM

By midcentury, Europe was in the midst of transformations that demanded radical responses. Every age has its changes and transitions, to be sure, but those faced by Europeans during this period rate as utterly momentous. The American and, particularly, the French revolutions challenged centuries-old political assumptions and practices of monarchical/aristocratic regimes, and raised the beacon of republican and democratic governments, replacing authoritarian principles with liberal freedoms and a bourgeois elite. For others, hopes for national independence or unity inspired activism. Italy, Poland, and the Balkans were divided under foreign imperial domination, and much of the Irish population felt subjugated under British rule.

At the same time, economic and demographic upheavals cracked and shifted the tectonic plates of society, creating a new geography of class, poverty, and prosperity. Nineteenth-century Europe experienced the industrial revolution, a fundamental transformation of production and life. The economic and social transformations of the period might be seen as progress to us in retrospect; however, at the time, they produced dislocation and disadvantage for workers overwhelmed by them.

This was magnified still further by exponential population growth and urbanization. Between 1800 and 1900, the population of Europe and the Russian Empire grew at what was then an unprecedented rate, more than doubling from 187 million to 401 million. However, city populations multiplied even more impressively: Paris grew fivefold, from 547,000 to 2,714,000; London sixfold, from 1,011,000 to 6,226,000; and Berlin nearly elevenfold, from 172,000 to 1,889,000. The loss of old ways and homes and the exploitation of dispossessed populations in industrial settings deepened disparities of wealth and well-being. The intense sense of injustice this sowed can be summed up as "the social question," which drove the dispossessed and those who championed them to take up arms.

A belief in the need for a new kind of society obsessed the European radical intelligentsia, although the exact form of that new world and the path by which to reach it were matters of contention. It was a volatile concoction of cause and conviction directed toward bringing down the status quo.

Radicals committed to a variety of causes, from nationalism to communism, adopted terrorism during the first wave. And from the start, first-wave radical terrorism of many stripes was transnational. A cohort of radicals and their works espousing terrorist strategies circulated in Europe, the Americas, and even other corners of the world.

Rationales for Radicals: Nationalism, Liberalism,
    Democracy, and Republicanism

The rationales for radicalism can be roughly divided between political and social, although the two often merged. Four causes stand out as being essentially political: nationalism in the form of desires for national independence or unification; liberalism as a pursuit for greater constitutionally guaranteed freedoms within a given state; democracy as the desire for representative political institutions chosen through a universal male electorate; and republicanism, meaning the replacement of traditional monarchical heads of state by representative constitutional institutions.

A traditional definition of nationalism still serves our purposes best here. Hans Kohn wrote: "Nationalism is a state of mind in which the supreme loyalty of the individual is felt to be due the nation-state."[33] Readers today are likely to see the terms *state* and *nation* as interchangeable, but they were quite distinct, although related, in the nineteenth century. The modern state came first, pretty much full-blown by the late seventeenth-century as a political reality with specific boundaries, common bureaucratic governing institutions, and sovereignty residing at the center, usually in the person of a monarch. The "nation" as a people, characterized by a shared self-perception and history, came later.

The concept of nationalism held that a nation should have its own state, its own authority over itself. The French Revolution turned a Bourbon-ruled state into one that represented the French nation. Nationalism was a *result* of revolution for the French; it would more likely be the *cause* of revolution in other parts of continental Europe. Nationalism could inspire terrorist violence in two circumstances above all: a desire to bring about national unification or a struggle to liberate a nation group from occupation or oppression by a government perceived as foreign. The first applied to Germany and Italy, the second to Greece and Ireland. When nationalism is the creed of an ethnic group without a state of its own, it seems apropos to speak of it as ethno-nationalism, a matter of aspiration.

There was another, more subtle implication of nationalism for terrorism. The historian Benedict Anderson describes the nation as an "imagined community," a matter of belief. "It is *imagined* because the members of even the smallest nation will never know most of their fellow-members, meet them, or even hear of them, yet in the minds of each lives the image of their communion."³⁴ The imagined community of the nation brought its members together as one, and as a result created a very large target community for terrorists who wished it harm. Attack a handful, and you have attacked the whole. A lesser act of violence is multiplied by the size of the nation. This is the nation as a victim, rather than as the aggressive agent, of terrorism.

The first wave of radical terrorism was inspired by the greatest range of causes and ideologies, but it was nationalism, or ethno-nationalism, that bookended the first wave in Europe. Heinzen was an ardent German nationalist; Felice Orsini, an Italian nationalist, attempted to assassinate Napoleon III in 1858; and the most consequential terrorist act of the first wave, the assassination of Archduke Franz Ferdinand in 1914, was the work of Serbian nationalist terrorists. In this last incidence of terrorism, the lowest level of warfare set in motion the doomsday machine that produced the greatest extremes of armed conflict that the world had yet seen—World War I.

Liberalism advocated a very different set of political goals, including freedom of the press, constitutional government, representative assemblies, and a more inclusive franchise. Democracy, defined as universal manhood suffrage, stood at the radical left of franchise. The cause of votes for women lagged behind; French women were not guaranteed the right to vote until 1944, although men won the vote a century before. Liberalism and democracy could be united with nationalism.

In a world of states still ruled by monarchs, republicanism was another revolutionary ideology, for it advocated the abolition of crowned rulers and their replacement by elected heads of state. During the period 1815–1914, France was the sole European great power under a republican form of government, first the Second Republic (1848–1852) and then the Third Republic (1870–1940), but for most of the century even France was ruled by crowned heads of state. However, thrones became less safe in an age of radical terrorism, as monarchs became targets of assassination.

Rationales for Radicals: Nihilism, Populism, Anarchism,
    Socialism, and Communism
Ideologies also developed during the nineteenth century in response to the social question. Radicals embraced the revolutionary principle that

the most fundamental structures, institutions, and practices of government and society could be challenged and changed. Nihilism, populism, anarchism, socialism, and communism espoused different ideologies that questioned the very foundations of values, class, and governance.

Nihilists rejected the validity of basic tenets of government, religion, and society, often insisting on science as the source of truth. As espoused by different individuals, nihilism encompassed differing focuses and levels of disbelief and dissent. There was something implicitly paradoxical in revolutionary nihilism, because to carry out radical action based on critical disbelief, nihilists had to believe passionately in something else.

In Russia, nihilism could lead to populism, meaning a strong faith in the peasantry as the critical revolutionary class, one that was hideously oppressed under czarist autocracy. This led the young, essentially student intelligentsia to "go to the people," as we will see below. While there certainly were differences between nihilism and populism, the paramount Russian terrorist group before 1890, Narodnaya Volya, merged elements of the two, along with principles similar to European liberalism, such as desire for constitutional government and civil liberties.

West of Russia, anarchism attracted the greatest number of violent revolutionary adherents in Europe before World War I. The first important radical figure to declare "I am an anarchist" was Pierre-Joseph Proudhon (1809–1865), who used these words in his 1840 essay "What Is Property?"[35] He also linked his distaste for central government with a denial of private property, declaring that "property is theft." A prolific proponent of anarchist thought, Peter Kropotkin, defined anarchism for the 1910 edition of the *Encyclopedia Britannica*: "a principle or theory of life and conduct under which society is conceived without government—harmony in such a society being obtained, not by submission to law, or by obedience to any authority, but by free agreements concluded between the various groups, territorial and professional, freely constituted for the sake of production and consumption, as also for the satisfaction of the infinite variety of needs and aspirations of a civilized being."[36]

Real revolution must involve the devolution of authority from a powerful central government toward voluntary organizations, such as community-based associations and labor unions. In an address given on May Day 1895, the anarchist theoretician and historian Max Nettlau (1865–1944) proclaimed his distress at state control: "Whether it be a little more democratized or not it does not matter, for we reject Democracy as well as Absolutism. . . . All we Anarchists want is equal freedom for all. The workers to provide for their own affairs by voluntary arrangements amongst themselves."[37]

Anarchists stressed freedom and self-discipline; however, a broad range of opinion and action created a considerable variety within the big tent of anarchism. Many combined anarchism with anti-capitalism and socialism in anarcho-socialism.

Socialism denied the validity of private ownership of the means of agricultural and industrial production and advocated instead some form of social ownership, from peasant or worker communes, at one extreme, to state ownership at the other. Like anarchism, socialism encompassed a spectrum of proponents.

Communism was a form of socialism of a particularly radical cast, which would fashion a classless society based on the common ownership of the means of production. Anarchists could hold communist views, but such anarcho-communists retained their distrust of an authoritarian state and would vest common ownership as much as possible directly in the peasants who worked the land and the workers who toiled in the factories. In contrast, the communism espoused by Marx (1818–1883), Engels (1820–1895), and, in its Russian avatar, Georgi Plekhanov (1856–1918) and Vladimir Lenin (1870–1924), argued that this profound and difficult transition would have to be managed by a revolutionary elite directing an authoritarian government functioning as the stewards of the workers—a dictatorship of the proletariat—at least for a time.

Identifying the ideological differences between revolutionary groups is made all the more challenging by the evolution and overlap of radical creeds. In reality, teasing out substantive but still subtle contrasts lay beyond the concerns of frightened and outraged target communities attacked by terrorism. During the period under discussion, authorities, newspapers, and general populations usually denounced all acts of terrorism as "anarchist."

THE CHARACTER OF FIRST-WAVE TERRORISM AND TERRORISTS

Radicals of several persuasions turned to terrorism as the most effective alternative in the repertoire of violent political resistance in a transnational revolutionary environment. This is basic, but there is more to say about the character of first-wave radical terrorism, including the role of new technologies of death, the link between action and publicity, and the romantic self-image of terrorists themselves.

The Technology of Murder

As we have seen in the work of Heinzen, the modern technology of explosives excited the terrorist imagination. The mercury fulminate so exalted by Heinzen in "Murder and Liberty" was more powerful than gunpowder, but so sensitive that a pile of it could explode under its own weight! Nitroglycerine, first synthesized in a laboratory in 1847, was so unstable and dangerous that its transportation was eventually banned. Albert Nobel labored to find a safer form of the explosive, and succeeded by mixing nitroglycerine with diatomaceous earth; in 1867 he patented this as dynamite, so stable that it required a detonator to explode, but many times more powerful than gunpowder. In 1875, he invented another, even more stable explosive, gelignite, which could be molded into different forms.

What Nobel intended as a boon to mining, construction, and industry was ecstatically embraced by terrorists. *The Alarm*, a Chicago radical newspaper edited by the anarchist Albert Parsons, crowed in October 1884: "One man armed with a dynamite bomb is equal to one regiment of militia, when it is used at the right time and place."[38] His wife, Lucy Parsons, a woman of color, put it more poetically: "The voice of dynamite is the voice of force, the only voice that tyranny has ever been able to understand."[39]

Anarchists shared their deadly secrets. The initial issue of *La révolution sociale*, the first anarchist journal published after the Paris Commune, appeared in Paris on 12 September 1880 and continued publishing for a year. Issues included a section on bomb manufacture, entitled Études scientifiques (Scientific Studies). *La lutte* (Struggle) appeared in Lyon in April 1883, not long after anarchists bombed a restaurant in that city. It included instructions on the making of explosives in a section called, with bitter humor, "Anti-Capitalist Products." Bombs meant to inflict maximum casualties commonly included nails and other bits of metal that became projectiles when the device exploded.

Bombs were not the only way "to proceed from words to actions," as the firearms industry had also obliged terrorists with the manufacture of small, easily concealed handguns. The first cartridge-firing revolver was produced in the mid-1850s by Smith & Wesson. The American John Browning designed an effective small semiautomatic pistol for a Belgian manufacturer in 1898. With some improvement, it became the FN Browning M1900, one of which was used by an assassin to shoot the Russian governor-general of Finland. Browning's later design, the FN 1910, was the pistol used to assassinate Archduke Franz Ferdinand on 28 June 1914.

When, in 1911, Leon Trotsky criticized what he condemned as the kind of "individual terrorism" committed by anarchists, he belittled their efforts by commenting, "The recipe for explosives is accessible to all, and a Browning can be obtained anywhere."[40] Any foolish enthusiast could resort to individual terrorism, because its means had become so available. Trotsky advocated the mass working-class–oriented Marxist approach to revolution.

It is common for historians to credit the new technologies of explosives and firearms as being essential to the rise of radical terrorism in the late nineteenth century. But this probably overestimates their impact. Hand-held bombs and small pistols were readily available in earlier ages. Gunpowder grenades were employed in siege warfare at least from the end of the sixteenth century. Small flintlock pocket pistols were quite available during the eighteenth century. If we want to identify the most important technological factors that brought terrorism to the fore, they are those that so advantaged the forces of order that mass crowd violence no longer promised success. Bombs and pistols simply facilitated what was made necessary by other factors.

Propaganda of the Deed
The principle of "propaganda of the deed" appealed to first-wave radical terrorists of all stripes. It was an advocacy for *action*, as opposed to cautious inaction, ideological debate, or popular education—the pistol over the pamphlet. Appeals to propaganda of the deed were, and still are, used to justify attacks by radical terrorists.

Heinzen did not use the term, but in its spirit, his work emphasized the violent act. The first to claim the importance of the deed over the word was Carlo Pisacane (1818–1857), who died in an ill-conceived Italian nationalist revolt. The year of his death he wrote his "Political Testament," in which he argued: "Propaganda of the idea is a chimera. The education of the people is an absurdity. Ideas spring from deeds not the other way around . . . as I see it, conspiracies, plots, and attempted risings are the succession of deeds whereby Italy proceeds towards her goal of unity. The flash of Milan's bayonet was more effective propaganda than a thousand volumes penned by doctrinaires . . . ."[41] The anarchist Mikhail Bakunin would do more to popularize the principle in his "Letters to a Frenchman on the Present Crisis," written in 1870, during the Franco-Prussian War: "All of us must now embark on stormy revolutionary seas, and from this very moment we must spread our principles, not with words but with deeds, for this is the most popular, the most potent, and the most irresistible form of propaganda."[42] When anarchists met in the International Anarchist Congress held in London during July 1881, they adopted a resolution that stated: "The International Workingmen's Association has regarded it as necessary to supplement spoken and written propaganda by propaganda by deed."[43]

This early enthusiasm for propaganda of the deed would eventually be criticized by *some* of its former advocates. In 1894, the old firebrand Peter Kropotkin wrote: "A structure based on centuries of history cannot be destroyed with a few kilos of dynamite."[44] In the 1890s mass labor demonstrations and strikes were showing more promise as a means of change.

Nonetheless, propaganda of the deed, under one title or another, has continued to inspire radical terrorists to this day. It is a creed of action, attractive to the committed and the desperate.

The Terrorist Mindset: Mystique and Martyrdom
The political extremists who turned to radical terrorism promoted a new mystique of resistance, encompassing its own ideals of virtue, heroism, and martyrdom. This melded ruthless prescriptions for violence and killing with romantic portrayals of the terrorist as an idealist who sacrificed his or her prospects for personal happiness in order to achieve the greater good of humanity. These ingredients proved to be basic to the terrorist mindset then and later.

We have already witnessed Heinzen's identification of the terrorist as martyr. One of the earliest and most famous, or infamous, Russian statements of the creed came from the pen of Sergey Nechayev in 1869.

He wrote this "Catechism of a Revolutionary" when he was close to Bakunin, and there is some debate as to whether it was a joint project. The "Catechism" begins: "The revolutionary is a doomed man. He has no personal interests, no business affairs, no emotions, no attachments, no property, and no name. Everything in him is wholly absorbed in the single thought and the single passion for revolution."[45] He is allowed "no friendship or attachment, except for those who have proved by their actions that they, like him, are dedicated to revolution." His revolution "destroys the entire State to the roots and exterminates all the state traditions, institutions, and classes in Russia." Nechayev died a revolutionary's death in 1882, imprisoned by the state he so wished to eradicate.

The will and testament written by Ignati Grinevitsky the night before he died in the same explosion that killed Alexander II expressed similarly dramatic notions of the revolutionary's fate. Soon after that assassination, Sergey Stepnyak-Kravchinsky, an anarchist militant who wrote under the name Stepniak, published *Underground Russia: Revolutionary Profiles and Sketches from Life*, a series of brief biographies of revolutionaries. His description of "the terrorist" rings with a tone even more romantic than found in Nechayev: "He is noble, terrible, irresistibly fascinating, for he combines in himself the two sublimities of human grandeur: the martyr and the hero. He is a martyr. From the day when he swears in the depths of his heart to free the people and the country, he knows he is consecrated to Death."[46]

Important literary figures such as Ivan Turgenev, Fyodor Dostoevsky, Émile Zola, Henry James, G. K. Chesterton, and Joseph Conrad also focused on terrorism. In 1878, Turgenev offered his portrait of a terrorist in his poem "The Threshold." The poem places "a young girl ... an ordinary Russian girl" before the threshold of a foreboding door. A disembodied voice asks if she is willing to endure what faces her: "Cold, hunger, hatred, derision, contempt, abuse, prison, sickness, and maybe even death?" To all these challenges she answers yes. The voice then asks, "Are you ready to sacrifice yourself?," and again she answers yes. She also protests that she is ready to commit a crime, if necessary. Finally she affirms her selflessness: "I need neither gratitude, nor any pity. I do not need a name." She passes all the tests, so the voice invites her to enter, and she does. The poem ends: "'Fool,' someone said from behind. 'Saint,' someone replied."[47]

Works of literature even influenced real-world terrorists: the anarchist terrorist Émile Henry quoted Zola's *Germinal* during his trial.

A surprising aspect of terrorist thought, from the beginning, is its religious tone, even when espoused by atheists. One reads the language of absolute good and evil, apocalypse and salvation, sacrifice and martyrdom. Such themes appear again and again, along with the conviction that violence alone can achieve the necessary good. Strong convictions that resemble religious faith are not the exclusive property of religious terrorism. We will look at this fact again in Chapter 8.

VARIATIONS ON THE THEME OF RADICAL TERRORISM

The phenomenon of terrorism was transnational from the start, in that national borders did not delimit the flow of ideas, individuals, and practices. But it is also true that the philosophies, actions, and chronologies of emergent first-wave radical terrorism differed from country to country. Therefore, we will consider a few case studies to illustrate commonalities and contrasts. This chapter deals directly with Europe, where modern radical terrorism was born. Russia and France will receive most of the attention. But first-wave radical terrorism also has an American history, and for that please go to our website, where we offer supplementary materials. As already noted, assassinations of prominent individuals typified this first wave of terrorism, and these attacks were not simply palace murders, but killings meant to unhinge policies and regimes. At the same time, there were indiscriminate attacks aimed not at particular individuals but at types, such as law enforcement and members of the hated bourgeoisie.

The First Radical Terrorist Campaign of the First Wave?

In concentrating on Russian and French terrorism from the late 1870s to 1920, we will not be focusing on nationalist-inspired terrorism; however, it remained a continuous terrorist theme among marginalized national groups. And a series of *attentats* by Italian nationalists operating in France arguably ranks as the initial terrorist campaign of the first wave of radical terrorism.

To understand this campaign, we need a little background. As part of the Revolutions of 1848, Italian nationalists took over the lands the papacy controlled as a state—Rome and the territory immediately surrounding it—and created the Republic of Rome in February 1849. The president of the new French republic, Louis Bonaparte, who would later seize power as Emperor Napoleon III, sent French troops to attack the Roman Republic and restore the pope to his political authority. This resulted in a siege of Rome and the downfall of the Roman Republic in July 1849. One of the most inspiring leaders of the Roman Republic and the cause of Italian unification was Giuseppe Mazzini. Mazzini and others regarded Napoleon III as a roadblock to Italian unification and concluded that he must be eliminated. The hope was that assassinating the emperor would precipitate a new republican revolution in France that would produce a government favorable to Italian unification.

After the defeat of the Roman Republic, Mazzini became a refugee, with one base in London, and he encouraged or engineered *attentats* against Napoleon III. On 28 April 1855, Giovani Pianori, a young Italian radical who had also drifted to London, attempted to assassinate the French emperor with pistol shots, but missed and was apprehended. In 1857, Mazzini wrote a letter urging: "Carrying out *attentats* is vital for Italy. . . . The Paris affair has become more urgent than ever."[48] A copy of this letter fell into the hands of Paris police, who identified and arrested three would-be Italian assassins. When taken into custody, they were in possession of a carton containing sixteen handguns and some knives that had been shipped to them from England.

Another *attentat* in this chain was carried out by Felice Orsini in 1858. He was a prominent member of the Carbonari, who had fought for Italian unification in the Revolution of 1848 and was elected to be a legislator in the Roman Republic. He too engaged with the London community of Italian emigrés. Orsini took advantage of modern chemistry and metallurgy to develop a new kind of bomb, one that exploded on contact rather than requiring a lit fuse to detonate the main charge. This Orsini bomb bristled with small projections filled with mercury fulminate that exploded when they struck a hard object, igniting the main explosive charge in the body of the bomb. Once the bombs were successfully tested in England, Orsini took several to Paris, where he joined with other conspirators. They then attacked Napoleon's carriage on the evening of 14 January, while the emperor and Empress Eugénie were on the way to the opera. Three bombs were hurled and detonated, but they failed to injure their intended targets; however, they killed eight other people and wounded 142, including Orsini. In his journal, *Pionier*, Heinzen saluted Orsini for his act.

In the complicated twists and turns of history, Napoleon III did commit French troops to the cause of Italian unification the next year. France joined with Victor Emmanuel, king of Piedmont-Sardinia, winning the battle of Solferino and compelling the Austrians to give up their hold on Lombardy—a critical step in Italian unification. In that sense, Orsini achieved his goal. However, the French still supported the pope's political authority in Rome, and for this, Italian nationalists once again targeted the emperor for assassination in January 1864. Four conspirators armed with bombs and pistols reached Paris, but the Parisian police arrested them before they could strike. A French garrison remained in Rome until it was recalled in 1870 to fight in the Franco-Prussian War. Only then were the papal lands absorbed into the new Italian state.

One aside: the armored carriage in which Alexander II was riding the day of his assassination was a gift from Napoleon III, meant to provide the czar with greater protection.

The Russian Experience
While the campaign of assassination attempts on Napoleon III can be seen as a terrorist harbinger in intent, organization, and method, it did not set off a continuous series of terrorist assaults. But Vera Zasulich's attempted assassination of the governor of St. Petersburg in 1878 did. Russian terrorism had deep roots. First came the sense of cause dating back to the early nineteenth century, followed by frustration with other routes toward change, and only then did radicals appeal to terrorist violence.

In this progression, we must mention the failure of the Decembrist Revolt in 1825, the disappointment with reform under Alexander II, disillusionment with propaganda of the word, and Narodnaya Volya's dedication to violence.

From 1816, a small band of forward-looking Russian Army officers favored the abolition of serfdom and the transition of Russia away from autocracy. The most assertive reformers hoped to establish a republican government, and they planned to stage a military-led revolution when the czar died and his successor was just taking power, often a time of confusion. Alexander I died on 1 December 1825, and on the morning of 26 December rebel officers led about 3,000 troops to seize Senate Square in St. Petersburg. However, they were overmatched by the new Czar Nicholas I, who soon rallied 9,000 loyal troops to crush the revolt. Shocked by the threat from liberal rebels, Nicholas pursued repressive, autocratic policies. Military coup had failed.

Nicholas died in 1855, and Alexander II succeeded his father. The new czar carried out substantial reforms, including the emancipation of the serfs in 1861. He also instituted important legal and military changes, as well as promoting local self-government in the countryside and large towns. However, his reforms did not satisfy those who held radical opinions, and opposition increased over time. Reform had disappointed.

The same year that Alexander II emancipated the serfs, a new word appeared in the Russian lexicon: intelligentsia. At first it referred to students, but by the late 1860s the word had been appropriated exclusively by revolutionaries, primarily sons and daughters of the middle class, self-defined as progressive. The intelligentsia embraced a form of populism that viewed the peasantry as the key revolutionary class even after the reforms of Alexander II. There was something earnest but also painfully naive in their faith that the people, the *narod*, could be mobilized by the young intelligentsia, who became known as "Narodniks."

In 1874, populist Narodniks ventured out into the countryside during the "mad summer" to make the peasants more conscious of their plight and how they might alleviate it. However, the Narodniks' efforts at propaganda of the word were unsuccessful, even ridiculous. Chastened, they formed the clandestine group Zemlya i Volya, or Land and Liberty, in 1876 to redirect their efforts to the immediate needs of the peasantry. During that year, they staged the first public revolutionary demonstration under the banner "Long Live the Socialist Revolution, Long Live Land and Liberty."[49]

Tensions within the group arose between those still interested in propaganda of the word and those dedicated to propaganda of the deed. The concept of terrorism was already there before a campaign of such violence actually began. Nechayev languished in prison, but his words were already well known, and violent Narodniks, notably Valerian Osinsky, were speaking of terrorism in 1876. And then Vera Zasulich fired the opening shot in a long terrorist campaign on 24 January 1878. This friend of Nechayev had been tried and imprisoned in 1869 for her radical opinions. Now, armed with a revolver, she seriously wounded the repressive governor of St. Petersburg. Zasulich's victim was so hated that a skillful defense at her trial made him the villain of the affair, and Zasulich was acquitted. She fled to escape being retried. It was the attempted assassination by Zasulich and her trial that inspired Turgenev to write his prose poem "The Threshold," which we have already cited. Some, including David Rapoport, date the beginning of the first wave of modern terrorism to Zasulich's act. Of course, I prefer to push the date back to the failure of the Revolutions of 1848 and the writings of Heinzen.

Osinsky and his confederates in Kiev carried out several assassination attempts soon after Zasulich's bold stroke. In May 1878, one of Osinsky's comrades killed Kiev's police chief. Stepniak, a member of Land and Liberty, stabbed and killed General Nikolai Mezentsov, chief of the czar's Third Section, the Russian counterradical police, in St. Petersburg on 4 August 1878. Stepniak eventually fled the country and settled in London, where he became a minor celebrity with the publication of *Underground Russia*.

Disagreements over the role of terrorist violence in the revolutionary process troubled Land and Liberty and were temporarily reconciled at a conference in June 1879. However, soon thereafter, Land and Liberty split into two groups with different philosophies. From this split emerged Narodnaya Volya, People's Will, which adopted a terrorist course. Narodnaya Volya embraced propaganda of the deed, but it also had a voice. The initial issue of the party's paper, *The People's Will*, appeared in October 1879; it would continue to be published sporadically until October 1885. Narodnaya Volya eventually created a network of chapters in nearly fifty Russian cities, but its total membership never included more than 500. The historian of terrorism Michael Carr terms Narodnaya Volya "the world's first self-styled terrorist organization."[50] But we must remember Mazzini's Italians.

Narodnaya Volya plotted to carry out the most dramatic attack possible in Russia, the assassination of Czar Alexander II. The successful assassination on 13 March 1881, the account of which began this chapter, was hardly the first attempt to kill the czar. Attacks on his life had been made in 1866, 1867, and April 1879, before the creation of Narodnaya Volya.

Narodnaya Volya was very much taken with explosives, establishing three "dynamite centers" in St. Petersburg to craft bombs. In December 1879 Narodnaya Volya terrorists attempted to bomb the czar's train as it traveled from the Crimea to Moscow; however, they failed to strike the train carrying the czar, although that carrying the court's servants was hit, but without serious injury to anyone. The next year, in February, a cadre of Narodnaya Volya employed as a carpenter at the Winter Palace smuggled in a large quantity of dynamite, from which he assembled a powerful bomb in a room below the palace banquet hall. Intending to kill the czar, the terrorist detonated the bomb during a royal reception. It caused great damage, killing eleven and wounding fifty-six; however, the czar was delayed and not present when the explosion tore the room apart.

Narodnaya Volya finally accomplished its goal by assassinating the czar in March 1881. While that attack shocked Europe and Russia, it accomplished little. Nine days later, the organization's executive committee addressed a letter to Alexander III, the son of the slain czar. The letter appealed for "an assembly of representatives of all Russian people, for the purpose of examining the existing forms of our state and society, and revising them in accord with the desires of the people."[51] But this was a pipe dream.

Instead of responding with liberal reforms, Alexander III intensified repression and eliminated what was left of Narodnaya Volya within a few years. In fact, the intensity of revolutionary violence abated for nearly two decades after the death of Alexander II, but discontent continued to fester. Hard economic times, the alienation of much of Russian society, and the rooting of socialist thought, notably of Marxism, prepared the way for a new resurgence of radical terrorism. This was predominantly the work of the new Socialist Revolutionary Party (SR) founded in 1901. The SR ascribed to a form of anarcho-socialist agricultural populism that went back to Land and Liberty and Narodnaya Volya, mixed with Marxist interpretations. However, the SR lacked the Marxist insistence on the need for a nationalized economy under a strong state. The SR quickly created its own Combat Organization, also known as the Terrorist Brigade, a small, semi-autonomous organization of violent extremists who undertook the deadly work. At its height, it numbered some sixty active terrorists, a fifth of whom were women.

As opposed to the score killed by Narodnaya Volya, this twentieth-century plague of terrorist attacks killed and wounded at least 17,000 from 1901 through 1916, according to historian Anna Geifman.[52] At the height of this carnage, the period beginning in October 1905 and lasting through December 1907, 4,500 Russian government officials were casualties, along with 4,710 private individuals. This tally was associated with the Russian Revolution of 1905.

Terrorists tried to assassinate the Russian prime minister, Peter Stolypin, on 25 August 1906. They struck at his country home, where he was holding a reception. The bombs they detonated killed twenty-eight, including his teenage daughter, and severely wounded his three-year-old son, but only slightly injured the prime minister himself.

The difference in the *quantity* of terrorist attacks by the SR amounted to a difference of *quality* as well. Unlike the assassination of Alexander II, the thousands of individuals assassinated from 1902 through 1916 added up to a mass attack on an entire class of officials, generating fear and outrage within a large target community. The Organization wielded an extremely broad brush in condemning individuals as guilty, including not just rulers and officials, but nearly everyone who wore a uniform, from grand princes to common policemen.

Along with government officials and agents, an increasing number of private individuals also suffered during this period. On 17 December 1905, anarchists bombed the Café Libman in Odessa, killing and wounding twelve, because they believed it was frequented by the bourgeoisie, although in fact it was also a haunt of the intelligentsia.

This era of revolutionary violence also involved what were called revolutionary "expropriations," that is, robberies intended to finance the revolutionaries, including their terrorist campaigns. We will see that radical terrorists have continued to engage in criminal activities including robberies, but also, in recent times, kidnapping for ransom and involvement in the drug trade to support themselves. During the year following October 1905, there were, according to Geifman, 1,951 robberies, of which 940 were committed against "state and private monetary institutions."[53]

Though he survived the Combat Organization's attack in 1907, Stolypin was fatally shot at the Kiev Opera House in 1911 by an anarchist revolutionary. This was not the work of the Organization, which had been disbanded in 1910.

The French Experience: The Attentats

Russian terrorism directed against czarist authoritarianism peaked twice, in 1878–1881 and 1905–1910, and French anarchist terrorism also had its high season, in 1881–1894, and then declined. Certainly, French anarchist terrorism flared under very different political circumstances—a republican constitutional regime, with a franchise and civil liberties that Russians could only envy. Yet there was also a well-remembered experience of repression, the defeat of the Paris Commune, where, once again, barricades had failed the radicals. Revolutionary violence and anarchism were native to France, and they found focus in the plight of industrial workers under the Third Republic. Socialism grafted onto anarchism, and Marxist conceptions of class and class warfare identified the bourgeoisie and its agents as the enemy.

Anarchism as a theory was forty years old in France by 1880, but propaganda of the deed only became its modus operandi after that year, brought to the fore by its prominence in Russia. In May 1881, Louise Michel, a veteran radical of the Paris Commune only released from imprisonment in 1880, spoke before a Parisian revolutionary group in praise of the assassination of Alexander II and propaganda of the deed: "Look what happened in Russia; look at the great nihilist party, see its members who know how to die so boldly and so gloriously! Why not do as they do? ... Imitate the nihilists, and I will be in the lead; only then will we be worthy of freedom, will we be able to seize it by conquest; on the remains of a rotten society that is everywhere breaking apart and that every good citizen must eliminate by iron and fire, we will establish the new social world."[54]

Within months of this address, Émile Florion set out to assassinate French prime minister Léon Gambetta on 20 October 1881, but was thwarted. An attempted assassination of an industrialist by a worker on the heels of a February 1882 strike in Roanne ranks as another of the first attacks of significance in a wave of *attentats*.

After the arrest of over fifty anarchists in Lyon, two bombs exploded in the Assommoir, an all-night restaurant thought to be frequented by bourgeois patrons. The blasts killed one and wounded several on 23 October 1882. This *attentat* stands out because it did not target a particular notable victim but intentionally struck indiscriminately at members of a class despised by anarchists.

The community of radical violent anarchists was not large during the early 1880s, but it was growing. There were perhaps thirteen Parisian anarchist groups in 1882, with a combined membership of only about 200. By 1893, a police estimate set the number of anarchists at 2,400. Authorities considered 852 of this number to be dangerous.[55]

French anarchist terrorism may have been undergirded by concepts of liberty and government by consensus, but it also had a strong element of revenge—of individual anarchists taking it upon themselves to enforce justice. This illustrates an aspect of radical terrorism as punishment as well as the pursuit of a political cause. Consider the chain of *attentats* that we can trace back to May Day 1891. On that occasion, French soldiers fired on a workers' holiday demonstration, killing nine and wounding thirty-five. The same day, anarchists from Saint-Denis, a suburb of Paris, mounted a small march of thirty participants, red flag in the lead, to Clichy. When police and demonstrators exchanged shots, the police arrested three. A trial found two guilty and sentenced them to hard labor for five and three years, respectively. They became known as the Clichy martyrs.

François Koenigstein, who styled himself Ravachol, took it upon himself to avenge the Clichy martyrs and in doing so detonated the opening blasts in a series of terrorist reprisals. A man with a sordid history of theft and murder, Ravachol arrived in Saint-Denis not long after the events at Clichy and embedded himself in the working-class anarchist community. In 1892, he bombed the homes of the judge and the prosecutor at the martyrs' trial. He failed to assassinate his intended victims, although he wounded six individuals in the second bombing. After that attack, Ravachol immediately had lunch at the Restaurant Véry, where he boasted of his deed within earshot of a waiter. The waiter denounced Ravachol to the police, who arrested the culprit a few days later, and the anarchist press lionized Ravachol. On 25 April, the eve of Ravachol's trial, an anarchist exploded a bomb at the Restaurant Véry as punishment for compromising Ravachol; two died in the explosion. Ravachol was tried for his bombings and sentenced to hard labor for life, but he was then tried for murders he had previously committed, and was sentenced to death. He cried, "Long live anarchy!" when the sentence was pronounced.

A year later, Léon-Jules Léauthier, a young anarchist shoemaker who admired radical martyrs, set his mind to avenging "the sublime Ravachol" by striking out at a bourgeois, any bourgeois. Léauthier sought his quarry in fine restaurants. He failed at his first attempt on 12 November 1893, but the next evening he stabbed a young, well-dressed young man who happened to be the Serbian ambassador. Léauthier was sentenced to imprisonment for life.

The chain added more links when Auguste Vaillant sought revenge for Ravachol by lobbing a small bomb from the visitors' gallery into the French Chamber of Deputies on 9 December 1893. He wounded forty, most with mere scratches. There were no fatalities, but Vaillant was, nonetheless, sentenced to death—the first person to go to the guillotine in nineteenth-century France without having actually killed someone. Vaillant's poor ten-year-old daughter appealed directly to the president of France, Marie François Sadi Carnot, but to no avail. Vaillant was guillotined on 5 February 1894, and within twenty-four hours of his burial, a small pyramid was found on the grave with an inscription, "Glory to thee, I am only a child, but I will avenge thee."[56]

Retribution would not be long in coming. A week later, the anarchist Émile Henry tossed a bomb into the Café Terminus at the Gare Saint-Lazare, killing one and wounding twenty. Henry tried to escape the scene of his attack but was seized in his flight. Soon after his arrest, he explained that his aim had been to attack not the specific people killed and injured at the Terminus, "but rather the entire bourgeoisie, of which the former was only a representative."[57] In a formal statement written for the trial, Henry referenced the executions of Ravachol and Vaillant and explained his action as class warfare: "[We will] spare neither women nor children because the women and children we love have not been spared. Are they not innocent victims, these children, who in the faubourgs [suburbs] slowly die of anemia, because bread is rare at home; these women who in your workshops suffer exhaustion and are worn out in order to earn forty cents a day, happy that misery has not yet forced them into prostitution?"[58] Thus, it was not the individual he aimed at, but the type: "I struck at random and did not choose my victims."[59]

In his micro-history of the bombing of the Café Terminus, John Merriman argues that Henry's *attentat* signaled the transition from assassinations of specific individuals to random killings of a much larger target audience; in fact, he titles his volume *The Dynamite Club: How a*

Bombing in Fin-de-Siècle Paris Ignited the Age of Modern Terrorism. But Henry's indiscriminate attack was hardly unprecedented; in the French experience recounted here, we have already mentioned the bombing of the Assommoir in Lyon in 1882 and Léauthier's efforts the next year. The most relevant previous attack struck in Barcelona, where the anarchist Santiago Salvador threw two Orsini bombs in the Liceu Opera House on 7 November 1893, killing twenty and injuring scores of others. This attack on the bourgeoisie received a good deal of press, including a front-page illustration in the tabloid *Le petit journal*.

The wave of attacks in France created an anti-anarchist hysteria throughout France and its capital, what Merriman calls a "dynamite psychosis."[60] This could be bizarre; witness the 1885 song "Dame Dynamite," a hit at the Montmartre Cabaret du Chat Rouge.[61] But the phenomenon was darker and more terrifying than amusing. Henry Vizetelly, translator and publisher of Zola's works, historian of anarchism, and an observer of this age, wrote: "Now the Parisians of 1894 felt that they . . . were on a volcano, and they lived in daily dread of some fresh eruption, which might occur at any moment, and in any part of the city. . . . 'Les Anarchistes! Une bombe!' were the exclamations heard at the least untoward incident which occurred in any place of public resort."[62]

The final grand *attentat* came when the Italian anarchist Santo Jeronimo Caserio stabbed the popular president of France, Sadi Carnot, who was visiting Lyon to give an address on 25 June 1894. The president died that night from his wound. Caserio had become incensed with the fact that Sadi Carnot had not commuted the death sentence handed down to Vaillant; the martyr was once more avenged.

The French anarchist terrorists who committed this series of related attacks and reprisals worked as lone wolves, or with minimal support. Anarchism created a terrorist culture onto which individuals could graft themselves and then act with terrorist goals even though they were not agents of an organized group. They appointed themselves as agents of revolutionary justice, mixing—perhaps confusing—their personal feelings with the demands of a greater cause. The acts of lone wolves today, such as Timothy McVeigh at Oklahoma City, Major Nidal Malik Hassan at Fort Hood, or the Kouachi brothers who gunned down twelve at the offices of *Charlie Hebdo* in Paris, have precedents at the very birth of radical terrorism.

After the assassination of Sadi Carnot, the pace of anarchist *attentats* abated. This shift was associated with three particular developments: the enactment of strict anti-terrorist legislation, the Trial of the Thirty, and a reevaluation of tactics and strategies among French radicals. One reaction to the series of anarchist attacks was the passage of strong, repressive anti-anarchist laws; three *lois scélérates*, or villainous laws, were adopted between 8 December 1893 and 28 July 1894. For a brief time, they effectively silenced the anarchist press and threatened to stifle the left. However, the *lois scélérates* were soon tested in the Trial of the Thirty, 6 August—31 October 1894, which put thirty alleged anarchists in court. Some of the sharp-witted defendants made the prosecutors look foolish. In the end, the jury acquitted all but three, who were sentenced as nothing more than common criminals. The trial highlighted and discredited the laws, but without creating any new martyrs to inspire further anarchist reprisals. The laws and the trial seemed to spur radicals to reevaluate their strategies.

By this point, important anarchist voices criticized propaganda of the deed, and when the radical press rebounded from the *lois scélérates*, some new messages were heard. Consider that this was precisely at the time when Kropotkin ridiculed the idea of changing the world "with a few kilos of dynamite." Jean Grave, who had edited the radical journal *La révolte* and been one of the thirty, established *Les temps nouveaux* in 1895. Its pages included an appeal by the labor union advocate Fernand Pelloutier (1867–1901), who wrote: "This entry into the trade union of some libertarians made a considerable impact. For one thing, it taught the masses the true meaning of anarchism, a doctrine which, in order to make headway, can very readily, let us say it again, manage without the individual dynamiter."[63] There would be stray acts of political violence in France, but the flood of acts and reprisals from 1892 to 1894 would not crest again.

COUNTERTERRORISM DURING THE FIRST WAVE

The first wave of radical terrorism was transnational. Important radical associations existed not only in Europe, but in North and South American, Australia, and even China and Japan. The fact that terrorism did not respect national borders eventually led threatened states to coordinate their counterterrorism efforts.

The example of terrorists active in the United States demonstrates the transnational character of the danger. Anarchist terrorism struck America, where European radicals had taken shelter even before the Revolutions of 1848. The continued arrival of immigrant workers spread the creed. German radicals played a role in the Haymarket Riot in Chicago on 4 May 1884. Gaetano Bresci, an Italian immigrant worker living in Paterson, New Jersey, returned to Italy to assassinate King Umberto I on 29 July 1900. Leon Czolgosz, the Polish-American anarchist who fatally wounded President William McKinley on 6 September 1901, claimed that he was inspired by Bresci's deed. On 16 September 1920, anarchists detonated a bomb on Wall Street that killed thirty-eight and wounded 143. It was the deadliest single terrorist attack on American soil until the 1995 bombing of the Murrah Federal Office Building in Oklahoma City by Timothy McVeigh. The radicals who carried out this attack were linked to the Italian anarchist Luigi Galleani. I argue that the Wall Street bombing was the concluding major attack of the first wave of radical terrorism. What began in Europe closed out in America. (See the website Supplements on anarchists in America.)

The transnational character of first-wave terrorism meant that this violence commanded international attention. Eventually this was powerful enough to bring governments together in search of ways to aid each other in combating terrorism. This important step was precipitated by the senseless assassination of Empress Elizabeth of Austria-Hungary in 1898.

The Assassination of Empress Elizabeth
On 11 September 1898, the aging but still regal Empress Elizabeth of Austria-Hungary walked toward a dock in Geneva, where she was to board a steamer. As she and her lady-in-waiting made their way, an Italian anarchist, Luigi Lucheni, armed with a small triangular file that he had sharpened into a stiletto, lunged at her and stabbed her in the chest, puncturing her lung and piercing her heart.

Elizabeth was a person of minimal political importance, but the outrage caused by her death compelled European states to recognize a need for international agreement and coordination in dealing with anarchist terrorism. The *New York Times* of 12 September announced, "All Europe Indignant: Antagonism to Anarchists Whetted by the Shocking Assassination of the Empress of Austria."[64] The London *Times* praised her as "an incarnation of charity and beneficence."[65] As a young woman she had been celebrated as the most beautiful woman in all Europe, and this increased her aura. Her assassination was condemned as "the most vile and most wicked among all the anarchist crimes."[66]

Lucheni, who portrayed himself as "the most convinced of anarchists,"[67] was quickly apprehended. He announced to a friend before undertaking his plan, "Ah! How I should like to kill somebody; but it must be some person of great importance, so that it might get into the papers."[68] He had intended to assassinate the Duke of Orléans, but the duke had left before Lucheni arrived in Geneva. Elizabeth was a convenient and symbolic second target. He hoped that his attack would forward the cause of anarchism, but it accomplished the very opposite. His widely publicized act incited outrage of such proportions that it compelled governments to meet in an international anti-anarchist, anti-terrorist conference within two months of Elizabeth's assassination.

The Rome Conference
The International Conference of Rome for the Social Defense against Anarchists, generally known as the Rome Conference, met in November and December 1898. It attempted to facilitate the capture and prosecution of terrorists through coordinating policies and practices.

Ruling regimes had already combated their own revolutionaries with legislation and law enforcement, including secret police, for decades. Different governments handled the problem of terrorism within their own borders in ways that fit their particular political and social circumstances. Some leaned toward prevention and others toward punishment. Prevention might sound kinder than punishment, but prevention involved political repression of dissidents, whereas punishment addressed only the violent acts committed by revolutionaries. The Russians emphasized prevention, but because the English traditionally respected divergent political views, the British were more prone to punish the crime and not the idea. Initial national responses to radical terrorism encompassed a predictable series of measures increasing physical security for likely targets and expanding the actions of secret police, including the use of inside informers. The Russians employed as many as 10,000 agents provocateurs from 1880 to 1917. In France, the police secretly funded anarchists, including their newspapers, to gain inside intelligence on their plans.

More than anything else, the need for international cooperation came down to three issues: expulsion of foreign radicals from countries where they sought refuge, extradition of those wanted for trial or punishment by other countries, and international arrangements to share information and coordinate police activities across borders. Before it could do any of this, the delegates at the Rome Conference had to define "anarchism" and "anarchist."[69] They shied away from identifying anarchism in terms of political ideology, so the protocol defined it by its deeds: "any act whose objective is the destruction of all social organization by violent means is an anarchist act." The anarchist was thus someone who committed an anarchist act, and anarchism was what such individuals practiced.

The protocol went on to *recommend* procedures for expulsion and extradition, including informing police authorities in neighboring states as to when and where expelled individuals would cross into other states. Should the country from which an anarchist was to be extradited not border on the country to which he was to be returned, the states through which he must pass were to assume the responsibility and cost of transit. Attempts on the lives of sovereigns and heads of state or their families were to be listed as extraditable offenses. Possession of explosives without legitimate reason was to be deemed a crime, as was membership in anarchist organizations, assisting anarchists, and provoking or defending anarchist acts. In addition, signatories deemed it criminal to propagandize anarchist doctrine in the army or to instigate "soldiers to indiscipline with an anarchist objective."

While diplomats discussed the public protocol, police authorities held secret parallel meetings. One useful result coming out of the police conversations was the adoption of precise and standardized descriptions of suspects. Given the difficulty of finding and sharing photographs, authorities were to rely on the *portrait parlé*, or verbal portrait, which emphasized features that could not easily be disguised. Sharing of information was also encouraged insofar as it was consistent with national laws and practices.

Anti-Terrorism after 1898

Other anti-terrorist efforts followed the Rome Conference. Even the Americans, who had not been invited to Rome, adopted anti-anarchist measures. In an address to Congress, Theodore Roosevelt, who had become president after the assassination of McKinley, condemned anarchists as "depraved" and declared, "Anarchy is a crime against the whole human race; and all mankind should band against the anarchist. His crime should be made an offense against the law of nations."[70] The next month, those attending the Second Pan-American Conference signed the Treaty for the Extradition of Criminals and for Protection against Anarchism.

The Germans and Russians embraced Roosevelt's call for more international agreements and continued to push for more severe approaches, and eventually this led to the St. Petersburg Protocol of March 1904. Germany, Austria-Hungary, Denmark, Romania, Russia, Serbia, Sweden, Bulgaria, and the Ottoman Empire signed on to the Protocol, and copies were dispatched to Belgium, France, Greece, Britain, Italy, Spain, and the United States in hopes that they might as well. The Protocol tightened procedures for extradition still further and required that each signatory establish "a Central Bureau of Police whose duties will be to gather information concerning anarchists and their doings" that would inform and coordinate with bureaus of other countries. The terms of the new agreement still were not enough to satisfy all anti-terrorist opinion. Kaiser Wilhelm II expressed particularly extreme views, writing in June 1906, "If, in response to an assassination, all countries would arrest and just behead known anarchists, this mess would soon end. But no government, including ours, has that kind of nerve."[71]

The history presented in this chapter becomes a reference point for the chapters to follow. Terrorism became an "ism" in the wake of the Revolutions of 1848. It developed a self-conscious sense of itself: shared challenges, shared methods, and a shared mindset. It became a transnational movement, or at least a transnational response to the political and social problems of its day.

There is no question that the first wave was a product of its age. Important contrasts separate the first wave from the radical terrorism we face today. Some of the most important political philosophies that inspired early terrorists—nihilism, populism, and anarchism—have since faded to the background. During recent decades, religious rationales—and non-Western ones at that—have come to the fore. Also, in contrast to the character of the first generations of terrorism, the strategies of terrorism have moved away from initiation and toward attrition and evolution.

And yet echoes of the anarchist discussion of terrorism can be found in much later radical classics, for example, Carlos Marighella's *Minimanual of the Urban Guerrilla*, written a century after Nechayev's "Catechism of a Revolutionary." Marighella stresses propaganda of the deed: "The coordination of urban guerrilla activities, including each armed action, is the primary way of making armed propaganda."[72] Marighella furthermore states that an "essential objective" of terrorists is the assassination "of the leaders and assistants of the armed forces and of the police." He insists on the necessity of violence and defines the struggle as war: "we are in a full revolutionary war and that this war can be waged only by violent means."

The romantic mystique of the terrorist as hero and martyr remains as well; it was certainly there in the hagiography of Che Guevara and the hunger-strikers of the Provisional IRA. Martyrdom has been translated to extremes by Islamists of al-Qaeda and Hamas, with their taunt that "we love death more than you love life."

In addition, the emergence of terrorism during the nineteenth century saw both group-based terrorism, as with Narodnaya Volya's assassination of Alexander II, and strikes by lone wolves, such as Émile Henry's bombing of the Café Terminus. This reminds us to consider not simply radical groups, but a revolutionary culture from which individuals emerge to act on their own, as did the Second Amendment extremist Timothy McVeigh in 1995.

As the following chapters will demonstrate, in the study of terrorism, the past certainly serves as prologue.

CHAPTER SIX

Second-Wave Ethno-Nationalist Terrorism

THE FLN AND THE PIRA

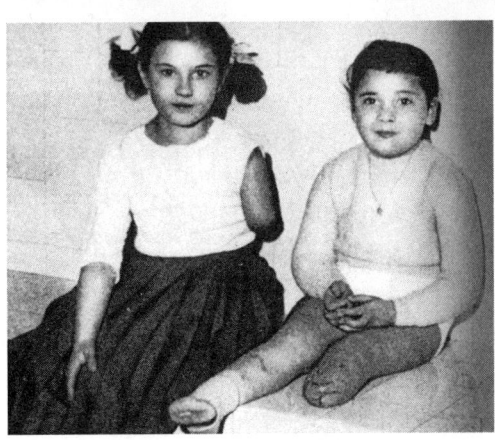

FIGURE 6.1. *Above:* FLN terrorist Zohra Drif placed a bomb in the Algiers Milk Bar in 1956; she is shown here after her arrest the next year. *Left:* Two of her victims, Nicole Guiraud and Danielle Michel-Chich. Wikimedia Commons.

NOT LONG AFTER 6 p.m. on 30 September 1956, a twenty-two-year-old Algerian law student, Zohra Drif, entered the Milk Bar, a popular stop for European residents of colonial Algiers returning from an afternoon at the beach. The place was full, many parents and children enjoying something cool. But Zohra had not come for a pleasant refreshment. She was there to place a bomb.

Her sense of the injustice suffered by the indigenous Muslim inhabitants of Algeria went back to her childhood. As a little girl, her parents had told her that the Nazi blitzkrieg that defeated France in 1940 had been "God's revenge on the Frenchmen for their treatment of the Muslims."[1] During the struggle for independence she strove to become directly involved, not simply to support male resistance fighters. She later recalled during an interview, "I wanted to work with a terrorist group, here in Algiers."[2] She became a cadre of the Front de Libération Nationale (FLN), the National Liberation Front in English. Drif and other young women who could pass for European were recruited by Saadi Yacef, the local commander, because they would find it easier to circulate among the European colonial population, the *colons*, without drawing attention. She was only one of three women dispatched on deadly missions that day. Another bombed the Cafétéria, an establishment popular with *colon* students, and a third placed her bomb at an Air France terminal in the city, but this last device failed to detonate. These were the opening blows in what would come to be known as the Battle of Algiers.

Zohra carried a basket that contained beach gear, but underneath the towel lay a bomb set to go off at 6:30. Drif shoved her basket under the counter at 6:20, paid her bill, and left the Milk Bar. The explosion killed three and wounded dozens, among them many children. The heavy glass on the walls shattered into shards that cut and severed. One of the survivors, Nicole Guiraud, wrote: "I was nearly cut in two, I lost an arm, I am crippled. I had just turned ten years old. My father . . . had a leg torn off and became deaf as a result of the explosion."[3] The blast that took off Danielle Michel-Chich's leg killed her grandmother. The images of maimed children stab at the heart; they were meant to (Fig. 6.1, bottom). Both Drif and Michel-Chich rose to prominence, the former as a politician and the later as an author. Michel-Chich would write a book *Lettre à Zohra D*, and they later were on stage together at a forum celebrating the fiftieth anniversary of Algerian independence. Michel-Chich could now address Drif face to face. She asked, "Was this the right thing to do to innocent people?" Drif gave a hard reply, "You are talking to the wrong person. Ask the authorities of your country [France]."[4]

The question and the answer had had been asked and answered before. In response to a friend who expressed qualms about the resort to terrorist tactics, the FLN revolutionary leader Ramdane Abane replied shortly after the bombing, "I see hardly any difference between the girl who places a bomb in the Milk-Bar and the French aviator who bombards a *mechta* [village]."[5] Both engaged in acts of war directed against civilians.

With this chapter the subject matter advances to radical terrorism in pursuit of ethno-nationalist goals. In the previous chapter we saw that ethno-nationalist causes explain much violent resistance during the nineteenth and early twentieth centuries, including the assassination of Archduke Franz Ferdinand in 1914. The two primary combatant organizations discussed in this chapter, the FLN during the Algerian War of Independence (1954–1962) and the Provisional Irish Republican Army (PIRA) during the Troubles (1968–1998), both conceived of their struggles as campaigns to end colonial occupations, by the French on the one hand and the British on the other. Their similar purpose lends a continuity to what we consider here the second wave of radical terrorism, from the close of World War II to the onset of the third wave around 1980. As noted before in this volume, this puts me at odds with those who see two distinctly different periods between the first and last waves, notably David Rapoport. If we consider ethno-nationalism to be one constant in the second wave, so too was Marxism of one intensity or another. This Marxism tended to be more traditional when espoused by ethno-nationalist terrorists. Revolutionary groups that combined struggles for national independence from colonial powers with socialist/Marxist principles commonly styled themselves as national liberation movements. The New Left Marxism later embraced by European and American terrorist groups was a different strain, but Marxism nonetheless. We will discuss it in Chapter 8. The fact is that the second wave was typified by a continuum of rationales running from extreme ethno-nationalism to exaggerated New Left Marxism at the poles, with different hybrids lying between.

While the FLN and the PIRA shared an ethno-nationalist focus, they and their experiences differed in important ways, and the contrasts explain the choice of these two groups here. One difference in goals between the FLN and the PIRA is that the former fought for the *liberation* of Algeria from French domination to create a new state, while the PIRA fought to expel the British and so bring about the *unification* of Northern Ireland with the existing Republic of Ireland.

Another matter of contrast between these campaigns of violent resistance was the role played by terror attacks within the broader menu of military options. The FLN lacked the capacity to face off against the French in conventional battle, but it could fight an insurgency in the countryside. In urban environments it relied on terrorism. The FLN was known to commit grisly, ostentatious atrocities designed to provoke the French into the kind of extreme reprisals that alienated the Muslim population and turned it against the colonizers. In contrast, the PIRA, even when engaged in terrorist jujitsu, operated within a culture of violence less accepting of headline-catching horrors. This made it wise for the PIRA to minimize death and injury to the innocent, which meant emphasizing military targets and giving civilians some warning when attacks were imminent. Lacking the capacity to launch a true insurgency, the PIRA was generally restricted to small-scale terrorism violence.

Of greatest interest, these terrorist campaigns concluded in very different ways. The FLN won its fight for independence without accepting any significant compromises with the French. But the leaders of the PIRA ended their armed conflict in an accommodation, the Good Friday Agreement (1998) that kept Northern Ireland as part of the United Kingdom, but gave it a government in which republicans and loyalists shared power. In this chapter, we will pay somewhat more attention to the PIRA in large part because its course of ultimate compromise may reveal more about how to bring terrorist violence to a reasonable end than does the experience of the FLN. But we must begin with the earlier, and more savage, struggle.

THE ALGERIAN WAR OF INDEPENDENCE AND THE FLN, 1954–1962

As a war of national liberation, the Algerian War of Independence typified the post–World War II decades; it came on the heels of a similar cataclysm for the French Empire in Indochina and coincided with the independence of neighboring French protectorates Morocco and Tunisia in 1956. However, the fact that the French state regarded Algeria not as a colony but as an integral part of France intensified the reality and the perception of the fighting there. The war lasted for nearly eight years, with changes of momentum in Algeria itself and shifts of opinion and politics in France. Currents of global attitudes and sympathies also affected the outcome of the conflict.

The Course of the Conflict
In considering the conquest of Algeria in Chapter 3, we discussed the origins of the animosity that explain the intensity of the country's War of Independence. Algerian Muslims were bludgeoned into becoming a colonial people, but the French embraced the convenient political fiction that Algeria was truly integrated as part of France over time. European immigrants to Algeria were granted full citizenship. Algerian voters sent representatives to the Chamber of Deputies in Paris. But although Algeria's Muslim population was offered the possibility of citizenship, relatively few Muslims applied for it, since it required decisions that separated them from their own community.

The scales were not fairly balanced in Algeria. In 1954, Europeans numbered about one million of Algeria's population of ten million. Of the European population, only about 20,000 lived in the countryside, but this 0.2 percent of the population owned 40 percent of the arable land, generally the best. Ninety percent of industry was in European hands. While many European colonists, or *colons*, were poor, on average the annual income of Europeans was twenty-eight times higher than that enjoyed by Muslims. The Muslim population had good reason to believe that it was dispossessed and exploited by the *colons*.

Muslim Algerians did not always suffer in silence. A major Islamic revolt struck in 1871, involving about 150,000 in jihad. During the 1920s and 1930s Algerian nationalist sentiment gelled, and the French spoke of reform programs, but they were not really implemented. During World War II, Charles de Gaulle, the leader of the Free French in exile, promised fundamental political and civil reforms for French colonies in the Brazzaville Declaration in 1944, but this too led to little.[6]

Desperation broke to the surface on 8 May 1945, the very day that Europeans celebrated victory over Nazi Germany. Clashes between Muslim demonstrators and local gendarmes escalated to mob violence that resulted in the massacre of 103 *colons* in and around the town of Sétif. In the kind of overreaction that would be so typical of the French authorities and *colons*, they responded by killing thousands of Muslims in reprisal.

British Army sources pegged the number at 6,000, but other estimates range as high as 45,000. It was a bloody harbinger of the future.

Yet the most pressing immediate colonial challenge to France came not from Algeria but from Indochina, where nationalist/Marxist guerrillas in Vietnam opposed French reassertion of their imperial mastery. The fighting there ended with French defeat and withdrawal; Cambodia and Laos became independent in 1953, and Vietnam was partitioned into North and South Vietnam in 1954. As the French pulled out, the United States inherited the sponsorship of South Vietnam over the next twenty years.

French humiliation in Indochina inspired armed revolt in Algeria, which began on 1 November 1954 with several attacks by the newly created FLN. With its armed force, the Armée de Libération Nationale (ALN), the FLN led the armed struggle, but it was not the only group pursuing Algerian independence. Notably, the Mouvement National Algérienne (MNA) fought the FLN in bitter and bloody rivalry, first in Algeria and then among the Algerian community resident in France. The FLN also targeted Algerians who were too cozy with the French, the so-called *Beni-Oui-Oui*, or "yes men." Moreover, the FLN, riven by divisions within its ranks, devoured some of its own cadres in deadly struggles over leadership and policy.

The French government deployed its police, gendarmes, and military units against the Algerian rebels; it also rallied certain Algerians to support it, including indigenous Algerian troops, or *Harkis*. The *colons* also took matters into their own hands, mounting their own vigilante and terrorist groups. Late in the war, when French president de Gaulle reluctantly realized that it was the best course for France to accede to Algerian independence, *colons* turned their violence against French officials and military commanders. Their primary organization in this was the Organisation de l'Armée Secrète (OAS). Historian Martin Evans sums up the war as "a complex and multilayered conflict": "It was not just French against Algerian. . . . It was also FLN against FLN. It was FLN against other Algerians. It was French against French. It was a war of the cities. It was a war of the countryside. It was a war of image and propaganda. It was a war of international diplomacy that transcended national boundaries and linked Algeria to metropolitan France, the French Union, the European Economic Community, the Arab World, and the cold war."[7]

From the outset, the FLN and the ALN grew in numbers and resources. Their hard-minded leadership recognized that they would be overmatched in head-to-head battles with the French, but the FLN could effectively fight a guerrilla insurgency in the countryside and mount terrorist campaigns in the towns. Things heated up in Algiers during the summer of 1956. The execution of two FLN operatives on 19 June brought quick reprisals in which ALN squads under Saadi Yacef gunned down forty-nine civilians, but avoided killing women, children, and the elderly. In revenge for the reprisal, on 10 August, *colon* terrorists blew up a house in the Casbah, killing seventy, including women and children. FLN leadership met later that month at Soummam. This Soummam Conference reached several key policy decisions, including the primacy of the civil authority over the military and the interior organization of the FLN over that part of the FLN based outside Algeria. At the Soummam Conference key leaders also advocated indiscriminate terrorism against all European *colons* without distinction as to age and sex.

So, on 30 September 1956 the FLN initiated the Battle of Algiers. Yacef commanded only about 1,500 urban operatives organized in a network of small cells, but it would require a great effort to defeat them over the next year. When police alone proved unable to suppress FLN attacks, the civil administration turned the task over to the army, calling upon elite French paratroops under General Jacques Massu. Massu divided the old center city, the Casbah inhabited by Muslim Algerians, into grid squares, isolated each with barriers and barbed wire, and established check points to control population and identify FLN cadres. The French also employed informers who resided on each block. To gain information and intimidate opposition, the French engaged in torture and summary executions; individuals simply "disappeared." Thirty to forty percent of the adult male population of the Casbah was arrested at some point or another. By September 1957 the French had won the Battle of Algiers, in the sense that they had decimated the FLN in the city; however, human rights abuses, particularly torture, discredited the French effort in the eyes of France's own population and around the world.

The French applied new tactics in the countryside. Some were harsh, including relentlessly hunting down insurgent groups and relocating populations into camps where they could be contained and controlled. Some were more benign, including dispatching dedicated young officers into the countryside to work with the locals and win their respect and allegiance. But the continued war was exhausting France. In 1954 the French maintained 50,000 troops in Algeria, but by 1956 the number soared to 400,000 and eventually peaked at 560,000, 90,000 of whom were Muslim *Harkis*. Many French reservists and conscripts resented being sent to Algeria, and protests erupted against this investment of young Frenchmen in a questionable cause. Monetary expenses also mounted. The French budget deficit doubled between 1955 and 1957. As the costs of war rose, public support for it fell, declining from 49 percent in February 1956 to 34 percent a year later.

Frustrated by the inability to bring the war to an end, the army command and much of the population hoped that a hero could be found to achieve victory. De Gaulle, who had abstained from politics since 1946, declared he would serve France once more. In a thinly veiled military coup with considerable popular support, he became premier on 1 June 1958 and rose to the office of president of the new Fifth Republic in January 1959. De Gaulle soon tried to negotiate with the FLN in an effort he titled the "paix des braves," or "peace of the brave," trying to appeal to the honor of the enemy. However, one of the tenets of the Soummam Conference was an inflexible demand for recognition of Algerian independence as a precondition for a ceasefire or negotiations, so the FLN refused de Gaulle's olive branches. De Gaulle's appeal to honor underestimated the FLN's revolutionary commitment to complete independence and disdain for compromise.

While leadership changed in France, the balance of power within the FLN also shifted, away from civil dominance over the ALN to assertion of the military's influence. The rising star, Houari Boumedienne, became chief of staff of the ALN in 1960. The conflict between civil and military precedence within the FLN led to the elimination of those who opposed the military, including Abane, who was assassinated by his erstwhile colleagues in December 1957. In addition, with the FLN within Algeria under such pressure and so isolated, the FLN organization outside Algeria in Tunisia exerted its authority, superseding a principle established at Soummam.

In order to finance its war effort, the FLN demanded that Muslims in Algeria support the war by contributing food, recruits, and funds. The need for money also led the FLN to demand payments from Algerians resident in France. The FLN demanded 500 francs per month from students, 3,000 from workers, and 50,000 or more from shopkeepers. Such heavy "taxation" could come down to extortion enforced by violence—more intimidation of the support community. Since the rival MNA remained strong among Algerians in France, the two organizations fought to the death on the back streets of working-class districts of Paris and other French towns. Over 4,000 Algerians died in this struggle, known as the Café Wars because attacks were often carried out in urban cafés.

Once in power, de Gaulle assigned a new and able general to command in Algeria, Maurice Challe, who conducted an intelligent counterinsurgency campaign in the countryside. In April 1959, Challe declared in an interview with the newspaper *Le monde* that the ALN had been essentially neutralized. This was an overstatement, but 1959 was the low point for the ALN in Algeria. Yet by then, simply surviving amounted to a kind of victory for the FLN.

Even with French military success on the ground, opposition to the war continued to mount in France. Unlike earlier French political leaders who regarded keeping Algeria as key to establishing France as a great power, de Gaulle came to realize that in order to reform and refashion the country to thrive in the modern world, France must cut free of the burden of maintaining Algeria. On 16 September 1959, in a broadcast address, de Gaulle declared: "Taking into account all these factors, those of the Algerian situation, those inherent in the national and the international situation, I deem it necessary that . . . [Algerian] self-determination be here and now proclaimed."[8] Infuriated *colons* felt betrayed and took to the streets of Algiers in "Barricades Week," 24–29 January 1960. During the first day's street battle, fourteen gendarmes died and 123 were wounded, as eight European demonstrators fell and twenty-four were wounded. But de Gaulle refused to back down and the protest collapsed.

Seeing the tide running against retaining Algeria, disgruntled army officers and *colons* dedicated to French control formed the OAS in January. It engaged in terrorism of its own in Algeria and in France, including attempts to assassinate de Gaulle.

Preliminary peace negotiations went nowhere in June 1960, but the momentum toward a settlement continued. The French population endorsed de Gaulle's efforts in a January 1961 referendum in which 76.35 percent of those voting endorsed his policy of self-determination. Peace talks with the FLN began anew in May 1961 and resulted in the Évian Accords in March 1962, marking triumph for the FLN. A truce between the French and the FLN came immediately, and in June the OAS put down its arms as well. Peace, on the FLN's terms, had arrived. With the ground cut out beneath them, *colons* fled Algeria, mainly for France. By the end of the year, 99 percent of the European *colons* had left.

Historians and governments dispute the numbers of those who died in the struggle. French figures for the numbers of French troops and European civilians killed are probably the most reliable. They list 24,614 killed in French forces, military and police, with an additional 450 unaccounted for and 64,985 wounded. To this should be added over 2,788 European civilians killed and more than 7,500 others injured in 42,090 acts of terrorism. Accounts of the human costs suffered by the Muslim population vary greatly and are more likely to have a political slant. A conservative estimate puts the total number of Algerian dead at 300,000, while the Algerian government claimed "one million martyrs."

The Character of Conflict
Several characteristics of the Algerian War of Independence deserve our attention. The complexity of the war meets the criterion of what modern military theory calls "hybrid warfare," a conflict that incorporates different kinds of warfare simultaneously. This can involve terrorism, insurgency, and conventional warfare, as did the Algerian conflict. In urban venues in Algeria and among the Algerian community in France, radical terrorism was the mode. Describing his conduct of the Battle of Algiers to the French ethnologist Germaine Tillion in July 1957, Yacef reluctantly, and tearfully, admitted his distaste for terrorist actions but argued that he had no choice: "Yes, Madame Tillion, we are assassins. . . . It's the only way in which we can express ourselves."[9] In the Algerian countryside, guerrilla bands could employ terrorist tactics as part of their insurgency against the French. For both the terrorists and the insurgents of the FLN, attrition served as a primary strategy. It exacted a toll that was unacceptable to the French, while winning international recognition for the cause of independence and for the terrorists and insurgents as legitimate political agents.

Across the borders, in newly independent and pro-FLN Tunisia, the FLN found sanctuary for its fighters and its leadership. There the ALN could take shape as a more conventional fighting force. The Tunisian sanctuary was so valuable that the French finally dealt with it by constructing the Morice Line, a barrier of electrified fencing, barbed wire, mines, and searchlights that effectively closed that border. It was a wall that worked. By the last stage of the war, the ALN commander, Boumedienne, ordered his forces to stop attacking the Morice Line and simply await becoming the armed force of an independent Algeria, and, it should be noted, an important player in the political struggles among Algerians that were to come. The FLN could be said to have followed a hybrid strategy in fighting a hybrid war: intimidation toward Algerians to enforce solidarity and to eliminate rivals, attrition within Algeria against the French, and evolution of its army and state organization within and outside Algeria in anticipation of victory.

The FLN and ALN committed acts that shocked Western eyes as barbarous; such ostentatious atrocities were calculated to provoke the French into frenzied reprisals that won over the Muslim population to the FLN. It was the terrorist jujitsu pointed out by Fromkin. The prominent writer François Mauriac bristled in *L'express*: "Horror calls forth horror. The FLN knows this, it looks for it, it will hesitate at nothing that will produce blind reprisals. Whatever happens on the streets of Algiers, let us say it very clearly, the FLN will have wanted it."[10]

In almost ritualistic fashion, fallen French soldiers would be discovered with their throats slit ear to ear, their genitals cut off and shoved in their mouths. Wounded men could be tortured by having their eyes gouged out. It was no surprise that rage gripped French troops who saw their comrades treated so.

The brutalization of European civilians by the FLN could be absolutely appalling. In a coordinated effort, several bands of Algerians attacked the European quarter of Philippeville and *colons* in the countryside around Constantine, notably at El-Halia on 20 August 1955. The murderous bands butchered all they could lay their hands on regardless of age or sex. Some women were raped before being disemboweled and decapitated. These massacres claimed a total of 123 killed, seventy-one of whom were European civilians. But the killing did not stop there. French soldiers sent to end the slaughter avenged it, killing 1,273 according to the governor general of Algeria, but 12,000 by the reckoning of the FLN. Of course, the French rampage alienated the Muslim population even more.

While the FLN directed its terrorism against the French forces and the *colon* community, its most important audience in Algeria was the native Muslim population. It won their allegiance by attacking the European oppressors, but it also eliminated those it saw as collaborating with the French, supporting other Algerian revolutionary groups, or simply not being aligned with the FLN. Loyal to the MNA, the villagers of Mélouza would not embrace the FLN; in fact, some killed ALN fighters in March 1957. In reprisal, on 29 May a party of ALN soldiers herded together about 300 men and boys and slaughtered them with guns, knives, axes, and pickaxes.

The French, besides their unrestrained retaliation, engaged in other policies and practices that alienated those they needed to win over. In order to cut off the FLN's access to recruits and resources, the French relocated villagers from the hinterland and confined them in camps. This program went by the innocuous title of *regroupement*. But it was anything but innocuous. Two million people were penned up in 1,250 camps by the fall of 1959. Living conditions were meager at best. Even Massu, a battle-hardened veteran, condemned "the level of life, and in particular the situation of the children" as "inferior to the most miserable I have known in Black Africa."[11] In his recent history, Vincent Joly argues that *"regroupement* forged a popular consensus among Muslims for independence."[12]

But torture proved even more corrosive to the French efforts in Algeria, both by creating enemies among the indigenous Muslims and by turning the French population against the war. Ultimately, knowledge of the extensive use of torture by the French made them international pariahs. As early as January 1955 articles in the French newspapers, *France-Observateur* and *L'express* denounced the French use of torture. It became a matter of national debate in France by 1957, with further revelations appearing in newspapers as varied as the Christian *Témoigne chrétien* and the left-wing *Les temps modernes*. Pierre-Henri Simon published his volume *Contre la torture* (Against Torture) that year. The leftist intelligentsia, such as Jean-Paul Sartre and Simone de Beauvoir, took up the cause, but it also drew the condemnation of the archbishop of Algiers, Léon Étienne Duval. The publication in English of Henri Alleg's stinging report of torture *The Question* in 1958, and of the anonymously edited collection of torture stories *The Gangrene* in 1960, caught the attention of American commentators and journalists. Stories of French excesses appeared in American newspapers, such as the *Chicago Tribune* and the *New York Times*.

The French employed a range of torture. General Paul Aussaresses spoke in an eerily matter-of-fact manner about his technique: "The methods I used were always the same: beatings, electric shocks, and, in particular, water torture, which was the most dangerous technique for the prisoner. It never lasted for more than one hour and the suspects would speak in the hope of saving their own lives. They would therefore either talk quickly or never."[13] Some of the tortured were killed and disposed of after suffering the ordeal.

Algerian victory over the French inspired later radical terrorists. Even those who could not visit Algeria and talk with those who had fought the French could have the illusion of doing so by seeing the important docudrama *The Battle of Algiers* by Gillo Pontecorvo, which appeared in 1966. The film portrayed the resolution, sacrifice, and triumph of the FLN and presented terrorism as the heart of the war, on both sides. To study the fight of the FLN is to study one paradigm of second-wave radical terrorism.

THE TROUBLES IN IRELAND AND THE PIRA, 1968–1998

The fight of the PIRA paralleled that of the FLN, in the sense that the Irish rebels also saw themselves as conducting an anti-colonial struggle; however, fundamental differences separated the two experiences. For one thing, the Troubles in Northern Ireland were not afflicted with the same intensity as the Algerian War of Independence. The loss of 3,500 killed during the Troubles was deplorable, tragic, but it was no more than 1 percent of the casualties suffered during the Algerian War of Independence. Of course, the Algerian fighting was more like a civil war than was the violence of the Troubles. But we also need to take into consideration that the terrorism committed on both sides of the Northern Irish conflict was restrained by a lower cultural tolerance for indiscriminate violence. Bear in mind that considering different cultural tolerances toward violence is a key analytical approach to understanding terrorism. We also need to recognize that in studying the Troubles, the issue of race was not as prominent as it was between European *colons* and Arab and Berber indigenous populations in Algeria.

Yet while conducted with less savagery, the Troubles greatly exceeded the Algerian war in longevity. The fighting in Algeria went on for eight years, but the Troubles consumed three decades. In the end, neither side won an unqualified victory, but they concluded a political compromise, the Good Friday Agreement in 1998.

The Long History of Irish Resistance
There is no way we can understand the origins of the PIRA without surveying the history of Irish opposition to English occupation of Ireland, which began in medieval times. Ireland was a kind of colonial possession of the English, inhabited by a people with a different culture who spoke a different language and, after the Reformation, adhered to a different religion. The PIRA saw itself as freedom fighters trying to throw off the last vestiges of foreign domination.

English intervention and occupation of parts of Ireland went back to the twelfth century. After the English crown became Protestant under Henry VIII, one strategy of exerting royal authority in Ireland became the creation of Protestant colonies, or plantations, in Catholic Ireland. The most important of these was the Plantation of Ulster in the north. Land seized from rebellious Irish chieftains was allotted to English and Scottish colonists, who were required to be English-speaking and Protestant.

The decades from 1640 to 1690 were a time of civil war, restoration, and revolution in England and, as a result, turmoil in Ireland. The ultimate resolution came with the Glorious Revolution of 1688 that installed the staunchly Protestant monarchs William III and Mary on the English throne. After securing his hold in England, William crossed over to Ireland to reassert the dominance of English authority and the security of Protestant settlement there in 1690. He crushed any hope of the rebellious Catholic Irish to assert their independence. Since William was a scion of the House of Orange, the color orange became symbolic of Protestant triumph and dominance.

Resistance to English dominion in Ireland festered during the eighteenth and nineteenth centuries. The Irish Rebellion of 1798 was the most important clash in which the Society of United Irishmen fought a conventional military campaign against the English, with aid from revolutionary France. Many Protestants formed the Orange Order and aided the British, who crushed the rebellion.

While the British made some movement toward reform, it was not enough to satisfy Irish nationalists in the nineteenth century, such as the radicals who formed Young Ireland in the 1840s. When the Great Famine struck Ireland between 1845 and 1852, many accused the British of heartlessly making things worse when people were starving. Such charges inspired the brief fiasco of the Young Irelander Rebellion in July 1848, one of the Revolutions of 1848.

Veterans of this rebellion who fled Ireland eventually formed the Irish Republican Brotherhood (IRB) in 1858. The IRB, popularly known as the Fenians, compiled a record of armed resistance, carrying out terrorist attacks and attempting a foiled Irish uprising in 1865. In May 1882, members of the Irish National Invincibles, a radical offshoot of the IRB, stabbed to death the new chief secretary for Ireland and his undersecretary in Dublin's Phoenix Park. This was very much in line with the first-wave radical terrorist practice of assassination. The Special Branch of London's Metropolitan Police—the unit charged with investigating terrorism to this day—was created the next year precisely to deal with the IRB.

The Parliament in London debated legislation meant to quell the resistance by granting greater autonomy to Ireland. Home rule bills were proposed but not passed in 1886 and 1893. A third home rule bill was introduced in 1912 and finally became law in September 1914, although it was immediately suspended owing to the outbreak of World War I. When it was first discussed, the third bill set the Irish Protestant community on edge. In January 1913, Protestants began recruiting an armed militia, the Ulster Volunteers. In November, a rejuvenated IRB mustered its own paramilitary, the Irish Volunteers.

When World War I broke out, the British war effort at first garnered Irish support, and eventually 200,000 Irishmen volunteered to fight. Still, the costs of the war and Irish animosity toward British rule led the IRB to stage the Easter Rebellion on 24–29 April 1916. Irish Volunteers, aided by other rebel groups, seized parts of Dublin. British troops quickly responded, even bringing artillery to bear, and within a few days they overwhelmed the rebels. The execution of the rebellion's leaders, followed by a stillborn British attempt to impose military conscription on Ireland in 1918, hardened opinion against British dominance among the Catholic population.

The Irish election of December 1918 resulted in a landslide for Sinn

Féin, the pro-republican party, which in January formed its own rebel government and declared a republic. The men who took up arms in its defense, many from the Irish Volunteers, were declared to be the Irish Republican Army (IRA) in service to the new Irish assembly. A bitterly fought insurgency followed, including terrorist attacks. Representatives of war-weary Great Britain and the Irish rebel government cobbled together a treaty in 1921. It created the Irish Free State, a self-governing country composed of the twenty-six predominantly Catholic southern counties of Ireland. Critically, the six predominantly Protestant counties of Ulster—Antrim, Armagh, Derry, Down, Fermanagh, and Tyrone—would remain united with Great Britain as Northern Ireland.

Republican purists rejected the treaty on the basis that the Free State acknowledged the British Crown and did not include all of the island. The IRA split between pro-treaty and anti-treaty factions, and civil war pitted the Free State's National Army against the anti-treaty IRA in June 1922. The National Army achieved victory by May 1923. Later, a new constitution of 1937 rechristened the Free State as Eire, or Ireland, and claimed Ulster as part of Eire. It also recognized the "special position" of the Catholic Church.

Meanwhile, the unreconciled rebel IRA became so much of a problem that the Irish government banned it in 1936. Past heroes had become present dangers. While the government of Eire remained neutral during World War II, it declared an emergency the day after war began in Europe. During the war years, Eire arrested and interned members of the declining IRA, even executing the IRA chief of staff for criminal actions against the government.

The IRA emerged from World War II banned and battered; by 1947 it claimed only about 200 activists. This rump IRA made two important decisions at this time. First, it forbade military operations against the southern Irish state, which declared itself the Republic of Ireland in 1949, breaking all ties with Britain. Second, the IRA took over Sinn Féin, or the tattered remains of it. The IRA rearmed itself largely through raids on British arms depots in the north during the early 1950s. It then undertook the Border Campaign of 1956–1962, an ineffective guerrilla conflict directed against the British Army and the Royal Ulster Constabulary (RUC). After the failure of the Border Campaign, the IRA needed a new direction.

Cathal Goulding, a charismatic figure with a long history in the IRA, became its chief of staff in 1962. He shifted the IRA to the left and advanced a strongly Marxist interpretation of the problems in Northern Ireland, seeing them as determined not by religious faith but by social class. He hoped to unite Catholic and Protestant workers. Goulding supported the rise of the Wolfe Tone Society, an organization created in 1964 to educate and raise the consciousness of its members concerning issues of economics, politics, and civil rights. Key to its development was Roy Johnson, a nationalist intellectual of Protestant background. Gerry Adams, later of such great importance, gained much of his initial political education in the Wolfe Tone Society.

Goulding, Johnson, and those who looked to them for leadership took heart from the South African anti-apartheid campaign and the American civil rights movement. In April 1967 the Northern Ireland Civil Rights Association (NICRA) emerged from discussions that included the Wolfe Tone Societies, north and south, and Goulding's IRA. The NICRA was intended to be nondenominational and politically unaligned, yet the civil rights movement it led would split the IRA and precipitate the Troubles.

Onset of the Troubles, 1968–1970
The NICRA carried out its first march on 24 August 1968, with 2,500 participants. When 400 constables of the RUC blocked the march from entering Dungannon, 1,500 Protestant counter-protesters, who considered the NICRA a front group for Catholic republicans, jeered. (Individuals favoring the merger of Northern Ireland with the Republic of Ireland into one Irish nation state are known as republicans or nationalists.) Some violence occurred when marchers tried to pass through the police lines. Violence escalated in October when the next march progressed through a predominantly Protestant part of Derry (Londonderry). This demonstration began with only 400 participants, some of whom were notable political figures, but the RUC quickly moved against it. Film crews recorded the baton-swinging police violence against unarmed protesters; it would change the climate in Northern Ireland. Historians generally date the beginning of the Troubles with these protests of 1968 or with the more violent repression of protest the next year.

Within days of the Derry march, students at Queen's University in Belfast formed the more radical group People's Democracy. They planned a march from Belfast to Derry for January 1969. Cooler heads, including Roy Johnson, opposed the march, rightly predicting that it would produce a bloody confrontation that would cripple chances for sectarian reconciliation. When the marchers reached Burntollet Bridge on 4 January, a mob of loyalists numbering several hundred attacked the protesters with stones, iron bars, and clubs. (Loyalists are Protestants loyal to Great Britain; they are also known as unionists for their desire to maintain the union with the British.) Police looked on without doing much. This mirrored the mayhem in Montgomery, Alabama, six years before; NICRA protesters even sang the American civil rights anthem "We Shall Overcome."

Battle lines formed between the Catholic and Protestant communities of Northern Ireland. This communal violence was turning cities and towns into warring ghettos, with minority Catholic families being driven out by majority Protestant neighbors in Protestant areas, while Protestants were expelled from Catholic-majority areas.

The greatest violence during the coming years would shake Derry and Belfast. There, the Catholic population had been disenfranchised by gerrymandering that gave Protestants control of the local government and the police. The news of the events at Burntollet sparked protests in Derry the next day. Police overreacted and Catholic vigilantes began patrols for their own protection. Mayhem peaked in the riots of 12–14 August, known as the Battle of the Bogside. This was not an affair of peaceful protesters, but a clash that pitted Irish republican protesters against police and violent loyalists. Overwhelmed RUC and reserve constables engaged in charges and countercharges against partisan crowds, and eventually resorted to tear gas. On 14 August, the prime minister of Northern Ireland asked the British prime minister to send troops, and the army was committed to a fight that would consume it for decades. No one died, but hundreds of people were injured during the Battle of the Bogside; however, other rioting in Northern Ireland left five Catholics and two Protestants dead. At this point, parts of Derry and Belfast became barricaded "no-go" Catholic areas that regular police and troops were prohibited from entering.

By late 1969, many within the IRA, which had not organized the Battle of the Bogside, believed they should return to armed militancy. Cathal Gounding not only emphasized a Marxist analysis, opposed sectarianism, and downplayed violence, but also advocated abandoning the traditional policy of "abstentionism"—refusing to take part in the regular governmental institutions of Northern Ireland. More radical members, led by Seán Mac Stíofáin, wanted to take up arms in defense of the Catholic population and to retain abstentionism. On 18 December 1969 these dissidents split off and elected their own executive, and the Provisional IRA (PIRA) was born. These "Provisionals," or "Provos," spearheaded the nationalist cause during the Troubles. Sinn Féin, the political party associated with the IRA, also split, with the Provisional Sinn Féin aligning with the Provos. Goulding's IRA now became known as the Official IRA (OIRA).

Adversaries and Allies

The battle lines were essentially drawn by 1970, but this was at least a three-sided war, with all the complexity that this implies. And the cast of players in this drama multiplied.

The PIRA stood as the most obvious leader in the armed struggle of Catholic nationalists, or republicans, against what they considered the British colonial occupation of Northern Ireland. The PIRA was organized in a hierarchical military style, with a disciplined rank and file that claimed to follow rules of engagement meant to minimize innocent casualties. Of course, to speak of the PIRA without mentioning the Provisional Sinn Féin misses one of the signature characteristics of the PIRA: its ties to a political organization that claimed not to be involved in violence and so could remain overt and capable of dealing with authorities.

But the PIRA was far from being the only republican organization. The OIRA continued an armed campaign until May 1972, when it announced a ceasefire that became permanent for the OIRA. In 1974, it split, with those who disapproved of its withdrawal from violence breaking off to form the Irish Republican Socialist Party, which had its own military wing, the Irish National Liberation Army (INLA). Not all nationalist groups took up arms. During the Troubles, the largest nationalist party was the Social Democratic and Labor Party (SDLP), which outdrew other republican competitors in elections. Formed in 1970, its most important leader was John Hume (b. 1937). The SDLP differed from the PIRA in major respects. At its founding it rejected abstentionism and participated in elections and government. Most important, while it was leftist and strongly republican, it was also resolutely nonviolent and open to pragmatic compromise.

The loyalists had their own array of organizations and paramilitaries, which opposed the republicans, victimized the Catholic community, and often opposed government policies that they considered too accommodating to the republicans. The year 1966 proved a time of loyalist genesis, because the unionists feared that burgeoning Catholic dissent would turn violent on the fiftieth anniversary of the 1916 Easter Rising. The fiery Protestant preacher and politician Ian Paisley cofounded the Ulster Constitution Defence Committee (UCDC) that year, and the paramilitary Ulster Protestant Volunteers (UPV) came out of the UCDC. Another paramilitary, the radical Ulster Volunteer Force (UVF), emerged in 1966. The UVF began its violent career in May and June 1966, causing three deaths. First blood was *not* drawn by the Provos. In 1971 another loyalist organization took shape, the Ulster Defence Association (UDA), which became the largest of the unionist paramilitaries. It also employed the name Ulster Freedom Fighters (UFF), so as to defect the claim that the UDA was terrorist. In addition, Paisley and Desmond Bell founded a new unionist party, the Democratic Unionist Party, in 1971. It grew to be the largest loyalist political organization in Northern Ireland.

Northern Ireland and Great Britain constituted two overlapping regimes. Northern Ireland was part of Britain, but began the Troubles with its own government, including a parliament that met at Stormont and its own prime minister, both of which it maintained until "direct rule" from Westminster was imposed in March 1972. Even after that date, matters could still be handled in Northern Ireland, but under direct rule, major decisions were made by the British Parliament, its prime minister, and a secretary of state for Northern Ireland. There were also short-lived Northern Ireland Assemblies in 1973–1974 and 1982–1986, created to return some self-government to Northern Ireland, but both were doomed by opposition from the unionists in the first instance and unionists and nationalists in the second.

The Northern Irish and British security forces included the Royal Ulster Constabulary, the Ulster Defense Regiment (UDR), and other units of the British Army. At the start of the Troubles, the RUC was backed up by the Ulster Special Constabulary, usually referred to as the B Specials. Because they had the reputation of being agents of the Protestant majority, the B Specials were dissolved in 1970 and replaced by the new UDR, which became the largest regiment in the British Army, with eleven battalions in 1972. Initially it was composed in the main of part-time soldiers, many of whom had previously been B Specials, but it evolved into a force about half composed of full-time troops. Regular army units were also rotated to police Northern Ireland in what was christened Operation Banner, from 1969 to 2007.

Crisis Years, 1971–1976

The crisis years of the Troubles, marked by the highest casualty rates, stretched from 1971 through 1976. During that six-year period half the 3,500 killed during the thirty years of the Troubles fell; 1972, far and away the costliest year, saw 480 slain. Although it does not count among the years of highest casualties, 1970 was hardly peaceful. On 27 June riots in Derry and Belfast climaxed in gun fights between republicans and loyalists that took seven lives. The enforcement of a curfew along the Catholic Falls Road by the British Army in Belfast led to more confrontations and deaths in July. The next year brought a large increase in violence. In August 1971 the British government introduced internment—arrest and detention without trial—to combat the republican paramilitaries in Northern Ireland. Only republicans were targeted in the sweep of 9–11 August, Operation Demetrius, when 342 were arrested. In this operation, British soldiers killed fourteen civilians, while three others died at the hands of unknown assailants. The worst violence came in West Belfast, at the Ballymurphy housing estate, where soldiers of the Parachute Regiment killed eleven in what came to be known as the Ballymurphy Massacre. On 4 December three loyalist terrorists of the UVF exploded a powerful bomb at McGurk's Bar, killing fifteen and injuring another seventeen. No other single bomb was as deadly during the three decades of the Troubles.

A rising spiral of action, reaction, and retaliation blighted 1972. Bloody Sunday, an iconic slaughter of the innocents, took place in Derry on 30 January 1972, when British troops fired on peaceful civil rights marchers, killing thirteen that day, with another dying of his wounds weeks after the shooting. The behavior of the edgy troops was inexcusable, and the fact that the British had put security in the hands of the Parachute

Regiment, a particularly rough unit that already had a record of deadly action in Northern Ireland, ranks as a monumental mistake. However, the PIRA had engaged in a campaign of provocation against the army in Derry over the preceding months, and seven soldiers had been killed. As the Provo Sean O'Hara explained, "[We] needed the whole situation to be escalated. The thing was always planned."[14] It was classic terrorist provocation, terrorist jujitsu. One of their leaders testified: "Bloody Sunday was a turning point. Whatever lingering chance had existed for change through constitutional means vanished. Recruitment to the IRA rocketed as a result. Events that day probably led more young nationalists to join the Provisionals than any other single action by the British."[15]

The OIRA, which was carrying out its own attacks, targeted the Parachute Regiment headquarters at Aldershot, England, on 22 February 1972 as retaliation. The PIRA employed its first car bomb in Belfast's Donegall Street on 20 March, killing seven and injuring 148. With the mounting casualties, the British government dissolved the government and parliament of Northern Ireland on 30 March, instituting direct rule from London. Because the Northern Irish government was viewed by the republicans as a tool of the loyalist majority, this act was considered a victory by the PIRA, and its confidence soared. The British and the PIRA held talks in London, accompanied by a PIRA ceasefire on 26 June. However, the assertive PIRA delegation, including Seán Mac Stíofáin and Gerry Adams, insisted that an agreement include a British promise to abandon Northern Ireland, a condition that was utterly unacceptable to the British. The PIRA ended its ceasefire on 9 July. It could be said that PIRA confidence encouraged a strategy of initiation at this time. The PIRA leadership believed that the momentum of events was on its side and all that was necessary to topple British dominion in Northern Ireland was one more great push.

That push came on Bloody Friday, 21 July 1972. Between 2:09 and 3:30 p.m., nineteen car bombs shook Belfast, killing seven men and two women. It was the largest single terrorist operation the PIRA would ever unleash on Belfast during the Troubles. New to the terrorist arsenal, car bombs proved to be ideal weapons of destruction. The cars could be loaded with a devastating amount of explosives, driven to and parked in the target area without arousing suspicion, and abandoned calmly by the escaping driver. At the Oxford Street bus terminal, a car bomb literally tore victims apart. TV reports of the scene showed firemen shoveling shredded remains onto tarps or into bags. The PIRA claimed credit for the bombings, but claimed they had phoned in warnings to limit civilian casualties. Phone warnings would become PIRA practice, part of their rules of engagement. However, on 21 July there was so little time and so many bomb sites, further complicated by hoax warnings, that it was virtually impossible for the authorities to respond to all the threats. It was horrific, but one PIRA official commented as he watched images of the carnage on TV: "This is how it has to be until they come to their senses."[16]

The British did not respond by retreat, but with assertion. Ten days later, in Operation Motorman, 12,000 soldiers moved into PIRA "no-go" areas that had been regarded as off-limits by the British since 1969. In reality, the destruction of barriers and barbed wire may have removed physical obstacles, but for years to come, the British and Northern Irish authorities only entered PIRA enclaves on occasion, and then only in force.

Sporadic killing continued in Ireland through 1973. In addition, the PIRA carried the war to England, beginning its string of bombings there with four car bombs detonated in London on 8 March, including one at the Old Bailey, the Central Criminal Court of England and Wales. One of the bombers, nineteen-year-old Marian Price, commented, "It doesn't seem to matter if it's Irish people dying" and stressed the need to "bring it to the heart of the British establishment."[17] The toll for that day in London amounted to one killed and 243 injured.

At the same time, principal parties pursued peace. The British created a more fairly elected Northern Ireland Assembly as a consultative body in May, and the first elections were held in June, with the SDLP taking part, although the PIRA abstained. In addition, there were plans to form a power-sharing Northern Irish Executive that would take part in a cross-border Council of Ireland with representatives of the governments of Britain and the Irish Republic. This plan was finally signed at Sunningdale in Berkshire, England, on 9 December 1973.

However, the Sunningdale Agreement was short-lived. Radical unionists plotted to scuttle it because they feared it constituted a sellout to Irish republicans and a slippery slope leading to a united Ireland. Loyalist labor unions declared a general strike on 15 May 1974, and the Sunningdale Agreement died an unnatural death on 28 May. Another twenty-four years would pass before a true power-sharing agreement would be accepted. The UVF contributed to the crisis by exploding car bombs in Dublin and Monaghan, Republic of Ireland, on 17 May. These attacks killed thirty-three and wounded 300. A month later, the PIRA bombed the British Houses of Parliament, injuring eleven. October and November would bring further PIRA bombings in England at pubs located in Guildford and Birmingham. The latter attack killed twenty-one civilians. On 22 December the PIRA bombed the house of former British prime minister Edward Heath, but no one was wounded.

The PIRA entered into a ceasefire from February 1975 to January 1976, but it led to nothing. Coming out of the ceasefire, the PIRA changed strategy. The expectation of initiating a quick victory receded, and the Provos switched to a strategy of attrition, which they labeled as the "long war," first mentioned in official IRA documents in 1977. It was described in the PIRA's own manual, known as the *Green Book,* as "a war of attrition against enemy personnel which is aimed at causing as many casualties and deaths as possible so as to create a demand from their people at home for their withdrawal."[18] PIRA leadership hoped that this strategy would produce new negotiations with the British, but they would be frustrated by the British reluctance to go back to the table. Recruits needed to be ready for the long haul. In a way reminiscent of Nechayev, the *Green Book* warns: "The Army as an organization claims and expects your total allegiance without reservation. It enters into every aspect of your life. It invades the privacy of your home life, it fragments your family and friends, in other words claims your total allegiance."[19]

Meanwhile, 1975 had marked the beginning of a particularly savage phenomenon, as a gang of loyalist partisans committed a series of twenty-three murders that continued to 1977 and then picked up again in 1982. These killers, known as the Shankill Butchers, randomly kidnapped Catholics off the street, subjected them to beatings and torture, and finally carved them up with meat-cutting knives, giving them their name. They can only be described as psychotic. The leader of the gang was finally killed by the PIRA in 1982, quite possibly with the connivance of the UVF, which had come to see him as a liability. The Shankill Butchers challenge the idea that sectarian violence can be explained solely in rational terms. However, their fate may also demonstrate that there were limits to what could be accepted by the Irish culture of violence.

The deadliest period of the Troubles had subsided and fatalities decreased to 111 in 1977, down from 294 the year before. The average annual toll would stand at eighty-eight from 1977 to 1994, when the peace process began. However, some of the most dramatic attacks were yet to come after 1977. These included the 1979 assassination of Louis of Mountbatten, a prominent World War II commander and a cousin to Queen Elizabeth II. A PIRA man secreted a bomb on a boat used by Mountbatten while vacationing on the coast of County Sligo in Ireland. The blast also killed four others, including Mountbatten's fourteen-year-old nephew, and injured three more.

Prison Protests: From Perpetrators to Victims
The experience of being imprisoned can be valuable for terrorists, as we will see repeatedly in the rest of this volume. First, imprisoned terrorists can use their court trial and imprisonment as public pulpits to preach their ideologies. Second, the experience can educate and radicalize those incarcerated with other terrorists. Third, those imprisoned together can develop networks with likeminded extremists. Fourth, in the public eye, imprisonment can transform individuals who have been arrested as violent criminals into idealistic victims of a repressive regime. Prisoners can engage in protests that make them objects of pity. The PIRA achieved this through prison protests and hunger strikes that publicized their presence and their "persecution."

The British and Northern Irish authorities initially responded to the violence of the Troubles by internment; accusation led directly to incarceration. Internment began in August 1971. Those interned were certainly prisoners, but they were not officially convicts and were not subjected to the usual prison rules and regulations. PIRA members who were tried and convicted in regular court for specific crimes protested that they *too* should be treated as political prisoners and not mere criminals. In 1972, forty such prisoners went on a hunger strike to win this status. The British did not accede entirely, but created Special Category Status for them. This allowed them to wear their own clothing, be excused from prison work, and have their own chain of command. Not long after instituting internment, the government concentrated internees and prisoners from the paramilitaries at the old Royal Air Force base, Long Kesh, at Lisburn. This facility was also known as Maze prison, or the Maze.

The British ended internment in December 1975, freeing the last individuals who had been interned. After internment ended, only prisoners tried and convicted by the courts as criminals would be incarcerated. To accommodate the influx of these criminalized prisoners, new cell blocks were constructed at the Maze; these were known by their shape as the H-Blocks.

PIRA prisoners sent to the H-Blocks mounted a series of escalating protests from the fall of 1976 through 1981 in hopes of gaining Special Category Status, as had convicted prisoners before. These began with the so-called blanket protest, in which prisoners refused to wear prison uniforms and simply covered themselves with their blankets. By 1978, about 250 PIRA men were "on the blanket." That March, the deteriorating relationship between the prisoners and the prison administration and guards raised the stakes. Protesting violence by guards, prisoners smashed cell furniture, and the authorities responded by removing all furniture from the cells, leaving the men with only mattresses and blankets. Next, prisoners refused to use the H-Block showers, and when the administration denied demands to put showers in the prisoners' cells, they ceased to wash at all. This was the "no-wash protest." In April 1978 things went further. Reacting to a fight between a guard and a prisoner, the other prisoners refused to leave their cells at all, meaning they did not use the H-Block toilets. They were given buckets as chamber pots in their cells, but disputes over emptying the buckets led to prisoners dealing with their urine by pouring it out of their cells under the doors and their feces by smearing them on the walls. This was the "dirty protest." Conditions within the PIRA-occupied H-Blocks became abominable. In July, Catholic archbishop Tomás Ó Fiaich visited the prison and reported, "The stench and filth in some of the cells, with the remains of rotten food and human excreta scattered around the walls, was almost unbearable."[20]

PIRA and INLA prisoners then upped the ante in 1980, electing to conduct a hunger strike. The IRA had used hunger strikes by individuals or groups as a tactic in 1917, 1920, 1974, and 1976. The republican hunger strikes at the Maze were not the work of individuals simply choosing this action on their own. The PIRA hierarchy was directing them. After strategy discussions, leadership opted for the strikes and then requested volunteers. This new action began in October, when seven prisoners began to fast. After they believed that they had won concessions, they stopped the strike in December, before any of them died. However, the expected gains were not realized, so a second hunger strike began when Bobby Sands refused food on 1 March 1981. The dirty protest now ended. Sands died on 5 May, and nine other hunger-strikers perished as well before the end of this protest on 3 October. By that time, some had already been force-fed and others simply ended their strike that day. Officially, the government made only one concession: the prisoners could wear their own clothes. But gradually, authorities granted other concessions that echoed Special Category Status.

While on hunger strike, Sands had been elected to the British Parliament in April 1981, a clear sign of the public's backing and sympathy. When he died, 100,000 mourners lined the route taken by his funeral procession. A fellow striker, Kieran Doherty, was elected to the parliament, the Dial, of the Republic of Ireland in June, before he too died in August. All this demonstrated the political power of public knowledge by Irish voters north and south, as did international statements of concern.

The repercussions of the hunger strike encouraged the PIRA leadership to seek gains by mobilizing political support as well as by violence. On 31 October, Danny Morrison, a PIRA stalwart who was then the director of publicity for Sinn Féin, gave a speech in which he famously declared, "Who here really believes we can win the war through the ballot box? But will anyone here object if, with a ballot paper in this hand, and an Armalite [rifle] in this hand, we take power in Ireland?"[21] This advocacy of the ballot signaled the greater influence of Sinn Féin, with its political status and its newspaper and propaganda organ, *An Phoblacht*. In 1983, Gerry Adams was elected president of Sinn Féin, an office he holds to this day. This prominent political wing of the PIRA would prove essential in the peace process.

The Peace Process, 1994–1998: The Fruit of Attrition
Despite a greater interest in the political arena, violence continued for more than another decade before the peace process began that led to the Good Friday Agreement. Attacks continued on British troops, enemy paramilitaries, and civilians. On 14 March 1984, Gerry Adams was attacked by UDA gunmen who riddled his car, hitting their mark with bullets to the neck, shoulder, and arm. The PIRA struck home against the government of Margaret Thatcher in October of that year, setting off a

bomb in the Grand Hotel at Brighton, where the Conservative Party was holding a conference. Thatcher escaped injury, but the blast killed five and injured thirty-one. PIRA cadres bombed a ceremony on Remembrance Day, 8 November 1987, at Enniskillen. The parade was meant to honor Northern Irish military dead, but the bomb turned it into a massacre, killing twelve and wounding sixty-three. The PIRA claimed that they were targeting soldiers, but the victims were overwhelmingly civilians.

Real progress toward a final peace settlement began in 1993 and 1994 with talks between the PIRA, Sinn Féin, the SDLP, and British government representatives. In December 1993 British prime minister John Major and Irish taoiseach, or prime minister, Albert Reynolds issued the Downing Street Declaration, guaranteeing self-determination for the people of Northern Ireland, who could decide by majority vote to stay united with Britain or merge into the Republic of Ireland. The declaration also promised that parties who renounced violence could take part in further negotiations. Eventually the negotiations required the participation of republican organizations, loyalist paramilitaries, the British government under two prime ministers, the government of the Republic of Ireland under three taoiseachs, and the United States during the administration of President Bill Clinton (1993–2001), represented by former Senator George Mitchell. The complexity of such multiparty negotiations is obvious.

To help the negotiations along, the PIRA declared a ceasefire on 31 August 1994, and on 13 October the loyalist paramilitaries followed suit. "Framing documents" that served as a basis for negotiations appeared in 1995.

However, by the start of 1996, the PIRA believed that the negotiations had stalled, and that it had lost its leverage at the table by agreeing to end violence. This exemplifies a paradox in some negotiations: a group ceases its violent campaign as a precondition to negotiations but then finds that without the threat of violence it loses its power at the bargaining table. Thus, on 9 February 1996 the PIRA ended its ceasefire, and within hours it exploded a truck bomb at the London Docklands, a riverside development in London near Canary Wharf. The PIRA phoned in multiple warnings before the blast, but the bombing still killed two and injured forty others. The PIRA continued this bombing campaign until July 1997, when it renewed the ceasefire.

Revived talks led to the Good Friday Agreement on 10 April 1998. This stated that most of the population of Northern Ireland wished to remain in the United Kingdom, but that Britain would abide by majority will in the future, meaning it did not declare a permanent claim on Northern Ireland. In fact, it had maintained this position ever since the Sunningdale Agreement of 1973. The agreement proposed a Northern Ireland Assembly and a power-sharing executive, concepts found in Sunningdale as well. There was also to be a vote in the Republic of Ireland to amend its constitution, removing claims on the six northern counties and simply stating that it is the "firm will of the Irish Nation" to achieve a united Ireland, but "only by peaceful means." On 22 May 1998 referendums were held in both the Republic of Ireland and Northern Ireland. Over 94 percent of those voting in the Republic approved the changes to the constitution, and 71 percent of those voting in Northern Ireland approved the Good Friday Agreement.

This was a great victory for peace, but not all were satisfied. Marian Price declared, "To suggest that a war was fought for what they have today, it diminishes anybody who partook in that war, anybody who died for it, and went out there and sacrificed their lives and their liberty."[22] In 1997, a die-hard faction among the Provos broke off from the PIRA to form the Real IRA (RIRA) to continue a campaign of violence directed toward driving the British out of Northern Ireland. To many it seemed tragic that the Troubles had continued for so long only to achieve what had been on the table a quarter century before. John Hume, head of the SDLP, commented, "When you look at the Good Friday Agreement, you're looking at Sunningdale II."[23]

Thirty long years had passed since the start of the Troubles and twenty-five since Sunningdale, which prefigured much that was in the Good Friday Agreement. Why did it take so long? The easy answer is that the major participants were not ready until 1998. Even if it is correct to argue that the long-war strategy was intended to bring the British back to the table again, it does not mean the PIRA was ready to concede. It is reasonable to assume that attrition eventually made both sides more willing to accept less. The circle of those encouraging negotiations had also grown, with the United States and the Republic of Ireland as players.

Based on extensive interviews, the political scientist Bonnie Weir, a specialist on the PIRA, argues, "In order to understand the occurrence, timing, and the process of the political transformation of violent opposition groups, we need to understand the role of the potentially conflicting interests *within* a violent opposition movement."[24] Roughly speaking, she frames these contrasting interests as being between idealists, who shun compromise, and pragmatists, who come to accept its necessity. Pragmatists are more likely to calculate the costs versus the benefits of continued violence as it affects the long-term goals of the group's actions and their own personal circumstances. There is much more to Weir's intriguing thesis, but if we accept its basic claim, we can invest attrition with a new dimension. It is not simply that attrition leads to general exhaustion, it heightens the divergence between idealists, like Marian Price, and pragmatists, like Gerry Adams and Danny Morrison. And the pragmatists ruled the day.

The Good Friday Agreement was hardly the end to the process, since its goals would only be realized when truces and ceasefires turned into permanent peace and a new workable power-sharing government formed. The RIRA was determined to continue the armed struggle and carried off a particularly deadly bombing in Omagh on 15 August 1998, killing twenty-nine and injuring 220. This attack can be categorized as a spoiling attack *and* an example of outbidding. Unable to tolerate the actions of RIRA idealists, PIRA pragmatists beat up some of them and warned others that they would pay with their lives if they refused to go along with the ceasefire. When RIRA hard-liners continued attacks, PIRA men killed the RIRA Belfast commander in broad daylight—no one was arrested. Some die-hards of the RIRA continue violent attacks to this day. The main-line republicans and loyalists still had to reach a level of confidence before they would decommission their weapons. The PIRA only rendered its weapons permanently inoperative in 2005, and the loyalist paramilitaries delayed doing so until 2009.

Creation of a functioning power-sharing government took years. Deadlocks and dissension caused the Northern Ireland Assembly to be suspended more than once, with the longest suspension running from 14 October 2002 until 7 May 2007. However, the Assembly that came back into being in 2007 succeeded. The first minister of the new executive was the old loyalist champion Ian Paisley, working in tandem with the deputy first minister, former PIRA commander Martin McGuinness.

In April 2014 Queen Elizabeth II visited Belfast, where she met McGuinness and they shook hands for the cameras.

Referencing Cronin's list of how terrorism ends, the FLN ended its campaign by achieving its goals: without compromising with the French, it won independence for Algeria and became the governing party of the new state. In contrast, the PIRA entered the political process by the 1980s, signed an agreement with those it had been fighting, and integrated into the government of Northern Ireland. Were we to qualify Cronin's list, we could consider Weir's argument that a terrorist group's transition away from terrorism and toward politics may result from splits within the group itself when, as in the case of the PIRA, pragmatists gain leverage over idealists. The attrition of the long war affected the PIRA as well as the British.

To demonstrate diversity among ethno-nationalist terrorist groups, we have presented two in this chapter. We might also have chosen terrorist groups arising from the communities of Armenians (ASALA), Basques (ETA), Kenyan Kikuyus (Mau Mau), Puerto Ricans (FALN), Kurds (PKK), or others. But trying to display the full diversity in an introductory work like this would simply produce a bewildering multiplicity of detail in which we could not see the forest for the trees. On the book website we make available another example of an ethno-nationalist group considered as terrorist. This case of the Liberation Tigers of Tamil Eelan (LTTE), or the Tamil Tigers, presents some striking contrasts, including the Tigers' reliance on suicide terrorism, their organization of wholly women's units, and their ultimate and utter elimination at the hands of the Sri Lankan armed forces after nearly twenty years of LTTE success. Like the FLN, the LTTE began as a radical terrorist group and evolved into a statelike organization with territorial control and an army of its own, but then crashed and burned.

In the next chapter we will present a study of ethno-nationalist terrorism that is central to the second wave and relevant to the third as well: that of the conflict between Jewish settlers and Palestinians from the 1880s through the 1980s. The Jewish community had its own paramilitaries that spun off terrorist groups before Israel became a state in 1948. The Palestine Liberation Organization (PLO) did not emerge as a terrorist organization until after Israeli victory in the 1967 war, but once active, the PLO became a new rallying point for transnational ethno-nationalist terrorism, one even the PIRA celebrated.

During the Troubles in Northern Ireland, the contending parties displayed their positions and their presence by painting murals, most famously in Derry and Belfast. Besides announcing allegiances to republican or loyalist paramilitaries, praising sacrifices, and denouncing betrayals, these omnipresent reminders of the struggle drew connections, marking out allies and adversaries. More than one mural concerned the sympathetic link between the PIRA and the PLO. One such painting in Belfast stands out. It dates from 1982, which we will see is a key year, for it was then that Israel invaded Lebanon. The mural shows a PLO and an IRA fighter side by side holding an RPG launcher above their heads. (A photograph of this mural can be found on this book's website.) The lettering is simple: "PLO-IRA ONE STRUGGLE." The artists of the mural insist that both are fighting against a stronger military power occupying their homelands.

CHAPTER SEVEN

Tales of Two Tragedies

PALESTINIANS AND ISRAELIS, 1881–1985

FIGURE 7.1. *Above:* In July 1946, Jewish terrorists from the Irgun, an organization led by Menachim Begin, bombed the King David Hotel in Jerusalem, killing ninety-one victims. *Below:* A generation later, PLO cadres, including Dalal Mughrabi, raided Israel in a plan that went wrong and resulted in the Coastal Road Massacre, in which thirty-eight civilians and nine terrorists were killed on 11 March 1978. The burned-out remains of the bus that was hijacked by the terrorists is now a memorial. *Above:* Imperial War Museum. *Below:* MathKnight/Wikimedia Commons, CC BY 2.0.

ON 29 NOVEMBER 1947 the General Assembly of the United Nations approved Resolution 181, a plan for the partition of Palestine into two independent states, one Jewish and the other Arab. Representatives of the Jewish community in Palestine accepted the partition, which was quite generous in setting the borders of the Jewish state; however, the leadership of the Palestinian Arab population rejected the resolution. Within days, civil war broke out.

December witnessed a series of attacks by the Irgun, a Zionist terrorist organization led at the time by Menachim Begin. In less than three weeks, Begin's cadres killed at least eighty victims (Fig. 7.1, top). The Irgun characteristically launched bomb attacks on Arabs thronged at markets or gathered for some other reason. In Jerusalem, at 9:55 a.m. on 29 December, a Jewish man flagged down a green taxi, claiming that he needed to take his pregnant wife to the Hadassah Hospital. The cabbie was forced from his taxi at gunpoint and taken away; he was released only in the afternoon. At 12:57 p.m., several Irgun cadres, dressed as Arabs, approached the Damascus Gate in the commandeered cab. There, at a bus stop, a crowd of Arabs waited. A bomb thrown from the cab arched into the group and exploded. The Irgun men then sprayed the Arabs with gunfire. Thirteen, including three children, died from the blast and bullets.

Events twist along unpredictable paths. In 1978, Begin, the former terrorist, played the part of peacemaker as the prime minister of Israel in negotiations with the Egyptian president Anwar Sadat. Although much of the world welcomed an accommodation between Israel and Egypt, the Palestine Liberation Organization regarded a potential peace treaty as disastrous, since it would strengthen Israel and weaken the leverage of the PLO. Fatah, the largest group within the PLO, resolved to sabotage the growing momentum toward accord before it could bear fruit, so it mounted the deadliest single terrorist attack in the history of Israel, the Coastal Road Massacre of 11 March 1978.

Fatah's original plan called for terrorists to strike by sea from their base in Lebanon, coming ashore at Tel Aviv, where they would seize a hotel and capture hostages to exchange for Palestinian prisoners held by the Israelis. The terrorists expected this to dominate the headlines and erode support for a peace accord—a stratagem of spoiling. In fact, navigational errors frustrated the plan, and the party of thirteen Palestinians came ashore short of their mark by some thirty miles. In addition, two of their number drowned while negotiating the heavy surf. The disoriented raiding party encountered an American tourist, Gail Rabin, taking nature photos on the beach. After finding out from Rabin exactly where they had landed, the reputed leader of the raid, Dalal Mughrabi, a nineteen-year-old woman born in the Sabra Palestinian refugee camp of Beirut, shot and killed Rabin.

Now sure of their location, the terrorists hijacked a taxi on the Coastal Road, killed its occupants, and then seized a bus. Further down the road they stopped another bus, crowded all the passengers into it, and continued toward Tel-Aviv. At this point they had seventy-one hostages, but the Israeli police were now alerted and finally stopped the bus as it approached the city. During the ensuing gunfight the bus exploded and burned. In all, thirty-seven Israelis and one American died, a total that included thirteen children. Nine of the terrorists in the bus also perished, including Mughrabi, who became revered as a martyred heroine (Fig. 7.1, bottom).

Three days after the massacre, the Israeli Defense Force (IDF) mounted a reprisal, Operation Litani. Yet the death and destruction of the PLO raid and the IDF reprisal did not halt the peace process that resulted in the Camp David Accords, signed on 17 September 1978. Three months later, Begin and Sadat were awarded the Nobel Peace Prize in Oslo, Norway.

The very different stories of Begin and Mughrabi converged in 1978, Begin as a senior state leader at that time striving to bring peace to one of Israel's borders, and Mughrabi as a passionate young militant intent on overthrowing the very state Begin wished to secure. Thus, both are iconic to the Israeli–Palestinian conflict. And both stories are part of the broader history of ethno-nationalism during the second wave of radical terrorism.

The Israeli–Palestinian conflict is fundamental to the history of terrorism after World War II. Both the creation of Israel and Palestinian resistance to it were tied up with the ideals of ethno-national identity and self-determination that so typified the second wave of radical terrorism. The Jewish community in British-administered Palestine wanted the British, with their limitations on immigration and land purchase, gone. The Palestinians regarded Israel as a colonial power that first drove them from their homes and then became an occupying power. Stark differences in power and perception continue to this day; political scientist Beverley Milton-Edwards and journalist Stephen Farrell observe: "Where Israel's supporters see a small, vulnerable Jewish state surrounded by Arab enemies, Palestinians see a nuclear regional superpower backed by the US which seeks to control, or even expel, them."[1]

At its base, the Israeli–Palestinian conflict was and remains a profound tragedy, a conflict between two abused peoples. Israelis can never forget the virulent anti-Semitism suffered by European Jews that climaxed in the Holocaust. Understandably, they regard having their own homeland as the best guarantee of their survival and happiness. Palestinians harbor their own memories as well, recollections of a land that was theirs for a millennium and from which they have been dispossessed. What Israeli's celebrate as their War of Independence (1948–1949) the Palestinians lament as their Nakba, the "Catastrophe."

The history of the Palestinians and their resistance, spearheaded by the PLO, warrants our attention when we focus on the third wave of radical terrorism as well. The Islamist narrative regards the fate of the Palestinians as proof that the West is at war with Islam, a war that requires Muslims to defend themselves through jihad. Eventually the secular PLO would have to contend not only with Israel but with the rival Palestinian Islamists of Hamas, but that is a story for Chapter 10.

No one interested in terrorism, past or present, can avoid confronting the hellish collision of opposing righteous causes in a land still revered as holy by Jews, Christians, and Muslims.

BACKGROUND, 1880–1949

To understand the creation of modern Israel, we must go far back into history. Jews became the dominant population of Palestine in Old Testament times. (Simply to avoid confusion, we will employ the word "Palestine" as a geographical term to describe the area that comprises modern-day Israel and the occupied territories. It was not termed Palestine in ancient times.) As punishment for rebellions against Roman rule, the Romans drove the great majority of the Jewish inhabitants out of their traditional homeland during the first and second centuries CE. These Jews of the Diaspora, "the scattering" or "the dispersion," constituted minority communities in other people's lands. Their well-being depended on tolerance, and that proved to be a weak guarantee. Jewish communities regularly suffered from prejudice and persecution that could escalate to mass murder during the Middle Ages and early modern eras.

The Enlightenment promised greater religious toleration, as reflected in pronouncements during the French Revolution and even under Napoleon. However, anti-Semitism grew more virulent during the nineteenth century, particularly in its last decades. In czarist Russia, reactions to the assassination of Alexander II in 1881 precipitated a series of pogroms, violent and deadly attacks on Jews that continued periodically through the remaining decades of imperial Russia and into the first years of the Soviet regime. Anti-Semitism infected "liberal" states as well, including France, where the National Anti-Semitic League appeared in 1889.

Slander and misinformation abounded, including the notorious forgery *The Protocols of the Elders of Zion*, a Russian version of which appeared in 1903, but which soon became available in several languages. It pretended to reveal a Jewish plot to rule the world through control of finance and the press. This anti-Semitic tide finally engulfed European Jewry in the Nazi genocide of the Jews, the Holocaust, during World War II.

Vicious anti-Semitism drove a great many European Jews to conclude that they would find no real tolerance or security in Europe. Those who wished to establish a Jewish homeland, Zion, found a leader in Hungarian-born Theodor Hertzl. He published *The Jewish State* in 1896, and the next year spearheaded the First Zionist Congress in Basel, Switzerland.

Before the Zionist immigration began, the number of Jews in Palestine, then ruled by the Ottoman Empire, was small. During the 1860s, it stood at about 14,000, or 4 percent of a total population of 350,000, 85 percent of whom were Muslim.[2] The first wave, or *aliyah*, of Zionist immigration to Palestine, from 1881 to 1903, numbered 20,000–30,000, the great majority of whom were from Russia. Successive *aliyahs* increased the population of the Yishuv, the Jewish community in Palestine, to 175,000 in 1931 and 630,000 in 1947. This last figure amounts to 32 percent of the two million people who inhabited Palestine by then.

Most immigrants chose to live in cities and towns; however, Zionist ideology emphasized not only returning to Zion but actually working its fields as agricultural pioneers. Under the Ottomans and during the British Mandate established by the League of Nations in 1923, Jews bought land upon which to establish agricultural communities. The money to do this came not only from settlers but from Jewish philanthropists; in 1901 the Zionist Congress created the still-functioning Jewish National Fund (JNF), the most important of the organizations that purchased land. But purchases that seemed benign had a sharp edge. Land bought from wealthy absentee Arab owners, as much was, dispossessed the Arab peasants who actually farmed it. Therefore, with good reason, the indigenous Arab community feared losing its patrimony.

The Zionists of the Yishuv harbored prejudices typical of other European colonists. They spoke of Palestine as if it were uninhabited; as one Zionist slogan put it, Palestine was "a land without people for a people without a land." Once they arrived and became aware that the land was in fact populated, most who joined the Yishuv regarded the Palestinian Arabs as, in the words of historian Benny Morris, "primitive, dishonest, fatalistic, lazy, savage—much as European colonists viewed the natives elsewhere in Asia or Africa."[3]

In general, the Yishuv regarded Palestine as their ancestral birthright where they would create a homeland, eventually a Jewish state. The indigenous Arabs believed that centuries of their presence consecrated Palestine as their own, not to be relinquished to Jewish newcomers from afar. Though relations were in some cases friendly, there simmered an inherent animosity born of contending goals and cultures.

Pilfering required Yishuv farmers to engage watchmen to guard their properties. In 1909, self-defense activists formed HaShomer to guard Jewish settlements; its motto was "In blood and fire Judea fell; in blood and fire shall Judea rise."[4]

During World War I the British government issued a series of promises, white papers, and proposals to win over the Yishuv and the Arabs as allies in the war against the Ottomans. To win Jewish support, the British government issued the Balfour Declaration of 1917 stating that it favored "the establishment in Palestine of a national home for the Jewish people," but insisting that "nothing shall be done which may prejudice the civil and religious rights of existing non-Jewish communities in Palestine."[5] Yet it is hard to imagine how this endorsement of Zionism could be realized without prejudicing the situation of Arabs.

After they had secured victory, the British gained Palestine as a mandate. They were the occupying power as troubles escalated. A series of Arab attacks and riots from March through May 1920 resulted in the deaths of sixty Jews and a similar number of Arabs. With such tumult, a new Jewish paramilitary, the Haganah, formed to guard the Yishuv. This was far larger than HaShomer, eventually growing to a force of some 20,000. Deadly rioting again struck Jerusalem, Hebron, and Safed from 23 to 29 August 1929, killing 133 Jews and 116 Arabs. At this point, the Irgun split off from the Haganah. Jewish and Palestinian acts of terrorism constituted exceptions to the rule that, in general, radical terrorism was relatively rare during the period from 1920 to World War II.

Within a few years an expanded and reorganized Haganah played a role in an even greater crisis, the Arab Revolt. The revolt began in May 1936 with demands to end Jewish immigration and the purchase of Arab lands by Jews. Violence escalated to a series of bombings, and London appointed the Peel Commission to look into the matter. In July 1937 it proposed a partition plan to create a small Jewish state and a larger Arab state associated with Transjordan, today's Jordan.

Much of the Yishuv's leadership welcomed the proposal or were at least willing to discuss it, but the Arabs rejected it out of hand. The Yishuv proved effective at bargaining, regarding small advantages as steps toward a greater goal. However, leaders of the Palestinian Arabs pursued an all-or-nothing strategy, passing up discrete gains for an ultimate victory that eluded them. The Israeli diplomat Abba Eban later commented that the Palestinians "never miss an opportunity to miss an opportunity."[6]

The Peel Commission's proposal included "transferring"—that is, uprooting and relocating—over 225,000 Arabs from their homes in what was to become the Jewish state. Many in the Yishuv had considered transfer essential from the start. The more optimistic, such as Hertzl himself, thought it could be accomplished through economic incentives.[7] The head of the JNF said to journalists in 1930 that to insure a truly Jewish state, "we must take over the land. We have a greater and nobler ideal than preserving several hundred thousands of Arab fellahin."[8] David Ben-Gurion, the most influential political strategist of the Yishuv and independent Israel's first prime minister in 1948, wrote an entry in his diary on 12 July 1937: "The compulsory transfer of the Arabs from the valleys of the proposed Jewish state could give us something which we never had . . . national consolidation in a free homeland."[9]

The British responded to escalating Arab violence with hard-handed counterinsurgency that enlisted support from the Haganah. The Irgun conducted its own campaign of terrorism. On 6 June 1938 its cadres exploded two large milk cans full of TNT and shrapnel at an Arab market in Haifa, killing twenty-one and wounding fifty-two.

By its end, the Arab Revolt resulted in the deaths of 300 Jews, but the roll of Arab casualties was much longer, with about 5,000 dead and 15,000 wounded. Of critical importance, many leaders of the Palestinian community were among those killed, captured, imprisoned, or exiled. Moreover, the Arab Revolt convinced a great many in the Yishuv that accommodation with the Palestinians was doomed to fail, and reinforced the opinion that a Jewish state could not incorporate a sizable Palestinian minority. Palestinians must be made to leave. In a 1941 memorandum Ben-Gurion made his position clear: "Complete transfer without compulsion—and ruthless compulsion at that—is hardly imaginable" because "the majority of the Arabs could hardly be expected to leave voluntarily within the short period of time which can materially affect our problem."[10]

When World War II broke out in 1939, the Haganah declared a cease-fire with the British so as to aid them against the Nazis. However, the Lehi, popularly known as the Stern Gang, spun off from the terrorist Irgun in July 1940 and continued its attacks on the British. As the war wound down, the Irgun began striking British targets as well; its most infamous, and deadly, attack was the bombing of the King David Hotel in Jerusalem on 22 July 1946, killing ninety-one and injuring a further forty-six. The hotel housed the headquarters of the British administration.

In February 1947 the war-weary British declared that they would end the mandate, and the problem of finding an equitable compromise passed to the newly created United Nations, which formed the United Nations Special Committee on Palestine (UNSCOP) to propose a formula. The Jewish Agency participated in the process, but the Palestinians and Arab states challenged its legitimacy and refused. In August 1947 UNSCOP recommended a partition between a Jewish state and Arab-held land in Palestine. While the Yishuv accounted for only about 32 percent of the population of Israel, and land ownership by Jews and Jewish corporations was no more than 20 percent (some estimates are much lower), UNSCOP assigned 50 percent of the land area to the Jewish state. These facts infuriated the Arab community. The Yishuv accepted the partition plan, but as Ben-Gurion stated, since the Arabs rejected it, the actual border "will be determined by force and not by the partition resolution."[11]

Civil war between Arab paramilitaries and the Yishuv soon broke out, but the better-organized and -trained Haganah defeated the local Arabs before Israel declared itself a state in May 1948. In response to the creation of Israel, the neighboring Arab states invaded. The Haganah became the Israeli Defense Force (IDF) and absorbed the Irgun and the Stern Gang. So complete was the mobilization of the Israelis in the IDF that it outnumbered the combined Arab forces marshaled against it and generally overmatched them in fighting ability. In addition, Israel secured weaponry and ammunition far more effectively than did the Arabs. During the fighting, which lasted until March 1949, the Israelis secured a larger area than that granted by Resolution 181. Meanwhile, Jordan established its authority over the Arab-held territory known as the West Bank, and the Egyptians occupied the Gaza Strip.

During the War of Independence, 700,000–750,000 Palestinians fled their homes and were not allowed by Israel to return. The result was a transformation of the percentage of the Jewish population in the new Israel. As a consequence of the 1948–1849 war, the percentage of Jews in Israel stood at about 80 percent.[12] This great gain for Israel reflects the great loss by Palestinian Arabs—their homes and homeland. The Nakba continues to cast a dark shadow across the modern history of the Middle East.

Officially, Israel insists that assurances were given to Arabs that if they peacefully remained they would not be abused by the IDF, whereas those who left would forfeit their property and be barred from Israel in the future. With these conditions understood, according to the official line, Arabs who abandoned their homes did so of their own volition, often encouraged by Arab authorities.

However, since the 1980s, revisionist Israeli historians and journalists have challenged this benign picture. Such revisionists point to the longstanding desire of Zionists to "transfer" Arabs, by force if necessary, in order to create a Jewish majority. Revisionists document attacks on Arab villages by the IDF, mass expulsions of Arabs from urban areas, and unjustified killings of Palestinian civilians, sometimes sinking to the level of massacres. However, they analyze these facts in different manners;

some, such as Benny Morris and Avi Shlaim, regard the violence toward Palestinian civilians as the self-directed actions of field commanders operating in a highly charged wartime atmosphere of mistrust and hostility. On the other extreme, Ilan Pappe argues that it was a premeditated campaign of "ethnic cleansing" outlined in the Israeli Plan D, drafted in March 1948.[13] This included instructions to attack Palestinian towns and villages, drive out the inhabitants, and eliminate their possible return by burning and razing the buildings, followed by planting land mines in the rubble.

This is not the place to resolve such a hotly contested debate. However, four points should be made. First, driving off Palestinian Arabs would have been entirely consistent with the Yishuv's historical desire to become a majority population and control more land to form a Jewish state. Second, the Palestinian population remains convinced to this day that it was expelled in a campaign of what we would now call ethnic cleansing, and a great deal of the world accepts the Palestinian charges. Third, belief in the Nakba and the ongoing refugee status of Palestinians provide strong motivations for Palestinian terrorism. And fourth, the perceived injustice to the Palestinians remains a primary claim among radical Islamists who believe that the West is engaged in a war on Islam. The *perception* of injustice dealt the Palestinians, whatever the *reality* might be, undergirds Middle East terrorism to this day, from the charter of the Palestine Liberation Organization to the *fatwas* of Osama bin Laden.

1949–1967

Between 1949 and 1967 Palestinians engaged in cross-border raiding into Israel, but not at the level of intensity that would follow. Meanwhile, major wars beat down the Arab states. Egyptian failure in the Israeli War of Independence helped precipitate the 1952 revolution that brought down King Farouk. Lieutenant Colonel Gamal Abdel Nasser played a key role in that coup, and in June 1956 he became president of Egypt. He also rose as the great hope of pan-Arabism, a movement for Arab peoples and states to unite for common causes. Egyptian nationalization of the Suez Canal, which had been under British "protection," precipitated the Suez Crisis and the Sinai War of 29 October–6 November 1956. Britain, France, and Israel allied to counter what they each saw as threats from a revitalized and more aggressive Egypt. Egypt found itself in an impossible situation during the Sinai War, with the IDF striking south into the Sinai and the European powers mounting an attack with warships and airborne troops on the canal. In a rare show of unity, both the United States and the Soviet Union vigorously protested, forcing the British and French to pull out of Egypt, while the Israelis had to withdraw from the Sinai. With the decline of British and French influence, the United States became the dominant Western presence in the Middle East.

Nasser's reputation did not suffer from defeat in the Sinai War, since he had battled an overpowering coalition. In the end he was able to hold on to the canal, win international recognition, and enhance his status as the champion of pan-Arab aspirations. In 1958 Egypt and Syria formed the United Arab Republic (UAR), although this only lasted until 1961, when a coup broke Syria's ties to the UAR. Still, the notion remained that Arab states would unite together, assert the identity and power of the Arab peoples, and destroy Israel.

Palestinians organized during the heady years of pan-Arabism. There were Palestinian resistance groups before 1964, but in that year the PLO was created as an umbrella organization to give the Palestinians a seat at the table alongside states of the Arab League. The PLO's two most important member organizations in its early years were Fatah, headed by Yasser Arafat, and the Popular Front for the Liberation of Palestine (PFLP), led by George Habash. Fatah has been the largest group, and in 1969 Arafat became chairman of the PLO as well as head of Fatah. The PLO is secular; while Arafat was a Muslim, Habash was an Orthodox Christian. As is commonly the case, Arafat was known by two names, his birth name and Abu Ammar. The second is a *kunya*, the kind of nom de guerre common among Arab radicals. When dealing with such radicals, we will refer to either the birth name or the *kunya*, whichever is most widely used. Both Arafat and Habash are usually referred to by their birth names. When we speak of Abu Bakr al-Baghdadi of the Islamic State, we are using his *kunya*. The use of noms de guerre among terrorists has not been limited to the Middle East, as we shall see in Chapter 8.

When, following rising tensions, the third Arab–Israeli war, the Six-Day War, broke out in June 1967, Palestinians had reason to hope for deliverance. Certainly, the most powerful Arab country, Egypt, led by the heroic Nasser and allied with Syria and Jordan, must defeat diminutive

Israel. However, land mass and total population alone do not determine military power, even though the Egyptians were now armed with modern Soviet equipment.

From the start, Israel's basic military doctrine has been to create a militia-style army, professional in its abilities but made large by mobilizing its population to the highest degree possible.[14] The Israelis would be able to surpass their enemies in manpower on the battlefield during each of their major wars.

The Six-Day War ranks as the most astounding victory in the IDF's embattled history. Along with its other advantages in 1967, the IDF was again better commanded and more capable. Within hours of its opening airstrike, the Israeli Air Force (IAF) eliminated the Egyptian Air Force, a feat that it would soon replicate with the Syrian and Jordanian air fleets. Israel not only defeated its enemies, it humiliated them. The IDF sent the Egyptian army reeling back, took Gaza, and advanced through the Sinai to the banks of the Suez Canal. The IDF drove the Syrians off the Golan Heights, regarded as key for the security of Israeli farms and towns in the northeast of the country. Jordan, which had essentially annexed the West Bank in 1949, lost it all, including the Arab-controlled part of Jerusalem.

A new exodus of Palestinians attended the Israeli conquest of the West Bank and Gaza. Some 200,000 fled the West Bank to Jordan, a transfer of population that Moshe Dayan, the minister of defense at the time, insisted that the Israelis must facilitate. Even with this displacement, slightly over one million Palestinians remained in the West Bank and Gaza, a substantial number in relation to the population of Israel itself, which stood just shy of two and a half million.

On 22 November 1967, the United Nations Security Council unanimously passed Resolution 242. After stating the "inadmissibility of the acquisition of territory by war," it insisted that a "just and lasting peace" must be based on two principles: first, "withdrawal of Israeli armed forces from territories occupied in the recent conflict," and second, "acknowledgement of the sovereignty, territorial integrity, and political independence of every State in the area."[15] This required concessions that neither Israel nor the PLO was willing to make. Israel refused to withdraw, and the Palestinian National Charter drafted by the PLO in July 1968 denied the legitimacy of Israel, considering it a "Zionist occupation."[16]

1967–1982

Israel's victory in 1967 disillusioned those who expected the Palestinian cause to be secured by the military forces of the Arab states. Abu Iyad, the second most important individual in Fatah, lamented: "I wasn't prepared for the overwhelming, crushing, humiliating defeat. . . . The Arab armies, all the Arab armies put together, hadn't been capable of keeping the little Israeli army at bay."[17] The PLO leadership realized that it must rely on its own efforts to regain the patrimony lost in the Nakba.

The primary base for Fatah terrorism became the Palestinian refugee community on the east bank of the Jordan River in the Hashemite kingdom of Jordan. In response to a Fatah bombing of an Israeli school bus in March 1968, the IDF attacked the Fatah stronghold of Karameh. The Israelis inflicted high casualties on Fatah during the resulting fight, but the stand of the Palestinians, supported by units of the Jordanian Army, won Fatah a major propaganda victory.

At the same time, the PFLP based in Jordan carried out a series of aircraft hijackings starting in July 1968. These events were intended to draw worldwide attention to the Palestinians' plight. While Israeli El Al flights were targeted, the other planes hijacked belonged to American, British, and Swiss airlines. Because these attacks were meant to have an international impact, we can call them "international terrorism," but be aware we are using the words in a special sense. "International" here signifies an *international* attack designed to draw attention to a *national or regional* conflict. As security commentators are apt to say, this terrorism is the result of "somebody else's civil war."[18]

The PFLP carried out a large-scale operation on 6 September 1970: it successfully hijacked TWA flight 741, Swissair flight 100, and Pan Am flight 93, while another hijacking failed in midair. The first two planes were flown to a small, remote airfield in Jordan; the third, a Boeing 747, was too large and ended up in Cairo. On 9 September a fourth hijacked plane, BOAC flight 775, joined the first two in Jordan. On 12 September the PFLP blew up the three planes at the remote airbase. All passengers and crew had disembarked, so there were no casualties.

The hijackings infuriated Jordan's King Hussein. Palestinian resistance groups had grown increasingly arrogant in Jordan, acting more and more like a state within a state. They set up roadblocks, disregarded Jordanian officials, and abused the king's subjects, including women.

The king declared martial law on 15 September and authorized attacks on Palestinian headquarters in Amman and several Palestinian refugee camps. After a ceasefire, fighting resumed in November and continued through July 1971, ending with Jordanian victory. Driven out of Jordan, the PLO regrouped in southern Lebanon, making it their new base of operations. The Jordanian expulsion of the PLO is known as Black September.

One consequence of the PLO's expulsion from Jordan was the spinoff of a new, and more radical, terrorist group that drew from Fatah cadres and called itself "Black September." Black September's most infamous attack struck the Israeli team at the Munich Olympics. In the early hours of 5 September 1972, eight cadres of Black September scaled the fence around the Olympic Village and forced their way into the apartments of the Israeli team. The terrorists killed two Israelis and took nine others hostage. In negotiations that followed, the Palestinians demanded the release of 232 prisoners held in Israel, and of two German terrorists of the German Red Army Faction (RAF). German negotiators agreed that the terrorists and their hostages could fly to Cairo, but first they were to be helicoptered from the village to a nearby NATO airbase. The Germans planned to ambush the Palestinians at the airbase, but the ambush/rescue went terribly wrong and terrorists killed the remaining nine Israelis. Five of the terrorists also died; the other three were captured. Responses to the massacre varied. The Israelis bombed PLO bases, killing as many as 200. In Libya, where the bodies of the slain terrorists were flown, they received heroes' welcomes.

In order to win the release of hostages taken in another airplane hijacking in October 1972, German authorities agreed to release the three Munich terrorists they held. The outraged Israelis then put in motion Operation Wrath of God to assassinate those involved with the Munich massacre. It claimed a number of victims from the fall of 1972 until July 1973, when operatives from Mossad, the Israeli intelligence agency, mistakenly killed an innocent Moroccan in Lillehammer, Norway. This error led the Israelis to suspend the operation, although it was revived several years later.

Meanwhile, warfare sputtered on between Egypt and Israel after the Israeli blitz of 1967. Russian military aid flowed to the Egyptians. When Nasser died of a heart attack on 28 September 1970, he was succeeded by Anwar Sadat, who prepared for a renewed armed struggle with Israel.

On 6 October 1973 the Yom Kippur War, also known as the Ramadan War or the October War, began with an impressive crossing of the Suez Canal by the Egyptian Army. Syria joined Egypt in this war and tried to retake the Golan. By the time the fighting stopped on 25 October, the Israelis had put armored forces on the Egyptian side of the canal and pushed the Syrians back from the Golan; however, the Egyptians regarded the war as a victory because they had carried out their initial crossing and still held positions on the east bank of the canal.

The fact that both sides believed they had achieved success gave them license to engage in talks that resulted in Israeli concessions and withdrawals from the Sinai. This progress finally brought Sadat and Begin to conclude the Camp David Accords in 1978. These accords also planted the seeds for the 1993 Oslo Accords. While Sadat was lionized in the West, his rapprochement with Israel enraged Islamist extremists, who assassinated him during an annual victory parade on 6 October 1981, celebrating the Egyptian crossing of the canal.

The PLO, it should be remembered, was not sectarian, not specifically Muslim, so it could work with other terrorist groups without religion being an obstacle. Israeli general Ariel Sharon described Lebanon, where the PLO was headquartered, as "the center of world terrorism."[19] To a degree, he was correct; terrorist groups were aided or inspired by the PLO. We have already mentioned Irish murals celebrating the PLO. Marxist radicals of the German Red Army Faction attended PFLP training camps and coordinated with that organization in the hijacking of a Lufthansa airliner in 1977. Revolutionary admiration seemed to flow back as well; the PFLP contained one unit named the "'Martyr Guevara" group, honoring the Cuban revolutionary Che Guevara.[20] Terrorism was transnational; its strongest bastion was now in the Middle East, not Europe, and the PLO was the central terrorist organization.

The PLO became powerful in its new home in southern Lebanon, creating a de facto state within a state, as it had in Jordan. Its presence and power, plus the population of over 300,000 Palestinian refugees, upset the balance between Christian and Muslim factions in Lebanon. The PLO presence became a major factor in precipitating the long and tragic Lebanese Civil War in 1975, which cost 100,000 lives before it waned in 1990. The PLO under Arafat's leadership increased its numbers and effectiveness, creating an insurgent army of 6,000–7,000 cadres capable of more than commando raids. By June 1982, the PLO bristled with about 250 canon and Katusha rocket launchers—not the stuff of simple terrorism. It is hard to consider the PLO as only a sub-state group when it had multiplied in numbers and increased in abilities to the degree that it could fight openly in the Lebanese Civil War. By intent or opportunism, it had come to follow a strategy of evolution.

During the 1970s, attacks by PLO fedayeen into Israel from Lebanon and Israeli reprisals made the border a war zone. A particularly dreadful massacre took place at Ma'alot on 15 May 1974, Israeli Independence Day that year. Dressed as Israeli soldiers, three cadres of the Democratic Front for the Liberation of Palestine, a group within the PLO, crossed into Israel from Lebanon and reached Ma'alot, where they killed four civilians and then took 115 hostages at a school. The Israelis tried to negotiate but were unable to get the terrorists to give them more time. When Israeli soldiers stormed the school, twenty-five hostages died and sixty-eight more were wounded.

International terrorism continued as well, and in these efforts the PFLP figured large. On 21 December 1975, PFLP cadres, led by the infamous Carlos the Jackal, raided the Vienna headquarters of the Organization of Petroleum Exporting Countries (OPEC). Carlos was, in fact, Ramírez Sánchez, a Marxist Venezuelan terrorist who joined the PFLP in 1970. The PFLP killed three during the raid and took sixty hostages. Carlos bargained with Austrian officials, who agreed to broadcast a Palestinian manifesto and fly his team and the hostages to Algiers.

On 27 June 1976, two PFLP cadres and two cadres from the German terrorist group Revolutionary Cells hijacked Air France flight 139 from Tel Aviv, eventually forcing the crew to land in Entebbe, Uganda. However, on 4 July an IDF team carried out a dramatic rescue. Three hostages died during the rescue; all the hijackers were killed, along with forty-five Ugandan soldiers. The Israeli commander, Yonatan Netanyahu, brother of Benjamin Netanyahu, also fell.

The next year, Fatah cadres staged the operation that resulted in the Coastal Road Massacre on 11 March 1978. As already mentioned, the Israeli response came quickly, when on the night of 14–15 March the IDF mounted Operation Litani against PLO bases in Lebanon south of the Litani River. The speed with which the IDF launched an invasion by 25,000 troops demonstrates that the incursion had already been planned.

The IDF withdrew in June, by which time 1,100–1,200 Lebanese and Palestinians had been killed in the conflict; twenty Israelis had lost their lives. PLO incursions declined.

But by 1981 the Israelis were carrying out strikes into Lebanon meant to bait the PLO to attack Israel. Once the peacemaker, Menachim Begin was now seeking a rationale to justify another war to destroy the PLO once and for all. But his American backers demanded clear "internationally recognized provocation" before they would accept an Israeli offensive.[21] Begin believed he had what he needed when, on 3 June 1982, Palestinians of the Abu Nidal group attempted to assassinate the Israeli ambassador to the United Kingdom, Shlomo Argov, seriously wounding him. Their leader, Abu Nidal, was not part of the PLO but, rather, an archenemy of Yasser Arafat. However, in a cabinet debate, Begin was not to be deterred by the facts; he insisted, "They're all PLO. Abu Nidal, Abu Schmidal. We have to strike at the PLO."[22]

On 6 June Israeli forces rolled forward in a full-scale invasion of Lebanon, ironically titled Operation Peace for Galilee.

1982–1985: THE LEBANON WAR

Israel had gone to war with neighboring states several times, but its military incursions into Lebanon in 1978 and 1982 were not really wars with the state of Lebanon per se, but attempts to destroy the PLO based in Lebanon. In another important contrast with past conflicts, while the IDF expected another quick victory, Israel found itself mired in Lebanon until 2000. What did change, however, was the identity of the primary enemy. Initially, this was the PLO, a second-wave ethno-nationalist terrorist group. However, within a matter of months Israel was facing a new foe, Hezbollah, a third-wave radical Islamist group. Hezbollah differed from the PLO in motivation and method. It would become more potent in insurgency and would add to the terrorist arsenal by employing suicide attacks.

The attempted assassination of Shlomo Argov was no more than a pretext for taking up arms in a war driven by much more extensive strategic goals. This was Begin's war, but he was in league with his strongly hawkish minister of defense, Ariel Sharon, who at times circumvented his prime minister. The first goal was to crush the PLO as thoroughly as possible and drive it out of Lebanon. Building on a long-held belief that

Israel shared common interests with the native Christian community in Lebanon, Begin hoped to install a Maronite Christian government headed by Bashir Gemayel that would agree to a peace treaty with Israel. The Israelis also hoped to drive Syrian forces out of Lebanon and undercut Syrian influence in Beirut.

Begin harbored another long-term motive. According to Benny Morris, "By invading Lebanon, Begin had hoped to neutralize Palestinian nationalism and facilitate Israeli annexation, at least de facto, of the West Bank."[23] Israel was entrenching itself in the occupied West Bank and East Jerusalem through the creation of Jewish settlements. The construction of settlements on this legacy of the Six-Day War at first moved slowly. In 1972 the number of Israeli settlers inhabiting the West Bank and East Jerusalem stood at less than 10,000, but by 1983 this number had increased to nearly 100,000. As of December 2015, the total had risen to about 800,000.[24] Critics condemn the establishment of settlements as a violation of international humanitarian law as set out in Article 49 of the Fourth Geneva Convention (1949), since the settlements amount to transporting the victor's population into territory it has occupied by conquest.

The Israelis did not expect as hard a fight as they got when their forces struck into Lebanon on 6 June 1982. Yet they still advanced to Beirut, overcoming opposition by the PLO and the Syrians, as well as from Palestinian fighters they encountered in the refugee camps. They began a siege of the city on 14 June. Begin had reassured the Americans that they would only advance forty kilometers, twenty-five miles, into Lebanon, but Sharon and Rafael Eitan, the IDF chief of staff, paid little regard to that promise.

The destructive brutality of the siege disillusioned and then appalled the administration of U.S. president Ronald Reagan, who did not favor war in the first place. On 9 June Reagan wrote to Begin: "I am extremely concerned by the latest reports of additional advances of Israel into central Lebanon and the escalation of violence between Israel and Syria. Your forces moved significantly beyond the objectives that you have described to me. . . . Menachem, a refusal by Israel to accept a ceasefire will aggravate further the serious threat to world peace and will create extreme tension in our relation."[25] A ceasefire with Syria materialized, but the siege of Beirut continued, and Begin and Sharon showed little intention of moderating it. Its worst intensity ravaged the city on 12 August, when the IDF subjected it to heavy artillery bombardment and the IAF launched seventy-two bombing sorties. Reagan telephoned Begin in dismay: "Menachem, this is holocaust. . . . It's got to stop."[26] The Americans pressed for a ceasefire.

Yasser Arafat agreed to it on 12–13 August, and French and Italian troops along with American Marines arrived on 21 August to facilitate and protect the withdrawal of 14,398 Palestinians and Syrians from Beirut. The PLO leadership reestablished itself in Tunis, Tunisia. Arafat returned to Lebanon the next year but was driven from the country again in December 1983, this time by Israelis and Palestinian rebels loyal to Syrian president Hafez al-Assad. Arafat and 4,000 of his PLO fighters left in ships escorted by vessels of the French Navy. Arafat would not come back to Palestine until 1994, after the signing of the 1993 Oslo Accords, to be discussed in Chapter 10. The Israelis had rid Lebanon of the PLO, but this would hardly be the end of terrorism; PLO cadres dispersed to other countries and the occupied territories, and new kinds of terrorists would also take up arms against Israel.

On 23 August 1982, during the PLO pullout, the Israelis seemed to achieve another of their goals with the election of the Christian candidate Bashir Gemayel as president of Lebanon, but the victory was short-lived. On 14 September an assassin in Syrian pay detonated a powerful bomb in an apartment immediately above a room where Gemayel was addressing a meeting. This killed twenty-six, including Gemayel. He was the only politician who could have really benefited the Israelis.

On 15 September the Israelis advanced into West Beirut, which had been a PLO stronghold. As part of the effort to solidify their position, the Israelis also wanted to clear out Palestinian fighters they feared were still harbored in the refugee camps. To do so in two camps bordering West Beirut, Sabra and Shatila, the Israelis called on the Christian Phalangist militia. At about 6 p.m. on 16 September, only two days after Gemayel had been killed, the Phalangists were given access to the camps and assisted by star-shell illumination from the Israelis. After entering the camps, the Phalangists, seeing the Palestinians as inveterate enemies and eager to avenge the killing of Gemayel, massacred men, women, and children. Estimates of the slain vary, but the Israelis themselves put the figure at 700–800.

The massacre shocked world opinion, and under pressure the Israeli cabinet established a commission led by the president of the Israeli Supreme Court, Yitzhak Kahan. On 8 February 1983 the Kahan Commission released its unanimous findings.[27] Although Israelis actually took no part in the killing, the Commission assigned some blame to Begin and found Eitan guilty of "a breach of duty and dereliction of the duty." The commission came down hardest on Sharon, declaring that that he bore "personal responsibility" and recommended that he be removed from office. Begin did dismiss Sharon as minister of defense, but kept him in the cabinet as a minister without portfolio.

The government of the United States pressured the Israelis to withdraw from Beirut in late September and dispatched an American-led Multi-National Force (MNF) to aid the Lebanese government in controlling the city. These moves simply marked the Americans as targets for violence by Shia fighters and religious extremists. As will be detailed in Chapter 9, Islamist radicalism was waxing, most obviously in the Iranian Revolution, leading to the flight of the shah in January 1979 and the creation of a Shia Islamic republic in April. When the Israelis invaded Lebanon, the Iranian government, now headed by Ayatollah Ruhollah Khomeini, supported the militant Lebanese Shia militias that fought against the IDF. A number of these militias coalesced into Hezbollah with assistance and finance from Iran. Officially, Hezbollah only formed in 1985, but its members were active well before then.

The Lebanese resistance attacked both the Israelis and Americans with terrorist suicide bombings, a major innovation in their terrorist repertoire. Robert Pape, an expert on this form of terrorism, credits Hezbollah with thirty-six suicide terrorist attacks in Lebanon between 1982 and 1986. On 18 April 1983, an Islamist suicide terrorist driving a truck bomb destroyed a section of the American embassy in Beirut, killing sixty-three, including eight from the CIA, and wounding another hundred. On 23 October of that year, a truck bomb demolished the building in Beirut being employed as barracks by U.S. Marines. This attack killed 241 Marines, sailors, and soldiers, and wounded another 128. At the same time, another suicide bomber detonated his bomb at the billet housing French paratroopers of the MNF, killing sixty-nine and injuring fifteen. And on 20 September 1984, a truck bombing of the relocated U.S. embassy in Beirut killed twenty-four. We will have much more to say about Hezbollah in Chapter 10.

A notable suicide attack against the IDF took place on 9 April 1985, when Sana'a Mehaidli, a sixteen-year-old woman, drove a bomb-laden white Volvo into an Israeli truck column and detonated her explosives, killing two Israelis and two Lebanese, and wounding two more. Mehaidli, a member of an Arab Greek Orthodox family, was not from Shia Hezbollah but a cadre of the Syrian Social Nationalist Party. She is credited as the first female suicide bomber, a phenomenon to be explored in Chapter 10.

On 17 May 1983, not long after the first bombing of the U.S. embassy, the Israelis agreed to a staged withdrawal from around Beirut and back toward Israel. They remained on Lebanese territory in a "Security Zone," a strip of territory along the border with Israel, encompassing about 10 percent of Lebanon. The withdrawal to the zone was completed in 1985, and the IDF continued to occupy it until 2000.

Important Israeli critics have condemned the Lebanon War and its consequences. For example, Ze'ev Schiff and Ehud Ya'ari characterize it as "anchored in delusion, propelled by deceit, and bound to end in calamity . . . There is no consolation for this costly, senseless war."[28]

The violent history of Palestine and Israel since the early twentieth century is essential to understanding the second and third waves of radical terrorism. The PLO arose in the context of the second wave, when it played an outsized role in transnational terrorism. And the third-wave narrative of a Western war on Islam feeds upon the Islamist interpretation of the Palestinians' fate. In February 1985, the newly constituted Hezbollah issued a manifesto that spoke of the horrors of the Lebanon War: "In a single night the Israelis and the Phalangists executed thousands of our sons, women and children in Sabra and Shatila." Israel posed the most immediate threat: "This enemy is the greatest danger to our future generations and to the destiny of our lands, particularly as it glorifies the ideas of settlement and expansion." But the manifesto targeted the United States as the ultimate evil: "We combat abomination and we shall tear out its very roots, its primary roots, which are the US." In 2004, Osama bin Laden even cited the Lebanon War as inspiring him to target the World Trade Center towers on 9/11: "As I watched the destroyed towers in Lebanon, it occurred to me to punish the unjust the same way: to destroy towers in America so it could taste some of what we are tasting and to stop killing our children and women."[29]

Worn down and weakened by ill health and ill fortune, Menachem Begin stepped down as prime minister in October 1983 and retired from politics altogether, telling his colleagues, "I cannot go on any longer."[30] He was succeeded as prime minister by another former terrorist, Yitzhak Shamir, a veteran of the Irgun who left it to join the more extreme Stern Gang. Begin spent the last nine years of his life in seclusion, rarely leaving his Tel Aviv apartment, and when he did, it was most often to visit the grave of his wife, who died in November 1982, another blow in that battered year. He died on 9 March 1992, at the age of 79. He had played so many different parts in his lifetime: terrorist, politician, peace laureate, and war-maker.

CHAPTER EIGHT

Urban Guerrillas

MARXIST TERRORISM DURING THE 1960S AND 1970S

FIGURE 8.1. The Italian Red Brigades (Brigate Rosse) kidnapped Christian Democracy Party head Aldo Moro on 16 March 1978. A photo taken by the terrorists (*left*) shows him seated in front of a Red Brigades banner. When negotiations for Moro's release proved futile, he was murdered on 9 May; his body was discovered under a blanket in the back of a Renault 4 in Rome (*below*). *Left:* Wikimedia Commons. *Below:* Paul Fearn/Alamy Stock Photo.

A MAN OF CONSCIENCE and regular habits, Aldo Moro began the day of 16 March 1978 by attending mass, after which he headed off to the Italian Parliament. He and his escorts proceeded in two cars, the first with Moro, a driver, and one bodyguard followed by the second with three more bodyguards. A former prime minister, Moro headed the centrist Christian Democracy, the largest party in the Italian government. At the time, he was trying to broker a coalition with the Italian Communist Party (PCI), to bring them into the government, after Communists had been excluded from any ministerial post for the past thirty years. This "Historic Compromise" was expected to bring the PCI more into the mainstream. Such moderation was detested by the terrorist Red Brigades, or Brigate Rosse (BR), and these radical Marxists plotted to scuttle the Historic Compromise by kidnapping Moro that morning. This amounted to classic terrorist spoiling.

The terrorists devised and executed an elaborate plan. They pre-positioned vehicles on the Via Mario Fani and placed armed cadres on the street. When they entered the street, Moro's cars were blocked front and back by BR vehicles, and gunmen killed Moro's driver and bodyguards without wounding Moro, who was quickly seized and spirited away to a safe house. During the next fifty-five days the story dominated the news. The BR wished to negotiate with the Italian government for the release of imprisoned terrorists, but the government, headed by Giulio Andreotti, refused. Despite written appeals from Moro, his wife, the pope, and others, Andreotti adhered to a hard line, *fermezza* (firmness).

As the weeks dragged on, the leader of the BR, Mario Moretti, feared that police might discover where Moro was being held, free him, and arrest or kill his captors. To avoid this dénouement, Moro must be released or executed, and Moretti favored the later. On the morning of 9 May, Moro was told he was to be transferred to another location, put in the rear of a Renault 4, and covered with a blanket. Moretti then shot him eleven times (Fig. 8.1, bottom). The hope of a Historic Compromise died with Moro; to this extent the terrorists had succeeded—but at a price.

The BR ranks among the radical groups characterized as urban guerrillas or New Left terrorists. In this chapter, we will deal with three such groups active on three continents: the Tupamaros in South America, the Weather Underground Organization (WUO) in North America, and the BR in Europe. This intercontinental spread emphasizes the transnational character of New Left terrorism, while also highlighting its Western center of gravity. Readers will find a fourth terrorist organization, the German Red Army Faction (RAF), discussed on this book's website. While the RAF achieved great notoriety in its day, we learn more by using the BR as our primary European example.

Some commentators, notably David Rapoport, consider New Left terrorism as constituting a separate wave of modern radical terrorism. However, I regard the urban guerrillas as part of our second wave, which is best envisioned as driven by a continuum of motivations, with ethno-nationalism at one extreme and Marxism of a New Left cast at the other. To separate this continuum does violence to the integration of motivations within the second wave, and it also sins against chronology. It is not as if ethno-nationalist terrorism came first but then gave way around 1960 to urban guerrilla terrorism, which predominated from that point on. The Marxist Tupamaros *predated* the formation of the nationalist PLO and PIRA. The Marxist Weathermen, RAF, and BR all came into being around 1970, well before the emergence of the ethno-nationalist Tamil Tigers, which remained important in South Asia until its extinction in 2009. And it is not simply that ethno-nationalist and New Left Marxist groups operated concurrently; they were interrelated and mutually supportive. This was most obvious in the case of the PLO, regarded as brother freedom fighters by the PIRA. RAF members trained with the PLO in Jordan and coordinated with the PFLP-EO, a spinoff of the older PFLP, on terrorist projects, including an airplane hijacking that was a paramount event in the history of the RAF.

One poster, drawn in 1970 by Holger Meins, a founding member of the RAF, graphically represents the sense of interrelationship between terrorist groups during the second wave.[1] (His poster can be viewed in our website's Gallery section.) Above bold letters spelling out "FREEDOM FOR ALL PRISONERS" sprouted a blood-red sunflower, with bullet-shaped leaves radiating from a grenade at its center. Meins gave the youth-culture catchphrase of "flower power" a menacing twist. Between the deadly leaves, he featured the names of thirteen revolutionary groups. Among these were the FLN, Fatah, the Tupamaros, and the Weathermen, along with nine other contemporary ethno-nationalist and Marxist terrorist groups. His appeal to release political prisoners embraced them all as part of a transnational movement for radical change.

Besides detailing the reality of urban guerrilla terrorism, this chapter deals with certain distinct themes. One is the way in which terrorists calculate their tactics in relation to cultural tolerances toward violence.

Early in their terrorist campaign, the Tupamaros carried out actions meant to startle, in the sense of surprise, but not to shock, in the sense of morally alienate. The WUO forswore violence against human beings, and while the BR did kill, it did not engage in indiscriminate attacks. To one degree or another, each terrorist group realized that the wrong kind of violence could alienate the very population to which they looked for support. Compare this with the extremely shocking violence perpetrated by the FLN, the PLO, and the Islamic State.

Yet ultimately, both the Tupamaros and the BR lost support by carrying out assassinations. The Tupamaros both alienated their base and so infuriated the Uruguayan government and military that the terrorist group was crushed by brute force. The BR likewise lost support, but it was also undone by a clever dose of leniency for those who aided the government in prosecuting terrorism. This kind of finesse is not really on Cronin's list. In contrast, although the WUO was put under considerable pressure, it was not really decimated, but rather dissolved. Even though its cadres were well aware of the need not to lose support, the end of the Vietnam War robbed it of its most compelling cause. The program of the WUO was broader than its anti-war theme, but its clearest, most substantial, and most attainable goal was to force the United States to abandon the war. So, in a sense it won, but attaining its objective weakened the WUO. In addition, divisive practices and ideological squabbling caused dissension and factionalism that broke down the WUO.

In fact, each of the groups set itself extreme objectives, but could not make up for lack of membership and resources, capacity, by intelligent calculation. The histories of the three groups discussed in this chapter highlight the strong role of ideology among the urban terrorists, although the Tupamaros made it a point not to commit to such dogmatic purity that they would drive off supporters. Ideology became part of a cultlike mindset among urban guerrilla terrorists that mirrored the intensity and patterns of religious thought, a similarity most revealed in studies of the BR. The isolation and conviction of the cadre led them to overestimate their power and underestimate the obstacles and resistance they would face.

Last, urban guerrilla terrorism reflected the characteristics of a relatively brief era. To appreciate this, we must look at the environment in which New Left terrorism arose and flourished.

CONTEXTS OF URBAN GUERRILLA TERRORISM

The urban guerrillas of this chapter emerged and thrived in a multifaceted context that characterized the 1960s and the 1970s. It was a time when revolution, or at least radical change, was in the air, especially in the mindset of young intellectuals and activists. Consider what had happened since the end of World War II: the triumph of the Chinese Communist Revolution in 1949 and of the Vietnamese rebels against the French in 1954; the success of the Cuban Revolution in 1959 and of the FLN in 1962; and the Chinese Cultural Revolution with the youthful Red Guards in 1966. The accomplishments of the civil rights movement demonstrated to Americans that dramatic social change could be accomplished by dedicated activists in service to a righteous cause. And it was a time of international disruptions. Consider 1968 alone. A rebellion against autocratic Communist rule in Czechoslovakia, styled the Prague Spring, shook the Communist Bloc from January through August. France experienced a severe labor and student revolt, most notably in Paris during May, when students marched and even raised barricades. Then the burgeoning anti-war movement in the United States turned the Chicago Democratic National Convention into mayhem during August.

And there was the Vietnam War itself. The Americans had become the sponsors of the South Vietnamese regime after the French pulled out of Vietnam. This sponsorship involved the Unites States in the turmoil of the regime, as it was opposed by factions within South Vietnam, most notably the Communist guerrillas, the Vietcong. American support escalated into the dispatch of American Marines in March 1965; it was now outright war. The United States mired itself in the conflict until 1973, during which time the greatest military power in the world rained down its awesome destructive force on one of the poorest countries on the globe. The Vietcong's Tet Offensive of early 1968 made the American military's claims of success ring hollow. For anti-war activists and radicals around the world, the war exposed the savagery of imperialism, the exploitation of the poor by the rich, but also the vulnerability of the international capitalist order. Opponents of the war across the globe censured the United States.

Fascination with radical change and protests against the war became staples of the youth culture of the time. Generalizations are very tricky here, but the youth culture was strongest in North America and Europe, areas relatively free of the immediate pressures of material want. Members of the post-war generation, the baby boomers, were caught up in the youth culture and believed they could fashion a new world. Sexual liberation challenged traditional mores and recreational drugs were raised from indulging hedonism to expanding consciousness. Social purpose and protest filled the music. Sex, drugs, and rock and roll. Terrorism was certainly a long way from "make love, not war," but for those increasingly dedicated to change and justice at any price, violence could promise more than could the formula of "turn on, tune in, drop out" espoused by counterculture gurus.

Many of those seeking revolutionary progress sought explanation and direction from Marxism. The post–World War II era was home to different strains of Marxism. Traditional Marxism emphasized the industrial, predominantly urban workers locked in a class warfare. In contrast, the victory of the Chinese Communists led by Mao Zedong gave his peasant-based form of revolution a great deal of influence. But there was also a Marxism of the New Left, championed by the likes of the German-born philosopher Herbert Marcuse and the American sociologist C. Wright Mills. The New Left was transnational, but more definably Western than the ethno-nationalist terrorism of our second wave. Moving away from traditional Marxism, New Left ideology put more emphasis on capitalism as alienation and consumerism than on naked class struggle and production. It focused less on the working class, and this made the New Left more relevant and approachable to college-educated youths—not the masters of the middle class, but their children. Marcuse even wrote on the subject of eroticism.

FOCOISM

The last contextual element that applies to urban guerrillas sprang from revisions in revolutionary theory and practices during the 1960s. We need to discuss this at more length because it relates directly to terrorism and to my argument that radical terrorism can be a form of entry-level warfare. Marx, who died in 1883, never actually led a proletarian revolution akin to what he talked about in theory. Lenin, who died in 1924, did, but the Russian Revolution was tarnished by 1960. Mao, who was still alive but in his seventies by the time of the Cultural Revolution, had led a successful violent revolution, but one based not on the industrial proletariat but on the rural peasantry. His success led to imitation, as in Vietnam. Maoist theory stressed the need to follow a methodical pattern of fostering a revolutionary movement. This Maoist sequence began with cultivating community support by the political education of the peasant population, because its aid was essential for the armed struggle to succeed. Mao used the metaphor of the guerrillas being the "fish" that must have the "sea" of a supportive populace in which to "swim." Only after this preparation could the armed struggle begin as guerrilla warfare and then evolve into forces large enough and strong enough to engage in conventional warfare to defeat the enemy. We will discuss his notions of evolution more in Chapter 11. Right now it is the switch to a rural base and the need for a great deal of spadework before beginning the armed struggle that matter most.

The Cuban Revolution, led by Fidel Castro, provided a different pattern of peasant-based revolution that promised results with much less extensive preparation. Although Castro's first act of the revolution occurred on 26 July 1953, it was a fiasco leading to the death or capture of the guerrillas. Castro found himself imprisoned, and upon his release in 1955, he fled from Cuba to Mexico, where he prepared for the next revolutionary assault. He arrived back in the eastern mountains of Cuba with a small band of supporters in December 1956, yet in only two more years he and his growing revolutionary forces would take Havana and drive the dictator Fulgencio Batista into exile. At the time of his triumph, Castro was thirty-two and his right-hand man, Che Guevara, one year older. They were the new revolutionaries, and they advocated a new kind of revolution. The speed with which Castro triumphed threw into doubt the necessity of Mao's methodical prescription.

Che, a towering revolutionary icon, published his *Guerrilla Warfare* in 1961. A more important work, *Revolution in the Revolution?* by Regis Debray, appeared in 1967, the year Guevara was killed in Bolivia. Debray was a French Marxist scholar who essentially spoke for Castro. Guevara and Debray argued that when a population already realized how corrupt and repressive its government truly was, small bands of guerrillas could take up arms and precipitate revolution without extensive preparation. These small bands, mere handfuls of fighters, were known as "focos," and the theory of precipitating revolution with them was "focoism." The focoism of Guevara and Debray held out the chance of ultimate success to revolutionaries who were strong in conviction but weak in numbers. For Guevara and Debray the foco was not a sufficient agent but the first step in an *evolution* advancing to fielding a conventional army. In *Guerrilla Warfare*, Guevara wrote, "Triumph will always be the product of a regular army, even though its origins are in a guerrilla army."[2]

Guevara was still talking about a rural revolution, so for Maoism and focoism to be relevant to an explicitly urban environment, more needed to be added to the mix. Two Latin American figures stand out here: the Marxist philosopher Abraham Guillén, *a* journalist and a veteran of the Spanish Civil War, and Carlos Marighella, a pragmatic Brazilian fighter who died a revolutionary's death in 1969. Marighella's *Minimanual of the Urban Guerrilla*, published the year of his death, became a must-read for urban guerrillas around the globe. Guillén and Marighella insisted that Guevara's Maoist emphasis on rural revolution did not fit countries with large urban populations, such as Argentina, Brazil, and Uruguay. Their prescriptions for focoism as an urban strategy encouraged little town-based groups to think big, to believe that they could precipitate a mass revolution with little preparation. It was seductive to revolutionaries with few numbers and resources, capable of little else than terrorism. And to such bands, the notion that a few could spark a mass movement looks more like a strategy of *initiation* than one of *evolution*. In fact, urban guerrillas were unable to advance beyond initiation.

THE TUPAMAROS

The name of the Tupamaros—more formally, the Movimiento de Liberación Nacional-Tupamaros (MLN-T)—referenced a hero of resistance: Túpac Amaru II, who led an indigenous uprising against the Spanish in Peru in 1780–1781. However, the Tupamaros' home turf was not Peru, but the relatively liberal and comfortable state of Uruguay, which boasted a history of progressive social reforms, freedom of expression, and democratic politics. Uruguay was also overwhelmingly urban—of its total population of about three million, 60 percent lived in the city of Montevideo and its surrounding area.[3] Historian Herbert Gatto points out: "What is . . . most surprising is not that Uruguay lacked some of the conditions for revolution . . . but rather, [that] it lacked all of them."[4] In a speech he gave in Montevideo on 17 August 1961, Che Guevara himself counseled his audience against turning to revolutionary violence:

"You have something worth preserving . . . the possibility of advancing through democratic channels as far as one can go."[5] And, he warned, "once the first shot is fired, you never know when the last one will be."

But long-term conditions and short-term hard times were not the same thing. A banking crisis struck in the mid-1960s. In 1968 the president of Uruguay, Pacheco Areco, instituted wage and price controls in hopes of securing support from the International Monetary Fund. Economic downturn brought on severe inflation. The exchange rate for one U.S. dollar increased from six Uruguayan pesos in 1959 to 400 in 1970.[6] Of course, for Marxist socialist intellectuals and their allies, there was an obvious cause for Uruguay's misfortunes: imperialism, its agents, and its beneficiaries. The United States was viewed as the ultimate culprit.

Individuals from the Uruguayan left coalesced into the MLN-T sometime in 1962–1963. They began their revolutionary campaign even before the group had a name. Its first act of violence came on 31 July 1963, when cadres raided a civilian shooting club in Neuva Helvecia, netting thirty-two weapons. On Christmas Eve of that year the group carried out what would become a kind of trademark act, holding up a truck operated by a large food chain and distributing the truck's chickens, turkeys, and candy among poor slum inhabitants.[7]

The next year brought another arms raid on a customs office, yielding another nineteen rifles, and at least two bank robberies at the Banco de Cobranzas in the fall.[8] From the start, then, the Tupamaros exemplified the actions that Marighella would counsel in his *Minimanual:* "The urban guerrilla must rob banks and armories, and seize explosives and ammunition wherever he finds them."[9] They also used violence as a political statement. The most notable action of 1965, the 9 August bombing of the offices of the Bayer chemical company, carried the radicals' signature for the first time, in a leaflet stating: "Death to Vietnam's Yankee assassins. The assassins' intervention in Vietnam must be answered by the union of all oppressed people. The common enemy must be crushed. Bayer, a Nazi enterprise, supports the gringos' intervention. Viva Vietnam. Viva la Revolución.—Tupamaros."[10]

In January 1966 leaders met in a secret Tupamaros Convention and adopted their first revolutionary slogan, "Arm yourselves and wait." The first major Tupamaro assault in Montevideo, an attempted robbery of the rubber manufacturer FUNSA on 22 December, led to a gunfight, leaving

Tupamaros dead and the operation aborted. The FUNSA fiasco caused the Tupamaros to regroup and rethink during 1967; they would not take up revolutionary violence again for eighteen months.

According to one Tupamaro, Efraín Martínez, this time was "the richest year for those inside the MLN-T. . . . We discussed Debray, Che Guevara, socialism, the realistic possibilities of pursuing a guerrilla [war] in Uruguay, the general outlines."[11] But the Tupamaros made a point of not becoming dogmatic; they wanted to set up as wide a tent as possible. Another of their slogans was "Words divide us, action unites us."[12] Too much attention to ideological sharpness would limit the appeal of the group.

The initial strategy that emerged from this reevaluation was "armed propaganda," which amounted to a form of propaganda of the deed in which revolutionary violence would speak for itself. A Tupamaro manifesto set out the principle of armed propaganda: "We follow one basic rule: Do not use violence that is not understood by the people. If the people don't understand it, the government can use it against us."[13] In order to limit harm to the innocent, Tupamaros believed that armed propaganda should only employ violence that was necessary or unavoidable.

Character of the Tupamaros

Although each of the three urban guerrilla organizations discussed in this chapter enjoyed a base of support greater than its active membership, the number of those personally engaged in violent actions remained small. When the Tupamaros began their campaign of armed propaganda in mid-1968, they only had about fifty members, and by mid-1970 this core had increased to about 1,000 active members, with about 2,000 more in Tupamaros Support Committees, who provided help in logistical matters. Individual attacks, however, usually involved only a handful of armed participants, with the largest investment of cadres being sixty-two for raiding the Uruguayan naval academy on 28 May 1970. This attack netted a large cache of weapons and badly embarrassed the government, but not a shot was fired. As would be expected, the great majority of active Tupamaros were young; about 50 percent of the cadres were students during the late 1960s.[14]

The Tupamaros' leadership was diverse. The most important of them, Raul Sendic, was a Marxist lawyer and labor leader. Another key personality, José (Pepe) Mujica, was the son of poor peasants.

As is typical of terrorist organizations, Tupamaros organized themselves in cells to limit the harm that could be done by the capture of any cadre of the group. However, Tupamaros went a step further by adopting a principle they christened "compartmentalization." Cadres went by noms de guerre and often did not know the real identities of their fellow Tupamaros. In some cases, they wore hoods at meetings to hide their appearance even from their comrades. Information was shared strictly on a need-to-know basis.

The Robin Hood Guerrillas
The era of armed propaganda produced several cleverly conceived, well-executed, and financially beneficial operations that won the Tupamaros a reputation as not only effective and careful of human life, but even artful and hip. We only have space here to mention a few of these.

Che Guevara had expressed a strong concern for radio: "The propaganda that will be the most effective in spite of everything, that which will spread most freely over the whole national area to reach the reason and the sentiments of the people, is words over the radio."[15] On 15 May 1969 twelve Tupamaros honored this principle by hijacking Radio Saraní while it was broadcasting an important soccer match, guaranteed to attract a huge audience. During the second half, listeners were regaled with Tupamaro propaganda instead of a play-by-play account of the match.

The catalog of Tupamaro armed propaganda included several audacious robberies that financed the group while also gaining publicity for its cause and a reputation for restraint in the use of violence. Notable among these was the robbery of the San Rafael Casino in Punta del Este on 18 February 1969. The actual robbery was the work of only a few Tupamaros, but the take was very large, $220,000, or about $1.5 million in current dollars. When Sendic, who commanded the operation, learned that the stolen money included the salaries and tips of the employees, he offered to return that amount. In May of that year, the American newsweekly *Time* took note of the Tupamaros' raid in an article entitled "The Robin Hood Guerrillas."[16] The magazine awarded them grudging praise: "Their daring, well-planned actions, their skillful public relations, their sense of humor and style have given them the romantic image of modern-day Robin Hoods, taking from the rich, giving to the poor, exposing wrongdoing and corruption—all the while thumbing their noses at the government." *Time* also noted correctly: "Perhaps the Tupamaros want to avoid hurting innocent bystanders and tarnishing their Robin Hood reputation."

The Turn to Greater Violence and Its Result
As the Tupamaros increased in numbers and resources, they adopted more aggressively violent tactics. Their Plan Satán marked this transition away from armed propaganda and toward rawer forms of terrorist violence.[17] It entailed kidnapping foreign officials in Uruguay and using them as bargaining chips to exchange for captured Tupamaros. On 31 July 1970, three teams of Tupamaros attempted simultaneous kidnappings. One of their targets was Dan Mitrione, an American working for the U.S. Agency for International Development. The Tupamaros believed him to be a CIA agent and dealt with him harshly. He was spirited off to what the Tupamaros called the "people's prison," an underground cell at a safe house. When the Uruguayan government refused to give in to the Tupamaros' demands, the revolutionaries tried Mitrione in a "people's court" and condemned him to death unless certain political prisoners were released by a deadline. Despite a flurry of appeals, Mitrione was executed, and his body, shot three times at close range, was left in a stolen car on 10 August 1971.

The execution of Mitrione undercut the Tupamaros' image of moderation and eroded their public support. Security analyst Pablo Brum summed it up: "The romantic Robin Hood warriors of just a few months before had forsaken their reputation."[18] The Tupamaros also kidnapped Uruguayans, at least five from March to July 1971 alone, and robberies continued. They killed policemen and soldiers, even murdering an inoffensive ranch hand who had inadvertently stumbled across a Tupamaro base. In Plan Hipólito, on 14 April 1972, Tupamaros gunned down another four victims, also wounding a custodian and the wife of one of those assassinated.

The government intensified its offensive against the Tupamaros. By 1972 the army superseded the police in carrying on the fight. Large-scale raids in April 1972 captured one major leader, killed several cadres, and seized an important trove of documents. Torture, which had been used somewhat before, became brutally common. Between mid-April and mid-November the authorities captured 2,873 people they claimed were Tupamaros and killed sixty-two others. The Tupamaros and their supporters were being decimated.

Once the army took over the effort to eliminate the Tupamaros, the military's power and influence increased, and those who now commanded such authority were loath to relinquish it. A new president, Juan Bordaberry, took office in 1972 and continued along a more authoritarian path. In June 1973 he suspended the constitution and dissolved both chambers of the Uruguayan congress. Bordaberry gave a free hand to the military and police to combat the MLN-T and ruled by decree, with the generals by his side. In 1976 the military forced his resignation and ruled until 1984, when the junta reluctantly stepped aside and allowed elections in November.

The ultimate failure of the Tupamaros combines two bullet points on Cronin's list of how terrorism ends. On the one hand, its turn to violence lost it much of its popular support base. On the other hand, its violence solidified the resolve of Uruguayan authorities to crush the revolutionary movement by brute force, which they did.

Considering their lack of success, it is surprising that the Tupamaros so inspired the spread of urban guerrilla terrorist groups on other continents. Part of this can be put down to timing: the Tupamaros were still in the ascendant from the mid-1960s into 1971, when other urban guerrilla movements were just taking shape. As one contemporary left-wing commentator put it, the Tupamaros "seemed to many revolutionaries throughout the world to provide a perfect model of what revolutionary activity should be."[19] It is also far from irrelevant that in 1972 the Tupamaros were romanticized in the film *State of Siege*, produced by Costa-Gavras and written by Franco Salinas, who had authored the revolutionary classic *The Battle of Algiers*.

One wonders what drives groups to escalate the level of their violence —perhaps overconfidence, perhaps frustration. Confidence in growing strength and support could encourage a terrorist group to escalate its tactics. Or disappointment that their revolution is not progressing quickly enough could convince terrorists to speed things up by becoming more extreme. And it may be that once a group turns to violence, it is more likely to intensify over time. Aversion to killing declines once a certain line is crossed.

There is little doubt that the Tupamaros' violent turn raised them from a troublesome hazard to an existential threat to the state, which responded with brutally effective military suppression. The success of this repression contradicted the analysis of the revolutionary guru Carlos Marighella, who argued that victory for the urban guerrilla would come when "the political situation in the country is transformed into a military situation" by an authoritarian regime.

History provides an ironic twist in the fact that José Mujica, who endured thirteen years as a prisoner of the Uruguayan junta, served as the country's president from 2010 to 2014. His wife, Lucía Topolansky, a veteran Tupamara, is currently vice-president of Uruguay. In the same period, Dilma Rousseff, who was a member of a revolutionary terrorist organization during her youth, served as president of Brazil from 2011 to 2016. Just as in Israel, old terrorists can be elected heads of government.

THE WEATHER UNDERGROUND ORGANIZATION

The Weather Underground Organization was very much a product of the contexts highlighted at the beginning of this chapter, and very much made in the U.S.A. It was unique in some ways, but it was not the only revolutionary group to emerge in the America of the 1960s and 1970s. In fact, the WUO splintered off from the Students for a Democratic Society (SDS). At its creation in 1960, the SDS agenda was oriented toward the civil rights movement, but as the decade progressed it focused on opposition to the Vietnam War and grew markedly more extreme. However, the honed edge of principle cut the burgeoning SDS into factions. During the June 1969 SDS convention in Chicago, one of these factions produced a manifesto that took its title from a verse in the Bob Dylan anthem "Subterranean Homesick Blues": "You don't need a weatherman to know which way the wind blows." Among the eleven people responsible for the manifesto were John Jacobs, Bernardine Dohrn, Terry Robbins, Bill Ayers, Mark Rudd, and Jeff Jones. The radical faction styled itself Weather*man* and eventually the WUO, but they are commonly referred to as the Weather*men*.

As made clear in the manifesto, the Weathermen advocated Marxist-Leninist-Maoist communism in a program that was anti-war, anti-imperialist, and pro-Black liberation. They supported the victory of the Viet Cong and North Vietnam as a way of defeating U.S. imperialism.

The manifesto also categorized the Black population of the United States as "an internal colony within the confines of the oppressor nation," victims of imperialism at home. The Weathermen extolled the cause of the militant Black Panther Party, although the Panther leadership could be harshly critical of the overwhelmingly white, middle-class, and college-educated SDS and Weathermen. The manifesto declared that the "most important task for us toward making the revolution" was "the creation of a mass revolutionary movement . . . akin to the Red Guard in China . . . with a full willingness to participate in the violent and illegal struggle." Ultimately, the goal amounted to nothing less than "the achievement of a classless world: world communism."

Chronology of the Weathermen and WUO
The Weathermen turned their efforts to staging a mass demonstration in Chicago, where in August 1968 some 10,000 anti-war protesters had seized streets, parks, and media attention during the Democratic National Convention. With the grandiose title "Days of Rage," the new protest was envisioned for 8–11 October 1969, with the intent to "bring the war home!," as the slogan penned by Jacobs declared. They expected a turnout on the level of 1968; however, only 600 protesters materialized. In its most dramatic scene, on the afternoon of 11 October, some 300 rampaged in the Chicago Loop, breaking windows, but they were quickly corralled and arrested. Days of Rage backfired, as it alienated public opinion. In contrast to this, the Vietnam Moratorium, a series of peaceful anti-war protests held on 15 October, mobilized millions of war protesters across the country and overseas.

Days of Rage was not really terrorism, but rather a violent public demonstration; however, terrorist acts were committed in other cities by radicals who shared the Weathermen's righteous fury. In New York, members of a likeminded collective led by Sam Melville conducted a series of bombings during the summer and fall of 1969. The collective's campaign reached a crescendo on 11 November with bombings of the Standard Oil offices in the RCA Building, the headquarters of Chase Manhattan Bank, and the General Motors Building, followed by the bombing of the New York Criminal Courts Building the next day.

Regrouping after the disappointing Days of Rage, the Weathermen held their first and only public national convention in Flint, Michigan, on 27–31 December. This meeting, attended by about 300, is usually referred to as the "War Council." A journalist from the *Fifth Estate*, a radical paper, reported that "an enormous cardboard machine gun symbolizing Weatherman's commitment to armed struggle . . . hung from the ceiling." He also observed that "part of the armed struggle, as Dohrn and others laid it down, is terrorism." It is worth noting that at the women's session, panelists stated that "the women who carry bombs under their dresses like in *The Battle of Algiers*" were the most valid examples to be emulated.[20]

The participants entirely severed the SDS connection and made plans for the most committed of the Weathermen to go underground, dedicating themselves to the work of revolution. Following the War Council, the new leadership called for culling out those thought insufficiently dedicated or suspected of being informers. This left about 150 active cadres divided into three primary collectives based in San Francisco, New York, and Chicago/Detroit.

The New York collective, headed by Terry Robbins, pursued a deadly track. On 21 February 1970 it firebombed the house of the judge presiding over the trial of Black Panthers in New York. The Molotov cocktails they threw did little damage, but Robbins was ready to go much further. His cadres plotted to bomb a noncommissioned officers' dance at Fort Dix and also strike the Butler Library at Columbia University. On 6 March, Robbins was assembling a bomb in a Greenwich Village townhouse. Cathy Wilkerson, who was at the townhouse, described the bomb as "a piece of ordinary water pipe, filled with dynamite, nails, and an electric blasting cap."[21] It exploded in the townhouse basement, killing Robbins and two others.

This fatal blast caused the Weathermen to reconsider their tactics. The WUO was in disarray, and the refugees filtered off to California, where they met in a "summit." Amid the debates, Bernadette Dohrn took the lead and advocated that the Weathermen reject attacks on people. Bill Ayers testified: "We were very careful from the moment of the townhouse on to be sure we weren't going to hurt anybody, and we never did hurt anybody."[22] However, a conservative scholar, Harvey Klehr, remarked, "The only reason they were not guilty of mass murder is mere incompetence."[23]

The WUO issued its first public communiqué on 21 May 1970, a taped declaration of war read by Dohrn and sent to a broadcasting station.[24] This followed President Richard Nixon's announcement of the U.S. incursion into Cambodia, which incited mass campus protests and the tragic killing of four demonstrators at Kent State University on 4 May and two protesters at Jackson State University on 15 May. The WUO declaration announced: "All over the world, people fighting Amerikan imperialism look to Amerika's youth to use our strategic position behind enemy lines to join forces in the destruction of the empire.... Revolutionary violence is the only way." (The *k* in Amerika was the German spelling, implying that the United States was a Nazi dictatorship.) The appeal referenced other revolutionary movements. "Now we are adapting the classic guerrilla strategy of the Viet Cong and the urban guerrilla strategy of the Tupamaros to our own situation."

From the summer of 1970 through the fall of 1975 the WUO carried out a bombing campaign against over twenty government and corporate buildings. On 9 June 1970, Weathermen exploded a dynamite bomb at the New York City Police Headquarters. In accord with their revolutionary morality, they phoned in a warning before the detonation of the bomb. Other targets of bombing attacks included the United States Capitol, government offices, and corporate headquarters.

In 1974 the WUO issued *Prairie Fire*, a book-length statement of its analysis and agenda. This work restated the WUO's ultimate aim as "the destruction of imperialism, the seizure of power, and the creation of socialism."[25] The documentary film *Underground*, filmed in 1975, exudes the same energy and confidence, but the WUO dissolved in 1976, just as the film was finally released.

The highly charged ideological environment of the group and the harsh means used to maintain "correctness" led to factionalism that bred disagreements and recriminations. Historian Jeremy Varon concludes, "By the time the dust cleared, alliances and friendships had been shattered, a whole subculture was in ruins, and the Weather Underground had fallen into oblivion."[26] Moreover, to the extent that its main glue was its resistance to the war in Vietnam, it is unlikely the WUO could have outlasted American withdrawal from the war in 1973 and the victory of the Viet Cong and North Vietnam in April 1975.

Several WUO cadres, including Dohrn and Ayers, turned themselves in to the authorities by 1980. By this point, many charges against them had been dropped because evidence supporting those charges had been illegally acquired. Those who gave themselves up were treated lightly by the law. Dohrn received some jail time and probation, while all charges were dropped against Ayers. Dohrn eventually became a professor in the Northwestern University School of Law. Ayers joined the faculty of the College of Education at the University of Illinois at Chicago.

However, other members remained in hiding well after 1976 or took up new violent resistance with other comrades. Notably, three former WUO cadres joined the May 19 Communist Organization and participated with members of the Black Liberation Army in robbing a Brinks armored car in 1981. This attack resulted in the deaths of one guard and two policemen. The three former Weathermen were captured and convicted of felony murder.

The Character of the WUO

The Weathermen were few; however, as is the nature of terrorist groups, their notoriety greatly exceeded their numbers. In October 1971 seven of fourteen people on the FBI's Ten Most Wanted List were left-wing activists; among them was one from the Weather Underground, Bernardine Dohrn. At that time, a total of sixteen Weathermen were regarded as highly sought fugitives by the FBI.

In pursuit of its program, the Weather Underground dismissed the White working class and emphasized the young, like themselves, and the Black community as allies in overthrowing the status quo. The *Fifth Estate* journalist commented: "Weatherman continues to promote the notion that white working people in America are inherently counterrevolutionary, impossible to organize, or just plain evil—'honky bastards,' as many Weathermen put it."[27] The WUO regarded race as more central than class in the United States.

Weathermen characterized those who represented the existing order as disgusting and subhuman, as "pigs." The WUO applied the term most specifically to the police. But this insult was further extended to vilify anyone who exemplified the current order. We see this use of "pig" in other urban guerrilla literature. Ulrike Meinhof of the RAF wrote: "Those in uniforms are pigs, not human beings . . . there is no use in talking to them, and naturally they can be shot."[28]

Two practices rendered the Weather Underground particularly harsh in eroding its members' sense of self and imposing revolutionary collective conformity. The first, compulsory participation in self-criticism sessions, derived from Maoist methods meant to impose correct revolutionary thought and principles. WUO collectives devoted considerable effort to long and abusive self-criticism sessions, known as Weatherfries. Individual members were berated for hours by their comrades. In later years, Dohrn commented: "I don't know if there's a good Maoism somewhere, but the Maoism that we adopted was stupid and lethal."[29]

The second, the "smash monogamy" campaign, mixed political radicalism with the sexual revolution coming out of youth culture. WUO ideology condemned exclusive personal and sexual relationships as "possessive" and "selfish." The leadership directed rotation of sexual partners. This could amount to forced sex. Susan Stern reported an incident in which a female collective member fought off the advances of Weather Underground leader Mark Rudd, sobbing, "No, no, no, please don't. . . . I want Mike . . . I can't help it, I love him." At this Rudd commanded, "You have to put the demands of your collective above your love. Nothing comes before the collective."[30] This echoes Nechayev's "Catechism of a Revolutionary": "All the gentle and enervating sentiments of kinship, love, friendship, gratitude, and even honor, must be suppressed in [the revolutionary] and give place to the cold and single-minded passion for revolution."[31]

Given the youth culture, it is not surprising that drugs were part of life in the WUO. The May 1970 declaration of war proclaimed, "We fight in many ways. Dope is one of our weapons. . . . Guns and grass are united in the youth underground."[32] Susan Stern described the use of marijuana and LSD in her autobiography as being pretty much standard.

The WUO's revolutionary program amounted to another strategy of initiation. They embraced Debray's concept of the foco, interpreted by Jeff Jones as a conviction that "a small group of very politically advanced, ideologically committed militant people can carry out revolutionary actions that will serve as an inspiration for other people."[33] The radical journalist attending the War Council summed up their position: "Weathermen now talk less about a 'strategy to win,' more about their historic role as *catalysts*."[34] Yet in believing that the United States was at a revolutionary tipping point and that a few symbolic blows could overthrow its equilibrium, the Weathermen were delusional. They made a mortal error in reading the widespread resistance to an unpopular war and the more assertive turn in racial politics by a minority within the Black community as proof of a fatally fractured society facing Armageddon. When writing about the WUO, the hard-edged feminist Susan Brownmiller described the cadres as "impatient, would-be revolutionaries in a non-revolutionary time."[35]

THE RED BRIGADES

The venue now changes to Italy and the Red Brigades during the 1970s and the early 1980s, a period known as the *Anni di piombo*, Years of Lead, meaning the lead of bullets. The noted political scientist Donatella della Porta has tabulated 13,550 violent political attacks committed in Italy during this period. In all this mayhem, 350 people were killed and 770 injured.

Complications, complexities, and convolutions characterize the Years of Lead. It was a war between left-wing extremists and the national government, marshaling its forces of order. But in addition, the Italian extreme right, the neo-fascists, fully engaged in the fray with their own political organizations and their own terrorist groups. The more conspiratorially minded also see the role of a conservative masonic organization, called P2 (Propaganda Due), maneuvering for an authoritarian regeneration of Italy. Even more exotically, other commentators believe that the United States made the situation worse by Operation Gladio, a plan to train and arm "stay-behind" guerrilla fighters should the Soviets advance into Italy in a future war. It is even claimed that the Americans pursued a "strategy of tension" meant to destabilize the country and discredit the strong Communist Party, which captured about 35 percent of the vote in 1976.

In this chapter, we will leave alone the daunting challenge of this three-dimensional chess game and limit ourselves to one player, the BR. It can be described as a left-wing paramilitary, but it clearly falls into the category of urban guerrilla terrorists.

The Seedbed

Of the three urban guerrilla groups discussed in these pages, the BR had to navigate the most troubled waters. Post-war Italy was a democratic, economically advanced country, but it was also a land of social alienation, labor unrest, and political turmoil. The economic boom that began in the 1950s attracted a mass exodus from the rural and impoverished south to the bustling industrial cities of the north. From the mid-1950s to 1970, nearly 20 percent of the population migrated from one region of Italy to another. Turin's population, for example, grew from 720,000 in 1951 to 1,125,000 in 1967. Italian cities were not ready for the great influx of new workers, who endured living conditions that could range from poor to wretched. Italy was fertile seedbed for Marxist thought. Workers who considered themselves underpaid and abused staged a series of massive labor strikes in 1969–1970.

The BR took as models earlier revolutionaries, among them the Tupamaros. The Italian radical millionaire publisher Giangiacomo Feltrinelli published works on the Tupamaros that, according to Paul Ginsborg, served as "a sort of do-it-yourself manual for the early Red Brigades."[36] Feltrinelli was fascinated with Latin American revolution and was the first to turn the classic Alberto Corda photograph of Che Guevara into a mass-produced poster, an image that became a transnational symbol of revolution during the second wave of radical terrorism. Feltrinelli also translated and circulated German Red Army Faction materials to Italian groups. He eventually went beyond words and acted as a revolutionary terrorist, dying in the explosion of a bomb he was placing to sabotage high-tension lines in 1972.

The BR's enemies list included the usual suspects. As serious Marxists, the BR vilified capitalism, the bourgeoisie, and the forces of order that maintained them. Imperialism explained misery, and for the BR, multinational corporations were the primary agents of imperialism. Thus, their great Satan was the "imperialist system of multinationals" and its servant, the state.[37] The BR even created its own acronym for it: "SIM," the Imperialist Multinational State (Stato Imperialista delle Multinazionali). The BR also expressed a hate of fascism, as Italian fascists were active and had their own violent organizations, such as the Nuclei Armati Rivoluzionari (NAR).

The United States sat as chairman of the board in the new multinational economy, and thus was the focus of protest. For the other urban terrorists, the war in Vietnam served as convenient and convincing proof of American hypocrisy and brutality. However, even though the BR appeared in 1970, it was several years before it turned more militant and the Italian population took note of it, and by then the Americans had withdrawn and victory had been secured by the Vietcong and the North Vietnamese. There was no longer a war to bring home. The anti-imperialist target for the BR was not a particular conflict, but the institutions of war-making: the U.S. military and NATO.

And the only effective tool to deal with these enemies was violence. BR chief Mario Moretti explained, "We chose the armed struggle because every other road was closed, we felt forced to it. Forced to do dreadful things. . . . Just as in war, where they do dreadful things because they're considered terrible and necessary."[38] Such "dreadful things" were done more easily because of ideology and enmity; the BR's enemies were reduced to subhumans, to "pigs," "rabid dogs," and "filthy worms," all of whom inspire "absolute revulsion."

The BR in the Field, 1970–1988
Several left-wing terrorist groups faced off against the Italian authorities and radical right-wing groups. The BR stood first among left-wing terrorists, mounting 648 actions and killing seventy-five victims during the Years of Lead. Among the other terrorist organizations on the radical left, Prima Linea (PL) was most active, with 599 actions.[39] Della Porta charts the curve of all left-wing terrorist events during the Years of Lead. It started slowly, and by 1974 the annual total of such events stood at fifty, but from that point things mounted at a faster pace, peaking in 1978 with a tally of about 250. After 1978 the curve fell as rapidly as it had climbed, decreasing to fifty in 1982 and virtually none in 1983.

The BR dealt in targeted violence, choosing specific victims. They might well injure or kill escorts or guards, but their goal was not to kill many "innocents." The deadliest event of the Years of Lead occurred on 2 August 1980, when a bomb killed eighty-five and wounded 200 at the main rail station in Bologna. However, this "Bologna Massacre" was not the work of the left wing, but is attributed to the neo-fascist NAR.

Scholars differ as to the number of cadres in the BR. David Moss gives the reasonable figure of 426 active members between 1970 and 1982, with the greatest concentrations in Rome, Milan, Turin, Genoa, and Naples.[40] Of this active, regular membership, only a limited number carried off violent operations, perhaps only about two dozen at any one time.

The BR was not prominent in its early years. Its first generation of leadership was arrested or killed between 1974 and 1976, and a second generation, led by Mario Moretti, directed the BR in a more extreme and violent course. Along with Moretti, Adriana Faranda and Valerio Morucci were notable cadres.

From the start, the BR engaged in robberies to finance its operations, and from 1974 it added other criminal activities to its repertoire. On 18 April 1974, in a complex operation involving twenty terrorists, the BR kidnapped a public prosecutor, Mario Sossi. They hoped to exchange him for imprisoned radicals, but failed. Sossi was released. The next year, the BR opted to increase its income by staging kidnappings for ransom. The violence further escalated in 1976 when BR cadres carried out the group's first assassination of a high official, killing state prosecutor Francesco Coco and two men in his security detail on 8 June. The killing of Coco proved to be a watershed, raising the visibility of BR violence. Assassinations became a hallmark of terrorism during the Years of Lead. On 16 November 1977, BR cadres gunned down Carlo Casalegno, the deputy editor of *La stampa*, a Turin newspaper that had attacked the BR in print many times.

The BR's most infamous act began with the kidnapping of Aldo Moro on 16 March 1978 and ended with his murder on 9 May, as described at the beginning of this chapter. The assassination of Moro ended the Historic Compromise, so hated by the BR, but the brutal killings of Moro and his bodyguards eroded support for the terrorists. The far-left newspaper *Lotta continua* (Continuous Struggle) suggested a motto for its readers: "Né con lo stato, *né con le Brigate Rosse*" (Neither with the state, nor with the Red Brigades). Eight months later, on 24 January 1979, the BR further undermined its standing with the left by assassinating Guido Rossa, a member of the Communist Party and a popular labor organizer. The murders of Moro and Rossa did not immediately eviscerate the BR, but it never again matched its earlier strength. In 1981 Mario Moretti was arrested and the BR split into two factions, the Communist Combatant Party (BR-PCC) and the Union of Combatant Communists (BR-UCC).

Even then the BR lumbered on through the 1980s. They committed a chain of kidnappings and killings. These included holding U.S. Army general James Lee Dozier from 17 December 1981 to 28 January 1982, when he was rescued by an Italian special operations team. They also gunned down Leamon Hunt, an American diplomat, in October 1984 and assassinated Italian officials in 1986, 1987, and 1988. After that, an extensive series of arrests all but ended the existence of the BR.

Organization, Recruitment, and Composition
The BR were organized in a hierarchical manner, but with some independence given to the local brigades established in major locales, notably Milan and Turin at first, with Genoa, Rome, and Veneto added after 1974. At the top of the pyramid, a centralized strategic command and an executive committee directed policy and practice across the brigades. The cadres were divided into two categories: the "irregulars," who maintained their normal lives—jobs and families—and were clandestine only in their membership in the BR; and the "regulars," who lived an entirely underground existence in cells. Irregular cadres and BR sympathizers were a literate crowd; brigadists authored many books, over twenty major texts, and had access to radical journals.

Violent acts were the work of the "column" in each brigade, the small number of regulars. For major operations the columns could work together. Daily existence for those underground was hard. One BR cadre explained that the life "isn't easy. You have to live a double life and keep the rules religiously and behave accordingly. . . . Going underground is a nightmare that follows you month after month and year after year, never changing."[41]

To maintain security, the brigades adhered to a networked cellular organization, with each cell composed of a handful of members who did not meet with the other cells. Knowledge and authority were compartmentalized, and cadres received information on a need-to-know basis. Adriana Faranda, who was a member of the Executive Committee at the time of the Moro kidnapping, later explained to surprised investigators that she was kept largely ignorant of the details of his situation in the People's Prison because the BR maintained "a criterion of the most rigid compartmentalization."[42] Once leaders made a decision, it was not debatable. As Faranda testified, "In the BR, the collective decisions are not questioned."[43]

The deeply clandestine nature of the BR complicated the recruiting of new members. It proved most effective to recruit associates, friends, and even family from within the social networks of current irregular members. Della Porta's study of a sample of 363 members of Italian leftwing terrorist groups found that 159 were recruited by a friend, seventy-three by a spouse or other relative, fifty-five by a political comrade, and thirty-four by a workmate, giving a total of 88 percent of the sample. As a Prima Linea member testified, recruitment "happened ... through completely personal ties. In this way the comrades of the [group] contacted people whom they knew for a long time."[44] We will have more to say about social networking in Chapter 9.

The breakdown of BR members by profession and gender shows a wide appeal. In a sample of 670 members for whom data was available, 153 (23 percent) were students, teachers, and lecturers, and 385 were classified as blue-collar workers, clerical workers, service workers, tradespeople, and artisans. Women constituted a quarter of the cadres of the BR.[45]

The Endgame

The BR were brought down by several developments. Most obviously, Italian law enforcement pursued its leaders and cadres with greater and greater efficiency. The founders of the BR were arrested or killed by 1976; Moretti, Faranda, and Morucci were all under lock and key by 1981. However, the Italians also adopted a policy of treating prisoners with some leniency if they renounced their past and aided law enforcement. The Repentance Law of 1980 created three categories: the *irriducibili* (irreducible), who refused to renounce their association and deeds, giving no information to the court; the *dissociati* (dissociated), who renounced their organizations and deeds but gave no information against others; and the *pentiti* (penitent), who both denounced themselves and testified against others. *Irriducibili* received no leniency; *dissociati* gained some leniency; and *pentiti* could win a pardon. The *pentiti* could be a good source of intelligence, but they also ran the risk of brutal reprisals by their former comrades.

In addition to state action, three other factors crippled the BR. First, their violence, particularly the assassinations of Moro and Rossa, eroded their public support. Second, ideological factionalism divided the group, most obviously in 1981. Third, BR violence led to no change; it had become pointless, save in exacting revenge. In 1984 many leaders, including the imprisoned Mario Moretti, even proclaimed that they renounced the armed struggle.

THE "CULT" CHARACTER OF THE TERRORIST MINDSET

By definition, terrorists carry out violent attacks that do not fit the parameters of generally accepted behavior. In the name of the highest cause, they commit the lowest acts, including murder. This has led some students of terrorist behavior to condemn them as psychopaths or, as Michael Burleigh would have it, "morally insane." Certainly, some who engage in terrorist violence are pathologically attracted to violence, but the real question is, how do people who profess, and practice, a heightened sensitivity to suffering and a desire for justice turn to terrorism? The cadres who carried out revolutionary attacks in the name of the Tupamaros, the WUO, and the BR did so as acts of conscience.

The fact that so many agents of revolutionary violence have been studied, often through their own testimony, interviews, or autobiographies, allows scholars to analyze the values and lives of urban guerrilla terrorists. The most convincing of these testimonies stress the interplay between the terrorists' initial idealism and the dynamics of living in small, clandestine communities of committed spirits, an interplay that fosters a moral universe with its own demands and logic. Della Porta calls this an "encapsulated-implosion process . . . characterized . . . by radicalization, all-pervasive militancy, and dramatic limitations on exchanges with the external environment." She argues that this "makes terrorist groups less and less like political organizations and more and more like religious sects."[46] The observation that terrorist groups resemble religious sects, or cults, is particularly relevant.

In his work on the BR, Alessandro Orsini explores the terrorist mindset, stressing that clandestine terrorist groups share important characteristics with religious groups. These characteristics include:

- a rejection of the real world as being inherently corrupt,
- a need to tear down the current reality in an apocalypse,
- an obsession with bringing perfection and purity, and
- a dualistic perception of the world as sharply divided between good and evil.[47]

Terrorists reject the present world as irredeemably vile, an intolerable reality that must be obliterated. Mario Ferrandi reports, "In those years, we never asked ourselves what base we had to build, the only thing we knew was that the present had to be destroyed."[48] This conviction that transformation required destruction approaches Christian and Muslim concepts of apocalypse, or, as Orsini calls it, "pantoclastic fury." A pure new world can only follow the annihilation of the corrupt world as it is. Valerio Morucci reminds his readers of the secular purity sought by the BR: "The politics on which our conduct was based was revolutionary, and the revolution would have led to a society without conflict. A society without the need for mediation, compromise, or filthy bourgeois politics. A pure politics."[49] Chapters 9 and 11 will comment on the importance of strictly religious apocalyptic thought among the Muslim community and in Islamist ideology.

For the cadres of the BR, killing in the name of virtue was consistent with their extreme dualism, their totalistic mindset. Morucci later blamed his personal tragedy on this "same fucking rigidity. . . . Always black or white, without gray areas, either friends or enemies, either love or hate, either moral or immoral."[50] Holger Meins, the radical author of the "flower power" poster and a leading cadre of the RAF, declared during the last days of a hunger strike that killed him: "The only thing that matters is the struggle—now, today, tomorrow, whether we eat or not. . . . Either a pig or a man / Either survival at any price or struggle unto death / Either problem or solution / There is nothing in between."[51] Contempt for compromise is part and parcel of this radical dualism, since compromise means selling out to the middle ground. In the melodramatic language of Morucci, "We could dirty our hands with blood, but never with the fetid fluid of compromise. That was the job of the 'bourgeois parties.'"[52]

Given the terrorists' dichotomy between good and evil, it is not surprising that they talked about love and hate. Faranda explained: "I considered that the armed struggle, the choice of taking up arms, could only go together with an implacable passion for humanity. And the love–hate bipolarity automatically implied hate for those who prevented the achievement of harmony and the different quality of life of which we dreamed."[53] Such a struggle for the good, conducted out of love for humanity—and a hatred of evil—demanded that the just accept risk in the performance of their moral duty. Patrizio Peci, a prominent BR cadre, interpreted political violence as "also a question of altruism and generosity: it means risking everything for a cause you believe is just, forgetting personal advantage."[54]

In a certain sense, the cohesion and standards of sacrifice maintained among underground terrorists resemble that typical of military combat units. In life and in art, soldiers describe their comrades as family: "We few, we happy few, we band of brothers." It is interesting that terrorists often use the same familial language. Weatherman Jim Mellen reported: "I was very close to [them]. They were my whole world."[55] Mario Moretti of the BR stated in an interview: "We feel nostalgia for the old patriarchal family, with everyone living in an enormous house. Our communes meet this need, they re-create a shared life, they save the single person from individual alienation."[56]

The closeness felt by terrorists of the clandestine Tupamaros, the WUO, and the BR derived in part from their isolation from their previous world of biological family, friends, coworkers, and the like. Such contacts could intentionally or unintentionally give away information as to the activities and whereabouts of terrorists, or interactions with people outside the organization could infect the revolutionary with opinions and values that ran counter to those of the group.

The terrorist groups became closed feedback loops. A cadre spoke and heard the same opinions and convictions repeated back to him or her by comrades. The group became an echo chamber repeating mutually held principles and collective slogans. As Peci reports, "You . . . don't talk with anyone else but the Red Brigades."[57] It is commonly and correctly stated that Marxist terrorists of this era overestimated the readiness of their societies to embrace revolution. This overconfidence can be explained by the fact that these groups referenced their own membership and the assertive youth culture in determining opinion.

Total absorption meant total discipline and self-discipline, as we have already seen with the PIRA doctrine expressed in their *Green Book*. Raffaele Fiore, one of the gunmen who took part in the Moro kidnapping, said, "If you wanted to carry out what they asked, you had to be very strict with yourself. This meant giving yourself rules; you needed an iron self-discipline, starting as soon as you got up."[58]

Work in social psychology tells us that groups tend to act differently than would their constituent individuals outside the group. This is the phenomenon of group polarization: "the tendency for group decisions to be more extreme than those made by individuals. Whatever way the individuals are leaning, group discussion tends to make them lean further in that direction."⁵⁹ In addition, the American social psychologist Leon Festinger pointed out that people are apt to judge their value and success by those around them: "When objective standards for self-evaluation are not available, people judge themselves in relation to others."⁶⁰ Combining these observations, one would expect that members of underground terrorist groups would naturally tend toward extremes in which their isolation engages them with each other in an escalating feedback loop of perception and opinion.

In this world of moral dichotomies in which the cadres of revolutionary terrorist groups judged themselves in relation to their radical comrades, virtue lay in being at the extreme. A kind of one-upmanship could take hold; witness Cathy Wilkerson's admission: "The competitive part of me wanted to be on the best team, the most passionate, the most sacrificing, the most uncompromising, and the most willing to follow each position to its extreme."⁶¹ This kind of competition between members is both evidence of and explanation for the drive to extremes in belief and action. Wilkerson also reports that support for such radical innovations as the smash monogamy campaign became important markers: "One's enthusiasm for these changes became a measure by which one's commitment was judged."⁶² Silke Mair-Witt remarked about her experience abandoning her standards and accepting those of her comrades in the RAF: "I've asked myself why I neglected my own moral standards even as I was envisioning social change. I learned how easy it is to listen to some ideology and to have an idea that gives you an excuse for anything."⁶³

During the second wave of radical terrorism, several New Left, urban guerrilla terrorist groups formed, fought, and faded. This included not only the three surveyed in this chapter but the likes of National Liberation Action in Brazil, the Symbionese Liberation Army in the United States, Prima Linea in Italy, the Revolutionary Cells in Germany, Action Directe in France, Revolutionary Organization 17 November in Greece, GRAPO in Spain, and the Japanese Red Army. Virtually all of these organizations were transnational, in that they referenced revolutionaries and terrorists in other parts of the world and at times worked with them. They shared similarly grand goals and in general had meager resources. Characteristically, they pursued strategies of initiation, hoping to act as catalysts for revolution. Most appeared in the late 1960s and 1970s, although some, like Action Directe, peaked in the 1980s.

Their fate was failure. Yet while they thrived, they commanded a great deal of attention despite their small numbers. The Germans marshaled an overwhelming police effort against the RAF and enacted new laws to suppress the small band of terrorists. The notably progressive writer Heinrich Böll insisted that the RAF threat be put in perspective, calling it "a war of six against sixty million."[64]

The nature of radical terrorism is to empower the weak, at least for a time; the course of the urban guerrillas demonstrates this. However, the next three chapters will deal with radical Islamist terrorist groups, which, unlike the urban guerrillas, have shown an ability to evolve into large statelike organizations that exert considerable power. The most obvious example is the Islamic State of 2014–2018, but Hamas and particularly Hezbollah have become formidable on their own turf. At the time these words are being written, the radical Islamist threat may show signs of receding—as evidenced by the decline of the Islamic State—but it still overshadows all other terrorist dangers.

CHAPTER NINE

Islamist Terrorism

IDEOLOGY AND RADICALIZATION IN THE THIRD WAVE

FIGURE 9.1. *Left:* A desolate Stéphane Charbonnier, editor of *Charlie Hebdo*, addressed the media after the satirical magazine's Paris offices were firebombed in November 2011. "Charb" would be killed, along with eleven others, when the Kouachi brothers attacked the new *Charlie* offices in 2015. *Below:* In reaction to the murderous attack on the offices of *Charlie Hebdo* in January 2015, "Je suis Charlie" demonstrations were held all over the world. This one is at the Place de la République in Paris, a site that has become the focus of memorials to the victims of terrorism. *Left:* Coyau/Wikimedia Commons, CC BY 3.0. *Below:* Olivier Ortelpa/Wikimedia Commons, CC BY 2.0.

AT 11:30 A.M. ON 7 JANUARY 2015, two heavily armed gunmen broke into the offices of *Charlie Hebdo* at 10 Rue Nicolas-Appert in Paris by forcing one of the staff, cartoon artist Corinne "Coco" Rey, to key in the door code so they could enter. Once inside they began their slaughter,

killing a maintenance worker at the reception desk with a burst of fire. The brothers Chérif and Said Kouachi next compelled Rey at gunpoint to lead them to a room on the second floor where staff members were gathered for a meeting. The assailants knew who they were after, calling out the name of editor Stéphane "Charb" Charbonnier to identify him before murdering him (Fig. 9.1, top); they also killed cartoonists Jean "Cabu" Cabu and eight others; eleven more were wounded. Shouting "Allahu Akbar!" (Allah is greatest), the killers fled the building and exchanged shots with policemen, wounding one who was then killed execution-style by one of the Kouachi brothers.

Over the next two days, a third terrorist, Amedy Coulibaly, killed a police officer in a Paris suburb and four patrons in a kosher grocery at the Porte de Vincennes; another eleven were wounded in Coulibaly's attacks and the hostage rescue at the grocery on the afternoon of 9 July. Coulibaly died in that police assault, and the Kouachi brothers were killed in a simultaneous attack staged by police where the two had holed up some twenty miles northeast of Paris. The actions of the Kouachi brothers and Coulibaly, all French-born men of Algerian descent in their thirties, constituted the worst terrorist attacks in France for over fifty years. Unfortunately, before the year was out, the death toll of 7–9 January would be surpassed nearly tenfold.

The attack on *Charlie Hebdo* demonstrated the deadly depth of feelings in a collision of cultural values. *Charlie*, published weekly, is harshly and often crudely satiric, known for its biting and inflammatory cartoons. For nearly a decade before the attack, the staff of *Charlie Hebdo* had used their sharp pencils to stab at Islam. In September 2005 a Danish newspaper published a cartoon that portrayed Muhammad wearing a turban that was, in fact, a bomb with its fuse lit. The cartoonist, Kurt Westergaard, became the target of threats and attempts on his life and appeared on an al-Qaeda hit list in 2010. This list also included *Charlie Hebdo*'s Charb, in part because *Charlie* had ridiculed the violent threats hurled at Westergaard.

And violence was directed against *Charlie Hebdo* in response to its disrespect for the Prophet. Some of the magazine's cartoons, though demeaning, were sarcastically inventive, but others were intentionally disgusting, one portraying a grossly naked Muhammad and implying sexually aberrant behavior. They insulted and infuriated many devout Muslims.

In November 2011, someone firebombed the offices of *Charlie*, then at 62 Boulevard Davout, destroying all its contents. Then Turkish hackers replaced the first page of the *Charlie* website with a declaration, in English and Turkish: "You keep abusing Islam's almighty Prophet with disgusting and disgraceful cartoons using excuses of freedom of speech. . . . Be God's curse be on you!"[1] Charb and Rénard "Luz" Luzier were placed under police protection. But Charb would not back down; he responded to threats with the declaration, "We have to carry on until Islam has been rendered as banal as Catholicism."[2] *Charlie Hebdo* renewed its offensive of offenses.

Of course, *Charlie*'s campaign of insult does not justify the murderous acts of 7–9 January, but it provides the necessary context for those attacks. It explains why one of the Kouachi brothers shouted as the two reached their car to escape, "We have avenged the Prophet Muhammad. We have killed *Charlie Hebdo!*"[3]

In the days following the attacks, the West focused on Parisian demonstrations mourning the victims, condemning the terrorists and celebrating freedom of speech and of the press (Fig. 9.1, bottom). The demonstrators carried the ubiquitous sign of support, "Je suis Charlie" (I am Charlie). But after *Charlie* published a cartoon satirizing the Prophet again on 14 January, anti-*Charlie* protests by Muslims, some bearing signs "Je suis Muslim," took place in Jordan, Chechnya, Somalia, Algeria, Niger, and elsewhere. Surveying these protests, Kyung Lah, reporting for the 19 January broadcast of *Erin Burnett OutFront* on CNN, concluded that they demonstrated "a division of culture, religion, and politics in an increasingly smaller, more globalized world."[4]

The attention now shifts to the third wave of terrorism, characterized by the predominance of radical Islamist terrorism. As we shall see, Islamists trace their interpretation of Islam at least to the writings of Taqī ad-Dīn Aḥmad ibn Taymiyyah (1263–1328). However, the emergence of radical Islamism as a major rationale for regional and global terrorism is associated with three events: the Iranian Revolution of 1979, the outbreak of the Russo-Afghan War that same year, and the Israeli invasion of Lebanon in 1982. The first created an Islamist regime that advanced a religious program within Iran and sought to undermine the influence of the United States. The second ushered in a decade of warfare in Afghanistan that became defined as a jihad between Islam and ungodly Russian communism. The third created a new front for Islamist struggle directed against the archenemy Israel. This struggle would be spearheaded in Lebanon by Hezbollah and, later, by Hamas in Israel.

In this environment, groups founded as terrorist groups have grown into statelike political entities, controlling territories, ruling populations, and fielding armies. This military/political evolution resulted from conscious decisions and from reactions to circumstance and opportunity, but in either case, the most prominent terrorist organizations of the third wave followed strategies of evolution. Along with Islamist ideology, this evolution has been the other most salient trait of the third wave.

This chapter will deal with conceptual issues, including the theology of Islam, the ideology of Islamism, the theory of a clash of civilizations, and hypotheses concerning radicalization. Here we will address background context and analytical approaches. After this, Chapter 10 will concentrate on histories of the regional Islamist organizations Hezbollah and Hamas. Chapter 11 will consider the global scope of Islamist terrorism characteristic of al-Qaeda and the Islamic State.

Because this chapter deals so much with the personal motivations and choices of violent extremists, it needs to begin with some caveats concerning generalizing about why individuals become radicalized. Compulsions that lead individuals to become terrorists could range from material need, to psychological fears or grievances, to moral outrage. Inspirations could include ideals of religious convictions or ethnic pride. Attractions could consist of romanticized notions of the rebel life, fantasies of adventure, or the pull of friends or family. The potential combinations of such factors approach the infinite, so to attempt to devise a formula that applies to all or most terrorists is impossible. Jeff Victoroff, an expert on the psychology of political violence, writes: "Terrorists are psychologically extremely heterogeneous. Whatever his stated goals and group of identity, every terrorist, like every person, is motivated by his own complex of psychosocial experiences and traits."[5] And it is not simply individuals who differ; terrorist groups do as well.

While numerous studies have tried to penetrate the complexities of terrorists' mindsets and motivations, we still lack a large body of works that apply rigorous standards of scientific inquiry. John Horgan, author of the most impressive work in the field, repeatedly criticizes studies for their insufficient sampling, often lacking control groups, and their authors' willingness to generalize from inherently special cases. Even among the growing number of inquiries based on interviews with terrorists, Horgan faults the tendency to accept terrorists' own evaluations of their motivations, accounts that may not be honestly revealing for one reason or another.[6] Victoroff observes, "The field is largely characterized by theoretical speculation based on subjective interpretation of anecdotal observations."[7]

Given the absence of definitive scholarship, this chapter will proceed with caution. It will offer information and observations, but will respect the complexity and uncertainty of reality.

MATERIAL INCENTIVES?

Those drawn to materialistic explanations of human conduct may want to explain membership in Islamist terrorist organizations by the need to survive in regions plagued with poverty and by the desire to gain financial reward. Certainly, poverty can influence perception and action, a fact of which terrorist recruiters are well aware. However, to see terrorism as a recourse reserved for the poor would be to go too far. Those who flew the planes into the World Trade Center and the Pentagon on 9/11 were hardly impoverished or undereducated. Marc Sageman states that the first generation of al-Qaeda in general were men of some substance in age, economics, and education.[8] On a different level, Ariel Merari reports that while Palestinian suicide bombers were hardly well-off, they were of average economic status among the Palestinian community.[9]

Still, poverty can create a vulnerability, and some Islamist terrorists appeal to, or exploit, material need. Jessica Stern points out, "Several studies have shown that states most susceptible to ethno-religious conflict are those that are poorer, unstable, and have a history of violence and conflict."[10] The head of a Pakistani madrassa associated with jihadists explained to Stern that he tried to reach the poor because "we need their children."[11] Stern explains that it can be a kind of extortion in Kashmir, where poor families are told to either give up a son or pay a large sum of money. Young boys sent off to a madrassa receive the essentials of life and an education, more than they might have had at home. Not all young men who come out of the madrassas commit themselves to jihad, but the madrassas can be fertile ground for recruiters.

This is not to say that all Pakistan jihadist organizations have similar recruiting patterns. A study by the Combating Terrorism Center at West Point concluded that Lashkar-e-Taiba (LeT) fighters were better educated than average young Pakistani men and that they did not have a particularly extensive religious education. One of the paper's authors, C. Christine Fair, stated to an interviewer, "It's a myth that poverty and madrasas create terrorism, and that we can buy our way out of it with U.S. aid."[12]

Nonetheless, financial compensation can serve as a valuable attraction. A BBC report concerning African jihadist groups in 2013—Boko Haram, al-Qaeda in the Islamic Magreb, and al Shabab—found that, owing to the region's poverty and lack of opportunity, "the pursuit of money is an issue that recurs in accounts of the reasons behind young men joining militant groups."[13]

Earthly reward has also perverted some who take on a holy cause. One terrorist confessed to Stern that he left terrorism because he saw what some terrorists had accumulated: "Soon after this I realized that everybody was making money . . . [a particular terrorist chief] started out an ordinary fellow, a teacher. But when I saw him in Pakistan he was driving around in a big jeep."[14] Stern concludes, cynically, "Whenever we face a terrorist threat, we should ask ourselves: Who stands to gain? Who is making money? Who is receiving benefits of any kind? Who is taking advantage of whom?"[15]

Thus, to disregard material want and reward as incentives for Islamist terrorists would be naïve. However, it is important to ask in specific circumstances whether money payment *caused* otherwise uncommitted individuals to join, or if it simply *allowed* individuals to maintain themselves within terrorist organizations once they were recruited. Stern reports, "In poor countries like Pakistan, militants say that their salaries play a key role, not in persuading them to join jihadi groups, but in keeping them there."[16]

And poverty can act in more subtle ways. Many recruits, notably foreign fighters, inflicted with feelings of cultural and social alienation, made worse by economic marginalization, can respond by forging a powerful identification with radical Islam. Even those who adopt life as a terrorist for material reasons will be exposed to a much more ideological level of reason and reaction once inside a radical Islamist group, and while the money may initially attract them, life with a terrorist group will radicalize them.

In any case, those sympathetic to the plight of the poor in troubled countries and inclined to believe that an assault on material want could bring terrorism to an end, should consider the very broad but relevant observation of Audrey Kurth Cronin, who has so much to say about how terrorism ends. She condemns as a myth the assumption "that dealing with the causes of terrorism is the way to solve the problem." Cronin's argument could be brought to bear on the issue of poverty by suggesting that eliminating poverty, even were it possible, would not end terrorist campaigns, because they take on a rationale and momentum of their own. "In short," Cronin concludes, "understanding the causes of terrorism may be no more important to ending a campaign than understanding the causes of war is to ending them; naturally the question has some relevance, but it is overshadowed by the dynamic of the conflict itself as it unfolds."[17]

CONSIDERING ISLAM

If attention to material benefit lies at one extreme of explanations of jihadist motivations, the long tradition of Islamist writings on resistance and jihad occupies the other. These writings are both theology and ideology, both a conception of divinity and a doctrine of earthly authority, society, and conduct. Not all Islamist terrorists have a deep understanding of the positions and arguments of their creed, but such understanding is not necessary to accept the demands of fundamentalism and jihad. And certainly, Islamist thought informs and inspires jihadi leaders. To deal with radical Islamism we must go beyond the actions of Hezbollah and the Islamic State and look at the beliefs of the actors. This section will consider certain basic tenets of Islam. We will later turn to a discussion of Islamist interpretations of the faith and the call to violence.

Bear in mind that with its current meaning, the word *Islamism* is relatively new to the analyst's lexicon. When Voltaire coined the French term *islamisme* in the eighteenth century, he applied it as a more enlightened way to identify what was generally referred to then as *mahométisme*, Muhammadism, a clumsy and misleading label for the religion of Islam. As scholars chose simply to use the term *Islam* in the early twentieth century, *Islamism* fell out of use. But during the last quarter of the twentieth century, largely owing to the Iranian Revolution, the phenomenon of ultraconservative interpretations of Islam stood front and center on the world stage, and in the Western press analysts began to talk of "Islamic fundamentalism." In light of the clear political intent of this militant Islam, they also discussed "political Islam." By the second half of the 1980s, English-language analysts adopted the term *Islamism* for this brand of militant Islam, and again the inspiration was French. French academics revived the term with its new extremist meaning since "fundamentalism" in French lacked the hard sense it had in English and *islamisme* was already in their dictionary. So, *Islamism* is a term imposed by Western commentators on what was by then a phenomenon in the Islamic world, particularly North Africa, the Middle East, and South Asia. With its insistence on political prescriptions, Islamism can be considered as an ideology, whereas Islam per se is a religion.

Let us make clear from the start that the religion of Islam must not be conflated with the beliefs of radical Islamists, any more than Christianity is fairly represented by the distortions of Christianity professed by some on the radical right wing in the United States—a subject to be discussed in Chapter 12. Whatever else we do to confront Islamist terrorism, those of us in the West should show respect for Islam as central to the lives of the 1.6 billion people who compose the *ummah*, the entire Muslim community worldwide. Disdain or condescension toward Islam in a globalized world is not only ill-mannered insult, it lacks essential wisdom. And it feeds the Islamist narrative that the West and Islam are locked in struggle calling for jihad.

The sources of Islamic theology, law, and social practice are the Quran, the *sunnah*, and the *hadith*. Muslims hold the Quran to be revelations directly from Allah and transcribed by his last prophet, Muhammad (570–632). This contrasts with the Old and New Testaments, which are acknowledged to have been authored by men. Another basis of Islamic belief is the *sunnah*, practices of life followed by Muhammad. These are drawn from the Quran and from the *hadith*, accounts of the Prophet's life and words. *Hadith* have been assembled in several multivolume collections by Islamic scholars over the centuries. As set out in the *hadith*, there are five pillars of the faith; these obligatory acts of all Muslims include: 1) *shahada*, testifying that there is no god but Allah and that Muhammad is his prophet; 2) *salat*, prayer; 3) *zakat*, compulsory giving of alms; 4) *sawm*, fasting during the month of Ramadan; and 5) *hajj*, pilgrimage to Mecca if able to do so.

Unlike Jesus, Muhammad stated that he was not divine but a messenger of Allah. When he was forty years old, Muhammad began to receive revelations, and in a few years he began to spread these teachings. The authorities who held power in Mecca, Muhammad's birthplace, viewed him and his followers as threats to the old ways, and in 622 he fled Mecca and made his *hijira*, or journey, to Medina. The *hijira* marks year one of the Muslim calendar. In Medina he united several tribes. Unlike Christianity in the time of Jesus, Islam grew in the days of Muhammad by force of arms as well as by power of faith. In 630 he returned with an army to conquer Mecca, but the city fell with little bloodshed. He then declared it to be the holiest of Muslim places.

The most important schism in Islam, that between the Sunni and Shia sects, came within fifty years of Muhammad's death in 632. He was followed as the leader of Islam by a succession of revered Four Rightly Guided Caliphs, the last of whom, Ali ibn Abi Talib, was assassinated in 661. Ali's closest followers wanted his son Hassan to succeed him, but Hassan's succession was disputed by a rival candidate, Muawiyah. This dispute was settled by a compromise that elevated Muawiyah to the caliphate, with the understanding that the position of the caliph would eventually return to the progeny of Ali. But by the time of his death in 1680, Muawiyah had chosen his own son, Yasid, to follow him as caliph. Hassan had died a decade before, but his younger brother, Husayn, stepped forward to claim the caliphate. Yasid refused to relinquish it, and his forces defeated and killed Husayn in the Battle of Karbala in October 680. The minority who were still loyal to Husayn split off to become the Shia, and the majority who supported the new caliph became known as the Sunni, in reference to the *sunnah*. Once in separate branches of Islam, the Shias and Sunnis developed their own traditions of belief and law. The separation between the two is great enough that many modern Sunni radical Islamists condemn the Shias as infidels.

Certain devout Moslems hope to re-create the form of Islam they believe to have been practiced by the first three generations of Moslems from the seventh through the early ninth centuries. These initial generations are known as the *Salaf*, the "predecessors." Those who advocate a return to the traditions of early Islam are known as *Salafi*, or Salafists. The Salafi movement that extends to this day is most associated with Muhammad ibn Abd al Wahab (1703–1792) and is important in Islamist ideology.

Islam honors the Old and New Testaments, although Muslims regard Jesus as a prophet, not as the son of God. As long as Jews and Christians under Muslim rule lived in order and peace, they could be allowed to pursue their religion while deferring to Muslim authorities. "There shall be no compulsion in religion," teaches the Quran, *Al-Baqarah* (The Cow), 2:256.[18] (The citation is to the *surah*, or chapter, of the Quran by name and number followed by the number of the verse in it.) There are other verses that endorse patience and tolerance in dealing with nonbelievers. "Say: 'Unbelievers, I do not worship what you worship, nor do you worship what I worship. . . . You have your own religion, and I have mine,'" *Al-Kafirun* (The Unbelievers), 109:1–6. And certainly, peace should reign among true followers of Islam. The Quran, like the Bible, forbids killing as a principle: "You shall not kill—for that is forbidden by Allah—except for a just cause," *Al-An'am* (Cattle), 6:152.

However, to state simply, as did President George W. Bush, that Islam is a religion of peace misses the sanction given righteous violence in the Quran. "Muhammad is God's apostle. Those who follow him are ruthless to the unbelievers but merciful to one another," *Al-Fath* (Victory), 48:29. Fundamentalists who take each verse literally and as of equal value to all other verses will find support for seemingly contradictory positions in the Quran. As well as counsels of peace, one will find exhortations to violence in the name of religion. "Slay them wherever you find them. Drive them out of the places from which they drove you. Idolatry is more grievous than bloodshed," *Al-Baqarah* (The Cow), 2:191. At times, verses taken out of context can seem very aggressive, but in context they are more moderate. "When the sacred months are over slay the idolaters wherever you find them," *Al-Tabwbah* (The Repudiation), 9:5, is quickly followed by "If an idolater seeks asylum with you, give him protection so that he may hear the Word of Allah, and then convey him to safety. For the idolaters are ignorant men," 9:6. A literalist could use these two verses to quite different purposes. And later in the same *surah*, we read, "Believers, make war on the infidels who dwell around you," 9:123.

Muhammad was a political figure and a military commander as well as a prophet. The contrast between the *hadith* and the Gospel stories of Jesus can be dramatic. They may be explained by the different circumstances of early Christianity and early Islam. The Christians could not overthrow Rome, so survival depended on tolerance, while the rapid victory of Islam depended on the success of Muslims in battle with infidel tribes.

Another contrast comes from differing concepts of the law. Christians, while accepting the Judeo-Christian tradition of religious law, as in the Ten Commandments, embraced the civil nature of law. Thus, one of the greatest legal traditions in the West is that of Roman law, which came out of a pagan society and was later adapted by Christian states and the Catholic Church itself. Western tradition also reveres the democratic principles of pagan ancient Greece, and holds that laws can be made by men. For Islamic conservatives, *sharia* law is divine in origin, with roots in the Quran and in the *hadith*. Law becomes inseparable from religion, and different legal traditions within Islam are important indicators of identity among Muslim communities. *Sharia* can be interpreted literally, leading to a demand by Islamists, for example, that punishments be those applied during the life of the Prophet—consequently, stoning and beheading. But it can also be seen as a spirit of the law more than a precise set of historical practices and punishments.

One last relevant aspect of Islam demands our attention before going on to explicitly radical Islamist thought: the concept of jihad. This term literally means struggle, but is generally translated into English as "holy war." It is argued that Islam distinguishes between a "greater jihad," which is a struggle within individuals to be better Muslims and fight their baser selves, and a "lesser jihad," which is physical warfare in the name of Allah. While there is some dispute as to the validity of this difference exalting inner jihad, there is no question of the quranic necessity to fight to protect Islam and defeat the infidels: to engage in holy war. And fighting in a true jihad is not voluntary, it is obligatory upon the *ummah*. During the late Middle Ages, an offensive jihad, declared to spread the faith, obligated Muslim rulers to participate with their armies, but a defensive jihad, fought to protect Islam, became a *personal obligation* on all able-bodied Muslim men. Islam ascribes great honor and reward to martyrs who die for the faith in battle. To be sure, the validity, even the sanctity, of using violence to defend religion is a common trait among religions. There is no question that Christians spread their religion by the sword from late antiquity through the imperialist rush of the late nineteenth century. Nonetheless, warfare is not integral to the New Testament in the way it is to the Quran and the hadith.

THE RADICAL ISLAMIST IDEOLOGY OF RESISTANCE AND JIHAD

Radical Islamists share an ideology of resistance and jihad that they can date back to the thirteenth century; however, what concerns us most here are their writings and actions since the early twentieth century. There is a rich historiography on this body of thought, which we can only note here briefly. Some argue that the literature of Islamism explains the appeal and strength of Islamist terrorists; Mary Habeck is among these scholars. I have problems with this. Islamist ideological writings may be critical in interpreting the leadership of Islamist groups, but the rank and file are probably driven more by gut feelings. However, we must begin by considering the ideology.

The first of the line of Islamist thinkers whose works are continually cited by modern Islamist ideologues was Ibn Taymiyyah. This devout and strong-minded legal scholar, who favored a return to the Islam of the *Salaf*, had to deal with Mongol forces that had destroyed the city in which he was born, Harran, and, in 1300, took Damascus, where he worked and taught. In 1303 he drafted a *fatwa* ordering a jihad against the Mongols and their allies. Since the Mongols had converted to Islam, the question was how they could become the target of a jihad. Taymiyyah essentially declared them *takfir*, apostates excluded from the true faith, because they still followed man-made laws—Mongol traditions—instead of true *sharia*. Such a regime was guilty of *jahiliyya*, that is, the pre-Islamic barbarous state of ignorance of Allah and of his guidance. *Jahiliyya* (adjective *jahili*) could then apply to peoples and even rulers who might claim to be Muslim, but were not acting as true Muslims. Taymiyyah's logic not only justified but required jihad against false or apostate Muslims, even if they were rulers. He declared fighting jihad to be the "best of all the voluntary (good actions) that man performs."[19]

Muhammad ibn 'Abd al-Wahhab (1703–1792) was an important and extreme *Salafi* who wished to purify Islam by stripping it of all innovations that had been accepted after the time of the Prophet. There was already a tradition of disdain for innovation in religion. The hadith of Jabir bin Abdullaah quotes the Prophet as stating that in religion "the worst of affairs are the newly-invented matters, every newly-invented matter is an innovation and every innovation is misguidance, and every [instance of] misguidance is in the [Hell] Fire."[20] Wahhab studied Taymiyyah and agreed on the necessity of jihad against heretical Muslims. In addition, Wahhab spoke out against Jews and Christians, arguing that they should be regarded as pagans. His uncompromisingly fundamentalist and harshly puritanical views resulted in his exile from his home, but he won allies in the Saudis, with whom he struck a pact in 1744: he would exert religious authority, while political power remained in the hands of the Saudis who rule Saudi Arabia to this day. They still maintain a Wahhabi form of Islam, and many also support Wahhabism through madrassas established outside of Saudi Arabia. Radical Islamist ideology shares a great deal with the Wahhabi interpretation of Islam. The Islamic State has even used Wahhabi textbooks in their schools.

Contact with Europeans who colonized North Africa and the Middle East in the late nineteenth and twentieth centuries led some Muslims to try to adopt and adapt to Western ways, but there were also those who advocated rejecting the West. Rashid Rida (1866–1935), an Egyptian, argued for a Salafist Islam free of Western influences to serve as a bulwark against the subversion of Muslim values and culture. He spoke out against Muslim rulers who turned away from Islam, who "abolish supposedly distasteful penalties such as cutting off the hands of thieves or stoning adulterers and prostitutes. They replace them with man-made laws and penalties. He who does that has undeniably become an infidel."[21] Egypt was the fountainhead of modern Islamist thought.

In 1928 Hassan al-Banna (1906–1949) formed the Muslim Brotherhood in Egypt. This began as a group pursuing spiritual renewal and social work within the Muslim community, but it also engaged in violent opposition to the Egyptian government, particularly in the wake of World War II. The motto of the Brotherhood became: "Allah is our objective; the Quran is the Constitution; the Prophet is our leader; jihad is our way; death for the sake of Allah is our wish." By 1948 the Brotherhood numbered half a million members, and that year one member of the Brotherhood assassinated the Egyptian prime minister, Nuqrashi Pasha. Al-Banna was assassinated the next year, apparently in retaliation. The Brotherhood grew not only in Egypt but by the spread of Brotherhood organizations to other venues, such as Palestine, Sudan, and Syria. The Egyptian Brotherhood renounced violence in the 1960s but remained a force for opposition to the government, and some of its more radical members spun off in more violent groups.[22]

In this progression of modern Islamist theology cum ideology, Sayyid Qutb (1906–1966), another Egyptian, ranks above the others. John Esposito, noted professor of Middle East studies, has dubbed Qutb "the godfather of modern revolutionary Islam."²³ Qutb was highly educated, became a teacher, and in 1939 joined the Egyptian Ministry of Education, where he remained during the 1940s. The ministry sent him to study American education from 1948 to 1950, but instead of admiring American culture and politics, he was appalled by what he saw. In *Milestones*, he proclaimed his shock "at this individual freedom, devoid of human sympathy and responsibility for relatives . . . ; at this behavior, like animals, which you call 'free mixing of the sexes'; at this vulgarity which you call 'emancipation of women'; at this evil and fanatic racial discrimination."²⁴ Rejecting Western modernity, he insisted on a reformed Salafist Islam. After returning from America, Qutb resigned from the Ministry of Education and joined the Muslim Brotherhood. Supportive of the 1952 coup that overthrew King Farouk, Qutb at first got along well with Nasser, but Nasser's nationalist agenda conflicted with Qutb's Islamist ideals.

Members of the Brotherhood, including Qutb, plotted to assassinate Nasser in 1954. When their attempt failed, Qutb was sent to prison, where he authored his most important works: a thirty-volume commentary on the Quran, *In the Shade of the Quran* (1954–1965), and *Milestones* (1964). In the latter he advocated an Islamist vanguard to overthrow the existing *jahili* regimes to create a true Islamic state. He remained behind bars for all but eight months of the rest of his life. He was convicted of complicity in a conspiracy to assassinate Nasser and other officials and was hung on 29 August 1966.

Qutb believed that a return to the proper practice of Islam "means destroying the kingdom of man to establish the kingdom of heaven on earth."²⁵ And this was cause for jihad. He stressed the necessity to abolish man-made laws in Muslim states: "It is necessary to revive that Muslim community . . . which is crushed under the weight of those false laws and customs which are not even remotely related to the Islamic teachings, and which in spite of all this, calls itself the 'world of Islam.'"²⁶ He insisted in his commentary on the Quran that the aim of jihad should be to "strike terror into the hearts of God's enemies who are also the enemies of the advocates of Islam throughout the world."²⁷

Qutb theorized that the West harbored a contempt toward Islam that dated back to the Crusades and had survived even through the Enlightenment to surface in a new intensity as Western imperialism. For him, "the Crusader spirit which runs in the blood of all westerners" was fundamental and irreversible.[28] Moreover, Qutb expressed a virulent anti-Semitism. In *In the Shade of the Quran* he argues, "The Muslim world has often faced problems as a result of Jewish conspiracies ever since the early days of Islam."[29] He believed that the aggressive Judaism of which he warned was most obvious in Zionism. Little wonder that violent radical Islamists rail against the Crusader-Zionist alliance against Islam.

Although he died young, Muhammad abd-al-Salam Faraj (1954–1982) became a noted exemplar of jihad. Trained as an electrical engineer, he founded an Islamist terrorist group in 1979 that merged with other extremists to become Tanzim al-Jihad, or simply al-Jihad, in 1980. A faction of it would later be known as Egyptian Islamic Jihad. Faraj took part in planning the 1981 assassination of Egyptian president Anwar Sadat, an attack that was carried out by one of Faraj's recruits, a lieutenant in the Egyptian Army.

Only after arresting Faraj did police discover the manuscript of his important work *The Neglected Obligation*, which soon appeared in installments and then as a complete volume. Faraj went even further than Qutb, elevating jihad to a sixth pillar of Islam, thus among its highest duties. His jihad meant warfare, not an inner spiritual struggle, and he firmly believed that jihad could win the entire world for Islam. This would establish a new caliphate to rule over a global *ummah*. He regarded the primary targets of jihad to be the corrupt Muslim regimes close at hand. He coined a term for such foes, the "near enemy." In contrast, he labeled infidel states, such as Israel and the United States, as the "far enemy," targets to be dealt with later.

The last Islamist extremist theorist discussed here, Abdullah Yusuf Azzam (1941–1989), has been credited as being the father of global jihad. He was a Palestinian who fled into Jordan because of the 1967 war. Azzam studied Islamic law and philosophy, earning his Ph.D. in 1973 from Cairo's Al-Azhar University, a highly respected institution. His religious ideas proved too extreme for Jordan, so he left to teach at the King Abdul Aziz University in Jeddah, Saudi Arabia. However, he was forced out of Saudi Arabia as well in 1979 and went to Pakistan. During the time when Azzam taught at Jeddah, the young Osama bin Laden studied there, and Azzam became his mentor. From Pakistan, Azzam issued the *fatwa* "Defense of the Muslim Lands, the First Obligation after Faith," in response to the Soviet invasion and repression of Afghanistan. Azzam aided fighters in Afghanistan and convinced bin Laden, who had joined him in Pakistan, to finance these efforts. Azzam lived by his motto of "Jihad and the rifle alone: no negotiations, no conferences and no dialogues."[30]

In *Join the Caravan* (1987), this learned Muslim scholar turned his talents to recruiting men to fight jihad in Afghanistan, by demonstrating how significant the arguments of traditional Islamic learning and of Islamist ideology were in the real world of jihadist warfare. His efforts contributed to a major transition from secular rationale to Islamist inspiration for armed struggle and terrorism in the Middle East. In his youth he had been with the PLO, but he found their Marxist nationalist "jihad" shockingly detached from Islam. By the time of the Afghan war, Azzam insisted that jihad was required not by national identity or political ideology but by Islam; it was global and religious. "Jihad today is individually obligatory, by self and wealth, on every Muslim, and the Islamic community remains sinful until the last piece of Islamic land is freed from the hands of the Disbelievers, nor are any absolved from sin other than the Mujahideen [those performing jihad]."[31] He condemned the *hadith* used to support the superiority of a greater—inner and spiritual—jihad as "a false, fabricated *hadith* which has no basis."[32] He cited Ibn Taymiyyah in support of his argument. Jihad is war for the sake of Islam and its *ummah*. Azzam pointed his readers to the words of Muhammad, as reported by Abu Hurairah, one of his companions: "Standing for an hour in the ranks of battle in the Path of Allah is better than standing in prayer for sixty years."[33]

Islamist theoretical exposition of resistance and jihad has an extensive history. Among Islamists, that history is not only long but honored, as demonstrated by references made to notable past contributors. However, the highly textual and rational arguments based on the faith of Islam can only provide some of the puzzle pieces. For one thing, a great many jihadis possess limited knowledge of Islam. Azzam himself spoke of illiterates among jihadis in Afghanistan and repeatedly stressed the need to attract educators—propagators—to teach: "You will become aware, on account of the profound signs left by the Arab youths of modest education . . . of the severe need for propagators, Imams, reciters of the Qur'an and religious scholars."[34] But there are also other factors, more visceral than rational, at work. Azzam spoke of debasement: "What then do you think about the millions of Muslims who are being humiliated with dreadful persecution, and are living the lives of cattle? They cannot repel attacks on their honor, lives and properties."[35] Grievances are calculated not only by physical injury and economic damage, but by insult and cultural humiliation.

Motivations are complex and can be, as Horgan cautions, beyond what even the individual realized him or herself. So, we must continue probing beyond base material factors and elevated matters of theology/ideology. We need to consider the more encompassing and fundamental, although elusive, issue of culture, which, of course, includes religious belief and practice, but much more as well.

A CLASH OF CIVILIZATIONS?

Since the early 1990s, academics, journalists, and security writers have lavished a great deal of attention on the theory that the world has become ensnared in a clash of civilizations. While the discussion is posed in more encompassing terms, it is usually employed to explain the rise in Islamist violence in a battle between the West and Islam.

The term "clash of civilizations" is most associated with Harvard political scientist, Samuel P. Huntington. Huntington first broached his clash thesis in an article published by *Foreign Affairs* in 1993 and then elaborated it in a book, *The Clash of Civilizations and the Remaking of World Order*, in 1996. He posited that since the 1600s, Europe, and increasingly the entire globe, have engaged in four eras of warfare, the last of which continues today. He differentiated these eras not by their military character but by the nature of the adversaries. From the mid-seventeenth century through the onset of the French Revolution in 1789, wars were fought between *dynastic princes*, who fought wars calculated to advance their states or their dynasties. The French Revolution ushered in a period in which populations came to see themselves as *peoples inspired by nationalism* to take up arms. The 1917 Bolshevik Revolution in Russia reset the board for a new era of warfare in which *political ideologies* drove conflict. Liberal capitalism confronted both authoritarian communism and fascism before World War II, and then a "free world" led by the United States stood against a "Communist Bloc" until the collapse of the Soviet Union in 1991.

After this, the great belligerent fault line changed radically. States played the key roles in the first three eras, but in the fourth, the warring entities can be sub-states, states, or coalitions, and the borders are not those of political units but of *civilizations*. In addition to Western civilization, Huntington lists eight others: Orthodox (Christian), Latin American, Japanese, Buddhist, Sinic (Chinese), Hindu, African, and, of course, Muslim. The essence of civilizations is identity, and as Huntington wrote: "The central theme of this book is that culture and cultural identities, which at the broadest level are civilization identities, are shaping the patterns of cohesion, disintegration, and conflict in the post–Cold War world."[36] Resurgent religion can be fundamental to cultural identity in an ever-shrinking world, and this is most striking in the Muslim world.

The phenomenon of globalization underlies both the theory of a clash of civilizations and the Islamist conception of a Western war on Islam. *Globalization*, like *terrorism*, is a term with a bewildering variety of definitions. One that is particularly apropos comes from an address by Eduardo Aninat, deputy managing director of the International Monetary Fund, in 2001: "Globalization can be defined as the increasing interaction among and integration of diverse human societies in all important dimensions of their activities—economic, social, political, cultural, and religious."[37] Globalization brings cultures closer together, but that does not necessarily bring understanding and harmony. A Hamas leader explained his view of globalization as oppression: "Globalization is just a new colonial system. It is America's attempt to dominate the rest of the world economically rather than militarily."[38]

Islamists speak in terms of a clash of civilizations, and it takes on the character of total war. Ajmal Qadri, head of a political/religious party in Pakistan that runs madrassas and has its own military wing, stated to Jessica Stern, "I believe that a clash of civilizations is inevitable. And in this clash, the fittest will survive. We are much more cultured than America and the West. The West is bereft of the strength that comes from families."[39]

Huntington offers reasons why differences breed hostility between civilizations. Perceived disadvantages, from poverty to powerlessness, are regarded as the products of an assault. Some external force must be to blame; we are poor because others have stolen our wealth. Inequality breeds envy, envy breeds resentment, and resentment breeds resistance, even revenge. And the language and metaphor of abuse, resentment, and resistance can become that of religion.

In his article "The Roots of Muslim Rage" (1990), the combative historian of the Middle East Bernard Lewis wrote: "This is no less than a clash of civilizations." Lewis argues that the Muslim world fell behind the West intellectually starting in the late Middle Ages. The ultimate result of this has been "a feeling of humiliation—a growing awareness, among the heirs of an old, proud, and long dominant civilization, of having been overtaken, overborne, and overwhelmed by those whom they regarded as their inferiors."[40]

It is not hard to see how injury can result from a military, political, or economic clash, but allow me to probe the impact of humiliation, as stressed by Lewis within the context of a clash in civilizations.

Insult as Injury: Insights from Terror Management Theory
Here I am going to climb out on a limb and suggest that a hypothesis from social psychology, Terror Management Theory (TMT), may enlighten us concerning the dynamics of a "clash of civilizations" and the Islamist narrative of a Western war on Islam.

TMT, first proposed by Tom Pyszczynski, Jeff Greenberg, and Sheldon Solomon, is not specifically about terrorism; rather, the terror in the title is that inflicted on humankind by the knowledge of our own approaching and inevitable deaths. TMT argues that culture functions to keep this fear at bay by promising literal or symbolic immortality. Religion is the most obvious example of that, but it goes beyond religion to other values through which we see our lives as meaningful and part of something greater and enduring. One could see oneself as justified by national identity—dying for one's country—or cause—dedicating one's life to the creation of a better society. We are nurtured to adopt a particular Cultural Worldview (CWV) that underpins our psychological well-being by providing a standard for enduring meaning. Self-esteem is the essential measurement of how we are seen, and how we believe ourselves to have lived up to the standards set by our CWV.

As a military historian, I have absolutely no problem accepting the importance of self-esteem, respect, and honor, the foundations of reputation. Men and women quite literally die for such values.

But self-esteem can be undermined either by a lack of reassurance that one is living up to the CWV or by a challenge to that CWV itself. Pyszczynski writes: "The effectiveness of both cultural worldviews and self-esteem depends heavily on consensual validation from others, and *those with different beliefs, values, and perceptions undermine this effectiveness, thus leaving us vulnerable to the core anxiety that is inherent in the human condition.*"[41]

To a person whose CWV is expressed primarily as religion, those who deny the validity of that religion's beliefs, values, and practices pose a threat to that person's psychological equilibrium. Such a threat need not be direct and bold; simply living by very different standards can be construed as a challenge. And examples of this other lifestyle need not be presented as polemic, they can come through entertainment or news. The globalization of communications provides conduits through which cultures can flow across borders between countries and continents. This could be read by some as enrichment, but it could also strike others as endangerment. How much worse is this when one culture's message to another is ridicule and insult to its most basic values?

So, adherents of a more puritanical creed that emphasizes restraint can be deeply offended by a lifestyle of sexual freedom, particularly if it is seen as a temptation that could lead right-minded people astray. And devout Muslims, who believe it is blasphemy to mock the Prophet through intentionally offensive cartoons, could regard a demonstration declaring "Je suis Charlie" on the Champs Élysées not as an affirmation of free speech but as proof of Western disdain for Islam. Thus, TMT offers perspective on why Muslims could see a clash of civilizations realized as a Western war on Islam in the cultural sphere, as well as being manifested in economic and political inequalities.

Beyond this, TMT also helps us understand not only the behaviors of terrorists but the reactions, all too often overreactions, of those they terrorize. The moral shock and sense of vulnerability generated by terrorism increase the target audience's awareness of impending death, what TMT terms "mortality salience." This leads the target audience to rally around its CWV and shore up self-esteem by aggressively asserting itself. Part of this is heightening one's own identity and excluding or condemning those who are not like you. So, after 9/11, Americans hung out their flags, put flag decals on their cars, listened to patriotic songs, and went to church—attendance on 21 September 2001 was greater than at any time since the 1950s.[42] And Americans retaliated vigorously—thus the war against the Taliban in Afghanistan and, I would argue, the invasion of Iraq in 2003. TMT may help us understand better the effectiveness of terrorism as provocation in terrorist "jujitsu."

I have brought up TMT because of its stress on CWV, self-esteem, and threats to both. You do not have to accept TMT in its entirety to grasp its disquieting elements of reality. It is certainly worth discussion.

Another approach to understanding how individuals uphold their worth and perceive threats comes from Social Identity Perspective (SIP), as explained and advanced by Sageman in his recent book *Turning to Political Violence*. To me it reads a bit like TMT without reference to the terror of death. SIP stresses that individuals self-categorize themselves as part of a group—for example, defining themselves as Muslims or as specific kinds of Muslims. Personally, I would question how much *self*-categorization is really a matter of the *self* or a result of choices presented or promoted by the dominant cultural worldview, but set aside that for a moment. Once self-categorized individuals perceive the nature and status of their chosen group as their own, and define themselves by its characteristics, strengths, and virtues, they personalize what they see as injuries, injustices, and insults inflicted on that group by others: for example, a Western war on Islam. We will return to more of Sageman's arguments below.

How Different Are We?
All this talk of contrasting and colliding civilizations, CWV, and group identities leads to the issue of just how different values held in the West are from those held in Muslim areas of the world. The answer is not simple. To argue that as human beings we all value essentially the same things does not take us far. First, it makes us too homogenous. Yes, we all care about our children, but that does not mean we all envision the same kind of education and the same kind of futures for them. Second, there is great variety within the West, and even greater within the Muslim world. Third, even when there are similarities in some areas, this may not affect religion or politics, both of primary concern here.

Hard data on cultural values and perceptions within the *ummah* refutes some stereotypes but still reveals real differences. In 2007 academic researchers John L. Esposito and Dalia Mogahed published *Who Speaks for Islam?: What a Billion Muslims Really Think*, based on polling data and face-to-face interviews with tens of thousands of participants in over thirty-five Muslim-majority countries between 2001 and 2007.[43] And the Pew Forum on Religion and Public Life has published two surveys of its own: *The World's Muslims: Unity and Diversity* (2012) and *The World's Muslims: Religion, Politics and Society* (2013).[44]

The 2012 Pew survey testifies to the very strong adherence to the religious beliefs of Islam in the Muslim world. Esposito and Mogahed present polling date establishing that in several Muslim-majority countries, about 90 percent of the populations insist that religion plays an important part in their lives.[45] (The Pew percentages are all stated as medians.) The adherence to Islam is confirmed in the distaste shown toward some aspects of Western culture. Thus while the 2013 Pew survey shows that a great number of Muslims "like Western entertainment" (for example, 52 percent in Morocco),[46] there is also a perception that Western entertainment weakens morality, ranging from 91 percent among Palestinians to 62 percent in Egypt.[47] Still, it is reassuring that the 2013 Pew survey found that among Muslims in the Middle East and North Africa, 60 percent state that there is "no conflict between religion and modern society."[48]

Muslims polled demonstrated a desire for *sharia*. We have seen that radical Islamists insist that laws should be divine in origin, based on the Quran and the *hadith*, and, therefore, man-made laws are by nature un-Islamic. The 2013 Pew survey found that 73 percent of all Egyptians polled believe that *sharia* is "the revealed world of God," and 74 percent favor "making sharia the official law of the country."[49] Of six national Middle Eastern and North African Muslim groups surveyed in the Pew study, the population least favorable to a *sharia*-based code is Lebanese (29 percent) and the most favorable is Iraqi (91 percent).

Esposito and Mogahed argue that support for *sharia* is based on a belief that it sets high moral principles, without having to entail seventh-century punishments. An *Al Jazeera* magazine article of October 2006 explained: "It's logical to install Sharia Law in Arab and Muslim states, where the majority of the population is Muslim. It's the only way for Muslims to escape the dictatorship and oppression of some of the Arab rulers, those who favor perceived self-interest over what's best for their nations."[50] However, unlike Esposito and Mogahed, the Pew researchers found a surprisingly high degree of support for traditional severe punishments, the *hudud*. Among those Egyptians who favored *sharia*, for example, 70 percent supported corporal punishments for theft, and 81 percent accepted stoning as a punishment for adultery.[51]

Yet the polling data used by Esposito and Mogahed show Muslim support for *sharia* law *and* democracy, a pairing of values that radical Islamists would find incompatible. Contrary to American perceptions, those more extreme in their religious views were *more* likely to invest their hopes in democracy than were the moderates; 50 percent of the more extreme, as opposed to 35 percent of moderates agreed with the statement that "'moving toward greater governmental democracy' will foster progress in the Arab/Muslim world."[52] As is the case elsewhere, here the Pew data support *Who Speaks for Islam?* The median among Middle Eastern and North African Muslims who "prefer democracy over strong leader" stands at 55 percent.

Americans are often scandalized by what they see as the treatment of women within Islam. The burqa or niqab (face covering) is read as a negation of a woman's rights, as a sign of slavery. But polling data studied by Esposito and Mogahed show that, "far from inspiring an eagerness to imitate, images of scantily clad young women may leave Muslim women believing that despite Western women's equal legal status, their cultural status is lacking."[53] However, status and power can be different things. The 2013 Pew survey found that 87 percent of Muslims in the Middle East and North Africa agree that "a wife must obey her husband," which is about the same figure for Egypt at 85 percent.[54]

However, the results analyzed by Esposito and Mogahed establish favorable majorities concerning four propositions that demonstrate more open attitudes: 1) women should have "the same legal rights as men," 57 percent in Egypt; 2) women should have the right to vote, 76 percent in Jordan; 3) women should have "the right to hold any job for which they are qualified outside the home," 85 percent in Egypt; and 4) women should have "the right to hold leadership positions at cabinet and national council levels," majorities in all countries surveyed except for Egypt (50 percent) and Saudi Arabia (40 percent).[55] Important Muslim-majority countries have elected women to top posts. The three most populous Muslim countries, Indonesia, Pakistan, and Bangladesh, have all chosen women prime ministers or presidents. The United States has yet to elect a female president.

Surveying their data, Esposito and Mogahed provide some important conclusions about Muslim views of the West: "When asked what they admire about the West, those politically radicalized and moderates registered these three spontaneous responses: (1) technology; (2) the West's value system, hard work, self-responsibility, rule of law, cooperation; and (3) fair political systems, democracy, respect for human rights, freedom of speech, gender equality."[56] But their responses to what they resented most about the West were very disturbing: 1) "sexual and cultural promiscuity," 2) "ethical and moral corruption," and 3) "hatred of Muslims."[57] The authors report that "across the Muslim world from Morocco to Mindanao" there is a "popular belief" that there is a "war against Islam," in the sense that the United States aims "to weaken and divide the Islamic world."[58] Later in their book, they present a distinctly unscientific piece of evidence, the remark of a minivan driver in Cairo: "America hates Islam; look at what they did to Iraq."[59] This is disturbing, in that it confirms that the global *ummah* largely accept a basic tenet of the Islamist narrative about a clash of civilizations. With a body of opinion already accepting that there is a Western hostility to Islam, buttressing that opinion by ill-considered words and actions is dangerous.

We will have more to say about surveys of Muslim religious opinions and values in Chapter 11.

RADICALIZATION

A consideration of the radical Islamist narrative and actual opinion among the global *ummah* leads us toward a consideration of radicalization. "Radicalization" has become something of a fashionable buzzword, so we had best be clear of its meaning from the start. Marc Sageman defines it as the "process of transforming individuals from rather unexceptional and ordinary beginnings into terrorists with the willingness to use violence for political ends."[60] "Radicalization" is most discussed in relation to radical Islamist terrorism, but the process is equally crucial to all forms of radical terrorism.

Sageman postulates that Islamist radicalization involves four "prongs."

One is "a sense of moral outrage at apparent crimes against Muslims both globally and locally." This can be related precisely to SIP. The second interprets the cause of that outrage as "part of a larger war against Islam." In the third, the ideology of a war on Islam "resonates with their own personal experience of discrimination, making them feel that they are also victims of this wider war." Fourth, "individuals are then mobilized through networks, both face to face and now more and more commonly online, to become terrorists."[61] The first three all relate directly to the Islamist narrative that there is a Western war on Islam, which is closely related to what Esposito and Mogahed revealed in their otherwise hopeful volume: most of the *ummah* believe that the West and America hate Muslims.

Sageman makes clear that the four prongs do not have to come in any particular order. Thus, it is quite conceivable that an individual can become involved with a terrorist group because of the pull of a social network in which he or she is enmeshed, and only become fully convinced of the general narrative stressing a Western war on Islam *after* entering the group. Moreover, both Sageman and John Horgan concur that transitions from "unexceptional and ordinary" to "terrorist" can occur at very different rates, and can be done little by little, rather than in one great surge of enlightenment and commitment. Horgan writes, "This sense that initial involvement in terrorism may develop from a series of incremental steps (each of which if taken in isolation would rapidly diminish in overall significance) is powerful."[62] During an interview, Adriana Faranda of the Red Brigades testified, "There were lots of little steps which led to where I ended up . . . it wasn't a major leap in the true sense of the word. It was just another stage . . . it was a choice."[63]

To my way of thinking, critical links in the chain are the conviction that the West is attacking Islam, that this abuse explains the *ummah*'s plight, and that such aggression prescribes that Muslims come to the defense of Islam in jihad. Horgan points to the research of M. Taylor and E. Quayle that in general "terrorists view their involvement as a *provoked reaction* requiring *defense* against an *enemy*."[64]

Social Networking: Face-to-Face and Virtual
Sageman's insistence that social networking matters fundamentally in the process of radicalization is widely shared. Horgan quotes Andrea

Elliott on this matter: "Increasingly, terrorism analysts have focused on the importance of social milieu. Some stress that terrorists are not simply loners, overcome by a militant cause. They are more likely to radicalize together with others who share the same passions and afflictions and daily routines."[65] Mark Juergensmeyer observes that an Israeli study headed by Ariel Merari established that Hamas suicide bombers "were recruited through friendship networks in school, sports, and extended families."[66] Much the same was true of face-to-face recruiting into the Red Brigades, as noted in Chapter 8.

The importance of social networks provides another perspective on the role of imprisonment in radicalization. Confined in close quarters with others, prisoners can form tight social networks. Should individuals in the networks be committed Islamists, others can be introduced to Islamism or strengthened in their existing commitment to it. The pull of the social network attracts and intensifies. This was the case for many, including Abu Musab al-Zarqawi, the infamous head of al-Qaeda in Iraq, which evolved into the Islamic State.

The ubiquity of the internet has altered the process of social networking. To real-world, face-to-face contacts, the internet adds virtual communities in the cyber world. In an age of online boards, chat rooms, and Facebook, the internet can be a source of the personal example and support of others so essential to radicalization. Radical groups of all kinds recognize this.

Sageman stresses the evolution of terrorist recruitment from personal contacts to virtual networks formed on the web. There, potential jihadis not only learn about organizations, but also read and see the kinds of accounts that incite moral outrage and advance the narrative of a clash of civilizations and a Western war on Islam. Jessica Stern shares this judgment: "Virtual networks enable violent individuals who are socially ill at ease to work together on a common political or religious cause without having to meet face-to-face."[67] Social networking on the web recruits members to established groups and also empowers lone-wolf terrorists with the sense that they are part of a jihadi community.

Sageman predicted that the effect of the internet on American Muslims would be less than it would be on Europeans. Certainly, American Muslims "can watch and read about atrocities against fellow Muslims around the world just as their European coreligionists do and, like them, also feel a sense of moral outrage at those acts. They read and chat about the global jihadi terrorist ideology on the Internet, just like their European counterparts."[68] However, since American Muslims on average are better educated, live a better life, and are more integrated than are European Muslims, they are much less vulnerable to jihadist appeals. But that does not mean they are immune, as illustrated by Major Nidal Hassan, who gunned down fellow American soldiers at Fort Hood in 2009, or Omar Mateen, who killed forty-nine at an Orlando nightclub in 2016.

The ability to recruit and mobilize Muslims already living in Western countries, Sageman argues, means that the major threats now come not from foreign Muslims crossing borders but from resident and even home-grown Muslims; therefore, border security actually provides little security. Hassan and Matteen were born in the United States, and the brothers who massacred the staff of *Charlie Hebdo* were both Parisian-born French citizens.

There is an implicit conflict between those who emphasize the theology and ideology of radical Islamism as motivating factors in the scourge of terrorism and those who consider radicalization through social networking to be more important. That exponent of social networking, Marc Sageman, offers a stern warning to those who see the centuries-old Muslim literature of resistance as the key to understanding Islamist terrorism: "I am not sure that this strong emphasis on ideology, religion, and fighting 'extremist Islam' is fruitful. . . . I have come to the conclusion that the terrorists in Western Europe and North America were not intellectuals or ideologues, much less religious scholars. *It is not about how they think, but how they feel.* Let us not make the mistake of over-intellectualizing this fight."[69] I take this as a caution to put ideology in perspective. Other things attract individuals. And Jessica Stern concludes about the draw of social networking in general: "In some cases, the desire to be with friends turns out to be more important, over time, than the desire to achieve any particular goal."[70] Still, Sageman himself stresses the narrative in his four prongs of radicalization, and, thus, to Sageman the narrative is a matter of strongly held convictions and SIP, not of mastering ideological debates. As Horgan insists, motivations are highly complex and should be examined from multiple perspectives. They can arise from inspiration and insult, from fanaticism and friendship. Do not expect formulas in such a complex matter.

Why Women Turn to Terrorism

To further complicate the matter, scholars debate if women become radicalized for different reasons than those affecting men. In a 1997 article, Mia Bloom argues that "women generally become involved, at least initially, for personal, rather than ideological, reasons."[71] She elaborated on this in her later book, *Bombshell: Women and Terrorism* (2011), where she explains the motivations of female terrorists by the four R's: revenge, redemption, relationship, and respect, to which she then adds another "R" for rape.[72] Among the women Bloom surveyed, "revenge for the death of a close family member is most often cited as the key factor that inspired a woman to get involved in the first place." Redemption moves women who believe they have transgressed sexual or social standards and must regain their honor. Bloom highlights "relationship," social networking, because "the best single predictor that a woman will engage in terrorist violence is her relationship with a known insurgent or jihadi." And "respect" for Bloom is the desire to be honored as being "just as dedicated and committed to the cause as men." Bloom adds rape because she sees rape as a matter of a woman being condemned not by actions of her choosing, but against her will. One redemption from the stigma of rape is sacrifice for a great cause.

Other analysts, such as Israeli counterterrorist authority Anat Berko, argue that women become terrorists as a form of empowerment in their own communities, communities that relegate women to inferior status and limited agency.[73] However, Bloom denies that women engage in terrorism to empower women in general or to strike a blow for gender equality, except in demonstrating the same dedication to cause. "Thus, participating in violence is not intended to level the playing field in their societies—this is not one of their goals."[74] She notes, "Almost all of the women whose stories have been examined in the course of my research for this book agreed on one thing: feminism was not the basis of their participation in the terrorist movement." In fact, "many of them were decidedly antifeminist . . . because the feminist agenda conflicted with nationalist agendas."[75]

SHARED ASPECTS OF RELIGIOUS TERRORISM

Before leaving a chapter that deals more directly with religion than does any other in this volume, we should ask how religiously inspired radical terrorists differ from those with secular motivations. My inclination is to argue that the two have more in common than you might suppose. We discussed this in Chapter 8, but we will go further here.

The two most significant books that deal with religious terrorism parallel each other in many ways, even in their titles: Mark Juergensmeyer's *Terror in the Mind of God* (2000) and Jessica Stern's *Terror in the Name of God* (2003). Both rely extensively on interviews with religious radicals from different faiths. At base, Juergensmeyer and Stern agree that forms of religious terrorism have much in common and that they diverge from terrorism in the name of other, more secular, causes. Their subjects pursue a religiously ordered government, society, and culture. Morality and immorality are defined by divine command, not human utility. Stern wisely centers on the sense of absolute certainty: "Although we see them as evil, religious terrorists know themselves to be perfectly good. To be crystal clear about one's identity, to know that one's group is superior to all others, to make purity one's motto, and purification of the world one's life's work—this is a kind of bliss."[76] Religious terrorists stress the language of sacrifice and martyrdom, and the promise of paradise.

Juergensmeyer emphasizes religious terrorists' perceptions of the conflict they undertake as "cosmic." "What makes religious violence particularly savage and relentless is that its perpetrators have placed such religious images of divine struggle—cosmic war—in the service of worldly political battles."[77] He notes three characteristics of cosmic war: 1) it "is perceived as a defense of basic identity and dignity"; 2) "losing the struggle would be unthinkable"; and 3) it is seen as unwinnable by human effort alone, but "if the struggle is seen as hopeless in human terms, it is likely that it may be reconceived on a sacred plane, where the possibilities of victory are in God's hands."[78]

However, upon examination, the differences between secular and religious clandestine terrorist groups seem less imposing than the similarities. If Islamist terrorists employ the language of religion, so have terrorists of a decidedly secular outlook. Juergensmeyer agrees with David Rapoport that religion and terrorism "fit together not only because there is a violent streak in the history of religion, but also because terrorist acts have a symbolic side and in that sense mimic religious rites."[79] Both the religious and the secular sacrifice themselves and count their martyrs.

Giving up one's comforts, earthly happiness, and even life for a greater cause amounts to a kind of sainthood, with the full range of iconography and hagiography. As Turgenev's "Threshold" ends, "'Fool,' someone said from behind. 'Saint,' someone replied."

Secular terrorists have not expected an otherworldly paradise as their reward, but they anticipate a kind of symbolic, and to them satisfying, immortality through the victory of the great cause to which they devoted themselves. Here the arguments of TMT apply. Society and posterity became inspiration and judge. If Islam constitutes the CWV that allays the terror of death, why could not the CWV of dedicated nationalists, anarchists, socialists, and communists do the same? The primary advantage religious terrorists stand to gain from their CWV might derive from the fact that it is shared and encouraged by the society from which the terrorists emerge, whereas a secular revolutionary CWV is probably not. However, the echo-chamber effect of the clandestine terrorist group reinforces the values and convictions of its members, be they religious or secular.

In considering and contrasting views of secular and religious terrorists, concepts of an apocalypse stand out as especially haunting. Christianity and Islam share a notion of a final apocalyptic battle between light and dark, good and evil. Those inclined to regard scripture as metaphorical may regard the apocalypse as symbolic, or at least remote. However, those of a more fundamentalist temperament seem far more adamant about the end of days. In Islam, one phenomenon of the end will be the return of the Mahdi, essentially a redeemer who will rule just before the Day of Judgment. A study by the Pew Research Center published in 2012 reveals that a surprisingly high percentage of Muslims surveyed believe that they will see the return of the Mahdi in their own lifetime.[80] Of all those surveyed, Afghans are most likely to expect an imminent return of the Mahdi; 83 percent of the population share this expectation. Perhaps such a view of the end of days among Afghans can be dismissed as a product of a war-shattered people hoping for relief. However, 68 percent of the population in far-more-developed Turkey also expect to see the Mahdi, as do 72 percent of Iraqis, 41 percent of Jordanians, and 40 percent of Egyptians. And the Egyptian figures are the lowest of all the North African and Middle Eastern populations studied. As we shall see in Chapter 11, the Islamic State has focused on these apocalyptic expectations and incorporated them in its own ideology and propaganda. Here the narrative of IS strikes a chord with beliefs strong among the Muslim *ummah* as a whole.

Yet, as made clear in the previous chapter, secular terrorists have espoused harshly apocalyptic convictions as well, believing in destruction —"pantoclastic fury." It could be argued that belief in divine sanction make this apocalyptic vision more powerful among religiously inspired terrorists, but I wonder. At times it seems to me that that the most important advantage of religiously based terrorism is that it can draw from a larger base of potential supporters, for example, the *ummah* of 1.6 billion, with a large percentage of it convinced of Western hostility to Islam. We will have more to say on this in Chapter 11.

JE SUIS CHARLIE?

Judged by the laws and morality of France, gunning down journalists at the offices of *Charlie Hebdo* amounted to cold-blooded murder. But judged by the ideology of radical Islamists in the mode of al-Qaeda or the Islamic State, the massacre was a legitimate act of jihad, an execution of the guilty, not a slaughter of the innocents. To say this is not to engage in moral relativism. Using bullets to erase drawings is beyond unforgivable. However, to deal with radical Islamism we must comprehend its rationales.

The information and arguments presented in this chapter should supply background and context for the moral choices made by the Kouachi brothers. Both had been networked and radicalized for years, mentored by extreme Islamists. Whether or not they were steeped in the writings of violent Islamism, they certainly knew the basic ideology of jihad. The Kouachis regarded their attack as righteous retribution against *Charlie* for repeatedly having published repulsive examples of the basest blasphemy: "We have avenged the Prophet Muhammad!" And they were prepared "to die as martyrs," as they proclaimed to negotiators before the final shoot-up in which they perished.

Charb also declared his willingness to face death, even if he did not embrace it. During an interview in 2012 he announced: "I am not afraid of reprisals. . . . This may sound a bit pompous but I would prefer to die standing than to live on my knees."[81] Like their editor, the staff of *Charlie* saw themselves as upholding freedom of speech and the press. Perhaps they did not choose to die for a cause, like martyrs, but they were killed because of their defense of a sacred principle.

But there is another lesson we might take away from this chapter. One of my principles in dealing with terrorism is "Do not feed the narrative." That is, avoid doing things or saying things that strengthen the terrorists' arguments and allow them to rally more support for their causes.

Freedom of speech must be defended, but does that legitimate saying anything at any time? As interpreted by the law, freedom of speech has never included the right to slander, and prohibitions on hate speech are common throughout Western states. U.S. law penalizes "fighting words," defined in an important Supreme Court decision as "those that by their very utterance inflict injury or tend to incite an immediate breach of the peace."[82] At their worst, the *Charlie* cartoons and articles were grossly insulting and hurtful to Muslims, and the fact that *Charlie* also lampooned Catholics, Protestants, and Jews is little defense.

Huntington closes his book on the clash of civilizations with a quotation from Lester Pearson's *Democracy in World Politics* (1955) advising that mankind was entering "an age when different civilizations will have to learn to live side by side in peaceful interchange, learning from each other, studying each other's history and ideals and art and culture, mutually enriching each other's lives. The alternative, in this overcrowded little world, is misunderstanding, tension, clash, and catastrophe."[83] Esposito and Mogahed plea for change in the West: "There should be rules and laws to respect people of other religions and not make fun of them. We must endeavor to relay the accurate picture of Islam to the West."[84] Principled civility, however, is probably a better instrument than compulsion by the law. The renowned Japanese film director Hayao Miyazaki, a man of another civilization, commented on the character of *Charlie Hebdo*'s cartoons of Muhammad, "I think it's a mistake to caricaturize the figures venerated by another culture. You shouldn't do it."[85]

Charlie's campaign to render Islam banal may simply have contributed to making the Islamic State anything but banal. Degrading ridicule of Muhammad can be expected to feed the Islamist narrative that points to a Western hatred of Muslims. To crowds declaring, "Je suis Charlie!," other crowds answered, "Je suis Muslim!"

CHAPTER TEN

Regional Jihad

HEZBOLLAH AND HAMAS

FIGURE 10.1. Hamas carried out the deadliest terrorist attack of the Second Intifada when a suicide bomber detonated his explosives at a Passover Seder held at the Park Hotel in Netanya, Israel, on 27 March 2002. Thirty died and 140 were injured in the Passover Massacre. Here, emergency personnel cope with the aftermath; bodies of the dead still lie under the wreckage. Havakuk Levison/Reuters Pictures.

THE SECOND INTIFADA, a Palestinian uprising against continued Israeli domination and Jewish settlements in Gaza and the West Bank, began in September 2000, following the failure of the Camp David Summit in July 2000. The fighting continued at least through February 2005. The striking image of a Palestinian combatant of the First Intifada was the stone-throwing youth facing down an Israeli tank; the suicide bomber became the archetypical agent of death during the Second Intifada.

Hamas, a creation of the First Intifada, committed the deadliest single attack of the Second. On the evening of 27 March 2002, the Park Hotel in Netanya, Israel, was hosting the traditional Passover meal, a Seder, for 250 guests in its dining hall. Many of the guests were elderly Jews who had no family in Israel with whom to celebrate this ceremony. Some had survived the Holocaust. About 7:30 p.m., a Hamas bomber, Tarak Zidan, disguised as a Muslim woman in full cover, entered the hotel carrying a heavy suitcase. Somehow, he got through security and then, bypassing the front desk, walked into the dining hall and detonated his bomb. The blast killed thirty and wounded 140 (Fig. 10.1). The oldest victim was ninety-year-old Chanah Rogan, born in Bessarabia in 1912, then part of the Russian Empire. She had emigrated to the United States after World War II, but had later moved to Israel. Widowed by 2002, she attended the Seder with a friend, Yulia Talmi, eighty-seven, who was also killed.

The Israeli military was poised to retaliate; in the fifteen months that preceded the Passover Massacre, the Second Intifada had taken the lives of over 300 Israeli civilians. On 29 March the IDF launched Operation Defensive Shield, storming into the West Bank to reoccupy territory that had been handed over to the Palestinian Authority for limited autonomous government. Defensive Shield was the largest IDF operation in the West Bank since 1967; nearly 500 Palestinians died and 1,450 were wounded. Thirty IDF soldiers were killed and 130 wounded.[1] The peace process was not only stalled, it was undone. As the scholar Asef Bayat notes: "Only when Israel invaded the West Bank in the spring of 2002 did ordinary people in the Arab world collectively explode with outrage. The millions of Arab citizens who poured into the streets of Cairo, Amman, Rabat, and many other cities to express sympathy with the Palestinians evoked memories of how Arab anticolonial movements in the postwar period were driven from below."[2]

It was a classic pattern: an act of Palestinian terrorism precipitated an overwhelming conventional military response by the Israelis, which physically succeeded because of the sheer power of Israel relative to the Palestinian population in the occupied territories. But on the world stage, Defensive Shield was met with condemnation in the Arab world and with accusations of war crimes by such groups as Human Rights Watch and Amnesty International.

This chapter considers the course of radical Islamist terrorism within Lebanon and Israel over the decades since 1985. The sectarian PLO plays a part, to be sure, but Hezbollah and Hamas occupy center stage. These two organizations espouse the Islamist ideology that characterizes the third wave of radical terrorism. They also evolved from terrorist groups in the 1980s to state-like organizations with large military forces. Such evolution is another important trait of the third wave. However, another obvious, but not universal, trait of the third wave, global scope, is not true of Hezbollah and Hamas, which are essentially regional in goals and resources, although Iran has recently used Hezbollah forces as shock troops outside of Lebanon. We will consider the first two traits in this chapter and add global scope in Chapter 11.

Both Hezbollah and Hamas consider the Israelis as primary enemies, and it is customary to merge the stories of the PLO with those of Hezbollah and Hamas. But I have chosen to separate them because they characterize two different waves of terrorism, PLO the second and the others the third. The conflicts between the PLO and Hamas, in particular, demonstrate the hostility between the secular second wave and the Islamist third wave, even when they are competing to represent and advance the interests of the same Palestinian population.

The material in this chapter, like that in Chapter 7, may disturb American readers not only because of the human suffering on all sides but also because the interpretations of the adversaries' attitudes and actions may challenge American assumptions about the Palestinians and the Israelis. But we need to face the debate in interpretations of violence in the Middle East. It is one of the theses of this volume that the Palestinian–Israeli conflict is fundamental to the history of terrorism since World War II. The PLO not only functioned as a major nationalist terrorist group of the second wave, but also became a hub of terrorist activity beyond Palestine through its symbiotic relationships with ethnonationalist and radical Marxist terrorists from the Americas, Europe, the Near East, and Japan. Moreover, perceived injustice toward the Palestinians became and remains a rallying cry for the radical Islamists of the third wave. An understanding of both the second and third waves requires an understanding of the Palestinian–Israeli conflict and recognition of the *perceptions* of that conflict among the Islamic *ummah* and the world community.

HEZBOLLAH

Hezbollah arose out of the almost unimaginably complicated political landscape of a Lebanon tortured by civil war and invasion. From the seventeenth century until World War I, the Ottoman Turks ruled over the territory that now comprises Lebanon. After their victory in 1918, the British and French divided between themselves the Ottoman lands that lay between present-day Turkey and Egypt. The British exercised mandates over Palestine, Transjordan, and Iraq, while the French held as their mandates what became Lebanon and Syria. The borders set for these domains reflected British and French convenience, not ethnic or political lines as they existed in reality.

The population of Lebanon was the most religiously diverse in the Middle East, and when it became independent in 1943, its constitution apportioned political authority to balance the power of different religions and sects based on the 1932 census, when Christians were in the majority, with 53 percent of the population. This style of government has been termed "confessionalism." According to the unwritten National Pact agreed at the time, the president must be Maronite Christian, the prime minister Sunni Muslim, the speaker of the parliament Shia Muslim, and the deputy speaker of the parliament and deputy prime minister Greek Orthodox. No official census has been taken since 1932, because its findings would upset the precarious political equilibrium. However, the CIA's *World Fact Book* estimates the 2015 population of Lebanon, divided into eighteen recognized sects, as 54 percent Muslim (equally split between Sunni and Shia), 40.5 percent Christian (broken down into 21 percent Maronite, 8 percent Greek Orthodox, 5 percent Greek Catholic, and 6.5 percent other Christian sects), and 5.6 percent Druze. The present constitution, following the Taif Agreement in 1989, requires that there be equal parliamentary representation between Christians and Muslims, apportioned between the sects of each religion.

Lebanese religious identity speaks not only to faith, then, but to political authority and affiliation. It also can correspond to military power, since the paramilitary militias that fought for power, most notably during the Civil War of 1975–1990, were commonly, but not exclusively, organized along sectarian lines. Hezbollah emerged during the Civil War and the fight against Israeli occupation as a militant Shia Islamist group, but it was preceded as an armed force by the military wing of Amal. However, rather than work as Shia allies, Hezbollah and Amal forces fought over control of Shia areas in Lebanon during the Civil War.

Politics are further complicated by the role of important families within the different communities and by the intervention of neighboring states. Certain linages have dominated sectarian politics; for example, the Maronite Christian Gemayel family, who created the Phalanges Party, commanded its militia, and provided two presidents for Lebanon.

Syria, Israel, and Iran have inserted themselves into Lebanese politics. The Syrian government under the al-Assads played kingmaker, or -unmaker, and occupied parts of the country from 1976 to 2006. As described in Chapter 8, the Israelis launched an incursion, Operation Litani, in 1978 and a full-scale invasion in 1982, which led to an occupation that only ended in 2000. Iran funded and armed Shia groups in Lebanon, and even dispatched Revolutionary Guards to train Shia fighters. Iran remains a strong backer of Hezbollah, which seems to be paying it debts by service to Iranian interests.

There are so many players on the board and the game is so complex that it would be impossible to trace the details from 1985, when we left it, to 2018 in the few pages of this section, so we will concentrate on Hezbollah as much as possible, but remain aware that is but a part of the story.

Leadership and Program
Different scholars treat the nature of Hezbollah from 1982 to 1985 differently. Augustus Norton, in his history of Hezbollah, writes, "From 1982 through the mid-1980s it was less an organization than a cabal."[3] The authority on suicide bombing, Robert Pape, describes Hezbollah during this period as a "loose federation of militant Shia groups."[4] Details on membership and leadership are blurry, as is the role of Iran, which some see as the puppet master of its proxies in Lebanon.

As the organization of Hezbollah gelled, it was headed by two of its founders from 1985 to 1992, when an Israeli targeted strike killed the second. Following his death, Hassan Nassrallah, a Shia religious scholar and activist, was chosen secretary general. He retains this top post to this day.

In 1985, Hezbollah published a manifesto declaring its goals, phrased in terms of ending colonial influence and imperialism, citing particularly Israel, United States, and France as threats. The manifesto decried the horror of the Israeli invasion of 1982, lamented the slaughter at Sabra and Shatila, and broiled at the lack of international sanctions against the perpetrators. The manifesto concluded by announcing that violence was the only proper response: "Thus, we have seen that aggression can be repelled only with sacrifice and dignity gained only with the sacrifice of blood, and that freedom is not given but regained with the sacrifice of both heart and soul."[5] The tone of the manifesto is strongly Islamist and sees Iran and its leader, Khomeini, as an example of resistance to the West. "Imam Khomeini . . . has repeatedly stressed that America is the reason for all our catastrophes and the source of all malice. By fighting it, we are only exercising our legitimate right to defend our Islam and the dignity of our nation."[6] But as shown in Chapter 8, Hezbollah's immediate enemy was Israel, and Hezbollah pressed for its elimination.[7]

Acts of Terror
Hezbollah is credited with a long list of terrorist attacks in Lebanon, beginning with the November 1982 suicide bombing of an Israeli headquarters in Tyre that killed seventy-five. Hezbollah was not the only Lebanese group to employ suicide bombers; it probably carried out less than a third, with the rest being the work of Shia Amal and secular nationalist groups, including the suicide car bombing by Sana'a Mehaidli in 1985.

The Beirut bombings of the U.S. embassy in April 1983 and the Marine barracks in October of that year demonstrate some of the difficulties involved when trying to ascribe responsibility for terrorist attacks. The Islamic Jihad Organization took credit for both attacks. But the authoritative journalist Robin Wright and others consider "Islamic Jihad" as simply a nom de guerre adopted by Hezbollah operatives.[8] Yet Robert Baer, a CIA agent knowledgeable about Lebanon, has insisted: "[Hezbollah] didn't do the US Embassy in 1983 or the Marines. It was the Iranians."[9]

Hezbollah has continued terrorist attacks during its over thirty-year career. Many credit it with the 1984 suicide truck bombing of the new U.S. embassy. In June 1985, Hezbollah cadres hijacked TWA flight 847, flying between Athens and Rome with 147 passengers and crew—an act of international terrorism in which one passenger, a U.S. Navy sailor, Robert Stethem, was killed.

The years from 1982 through 1992 also witnessed nearly 100 kidnappings of foreigners in Lebanon; journalists labeled this the "Hostage Crisis." Norton credits "groups linked to Hezbollah" with kidnapping "dozens of foreigners."[10] While some kidnappings were undertaken for ransom, most were politically driven. Terry Anderson, correspondent for the Associated Press, holds the unenviable distinction of having been held for the longest period—from 16 March 1985 to 4 December 1991, nearly seven years.

Hezbollah operations were not restricted to Lebanon. The Israeli embassy in Buenos Aires, Argentina, was bombed on 17 March 1992 and another deadly terrorist attack struck a Jewish Community Center there on 18 July 1994, killing eighty-five and injuring hundreds. There is controversy over who actually carried out these attacks, but the Argentine government holds Hezbollah and Iran responsible. A day after that on the community center, a bomb brought down Ala Chiricanas flight 901 as it was flying from Colón, Panama, to Panama City. It is alleged that this was also the work of Hezbollah.

At War with Israel
Above all, Hezbollah focused on Israeli forces in Lebanon. It combined terrorism with what can be best considered as insurgency. Hezbollah attacks were so frequent during 1984 that Israeli soldiers were dying at the rate of one every three days, a rate that shook the Israelis. In July 1993, Israel and Hezbollah reached an oral agreement brokered by the United States: Israelis would not strike civilian targets and resistance groups would restrict their actions to Israeli armed forces in the Security Zone.

The agreement reduced but did not eliminate civilian casualties. In early April 1996, Hezbollah fired Katyusha rockets into Israel in retaliation for the killings of Lebanese civilians by Israeli troops. Although these rockets killed no one, Israel retaliated with a major attack, Operation Grapes of Wrath, killing over 150 Lebanese civilians and wounding 350 others. The most egregious attack during the operation was the Israeli shelling of a United Nations compound in the Lebanese village of Qana on 16 April. This bombardment killed 106 and wounded another 116; four Fijian UN peacekeepers were among the casualties. In 2007 Norton wrote that "no incident in recent memory has inspired more hatred for the Jewish state than the Qana attack."[11] Bin Laden would include a reference to Qana in his 1996 *fatwa*.

Human Rights Watch calculates that during the years from the invasion of Lebanon by the IDF in June 1982 until its withdrawal from the Security Zone in May 2000, at least 500 Lebanese and Palestinian civilians were killed in southern Lebanon, as compared to fewer than seventeen Israel civilians struck down along the Lebanese border during the same period. The disparity between Israeli casualties and those of its enemies would be issues in Islamist literature, as we shall see in the case of Hamas discussed below.

Preparation and Politics
Through the years of Israeli occupation and after, Hezbollah provided relief and social services for the Lebanese Shia community. The government of Lebanon itself has historically offered minimal social services. Hezbollah fills in by creating schools, clinics, and hospitals. In addition, it funds repairs or reconstruction of homes destroyed in the fighting. On top of this, from 1984 it began offering small loans through a program called Qard al-Hassan, "good loan," which now issues roughly 750 loans each month. Hezbollah receives funding from Iran that has grown to as much as $2 million annually, and some of this largess is passed on to Shia civilians.[12] Hezbollah cultivates community support through its acts of aid and charity. Thus cultivation of community support has served some of the same purpose as the political education advocated by Mao: it is a valuable way to gain and maintain the good will of the population upon which a successful revolutionary armed struggle depends. And it fosters a strategy of evolution.

When Mao argued that the revolution must begin by winning over the people, who would provide the sea of support required by guerrillas, he was advocating the cultivation of community support. As discussed in Chapter 8, the theory of focoism downplayed this process of preparation, but it returned as an important element of terrorism for the third wave. The contrast is that while Mao saw preparation as preceding the armed struggle, Islamists have used it more to secure continued support during the fighting. (See the Appendix for Figure A.1, a graphic displaying terrorist strategies and including the role of creating and maintaining community support.)

Enjoying considerable popularity, as well as military force, Hezbollah abandoned its earlier position of eschewing the political system and entered the political fray in 1992, winning two seats in the 128-seat Lebanese National Assembly. It can be argued whether this is best understood as Hezbollah becoming part of the regular political process or evolving from a terrorist "group" toward a state within a state. In 2009, the most recent full election, it garnered twelve seats. It joined the political coalition, the 8 March Alliance, which held power from June 2011 to March 2013. In the world of shifting alliances that is Lebanese politics, Hezbollah has maneuvered well. Daniel Byman, the current research director of the Center for Middle East Policy at the Brookings Institution, has declared that Hezbollah is "a very skilled terrorist group, it's a very formidable guerilla organization, it's the most powerful single political movement in Lebanon, and it's a large social provider."[13]

2006 Lebanon War
Things were more peaceful on the Israeli-Lebanese border after Israel's withdrawal, but tensions grew again between Israel and Hezbollah. Following Hezbollah raids and rockets in May and June 2006, full-scale fighting broke out again on 13 July, when ground forces of the IDF drove into southern Lebanon, as the navy blockaded the Lebanese coast and the air force hit targets throughout the troubled country. Though both sides had been spoiling for a fight, both got more than they had bargained for. Hezbollah held well-placed defensive positions manned by cadres who died rather than surrender. They could not maneuver, but they made the Israelis pay a price that the invaders did not expect. Not long after the war, Brigadier General Guy Zur, the commander of the 162nd Division, one of the formations that carried out the incursion, grudgingly praised Hezbollah: "This is by far the greatest guerrilla group in the world."[14] This war was certainly asymmetrical, but it was not a terrorist campaign.

The performance of the IDF was not up to previous standards. This is thought to have been the consequence of devoting long years to policing the occupied territories, causing the IDF to neglect practicing the skills and coordination required in conventional warfare. An Israeli commission, empaneled after the war, concluded that Israeli political and military leaders were guilty of "grave failings" that had created a situation in which "a semi-military organization of a few thousand men resisted, for a few weeks, the strongest army in the Middle East, which enjoyed full air superiority and size and technological advantages."[15]

If the Israelis did not achieve the walkover they expected, Hezbollah did not expect such a large and destructive Israeli campaign. There were those in Lebanon who sharply criticized Hezbollah for bringing on such a storm. Human Rights Watch counted 1,109 Lebanese dead and 4,399 injured, figures that include noncombatants as well as combatants. One million people were displaced. Israeli losses included twelve IDF soldiers and forty-three civilians killed with "hundreds" of Israeli civilians wounded.[16] Norton concluded that, despite the costs, "since the 2006 war with Israel, an overwhelming majority of the Shia have embraced Hezbollah as the defender of their community."[17]

Hezbollah issued a new manifesto in November 2009, its first such pronouncement since 1985. This was a more mature declaration in substance and tone. It attacked sectarianism and preached Lebanese unity. Reflecting Hezbollah's evolved reality, the manifesto centered on Lebanon: "Lebanon is our homeland and the homeland of our fathers, ancestors. It's also the homeland of our children, grandchildren, and the coming generations. It is the country to which we have given our most precious sacrifices for its sovereignty and pride, dignity and liberation."[18] Not surprisingly, it still railed against Israel, condemned American policy, and insisted on the liberation of Palestine. But importantly, the Hezbollah declaration was national, not global, and less strident in its Islamist principles than the manifesto of 1985.

The war of 2006 did not solve anything, but it further established Hezbollah as Israel's most inveterate enemy. The *Christian Science Monitor* reported in 2014 that General Benny Gantz, then chief of staff of the IDF, declared that "Hezbollah is like a state" and only few militaries have more firepower.

Hezbollah has gone from a terrorist cabal to a force that can fight with considerable parity on its chosen ground against one of the world's most impressive military powers. Hezbollah's evolution is both military and political. Since the Shia community amounts to only about a quarter of the population of Lebanon, Hezbollah would be unwise to try to dominate Lebanon as a whole, but it has successfully become a state within a state in the areas it dominates. It even maintains a kind of foreign policy, not only in its hostile relations with Israel, but through its armed intervention in the Syrian Civil War that followed the Arab Spring of 2011.

Its success and its dependence on Iran have led the latter to call on Hezbollah to field troops in Syria to support Bashar al-Assad. It has also deployed fighters to Yemen and Nigeria. So, while maintaining its focus on Lebanon, Hezbollah has become a factor beyond its home ground.

HAMAS

When we left the history of the Israeli–Palestinian conflict in Chapter 7, the Israelis had invaded Lebanon and exiled the PLO leadership from Lebanon to Tunisia. Now we shift our focus to Hamas, a radical Islamist Palestinian terrorist group, from its beginning during the First Intifada in 1988 to the 2014 Gaza conflict. Hamas has much in common with Hezbollah, including Islamist ideology and enmity with Israel; however, Hamas has a very different history.

Hamas's Islamist Roots

Hamas emerged from a service-based organization that existed for fifteen years before Hamas took up arms in the First Intifada. In fact, one can trace the lineage of Hamas back to the years immediately after World War II, when the Egypt-based Muslim Brotherhood set up branches in Palestine. The Israeli War of Liberation left Gaza in Egyptian hands, and the Brotherhood stayed. Sheikh Ahmed Yassin, pivotal to the rise of Hamas, was born in the Palestinian village near Ashkelon and came to Gaza as a refugee. A boyhood accident left him a wheelchair-bound quadriplegic for the rest of his life. He became involved with the Brotherhood in his youth. The rise of pan-Arabism did not attract Yassin; his hopes for Palestinian liberation and independence grew from religious, not secular, roots. After the wars of 1967 and 1973, the Brotherhood's appeal to Islam as the more promising path to Palestinian political redemption attracted greater numbers of followers.

In 1973 Yassin and some likeminded comrades set up an Islamic charity, al-Mujamma' al-Islami (The Islamic Center). This organization rejected the secular PLO, with its Marxist cast, and devoted itself to religious and social work, founding mosques, schools, and clinics and granting loans and scholarships. Yassin fervently desired Palestinian liberation, but he was not ready to confront Israel militarily. As an influential Gaza nationalist commented: "They emphasized that the only path to liberation was through the realization of *an Islamic state*. Even at this stage they were voicing political ideas—they belittled fighting the occupation."[19]

However, neither the spiritual goals nor the welfare mission of Mujamma kept it from employing violent means to combat secularism and the PLO in Gaza. Mujamma cadres resorted to physical attacks on what they regarded as un-Islamic behavior by individuals and businesses, including mob action against bars, cafés, and movie theaters. Mujamma also took control of the new Islamic University of Gaza. Mujamma supporters ousted the president of the university, who was a Fatah loyalist and enforced quranic codes. Sexes were strictly segregated and dress codes imposed, including the wearing of "*sharia* dress" by women.

Regarding it as a rival to the PLO, the Israelis tolerated Mujamma in the time-honored practice of divide and rule. In 1978, Israel officially recognized Mujamma, which allowed it to expand its activities. Thanks to Yassin's patience in confronting Israel, the beneficence of Mujamma succeeded in cultivating community support and, eventually, aiding a strategy of evolution.

The First Intifada
In 1987 incidents in Gaza ignited the First Intifada. On 8 December an IDF tank transporter truck plowed into a line of cars, killing four Palestinians and injuring seven near a refugee camp in Gaza. While Israeli news proclaimed this an accident, many Palestinians regarded it as an act of revenge for the fatal stabbing of an Israeli in Gaza two days earlier. Violent Palestinian protests began on 9 December; it was the start of the First Intifada, which would continue until preliminary peace talks began in Madrid during the fall of 1991.

Several different Palestinian organizations participated in the First Intifada. When the uprising broke out in the West Bank as well as Gaza, the PLO was still headquartered in Tunis. As the resistance spread, the PLO played catchup rather than taking the lead. That fell to the United National Command (UNC), a bottom-up organization put together for this rebellion. At first the PLO favored *armed* resistance, but Palestinians in the streets found that what stymied Israeli forces most were attacks by groups armed only with rocks and bottles. These put Israel in the role of the "heavy." Israel, which had courted the image of the diminutive David bravely confronting the Arab Goliath, was now the bedeviled giant itself.

Faced with this new reality, Yitzhak Rabin, then serving as minister of defense, exclaimed to his colleagues, "This Intifada, what tanks and warplanes couldn't do to us, women demonstrating and stones did, because the world cannot tolerate seeing these demonstrations."[20]

As the rebellion gained momentum, Yassin reversed his policy of not openly resisting Israeli occupation in Gaza, and Hamas, formally the Islamic Resistance Movement, emerged from the Muslim Brotherhood and Mujamma. The preface of Hamas's Covenant, or Charter, of 18 August 1988, announces its cause and does so by quoting the founder of the Muslim Brotherhood, Hassan al-Banna: "Israel will exist and will continue to exist until Islam will obliterate it, just as it obliterated others before it."[21]

Echoing Azzam, the Covenant commands, "The day that enemies usurp part of Muslim land, jihad becomes the individual duty of every Muslim." Thus, "the question of the liberation of Palestine is bound to three circles: the Palestinian circle, the Arab circle, and the Islamic circle. Each of these circles has its role in the struggle against Zionism." The Covenant proclaims that Hamas shares the goal of a liberated Palestine with the PLO, but cannot accept the latter's secular nationalism: "Secularism completely contradicts religious ideology." Hamas must oppose the PLO, but the real enemy is Jewish Israel, the Zionists: "Their plan is embodied in the 'Protocols of the Elders of Zion.'"

Only in 1989 did Hamas undertake its first actual attacks, which included kidnapping and then killing two Israeli soldiers. Israel responded by outlawing Hamas and rounding up 300 cadres and supporters, Sheikh Yassin being one of them. He would not be released until 1997. Hamas created a special military wing, the Izz al-Din al-Qassam Brigades, in 1991; these were named after the Palestinian hero al-Qassam, who fought against the Zionist settlement of Israel and died in a firefight with British police in 1935. The al-Qassam Brigades operate with considerable independence from Hamas's leadership.

Hamas and its al-Qassam Brigades were just coming on line as a military force when negotiations between the Israeli government and the PLO began tentatively in Madrid from 30 October to 1 November 1991; bilateral and multilateral talks followed this opening. Weakened by its support of Iraq and by the demise of the Soviet Union, its old sponsor, the PLO sought to regain what leverage it could from the First Intifada.

Eventually negotiations led to important agreements concluded at Oslo during August and September 1993. In an exchange of letters on 9 September, the PLO recognized the right of the Israeli state "to exist in peace and security," and Israel accepted the PLO as "the representative of the Palestinian people."[22] Within days, President Bill Clinton hosted Yitzak Rabin and Yasser Arafat at the White House for the official ceremony accepting the Oslo I Accord, an interim agreement designed to make progress toward Palestinian self-government.

Rabin, Shimon Peres, and Arafat won the 1994 Nobel Peace Prize for their efforts, just as Begin and Sadat had sixteen years before. So, in 1994, Arafat returned from his exile in Tunis to Gaza. The Palestinian Authority (PA) was created as the instrument of Palestinian self-government, and Arafat set up his headquarters at Ramallah on the West Bank.

Casualty figures for the First Intifada vary.[23] Israeli forces killed about 1,200 Palestinians, a number that includes 200 under the age of sixteen. Tens of thousands of Palestinians were wounded. In addition, nearly 1,000 Palestinians were killed by other Palestinians who believed their victims to be political rivals or to have collaborated with the Israelis. Israeli losses were much smaller. The Ministry of Foreign Affairs puts the number of Israelis killed at 200, while the Israeli human rights group B'Tselem lists 179. During the same period 3,100 were injured. Characteristically, Palestinian losses far surpassed those of Israelis. Palestinians point to casualty figures to buttress their portrayal of the Israelis as cruel oppressors.

Continuing the Oslo Process
Hamas did not support the negotiations between the PLO and Israel. The two resistance organizations were so locked in struggle that one of Yassin's earliest followers, Mahmoud Zahar, asserted, "We'll defend ourselves against Israel and the PLO."[24]

But opposition to the Oslo I Accord also came from Israeli religious radicals. Early on the morning of 25 February 1994, Baruch Goldstein, a Jewish religious extremist, dressed in his reserve officer's uniform and carrying his assault rifle, entered a section of the Cave of the Patriarchs at Hebron reserved for Muslim prayer. Goldstein opened fire, massacring twenty-nine and wounding 125 before his rifle jammed and he was seized and beaten to death. Scholars Ami Pedahzur and Arie Perliger insist that Goldstein was not a lone-wolf terrorist, but a member of an organization and a community entirely set against concessions to the PLO.[25] Reflecting the views of such extremists, Rabbi Yaacov Perrin proclaimed in his funeral eulogy for Goldstein, "One million Arabs are not worth a Jewish fingernail."[26]

Hamas responded to the massacre at Hebron by adopting terrorist stratagems that were intended both to *outbid* the PLO in Palestinian eyes and to *spoil* the Oslo process. After the traditional forty-day mourning period for those who died, Hamas struck at the Israeli town of Afula on 6 April 1994. There a suicide bomber killed eight Israelis and wounded another thirty-four. Suicide bombing became a characteristic form of violence by the al-Qassam Brigades in their attempt to assassinate the Oslo process.

After the Cave of the Patriarchs massacre, Rabin struggled forward in pursuit of a lasting peace settlement. As part of that effort, he addressed a peace rally on 4 November 1995, where Yigal Amir, an Orthodox Jew totally opposed to the Oslo process, gunned down Rabin. Amir's opposition typified the radical religious extreme, and although he was not part of any established group, he was nonetheless a terrorist who had put together a small group bent on assassinating Rabin.

Hamas attacks continued. In a notably deadly set of attacks during 1996, Hamas suicide bombers twice struck No. 18 busses on Jaffa Road in Jerusalem: the 25 February 1996 bombing killed twenty-six Israelis and injured forty-eight more, and the second attack killed nineteen Israelis and injured seven exactly a week later, on 3 March.

The last major attempts to achieve a two-state solution in line with Oslo came at the Camp David Summit, 11–25 July 2000, and at the Taba Summit, 12–27 January 2001. The Israelis, led by Prime Minister Ehud Barak, put what they regarded as major concessions on the table and claim Arafat was intransigent. Arafat insisted that the PLO could not accept some of the terms, such as the Israeli refusal to grant the PLO sovereignty in East Jerusalem. The Israeli and American press largely regarded Camp David as another opportunity squandered by the Palestinians. However, Shlomo Ben Ami, the foreign minister of Israel at the time, later stated in an interview, "Camp David was not the missed opportunity for the Palestinians, and if I were a Palestinian I would have rejected Camp David, as well."[27]

The Second Intifada

On 28 September 2000, just two months after the Camp David Summit collapsed, Israeli hard-liner Ariel Sharon conducted a visit to the Temple Mount, or the Haram al-Sharif, by a delegation of rightist Likud Party members, with about 1,000 Israeli police as security. In Palestinian memory, Sharon would be forever associated with the Sabra and Shatila massacres of refugees in 1982, and his presence at this revered Muslim site, with the Dome of the Rock and the al-Aqsa mosque, was incendiary. Tensions skyrocketed and the growing Palestinian crowd threw rocks at the police, who responded with rubber bullets and tear gas. The Second Intifada ignited, to burn through 2005. On 6 February 2001, Sharon was elected prime minister, to remain in office for the rest of the Second Intifada.

It is still debated where blame for starting the Second Intifada lies. Palestinians point to the provocative act of Sharon, and there is no question that his visit to the Haram al-Sharif was incendiary. On the other side, there is the argument that the PLO was looking to launch another intifada after the failure of Camp David, and Sharon's actions were simply an excuse to begin the struggle. Among the testimony that buttresses the latter charge is that of Arafat's own widow, who in 2012 stated that immediately after returning from Camp David her husband told her that he had resolved to start another intifada.[28] A commission created in 2001 and chaired by George Mitchell, who had played a positive role in the Good Friday Agreement, could reach no definitive conclusions as to the existence of plans before the opening shots. However, it pointed to the poisoned atmosphere in which the violence began and then so rapidly escalated: "Amid rising anger, fear, and mistrust, each side assumed the worst about the other and acted accordingly."[29]

The First Intifada had begun from the bottom up, and its iconic violence pitted unarmed youths against tanks. In contrast, the Second Intifada was directed from the start by the PLO and Hamas, and the deadliest agents of Palestinian violence were suicide bombers. The Israeli Security Agency reported 151 suicide bombings. A study based on a sample of 135 of these attacks by Palestinians during the Second Intifada ascribes fifty-four, or 39.9 percent, to Hamas, 25.7 percent to Palestinian Islamic Jihad, 26.4 percent to Fatah, and 5.4 percent to the PFLP. In 2001 alone, Hamas carried out a series of suicide bombings that killed twenty-one at a Tel Aviv disco (1 June), fifteen at a Sbarro Pizzeria in Jerusalem (9 August), and eleven at Ben Yehuda Street pedestrian mall in Jerusalem (1 December). The greatest annual toll of bombings plagued 2002, with fifty-five.[30] As described at the start of this chapter, on 27 March 2002 a Hamas suicide bomber killed thirty Israelis at a Seder in Netanya. In response to this Passover Massacre, the IDF undertook Operation Defensive Shield, from 29 March to 7 May. The casualties were again disproportionate during this large-scale operation: 30 Israelis were killed and about 500 Palestinians.[31]

Along with the suicide bombing, the rocket attack became a signature of Hamas. In September 2001, Hamas fired the first of its homemade Qassam rockets from Gaza into Israel. As one student remarked to author David Pratt, "Why should we be the only ones who live in fear? With these rockets, the Israelis feel fear, too. We have to live in peace together, or live in fear together."[32] Hamas was not the only group firing rockets, but it was the most prolific. During 2003 and 2004 a total barrage of 450 Qassam rocket attacks struck Israel.

Israel responded to the rocket attacks with Operation Days of Penitence, 29 September—16 October 2004. The IDF brought not only its full array of weaponry, but armored bulldozers to flatten homes it claimed were being used by Hamas cadres. According to B'Tselem, 133 Palestinians were killed by the IDF, including about fifty civilians, about half of whom were children under age eighteen.[33] During the operation, a single Israeli soldier was killed. Also, the IDF demolished or severely damaged 235 homes in the north. The pattern of Israeli incursions into Gaza as retaliation and retribution for Hamas violence was set, and they would come again in 2008–2009, 2012, and 2014.

Israelis also employed the tactic of targeted killing, essentially assassination. Among those targeted were high-ranking leaders of Hamas. Ahmed Yassin, his two bodyguards, and nine others died in the blasts of helicopter-fired Hellfire missiles on 22 March 2004, and less than a month later his successor as the head of Hamas, Abdel Aziz Rantissi, was killed by Israeli missiles. According to B'Tselem, in the ten years following 27 September 2002, 240 Palestinians killed "were targets of assassinations."[34]

Authorities debate when the Second Intifada ended, but the best case points to the downturn in the conflict during 2005. Yasser Arafat became ill and died in a Paris hospital on 11 November 2004, and with his death the PLO suffered not only the loss of its leader, but also a lessening of its leverage. In February 2005, the newly elected president of the PA, Mahmoud Abbas, met with Ariel Sharon, President Hosni Mubarak of Egypt, and King Abdullah II of Jordan at the Sharm el-Sheikh Summit. Abbas and Sharon announced an end to violence between their peoples.

Between 29 September 2000 and 15 January 2005, about 3,200 Palestinians and 950 Israelis died as a result of the Second Intifada.[35] Beyond the cost in dead and wounded, the Second Intifada witnessed the destruction and damaging of Palestinian homes and property. From October 2000 through January 2005, Israeli forces destroyed 664 houses as punishment of Palestinians, leaving 4,182 people homeless.[36] Critics charge that the destruction of the homes of terrorists' families or of local communities where terrorist resided amounts to collective punishment, which is condemned by international law. If the Israeli government ordered the destruction of these homes as punishments against innocent individuals, not terrorists themselves, in order to intimidate other such families and communities, is it unreasonable to regard these acts of destruction as state/military terrorism by Israel? Only at the end of the Second Intifada, on 17 February 2005, did Israelis officially declare they would no longer engage in the punitive demolition of homes. However, the Israelis resurrected the policy of demolitions in the summer of 2014.

At the start of the Second Intifada, the Israelis also reduced Gaza International Airport to ruins and destroyed Gaza Seaport, then under construction. Neither has been rebuilt.

In August 2005, Israel unilaterally withdrew its Jewish settlers and troops from the Gaza Strip, dismantling the twenty-one Israeli settlements there. This disengagement from Gaza was not a concession to the Palestinians but part of a complicated plan to concentrate Israeli population in territory where Israel intended to maintain Jewish demographic dominance. Gaza was viewed as a wholly Palestinian enclave to be boxed in.

Hamas Victory in Gaza, 2005–2008
Hamas and Fatah had been feuding over the proper course of Palestine liberation since Mujamma battled Fatah for influence in Gaza during the 1970s. Hamas believed Salafist Islam to be fundamental to Palestin-

ian success, and considered Fatah to be religiously null and financially corrupt. Attesting to the moral superiority of Hamas, one of its stalwarts boasted: "We are clean, we actually fight the occupation when they raid our homes and those of our neighbors . . . we are the true defenders."[37]

In April 2005 Hamas and Fatah agreed to reform the PLO, and Hamas, which had boycotted electoral politics before, decided to run candidates in the May 2005 PA municipal elections. Hamas did well in Gaza. Then Hamas scored an utterly unexpected success, winning a majority of the seats in the PA parliamentary elections of January 2006.

What was welcomed as a surprise for Hamas struck Israel and the "Quartet" of the UN, the European Union, the United States, and Russia as a disaster. The Quartet had been underwriting the PA in hopes of resolving the Israeli–Palestinian conflict. Now the Quartet withdrew aid and refused to reinstate it unless Hamas agreed to recognize Israel, renounce violence, and uphold commitments agreed to by previous PA regimes. Hamas would not. Hamas and Fatah battled each other in words and actions, a crisis that escalated until 10–15 June 2007, when Hamas staged a coup, called by some the Battle of Gaza, taking over the Strip by coordinated and deadly attacks. PA president Abbas declared an emergency and expelled the Hamas prime minster. Essentially, the West Bank under Fatah separated from Hamas-held Gaza. Israel and Egypt blockaded Gaza, and that blockade continues.

Certainly by 2005–2006, Hamas, like Hezbollah, had evolved into a political entity that that must be considered a state, or proto-state, governing Gaza and mounting military forces—al-Qassam Brigades and regular security forces within Gaza. To call it a "terrorist group" confuses its real identity. However, its turn to politics was not a turn away from violence. As Jamila al-Shanti, a leading Hamas woman cadre, commented, "The difference between us and Sinn Fein is that when we entered the election we entered it with the intention of sheltering the [armed] resistance. It wasn't a choice between resistance and politics, it was to protect the resistance."[38]

Operation Cast Lead, 2008–2009
Hamas and Israel were at a kind of standoff through 2007 and 2008, but in late December 2008, Palestinians in Gaza began bombarding Israel with rockets, with more than sixty launched on 24 December alone.

Hamas employed its Qassam rockets as well as new Grad rockets, originally a Soviet design, with a range of twenty kilometers. This sparked a major reprisal, Operation Cast Lead, on 27 December, when air strikes targeted installations across the Gaza Strip. IDF ground forces then invaded on 3 January 2009, and fighting ended with an Israeli ceasefire on 18 January, after which the IDF withdrew. The casualties in Operation Cast Lead were even more disproportionate than usual. The Israelis lost thirteen, of whom four fell to friendly fire, while B'Tselem lists 1,391 Palestinians killed in Gaza, of whom 110 were women and 344 were minors; of this last category only twenty-two were combatants.[39] The contrast in casualties drew criticism. The Report of the United Nations Fact Finding Mission on the Gaza Conflict, known as the Goldstone Report after its lead author, charged Israel with "grave breaches of the . . . Geneva Convention" for the willful "targeting and arbitrary killing of Palestinian civilians."[40]

Once again Israel chose to meet a terrorist threat with a conventional response that generated mass casualties. By doing so the Israelis had the satisfaction of revenge and the hope of deterrence, while their government retained support from a population that wanted retribution. However, Hamas gained by advertising the callous brutality of the Israelis, much as the FLN had provoked the French retaliation to the same purpose. In a sense, a strong response by Israel served the purposes of both Israel and Hamas in playing to their own domestic audiences and, for Hamas, a transnational audience as well.

Pillar of Defense and Protective Edge, 2012–2014
The Israelis staged Operation Pillar of Defense, another invasion of Gaza, from 14 to 21 November 2012. In June, the kidnapping and murder of three Israeli boys on the West Bank spiked tensions; the Israelis saw this as a Hamas attack. However, the accelerating pace of rocket attacks from Gaza was more fundamental. During 2010, Palestinians fired 146 rockets into Israel, a figure that climbed dramatically to 418 in 2011 and rose to 422 for the first ten months of 2012.[41] These all qualify as terrorist attacks. Operation Pillar of Defense was less intense than Cast Lead. The IDF killed 167 Palestinians, including at least sixty-two combatants and seven who were targeted for assassination by the Israelis.[42] The IDF lost two soldiers during the operation, and four Israeli civilians were killed.

In 2011 the Israelis brought a new missile defense system on line. Given the name Iron Dome, it has proven remarkably effective at intercepting short-range missiles headed for populated areas. The system was developed by the Israelis, and the United States provided as much as $1 billion of funding for Iron Dome by 2014.

Not long after Pillar of Defense, both sides were accusing one another of breaking the ceasefire that ended that operation. Tensions ratcheted up again in 2014. On 5 March, Israeli naval vessels captured a ship carrying dozens of Syrian-made M-302 rockets, meant for Hamas. The M-302 has a range of over sixty miles, putting Tel Aviv well within striking distance of Gaza. On 12 March, a barrage of sixty less advanced rockets was fired into southern Israel by Palestinian Islamic Jihad in revenge for the IDF killing three of his cadres. And once again, rocket fire greatly increased in early July.

On 8 July, the Israeli Operation Protective Edge began and continued until 26 August, at which point 2,220 Palestinians had perished. The IDF lost sixty-six soldiers; four Israeli civilians also died, and one foreigner.[43] Once again much was reduced to rubble, and accusations of war crimes committed by the IDF and by Hamas shot back and forth like artillery barrages. Both sides regarded the conflict as a victory, Israel because it had punished Hamas for its attacks and Hamas because it had demonstrated that it remained defiant and undeterred.

HAMASTAN AND HEZBOLLAH

From its beginning, Hamas has held to its principle that all of Palestine by rights should be Muslim land, not ruled by a Jewish population. The one modification to its program has been a willingness to consider a long-term truce in return for several conditions, notably the creation of a Palestinian state with all lands that Israel occupied in 1967: the entire West Bank, the Gaza Strip, and East Jerusalem. This Israel will not do. Of course, the PLO has already reached compromises with Israel, including recognizing Israel as a legitimate state, and Hamas ridiculed Fatah for doing so.

When Hamas emerged from Mujamma and the Islamic Brotherhood, it was a terrorist group taking part in, but not dominating, the First Intifada. A rival of the PLO, Hamas was clearly not its equal. Twenty years later, it faced off against the PLO in elections and in open combat, and took over the Gaza Strip as its own territory. Israeli prime minister Benjamin Netanyahu refers to Gaza with disdain as "Hamastan," a separate country.

To a degree Hamas has paralleled Hezbollah, in that both have grown and shown surprising staying power. In their 2007 study of Hamas, Beverley Milton-Edwards and Stephen Farrell listed the combined strength of the al-Qassam Brigades and the Hamas Executive Forces at perhaps 16,000.[44] A more recent source estimates 20,000–40,000.[45] Still, while the al-Qassam Brigades are capable of bloodying the Israelis and inciting them into marshaling their impressive military might to invade Gaza, Hamas lacks the ability to either break the blockade or repel the IDF. Hezbollah is better able to resist the IDF effectively, as Israeli testimony confirms. In 2016, Haaretz credited Hezbollah with 45,000 fighters, 21,000 of them "in regular service."[46] Hamas has become the Palestinian state in Gaza; Hezbollah has become a state within a state in its Lebanese areas and a major player in the government of Lebanon as a whole. To call either a mere "group" distorts reality.

Both Hamas and Hezbollah elevated the level of warfare they conduct, entered the political system, and achieved some of their goals. I would say that both adopted strategies of evolution, although the interplay of circumstance, opportunity, and conscious design differs. Hezbollah has been better in regularizing and legitimating its power; Hamas is more rogue. They both fight asymmetrical wars with Israel. Hezbollah has exploited the topography of southern Lebanon to take on the IDF. Hamas fights with urban tactics and its rockets. Israel has won engagements against both, but it has not been able to eliminate them.

There is no way to predict where this will lead. Hamas will continue to exist in Gaza unless the Israelis decide to eradicate it, but this can only be done at a heavy price internationally. Hezbollah has done well in Lebanon and, again, even if Israel were able to eliminate it, the price would probably be more than the Israelis are willing to pay. And Israel has a poor history in Lebanon.

Hamas and Hezbollah have been regional in focus and in resources, although, in recent years, Hezbollah has proven itself useful to Iran outside the borders of Lebanon. We must now turn to Islamist terrorists who have adopted global scopes, "global" either in identifying and attacking enemies or in pursuit of recruits and resources.

CHAPTER ELEVEN

Global Jihad

AL-QAEDA AND THE ISLAMIC STATE

FIGURE 11.1. New York City tabloids featured screenshots from the video showing the beheading of James Foley by an ISIS "monster." Both papers screamed "SAVAGES," but ISIS dominated the news cycle as it had intended. Richard Levine/Alamy Stock Photo.

ON 19 AUGUST 2014, the Islamic State (IS) posted a video of the beheading of James Foley to YouTube. Entitled "A Message to America," the video is staged, but the execution is nonetheless real.[1] An American freelance journalist, Foley had been kidnapped in northern Syria on 22 November 2012, most likely by Shabiha, an ethnic militia favorable to president Bashar al-Assad, but Foley changed hands and was held by the IS when he was murdered (Fig. 11.1).

The video begins with a clip of President Barack Obama announcing on 7 August that the United States was beginning air operations against the IS. The killing of Foley is presented as retribution for these U.S. attacks. Clad and hooded in black, the executioner in the video grasps a combat knife. He speaks with an English accent. We believe him to be

289

Mohammed Emwazi, born in Kuwait but raised in the United Kingdom. The press dubbed him "Jihadi John." He stands beside Foley, who is kneeling, handcuffed, and dressed in orange, mimicking the jumpsuits worn by American-held prisoners at Guantanamo Bay.

Foley delivers a long denunciation of the United States: "I call on my friends, family, and loved ones to rise up against my real killers, the U.S. government, for what will happen to me is only a result of their complacency and criminality." He continues, addressing his brother, a USAF officer, "I call on you, John, think about who made the decision to bomb Iraq recently to kill those people whoever they may have been. . . . I died that day, John. When your colleagues dropped that bomb on those people, they signed my death certificate."

Then Jihadi John delivers his own bitter denunciation of America. "You are no longer fighting an insurgency. We are an Islamic army and a state that has been accepted by a large number of Muslims worldwide." Finally, Emwazi grabs Foley and saws at his neck with the knife. The screen goes black. The next images are of Foley's blood-spattered, decapitated head, lying on the back of his lifeless body.

The video ends with Jihadi John holding the collar of still another kneeling prisoner in orange, Steven Sotloff, and threatening, "The life of this American citizen, Obama, depends on your next decision." A video of Sotloff's beheading would be discovered on 2 September.

The brazen execution of James Foley horrified us. But the video won for the IS, still mainly called ISIS (the Islamic State of Iraq and Syria), the kind of notoriety it craved, trumpeting itself and its message. The American media condemned ISIS as "monsters" and "savages," but ISIS ultraviolence took the news cycle hostage. And what we saw as abominable the IS leadership regarded as useful in spreading fear and outrage among its enemies, while also attracting potential radical recruits to the new, self-proclaimed caliphate.

A U.S. air strike killed Jihadi John in November 2015, but that stopped nothing but one heartless heart. He was easily replaced; the IS was a legion of executioners.

This chapter describes the metamorphosis of two radical Islamist terrorist groups of the third wave, al-Qaeda and the Islamic State. They are related, the IS being an outgrowth of al-Qaeda, but they are not the same. In the following pages, we will explore their similarities and differences, born of ideology, history, and personality.

GLOBAL ISLAMIST STRUGGLE AND THE CALIPHATE

The fundamentals of the Islamist ideology discussed in Chapter 9 remain essential to al-Qaeda and the Islamic State. However, we need to consider additional ideological developments when dealing with al-Qaeda and the IS. These include 1) differing emphases on the global scope of radical Islamist jihad and 2) development of self-conscious theories of the way in which Islamist terrorist groups can evolve into large state or state-like entities.

Global Scope: Conflict and Participation

The literature on al-Qaeda and the Islamic State often contrasts the global jihad pursued by al-Qaeda with the "jihad-in-one-state" thrust of the IS and its earlier avatars. However, both al-Qaeda and the IS have thought and acted with a *global scope*: global conflict for al-Qaeda and global participation for the IS.

As noted in Chapter 9, Muhammed abd-al-Salam Faraj, in his *The Neglected Duty*, prioritized the "near enemy," *jahili* Muslim regimes, over the "far enemy," unbelievers, which included Israel and Western countries. But al-Qaeda's leader, Osama bin Laden, believed the near enemy, such as the Saudi state, would never fall as long as it enjoyed the support of the most powerful far enemy, the United States. Therefore, he argued for attacking the far enemy first, even though that enemy was a world away from the Middle East. This marked a change from national or regional jihad to global jihad, in the sense of *global conflict*.

Al-Qaeda's shift toward prioritizing the far enemy became public in bin Laden's August 1996 *fatwa* "Declaration of War against the Americans Occupying the Land of the Two Holy Places."[2] This rambling, lengthy document expressed bin Laden's outrage at the presence of U.S. military forces in Saudi Arabia, which he referred to as "the land of the two Holy Places" (Mecca and Medina). He again condemned the Saudi regime, a near enemy. However, he identified the primary task as defeating the Americans, because "the occupying American enemy is the principal and the main cause of the situation. Therefore, efforts should be concentrated on destroying, fighting and killing the enemy until, by the Grace of Allah, it is completely defeated."

Two years later, bin Laden put out another *fatwa*, this time as part of the "World Islamic Front."[3] This document stressed grievances against the Americans "that are known to everyone": occupation of the Arabian Peninsula, devastation and massacres of the Iraqis, and support for Israel in "its occupation of Jerusalem and murder of Muslims there." The *fatwa* concluded: "All these crimes and sins committed by the Americans are a clear declaration of war on Allah, his messenger, and Muslims." Because this jihad is fought to defend Muslims against those who attack Islam, "the ruling to kill the Americans and their allies—civilians and military—is an individual duty for every Muslim who can do it in any country in which it is possible to do it." Ayman al-Zawahiri, bin Laden's second in command of al-Qaeda, echoed this in his own manifesto, *Knights under the Prophet's Banner* (2001): "This is the stage of the global battle, now that the forces of the disbelievers have united against the mujahideen."[4]

It is true that because of the notoriety of al-Qaeda's 9/11 attack, terrorist groups with narrower focuses chose to associate themselves with al-Qaeda. Marc Sageman, in his study *Leaderless Jihad*, describes this transformation as one from a hierarchical "al-Qaeda Central," run by bin Laden, to one in which al-Qaeda became a franchise, in which al-Qaeda leadership only loosely directed an association of Islamist terrorist groups. He called this "al-Qaeda the social movement." Groups affiliated with al-Qaeda included al-Qaeda in the Arabian Peninsula (AQAP) and al-Qaeda in the Islamic Maghreb (AQIM). Another was al-Qaeda in Iraq (AQI), which would evolve into the IS.

Bin Laden, however, remained concerned with the far enemy in a global conflict.

In contrast to bin Laden's preoccupation with global conflict, the IS and its precursors focused on *global participation*, a concept that predated bin Laden's shift to the far enemy. The primary examples of global participation have been the mujahideen who fought during the Soviet–Afghan War and the recruits who came to the IS from over eighty countries to fight in Iraq and Syria. As discussed in Chapter 9, works by the Jordanian religious scholar Abdullah Azzam, the "father of global jihad," argued that Muslims from *around the world* should unite to defend Muslims under attack *any place in the world*. When, in an internal al-Qaeda memo, he later described the accomplishments of his effort during the Soviet–Afghan War, he listed first and foremost that "it has contributed in transforming the issue of the Islamic Jihad in Afghanistan into an international Islamic one."[5]

This quotation from Azzam clearly points to the fact that global participation was entirely consistent with an emphasis on fighting the near enemy in a localized jihad—quite different from bin Laden's globalization. We will discuss IS global participation at greater length later in the chapter, but it is enough now to distinguish it from global conflict. Both are important aspects of global scope, but I am convinced that global participation will ultimately prove to be more important than a fixation on global conflict.

Certainly, global participation proved to be a major factor in the ability of ISIS to become the IS, to combat near enemies and create its new caliphate. And future jihadis will remember this.

Creating the Caliphate through Regional Jihad
Both al-Qaeda and the precursors of the IS talked of a return of the caliphate. Although al-Qaeda saw this as something coming in the long term, IS precursors demanded it immediately. The result was the proclamation of the Islamic State, and the caliphate, in June 2014. A caliphate is an Islamic government that unites political and religious authority within a territory in the person of a caliph. In addition, it can imply religious authority over Muslims exerted by a caliph well beyond the area of his political control. A caliph must be descended from Muhammad, which the IS leader Abu Bakr al-Baghdadi claims to be. In 1924 the Turkish leader Kemal Ataturk abolished the last generally recognized caliphate, based in Istanbul, but radical Islamists hope to recreate the office. They declare the old boundaries, particularly those imposed after World War I by Great Britain and France, to be invalid. These are to be replaced by a caliphate ruling over a growing domain.

Bin Laden spoke repeatedly of a new caliphate, and he condemned America as the last barrier to its creation. But his caliphate, though desirable, need not be rushed. In July 2005, al-Zawahiri wrote to offer counsel to Abu Musab al-Zarqawi, then head of al-Qaeda in Iraq (AQI), a predecessor of the IS. In this letter he outlined what the Iraqi jihad should be. It must begin by expelling the Americans from Iraq and then creating an emirate, which in time "achieves the level of a caliphate." Then would come further expansion and "the clash with Israel, because Israel was established only to challenge any new Islamic entity."[6] Al-Zawahiri prescribed a long process; al-Zarqawi and his successors fixed on a rapid transformation. That conflict was by nature geographically regional, thus the validity of considering the IS as engaged in regional jihad, as opposed to al-Qaeda's pursuit of global jihad. However, the IS achieved its regional goal by enlisting global participation.

In a chilling prophecy made the same year that al-Zawahiri wrote his letter, Fouad Hussein foresaw six stages leading to ultimate Muslim triumph by 2020. His book *Al-Zarqawi: The Second Generation of Al-Qaeda* is based on interviews with al-Qaeda militants, including al-Zarqawi. Hussein's first stage began with 9/11. In the fourth phase, 2006–2013, al-Qaeda was to cause the fall of Arab governments, and in the fifth, 2013–2016, an Islamist caliphate would be declared. During the sixth, 2016–2020, an Islamist army would carry on a global conflict between Muslims and infidels leading to "definitive victory."[7] When the leader of the IS, Abu Bakr al-Baghdadi, declared the IS a caliphate with himself as the new caliph, Caliph Ibrahim, he was right on Hussein's timeline.

AN ISLAMIST THEORY OF EVOLVING STAGES IN WARFARE

The ideology of al-Qaeda, as further implemented and expedited by the Islamic State, prescribes growth from a small but highly dedicated core of jihadists with grand aspirations to a caliphate with territorial control, large military forces, and great religious authority. The role of terrorism in such growth is best characterized as a strategy of evolution to higher levels of warfare. In framing this strategy, prominent Islamist theorists have been influenced by Western military classics and by writings on revolutionary warfare, including the works of Mao Zedong. This may come as a surprise to many readers, but it is clear evidence of the ability of radical terrorists to learn and adapt.

A chain of Islamist military writers linked Western and Asian military classics to the radical Islamist practice of jihad. These key modern figures include Abu Ubayd al-Qurashi, Abdel Aziz al-Muqrin, Abu Musab al-Suri, and Abu Bakr Naji. Of these, only al-Suri may still be alive.

All of these individuals wrote their key works between the late 1990s and 2005; consequently, they all wrote when al-Qaeda was the most important example of global Islamist jihad. However, their works influenced the groups that grew into the IS; in fact, Naji's *The Management of Savagery* (2004) is usually regarded as the most important military/political treatise for the IS.

The Islamist authors were generally familiar with a wide range of works, from Clausewitz's *On War* to Marighella's *Minimanual* and others, either through their own reading or through studying the writings of others. There seems to be no reluctance to gain from secular military literature. Even Naji, who is particularly careful to deal with everything in terms of Islam, advised reading "general books on the art of war, especially guerrilla wars, as long as the student is able to correct the Sharia mistakes that are in them."[8] It comes as a particular surprise that Naji even quotes Paul Kennedy, the noted historian of international relations at Yale University: "It is just as . . . Paul Kennedy says: 'If America expands the use of its military power and strategically extends more than necessary, this will lead to its downfall.'"[9]

Naji also specifically counsels studying "the writings of Abu Ubayd al-Qurashi." Qurashi was himself widely read in military literature, and cited Sun Tzu, Clausewitz, Mao, North Vietnamese general Vo Nguyen Giap, Che Guevara, Régis Debray, Marighella, and even the American authority on guerrilla warfare Robert Tabor, author of the classic *The War of the Flea*.[10] Al-Qurashi's interests also included what at the time were avant-garde topics within the U.S. military.

We have already discussed Mao's theories in Chapters 1 and 9, and these theories become important again here. His paradigm of evolving states of warfare definitely influenced Islamist military and political thought. The noted scholar and commentator William R. Polk concludes: "The politico-military doctrine Naji lays out can be described as a Muslim version of what Mao Zedong and Ho Chi-Minh proclaimed as their kind of war: a combination of terrorism, when that is the only means of operation: guerrilla warfare, when that becomes possible as areas of operation are secured; and ultimately, when the conflict 'matures,' the creation of a warlike but independent state-society that he thinks of as a new caliphate."[11]

Mao framed his concepts of progressive phases of revolutionary warfare in different ways. In his classic work *Guerrilla Warfare* (1937), he mentions three *military* stages: guerrilla, mobile, and positional. Guerrilla is the most basic, requiring the least in manpower and resources; mobile warfare evolves as a combination of guerrilla warfare and larger regular units coordinating their actions. Finally, the revolutionaries command enough population and resources to field a conventional army capable of taking and holding positions, lines, in an orthodox manner. He constantly insists that victory comes only with a full transition to conventional military forces following an offensive strategy in a final stage. In *Problems of Strategy in China's Revolutionary War* (1936), Mao speaks of "the period of strategic defensive" and the "stage of strategic counter-offensive," and at the same time contrasts "mobile warfare" with "fixed battle lines and positional warfare."[12] The critical point is that Mao wrote of starting small and then self-consciously and systematically building up over time, shifting into different, higher, levels of warfare.

A Practical Course for Guerrilla War by al-Muqrin labels the three phases: attrition (strategic defense), relative strategic balance (policy of a thousand cuts), and military decision (final attack).[13] In his crucial *The Management of Savagery*, Naji reworks the phases into his three, which are more idiosyncratic: "the stage of vexation and exhaustion," "the stage of the administration of savagery," and "the stage of the power of the establishment of an Islamic state."[14] Roughly speaking, Naji's could be seen as attrition, consolidation, and statehood.

So, it is clear that Islamist military writers read the world library of military works, particularly those dealing with revolutionary and guerrilla warfare, and that they read one another. As stated before, terrorists have learned from each other, and terrorism is a methodological "ism," innovated, copied, and shared. Radical Islamists developed a literature that translated classical military studies into the language of jihad.

In sum, the military literature of radical Islamism features the concept of warfare that evolved in means and levels. How much that theoretical conception of warfare actually provided the blueprint for what, in fact, occurred can be debated. However, the evolutionary conception at least supplied broad goals that effort and opportunity were then able to transform into reality. There is also no question that the model of evolutionary stages of warfare has been used by the IS to explain its own success.

The terrorism that served Islamists as entry-level warfare suggested itself not only because it was a form of warfare available to them, but because it was considered as the first step along an evolving the path to victory. Moreover, violent radical Islamist groups would have to be deaf and blind not to realize the role terrorism has played as a form of resistance since World War II. Even if they restricted their horizons to the Islamic world, they could see the terrorism of the FLN and the PLO, to say nothing of what was learned in Lebanon and Afghanistan as time progressed and al-Qaeda became the most prominent face of radical Islamism.

AL-QAEDA

Al-Qaeda ranked the United States as its primary target, the far enemy that maintained Israel and the hated *jahili* Muslim near enemies. Security analysts, journalists, and scholars still debate the degree to which al-Qaeda conducted attacks against America before 1998, such as the bombing of the World Trade towers in 1993. However, the bombings of two U.S. embassies in Dar es Salaam, Tanzania, and Nairobi, Kenya, on 7 August 1998 moved al-Qaeda toward the top of the Clinton administration's security agenda. Three years later, the al-Qaeda attacks of 9/11 drove President George W. Bush to declare a "war on terror." Immediately, the United States intervened in the Afghan civil war in an attempt to overthrow the Taliban. Continued outrage over 9/11 played an important role in bringing on the Iraq War in 2003. Al-Qaeda was certainly not the first Islamist terrorist group, but it struck with the longest reach and inflicted the most devastating blow. And it provoked the most extreme reprisals from the United States.

Osama bin Laden
Al-Qaeda is more than bin Laden, but its history is closely tied to its former leader and his personality. Bin Laden was affected by all three of the major events that brought on the third wave of radical terrorism: the Iranian Revolution of 1979, the Soviet invasion of Afghanistan in 1979, and the Israeli invasion of Lebanon in 1982. By then he was in his twenties and already influenced by the jihadi theorist Azzam.

Osama was born in 1957, the seventeenth son of Mohammed bin Laden, a billionaire construction contractor closely linked to the royal family of Saudi Arabia. Osama's mother, Alia, was perhaps the tenth or eleventh among Muhammad's wives. Alia married Muhammad in 1956, and he divorced her when Osama was four or five. Muhammad arranged for her to marry one of his employees, with whom she had four other children. Osama grew up in this second household, although he always enjoyed the wealth and privilege of his father's family. Osama is remembered as a shy, gentle, and devout boy.

Osama was the only one of Muhammad's sons who did not go abroad for at least part of his education. He eventually attended a university in Saudi Arabia, where Azzam taught. Coming just months after the Iranian Revolution, the Soviet invasion of Afghanistan would have a great impact on his life. Bin Laden worked to support the Afghan resistance, relocating to Pakistan in the early 1980s to aid the effort. There, he labored with Azzam to support the mujahideen, the jihadis fighting to expel the Soviets. In 1984, bin Laden and Azzam formed the Maktab al-Khidamat (MAK), the Afghan Services Bureau, to support the Afghan resistance. MAK did everything from fundraising, to purchasing and distributing supplies, to establishing schools and orphanages.

As the war drew down, bin Laden, Azzam, and others joined to form al-Qaeda in 1988 with the goal of continuing jihad after Afghanistan. The name comes from the Arabic *qaeda*, meaning "base." This new effort benefited from the network of foreign jihadis in which bin Laden was embedded. Early on, al-Qaeda numbered only a few hundred. Bin Laden returned home to Saudi Arabia in 1990. Azzam was assassinated in 1989, some say on bin Laden's orders because the two had a falling out over determining the next target of jihad. Once back in Saudi Arabia, bin Laden became an irritant to the Saudi government. After the Iraqi invasion of Kuwait in August 1990, the Saudis appealed to the United States to defend it against potential aggression from Saddam Hussein. Osama bin Laden argued that the Saudis should instead rely on him and his mujahideen for defense, but the Saudis reasonably ignored his pleas. Bin Laden's public harsh criticism of the Saudi government for welcoming in an army of infidel Americans into sacred land made him persona non grata.

Bin Laden left Saudi Arabia in 1992, never to return. He took refuge in Sudan, where the head of government, Hassan al-Turabi, offered sanctuary to Islamists. Bin Laden ingratiated himself with the Sudanese regime not only by his ideology but also by his useful aid, undertaking construction projects for the government at his own expense. Meanwhile, he rallied members of al-Qaeda to Sudan and recruited more. He remained in Sudan until 1996, when his welcome ran out due to pressure on the Sudanese government from the Americans, the Saudis, and the Egyptians. Bin Laden next set up al-Qaeda in Afghanistan in May 1996.

There he was the natural ally of the Islamist Taliban. In the wake of the Soviet withdrawal and the collapse of the Soviet Union, rival warlords had engulfed the country in fractious civil war. Within this armed chaos, the Taliban arose in the Pashtun south of Afghanistan. *Taliban* is the Pashto word for "students," referencing Taliban recruitment of young extremists from the madrassas. In 1994 the Taliban, led by Mullah Mohammed Omar, took Kandahar and soon controlled twelve of the thirty-four provinces of Afghanistan. After a long siege, the Taliban finally took the Afghan capital, Kabul, in 1996, and proclaimed the Islamic Emirate of Afghanistan, with Mullah Omar as emir.

Bin Laden benefited greatly from the sanctuary al-Qaeda enjoyed in Afghanistan under the protection of Mullah Omar. Among those who joined bin Laden, Ayman al-Zawahiri was an Egyptian physician turned terrorist, whose organization, Egyptian al-Jihad, had experienced repeated failures. He threw in his lot with bin Laden in 1998, becoming al-Qaeda's number-two commander. According to author Lawrence Wright, "each man filled a need in the other. Al-Zawahiri wanted money and contacts, which bin Laden had in abundance. Bin Laden, an idealist given to causes, sought direction; Al-Zawahiri, a seasoned propagandist, supplied it. They were not friends but allies."[15]

Bin Laden and al-Zawahiri recruited more fighters, set up training camps, and directed international operations. The number of al-Qaeda fighters directly under bin Laden's command peaked at perhaps 2,500 immediately before 9/11, a strength that would not be equaled again.[16] With the American counterstroke against Afghanistan in October and November 2001, bin Laden retreated to a mountain stronghold in Tora Bora, until he was driven from there in December 2001. His exact whereabouts over the next years remain a matter of conjecture, but it is most probable that he set up in the tribal areas of Pakistan near the Afghan border. Following a decade-long manhunt, U.S. intelligence finally tracked him to a compound in Abbattabad, Pakistan. There, at about 1 a.m. on 1 May 2011, special forces from Navy Seal Team Six struck the compound, killing bin Laden and four others. He was later buried at sea, an anonymous grave that could not attract pilgrims.

The Terrorist Career of al-Qaeda before 9/11
Al-Qaeda would command the world's attention more than any other Islamist terrorist group after 9/11, but there were other Islamist assaults on America and American interests before al-Qaeda dominated the stage. Islamist terrorist strikes against the United States began in 1992, although they do not appear to have been the work of al-Qaeda. In December of that year, two bombs exploded at hotels in Aden, Yemen. These were meant to kill American troops in transit to Somalia. However, the bombers had poor intelligence and struck hotels where Americans were not resident at the time. Nonetheless, two died, an Australian tourist and a hotel employee. In 2008 bin Laden claimed credit for the bombing, but it may well have been a false claim.

In February 1993 radical Islamists detonated a truck bomb in the underground parking area of the North Tower of the World Trade Center in New York. They intended to bring both the towers down, with the undermined North Tower collapsing into the South Tower. Fortunately, while the bomb caused serious damage and killed six, it failed to topple the North Tower. It is true that the mastermind of the bombing, Ramzi Yousef, was the nephew of Kahalid Sheikh Mohammed (KSM), who later played such a role in 9/11; however, KSM is on record as denying that Yousef ever was a member of al-Qaeda or that Yousef ever met bin Laden.[17]

Yousef next took part in the Bojinka Plot to bomb eleven jet airliners in midair and crash a twelfth into CIA headquarters. This plot involved both him and his uncle, KSM. But a chemical fire in Yousef's Manila apartment on 6 January 1995 alerted the Filipino police, and Yousef fled before the plot could be carried out. He was traced to Islamabad, where he was arrested on 7 February. In 1996, Islamists bombed the Khobar Towers in Saudi Arabia. U.S. Air Force personnel were billeted in the bombed structure, and nineteen airmen were killed. The attack has been attributed to a Saudi Hezbollah operative.

Although some commentators credit one or more of these attacks to al-Qaeda, notable authorities such as Lawrence Wright and Fawaz Gerges do not see these as the work of al-Qaeda. They see Al-Qaeda as a major terrorist actor only after bin Laden returned to Afghanistan. Nevertheless, the attacks of the early and mid-1990s clearly demonstrate that the United States had become a target for radical Islamist terrorists before 1998.

On 7 August 1998, after months of planning and preparation, al-Qaeda cadres carried out the major truck bombings of two U.S. embassies in Africa, at Dar es Salaam and Nairobi. The explosives were detonated at 10:35 a.m. in Nairobi and 10:39 a.m. in Dar es Salaam—impressive coordination. The Nairobi bomb killed twelve Americans and 201 others; it wounded a total of 5,000. The bomb in Dar es Salaam killed eleven, none of whom were American, and wounded eighty-five. Bin Laden expected American reprisals, and he and his immediate retinue left Kandahar and went off into the countryside to escape the retribution.

President Clinton ordered cruise missile strikes on al-Qaeda; these hit camps and installations in Afghanistan and Sudan on 20 August. Thirteen Tomahawk missiles demolished the al-Shifa pharmaceutical plant at Khartoum in Sudan, where American intelligence believed al-Qaeda was manufacturing VX poison gas. The al-Shifa attack caused a storm of controversy. Sudanese authorities claimed the facility simply produced medicines for human and veterinary use, and Clinton's domestic critics argued that the president was trying to draw attention away from the public scandal over his liaison with White House intern Monica Lewinski. But Richard Clarke, counterterrorism czar at the time, insists that the chemical evidence was solid.[18]

Al-Qaeda planned a series of operations meant to coincide with the dawn of the new millennium, the Millennium Plot. Al-Qaeda cadres conspired to bomb four sites in Amman, Jordan, but their intentions were discovered and the participants were arrested on 12 December 1999. An operation to bomb Los Angeles International Airport was foiled on 14 December, when an astute border guard caught the cadre trying to cross into the United States from Canada in a car laden with explosives. A third blow, the bombing of the USS *The Sullivans*, an Arleigh Burke–class destroyer, failed on 3 January 2000. The bombers, trying to attack the ship in the port of Aden, overloaded their suicide boat with explosives and it sank under the weight. However, on 12 October al-Qaeda carried out a successful attack on the USS *Cole*, another Arleigh Burke, while it was refueling in Aden. The suicide bombing blasted a forty-by-sixty-foot hole in the port side of the ship and killed seventeen sailors, with another thirty-nine wounded. The ship, which was in danger of sinking, was kept afloat, transported back to the United States, and back with the fleet by 2003. Al-Qaeda did not advertise its attacks before that on the *Cole*, after which bin Laden brought al-Qaeda into full light.

9/11 and Its Immediate Consequences
Al-Qaeda's malevolent masterstroke came on 11 September 2001. This scheme to use planes as cruise missiles piloted by suicide bombers originated with KSM. He had known of bin Laden before, but it was only in mid-1996 that the two met in Afghanistan and discussed plans for future attacks by al-Qaeda. KSM officially committed himself to al-Qaeda after the embassy bombings. His original plan involved ten planes, but bin Laden rejected it as too complicated. Preparations for the actual 9/11 attack began in 1999, with the planning led by bin Laden, KSM, and Mohammed Atef, the chief military commander of al-Qaeda. The planes leaving from Boston, Newark, and Washington, D.C., all bound for Californian destinations, would be hijacked after takeoff and directed at targets in New York City and Washington. The terrorists chose planes intended for long flights because they would be carrying large fuel loads that would become incendiaries when the planes crashed into their targets. The four suicide pilots would have to attend U.S. flight schools to learn how to handle Boeing 757 and 767 airliners, models with very similar controls. Fifteen other jihadis would also be sent to the United States to supply the "muscle" to aid the pilots and control the passengers and crew. All this needed to be worked out in detail, financed, and accomplished without attracting attention. Not everything went smoothly; the first two men chosen to become pilots failed to learn how to fly and were downgraded to serve as muscle.

U.S. authorities in different agencies uncovered troubling patches of intelligence, but relevant warnings were not shared. For example, FBI information about the possibility of Middle Easterners in U.S. flight schools was not passed on to the Federal Aeronautics Administration. There was vague intelligence about "spectacular" terrorist attacks in the works, but nothing specific enough as to method, time, or place. The 9/11 Commission Report concludes: "In sum, the domestic agencies never mobilized in response to the threat."[19]

On 9 September 2001, American Airlines flight 11, piloted by Mohamed Atta, the chief among the hijackers, struck the North Tower of the World Trade Center at 8:46 a.m., setting off a catastrophic fire. United Airlines flight 175 crashed into the South Tower at 9:03. At 9:37 American Airlines flight 77 ploughed into the Pentagon in Washington. After the fire had weakened its structure, the South Tower of the World Trade Center collapsed on itself at 9:59; the North Tower cascaded down at 10:28. Meanwhile, the passengers aboard the fourth plane, which had taken off only after a delay, learned of the crashes of the other planes via cellphone and decided to move against the terrorists who had taken over their flight. During the battle in the cabin, the plane plummeted to the ground, burying itself in a field near Shanksville, Pennsylvania. The toll of all those killed reached 2,977, plus the nineteen hijackers. The magnitude and meaning of the day make this terrorist attack an act of war. Putting this in perspective, only the number of Federal plus Confederate troops killed at Antietam on 17 September 1862, 3,700, surpasses 9/11 as a one-day death total in an American military engagement.

The great cost of 9/11 has skewed our view of terrorism and of al-Qaeda. That day was a one-off, not equaled before or since. Terrorist attacks characteristically inflict a small number of casualties; a death toll of a hundred is regarded as particularly grievous. Before 9/11 the costliest attack on American soil was the work of Timothy McVeigh: his bombing of the Murrah Office Building in Oklahoma City, which killed 168 people in 1995. And until Oklahoma City, the deadliest terrorist attack was the Wall Street anarchist bombing of 1920, when thirty-eight perished.

After Americans grasped the full horror of what had happened on the morning of 9/11, the wounded nation braced to strike back. The Bush administration, which had been slow to appreciate the terrorist threat when the new president came into office eight months before, recognized that its primary enemy was al-Qaeda. The military hurriedly drafted plans for retaliation. After bin Laden's Taliban protectors refused to hand him over, the war to destroy the Taliban began on 7 October. The conflict, dubbed Operation Enduring Freedom, initially employed a surprisingly small number of boots on the ground. The first deployment consisted of only 115 CIA agents and 300 special forces troops. These personnel marshaled Afghan opposition to the Taliban and coordinated U.S. air operations in support of the Northern Alliance, an Afghan force that had been battling the Taliban for years. By 13 November, Northern Alliance fighters entered Kabul. Kandahar, the Taliban capital, fell in December. By this point, the United States and its allies had dispatched significant numbers of troops to Afghanistan, including the 101st Airborne and Marines. Bin Laden took refuge in the mountains and caves of Tora Bora, and when U.S. forces attempted to capture him in December, he escaped, most probably into Pakistan.

Experts still disagree over whether bin Laden expected the United States to retaliate by invading Afghanistan. Peter Bergen, in *The Longest War: The Enduring Conflict between America and al-Qaeda* (2011), argues that bin Laden did not. However, Lawrence Wright disagrees: "Bin Laden wanted to lure the United States into Afghanistan, which was already being called the graveyard of empires. The usual object of terror is to draw one's opponent into repressive blunders, and bin Laden caught America at a vulnerable and unfortunate moment in its history."[20] There is strong testimony supporting Wright's opinion. In a 1996 interview, bin Laden announced, "We want to bring the Americans to fight us on Muslim land. If we can fight them on our own territory we will beat them, because the battle will be on our terms in a land they neither know nor understand."[21] In February 2001, Mohammed Atef outlined al-Qaeda strategy to a Pakistani correspondent for Al Jazeera: "There are two or three places in the world which [are] the most suitable places to fight Americans: Afghanistan, Iraq, and Somalia. We are expecting the United States to invade Afghanistan. And we are preparing for that. We want them to come to Afghanistan."[22]

But whether or not bin Laden wanted an American intervention in Afghanistan, there is little doubt that the strength and effectiveness of the U.S. intervention surprised him. Many within the jihadi community were furious with bin Laden for bringing down such a disaster upon his hosts, the Taliban. But given the failure of the U.S.S.R. in Afghanistan, bin Laden would not have expected that the Taliban would be so quickly decimated and al-Qaeda expelled from its sanctuary.

The war in Afghanistan did not end with the flight of bin Laden from Tora Bora in December 2001. It continues to this day, and despite initial American successes, the possibility of victory against a resurgent Taliban now seems remote. We will learn about this in Chapter 14.

Al-Qaeda Terrorism after 9/11

Al-Qaeda has never again come close to causing the level of death and destruction it inflicted on 9/11, but it has continued to conduct, or inspire, terrorist operations. On 12 October 2002, Jemaah Islamiyah, a Southeast Asian Islamist group with links to al-Qaeda, carried out a coordinated suicide bombing in Bali that killed 202 and injured another 209. Islamists said to have sympathized with al-Qaeda carried out a suicide bombing of an Israeli-owned hotel in Mombasa, Kenya, on 28 November, killing thirteen. In 2003, al-Qaeda cadres attacked a housing compound in Riyadh, Saudi Arabia, killing thirty-nine by a suicide car bomb and gunfire on 12 May. The year brought two other major bombings in Jakarta, where twelve died, and Istanbul, where al-Qaeda bombers killed fifty-seven on 15 and 20 November.

On 19 March 2003 coalition forces, predominantly U.S. and British, with Australian and Polish units as well, invaded Iraq in Operation Iraqi Freedom. The war as a whole is beyond the scope of this volume, but it is important to discuss its relationship to terrorism. American commitment to the overthrow of the Taliban in Afghanistan after 9/11 seems both inevitable and justified. But the campaign to overthrow Saddam Hussein was neither necessary nor wise. The Bush administration seemed obsessed with Iraq, and immediately after the 9/11 attacks, it tried to tie them to Saddam in a way that would support invading Iraq.

The explicit argument during the runup to the war in 2002 and 2003 concerned American charges that Saddam was developing chemical and nuclear weapons of mass destruction.[23] But beyond this, a great many Americans blamed Saddam for 9/11. A 13 September 2001 *Time*/CNN poll revealed that a surprising 78 percent of those polled suspected that Saddam was in some way responsible for 9/11.[24] A *Washington Post* poll published on 6 September 2003 reported that 69 percent of those polled *still* believed that it was "at least likely that Hussein was involved."[25] It can be argued that Saddam made a convenient proxy for those dismayed that bin Laden was still at large.[26] As the experienced journalist Patrick Cockburn put it: "The shock of 9/11 provided a Pearl Harbor moment in the US when public revulsion and fear could be manipulated to implement a preexisting neo-conservative agenda by targeting Saddam Hussein and invading Iraq."[27]

The destruction of Iraqi political infrastructure and the inability of the United States and its allies to create a viable new regime resulted in an insurgency against the Americans and their allies. This included vicious sectarian terrorism between Sunnis and Shias. Al-Qaeda benefited from the deepening crisis, gaining new recruits for its various local subsidiaries, such as AQI.

The war in Iraq also provoked terrorist attacks meant to punish those aiding the U.S. effort there. Accounts of two of such al-Qaeda–inspired attacks began this volume: the 11 March 2004 bombings of four Madrid commuter trains that killed 191, and the 7 July 2005 suicide bombings of three lines of the London Underground and one double-decker bus that killed fifty.

A suicide terrorist detonated a truck bomb at the Islamabad Marriott Hotel on 20 September 2008, killing fifty-four. The motive for the bombing is still unclear, but this seems to have been intended as an attack on the new Pakistan government under President Asif Ali Zardari, which cooperated with the United States. The identity of the group responsible is still a matter of contention; however, immediately after the explosion, a U.S. military intelligence official observed that the attack "bears all the hallmarks of a terrorist operation carried out by al-Qaeda or its associates."[28]

Al-Qaeda Lone Wolves

As al-Qaeda Central gave way to al-Qaeda the social movement, lone-wolf attacks by individuals or small independent cells came more to the fore. The media often talk about lone-wolf terrorism as a recent development, but the concept was there from the start of radical terrorism, as shown in Chapter 5. Bin Laden explicitly advocated it before 9/11. His 1998 *fatwa* can be read as a call for attacks by individuals: "We—with Allah's help—call on every Muslim who believes in Allah and wishes to be rewarded to comply with Allah's order to kill the Americans and plunder their money wherever and whenever they find it." In his 2001 tract *Knights under the Banner of the Prophet*, al-Zawahiri made a similar appeal, as did al-Suri in *The Global Islamic Resistance Call* (2004). Al-Suri wrote: "Hence, our method should therefore be to guide the Muslim who wants to participate and resist, to operate where he is, or where he is able to be . . . and to pursue jihad and Resistance in secrecy and alone, or with a small cell of trustworthy people."[29]

After 9/11, individuals claiming loyalty to al-Qaeda engaged in lone-wolf attacks. Richard Reid attempted to blow up an American Airlines flight from Paris to Miami on 22 December 2001 with an explosive hidden in his shoe. He was unable to ignite the bomb and was overpowered by other passengers. On 5 November 2009, U.S. Army major Nidal Malik Hasan killed thirteen and wounded thirty at the Readiness Center at Fort Hood, Texas. He was not directly tied to al-Qaeda, but was strongly influenced by the American-born imam Anwar al-Awlaki, who went to Yemen and became a figure in AQAP. The *New York Times* would call Awlaki "perhaps the most prominent English-speaking advocate of violent jihad against the United States."[30] On Christmas Day of that year, Umar Farouk Abdulmutallab, a Nigerian trained by al-Qaeda in the Arabian Peninsula and inspired by Awlaki, tried to bring down a Northwest Airlines flight from Amsterdam to Detroit. Abdulmutallab was equipped with a bomb sewn into his underwear. As in the case of Reid, the bomb failed to ignite and passengers subdued him. Faisal Shahzad, a Pakistani who became a naturalized American citizen, tried to detonate a car bomb in Times Square, New York City, on 1 May 2010. The bomb failed to explode. Like Hasan and Abdulmutallab, Shahzad claimed to be inspired by Awlaki and contacted him over the internet, but he did not meet him face to face. Shahzad received training in Pakistan, probably by the Taliban.

The Tsarnaev brothers acted together in bombing the Boston Marathon on 15 April 2013. Although not connected in any way with al-Qaeda, they learned to make the pressure-cooker bombs they used from AQAP's online magazine *Inspire*, which featured an article titled "How to Make a Bomb in the Kitchen of Your Mom" in its summer 2010 issue.

The Victory over al-Qaeda?
Some held that the resort to lone-wolf terrorism was not a sign of al-Qaeda's strength, but a symptom of weakness. No later than 2008, a body of journalism and scholarship argued that al-Qaeda was on a downward track. This direction of opinion would be reinforced by the killing of bin Laden in 2011. In *Leaderless Jihad: Terror Networks in the Twenty-First Century* (2008), the security authority Marc Sageman argued that the power of al-Qaeda Central was waning as it was overtaken by al-Qaeda the social movement. He stressed the emergence of a leaderless jihad that

conducted terrorist attacks without resources or orders from the center, like the individuals just discussed. But he also predicted, "The leaderless jihad will probably fade away for . . . internal reasons. The danger is that too vigorous an eradication campaign might be counterproductive and actually prolong the life of the social movement."[31]

Expressing confidence that Islamism was in decline, and the Muslim world was entering a post-Islamist era, the academic sociologist Afez Bayat published *Life as Politics: How Ordinary People Change the Middle East* in 2010. This Iranian by birth proposed that "the Iranian experience of 1979 may well remain the first and last Islamic Revolution of our time."[32] In this book he told his readers that the actions of a great number of individuals tending in the same direction, but without formal organization or leaders—what he refers to as "nonmovements"—can and have had a positive impact on politics and law in the Middle East. He further proclaimed that "a new post-Islamist trend has begun to emerge, attempting to accommodate aspects of democratization, pluralism, women's rights, youth concerns, and social development with adherence to religion."[33]

Bayat's book seemed prescient with the outbreak of rebellions that were soon labeled the Arab Spring. These began in December 2010 with the Tunisian Revolution that ousted President Zine El Abidine Ben Ali. On 14 January 2011, the last day of Ali's regime, *Al Jazeera* optimistically observed, "it's pretty much obvious that the glass ceiling of fear has been forever shattered in Tunisia and that the police state that Ben Ali created in 1987 when he came to power in a coup seems to be disintegrating."[34] Within the next fourteen months, other rulers were deposed or resigned in Egypt, Libya, and Yemen, and major uprisings occurred in Bahrain and Syria. Demands for the end to tyranny and the adoption of reforms and democracy seemed to undermine radical Islamists' claims that the "near enemy" could only be overcome by terrorist violence.

Eventually, the exhilaration of victory would give way to disappointment. With the election of a Muslim Brotherhood candidate as president of Egypt, Mohamed Morsi, his grab for greater powers, and his overthrow by a military coup in July 2013, Egypt circled back toward an authoritarian government. Following the end of the Muammar Gaddafi regime in August 2011, and his killing in October, Libya descended into chaos. Yemen is embroiled in civil war.

But the Arab Spring was still promising a better future when the United States withdrew its last troops from Iraq in December 2011. The brutal sectarian chaos, with its terror campaigns by Sunni and Shia militia that followed American conquest in 2003, had waned with the rising of Sunni tribes against AQI in 2006 and 2008 (the Sunni Awakening) and the U.S. troop "surge" in 2007–2008. By the time of the U.S. withdrawal, a seemingly stable government under Nuri al-Maliki, a Shia, ruled from Baghdad. Al-Maliki was soon to adopt oppressive measures against the Sunni minority, but the consequences of this were not yet clear.

In September 2011 Fawaz Gerges, a well-respected author, published *The Rise and Fall of Al-Qaeda*. By then, bin Laden had been killed, and his death was not the last of the year. Not long after the publication of Gerges's book, Anwar al-Awlaki was killed in a drone strike on 30 September. Gerges confidently announced that "like Osama bin Laden himself, the world's most feared and hated terrorist organization [al-Qaeda], indeed the very embodiment of what 'terrorist organization' has come to mean in the minds of Americans and Westerners . . . no longer exists. It has all but vanished, or at least dwindled to the palest shadow of its former self."[35]

Opinion among the *ummah* even added weight to this sense of al-Qaeda in decline. Pew Research Center studies found that in Jordan, confidence in bin Laden fell from 61 percent in early 2005 to 24 percent after the 2005 Amman bombings, and it continued to plummet to 13 percent shortly before his death in 2011.[36] Another Pew survey of 2013 discovered that most of the *ummah* disapproved of al-Qaeda, a tally that reached 96 percent in Lebanon, 69 percent in Egypt, and 57 percent overall.[37]

On the campaign trail in 2012, President Barack Obama delivered stump speeches that hammered at the same theme: victory over al-Qaeda: "And while a new tower rises above the New York skyline, al-Qaeda is on the path to defeat, and Osama bin Laden is dead," and "Al-Qaeda has been decimated."[38] A month after Obama's reelection, Fareed Zakaria, a noted journalist close to Gerges, published an opinion piece in the *Washington Post* entitled "End the War on Terror and Save Billions."[39] In his argument, Zakaria quoted a recent speech by Jeh Johnson, then the outgoing general counsel at the Pentagon: "[A]l-Qaeda as we know it, the organization that our Congress authorized the military to pursue in 2001, has been effectively destroyed."[40]

It seemed that terrorism as a whole was on its heels. In January 2014, President Obama sat for a now-infamous interview with David Remnick, editor of the *New Yorker*. Still confident that al-Qaeda had been degraded down the scale of dangers, Obama refused to be too concerned with ISIS, which would soon become the IS. Using the basketball references he finds comfortable, the president described ISIS: "The analogy we use around here sometimes, and I think is accurate, is if a jayvee team puts on Lakers uniforms that doesn't make them Kobe Bryant." ISIS simply fell short of the threat posed by al-Qaeda: "I think there is a distinction between the capacity and reach of a bin Laden and a network that is actively planning major terrorist plots against the homeland versus jihadists who are engaged in various local power struggles and disputes, often sectarian."[41]

And then came June.

THE ISLAMIC STATE

ISIS shocked the world that month. After six days of combat, its fighters seized the city of Mosul in Iraq on 10 June 2014. News media reported the unbelievable: a mere 1,500 ISIS forces destroyed or drove off fifteen times their number of Iraqi troops guarding the city. Tikrit, the birthplace of Saddam Hussein, fell later that month. The Iraqi Army was revealed as a hollow shell, rotted out by corruption. Commanders had been selling government ammunition for personal profit and pocketing money meant to pay for food. It was so dreadful that only a third of the nominal troop strength was even with military units; the rest had bribed their officers to remain on "permanent leave" from the army. On 29 June, ISIS declared that it was constituting itself as a new caliphate, with its leader, Abu Bakr al-Baghdadi, assuming the title of Caliph Ibrahim. It became the Islamic State. Days later, the self-declared caliph himself delivered a sermon to those gathered for prayer at the Grand al-Nuri Mosque of Mosul.

A terrorist group, through a strategy of evolution, had gained the command over territory, population, and resources that define a state. Yet the change in status did not transform the character of the IS, which continued to commit the kinds of ostentatious terrorist atrocities that defined it before. There is more to the IS than terrorism, but the discussion in this chapter will center primarily on its terrorist acts, rather than on its conduct as a state at war.

The sudden triumph of the IS, the political entity that Americans usually still called ISIS, startled the Obama administration. To understand that triumph we must go back at least a decade and a half before the fall of Mosul.

From Jama'at al-Tawid wal-Jihad to the Islamic State, 1999–2018
The earliest avatar of the IS, Jama'at al-Tawid wal-Jihad (JTJ), appeared in 1999. Its founder, Ahmad Fadeel al-Nazal al-Khalayleh, known by his *kunya* as Abu Musab al-Zarqawi, was born in 1966 in Jordan. He was attracted to jihad in the late 1980s, after a dissolute youth. He went off to Afghanistan in 1989 but was too late to take part in the war against the Soviets. Nonetheless, he was involved in some of the fighting that followed the Soviet withdrawal. He returned to Jordan in 1993 and engaged in some failed terrorist actions, which led to his arrest that year. As has been the case for many terrorists, his years in prison provided time for self-education and further radicalization. After being released in 1999, he took part in the foiled Millennium Plot to bomb sites in Jordan. When the plot was discovered and suspects rounded up in December, he slipped the net and escaped, first to Pakistan and then to Afghanistan. There he appealed to bin Laden for help in setting up JTJ. (The name of the group translates as "Organization for Monotheism and Jihad.") Al-Zarqawi and bin Laden did not get along well, as the younger extremist was too brazen and bloodthirsty for bin Laden. Still, al-Zarqawi was allowed to establish a training camp in Herat, Afghanistan. He fought against the Americans in Afghanistan after 9/11, but crossed into Iran in 2002. By 2003 he had surfaced in Iraq. Even before the U.S. invasion of Iraq, al-Zarqawi benefited from an unexpected source. In his address to the UN Security Council on 5 February 2003, Secretary of State Colin Powell raised al-Zarqawi as a major terrorist threat: "Iraq today harbors a deadly terrorist network headed by Abu Musab al-Zarqawi, an associate and collaborator of Usama bin Laden and his al-Qaeda lieutenants."[42] Powell went on to mention al-Zarqawi's name twenty more times in his address, lending al-Zarqawi international notoriety. Once the war began,

JTJ fomented sectarian violence. Al-Zarqawi also attacked American targets, including contractor Nick Berg, whom he beheaded on 7 May 2004. Al-Zarqawi posted a shocking video of the brutal execution on the internet.

Al-Zarqawi gained something approaching star status. In a video shown on Al Jazeera, one of the 2005 London subway suicide bombers, Mohammad Sidique Khan, hailed "today's heroes, like our beloved Sheikh Osama bin Laden, Dr. Ayman al-Zawahiri, and Abu Mus'ab al-Zarqawi, and all the other brothers and sisters who are fighting in Allah's cause."[43]

In 2004, al-Zarqawi swore *bayah*, loyalty, to bin Laden, and with this commitment, JTJ became al-Qaeda in the Land of the Two Rivers, generally referred to in the West as al-Qaeda in Iraq. The number of fighters he commanded at this juncture was small. AQI grew but probably never was large; in an authoritative estimate, Malcolm Nance put the figure at about 850 full-time fighters and described it as "a microscopic terrorist organization" in the context of the large insurgency ripping Iraq apart in late 2006 and early 2007.[44]

Bin Laden and al-Zarqawi shared a devotion to jihad, but differed greatly in their choice of goals, targets, and tactics. Bin Laden regarded defeating or exhausting the Americans and the West as primary, while al-Zarqawi was more concerned with striking the near enemy. Bin Laden was willing to pitch a big tent, to compromise and coordinate with others so as to work together in the great jihad against latter-day Crusaders and their Zionist allies. But al-Zarqawi was not so obliging; he preferred to dominate, not cooperate, and he detested the Shias. Moreover, al-Zarqawi reveled in publicizing hideous atrocities, like the beheading of Berg, while bin Laden and al-Zawahiri objected to such overt savagery, believing it would alienate most Muslim opinion.

On 7 June 2006, al-Zarqawi was killed in an American airstrike. Days after his death, a close collaborator of al-Zarqawi, Abu Ayyub al-Masri, became head of AQI. In the months that followed, AQI came together with other jihadis to form the Islamic State of Iraq (ISI) in October 2006, with al-Masri as its leader. The declaration of itself as a "state" without the prior approval of bin Laden proved to be a further bone of contention between al-Qaeda leadership and what was now ISI.

More an apocalyptic zealot than a strategist, al-Masri was not up to the difficult situation that faced ISI. Some Sunni tribes supported AQI, because the Sunnis were threatened by the Shia majority in the sectarian violence that plagued Iraq following the American-led invasion. However, al-Zarqawi did not treat his Sunni allies as partners but as subjects. If they faltered in their support, awful things could happen to them. As a consequence, resentful Sunni tribes began to resist AQI by 2005 and 2006. This resistance swelled into what is called the Sunni Awakening. David Petraeus served as commanding general of the allied forces (Multi-National Force—Iraq) as the Awakening gained momentum, and he supported it. Terrorism scholar Audrey Kurth Cronin bluntly insists that ISI "was nearly wiped out when Sunni tribes decided to partner with the Americans to confront the jihadists."[45] Petraeus also instituted a new counterinsurgency doctrine that stressed increasing the security of the Iraqi people and was able to pursue this goal with an additional 30,000 U.S. troops deployed in Iraq 2007-2008: the "Surge." Peter Mansoor, Petraeus's executive officer at the time, insists there were two surges: "the surge of ideas—the new concept for the employment of forces; and the surge of forces—the reinforcements that enabled the implementation of the new strategy quickly."[46]

One of al-Masri's decisions was to promote an individual about whom we know little, Abu Omar al-Baghdadi. He would come to be revered as "commander of the faithful," a term associated with the Mahdi, or savior, prophesied to lead Islam in the end days. On 10 April 2010 a joint American-Iraqi operation killed al-Masri, al-Baghdadi, and three of their companions.

The death of the two ISI leaders left a void at the top that Abu Bakr al-Baghdadi rose to fill. He headed the organization as it reestablished its numbers and power. Al-Baghdadi was born Ibrahim Awad Ibrahim al-Badri in Samarra, a town about seventy-five miles north of Baghdad, in 1971. A devout youth, he is reputed to have earned a Ph.D. in Islamic studies at the Islamic University of Baghdad in 2007. But before that, he received another kind of education when he was imprisoned by Americans from February to December 2004 at Camp Bucca, known as the "Academy" by the terrorists. One of al-Baghdadi's fellow prisoners, Abu Ahmed, testified, "Here, we were not only safe, but we were only a few hundred meters away from the entire al-Qaeda leadership. . . . We had so much time to sit and plan. It was the perfect environment."[47]

The presence of U.S. combat troops ended in December 2011, by which point al-Baghdadi had rebuilt ISI to a force of 800–1,000 full-time fighters. He unquestionably saw the U.S. withdrawal as a great opportunity. The "Strategic Plan for Reinforcing the Political Position of the Islamic State of Iraq," a work that was available to him no later than January 2010, argued: "When the Americans withdraw within two years ... the situation will be strongest politically and militarily for the Islamic plan to prepare to completely seize the reins of control over all Iraq."[48]

Al-Baghdadi expanded the reach of ISI into strife-torn Syria. Protests against the government of Bashar al-Assad began in March 2011 as a manifestation of the Arab Spring and exploded into civil war by September. Syria became a war zone that presented radical Islamists with the possibility of advancing their cause. Al-Baghdadi exploited the turmoil by dispatching some of his cadres to Syria in August 2011 to create a resistance force loyal to him and al-Qaeda. The men deployed to Syria became the core of Jabhat al-Nusra, or the al-Nusra Front, in January 2012. It attracted experienced fighters and soon became a major player in the brutal contest.

Things heated up in Iraq as well. The actions of the Baghdad government headed by Nouri al-Maliki favored the Shias, alienated the Sunnis, and reignited the sectarian violence of 2004–2008. Government forces shot down Sunni protesters, their leaders "disappeared," and Shia militias killed with impunity.[49]

In Syria, the link between al-Nusra and ISI was not widely known. But, driven by ambition or jealousy, al-Baghdadi declared in April 2013 that al-Nusra was merging with ISI under his command. With this putative merger, al-Baghdadi gave ISI a new name, the Islamic State of Iraq and the Levant. Obama referred to it by the acronym ISIL, although most of the Western press and public referred to it as ISIS. Arabic-speakers use the term Daesh to denote and demean ISIS and, now, the IS.

The leadership of al-Nusra, caught off-guard, refused al-Baghdadi's incorporation of al-Nusra and proclaimed their loyalty to al-Qaeda. One of the disputes between them was the split of oil revenues from territory al-Nusra had conquered.[50] Al-Zawahiri tried to intervene on al-Nusra's behalf in June, but to little avail. Relations became strained to the breaking point, and al-Qaeda dissolved its relationship with ISIS in February 2014. ISIS and al-Qaeda, through its loyal affiliate al-Nusra, would now be adversaries. From this point on, global jihadists split into two camps, one associated with al-Qaeda and the other affiliated with ISIS.

Many al-Nusra fighters came over to ISIS, and with the addition of these men, the influx of foreign fighters, and the gain of other recruits, the ranks of ISIS swelled. From about 2,500 in 2012, it mounted to 7,000–10,000 in 2013. Al-Baghdadi commanded his organization's most deadly operation to date on 23 July 2012. Thirty-two suicide bombers struck across Iraq, killing 116. The next year witnessed a shockingly bloody toll throughout Iraq, with over 8,000 killed by *all* terrorist actors.[51]

Al-Baghdadi's forces doubled in size again during the critical year of 2014. By September, the CIA estimated that the new IS, the caliphate, could muster 20,000–31,500 fighters.[52] With its conquests, the IS commanded extensive resources. Jessica Stern and J. M. Berger state bluntly, "No one disputed that ISIS had become the richest terrorist organization in the world, and was getting richer by the day."[53] By the end of 2014, its income was believed to be $1–3 million *a day*, largely by oil sales.

Because of the great initial success of the IS, other Islamist terrorist groups from Africa to East Asia latched on to it, much as groups had previously associated themselves with al-Qaeda. These new recruits offered *bayah* to al-Baghdadi. If it was accepted, the group and its area of control would be recognized as a *wilayah*, or province, of the new caliphate. This gave the IS the appearance of an international presence.

With the fall of the Iraqi city of Sinjar to IS forces in early August 2014, the horrendous plight of the local Yazidi people at the hands of the IS, and the increased threat to Iraqi Kurds, the United States began its own air strikes against IS forces on 8 August. At the same time Iran undertook air operations against the IS in Iraq. From September of that year, the United States led a coalition air offensive to degrade IS forces. This coalition has included the United Kingdom, France, Australia, Bahrain, Belgium, Canada, Denmark, Germany, Italy, Jordan, Morocco, the Netherlands, Qatar, Saudi Arabia, Turkey, and the United Arab Emirates. Syria, Russia, Iran, and Hezbollah also battled the IS; however, they were more intent on reestablishing Bashar al-Assad's control over Syria than with defeating the IS.

In August 2014, Patrick Cockburn summed up the allied nightmare that the IS had become: "For America, Britain, and the Western powers, the rise of ISIS and the caliphate is the ultimate disaster. Whatever they intended by their invasion of Iraq in 2003 and their efforts to unseat Assad in Syria since 2011, it was not to see the creation of a jihadi state spanning northern Iraq and Syria, run by a movement a hundred times bigger and much better organized than the al-Qaeda of Osama bin Laden."[54] The IS appeared to be unstoppable in the summer and fall of 2014. Its victories seemed nearly miraculous, and the spell of that magic drew more foreign jihadis to its cause.

Fortunately, the tide of IS gains ebbed, a reality that became clearly apparent as early as 2016. A chain of defeats cost the IS the cities it had taken. In Iraq, Ramadi fell in February 2016 and Fallujah in June. By late August, the IS had lost Manbij, a critical hub in Syria. In July 2017, Mosul, the greatest conquest by the IS, was retaken by forces that included Iraqi government troops, Kurdish Peshmerga, Shia militia, Iranians, and Americans. Tal Affar in Iraq was declared liberated on 2 September 2017, and Hawija on 4 October. The IS "capital" in Syria, Raqqa, was recaptured after a siege of over four months on 17 October. In November, the IS lost Al Qaim in Iraq, and Abu Kamal and Deir ez-Zor in Syria.

IS troops put up a very stout defense of Mosul, in fighting that continued over nine months. However, as the string of defeats continued, IS jihadis proved less bent on fighting to the death than on escaping. Their intent seems not to give up the war but to regroup for continued conflict. An article in the December 2017 issue of the Combating Terrorism Center's journal *CTC Sentinel* was entitled "Insurgents Again: The Islamic State's Calculated Reversion to Attrition in the Syria-Iraq Border and Beyond."[55] The author, Hassan, argued that the Islamic State had decided to abandon conventional warfare and return to insurgency, fighting as it had before 2014. A *New York Times* front-page feature published on 5 February 2018 declared, "Thousands of ISIS Fighters Flee in Syria, Many to Fight Another Day."[56] We shall see below that the leadership of the IS began considering how it would deal with military failure when it still looked very strong. The battle would continue by returning to the "desert."

The IS evolved under al-Baghdadi from a terrorist group to a state, or state-like political entity, but what evolves can devolve. However, no matter what happens to the IS in the future, the example of its striking metamorphosis from terrorist group to state will survive and inspire radical Islamists. It will also be studied by counterterrorists. We were surprised in June 2014, and we must be more aware and better prepared in the future.

Certainly, the dream of a new caliphate, so important to the ideology of radical Islamists, was embedded in al-Baghdadi's consciousness, as was the knowledge that he had to win control over a territory and its population before he could declare a caliphate. This studious man also read that a struggle begun on a low level with few resources could evolve into something powerful enough to conquer land and people, as he needed to do. He achieved his goal not simply by embracing ideology and envisioning a path to greater strength, but also by seizing opportunity. Like many a successful strategist in the past, he was a savvy opportunist. He pondered and planned, but he also pounced. Now what will he do?

The IS Outside the Caliphate: Networks, Cells, and Lone Wolves
The IS and its predecessors have long appreciated the values of lone wolves striking in their own lands on their own initiative. In response to the U.S. bombing campaign that began in August 2014, the IS issued a call to lone wolves. In his long and rambling appeal "Indeed Your Lord Is Ever Watchful," the leading IS spokesman, Abu Muhammad al Adnani, voiced a confident appeal on 9 September: "So O muwahhid, do not let this battle pass you by wherever you may be. . . . If you can kill a disbelieving American or European—especially the spiteful and filthy French . . . including the citizens of the countries that entered into a coalition against the Islamic State . . . do not ask for anyone's advice and do not seek anyone's verdict. Kill the disbeliever whether he is civilian or military, for they have the same ruling [of guilt and deserve death]."[57]

Amedy Coulibaly, who coordinated his deadly attack on a kosher market in Paris with that of the *Charlie Hebdo* killers in January 2015, pledged his loyalty to the IS. In little more than a month, during the fall of 2015, IS or IS-inspired terrorist networks, cells, and individuals carried out five major terrorist attacks. On 13 November, terrorists from a Belgian-based IS network stunned France, killing 130 with bullets and bombs in Paris. The IS claimed responsibility. And on 2 December, a married couple, lone wolves inspired by the IS, shot down fourteen in San Bernardino, California. The IS called them soldiers of the caliphate.

Another IS-inspired, American-born terrorist, Omar Mateen, shot and killed forty-nine at a nightclub in Orlando, Florida on 12 June 2016. This mass shooting supplanted the Wall Street bombing of 1920 as the third most deadly terrorist attack on American soil. The French city of Nice suffered another tragedy on 14 July when Mohamed Lahouaiej-Bouhlel, a Tunisian living in France, plowed a large truck through a crowd drawn by Bastille Day fireworks. He killed eighty-six and injured another 434. The IS claimed credit for the attack.

On 28 November 2016, an IS-inspired Somali refugee injured eleven on the campus of Ohio State University. He drove his car into students and then jumped out of the vehicle wielding a butcher knife, stabbing two before being shot dead by a policeman. A Tunisian asylum seeker in Germany, who had pledged *bayah* to al-Baghdadi, hijacked a large truck and shot its driver on 19 December. He then drove it to a Berlin Christmas market, where he plowed into the crowd, killing twelve and injuring fifty-six. The new year began grimly in Istanbul when, shortly after 1 a.m. on New Year's Day, a gunman killed thirty-nine revelers and wounded seventy at a crowded nightclub.

Sayfullo Saipov, an immigrant from Uzbekistan who had become a permanent resident of the United States, rented a pickup truck and ran down nineteen victims in New York City on 31 October 2017. Eight died. This was the bloodiest day of terrorism the city had experienced since 9/11. Saipov had an ISIS flag in the cab of his truck.

During his last official public address, delivered on 21 May 2016, Adnani again encouraged lone-wolf attacks in the lands of IS's enemies, but now the IS was on the defensive: "The smallest act you do in their lands is more beloved to us than the biggest act done here.... Know that your targeting those who are called 'civilians' is more beloved to us and more effective, as it is more harmful, painful, and a greater deterrent to them."[58] Adnani was mortally wounded in an airstrike in August 2016. One can expect more lone-wolf attacks in Europe as some IS fighters choose to, or are ordered to, return from Syria and Iraq to their homes. America is in much less danger from this, since so few U.S. citizens or residents went to fight with the IS.

ZARQAWISM: PART OF THE DNA OF THE ISLAMIC STATE?
The IS has committed, supported, or inspired ostentatious atrocities and then multiplied their shock value by publicizing them in lurid videos.

Savagery seems to be their signature. Some commentators use the term "Zarqawism" as shorthand for the brutal practices of the IS. The IS ideology encapsulates Zarqawi's extreme anti-Shia sectarianism, the barbarities committed by his own hand, and his desire to advertise such brutal excesses to the world. Security journalists Michael Weiss and Hassan Hassan credit al-Zarqawi as "a dire pioneer" because of his "marriage of horrific ultraviolence and mass media," initially demonstrated worldwide with the videotaped beheading of Nick Berg on 7 May 2004.[59] It is believed that al-Zarqawi actually carried out the beheading himself, although the executioner wore a mask.

To label the extremes of violence typical of JTJ, AQI, ISI, ISIS, and the IS as "Zarqawism" implies that al-Zarqawi set the tone for the violent excess that continued to characterize these groups. He could have done so by setting a striking example that attracted and inspired radical recruits who then passed on his mentality, means, and methods to others. The death of any one man, even al-Zarqawi himself, need not bring his legacy to an end.

Al-Zarqawi's JTJ was not the first radical Islamist terrorist group to decapitate its victims. Chechen rebels reputedly beheaded a Russian soldier in the 1990s, and Abu Sayyaf, a Filipino militant group linked to al-Qaeda, beheaded captives as early as 2001. Most important, Islamist radicals kidnapped and beheaded American journalist Daniel Pearl on 1 February 2002 and posted a gruesome video of the murder three weeks later. Years later, Kahalid Sheikh Mohammed would claim to have actually carried out the execution. However, the beheadings that most shocked the world were the series of such murders committed by the IS in 2014: American journalists James Foley (around 19 August) and Stephen Sotloff (around September 2), British aid workers David Haines (13 September) and Alan Henning (around 3 October), and American soldier turned medical aid worker Peter Kassig (around 16 November). The victims usually wore orange jumpsuits, as worn by the prisoners held at Guantanamo. They read statements condemning allied governments and airstrikes, after which the executioner put his knife to their necks.

Adding to their collection of horrors, the IS also burned individuals alive. The Jordanians joined the air offensive against ISIS, and on 24 December 2014, one of their F-16s crashed due to mechanical problems. The pilot, Muath al-Kasasbeh, was captured. The IS conducted a kind of perverted contest in which people Tweeted their ideas to #Suggest a Way to Kill the Jordanian Pilot Pig. In February 2015, the IS posted a video of Lieutenant al-Kasabeh confined in an iron cage, doused with gasoline, set afire, and writhing until his death. Al-Kasabeh was not the only one to suffer this fate. In August 2015, IS fighters suspended four Shia enemies by chains, set the gasoline-soaked ground underneath them afire, and lowered them into the flames.

It is understandable that the deaths of individuals by knife and flame shock us, but seeing the deaths of those whose faces we recognize should not distract us from the numerous massacres perpetrated by the IS against those unknown to us. Hundreds of prisoners captured by the IS when it took Mosul and Tikrit were massacred. In Tikrit the prisoners were separated, Sunnis from Shias, and a video showed many of the Shias standing before a trench that would be their grave as they were machine-gunned down. Other videos display captured Iraqi troops trucked to their final destination, marched to a shallow ditch, forced to lay down in it, and shot where they lay.[60]

Even Sunni tribesmen in Syria and Iraq, thought to be potential allies of the IS, felt its wrath if they did not cooperate with the IS to the fullest degree. Consider the violence in Syria's Deir ez-Zor province. In August Al Jazeera reported that the IS had killed 700 members of the Sunni al-Sheitat tribe. Only 100 of the dead were fighters, many of whom were beheaded, and the rest civilians. In December a mass grave of 230 from this tribe was discovered. This avalanche of murder shocked even the jihadi community, turning many against the IS.[61]

The IS and Hudud *Punishments*

The most omnipresent form of violence impinging on the lives of all who lived in controlled areas was the strict imposition of *hudud*, the harsh punishments prescribed in the Quran and the *hadith* for such crimes as adultery, fornication, false accusation, apostasy, drinking alcohol, rebellion, and theft. This was briefly discussed in Chapter 9. Historically, such a high burden of proof was put upon the accuser that the full vigor of *hudud* punishments was not particularly common. However, IS authorities accepted much lower standards of proof, making these severe punishments prevalent. Adulterers were stoned to death, fornicators were whipped, common thieves had a hand or foot cut off, and thieves who killed were beheaded or crucified. What may be more a matter of shock and dismay is not the enforcement of these penalties but their *public* enactment and subsequent publication. Even children could see the rotting remains of those executed and left as moral reminders. Public punishments served to advertise the rigor of the IS, to outbid its Islamist rivals, and to intimidate populations under its authority.

The IS was also stern about enforcing propriety upon its Muslim women. In Raqqa and Mosul, the IS established the al-Khansa Brigade, an all-female unit tasked with policing the dress and conduct of women. An official explained, "We have established the brigade to raise awareness of our religion among women, and to punish women who do not abide by the law. There are only women in this brigade, and we have given them their own facilities to prevent the mixture of men and women." The women, who carried weapons, were empowered to "arrest and punish women who do not follow the religion correctly. Jihad is not a man-only duty. Women must do their part as well."[62] The punishments inflicted by women of the al-Khansa can be very harsh, including whippings and disfigurement.

Some observers argue that *hudud* punishments serve another function in addition to intimidation: they desensitize the IS population to brutality. Stern and Berger argue: "ISIS's psychological warfare . . . is deliberately attempting to blunt its followers' empathy by forcing them to participate in or observe acts of brutality. Over time, this can lead to secondary psychopathy, or a desire to harm others, and contagion of violence."[63] This is an argument that exposure to atrocities breeds more atrocities.

The IS Theology of Rape
Given the IS's emphasis on a strict fundamentalist interpretation of *sharia* law and *hudud* punishments, including the stoning of adulterers, as well as its concern for religious propriety among Muslim women, it seems bizarre that the IS formally advocated the rape of enslaved women. This issue rose to the world's attention with the fate of Yazidi women captured by the IS in the course of its Northern Offensive in August 2014.

Living in Iraq, close to its border with Syria, the Yazidis practice a religion condemned and detested by the IS as devil worship. This excluded

Yazidi civilians from any protection from the IS forces as they expanded and consolidated their hold on northern Iraq. Yazidi refugees fleeing the IS suffered unendurable conditions in the nearby mountains. A UN observer in Iraq condemned the IS: "We believe that what they have done may be classified as genocide and a crime against humanity."[64] Figures are not exact, but it is estimated that during the IS conquest, 5,000 Yazidi men were executed and more than 7,000 women and girls taken off to be sex slaves.

The IS regarded the rape of captured infidel women as just, even as an *act of reverence*. An article in the *New York Times* described the rape of a twelve-year-old enslaved Yazidi girl by an IS warrior who owned her. "He bound her hands and gagged her. Then he knelt beside the bed and prostrated himself in prayer before getting on top of her. When it was over, he knelt to pray again, bookending the rape with acts of religious devotion."[65] IS authorities argued that an unmarried man preserves his sinless chastity by having sex with a slave, who by definition is not a Muslim. The fourth issue of *Dabiq* carried an article titled "The Revival of Slavery before the Hour," which argued that pagan women should be enslaved as a portent of the end times.

The IS distributed captured women from the Yazidi and other religious minorities as rewards to fighters, and women were bought and sold at slave markets. Some were purchased by human traffickers.

It could be argued that young men, offered the opportunity of having sex with a female slave without any threat of punishment, are little concerned with the niceties of *sharia* law. However, the IS defended the practice as consistent with *sharia*. The Research and Fatwa Department of the Islamic State even published a pamphlet, *Questions and Answers on Taking Captives and Slaves*.[66] It was a kind of theology of rape that argued, "It is permissible [for devout Muslim men] to have sexual intercourse with the female captive" in order to "guard their chastity," and in doing so "they are free from blame."

The ultraviolence of Zarqawism testifies to a culture within the IS and its predecessors that tolerates and promotes the most inhumane barbarity. To what extent this culture of violence is defined by ethnicity or religious extremism, or simply the product of a brutal taste for savagery in al-Zarqawi and his successors, can be debated. In any case, the controversy between the IS and al-Qaeda over Zarqawism argues against generalizing too broadly about the lack of restraint and the exultation of excess among radical Islamists.

FITNA: CONTRASTS AND CONTROVERSIES BETWEEN AL-QAEDA AND THE IS

As radical Islamist groups with pretensions to a global scope, al-Qaeda and the IS share much; after all, the latter declared its loyalty to the former when it became AQI in 2004. However, the association of the two was basically a marriage of convenience, not a coming together of soul mates. Their relationship degenerated into *fitna*, a fractious dispute, leading to open conflict. The contention went back at least to 2005 and extended past bin Laden's death. As we have seen, ISIS formally broke with al-Qaeda in 2014. We need to consider some fundamental issues of dispute.

Bin Laden and al-Zawahiri Criticize al-Zarqawi's Ultraviolence
Under bin Laden and al-Zawahiri, al-Qaeda advocated gradualism, accommodation, and compromise with other Muslims willing to support al-Qaeda's greater goals. And it condemned savagery and the publication of such brutality as something that would trouble, disgust, and alienate the *ummah*. Thus, instead of proceeding to enforce extreme *hudud* from the first, al-Qaeda advocated an incremental approach. As the head of AQAP, Abu Basir, counseled the emir of AQIM, "You have to take a gradual approach with them when it comes to their religious practices. You can't beat people for drinking alcohol when they don't even know the basics of how to pray."[67] Teaching must precede punishment.

Abu Basir's letter expressed the hope of al-Qaeda to win over Muslims through a hearts-and-minds approach. This is also exemplified by a letter written by the emir of AQAP to a fellow al-Qaeda emir in North Africa: "Try to win them over through the conveniences of life and by taking care of their daily needs like food, electricity and water. Providing these necessities will have a great effect on people, and will make them sympathize with us and feel that their fate is tied to ours."[68] Such advice is, of course, consistent with the concept of cultivating community support as part of the strategy of evolution, as discussed in Chapter 10. In contrast, the IS and its predecessors sought to grow by domination.

In the words of William McCants, the IS believes that "cutting out the hearts and minds of a population," quite literally if necessary, "can subdue them faster than trying to win them over."[69]

Within a year of al-Zarqawi's *bayah* to bin Laden, al-Zawahiri wrote al-Zarqawi a letter of advice and reprimand on 11 October 2005. Al-Zawahiri stated the general goals of al-Qaeda and praised al-Zarqawi's efforts to a degree, but his rambling dissertation ended with appeals for cooperation, criticism of al-Zarqawi's attacks on the Shias, and condemnation of his graphic bloody public violence. Al-Zawahiri was protesting Zarqawism. It was al-Qaeda's goal to spearhead a great effort against the enemies of Islam, not create irreconcilable conflict within the *ummah*: "Many of your Muslim admirers amongst the common folk are wondering about your attacks on the Shia. The sharpness of this questioning increases when the attacks are on one of their mosques. . . . My opinion is that this matter won't be acceptable to the Muslim populace however much you have tried to explain it, and aversion to this will continue."[70] And al-Zarqawi must bridle his penchant for public violence: "Among the things which the feelings of the Muslim populace who love and support you will never find palatable . . . are the scenes of slaughtering the hostages. You shouldn't be deceived by the praise of some of the zealous young men and their description of you as the sheikh of the slaughterers, etc."[71]

Al-Zawahiri's criticisms had little effect on al-Zarqawi, but he might have been wise to take them more seriously. IS savagery did ultimately unite its enemies, isolate it from potential allies, and alienate Muslim opinion. A Pew Research Center report of November 2015 revealed that a large majority of Muslims surveyed expressed disfavor with the IS. This unfavorable rating reached nearly 100 percent in Lebanon, 94 percent in Jordan, and a surprising 84 percent in the Palestinian territories occupied by Israel.[72]

Contesting the Caliphate and the Apocalypse
In another contrast, the leaders of al-Qaeda focused on attacking the United States, the far enemy, as they believed success in the Middle East could be achieved only if the *jahili* regimes could be deprived of American support. However, al-Zarqawi and those leaders who came after him in the IS concentrated on regional and local enemies, which included

Americans in Iraq, but did not encompass major attacks on the American homeland. *Jahili* regimes, the near enemy, ultimately dominated IS's concerns, albeit with global participation.

Also, as already explained, al-Qaeda and the IS differed over the resurrection of a caliphate. For bin Laden and al-Zawahiri, it was important to lay a foundation for a successful caliphate by winning mass support within the *ummah* and by driving off the United States through exhausting its will and diminishing its resources. McCants concludes: "Al-Qaeda leader Osama bin Laden and his deputy Ayman al-Zawahiri wanted to build popular Muslim support before declaring the caliphate. The Islamic State wanted to impose a caliphate regardless of what the masses thought."[73]

From its beginnings, the IS leadership regarded the creation of an Islamic State and a caliphate within the context of apocalyptic prophecy. Bin Laden and al-Zawahiri were cognizant of prophecy, but to them the end days lay in a more distant future. But to the IS leadership the apocalypse was imminent, and since the creation of a caliphate presaged the end times, it ought not to be delayed.

There were plenty of precedents for belief in an impending apocalypse and the coming of the Muslim savior, the Mahdi. One had even occurred in 1979, when a Muslim sect that believed the end days were arriving seized the Grand Mosque in Mecca and had to be driven out by deadly force. Al-Qaeda hardly referred to the end times and never said the arrival of the Mahdi was close at hand. However, the scholar of modern Islamic apocalypticism, Jean-Pierre Filiu argues that within the Sunni community as a whole, the U.S.-led invasion of Iraq in 2003 greatly increased what had been only slight interest in the apocalypse.[74] By 2012 a belief that the apocalypse was near became a strong sentiment, as shown in the Pew Research Center survey discussed in Chapter 9. In *The Global Islamic Resistance Call*, Abu Musab al-Suri writes: "The earth is filled up with oppression and injustice, and events are tumbling toward the appearance of the Mahdi. He will emerge to lead the confrontation and fill the earth with justice."[75] According to one important interpretation, the Grand Battle, the final armed clash between Islam and the infidels, is to take place at Dabiq in Syria. This explains why the IS titled its online journal *Dabiq* when it first appeared in July 2014.

The IS leadership viewed the immediate future through an apocalyptic lens. Al-Zarqawi wrote of establishing a "caliphate according to the prophetic method."[76] For the prophecies speak of a final caliphate just preceding the apocalypse. His successor, al-Masri, was, if anything, too fixated on the end days and the Mahdi. Al-Baghdadi, of course, went so far as to declare the IS to be a caliphate. And jihadis fighting in Syria shared this vision. As Abu Omar, a jihadi in Aleppo, testified: "If you think all these mujahideen came from across the world to fight Assad, you're mistaken. They are all here as promised by the Prophet. This is the war he promised—it is the Grand Battle."[77]

IS Triumphalism
In contrast to al-Qaeda, the IS added a new triumphalism to the established Islamist narrative. The Islamist narrative stresses that the West is at war with Islam, and, consequently, Muslims must defend themselves by jihad. However, as Jessica Stern and J. M. Berger point out in *ISIS: The State of Terror*, while al-Qaeda propaganda "brimmed over with talk of 'the plight of Muslims,'" IS propaganda eschewed pathos and exalted victory, inviting recruits to join in the triumph.[78] The IS pointed to its phenomenal evolution to a powerful army and a state and to its success in battle as proofs that it had received the blessing, *barakah*, of Allah.

But triumphalism requires triumph. With the loss of its territory won by conquest, the bright but brutal confidence of the IS dimmed.

TERRORISM IN THE DIGITAL AGE: THE MEDIA AND THE MESSAGES
Another difference between al-Qaeda and the IS lies in their concern for and mastery of the media. Whatever the fate of the IS, its reliance on videos with high production values that play to the emotions and its manipulation of social media will remain a standard for terrorist groups in the future, even if those groups reject the ultraviolence portrayed in IS propaganda.

Al-Qaeda took a restrained, even stodgy approach to the media. Stern and Berger put it in rather flip terms: "For the first decade of its life, al-Qaeda was publicity-shy. . . . ISIS, in contrast, is a publicity whore."[79] Abu Bakr Naji in *The Management of Savagery* put considerable stress on media, both condemning what he termed the "deceptive media halo" of the terrorists' powerful enemies, mainly the United States, and stressing the need for the jihad to pursue an effective media strategy. "Therefore, understanding the media politics of the adversaries and dealing with them is very important in winning the military and political battle. One of the most important things that will assist our media policy is to communicate our media material to its intended audiences."[80] The word "media" appears over eighty times in the English translation of his text. The IS was not the first to exploit publicity, but they have been the best at it.

Their most striking medium has been video transmitted on the internet. Images of their ultraviolence horrify and repel the great majority of people, Muslims included; however, they also excite and attract individuals that the IS wants, those inspired by radical Islamism and excited by bloodshed. The grandest of their videos have been part of the series *Salil al-Sawarim*, or *The Clanging of the Swords*. The particularly noteworthy fourth video of the series shows killings and executions, leaving little to the imagination, all to the accompaniment of a soundtrack of IS *nasheed* songs, rhythmic and jubilant. Interspersed with the upbeat carnage are enthusiastic speeches supporting jihad. All the victims shown are Muslims: Shias, condemned as *rafidah* (those who have rejected the true faith), and Sunnis whom the IS holds to be traitors or apostate. In contrast, al-Qaeda videos tend to be long, talking-head lectures and cannot compete with the action of *The Clanging of the Swords*.

IS "print" media, seen on the internet, has a real professional flair. There was precedent; in 2008 AQAP first produced its own internet magazine, initially entitled *The Echo of Battles* but soon changed to *Inspire*. The IS began the English-language *Dabiq* in July 2014, and it has been quite slick. Its pages display images of savage violence similar to IS videos, but also articles on IS ideology.[81] With its fortunes declining in Syria, the IS had to retreat from Dubiq during October 2016. Having lost Dubiq, the IS renamed its journal *Rumiyah*, or Rome. This references the fact that the prophecies that foretold victory at the apocalyptic Grand Battle described the defeated enemy as "Rome."

IS propagandists use the internet as much more than a medium to distribute videos and printed materials. Here the IS shows great ingenuity and expertise. They have propagated malware bots on the computers of unsuspecting individuals. These bots then make postings to Twitter and other sites to give the impression that the IS has a monumental following. This is part of seeming to be a major presence before you actually are: a "fake it till you make it" strategy. Social media allows feedback between interested parties and the IS itself to generate and measure support. Social media also steers people to the videos and other media IS posts. In certain circumstances it can also be used to coordinate "smart mobs," in which networks spread information and coordinate action. Between September and November 2014, there were more than 45,000 pro-IS accounts on the web. Stern and Berger award grudging respect: "Within a short span, ISIS leader Abu Bakr al Baghdadi and his fanatical followers have sketched out a new model for fringe movements to exploit changing social dynamics and new technologies, exerting an influence over world politics that is wildly disproportionate to its true size and strength."[82]

Recruitment and Provocation

As we have seen several times in this book, terrorists tend to defend their recourse to attacks on the innocent and the defenseless, often resulting in ostentatious atrocities, as forced upon them by their lack of the ability to do otherwise. Terrorists must resort to suicide bombers because "we don't have jets, we don't have tanks."[83] It might be expected that a terrorist group that becomes powerful enough to claim to be a state would turn to more conventional kinds of warfare, if only to appear more legitimate. The IS showed no signs of moving in this direction. Its dedication to ultraviolence could be explained in several ways, most of which come down to "old habits die hard." But I am inclined to see IS ultraviolence as neither habit nor psychosis, but as purposefully fulfilling two necessities: recruitment and provocation.

For the IS to maintain its forces, it absorbed what manpower it could find locally, but it also *had to* attract foreigners: global participation. No one knows for sure how many full-time fighters the IS recruited or exactly how many of these were and are foreign. In its December 2015 report on foreign fighters, the Soufan Group estimated the number of such volunteers in Syria and Iraq at over 24,000 from eighty-six countries.[84] These foreign fighters were not marshaled in IS forces alone, but they were primarily IS volunteers. It is no surprise that the IS tailored its internet propaganda to bring in foreign recruits.

The nature of IS propaganda, particularly the videos, seems designed to attract *a certain kind* of foreign fighter: those drawn to the Islamist message, excited by the sense of power projected by its ultraviolence, and enticed, or at least not deterred, by its savagery. Undoubtedly, the vast majority of Muslims are horrified by beheadings, massacres, and sexual slavery. However, the IS does not need to win over all 1.6 billion Muslims worldwide. Extrapolating from the Soufan figures, in the eighteen months between June 2014 and December 2015 the number of foreign fighters in Syria doubled from 12,000 to over 24,000. These figures do not expressly consider wastage from casualties, so generously assume that the increase of 12,000 would have required 20,000 new recruits. This would mean an influx of only about 1,100 recruits per month to all groups fighting against the Assad regime, a barely visible 0.00007 percent of the *ummah*.

To net its recruits in the deep and wide ocean of the *ummah*, the IS cast its net broadly, but it only had pull in a small catch who fit the IS profile. IS videos both attracted and screened potential fighters, producing what the IS wanted. *The Clanging of the Swords, Part 4* (May 2014) provided intensely gruesome images of its violence and directly praised and appealed for foreign volunteers. It included an oration by a bearded IS warrior: "Praise be to Allah who has granted us the blessing of emigrating for His sake. . . . We praise Allah for his blessings and for gathering us together with the lions of the Islamic State from every corner of the world."[85] As McCants alerts us: "The [Islamic] State revels in gore and wants everyone to know it. And yet it has been remarkably successful at recruiting fighters, capturing land, subduing its subjects, and creating a state. Why? Because violence and gore work."[86]

Beyond recruitment, the global distribution of IS propaganda was also intended to provoke the West. Accept that the leadership and a significant proportion of IS forces believed IS ideology concerning the blessing of Allah upon its jihad and the imminent coming of the apocalypse and the Grand Battle. Allah will intervene; victory is promised in this great clash of arms. So the IS very much wanted to precipitate this victory by provoking the intervention of their Western (Christian and Jewish) enemies. And given the IS's sense of urgency, the sooner the better. The IS could look to previous successes over infidels, the Russians in Afghanistan and the Americans and their allies in Iraq. Therefore, the images of savagery that the IS presented, such as beheadings of Westerners, were not meant to make the United States and its allies cower but to charge into battle. They were not meant merely to inflict fear but to incite outrage.

In this campaign of provocation, the actions of lone wolves in the United States, Europe, and elsewhere were also a kind of propaganda of the deed, designed to further the campaign to make enemy governments invest more resources and forces on the battlefields of Syria and Iraq.

It could be argued that the campaign of public ultraviolence ultimately rebounded against the IS. We have already noted the low IS approval ratings among the *ummah* by late 2015. Surely the extreme public violence of the IS explains this in large part. Cronin's list of how terrorism ends includes collapse of a terrorist group because of a fall in popular support. Bin Laden and al-Zawahiri may have been proven right: al-Zarqawi and those who followed him went too far. And IS provocation did not bring the Grand Battle of the end days, but the battles that ended the IS. It was overcome by a coalition of forces who may have not agreed on much, but they were in accord about the need to eradicate the IS. Another item on Cronin's list was the destruction of a terrorist group by brute force; the IS as a *state* has been hammered into the ground in Iraq and Syria. At least for now.

In considering the pasts of al-Qaeda and the Islamic State, we are tempted to speculate about their futures. But in a work of history such as this, it is best to be modest in predicting what is to come.

The IS, despite its astounding victories in 2014, has suffered a string of defeats. IS forces fought with desperate determination but failed to hold what they had won. In November 2016, U.S. Secretary of Defense Ashton Carter declared, "We're going to destroy the idea that there is an Islamic State. . . . And that magnetism that two years ago brought many foreign fighters—there'll be no magnet left."[87]

Yet Adnani's final address in May 2016 warned: "Or do you, O America, consider defeat to be the loss of a city or the loss of land? . . . Certainly not! . . . We would be defeated and you victorious only if you were able to remove the Qur'an from the Muslims' hearts."[88] He was announcing that should the IS suffer a setback it would again simply regroup, as it did after the American surge in Iraq. "We fight in obedience to Allah and to become closer to Him. And victory is that we live in the might of our religion or die upon it. It is the same, whether Allah blesses us with consolidation or we move into the bare, open desert, displaced and pursued."[89] For the IS, defeat in the cities may not mean destruction but redeployment as it returns to insurgency and terrorism. And it could mean changing its major effort to another venue.

Adnani was not simply papering over defeat with brave words. The IS has established *wilayahs* outside of Syria and Iraq; perhaps it could regroup there, attracting the same kind of fighters who once journeyed to Syria. Or radical Islamists could find another champion. IS defeat could allow an al-Qaeda resurgence. As a senior American counterterrorism official told the foreign affairs analyst Robin Wright even as the IS was crumbling: "There's always been this dream of recapturing and bringing back the caliphate. . . . Who's going to tap into that next?"[90]

In discussing the Islamic State, I have used the past tense much of the time. It seemed a reasonable choice as I revised my manuscript in early 2018. But it is risky to expect a particular future; consider the shock of June 2014. In 1953, the novelist L. P. Hartley penned a statement much used by historians: "The past is a foreign country: they do things differently there." Yes, and the future is unexplored territory; who knows what they'll do *there*.

Ultimately, the ability of terrorist groups to achieve their goals depends on their ability to mobilize and keep support. The extreme political ideologies of the radical Marxist urban guerrillas disrupted but could not destroy the regimes they attacked. They never really had the numbers. Ethno-nationalist terrorist groups succeeded by bringing to bear a national or ethnic population, as did the FLN and the LTTE. However, radical Islamists perform on a much larger stage, and their target audience is huge, an entire worldwide religious community. We should avoid policies and proclamations that increase their ability to draw from it.

In any case, radical Islamism is not the only terrorist threat that confronts us. We must move on to two others now: radical right-wing violence in the United States and narcoterrorism in many venues.

CHAPTER TWELVE

Radical Right-Wing Violence in the United States

FIGURE 12.1. Timothy McVeigh targeted the Murrah Federal Office Building in Oklahoma City with a truck bomb on 19 April 1995. His act of right-wing terrorism killed 168 people, making it the deadliest act of radical terrorism on American soil until the 9/11 attacks. AP Photo/File.

TIMOTHY MCVEIGH, A DECORATED VETERAN of the First Gulf War, fervently believed that the U.S. government was trying to void the Second Amendment of the Constitution in order to impose tyranny on American citizens. He shared a conviction common on the right wing that that the Second Amendment was the best guarantee against oppression. To McVeigh, the actions of the Bureau of Alcohol, Tobacco, and Firearms (ATF) and the Federal Bureau of Investigation (FBI) at Ruby Ridge in 1992 and during the siege of the Branch Davidian compound at Waco, Texas, in 1993 proved that the government was, indeed, assuming dictatorial powers. It must be compelled to cease and desist.

Inspired by the far-right manifesto *The Turner Diaries*, McVeigh plotted to bomb the Alfred P. Murrah Federal Office Building in Oklahoma City. He chose the building as his target because it housed offices of the ATF and the Drug Enforcement Agency (DEA), because its glass front would maximize casualties, and because the site of the building would provide the most startling images of destruction for propaganda reasons. He fixed on 19 April 1995 as the date for his attack for symbolic reasons. It was the second anniversary of the final attack and inferno that killed the Branch Davidians at Waco. In addition, it was the anniversary of the "shot heard 'round the world" at Lexington, Massachusetts, in 1775. McVeigh regarded himself as an embattled patriot opposing despotism.

He enlisted the support of an army buddy, Terry Nichols. Two others also knew of his plans, but McVeigh acted essentially as a lone wolf. With great care to escape detection, he secured and stored the necessary bomb-making materials. The day before the attack, he and Nichols packed a rented Ryder truck with three tons of ammonium nitrate fertilizer and nitromethane, a high-energy racing-car fuel, along with other explosives. At 9 a.m. on 19 April he parked the truck bomb in front of the Murrah Building, exited the cab, and walked toward a getaway car he had stationed not far away. As planned, the fuses he had lit to set off the blast detonated the explosives while he was walking to the vehicle.

The explosion, equivalent to 5,000 pounds of TNT, demolished the front of the building, killing 168 people and injuring another 680 (Fig. 12.1). McVeigh intended to destroy federal offices and kill federal workers, but the building also housed a day care center for children. The most heartbreaking image of the tragedy showed a fireman cradling in his arms the bloodied body of an infant, one of nineteen children who perished. Up to that point in time, the Oklahoma City bombing was the deadliest single terrorist attack on American soil; its toll of misery would only be exceeded by that of 9/11.

McVeigh drove north from Oklahoma City on I-35, but an Oklahoma state trooper stopped him because his car had no rear license plate. The trooper arrested McVeigh for having a loaded handgun without a license, and authorities soon identified him as having rented the truck used for the bombing.

Recognizing that he could be killed or captured during his escape, McVeigh had put a thick packet of articles and papers in the trunk of his car, documents he hoped would reach the press. His was a political act, and he wanted it properly understood. Among these papers was a quote from *The Turner Diaries*: "The real value of our attacks today lies in the psychological impact, not in the immediate casualties."[1] Classic terrorism.

Tried and convicted, Timothy McVeigh was executed three months to the day before 9/11. He had dropped his appeals and accepted his fate. Concerning those killed in the bombing he commented: "I am sorry these people had to lose their lives, but that's the nature of the beast."[2]

Radical Islamism and the evolution of the Islamic State have recently posed the most pressing terrorist threats to the global community, but these are not the sole forms of terrorism that haunt the world. Within the United States, the radical right has engaged in a great deal of violence against people and property during the past fifty years. Much of this is best considered as hate crimes or acts of sheer rage; some of it qualifies as terrorism by our criteria. This chapter will discuss this range of violence. The ideology and actions of the extreme right differ sharply from those of radical Islamists, but there are disturbing similarities as well, including the powerful role of fundamentalist religion. The record of radical right violence serves as a cautionary tale to those who see terrorism as essentially foreign. In fact, the cost in lives exacted on American soil by the radical right, from the morrow of 9/11 until June 2016, exceeded that inflicted by Islamist terrorists. And given the increasingly bitter political polarization in the United States, it is not unreasonable to fear that we might see a real increase in right-wing extremism.

VARIETIES OF RIGHT-WING VIOLENCE

In discussing right-wing terrorism we must begin by pointing out what should be obvious: conservatism is not inherently extremist. An old and honorable tradition of conservatism in the United States privileges individual liberty and is suspicious of authority, particularly that of the federal government. The radical right is something different.

Arie Perliger has written one of the most useful surveys of right-wing terrorism, *Challengers from the Sidelines: Understanding America's Violent Far-Right* (2012). He divides right-wing extremist movements into three categories. We will too, although we will label them in a somewhat different manner. Ours will be 1) hate groups, including the Ku Klux Klan and the Aryan Nations (AN); 2) anti–federal government groups including militias; and 3) Christian anti-abortion groups like the Army of God and committed individuals. Lines between hate groups, anti-federalists, and anti-abortion groups blur, and all three tend to share some core beliefs. Consider the AN, which has been labeled by the RAND Corporation as the "first truly nationwide terrorist network" in the United States.[3] It advocates fundamentalist Christian Identity convictions of White supremacy (see below) and promotes race hatred; at the same time, it regards the federal government as an enemy that is dominated by Jews, in what it calls the Zionist Occupation Government. Moreover, as journalist James Ridgeway showed in his 1995 work *Blood in the Face*, the same prominent people often belonged to radical-right groups of different stripes at one time or another.[4]

Perliger argues that a form of extreme nationalism is most important for "understanding the far-right worldview." This stresses "internal homogenization, i.e., the aspiration that all residents or citizens of the polity will share the same national origin and ethnic characteristics" and "external exclusiveness, the aspiration that all individuals belonging to a specific national or ethnic group will reside in the homeland."[5] This form of nationalism is infused with a great deal of racism, buttressed by particular twists on Christianity. Still, as always in discussing terrorism and terrorists, there are exceptions. McVeigh, the deadliest right-wing terrorist, certainly saw himself as a patriot, but he denied being racist, although he resented what he saw as the preferential treatment given Blacks.[6] Concerning religion, he declared, "Science is my religion."[7]

In this chapter we will begin by discussing underlying ideologies of racism and religion, which relate to earlier treatments of the Ku Klux Klan in Chapter 4 and display certain parallels with the religious intensity of radical Islamism discussed in Chapters 9–11. We will then devote separate sections to hate groups, anti-federalist extremists, and anti-abortion terrorism.

THE MAGNITUDE OF THE THREAT POSED BY RIGHT-WING VIOLENCE

It is understandable that Americans fear the IS as a global threat and as a danger within the United States. However, far-right extremists have also been deadly. According to New America, a Washington think tank, the death toll inflicted by "jihadist terrorists" in the United States after 9/11 and through May 2016 stood at forty-five, while the number killed by "far right wing" violence during the same period was significantly *higher*, at sixty-four. Only the killing of forty-nine people by an IS-inspired gunman at an Orlando nightclub on 12 June 2016 raised the toll of those murdered by radical Islamists above that by the radical right. By August 2017 the total number of those killed in radical Islamist terrorist attacks had reached ninety-five, while those who had died at the hands of radical right-wing terrorists climbed to sixty-eight.[8]

Perliger, who considers the broader category of right-wing violence as a whole, not simply terrorism, includes 4,420 incidents against property and persons that can be considered as right-wing violence in the United States from 1990 to 2012. These resulted in 670 fatalities, as well as injuring some 3,053.[9] A bit less than a quarter of the 4,420 incidents included by Perliger's count can be ascribed to particular groups or causes, and, among these, 593 are attributed to racist groups, while militias and other anti-federalists are credited with eighty-seven, and 227 were carried out by anti-abortionists.[10]

Since the 1990s, the radical right has been a long-term growth industry. According to the Simon Wiesenthal Center, when McVeigh bombed the Murrah Office Building in 1995, only one hate group was on the web.[11] Estimates of the growing number of hate groups differ, but the Southern Poverty Law Center (SPLC) reports the count at 602 in 2000, 803 in 2005, 1,002 in 2010, and 954 in 2017.[12] At the same time, the number of what the SPLC considers to be right-wing "Patriot Groups," including militias, rose from an annual average of 148 during the presidency of George W. Bush (2001–2009), to 512 in 2009, with the new Obama administration, and 1,360 in 2012, when Obama was running for reelection.[13] Obviously the election of America's first African-American president caused a great rise in "patriotic" enthusiasm.

The far right has attracted a great number of supporters, including those actually engaged in violence and those in sympathy with them. In 1988, the Center for Democratic Renewal, an organization that tracks such organizations, set the number of right-wing activists at 15,000–20,000 and of those who attended right-wing gatherings at 150,000.[14] Stormfront, a website that touts "White Pride World Wide," was created in the mid-1990s. It provides a striking barometer of the far right. By January 2002, it boasted 5,000 registered users; this number increased dramatically to 23,000 in 2004, 100,000 in 2007, and 165,000 in April 2009.[15]

In short, far-right ideology, groups, and violence have been and are serious matters in the United States, even if they have not attracted the attention that Islamist terrorism has garnered since 9/11.

APOCALYPSE

Although the grievances and causes that motivate far-right extremists vary, it is surprising how much they share a common culture. Most prominent are a form of White supremacism entwined with untraditional readings of Christian scripture, conspiracy theories that mix racism with fear of government authority, and an apocalyptic vision of inevitable conflict between races or/and between individual liberty and tyranny. These can be seen as the radical right's version of the terrorism mindset we have seen before.

Christian Identity: White Supremacist Religion

Just as radical Islamists base their morality and ideology on a particular fundamentalist literal interpretation of the Quran and the *hadith*, so a great many on the radical right in the United States have found inspiration, or justification, in fundamentalist interpretations of the Bible that advance White supremacist convictions. Although not all extremists adhere to any one creed, a warped form of apocalyptic Christianity, called Christian Identity, stands out as a bastion of the radical right. By about 2000, the Christian Identity movement in its several guises was estimated to command tens of thousands of adherents; one estimate put the number at 20,000–30,000; another, by widely published religious scholar Rosemary Reuther, set it at 50,000.[16] The following discussion of Christian Identity should make clear that it is not just Islam that can be twisted into strange and menacing shapes.

Christian Identity holds that the Book of Genesis describes two entirely different creations, not simply two tellings of the same creation. For those who embrace Christian Identity, the first creation, Genesis 1:26–28, was of inferior races, what Christian Identity adherents condemn as "mud people." Only the second creation, Genesis 2:7–25, brought White people, Adam and Eve, into being. So, Whites are entirely separate from, and superior to, the "colored" races. One strain of Christian Identity thinking—seed-line doctrine—argues that Eve's original sin was to be seduced by Satan, the snake, who fathered Cain, while Adam fathered Abel. Cain was, thus, the child of the devil and killed Abel. He then fled and fathered the Semitic Jews with the mud people. So, according to this interpretation, the battle between Whites and Jews is primeval, a struggle between God and Satan. American Christian Identity exalts the White race, detests the mud people, and combats the Satanic Jews.

Christian Identity goes even further in its reinterpretation of the Bible. The Jews of the present world are not the chosen people of God. The true chosen are the descendants of the lost ten tribes of Israel, who were, in fact, White and migrated to northern Europe. Christian Identity developed from mid-nineteenth-century British Anglo-Israelism, which held that the Anglo-Saxon British were God's real Jews. The original version of this belief was not intrinsically anti-Semitic, but that which rooted in America in the 1880s took a strong anti-Semitic turn. Its most important American spokesmen included Wesley Swift, who was at one point an organizer for the KKK. Swift founded the White Identity Church of Jesus Christ-Christian in 1946. Richard Girnt Butler adopted Christian Identity and in the 1970s established the White supremacist and neo-Nazi Aryan Nations (AN) at Hayden Lake, Idaho. The emphasis on the Aryan race clearly associated AN with Hitler's regime, from which it borrowed uniforms and ceremony, as well as beliefs.

Christian Identity is not the only fundamentalist sect on the extreme right. The Christian anti-abortion movement, for example, is permeated with ideas from Dominion Theology. At the extreme of Dominianism stand the Christian Reconstructionists, who want to create a theocratic totalitarian state in line with Old Testament laws. An advocate of Reconstructionism, Gary North, stresses "the moral obligation of Christians to recapture every institution for Jesus Christ."[17] Christian Reconstruction's advocacy of theocracy seems eerily like the radical Islamist desire to return to the *Salaf.*

Conspiracies of Race and Power
The term ZOG—Zionist Occupation Government, or Zionist-Occupied Government—became current in the AN by the mid-1970s. The concept

of ZOG adopted and adapted older anti-Semitic conspiracy theses, going back at least to the *Protocols of the Elders of Zion*, that Jews were secretly running governments for their own benefit. James Ellison, leader of the Christian Identity cult the Covenant, the Sword, and the Arm of the Lord (CSA), declared in 1976: "The Jews have declared war on our race, promoting race-mixing and thereby polluting the pure seed of God.... This ZOG, this Zionist Occupied Government, is killing our white babies through abortion! It is destroying white minds with its humanistic teachings of evolution!"[18] The 1996 Aryan Nations and the Church of Jesus Christ-Christian Declaration of Independence announced the need for White self-defense against the ZOG: "The history of the present Zionist Occupied Government of the United States of America is a history of repeated injuries and usurpations.... The United States and its 'New World Order' has as one of its foremost purposes, the eradication of the White race and its culture."[19]

Many radical-right extremists believed that a New World Order (NWO) plotted to absorb the United States into a tyrannical global regime. This would begin by an accretion of power in the federal government, thus the creation of a national police force, for example. International "peacekeeping" forces would then deploy in the United States to impose their will on America. These military units, sometimes described as UN troops, would build up secretly, using unmarked "black helicopters," according to one version of the myth. In an odd twist, the proclamation of a post–Cold War NWO by President George Herbert Walker Bush in his 11 September 1990 address to a joint session of Congress lent a superficial weight to this conspiracy theory.

An Apocalyptic Vision: The Turner Diaries
Among the works authored by members of the White supremacist, antifederalist, and fundamentalist radical right, none surpasses in its popularity and influence *The Turner Diaries*, published in 1978 by William Pierce, under the pseudonym of Andrew MacDonald. A *New York Times* article published shortly after the Oklahoma City bombing reported that federal officials called the book the "Bible of the extremist right."[20] Although Pierce, a neo-Nazi, was not connected to the Church of Jesus Christ-Christian, he was influenced by Christian Identity ideas, and his *Turner Diaries* was and is read by Christian Identity adherents. Among a

great many others, Timothy McVeigh was also caught up in *The Turner Diaries*, read it, gave copies to friends, and sold the book at gun shows, although he claims to have been most concerned with its gun-rights message, and not its racism. *The Turner Diaries* certainly appealed to anti-federalist Second Amendment enthusiasts: a promotional tagline on the back of the first edition read: "What will you do when they come to take your guns?" The symbolic importance of gun ownership is central to the anti-federalist strain on the right, but the confiscation of guns is also seen as a threat to those committed to Christian Identity. For them gun control is a means by which the "Jewish-UN-liberal conspirators" can render their opponents powerless.[21]

The book of radical fiction takes the form of a diary written by Earl Turner, a participant in an uprising that has overturned the U.S. government. The Cohen Act, a law ordering the seizure of all privately owned firearms, precipitated the violent rebellion. This is only one of a series of laws that a Jewish-dominated government enacted to render Whites defenseless. In response, persecuted White supremacists form "The Organization" to conduct an escalating guerrilla war against the government. In one of its early operations, Turner's band demolished the FBI headquarters building in Washington, D.C. with an ammonium-nitrate and fuel-oil truck bomb. This fictional bombing is thought to have been the inspiration for McVeigh, who used a similar truck bomb in Oklahoma City. Eventually this rebellion secures control of southern California and takes racial revenge, as described in Turner's diary: "Today has been the Day of the Ropes. . . . The first thing I saw in the moonlight was the placard with its legend in large, block letters: 'I defiled my race.' Above the placard leered the horribly bloated, purplish face of a young woman. . . . There are many thousands of hanging female corpses like that in this city tonight. . . . They are the White women who were married to or living with Blacks, with Jews, or with other non-White males."[22]

The Organization launches nuclear attacks on New York and Israel; other American cities are destroyed. In 1999, to combat an invasion by the U.S. military dictatorship, Turner undertakes a suicide mission, flying a small plane with an atomic weapon into the Pentagon. Much of the world has descended into destruction and chaos, but White Aryans prevail and create a new world. To do so they use nuclear, chemical, and biological weapons to eradicate non-White enemies, such as the Chinese.

In victory, the Aryans create their own new dating system for the world, beginning with 1999 as year 1: "It was in the year 1999, according to the chronology of the Old Era—just 110 years after the birth of the Great One [Adolf Hitler]—that the dream of a White world finally became a certainty."[23]

The Turner Diaries is an apocalyptic fantasy. Another notion of a necessary cataclysm, a Racial Holy War, or RAHOWA, survives among radical racists. RAHOWA as a term was propagated by Ben Klassen, the White supremacist who founded the World Church of the Creator in the early 1970s.[24]

As appalling as the vision of such right-wing extremists is, it gives the comfort of certainty: a simplified struggle between absolutes, good and evil. And of clear duty—they believe their communities to be under attack and they are morally bound to defend them by any means necessary. As one Christian Identity believer testified, the Bible is "a book of war, a book of hate."[25]

HATE GROUPS

Hate groups are those whose primary focus is their hostility to others based on their race, ethnicity, religion, sexual orientation, or gender identity.[26] The dominant, but not only, theme in violent hate groups in the United States is White supremacy. Organizations and individuals within the radical anti-federalist category often also harbor extreme racial hatred, but their primary emphasis is on what they perceive as the dangers of growing government tyranny. Groups with an organizing principle of hate for the "other" can pursue terrorist campaigns, but they can also express or inspire violence that has little purpose other than venting rage and celebrating dominance. Hate crimes are deplorable and vicious, but we need to ask if individual cases are best considered as terrorism, or simply as detestable violence. Such a distinction matters little to the immediate victims and their loved ones, but it is significant in a study of terrorism per se.

Hate groups are too numerous and varied to be considered here at length. Older forms persist, notably the KKK and various neo-Nazi groups. As explained in Chapter 4, membership in the Ku Klux Klan declined sharply after the victories of the civil rights movement; in the 1980s it sank to no more than 1,000. But Klan regalia and ceremony seem irresistible to racists, and the KKK has rebounded a bit. The Southern Poverty Law Center estimated the membership of the smaller but more overt Klans in 2012 at 5,000–8,000. And with the approach of the presidential campaign of 2016, the number of Klan chapters increased from seventy-two in 2014 to 190 in 2015.[27]

The neo-Nazi genre of hate groups also has a long history. American Nazi groups existed in the 1930s, and neo-Nazi sentiment surfaced after World War II. George Lincoln Rockwell founded the American Nazi Party in 1959. Rockwell retitled the group the National Socialist White People's Party in 1967, but he was assassinated by one of his own disaffected followers in August of that year. The party splintered, and the most powerful of neo-Nazi organizations was the National Alliance, founded in 1970 by William Pierce. According to the SPLC, the largest and most important neo-Nazi group is now the National Socialist Movement; by 2009 it had sixty-one chapters in thirty-two states; its membership still numbered in the hundreds, not the thousands.[28] They adhere to Christian Identity and declare as one of their "25 Points" that "all non-White immigration must be prevented. We demand that all non-Whites currently residing in America be required to leave the nation forthwith and return to their land of origin: peacefully or by force."[29]

But we will now look more closely at three examples of hate groups: the AN, the CSA, and the right-wing skinheads.

Aryan Nations and the Silent Brotherhood
Founded by Richard Butler as an outgrowth of the Church of Jesus Christ-Christian in 1971, Aryan Nations is an arm of White supremacist fundamentalism that also incorporates the ideas and the trappings of neo-Nazism. In his study, it is said, Butler kept both the Bible and Hitler's *Mein Kampf*, along with a framed picture of the Führer. The annual AN World Conferences at Hayden Lake brought together members of several White supremacist organizations, including Klansmen, neo-Nazis, and skinheads. These meetings peaked in the 1980s, when the congresses drew as many as 200 participants. Butler preached White-separatism, a White migration to the Pacific Northwest, where he hoped to establish an Aryan homeland in five of the fifty United States.[30] He believed the government and media to be dominated by Jews and condemned the U.S. Army as "creating an empire for the anti-Christ, the Jews."[31]

The AN advocated, and thus inspired, violence, but it apparently did not directly organize and dispatch its members to commit major crimes and murders. However, individuals associated with the AN in one way or another did do so. The most prominent example of this is the group led by Robert "Bob" Mathews in 1983 and 1984. This group had no formal name at first, although it was called at times "the Order," a name taken from *The Turner Diaries*. When Mathews crafted a name, a creed, and an emblem, he titled his band the Silent Brotherhood. It never claimed more than twenty or so active cadres, recruited from AN members along with some from the neo-Nazi National Alliance. Mathews associated with Butler, but considered him insufficiently extreme. Also, he did not entirely subscribe to Christian Identity but espoused his own idea of a Nordic belief system that he called "Odinism."

Mathews obsessed over the need to secure funds for the White separatist cause in its war against the ZOG, so the Silent Brotherhood turned to robbery. After clumsy and unproductive efforts, it moved on to attacking armored cars. On 19 July 1984 a crew of twelve, led by Mathews, robbed a Brinks armored car in an elaborate operation at Ukiah, California. This heist netted $3.8 million, some of which they distributed as gifts to other White supremacist organizations. But it was not just robbery. A month before Ukiah, on 18 June, members of the Silent Brotherhood assassinated Alan Berg in Denver, Colorado. Berg was a sharp-tongued Jewish shock jock who had infuriated them.

But the FBI was on Mathews's trail, aided by an informant within his circle. On 7 December 1984 agents surrounded Silent Brotherhood safe houses near Freeland, Washington. Other members of the group surrendered, but Mathews held out, perishing in a fire that consumed his house.

Other individuals associated with AN who turned to violence include Buford Furrow, who had served as one of Butler's bodyguards. In August 1999 he attacked the North Valley Jewish Community Center in Grenada Hills, California, wounding five people. He then fled and later shot to death a Filipino-American mail carrier. Furrow turned himself in and was sentenced to two consecutive life sentences plus 110 years.

Leadership squabbles plagued the AN during the 1990s, but through this, the group stayed solvent with membership payments and the financial backing of two Silicon Valley millionaires, Carl Story and Vincent

Bertollini, who left California for northern Idaho in 1995. But then AN suffered a severe blow in a legal action pursued by the SPLC. In July 1998, AN security guards, spooked by a car's backfire that they interpreted as gunfire, shot at a car carrying Victoria Keenan and her son Jason, Native Americans. The guards chased the car, peppering it with bullets. When the car spun off the road, the guards dragged Keenan and her son out of the vehicle and terrorized them, putting a gun to her head. Led by Morris Dees, the SPLC sued the AN, and in September 2000 the court awarded the Keenans a judgment of $6.3 million. This bankrupted the AN.

The AN continued on, but was torn by leadership disputes. In 2004, Butler died and the AN split into different factions and continued to decline. One of the new leaders, August Kreis, grabbed some headlines in 2005 when he advocated an alliance between AN and al-Qaeda, since they shared common enemies, the Jews and the U.S. government. Kreis testified, "I want to instill the same jihadic feeling in our peoples' heart, in the Aryan race, that they have for their father, who they call Allah."[32]

The use of the word "Aryan" in the names of other groups usually indicates White supremacist orientation, as with the Aryan Brotherhood, a White supremacist prison gang with about 10,000 members across the United States, and the Aryan Republican Army, a White supremacist criminal group that committed some twenty-two bank robberies during the 1990s. The Aryan Brotherhood came under scrutiny during the trials of the three men who viciously murdered James Byrd, Jr. in June 1998. This African-American man was horribly beaten and then dragged to his death behind a pick-up truck in Jasper, Texas. The brutal killing was not a calculated act of terrorism, but a despicable hate crime committed by three White men, two of whom either had ties to the Aryan Brotherhood or shared its ideology.[33]

The Covenant, the Sword, and the Arm of the Lord
The history of another hate group, the CSA, which existed from 1971 until 1985, has more bizarre, and dangerous, dimensions. Its acronym is an obvious reference to the Confederate States of America. The new CSA took on traits of a religious cult. As was the case with AN, the Covenant, the Sword, and the Arm of the Lord adhered to Christian Identity, but with a particularly strong apocalyptic aspect. Members sold their

homes, donated their money to the cult, and were instructed to destroy all mementos of their pasts. CSA founder James Ellison saw himself as a religious leader, but went too far. At one point in 1982 he even endorsed polygamy, when he wanted to enjoy the favors of another man's wife.

Ellison and his seconds, Kerry Noble and Richard Snell, had close relations with other White supremacist organizations, including the KKK and the AN. Butler was an honored guest of the CSA, even appearing as a featured speaker at its national convention in 1982.

A decade before McVeigh's attack in Oklahoma City, Ellison and Snell conspired to blow up the Murrah Office Building, but the plot was never realized. The authorities were closing in, and on 19 April 1985, 200 FBI, ATF, and state law enforcement agents surrounded the CSA compound. After negotiations, the occupants surrendered, although the compound had supplies to withstand a long siege. On the grounds, authorities discovered a large drum of cyanide intended for poisoning the water supplies of American cities, an act that would have resulted in mass casualties. Noble would later explain: "The major cities to us were like Sodom and Gomorrah, like the Tower of Babel. Who would be judged? The homosexual; the liberal, idolatrous preachers; those officials in high places; the merchants of trade and usury; and all those who refused the word of the Lord. They were the enemy. And so they would have to die."[34] Ridding the world of such "abominations" would facilitate the arrival of the apocalypse.

Ellison and Noble received prison sentences. To reduce his sentence, Ellison turned informer. Snell had already been arrested for the April 1984 murders of a pawnbroker, who Snell mistakenly believed was Jewish, and a Black Arkansas state trooper. In an odd turn of fate, Snell was executed on 19 April 1995, the very day that McVeigh detonated his truck bomb.

Racist Skinheads
Although White supremacist ideology was not part of the original British skinhead youth and music culture of the late 1960s and early 1970s, White power advocacy became an important characteristic of the second skinhead surge that began in the late 1970s and continues to this day. White power rock was and remains a defining expression for racist skinheads, as is Nazi symbolism. During the mid-1980s, racist skinhead or-

ganizations appeared in the United States. By 1988, the Anti-Defamation League estimated that there were 2,000 "neo-Nazi skinheads" across the country, according to the *New York Times*.[35] From this base, the phenomenon continued to grow. The SPLC reported that in 2012 there were 133 skinhead groups of all varieties in the United States. Among the White power skinhead groups, Hammerskin Nation, formed in 1988, is the largest and most important. Its creed includes: "We must secure the existence of our people and a future for White Children."[36] It has become an umbrella organization for many local skinhead groups.

The radical right soon recognized that the skinheads provided a new means of youth recruitment. Thomas "Tom" Metzger, who created White Aryan Resistance (WAR) in 1983, was one of the first to realize this. He began his right-wing career in the Christian Identity church and joined the KKK in 1975, rising to become California Grand Dragon of the Knights of the Ku Klux Klan. The SPLC called him "one of the most notorious living white supremacists in the United States."[37] In a 1988 WAR Hotline message, we can see his prejudice displayed: "You ask: What is WAR? We are an openly white-racist movement—Skinheads, we welcome you into our ranks—The federal government is the number one enemy of our race. When was the last time you heard a politician speaking out in favor of white people? . . . You say the government is too big; we can't organize. Well, by God, the SS did it in Germany, and if they did it in Germany in the thirties, we can do it right here in the streets of America. We need to cleanse this nation of all nonwhite mud-races for the survival of our own people and the generations of our children."[38]

In Oklahoma that year Metzger organized the first hate-rock festival, Aryan Fest, appealing to racist skinhead tastes in music and violence. On 13 November an Ethiopian graduate student, Mulugetta Seraw, was beaten to death with a baseball bat in Portland, Oregon; three skinheads from East Side White Pride eventually pleaded guilty of hate-crime murder. In 1989, the SPLC and the Anti-Defamation League sued Metzger and WAR for inciting the act. The jury awarded the Seraw family $12.5 million in October 1990. The suit bankrupted Metzger, and although it did not eliminate WAR, it has been reduced to little more than a soapbox for Metzger, who has continued his racist rhetoric.

Racist skinhead violence characteristically focuses on direct violent personal attacks on minorities. For example, skinheads murdered homeless men in 1992, 1995, and 2003. In 1995 two skinheads, U.S. Army paratroopers at the time, killed a Black couple whom they apparently chose at random; and in 1999 Florida skinheads assaulted inter-racial couples, killing a woman and a child. In 2012, Wade Michael Page killed six Sikhs and wounded four others at a Sikh temple in Oak Creek, Wisconsin. Wounded by a police officer, Wade took his own life. Page was a White supremacist, a White Pride rock musician, and a Hammerskin.

ANTI-FEDERALISTS: THE MILITIAS

Anti-government extremists describe themselves as akin to the founding fathers of the United States, but today's violent anti-federalism is not related to the birth pangs of the United States. It has far more in common with the White supremacist secession of the Confederate States in 1861 and the appeals to "states' rights" voiced by opponents of the civil rights movement during the 1960s. In addition, the anti-government movement is wrapped up in the gun culture of the extreme right. This holds that the private ownership of firearms is essential to the maintenance of liberty because an armed populace can resist a tyrannical government. We will center on the militia movement as representative of anti-federalists, but they are not alone.

Posse Comitatus

The new face of the anti-federalist far right appeared in 1969 with the group Posse Comitatus. The Latin name refers to a county sheriff's right to conscript citizens to aid him in enforcing the law, to form a posse. This organization, based in Oregon, insisted that according to the common law tradition the highest level of authority is the county and its sheriff. Members of Posse Comitatus refused to accept the authority of the federal government. Posse Comitatus and Christian Identity proved to be quite compatible; in fact, the group's leader, William Potter Gale, was a Christian Identity minister. Posse Comitatus embraced virulent anti-Semitism, as in its 1985 declaration: "Our nation is now completely under the control of the International Invisible government of the World Jewry."[39]

As economic crisis struck American farming in the 1980s, Posse Comitatus tried to take advantage of it by spreading its anti-government creed among the agricultural community. However, the populist appeal of the group was limited by its extremism and propensity to criminal violence. By the early 1980s, Posse Comitatus was on the federal government's radar. In February 1983, Gordon Kahl, a member, killed two federal marshals in North Dakota. Kahl went on the run and was eventually cornered and killed in June. Prosecutions of those who chose not to file tax returns because they considered federal taxes illegitimate further embarrassed Posse Comitatus. The group dwindled to the point of virtual collapse by the late 1980s.

The so-called sovereign citizen movement also denies the authority of the federal government. This movement is less hierarchical than Posse Comitatus, and less defined by group membership, but it still falls within the anti-federalist classification. Its most common form of protest is an unwillingness to pay taxes. However, individuals within this movement have turned to deadly violence, as when Jerry and Joseph Kane, father and son, murdered two police officers who had simply stopped them along an interstate near Memphis in 2010. Later that same day, the Kanes died in a firefight with police.

The Militia Movement
In a sense, the militia movement repackaged the far right with a patriotic label. These armed right-wing groups envision themselves as descendants of the "minutemen" who fought to establish American liberty. Posse Commitatus can be seen as a precursor to the militias, but the armed paramilitary bands arose particularly as a response to two events of the early 1990s that were read as demonstrating a growing attempt to impose authoritarian government within the United States. What happened at Ruby Ridge and at Waco greatly alarmed people already attracted to conspiracy theories about the Zionist Occupation Government and the New World Order. It was clear to such true believers that the government was conspiring to disarm the population.

In August 1992, agents of the U.S. Marshals Service and the FBI besieged Randy Weaver and his family at his home on Ruby Ridge in northern Idaho. Weaver, who associated with the Aryan Nations, came under investigation by the ATF. In an attempt to get leverage over Weaver, whom the ATF wanted to turn into an informant against the AN, an ATF informant bought two shotguns from Weaver, who is alleged to have sawed off the barrels to an illegal length. Weaver was arrested on these charges in 1991 but missed the court date owing to a clerical mistake on the part of the authorities. Because of the mix-up, a judge issued a bench warrant to arrest Weaver. The mishandling of the court appearance left Weaver convinced he would not receive a fair hearing, and he hunkered down at Ruby Ridge. Marshals negotiated with Weaver for a voluntary surrender, but the U.S. attorney refused to accept the agreement. Finally, on 21 August 1992, marshals reconnoitered Weaver's property in preparation for a raid. Their presence alerted the Weavers' dog, so his fourteen-year-old son Sammy and a family his friend, Kevin Harris, both armed, went out to investigate. Marshals shot the dog. Accounts vary, but what is certain is that in an exchange of gunfire a marshal was mortally wounded and Sammy, while retreating, was shot in the back and killed. Weaver and Harris later retrieved Sammy's body and placed it in a shed by the house.

Marshals called in the FBI. The next day, FBI sniper Ron Horiuchi fired at Weaver, who, with his daughter and Harris, was visiting his son's body. Horiuchi hit Weaver in the shoulder. The three fled back to the house and Horiuchi fired again; this bullet wounded Harris and hit Weaver's wife Vicki in the face, killing her. Again, accounts vary, but apparently she was standing behind a door and was stuck by the bullet meant for Harris. The siege continued for another ten days, when Weaver finally surrendered.

In the ensuing trial, Harris was cleared of all charges. Weaver was convicted only of missing his court appearance and was released a few months after the verdict. The U.S. government settled out of court in a civil lawsuit filed by Weaver over the deaths of his wife and son. The government paid $3.1 million to Randy and his three surviving daughters; Harris received a settlement of $380,000. There is no question that the agents of the U.S. government horribly mishandled the entire affair, and because of it, three people were dead. But to many extremists on the radical right, this simply proved the length to which the government would go in persecuting its opponents. *The Turner Diaries* were becoming reality.

Six months after the tragic fiasco at Ruby Ridge, the siege of the Branch Davidian complex near Waco, Texas, offered additional proof to far-right anti-federals that their predictions of a tyrannical, heavy-handed government were on target. And once again, they could read it as an attempt to seize firearms in private hands.

The sect of Branch Davidians split off from the Davidian Seventh-Day Adventists in the 1950s. By the late 1980s David Koresh had become the sect's leader at its Mount Carmel Center on seventy-seven acres a few miles northeast of Waco. Koresh's behavior became increasingly cultish, including his claim to be able to have multiple wives through "spiritual marriage." One of these was reputedly a thirteen-year-old girl. The ATF moved against Koresh and the Branch Davidians because they were suspected of owning illegal weapons. This, combined with other concerns, led ATF agents to stage a poorly conceived and badly executed raid on 28 February 1993. Owing to an intelligence breach, Koresh learned that the ATF were coming to Mount Carmel and prepared to resist. The agents carried out their raid even after learning that Koresh knew it was imminent. A gunfight ensued. Four ATF agents were killed and sixteen wounded; six Branch Davidians were killed, and Koresh and several others were wounded.

The subsequent siege dragged on until 19 April, when the FBI and Texas and Alabama National Guard attacked. The plan was to use tear gas to drive the Branch Davidians out. Combat vehicles punched holes in the walls of the buildings to allow the tear gas rounds to penetrate. After six hours, fires broke out at three different sites in the compound and rapidly engulfed the buildings. It seems that these were set by the Branch Davidians themselves in a mass suicide. Only nine people exited the building as the flames raged. Seventy-six other Branch Davidians, including five children under age fourteen, perished in the inferno. It was another, even more ghastly, disaster.

The militia movement surged in response to what the radical right regarded as "evidence" of a government run amok. The Militia of Montana (MOM) formed late in 1992. During a 1995 interview, the founders of MOM, John and David Trochmann, adhered to an essential tenet of the far right, insisting, "Gun control is people control." In the same interview, the Trochmanns claimed a membership of 12,000. MOM invested its credibility in the Y2K hysteria that a computer collapse generated by the advance of the clock to the year 2000 would cause chaos, for which militia members must prepare. When the scare fizzled, MOM faded, although it continues to publish its newsletter *Taking Aim*.

MOM stayed within the limits of legal conduct, but the Michigan Militia, which emerged in 1994, skirted the bounds. It formed paramilitary units and stockpiled arms, circumventing regulation and monitoring by exploiting the gun-show loophole in gun-control legislation. Arie Perliger argues that MOM and the Michigan Militia represented two poles of the militia movement, the one more devoted to legal advocacy in defense of what it saw as legitimate rights, the other more extralegal and focused on military readiness to survive repression or chaos.[40] Some went further, operating as terrorist groups. Members of the Oklahoma Constitutional Militia planned an attack on the offices of the SPLC, but were arrested in November 1995. Twelve others from the Arizona Viper Militia plotted to bomb IRS, ATF, police, and National Guard facilities in Phoenix, but were found out and apprehended in July 1996. In addition, the Mountaineer Militia intended to destroy the FBI's Criminal Justice Information Services Division, but were foiled in October 1996.

Militias were active in all fifty states during the mid-1990s. No exact figures are available, but scholars Chip Berlet and Mathew Lyons estimate the total membership of the militias as 20,000–60,000.[41] Linda Thompson, the self-proclaimed acting adjutant general of the "Unorganized Militia of the United States," warned: "This is the coming of the New World Order. A one-world government, where, in order to put the new government in place, we must all be disarmed first."[42]

The militia movement sharply declined in 2000, but it did not disappear, and it again grew after the 2008 election. The SPLC states that while there were only forty-two militia groups in 2008, this number soared to 334 in 2011.[43]

If the militia movement as a whole cannot be condemned as terrorist, some groups, as we have seen, planned terrorist attacks. Most important, the militia movement fosters a radical-right ideology that has inspired terrorism. The case of Timothy McVeigh must be seen in the context of the militia movement, since he shared so much of the ideology of the militias and lived in their world of guns and conspiracy theories.

ANTI-ABORTION VIOLENCE AND TERRORISM

Beyond racist extremism and anti-federal radicalism, we need to focus more narrowly on a cause that has inspired violence and threats of violence—anti-abortion. National Abortion Federation statistics show that between 1977 and 2015, eleven murders, twenty-six attempted murders, forty bombings, 185 arsons, and ninety-eight attempted bombings and arsons were committed by anti-abortion extremists.[44] In addition, there were 516 threats of death or physical harm. Because such violence is not simply meant to punish offenders, but to dissuade abortion providers and the women they serve, this record amounts to terrorism. If we add other acts of disruption, including invasions, trespassing, and vandalism, the total reaches 7,214 incidents. And this does not count hate calls, mail, and email, which number in the tens of thousands.

Deadly violence peaked in the 1990s and has markedly declined since. That decade witnessed seven murders and sixteen attempted murders, while the years 2000–2009 saw only one of each. Still, the one attack at Planned Parenthood in Colorado Springs on 27 November 2015 by Robert Dear killed three and injured nine—an awful toll, even if these were the only such casualties since 2010.

Anti-abortion activism and terrorism arose in response to the 1973 Supreme Court decision in *Roe v. Wade*, which declared abortion in the first two trimesters of pregnancy to be protected by the Constitution, citing what the court believed to be a Fourteenth Amendment guarantee of privacy. Opposition to abortion is obviously not restricted to the extreme right or any particular faith. Such opposition has been a basic doctrine of the Catholic Church and its popes, even the humane John XXIII and Francis I.

Perliger points out that the majority of violent anti-abortion attacks involved individuals or very small cells, not larger organizations. However, there have been organizations that advanced the anti-abortion agenda by protest and harassment, such as Operation Rescue and Operation Save America. The group that has played the most prominent role in advocating anti-abortion violence is the Army of God (AOG), formed in 1982 and still active. It has been highly secretive even among those who consider themselves members.

The most notable individual in AOG is the Reverend Michael Bray, who espouses Reconstruction Theology, which holds that the United States should become a Christian theocracy.[45] He was sentenced to ten years' imprisonment in 1985 for possession of explosives in regard to ten bombings, but served less than four years. The *Army of God Manual*, discovered in 1993, contains instructions for bombing and arson, which it states are "powerful, appropriate and discriminate."[46] In 1994, Bray wrote *A Time to Kill*, justifying and lauding anti-abortion violence, including the killing of doctors who performed abortions. AOG held

"White Rose" banquets, which celebrated the anti-abortion cause and revealed the organization's tolerance of deadly violence. At the 2001 banquet, Bray received an award for his efforts. In the words of a reporter, "During the event, numerous speakers called for violence against abortion clinics, approved of murdering abortion providers, and made jokes about killing homosexuals."[47]

AOG carried out its first assault in August 1982, when three men claiming membership in the organization kidnapped Dr. Hector Zevallos and his wife Rosalee in Granite City, Illinois, where Zevallos performed abortions. The couple was threatened with death but released unharmed eight days after being seized. Those who associated themselves with AOG were not always so kind. On 19 August 1993, Rachelle "Shelley" Shannon shot Dr. George Tiller in both arms at his Women's Health Care Services in Wichita, Kansas. His was one of only three clinics in the nation providing late-term abortions. Shannon later pleaded guilty to committing arson at several other abortion clinics. Her combined sentences totaled thirty-one years. On 29 July 1994, Dr. John Britton, aged sixty-nine, fell to a shotgun blast fired by Paul Jennings Hill, a man influenced by Bray. The gunfire also killed Britton's escort, James Barrett, aged seventy-four, and wounded Barrett's wife. Hill stated in 1997 that "the abortionist's knife" is the "cutting edge of Satan's current attack."[48] Hill, believed to have had ties to AOG, was found guilty and executed in 2003. Years after surviving Shannon's attack, Tiller was assassinated while serving as an usher at a church service on 31 May 2009.

It was not simply the doctors who died in anti-abortion violence. On 30 December 1994, John Salvi shot and killed receptionists at two abortion clinics in Brookline, Massachusetts. As well as murdering these two women, Salvi wounded five others. He would later be captured at Norfolk, Virginia, where he had fired at another abortion clinic, but without injuring anyone. That clinic had been picketed by well-known AOG advocate Donald Spitz, with whom Salvi had contact. Salvi had also protested Spitz's earlier arrest.

Eric Rudolf set off an explosive device composed of three pipe bombs and masonry nails on 27 July 1996 at Centennial Olympic Park in Atlanta during the 1996 Summer Olympics. Although he phoned in a warning and there was an effort to clear the park, the bomb killed Alice Hawthorn and injured 111 others. Another victim died of a heart attack. Rudolf avoided capture until May 2003, and during his time on the run he bombed three other sites: an abortion clinic in an Atlanta suburb on 16 January 1997; an Atlanta lesbian bar on 21 February 1997; and an abortion clinic in Birmingham, Alabama, on 29 January 1998. According to the *Washington Post*, Rudolf "had a long association with the Christian Identity movement."[49] In his explanation for the bombing, Rudolf strangely linked abortion with "global socialism." Michael Bray testified that Rudolph was also incensed by the fact that Olympics officials diverted the carriers of the torch from a North Carolina county that had passed an ordinance against sodomy.

LONE WOLVES LURKING ON THE FAR RIGHT

On the far right, unaffiliated individuals can be as dangerous as or more dangerous than those who are formally members of one or another organization. Most obviously, Timothy McVeigh had no formal relationship with any group except for a trial one-year membership in a North Carolina Klan group, a membership he chose not to renew. He mused about heading his own militia, but this never came to pass. Some speculate that he had some contact with the Michigan Militia, but he was not a member.

A highly dangerous loner, William J. Krar, is little known by the public, but came close to being instrumental in mass murder. In April 2003, Krar, his partner Judith Bruey, and his associate Edward Feltus were arrested in Tyler, Texas. The authorities discovered a cache that included a cyanide gas-generating device and other deadly chemicals, machine guns, 500,000 rounds of ammunition, sixty conventional pipe bombs, and much more.[50] Krar served as a free-lance suppler of weaponry and documents for far-right groups and individuals. His intense anti-government commitment was part and parcel of the same gun culture that motivated McVeigh. Among Krar's belongings were copies of *The Turner Diaries*. Krar's possession of chemical weapons and his potential for facilitating disaster earned him a sentence of 135 months. He died of a heart attack in May 2009 while serving behind bars.

RADICAL RIGHT-WING TERRORISM AND THE STRATEGY OF INTIMIDATION

This book has adopted terrorist strategy as a category of analysis, as a way to understand and differentiate terrorisms. I have proposed four basic strategies, with the proviso that the same terrorist organizations can apply combinations of strategies in dealing with different audiences. I have argued that the primary strategy of intimidation best suits strong-capacity terrorism—state, military, and social—while weak-capacity terrorism depends most on initiation, attrition, or evolution. Thus, the Stalinist purges relied on intimidation; Marxist urban guerrillas placed their hope in strategies of initiation; the PIRA pursued long-war attrition; and radical Islamist terrorist groups have been distinguished by the success of evolution. Where can we place far-right terrorist groups?

The first response to this question is to make clear that the far right encompasses a range of nonviolent and violent resistance, and that despite important similarities, one should not expect uniformity of goals or methods. That being said, I would argue that these *sub-state groups and individuals* have relied primarily on intimidation, as opposed to the more common weak-group initiation, attrition, and evolution. Moreover, the extreme right has combined intimidation with different measures of punishment and sheer abuse. This diverges from the patterns discussed in the preceding chapters of this book. It fits their tendencies toward deep visceral feelings and strong commitment to outlandish conspiracy theories. Moreover, it reflects their *lack of realistic scenarios for success* in American society as a whole. The extreme right are greater dreamers than even Narodyna Volya or the Weathermen, although the dreams of the right seem more like nightmares. Of all the violent right-wing groups surveyed in this chapter, the anti-abortion extremists are most solidly grounded in the possible, since there is a large body of pro-life sentiment in the general population. Still, even violent anti-abortion extremism relies most on intimidation and punishment.

Consider the rationale McVeigh expressed for his act of terrorism. On 26 April 2001, six weeks before his execution, he sent a letter to Fox News correspondent Rita Cosby explaining why he had bombed the Murrah Federal Office Building.[51] He gave three reasons. "Foremost, the bombing was a retaliatory strike; a counter attack, for the cumulative raids" by federal agents whose actions had become "increasingly militaristic and violent," to the point of "deploying tanks against its own citizens" at Waco. McVeigh's bombing was also a "pre-emptive . . . strike against these forces and their command and control centers within the federal building." Last, "borrowing a page from U.S. foreign policy, I decided to send a message to a government that was becoming increasingly hostile, by bombing a government building and the government employees within that building who represent that government." The bombing of the Murrah Federal Office Building was a reprisal meant to punish, a pre-emptive strike meant to weaken, and a warning meant to intimidate the government. In this last sense, it had much in common with the assassinations of Alan Berg by the Silent Brotherhood or those of Dr. John Britton in 1994 and Dr. George Tiller in 2009 by right-to-life radicals. Such acts were meant as deterrence through fear.

Hate-group henchmen can go beyond intimidation to naked abuse, attacking individuals with little other purpose than to revel in the violence of hurting "undesirables." Beatings and killings inflicted by Klansmen, neo-Nazis, and skinheads upon minorities can be a kind of affirmation through violence, satisfying in itself without any grand purpose—more like crime than terrorism.

White supremacist Dylann Roof shot and killed nine parishioners of the Emanuel African Methodist Episcopal Church in Charleston, South Carolina, on the evening of 17 June 2015. In a statement he wrote in jail, he expressed no regret: "I am not sorry. I have not shed a tear for the innocent people I killed. . . . I do feel sorry for the innocent white people that are killed daily at the hands of the lower race."[52] The manifesto he published on his website before the murders was full of frustration and hate for African-Americans. It is said that Roof wanted to start a race war. Surely, he was not the first to fanaticize about a race war; that is the theme of *The Turner Diaries,* after all. But was he bent on initiation or simply striking out that evening in Charleston? My guess is the latter. It was not even about intimidation; he was venting his fury.

A RIGHT-WING SURGE WITH PRESIDENT TRUMP?

Because of the 2016 election, the American public learned of the alt-right, short for "alternative right." This is a movement of relatively recent origin. Richard B. Spencer, regarded by many as its creator, founded his website Alternative Right in 2010. It not only takes issue with the left and center, but disdains traditional conservatism, which is why it is self-described as alternative. The alt-right can be characterized as White nationalist and nativist, meaning that it generally believes that national identity entails the predominance of White ethnicity and reviles immigrants of other races. This predominance should be maintained not only in demography but in culture as well, so it sneers at multiculturalism. President Donald Trump's reliance on Steve Bannon, a champion of the alt-right whom Trump appointed as his senior Counselor and chief strategist, seemed to guarantee the alt-right a seat at the table. And Trump's reaction to the events of the "Unite the Right" rally on 11–12 August 2017 in Charlottesville, Virginia, were read as support by the far right, including the KKK and neo-Nazis.

Only time will tell whether the far right is experiencing a temporary spike in publicity or a lasting surge in numbers and strength.

NOT JUST IN AMERICA

The focus here has been on extremists in the United States, but the right-wing resurgence is not limited to America. Europe is also suffering such a political shift. Italy was plagued with major fascist violence during the Years of Lead, 1968–1982, its most egregious action being the bombing of the Bologna railroad station in August 1980, killing eighty-five and injuring over 200. And Italy is again seeing a resurgence of the right, now particularly directed against African immigrants.[53] Germany is also experiencing growth in the right wing, with the electoral success of the Alternative for Germany Party.[54] In 2017, the British right reveled in the attention to its internet posts given them by President Trump.[55] In France the right-wing National Front (now the National Rally Party), then led by Marine Le Pen, did well in the first round of the French presidential election of 2017, even if Le Pen was defeated by Emmanuel Macron in the final election. The National Rally is *not* a terrorist organization to be sure, but it represents the presence of a strong right wing in French politics. The right wing is also gaining strength in other countries, including Hungary and Poland.

In 2011 the world was shocked by what happened in progressive Norway. Anders Behring Breivik perpetrated a particularly horrendous terrorist act on 22 July. He detonated a truck bomb at the Regjeringskvartalet (government quarter), a complex of government buildings in Oslo, killing eight. He then went off to the Workers' Youth League summer camp at Utøya, where he shot and killed sixty-eight victims, many face to face. Breivik was a fiercely anti-immigrant Islamophobe who also hated the culture of the left—"cultural Marxism," as he called it.

In contrast to Timothy McVeigh, who seemed coldly rational, Breivik is narcissistic and unbalanced. Both had messages to spread. McVeigh did it through his statements and through interviews he granted to authors Lou Michel and Dan Herbeck, who wrote *American Terrorist* about him. Breivik assembled a rambling and disjointed 1,500-page manifesto. But whatever his state of mind, Breivik's actions reflected the anti-immigrant resentment that so troubles Europe and so characterizes the American far right.

Right-wing terrorism in the United States provides one more example of how terrorism is an "ism" of totalist mindsets and deadly methods in the service of many masters. Radical Islamists and ultra–right-wing Americans who turn to terrorism justify themselves in the name of self-defense and retaliation. And adherents of radical Islamism and of Christian Identity claim high moral purpose with divine sanction.

The last kind of terrorism we will discuss in this volume is removed from such high purpose. It employs the means without the morals, but it can be terrorism nonetheless. And like terrorism of the radical right in the United States, it adopts a strategy of intimidation. Let us turn now to narcoterrorism.

CHAPTER THIRTEEN

Narcoterrorism

FIGURE 13.1. *Left:* A cocky, smiling Pablo Escobar poses like a movie star for a mugshot in 1977, when he was already enjoying the spoils of the cocaine trade. *Below:* Those smiling as they crowd around his body are men of the team that traced the narcoterrorist down and killed him on 2 December 1993. Wikimedia Commons.

PABLO ESCOBAR AND JOSÉ GACHA, leaders of the Medellín cartel, waged war against the state. They targeted the headquarters of the Departmento Administrativo de Seguridad (DAS) in Bogota with a truck bomb on the morning of 6 December 1989. The DAS was the Colombian equivalent of the FBI, and it was then led by General Miguel Maza, an inveterate enemy of the drug lords. The explosion of 1,000 pounds of dynamite, packed into a bus parked in front of the DAS building, excavated a four-foot-deep crater where the bus had stood, demolished the front of the building, and leveled surrounding structures. Seventy victims died and about 1,000 others were wounded. Doubtless, Escobar and Gacha had hoped to kill Maza; it was not the first time they had tried to assassinate him. But he miraculously escaped injury in the bombing of the DAS.

The previous week, on 27 November, Avianca flight 203 exploded in the air, causing the death of all 107 aboard. There is some dispute as to what caused the catastrophe, but it is most widely believed to have also been the work of the cartel in an attempt to assassinate presidential candidate César Gaviria, who was supposed to be a passenger on the ill-fated flight but had not boarded the plane. Gaviria was a target because had taken up the candidacy after his friend and mentor, Luis Carlos Galán, had been gunned down in August of that year.

Escobar and Gacha were fully engaged in criminal enterprise. They pursued their goals of wealth and power through the production, shipment, and sale of cocaine. These ruthless men stopped at nothing to pursue their illicit drug trafficking. Yet the criminal status of these perpetrators does not disqualify the bombings of the DAS and of Avianca flight 203 from consideration as terrorist acts, because Escobar and Gacha ordered these horrific attacks in order to achieve a political goal.

Escobar and those like him believed that their ability to bribe, coerce, or kill Colombians left them immune from penalties imposed by the justice system within their own country, but they greatly feared being extradited to the United States. Gavaria had declared his willingness to uphold Colombia's extradition treaty with the United States, and the DAS led by Maza was working to bring Escobar down.

In 1989 Escobar posed a deadly threat to the Colombian government and society, but only a few years later he would die in a hail of gunfire at the age of forty-four (Fig. 13.1, bottom). His death struck a blow at the Medellín cartel, but it hardly brought down the drug trade; it and the narcoterrorism associated with it continue. Popular culture has romanticized him as the epitome of the drug lord, with his great wealth, flamboyant life style, and limitless violence. A March 2018 article in the *New*

Yorker was titled "The Afterlife of Pablo Escobar: In Colombia, a Drug Lord's Posthumous Celebrity Brings Profits and Controversy."[1] Apparently, evil has its rewards.

This chapter confronts narcoterrorism, a subject that forces us to reexamine the interplay of tactics, intentions, and results in defining terrorism. Narcoterrorism demands our attention because it is tied in with second- and third-wave terrorism and is much discussed in the news. This relatively recent manifestation of terrorism only caught the world's attention in the 1980s; in fact, it did not even have a name until then. As prominent as it has become, the term *narcoterrorism* can mislead by imputing unity to what is quite diverse. We need to realize that it encompasses different admixtures of crime, power, and purpose among organizations ranging from small groups to large insurgent forces. Let us begin by considering the links between crime and terrorism in general.

CRIME AND TERRORISM

The existence and actions of radical terrorist groups are by nature illegal, thus criminal. Fundamental to most terrorist groups is the need to finance their campaigns, and this is most commonly achieved through robbery, ransom, and extortion. So, for example, Carlos Marighella incorporated armed robbery as an element of his practical revolutionary theory in *The Minimanual of the Urban Guerrilla*: "The most popular mission is the bank assault," which he called "a typical expropriation."[2]

In the present-day environment, tapping the drug trade presents another, and far more lucrative, way to raise funds outside the legitimate economy. In 2011, the United Nations Office of Drugs and Crime (UNODC) estimated the worldwide drug market at $400 billion, with U.S. drug sales alone standing at $65 billion. Its *World Drug Report* for 2015 states that 246,000,000 people, or 5 percent of world population aged fifteen to sixty-four, used an illicit drug in 2013. Historically, the draw of drug money has exerted an irresistible pull on terrorist organizations; for example, fourteen of the thirty-six foreign terrorist organizations listed by the U.S. State Department in 2004 were identified as involved with drug production and distribution. By the fall of 2017, Western officials estimated that the Taliban depended on proceeds from the drug trade for 60 percent of their income.[3]

Geography also helps explain the importance of trafficking to terrorism. In a cursed coincidence, traditional drug production tends to thrive in conflict-ridden areas. Nearly all the coca plants whose leaves are the raw material for producing cocaine grow in Colombia, Peru, and Bolivia, countries that have known political turmoil, military coups, and armed rebellion. Nearly 90 percent of the opium poppies that go into heroin production grow in Afghanistan today. Terrorist groups that are not located in prime growing areas for coca and opium can take advantage of the drug economy by providing transportation and distribution, as do the Mexican cartels. Colombia, Afghanistan, and Mexico will be subjects of discussion during the course of this chapter. Even terrorist groups off the major drug highways engage in retail trafficking. This has included groups as varied as the PIRA in Northern Ireland, the Tamil Tigers in Sri Lanka, Hamas in Palestine, and Abu Sayyaf in the Philippines.

Narcoterrorism ranks as the most important current example of a more general phenomenon that we must consider: the convergence between criminal organizations and terrorist groups. Security analyst Tamara Makarenko proposes an intriguing descriptive theory about what she calls the "crime–terror continuum." She represents this graphically, and I have reworked her graphic in the interest of increased clarity (Fig. 13.2).[4] At one pole on the continuum stands organized crime and at the other terrorism; they converge along a path that can lead to mergers of crime and politics at the center. Criminal organizations can supply money and weapons to terrorist groups, which, in turn, can provide security in areas where the terrorists are strong. Although the crime–terror continuum could apply to any large-scale illicit activity, Makarenko notes that "the most commonly cited alliances exist in the realm of the international drug trade."[5]

The problem with alliances, her first stage of convergence, is that the allies can have different, even conflicting goals. Therefore, it can become advantageous for criminal organizations to adopt terrorist methods of their own for what Makarenko calls "operational purposes," her second stage, without being dependent upon a terrorist group. Likewise, terrorist groups may choose to engage in criminal operations themselves, independent of criminal allies. The criminal and the terrorist become more like each other. In Makarenko's schema, the mix of criminal and terrorist activities can yield "hybrid groups": criminal organizations heavily

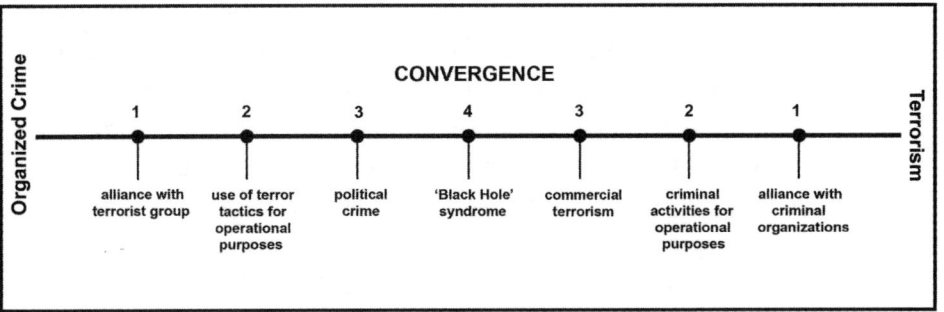

FIGURE 13.2. This graphic representation of the "crime–terror continuum," based on that offered by Tamara Makarenko, portrays the tendency of criminal and terrorist groups to become more like one another in certain circumstances, to converge. It is most apropos in the case of narcoterrorism.

engaged in "political crime" and terrorist groups devoting themselves to "commercial terrorism," her third stage. According to Makarenko's thesis, if hybrid groups become powerful enough to undermine the state regime of a country, we reach a fourth stage, the "black hole" syndrome, which "encompasses two situations: first, where the primary motivations of groups engaged in a civil war evolves from a focus on political aims to a focus on criminal aims; second, it refers to the emergence of a 'black hole' state—a state successfully taken over by a hybrid group."[6] Makarenko's thesis appears elegant and symmetrical, but it certainly has its critics.

Convergence between criminal organizations, with their pursuit of private material benefit, and far more high-minded radical terrorist groups and revolutionaries may seem odd. However, criminal and terrorist organizations have much in common. To the extent that both are illegal, they are likely to be at war against the same ruling regime. They may not be friends, but they may share a common enemy. Most important, as illicit organizations they may be forced to work with each other to secure what they need outside the legal marketplace, financial institutions, and security apparatuses.

FOUR MANIFESTATIONS OF NARCOTERRORISM

Peruvian president Fernando Belaunde is credited with coining the term *narcoterrorism* in 1983 to label terrorist attacks by drug traffickers against his government and its anti-narcotics police. *Narcoterrorism* as employed today by the Counter Narcoterrorism Operations Center of the Drug Enforcement Administration (DEA) covers different phenomena. On the one hand, "narco-driven terrorism" is the use of terrorist-style tactics, "high-profile violence and intimidation," by drug-trafficking organizations "to advance or protect their drug trafficking activities." On the other hand, the DEA label "narco-supported terrorism" encompasses "terrorist/insurgent organizations that use drug trafficking proceeds to advance their political agenda."[7] This is a useful dichotomy, but it does not capture the full range of possible relationships between trafficking and terrorism that we should discuss here.

For the purposes of this chapter, we will distinguish between four manifestations of the nexus between terrorist violence and the drug trade. These four manifestations are not particular points on Makarenko's continuum; instead, they represent forms of violence in the real world that are referred to as "narcoterrorism" by journalists, scholars, and policymakers. Still, in analyzing these manifestations, we will find Makarenko's continuum useful.

The first and second manifestations include terrorist and insurgent organizations *with political intent* that finance themselves, in part or primarily, with income from the drug trade. The first involves radical terrorist groups that employ funds gained from drug production and/or trafficking to fund themselves. The example presented below is the Fuerzas Armadas Revolucionarias de Colombia (FARC), which began as a small radical terrorist group. Such groups that finance themselves through the drug trade can pursue strategies of intimidation, initiation, attrition, or evolution, as suits their ideology, strength, and strategy. The second manifestation encompasses major guerrilla or regular forces that depend upon funds gained from the drug trade to finance their military campaigns in civil wars. These groups differ from terrorist groups by virtue of their greater size and territorial control, characteristics that define them at least as insurgents. The example discussed here is the Taliban.

The third manifestation comprises drug cartels that, in addition to criminal activity, act *with political intent* to shape governance and policy. We will discuss Escobar's Medellín cartel as an example of this. The fourth includes cartels *without political intent*, but whose tactics of intimidation and corruption nonetheless *result* in undermining governance. Their political impact is ultimately incidental, a result of doing business, rather than primarily intentional. Here we will consider the Mexican drug cartels, especially Los Zetas. These last two manifestations each concern criminal organizations that adopt terrorist-style tactics to coerce and control populations and governments. Their strategy is intimidation above all. Without effective, and ruthless, strength they could not function. In certain circumstances, they seek public tolerance or even support within their own locales, but they are fundamentally about power.

Beyond these four manifestations are drug-producing and/or -trafficking organizations that engage in terrorist-style ostentatious atrocities with no other purpose or result than to advance their criminal enterprise. These lie beyond our discussion of political terrorism.

PABLO ESCOBAR AND THE MEDELLÍN CARTEL

For reasons of chronology and narrative, we will shuffle the deck of our four manifestations and begin with the example of the Medellín cartel, followed by that of FARC. I deal with these two examples together because both grew out of a common Colombian background and then converged from the opposite extremes of Makarenko's crime–terror continuum. The Medellín cartel and its most prominent chief, Pablo Escobar, though ruthless cocaine traffickers, engaged in political violence to defend their interests and to protect major players in the Colombian drug trade from extradition to the United States. At the other pole stands FARC, which began in the 1960s as a Marxist radical group focused on revolutionary regime and social change. It evolved into a sizable insurgent force with terrorism as part of its violent repertoire, and eventually it became a player in the drug trade, exploiting it to earn hundreds of millions of dollars annually to support its cadres and campaigns. After dealing with convergence in Colombia, we will turn to the resurgent Taliban's mining of the opium trade in Afghanistan to support its large-scale conflict with the Afghan government, the United States, and its allies. Last, we will consider the chaotic and barbaric struggles between drug cartels in northern Mexico, which threaten to undermine the Mexican state and may even pose a serious threat to security in the United States just across the border.

La Violencia *in Colombia*
The conditions that allowed the rise of the Colombian drug cartels and explains the emergence of FARC must be traced back to *La Violencia*

(Violence), a period of political turmoil that engulfed Colombia from 1948 to 1958. During this civil war between political factions and armed paramilitary groups, some 200,000 perished. Blessed and cursed by its beautiful mountainous topography, Colombia is subdivided into local bastions; it has been characterized as "ungovernable" and "a land that breeds outlaws."[8]

We have spoken of different cultures of violence, what would be tolerable and what would alienate a population. Mark Bowden dramatically describes the culture of violence during *La Violencia*: "Terror became art, a form of psychological warfare with a quasi-religious aesthetic. In Colombia it wasn't enough to hurt or even kill your enemy; there was ritual to be observed. Rape had to be performed in public, before fathers, mothers, husbands, sisters, brothers, sons, and daughters. And before you killed a man, you first made him beg, scream, and gag . . . or first you killed those he most loved before his eyes."[9] This culture of violence set a high bar for the level of brutal excess that could inflict shock on the Colombian population.

La Violencia ended when the warring Liberal and Conservative parties agreed to share power, but it also left a legacy of paramilitary groups fighting for conflicting interests and principles. The toll of death waned after *La Violencia*, but conflict between the government, private right-wing paramilitaries, and radical guerrillas continued and eventually intensified. During the 1970s, human rights groups counted 1,053 victims of political killings, but that number soared to 12,859 during the 1980s.

Escobar and Terrorist Violence to 1992
Illicit activities and the drug trade were not new to Colombia, but the boom in the American demand for cocaine starting in the mid-1970s created a market that Colombian drug traffickers were quick to exploit. It yielded phenomenal profits. Pablo Escobar became the most notorious of these new drug lords. His life makes for an engrossing story, and it has been well told by Mark Bowden in his book *Killing Pablo*. Escobar began as little more than a heavy-handed tough with special skill as a car thief. But through his street smarts, utter ruthlessness, and good luck he eventually rose to head the Medellín drug cartel. At the peak of his power and wealth, around 1990, he is reputed to have been one of the richest men in the world. In 1989, *Forbes Magazine* estimated his net worth at

$3 billion (nearly $6 billion in 2017 dollars), although it is common to see his fortune estimated at as much as $30 billion. He owned nineteen homes in Medellín alone (each equipped with a heliport), considerable real estate holdings, and a dazzling array of possessions, including large zoo animals at his country estate, Hacienda Los Nápoles, on 7,400 acres.

Escobar did whatever it took and whatever he wanted. He is reputed to have described the drug business as "simple—you bribe someone here, you bribe someone there, and you pay a friendly banker to help you bring the money back."[10] However, bribery carried with it the threat *"plata o plomo,"* take my silver or get my lead—my bullets. It is said that his favorite manner of executing his enemies was to hang them upside down and then burn them. Thugs from the Medellín cartel employed abominable excesses; one of their atrocities involved slitting their victims' throats and pulling their tongues out though the openings in what was known as the Colombian necktie, a legacy of *La Violencia.*

Despite his incredible brutality, Escobar commanded popular adulation in his home town, Medellín. He gave millions for public projects, including new housing for slum dwellers, roads and power lines for badly served areas, and soccer fields, lighted so working folk could play in the evenings. By investing more than the government in public welfare and publicizing his generosity, he became a local hero. In 1982, at the height of his popularity, he won election as an alternate representative to the Colombian Congress. He enjoyed the public spotlight, and the Bogotá press lauded him as a kind of Robin Hood.

Escobar's charisma, riches, and swagger made him, and continue to highlight him, as a kind of malevolent hero. Even today, one can buy T-shirts emblazoned with his image, including that of the smiling and confident young Pablo shown in Figure 13.1 (top) above. Netflix has even produced a dramatic series, *Narcos*, the first two seasons of which focus on the life and death of Escobar.

Despite his power and wealth, he was also a troubled man. Escobar was confident that his policy of *plata o plomo* intimidated the Colombian justice system, but he and other drug traffickers were unnerved by the possibility of extradition to the United States. In 1979 Colombia had signed an extradition treaty with the United States. Escobar brought together a loose association of drug lords, "the Extraditables," who cynically argued that the extradition treaty was a treasonous betrayal of Colombian national sovereignty. Of course, their own private interests and fears are what drove them to oppose it by any means necessary.

On 30 April 1984, two assassins on a motorcycle gunned down Colombian minister of justice Rodrigo Lara, almost certainly on Escobar's orders. In the first application of the 1979 treaty, Lara had moved to extradite the drug kingpin Carlos Lehder. Moreover, Lara was conducting a campaign against Escobar and cooperating with U.S. authorities. However, killing Lara turned out to be a disastrous mistake for Escobar, because it enraged public opinion and drove President Belisario Betancur to adopt Lara's cause as his own, and enlist U.S. help to do so.

In July 1984, drug heavyweights Escobar, Gacha, and Jorge Ochoa were indicted for trafficking by a federal grand jury sitting in Miami. Ochoa was arrested in Spain on 15 November, and the United States and Colombia moved to extradite him. The Extraditables reacted with a deadly threat, faxed to the public media in Colombia: "We have found out that the government is trying by whatever means possible to extradite citizen Jorge Luis Ochoa to the United States. For us, this is the vilest of outrages. . . . In case Jorge Luis Ochoa is extradited to the United States, we will declare absolute and total war against this country's political leaders. We will execute out of hand the principal chieftains."[11]

In the eighteen months following Lara's assassination, more than thirty judges were killed, and on 6 November 1985, some forty cadres from the guerrilla group M-19 stormed the Palace of Justice in Bogotá. M-19 took hundreds hostage, including members of the Colombian Supreme Court. The revolutionaries made political demands, including the arrest and trial of President Betancur. In addition, M-19 insisted that the government abrogate the 1979 treaty. It is still a matter of debate, but it has been charged that Escobar and other traffickers supported the attack by paying M-19 $1 million. The army surrounded the Palace of Justice and retook it with heavy casualties: 100 died, including eleven members of the Supreme Court.

Escobar's violent campaign against the government and the judiciary continued. As discussed at the beginning of this chapter, Avianca flight 203 went down on 27 November 1989, and nine days later henchmen from the Medellín cartel exploded a massive truck bomb at the headquarters of the DAS. Authorities struck back, and on 15 December police cornered José Gacha and killed him in a gunfight.

Still, the terror campaign against extradition seems to have borne fruit, because a new Colombian Constitution prohibited extradition in 1991, and Escobar took the opportunity to negotiate his surrender. He agreed to serve a prison sentence in Colombia. The government allowed Escobar to create his own prison, known as La Catedral, by renovating at his expense and to his specifications an unused drug rehabilitation center in the hills overlooking Medellín.[12] It was more mansion than prison, and the guards were essentially on Escobar's payroll. He ran his business from La Catedral and trucked in everything for lavish parties, including women.

Escobar's imprisonment, such as it was, lasted only from June 1991 to September 1992. The authorities, having become aware of his continued criminal dealings at La Catedral, resolved to move him to a real facility. Not surprisingly, Escobar received warning of the plans and escaped, just as army units surrounded and occupied his luxury lockup.

Escobar was on the run for the next fourteen months. More than once, he was almost caught, but slipped the trap. Still, the noose grew tighter. Government and army authorities who refused to be bought with his *plata* gained in expertise. The United States aided the search with a special electronic surveillance unit, Centra Spike, and dispatched Delta Force Special Forces. Colombia devoted its own elite unit, Search Bloc, to the chase. Then, seemingly out of nowhere, an illicit vigilante organization of Colombians appeared: Los Pepes, short for Perseguidos por Pablo Escobar (People Persecuted by Pablo Escobar.) Its membership and support have been alleged to have come from Escobar's enemies in the Cali cartel and from the Colombian National Police. What is absolutely clear is that Los Pepes operated outside the law, committing the kind of murder and ostentatious atrocities typical of Escobar himself.

All this wore Escobar down. Finally, on 2 December 1993, his propensity to talk with his son by radio betrayed his location in a middle-class barrio of Medellín. Cornered by the Search Bloc, he was shot down while trying to escape over a roof. There is little reason to doubt that his pursuers wanted to do anything but kill Escobar. He died from a shot through his ear, suspiciously like an execution. The jubilant team that had located and killed him posed for photographs with his lifeless body where it lay on the tiles (see Fig. 13.1, bottom).

The most famous of the cartel bosses had undertaken a campaign of violence and the threat of violence with the intention of changing Colombian political policy. As a terrorist, Escobar's strategy was intimidation, but that intimidation finally led not to capitulation but to effective resistance, which included terror tactics by Los Pepes. Ultimately, Escobar failed and perished. An important point to be made is that while Escobar was vehemently attached to his cause, it was clearly *his* cause and not something that inspired the rank and file of his cartel. His henchmen were not driven by higher motives. However, there were such men and women in Colombia, and many of them joined together in FARC.

FARC

Founded in the mid-1960s, the Fuerzas Armadas Revolucionarias de Colombia conducted the longest ongoing insurgency in modern history until FARC was disbanded as an armed paramilitary in 2017. FARC appeared on the U.S. Department of State list of foreign terrorist organizations at the creation of that list in October 1997. It adhered to a Marxist-Leninist ideology promising to benefit the peasants who had been so mauled by *La Violencia* in Colombia's rural areas. In contrast to many other revolutionary groups, FARC was led by individuals coming from the very peasantry they wished to protect and advance.

There is no question that FARC employed tactics that meet our criteria for radical terrorism. However, FARC grew to such numbers, became so wealthy, and convincingly controlled large enough expanses of territory that, like the LTTE and the IS, it can be regarded as having followed a strategy of evolution. It grew from a terrorist band to a kind of proto-state engaged in a major insurgency against the Colombian government. The more it evolved into a state or a military force, the more important intimidation became as its strategy.

At the outset, in 1964, some fifty individuals formed the group; by 1966 FARC had grown to 350 cadres. By 1970 its numbers are estimated to have increased to 800–1,000. This number is believed to have doubled by 1978 and further increased to something over 4,000 by 1986—still a large group rather than an army. But over the next decade FARC expanded dramatically. One authority puts FARC strength at 20,000 in 2000 and credits the insurgents with controlling 40 percent of Colombian territory and committing over half of the terrorist attacks on U.S. interests in Colombia. FARC maintained its strength for a decade, but then

Colombian government offensives backed by the United States set the organization back on its heels. From 2009 through its disarmament in the spring of 2017, FARC seems to have commanded only 7,000–8,000 cadres.

We will consider FARC as an example of our first manifestation, a radical terrorist group that supports itself by takings from the drug trade. But at its height, FARC grew to something larger than a "group," something more like a small army. This blurs the difference between it and our example of the second manifestation, the Taliban. We recognize this muddying of the waters, but FARC was clearly a radical terrorist group that evolved; the Taliban at the time we will consider it was and is a major, and potentially victorious, army fielding an estimated 60,000 fighters by 2014. I consider FARC and the Taliban to be in different leagues, although they both have resorted to terrorist tactics.

The FARC's appearance, rise, fall, and negotiated transition back into Colombian politics and society is a story that must be told. And its involvement in the drug trade is a big part of that story.

As the FARC grew, maintaining its forces required considerable resources, and FARC relied on criminal activities to do so. These included kidnapping, extortion, and, of course, the drug trade. Kidnapping for punishment, negotiation, and ransom was an all too common mode of radical violence in Colombia, and FARC participated in it on a large scale. Thus, of the nearly 3,000 individuals kidnapped in 1999, about a quarter are considered to have been taken by FARC. Both murders and kidnappings peaked in 2002 and then declined. However, a 2010 publication claims that FARC pocketed nearly $92 million from its kidnappings annually.

As a developed organization in control of territory, FARC imposed "taxes" on the wealthy. FARC's Law 002 required all wealthy individuals or businesses with assets of $1 million or more to pay a tax. This extortion played into kidnapping, because those who failed to make the payments or fell behind on them could be kidnapped, and their "ransoms" simply amounted to "back taxes." Money raised from Law 002 and from taxing drug production in FARC areas went to finance military operations. However, revenues extorted from local small commerce funded local projects intended to benefit the community. FARC carried out some construction, maintained its own law courts, and established hospitals for its own cadres and often to serve the local community. As with radical Islamist groups, public programs ingratiated FARC with the surrounding population.

The amount of money FARC raised from impositions on coca-growing peasants and drug traffickers is nothing short of phenomenal. Different experts state different figures, but the tallies of income are universally staggering. Left-wing journalist and scholar Garry Leech estimates that FARC pulled in $60–$100 million annually in the early 1990s by taxing 7–10 percent of the market price of a kilo of coca paste.

A Brief Chronology of FARC at War and in Search of Peace in Colombia
Although it only called itself FARC in 1966, the group claimed that its history began in a fight between guerrillas and the Colombian Army troops who assaulted the self-declared Communist-run rural enclave of Marquetalia in May 1964. FARC functioned as the armed wing of the Colombian Communist Party (PCC). At the outset, the FARC's leader was Pedro Antonio Marín, a man of peasant origins who adopted the nom de guerre Manuel Marulanda. He remained its military commander until his death in 2008. Marulanda was joined at the head of the organization by Luis Alberto Morantes, who took the nom de guerre Jacobo Arenas. Arenas directed FARC as its political chief, making an effective duo with Marulanda. In 1982, when the FARC numbered a few thousand fighters, it altered its name to FARC-EP, the EP standing for Ejército del Pueblo (Army of the People); however, it was still generally referred to as FARC.

Growing FARC power in the countryside led to open conflict with the drug cartels. This enmeshed it in a complicated four-sided war in which FARC contended with the Colombian Army, local anti-guerrilla paramilitaries financed by land owners, and the cartels.

FARC became such a force that the Colombian government had to take notice. Peace talks began in 1984, leading to a ceasefire between the parties that lasted from 1984 to 1987. FARC, aided by the PCC, took the opportunity afforded by the pause in hostilities to ally with other leftist groups, forming a new and broader opposition party, the Unión Patriótica (UP). However, by 1990, more than 2,000 members of the UP had been assassinated. This attempt to join the political process came to little.

After the failure of the peace talks in 1987, further attempts were made in 1991 but led to nothing. Negotiations began again in 1998 and continued into 2002. As a confidence-building measure, the new president, Andrés Pastrana, ceded FARC a sanctuary. It covered 16,200 square miles, roughly the area of Massachusetts and Connecticut combined. At the same time, the governments of Colombia and the United States instituted Plan Colombia, an aid program to fund counter-drug and counter-insurgency programs. This led to a flow of $500 million to Colombia, some of which was devoted to spraying defoliants on coca fields. Meanwhile, FARC, reacting to what it considered abuse of the peasantry, carried on its own terrorist actions, including kidnapping and attacks on towns. Pastrana ended the peace talks in February 2002 and commanded the army to take back the sanctuary area.

Under renewed assault by Colombian forces now enjoying American backing through Plan Colombian, the FARC suffered reverses over the next decade. It lost territory and its numbers declined roughly 60 percent. Once gain it pursued negotiations.

After tentative feelers, peace talks began in 2012, first in Oslo and then in Havana. This time they led to success. Fighting continued during the talks, interrupted only briefly by fragile ceasefires, until both sides reached an agreement in June 2016. An enduring bilateral ceasefire took hold on 29 August. With great flourish, Colombian president Juan Manuel Santos and FARC leader Rodrigo Londoño Echeverri, known as Timochenko, signed a peace deal in September. However, Colombian voters turned down this agreement in a referendum on 2 October. The majority rejected it as being too generous to FARC. After being modified, a new peace accord was signed on 24 November and approved by the Colombian Congress six days later. By June 2017 FARC had disarmed. The world's longest-running insurgent civil war, which killed over 200,000 people and displaced over five million, had finally come to an end.

FARC Terrorism
FARC regarded itself as a revolutionary army fighting a guerrilla insurgency against the Colombian government, while defending itself from right-wing paramilitaries and, if necessary, drug cartels. But in fighting its wars it employed terrorism, and it is that aspect of FARC the concerns us here.

Human Rights Watch (HRW) charged Marxist guerrillas in Colombia with human rights violations on a major scale. The HRW *World Re-*

port 1995 stated, "For their part, guerrillas continued to violate international humanitarian law by engaging in murder, indiscriminate attacks, kidnapping, and the mining of civilian areas."[13] As an example of such actions, the Report noted that FARC cadres "attacked a local fundraising party in the La Chinita neighborhood of Apartadó, Antioquia, killing thirty-five." Year after year abuses were condemned. The *World Report 2010* echoed what had been said before and emphasized particular outrages: "The FARC . . . is frequently involved in massacres, killings, threats, and recruitment of child combatants. In February the FARC massacred 17 Awá [an indigenous people] in Nariño."[14] A witness testified that Awá were tortured before being killed. FARC was also believed to have killed "human rights defender" Islena Rey in the state of Meta.

FARC and the Cartels
Coca growing and the cocaine market boomed in the late 1970s, and avaricious drug lords sought to increase their control over growing areas. This put them on a collision course with FARC, based as it was in rural Colombia. At first, FARC opposed and tried to suppress the growing of coca because the production of drugs was inconsistent with its ideological message. However, a CIA intelligence estimate of June 1983 reported, "The FARC in some areas established quotas, taxes, wages and rules for workers, producers and owners of the coca fields." Rather than eradicating the drug trade, FARC had decided to regulate and profit from it.

This could lead to conflict as well as convergence. As insurgents began to extort "taxes" from growers and traffickers, the guerrillas resorted to kidnapping the delinquent "taxpayers" or members of their families. When the M-19 guerrillas kidnapped the sister of Medellín cartel drug barons Juan David Ochoa and his two brothers in 1981, the major traffickers, including Escobar, formed their own paramilitary, Muerte a Secuestradores (Death to Kidnappers), to combat the left-wing guerrillas, including FARC. Drug traffickers fought not only to protect their own but to assert control over coca-growing areas.

As the Colombian state's campaigns beat down the Medellín and Cali drug cartels, a series of "mini-cartels" emerged, and some relied on FARC for protection. This happened just as coca production shifted more and more to Colombia, because the flow of coca paste from Peru and Bolivia was declining. FARC's particular stronghold was over the coca-growing areas in the remote southern jungles of Colombia. FARC became an agent and middle-man for the peasants in its territories, negotiating prices and establishing relationships with drug traffickers in Colombia, Peru, Bolivia, Venezuela, and Mexico.

As FARC became more and more deeply involved in the drug trade, making millions, some critics claimed that it was motivated more by profits than by principles. Not surprisingly, FARC leaders protested that they maintained their ideological principles despite the pull of drug money. In 2000, Simón Trinidad, a high-ranking commander, stressed that FARC intervened for the benefit of the peasantry, "providing a better life for the poor campesinos through agrarian reform, by giving them good lands, technical assistance and low-interest loans to change from growing illicit crops to legal crops, such as coffee, yucca, bananas, sugarcane and ranching."[15] In some areas, FARC required that coca-growing peasants devote 30 percent of their fields to traditional food crops; in others that proportion rose as high as 75 percent. Acting in accord with its ideological underpinnings, FARC broke up ten large ranches in the central province of Meta, redistributing the land to poor peasants.

In contrast to this protestation of principle, security authority Jorrit Kamminga argued in 2013: "FARC could be considered a prime example of a guerrilla movement that has (partly) shifted from grievances to greed to motivate its struggle against the Colombian government. Its involvement in the illicit drug trade . . . may indeed have become an independent motivational force in itself."[16]

On the crime–terror continuum, FARC advanced through illicit alliances to commercial terrorism. To thrive in the violence-ridden and cocaine-rich environment of Colombia, it had to ally with criminal drug traffickers motivated by power and greed, not politics and principles. Eventually, FARC had to get its hands dirty to do its work. It was not so much a transformation as a merging, a convergence. A director of the Colombian National Police admitted the complexity and confusion: "One does not know if the drug trafficker is a guerrilla or if the guerrilla is a drug trafficker. The line is now blurred."[17]

Endgame?
FARC officially put down its weapons in 2017, ending a history of violence that went back half a century. It did so as a result of negotiations,

and its cadres reentered society as full citizens. It began as a small group, but evolved into a major force estimated at 20,000 at its height, with control over populations and resources. As part of the peace agreement, FARC cadres received amnesty, unless they were guilty of serious war crimes. Although there are to be trials for those accused of human rights violations, those found guilty are not to serve traditional prison sentences but to be compelled to provide reparation services, such as mine clearing. FARC was recognized as a political party, with ten guaranteed seats in the Colombian House of Representatives and Senate. FARC leader Timochenko was even slated to run for president of Colombia in the 2018 elections, but had to withdraw for health reasons. So, FARC ended the terrorist campaign by reentering the political process of Colombia.

It is too soon to judge the fallout from the dissolution of the FARC as a terrorist and insurgent force. Might some FARC members stay attached to the drug trade? Might some launch out in their own resistance or join the remaining left-wing terrorist group in Colombia, the Ejército de Liberación Nacional (National Liberation Army)? Concern with the future of FARC dropouts began soon after the agreement. Defense Minister Louis Carols Villegas stated in the fall of 2017, "Those who declare themselves in dissent from the FARC or simply become bandits because of the ambition of money, gold and dollars are high-value targets, we will persecute them."[18]

FARC's soft landing after a hard war was not the fate of its neighboring Communist resistance group in Peru, Sendero Luminoso, or Shining Path. It began terrorist attacks in 1980 and grew to a strength of several thousand fighters. It, too, profited from the drug trade. However, Shining Path declined sharply after the capture of its charismatic leader, Abimael Guzman, in 1992. Thus, the fate of Shining Path illustrates the dangers of being too dependent upon a charismatic chief. An account of Shining Path can be found on the website for this book.

The histories of the Medellín cartel of Pablo Escobar and of FARC provide two case studies of convergence between drug organizations and terrorist groups in one country, Colombia. The reality is more convoluted than Makarenko's schema, but the main lines apply. Moving now to Afghanistan, we consider the Taliban, which rose to rule most of the country from 1996 to 2001, met defeat in 2001–2002, and then staged a resurgence that continues to this day. The saga of the Taliban stands as an extreme case of what the DEA would classify as drug-supported terrorism. We consider it as our second manifestation, the exploitation of the drug trade to finance a major civil war.

THE RESURGENT TALIBAN, 2003–2016

After its initial defeat by the United States and its allies, in league with the Afghan Northern Alliance, the Taliban reasserted itself in Afghanistan. It now fields a large military force that employs terrorist tactics but also seizes and holds ground in positional war against the government in Kabul and its American backers. The cultivation of opium poppies and the consequent processing and trafficking of opiates in Afghanistan finance this resurgence. Like FARC, the Taliban demonstrates how a political organization can benefit from the drug trade, but the Taliban's size and power are far greater than FARC's ever were.

It is in Afghanistan that the interdependence of drug trafficking and deadly political conflict most immediately impacts U.S. military and geopolitical strategies. The Afghan Taliban has once again become an army and proto-state engaged in a civil war. Interestingly, the U.S. Department of State does not list the Afghan Taliban as a foreign terrorist group, but the Department of the Treasury includes it as a "specially designated global terrorist." The charge of narcoterrorism has been repeatedly levied against the Taliban by journalists and policymakers.

As we saw in Chapter 11, the Taliban commanded such power and territory that it could offer sanctuary to Osama bin Laden and al-Qaeda in 1996. And, of course, it became the base for his attacks in 1998, 2000, and 2001. When the Taliban leader Mullah Omar refused to turn bin Laden over after 9/11, the United States formally began its war on the Taliban, Operation Enduring Freedom, on 7 October 2001. At that time the Taliban fielded about 50,000 fighters, but it was quickly defeated and decimated.

However, the Taliban rebounded before long. By 2003 it had resurfaced and made significant gains. By 2006, Taliban strength grew; even low appraisals put it at 4,000–5,000 combatants. A U.S. intelligence report stated the size of Taliban forces at 25,000 in 2009. Taliban expansion continued at an alarming rate; in 2014, its forces were estimated at more than 60,000 by Matt Waldman, an expert on Afghanistan. At the time of writing this chapter, it appears that the war in Afghanistan is "unwinnable" from the U.S. perspective, as a *New York Times* article declared in February 2018.[19]

The phenomenal growth and success of the Taliban have been largely funded by exploiting the opium trade. Opium poppies have long been cultivated in Afghanistan, and during the 1990s Afghanistan became the world's leading source of opium, surpassing Myanmar. According to estimates by the United Nations Office on Drugs and Crime, Afghanistan produced a total of 4,600 metric tons of opium in 1999, amounting to 80 percent of the world's production. Fully 97 percent of the Afghan production that year came from Taliban-controlled areas. After a major decline in opium production in 2001, the crop came back strong, peaking with a bumper crop of 8,200 metric tons in 2007, with an export value of $4 billion and constituting 93 percent of world production. The 2014 crop reached 6,400 metric tons, a total that, as usual, was produced mainly in areas where the Taliban was and is strong. In short, the Afghan opium trade is a monstrously lucrative low hanging fruit with which the Taliban has nourished itself.

Given Islam's prohibition of intoxicants, alcohol and drugs, it may appear hypocritical that the Taliban fosters and profits from the opium trade. In fact, the Taliban has harshly punished the consumption of drugs by Muslims. But except for 2001, it has not banned opium production. It only did so that year because the U.S. government paid the Taliban $43 million to eradicate poppy growing as part of the American war on drugs. This was, of course, before 9/11. In 2007 one common Taliban cadre explained the logic of growing what the organization did not allow to be consumed: "It is obvious to everyone that the Americans hate poppies, and if we grow it . . . it will be better for us and worse for the Americans."[20] In fact, supplying the West with opiates facilitates drug addiction in the West, and the money brought in by the flow of drugs finances the Taliban's conflict with the Afghan government and its Western allies.

Drug-Related Revenues of the Taliban
In her book *Seeds of Terror: How Drugs, Thugs, and Crime Are Reshaping the Afghan War*, Gretchen Peters draws a direct relationship between the increased level of military operations by the Taliban in 2006 and the large opium crop harvested that year: "It's no coincidence that it was also the bloodiest fighting season since Mullah Omar's regime was toppled

five years earlier, with about four thousand deaths."[21] U.S. casualties in Afghanistan peaked in 2010, and although other factors were certainly involved, the Taliban's ability to finance itself through the drug trade must be weighed in the balance.

Major drug traffickers funneled money to the Taliban. For example, Haji Juma Khan, the king of the Afghan opium trade, gave them huge sums. DEA undercover agent, Edward Follis, who knew him well, writes, "Haji Juma Khan's personal wealth was staggering, his profits calculated in the billions. The DEA believed that several hundred million of his narco-dollars went straight to the Taliban and Al-Qaeda."[22] He was also a confidant of Osama bin Laden and Mullah Omar, although Haji Juma was not fundamentalist in his Islam. Eventually, he was arrested and rendered—that is, spirited off—to the United States and confined in New York, where as late as 2017 he was still awaiting trial.

Money came from several sources, not simply the kingpins. In 2007, the 10 percent tax that the Taliban levied on opium farmers would have yielded roughly $56 million. At the same time, the fifty heroin refineries then operating in Taliban territory would have generated another $133 million. On top of this, the Taliban could have netted as much as $250 million for using its forces to protect drug shipments. The DEA, which has carried out anti–drug trafficking operations in Afghanistan, estimated that by about 2009 the Taliban drew 70 percent of its financing from the opium trade.

Pakistan, Dawood Ibrahim, and the D-Company
In exploring Taliban terrorism, it is important to note the political relationship between Afghanistan and Pakistan. This involves institutions and individuals in the Pakistani government and armed forces that regard the Taliban as a Muslim ally in limiting the influence of Pakistan's archrival, India. Elements within the Pakistani military intelligence agency, the Directorate of Inter-Services Intelligence (ISI), have supported terrorist activities in a devious double game that leads many American foreign policy commentators to call Pakistan a "frenemy." Pakistani support for terrorism has also involved Dawood Ibrahim, leader of the largest crime syndicate in South Asia, known as D-Company. This crime boss and drug trafficker grew up in Mumbai and relocated to Pakistan.

Ibrahim was infuriated by the destruction of a historic mosque by a Hindu mob and the consequent riots that pitted Hindus against Muslims in December 1992 and January 1993. In retribution, he masterminded a series of car bombings that struck Mumbai on 12 March 1993, killing 257 and injuring 713. It is also suspected that Ibrahim supported the Pakistani Islamist terrorist group Lashkar-e-Taiba (LeT) in its 2008 terror attacks in Mumbai that killed 166 plus the terrorists. One thesis for Ibrahim's involvement proposes that his was a symbiotic relationship with LeT in which LeT benefited from financing, weapons, and knowledge from the D-Company, and Ibrahim could bask in some of the glow of jihadism. It is also possible that the ISI takes advantage of Ibrahim to advance its own program.

It is clear that Ibrahim had a relationship with the Taliban and Osama bin Laden, which may have had something of the same benefit for him. A former CIA official counseled Peters at the time, "If you want to understand what Osama bin Laden is up to, you have to understand what Dawood Ibrahim is up to."[23]

Taliban Terrorism in the Context of the Broader Afghan Conflict
The Taliban arose in a very brutal and bloody environment of civil war following the Russian withdrawal from Afghanistan, the dissolution of the Afghan Communist regime, and the onset of a multisided power struggle among warlords. From 1994 to 2001, the Taliban engaged in horrendous violence, including massacres. The resurgence of the Taliban that began in 2003 brought a new wave of terrorism.

The number of civilian casualties inflicted by the Taliban can be regarded as a measure of the degree to which it employed terrorist tactics. Since 2009, the United Nations Assistance Mission in Afghanistan (UNAMA) has registered and reported these civilian casualties annually. With one exception, the annual number of civilian casualties increased each year; nearly 6,000 were killed and injured during 2009 and 11,000 in 2015.[24] UNAMA identified "Anti-Government Elements," that is, the Taliban and other rebel groups, as responsible for 77 percent of the deaths in 2011 and 74 percent of civilian casualties in 2014, when only 8 percent were attributable to Afghan national forces and 3 percent to international forces.

Bare figures turn terrorism into statistics rather than human suffering. More specific accounts emphasize the human toll. Writing in 2006, journalist Sebastien Junger reported, "I was told about one man whom the Taliban skinned alive and left in a field to die. I was told about another man who was forced to watch as his wife was gang-raped in front of him; his eyes were then stabbed out so that it would be the last thing he ever saw."[25]

The Taliban has also conducted a campaign against education, particularly girls' education. Among its myriad of attacks in 2006, the Taliban destroyed 187 schools, murdered eighty-five teachers, and killed 600 policemen, as well as conducting 141 suicide bombings that inflicted nearly 1,200 casualties. During 2007, Taliban attacks and threats forced the closing of 450 schools in what Human Rights Watch called "part of their campaign of terrorizing the civilian population." In one such attack on a girls' school on 12 June, the Taliban murdered two schoolgirls and injured three others, along with a teacher, in front of their school near Kabul.[26]

Perhaps the best-known Taliban atrocity is the shooting of the then fifteen-year-old Malala Yousafzai in Pakistan's Swat Valley. Despite her youth, she crusaded for girls' education, drawing the wrath of the local Taliban. In October 2012, a gunman boarded the bus on which she was riding and demanded that she identify herself or he would kill everyone. He shot her in the face with a bullet that passed through her head and neck into her shoulder. Miraculously, she survived and has become a heroine for her courage, her survival, and her ongoing advocacy. Her assailant belonged not to the Afghan Taliban, but to its independent cousin, the Pakistani Taliban.

The pace of ostentatious atrocities has not slackened. Kunduz, a city in northern Afghanistan, was taken by the Taliban in September 2015, and accounts of their conduct after they took control are shocking. Amnesty International reported: "Mass murder, gang rapes and house-to-house searches by Taliban death squads are just some of the harrowing civilian testimonies emerging from Kunduz."[27]

The war being waged by the Taliban has multiple dimensions: it is conventional in the taking and holding of territory, terrorist in its attacks in government areas, and criminal in its engagement with the opium trade. This fits the concept of "hybrid warfare." In 2010, Frank G. Hoffman, an authority on the subject, defined a hybrid threat as "any adversary that simultaneously and adaptively employs a fused mix of conventional weapons, irregular tactics, terrorism and criminal behavior in the battle space to obtain their political objectives."[28] Such an idea of warfare makes the inclusion of terrorism as a form of war all the more valid.

The career of the Taliban has led some to argue that it has been diverted from its political purpose by the draw of illicit profit along the crime–terror continuum. Doug Wankal, who headed the U.S. embassy's counter-narcotics task force until 2007, went so far as to caution, "People should be concerned about the FARCification of the Taliban," implying that both had become drug cartels.[29] Drug money certainly supported FARC's Marxist cause and supports the Taliban's Islamist jihad, but does money alone draw cadre to fight or simply enable them to maintain themselves as they engage in a war they have taken up for other reasons?

Whether carried on for principle or profit, there is surprising extremism in the violence of narcoterrorism in the three manifestations discussed so far. Our discussion of the fourth manifestation centers on the Mexican drug cartels. Their cruelty is all the more shocking because it lacks any shred of legitimation through grand political purpose.

MEXICAN DRUG CARTELS

The Mexican drug cartels carry on violent campaigns, including terrorist-style ostentatious atrocities, but they fight to achieve criminal, not essentially political, purposes. Yet as a byproduct of their campaigns of violence and corruption, the cartels have undermined governance. Thus, they exemplify our fourth manifestation of narcoterrorism.

Just as in other cases discussed in this chapter, the Mexican cartels gain a phenomenal amount of money from the drug trade. The DEA put the take from Mexican and Colombian drug sales in the United States in 2012 at $18–39 billion. For comparison, General Motors claimed a net income of $4.9 billion that year, after interest payments and taxes. Mexican cartels traffic in marijuana, cocaine, heroin, and synthetic drugs such as methamphetamine and fentanyl. The cartels are surprisingly agile, adapting to demand and profit. They produce some of their own product, such as marijuana and some heroin, while in the case of cocaine and some synthetic drugs they transport and wholesale what is made elsewhere. Their great market is the United States, where they commonly supply urban street gangs who retail the drugs.

In their wars over territory and trade, the cartels fight each other, the Mexican authorities, the army, and the police. As they do so, great numbers of the innocent die as well. Experts differ, but it is reasonable to number those who have perished in the drug wars during the past decade at more than 100,000.

As Sylvia Longmire puts it in her 2011 book on the cartels, "While not interested in taking the political reins themselves, cartels actively manipulate governments through bribery and intimidation."[30] They employ their assets for influence. One exceptional document from the Monterrey branch of the Mexican cartel Los Zetas bears witness both to their meticulous bookkeeping (there were penalties for letting money go astray) and to their outlays for bribes. The captured ledger recorded expenses of $646,000 for one month in 2007. Amounts of $18,400 and $1,000 went for lookouts and security, respectively. "Gifts" were recorded at $50,000, but "payoffs to police" cost $552,350, or 85 percent of the funds detailed in the ledger.[31]

But the most detestable resource of the cartels is their bottomless pit of ultraviolence, much of it ostentatious atrocities employed to render local government compliant and local police impotent. Assassinations of Mexican mayors exemplify this brutality. During 2010 at least fifteen mayors were murdered by drug cartel hitmen, and three more fell in January 2011. An especially shocking assassination struck down Dr. Maria Santos Gorrostieta in 2012. This brave physician, mother of three, served as mayor of Tiquicheo, a town of about 13,000, from 2008 to 2011. She stood up to the local drug traffickers and was targeted in other gun attacks before she was killed. On 15 October 2009, gunmen killed her husband and wounded her. On 23 January 2010, she was targeted again and shot multiple times; somehow, she survived this vicious assault. She left office in 2011, but the gang still had something to prove. On 15 November 2012, two men dragged her from her car as she drove her daughter to school. She begged them to leave her daughter alone and went with them willingly so that they would spare the girl. Eight days later, farm workers found her lifeless body, beaten and burned.

History and Variety of the Cartels
Mexican criminal organizations have been engaged in drug trafficking for many years, but the emergence of the drug cartels as we know them

today only began when the primary pathway for the shipment of Colombian cocaine coming to the United States switched from Florida to Mexico. In the early 1980s Miami was the epicenter of the cocaine trade and the Colombian cartels imported their drugs directly. But more aggressive drug enforcement in the United States and the breaking up of the Medellín and Cali cartels in Colombia made the remaining smaller Colombian producers more and more dependent on transshipment through Mexico. Mexican cartels grew to overshadow their Colombian suppliers.

Until the end of the 1980s, the Guadalajara cartel exercised a virtual monopoly on drug trafficking in Mexico. Félix Gallardo became its head by late 1985. Owing to the greater flow of drugs and increased law enforcement pressure, Gallardo decided to subdivide the cartel into four organizations based on drug-trading routes. These organizations would become the Sinaloa, Tijuana, Juarez, and Gulf cartels. Although Gallardo intended this reorganization to provide greater efficiency and security, it triggered deadly rivalries and set off wars between cartels.

The map of Mexican cartels, in terms of their territory, power, and leadership, has changed over the years as existing cartels decline or split and new organizations emerge to challenge established organizations. A Congressional Research Service survey states that as late as 2006, the same four cartels dominated drug trafficking in Mexico. However, that stability gave way to considerable flux. By the summer of 2015, the DEA identified eight major cartels: Los Zetas, Sinaloa, Jalisco New Generation, Beltran-Leyva Organization, Gulf, Juarez, La Familia Michoacana, and Los Caballeros Templarios. But, as noted, the map is always changing. The much-publicized arrest of Joaquín "El Chapo" Guzmán, head of the Sinaloa cartel, by Mexican authorities in January 2016 could lead to further instability. He was extradited to the United States in January 2017 and was set to stand trial in November 2018.

Los Zetas
There is not sufficient room here to describe at length the career of each of the cartels, but we will take a brief look at one, Los Zetas. When Osiel Cárdenas rose to head the Gulf cartel in 1999, he insisted on greater protection from rival cartels and from the Mexican military. His anxiety rose to the level of paranoia, and Cárdenas recruited soldiers and veterans from the Mexican Army's special forces to serve as his personal security

detail. This force of about thirty highly trained professionals, drawn by the high pay and adventure, became narcomercenaries. Their original commanders were Antonio Javier Quevedo and Arturo Guzmán. They took the name Los Zetas, "the Z's," probably because of Guzmán's radio call sign "Z." He would be "Z-1," with others having their own numbers. Los Zetas grew to a few hundred cadres, a surprisingly small number given their clout among the cartels.

By 2002 they were led by two new commanders who would be in charge for a decade: Heriberto Lazcano and Miguel Treviño. In 2007 the U.S. National Drug Intelligence Center evaluated the group as "maybe the most technologically advanced, sophisticated, and violent of these paramilitary enforcement groups."[32] The independence with which Los Zetas operated in the cartel grew until it separated from the Gulf cartel in 2010, and the two became enemies.

Both Lazcano and Treviño were ferocious. Before Los Zetas, criminal organizations in Mexico had respected a code that regulated conduct between cartels, limited executions of rivals, and put civilians out of bounds. Then Los Zetas raised the bar on barbarity. Their repertoire of torture and murder includes beating victims to death with two-by-fours, suspending them upside down and castrating them, skinning them alive, and burning them to death in barrels of oil. They seem to take pleasure in the extremes of their violence and in exhibiting it to the world with videos of executions and public displays of severed heads and dismembered bodies. In May 2012, drivers in Nuevo Laredo were confronted by the sight of nine bodies hanging from a bridge. A sign displayed with the bodies made it clear that these killings were part of a drug war, most certainly between Los Zetas and the Sinaloa cartel. But that was not the end of the day's gruesome discoveries. Fourteen severed heads were found in coolers outside the city hall; their bodies were stashed in a vehicle parked by another bridge.

The kind of savagery exploited by Los Zetas is wrapped up in the Mexican popular culture of violence. The ultraviolence of the drug wars is celebrated in *narcocorridos*, or narco ballads. One *corrido*, "Sanguinarios del M1," memorializes a Sinaloa cartel enforcer. The song is a boast by heavily armed "bloodthirsty crazies" who "love to kill" and chop off the heads of all who get in their way.[33] Crime and death are even given a place in popular Catholicism. There is a cult of Jésus Malverde, a mythologized bandit in the Robin Hood mode. This predated the drug wars, but he has become a kind of patron saint of drug criminals. And there is the cult of Santa Muerte, Our Lady of the Holy Death. This saint has some Aztec roots and is revered or worshipped as a woman's skeleton in colorful robes. She has been appropriated as an even more important saint of the drug trade. In one case, police arrested suspects in a human sacrifice made before the image of Santa Muerte.

The tide seems to have turned against Los Zetas. While the individual cartels fight for their own interests, they also form shifting alliances of convenience. So, the Sinaloa and Gulf cartels, former enemies, allied against Los Zetas. The killing in Nuevo Laredo was apparently part of this war. Lascano died later in 2012 during a shootout with Mexican marines. Miguel Treviño was arrested in July 2013. Los Zetas' loss has been the Sinaloa cartel's gain.

Beheading

Mexican ultraviolence provides us with another case of terrorists copying other terrorists. The practice of decapitation was not original to the Mexicans but an import from Islamist terrorism. Terrorism authority Ioan Grillo states that "decapitations were almost unheard of here before 2006," when the first major publicized instances occurred.[34] Explaining the Mexican drug lords' 2006 turn to beheading, Jorge Chabat, a justice expert at the Center for Research and Teaching of Economics in Mexico City, traced a line from Islamist terrorism to Mexican narcoterrorism: "These guys are copying the methods of al-Qaeda."[35] As already noted, Daniel Pearl was beheaded in Pakistan by Islamist radicals in 2002, and al-Zarqawi beheaded Nick Berg in 2004. Both these murders were broadcast world-wide by videos on the web. Apparently leaders of Mexican drug cartels were watching.

On 6 September 2006, members of La Familia Michoacana, a group that split off from Los Zetas, stormed into a disco bar in Uruapan, a city in the central Mexican state of Michoacán, and emptied a bag of five severed heads on the dance floor, to the horror of the partiers. The victims were methamphetamine peddlers who drew the wrath of La Familia. *Time* magazine featured the beheading of twelve rival drug dealers by Los Zetas in October 2008. The innocent were also targeted: on 16 May 2011, a Los Zetas gang butchered twenty-seven farmhands in Guatemala, just over the Mexican border. Los Zetas have a long reach. Twenty-five of the slaughtered were beheaded. The massacred workers were killed because they did not tell the Zetas the location of their boss, a smuggler sought by the Zetas.

The Cartels and the Mexican State
Mexican drug cartel violence clawed its way up the scale of savagery in 2006, but that was also the year that the new Mexican president, Felipe Calderón, began the Mexican Drug War in December with a military offensive against the cartels in Michoacán. Part of his strategy was to rely on the Mexican military, rather than the police, because of the corruption of local police forces. Calderón eventually committed 45,000 troops to the Drug War. In 2007, the U.S. government announced that it was partnering with Mexico in the Mérida Initiative. This effort in the war on drugs became law in June 2008, with an initial grant of $400 million. From 2008 through 2015, Congress appropriated a total of $2.3 billion to the initiative.

The growing danger posed by the cartels was plain to observers on both sides of the border. In his study for the U.S. Army's Strategic Studies Institute in 2009, Hal Brands declared, "Narcotics-driven corruption is rampant, government control of large swaths of the country is tenuous at best, and predictions that Mexico is on the way to becoming a failed state are frequent."[36] In remarks delivered on 4 August 2010, President Calderón bluntly assessed the threat: "Their business is no longer just the traffic of drugs. Their business is to dominate everyone else. . . . This criminal behavior is what has changed and become a defiance to the state, an attempt to replace the state."[37] Clearly, the cartels constituted not only a criminal menace but an even greater political threat, even though they did not espouse a political ideology.

There are even more disturbing scenarios that are best encompassed by Hoffman's idea of hybrid warfare. The Mexican government has been engaged in a multilevel armed fight with the cartels, involving insurgency, terrorism, and criminal activity now and perhaps other dimensions in the future. U.S. defense intellectuals worry about this war crossing the border if northern Mexico descends into utter lawlessness, causing refugees to stream into the United States to fill refugee camps in California, Arizona, New Mexico, and Texas. These camps would then become new theaters of conflict for the cartels. U.S. forces would be dragged into such a hybrid war on both sides of the border.

The level of violence perpetrated by Mexican drug cartels ratcheted up even though the killers were not compelled by any great cause. For their ostentatious atrocities to continue to shock, they had to become more extreme.

The extreme forms of ultraviolence typical of each of the narcoterrorist organizations discussed in this chapter may lead us to suppose that it is intrinsic to the drug trade. I am of two minds on this. On the one hand, it seems that the less principled the terrorist, the more unrestrained the violence, as if the only leverage terrorists have comes from the fear generated by atrocities. On the other hand, the reason that such ultraviolence is effective lies in culture; the more an audience expects and is tolerant of atrocities, the more extreme they must be to intimidate that audience. It is worth remembering that *La Violencia* set the tone of ultraviolence in Colombia before the rise of the modern drug trade. But that is a subject for a different book than this. The violence performed by terrorists reflects not only by their own ruthlessness, but also the audiences for whom they are performing.

The very word *narcoterrorism* implies a convergence of drug-related crime and terrorism. This is generally discussed in two senses: how criminal groups become more political, and how political terrorist groups become more dependent on the drug trade to finance their campaigns. But there is another aspect, most obviously evident in the case of the Mexican cartels, and that is a convergence of violence, as criminal organizations take on the extreme forms of violence characteristic of terrorists, even when the criminal organizations have no political ideology or cause. What is clear from the case of narcoterrorism is that ruthless repertoires of violence inflicted by terrorists can be transshipped like drugs, and, like drugs, they can vitiate restraint. There is good reason for the media to define narcoterrorism by its tactics.

CHAPTER FOURTEEN

Homeland Security

FIGURE 14.1. This poster, issued by the American Civil Liberties Union, warns of the threat to constitutional freedoms and protections posed by the Patriot Act. The "patriot" is the Terminator. Note him pulling down the Statue of Liberty and rifling through someone's private files in the background. ACLU, used with permission.

EVERY PREVIOUS CHAPTER of this book began with a story of the human costs of the violence discussed in that chapter, from the beheading of a single man, John Foley, to the incineration of tens of thousands in Dresden. The phenomena discussed in this chapter—counterterrorism laws and practices in the United States of America—have also produced victims, but in more subtle ways. Organizing and acting to prevent and prosecute terrorism in and against the United States is undoubtedly necessary. In the name of increased security, we sacrifice convenience—for example, by standing in TSA lines at airports—and a degree of privacy—as represented by security cameras and more obtrusive monitoring. But our values and freedoms are also at risk when our government increases its powers of investigation, interrogation, and incarceration. To what extent will we change, or warp, our principles in the name of defending ourselves from a real but elusive threat? We should heed the warnings of those like the American Civil Liberties Union, who caution us against the dangers we create when we rashly contrive to protect ourselves (Fig. 14.1).

Sami Omar al-Hussayen, his wife, Maha, and their three young sons lived in Moscow, Idaho, where he pursued a Ph.D. in computer science at the University of Idaho. In the early-morning hours of 26 February 2003, as many as 100 law enforcement agents in flak jackets descended on the campus and arrested Sami. Al-Hussayen is Saudi and was in the United States on a student visa that allowed him to study but not to work. While in the country he volunteered his services as a webmaster to a Muslim charity, as well as donating his time to other good causes. Anxious about charitable funds being diverted into terrorist coffers, the FBI had put al-Hussayen under surveillance during the preceding year, listening to 10,000 phone calls and reading 20,000 emails. Sami was jailed on suspicion of offering "material support" to terrorists. His wife and children were forced to return to Saudi Arabia before he had his day in court. When al-Hussayen was finally put on trial in April 2004, the jury acquitted him of any charge of terrorism. One juror stated to the press, "There was no clear-cut evidence that said he was a terrorist, so it was all on inference."[1] However, al-Hussayen was then deported because the government claimed that he had lied on his immigration forms when he said he would only be studying and not working; authorities decided to count his volunteer contributions as work. Sami Omar al-Hussayen was jailed for fifteen months, his family traumatized, his name sullied. Fortunately, he had a future waiting for him after he was deported to Saudi Arabia, where he reunited with his family and ultimately became a professor at a Saudi technical college. But he was not the only casualty of overzealous prosecution.

Abdullah al-Kidd was arrested only days after al-Hussayen. Al-Kidd was born Lavoni T. Kidd in Wichita, Kansas, and attended the University of Idaho, where he was a football star in the 1990s. While at the university he converted to Islam, and as he became more deeply engaged in Islam, he decided to study Arabic and Islamic law in Saudi Arabia as he pursued a doctorate in Islamic studies. Authorities arrested him while he waited for his flight to Saudi Arabia at Dulles International Airport in Washington, D.C. While they were not close friends, al-Kidd knew al-Hussayen, and the FBI was suspicious of an American convert to Islam who was "tied" to a suspected terrorist and was flying to Saudi Arabia. The FBI presented manufactured or misleading information to a judge to secure a warrant, and al-Kidd was taken into custody as a "material witness." Held prisoner for fifteen days in harsh and degrading conditions, he was finally released with restrictions that imposed great strain on his family and ruined his own life. Al-Kidd lost his scholarship. He went from aspiring scholar to working on a crew of furniture movers. His wife left him, taking their daughter with her. In 2004 al-Kidd lamented, "'My reputation is destroyed. I keep getting nos from jobs as if I'm an ex-felon. And I'm not an ex-felon." He went on, "I lost a good wife. I'm not with my daughter anymore. How painful is that?"[2]

The FBI never charged al-Kidd with any crime, nor did they call him to testify in al-Hussayen's trial. He eventually received some measure of justice, enough to prove that he was unjustly harmed. In 2008 and 2009 he received a monetary settlement for abuses at three facilities in which he was held. And in 2015, nearly twelve years after being seized as a material witness, the U.S. government reached a final settlement with al-Kidd, issuing a formal statement of regret and monetary compensation of $385,000.

These two related stories of government action and personal suffering do not equal the lurid extremes of violence highlighted at the start of the preceding chapters. Yet U.S. counterterrorism has produced its own shocking stories. With the decision of the George W. Bush administration to legitimate torture, prisoners held outside our borders were abused and degraded, most notoriously at Abu Ghraib. There, captured Iraqis were humiliated, beaten, tortured, and sodomized; at least one prisoner, Manadel al-Jamadi, died under torture. However, much more surreptitiously, the CIA colluded with at least fifty-four countries either to set up "black-site prisons" of its own, as in Poland and Romania, or to turn over prisoners to the not-so-tender mercies of foreign security forces to carry out brutal interrogations, as in Egypt, Morocco, Syria, and Jordan. In a process of "rendition," captured suspects were spirited off to detention outside U.S. jurisdiction. The United States became infamous for declaring that waterboarding was not a torture, even though the U.S. had participated in war crimes trials that pronounced death sentences for Japanese who had waterboarded Americans in World War II.

This is not a chapter on how to defeat terrorism. Rather, it focuses on some of the ways in which the fervor to protect ourselves from terrorism have affected, or threaten to affect, life and liberty in the United States. Matters considered here include: 1) the American history of sacrificing civil liberties in wartime; 2) the growth of a counterterrorism regime consisting of departments, agencies, and offices before and after 9/11; 3) adoption of anti-terrorist laws, most notably the Patriot Act, and their application; and 4) the expansion of presidential powers and prerogatives in the name of national security. The chapter ends with an appeal to resist the pull of militarization and militarism in the name of buttressing our perception of safety.

The discussion of domestic counterterrorism fits the purpose of this book, since this volume is ultimately designed to advance the kind of rational understanding of terrorism that will aid us both in evaluating the dangers posed by terrorism and in putting into perspective our counterterrorism efforts and the sacrifices that we are asked to make in order to assure homeland security.

THE SECOND CASUALTY OF WAR

It is often said that in war, truth is the first casualty. Yes, but in the United States, civil liberties and protections have also fallen victim soon after armed conflict flares up. Safeguards against unwarranted search and seizure and guarantees of habeas corpus, due process, and speedy trial have suffered as we have rallied around the flag. Distinguished law professor Geoffrey Stone concludes, "The United States has a long and unfortunate history of overreacting to the perceived dangers of wartime. Again and again, Americans have allowed fear and fury to get the better of them."[3]

During the Civil War, President Abraham Lincoln repeatedly suspended the right of habeas corpus. Habeas corpus, Latin meaning literally "you shall have the body," is the right of an arrested person to appeal before a court and contest the legitimacy of his or her arrest. Thus, it is a right against being arrested and held without trial. We call such confinement on suspicion alone "internment," as discussed in Chapter 6 vis-à-vis the Troubles in Northern Ireland. The Constitution specifically mentions habeas corpus only in Article 1, Section 9, defining the terms under which it can be suspended: "The Privilege of the Writ of Habeas

Corpus shall not be suspended, unless when in Cases of Rebellion or Invasion the public Safety may require it."

While the Constitution allows for suspension, Article 1 deals with the legislative branch, so it can be argued that suspension is ascribed to Congress, not to the president. Lincoln's initial decision to suspend habeas corpus came on 25 April 1861, two weeks after Confederates bombarded Fort Sumter. On 26 May 1861, Roger Taney, chief justice of the Supreme Court from 1836 to 1864, declared that the president lacked the right to do so, but Lincoln ignored his ruling and continued to suspend habeas corpus and enforce martial law as he chose. Only in March 1863 did Congress give its blessing to Lincoln's suspensions and authorize him to exercise this authority as he deemed necessary. In September of that year, the president reasserted a nationwide suspension of habeas corpus in cases concerning the prosecution of the war. He also closed down newspapers he accused of obstructing the war effort.

Although a great many Americans had been reluctant for their country to become a belligerent in World War I, a wave of hyperpatriotism swept through the country when the country declared war on Germany in April 1917. Congress passed the Espionage Act of 1917 in June. It was directed against potential hostile foreign agents in the United States and those who would hinder the war effort, including wartime conscription. Though controversial in some of its provisions, the Espionage Act remains part of U.S. law to this very day, as United States Code, Title 18, Chapter 37. Both Chelsea (formerly Bradley) Manning and Edward Snowden have been charged with violating this law by disseminating classified documents on public media.

In 1918, Congress extended provisions of the Espionage Act by passing the Sedition Act. This law penalized free speech by criminalizing "disloyal, profane, scurrilous, or abusive language about the form of government of the United States or the Constitution of the United States, or the military or naval forces of the United States, or the flag of the United States." The Sedition Act remained in force after the war and was used to punish leftists during the Red Scare of 1919–1920, but it was finally repealed in December 1920.

The most extensive and wrongheaded single act denying Americans their constitutional rights because of wartime "necessity" struck the Japanese-American community during the opening months of World

War II. On 19 February 1942, President Franklin D. Roosevelt issued Executive Order 9066 authorizing "Military Commanders . . . to prescribe military areas in such places and of such extent as [they] . . . may determine, from which any and all persons may be excluded."[4] This permitted the military commander of the Western Defense Command, Lieutenant General John L. DeWitt, to remove anyone of Japanese ancestry from a band of territory encompassing the western coast from the Canadian to the Mexican borders. Neither the U.S. Navy nor the FBI thought this was necessary, but DeWitt testified before Congress that "a Jap's a Jap" and insisted that they were "a dangerous element."[5] This led to the uprooting and internment of 110,000–120,000 Japanese-Americans behind barbed wire in "relocation camps." They were stripped of their rights, their homes, and their livelihoods. The exclusion order was not rescinded until January 1945. The internment was a reflection not of a real danger, but of racially induced hysteria. No Japanese-American was ever convicted of espionage or aiding the enemy in the United States during World War II. In fact, the Japanese-American 442nd Regimental Combat Team, composed of Japanese-American rank and file, is regarded as the most highly decorated U.S. Army unit of its size during World War II. Its men came from the Japanese-American community of Hawaii and from the relocation camps to fight in the European theater of the war.

Within a few years after Allied victory in World War II, suspicions and tensions between the United States and the Soviet Union escalated to such an extent that we speak of a new conflict, the Cold War, beginning in the late 1940s and continuing until the dissolution of the Soviet Union in 1991. One early phenomenon was a second Red Scare, akin to but deeper than that which followed World War I. This scare is dated differently, but it is commonly seen as lasting from 1947 to 1957. On 22 March 1947, President Harry S. Truman issued Executive Order 9835, which established a loyalty program to identify and take action against anyone who was seeking to be hired or was already employed by the federal government and found to be linked with any "totalitarian, fascist, communist, or subversive" organization. Truman later admitted to confidants that instituting the loyalty program had been a grave mistake: "Yes, it was terrible."[6] The House Un-American Activities Committee (HUAC) became instrumental in the American anti-Communist crusade. In the other house of Congress, the most infamous voice of Red Scare hysteria was Senator Joseph "Joe" McCarthy of Wisconsin. McCarthyism, a term coined in 1950 by the political cartoonist Herblock, became synonymous with making unfounded accusations, stifling political dissent, and imposing loyalty oaths, which would later be declared unconstitutional. McCarthy was finally censured by the Senate in December 1954.

THE GROWTH OF THE COUNTERTERRORISM REGIME BEFORE 9/11

As key as 9/11 was in escalating the government's counterterrorism campaign, that effort dated back three decades before the destruction of the World Trade Center towers. The two events that first caused the U.S. government to concentrate on terrorism both occurred in 1972, and both involved Israel: the Japanese Red Army/Popular Front for the Liberation of Palestine assault on Israel's Lod Airport (now Ben Gurion International Airport), which killed twenty-six on 30 May; and the Black September killing of Israeli Olympians at Munich on 5–6 September. On 25 September, President Richard Nixon issued a memorandum creating a cabinet-level Committee to Combat Terrorism, to be chaired by the secretary of state and include ten others, including the secretary of defense and the heads of the CIA and the FBI. Quickly on the heels of this, the government created the Office for Combating Terrorism within the State Department to deal with day-to-day matters. In 1976 the Ford administration created the position of coordinator for counterterrorism in the State Department.

In 1978 Congress passed legislation that would become extremely important in determining the legitimacy of wiretaps, searches, and seizures in counterterrorism efforts. The Foreign Intelligence Surveillance Act (FISA) of 1978 was enacted to put more controls on electronic surveillance by establishing a procedure by which proper warrants could be issued. It allowed surveillance on agents of foreign powers operating in the United States and provided for the creation of special FISA courts to consider and approve warrants for such surveillance. Its provisions would be extended over the years to make it easier to get information by intercepting telephone and computer-based exchanges.

Terrorism struck at American targets abroad during the 1980s and 1990s and at targets within American borders, notably when radical Islamists struck the World Trade Center towers in New York City in February 1993 and Timothy McVeigh bombed the Murrah Federal Office Building in Oklahoma City in April 1995. In January 1995, President Bill Clinton issued Executive Order 12947 to prohibit financial transactions of "terrorists who threaten to disrupt the Middle East peace process."[7] This order caused the Treasury Department to issue a list of Specially Designated Terrorists as identified by the department's Office of Foreign Assets Control. More and more names have been added, until today the list, now called the Specially Designated Nationals List, runs to nearly 1,000 pages. The Department of State created its own Foreign Terrorist Organizations list in 1997.

Only days after McVeigh detonated his bomb, Senator Robert Dole brought a hurried bill to the floor of the Senate. This legislation, the Anti-Terrorism and Effective Death Penalty Act (AEDPA), contained proposals that had been discussed earlier but were only brought to the floor now.[8] AEDPA increased federal authority and police powers, while weakening habeas corpus protections. After a year of consideration and debate, the bill passed Congress, and on 24 April 1996 President Clinton signed it into law. Randy Hertz and James S. Liebman write in their authoritative *Federal Habeas Corpus Practice and Procedure*: "AEDPA, enacted at the crest of the shock wave set off by the Oklahoma City bombing, reflected a passion-fueled, extreme, and not well thought-out form of habeas corpus bashing."[9] In a 2015 *New Yorker* article, "The Destruction of Defendants' Rights," Yale Law School scholar Lincoln Caplan condemned AEDPA as "one of the worst statutes ever passed by Congress and signed into law by a President."[10]

The U.S. government continued to refashion agencies and offices to deal with the terrorist threat. By 1989, Nixon's Office for Combating Terrorism had evolved into the Office of the Coordinator for Counterterrorism, which would morph into the Bureau for Counterterrorism in 2012. President Clinton created the office of National Coordinator for Security, Infrastructure Protection and Counter-Terrorism as part of his Presidential Decision Directive 62 (PDD-62) on 22 May 1998. Clinton appointed Richard A. Clarke to this office; Clarke soon became known as the "terrorism czar."

All of this was done before the great shock of 7 August 1998: the bombing of U.S. embassies in Dar es Salaam and Nairobi. This marked the point at which al-Qaeda rose to the top of the list of international terrorist threats to the United States. Clinton reacted with cruise missile strikes on Sudan and on al-Qaeda sites in Afghanistan, as discussed in Chapter 11. The danger posed by al-Qaeda became all the more apparent in 2000. Al-Qaeda millennial attacks against American targets failed, but on 12 October suicide bombers attacked the USS *Cole*, killing seventeen on board. Eleven months later far worse would befall the United States.

THE PATRIOT ACT

This volume began by invoking the al-Qaeda attacks of 11 September 2001, soon labeled as "the day that changed the world." Some have used the phrase not as a statement but a question: "What did 9/11 really change?" It certainly magnified the American focus on terrorism, with President George W. Bush declaring a "war on terror." In short order, it also resulted in what many regard as challenges to the rights and protections accorded U.S. citizens by legal precedents, enforcement practice, and constitutional promises. Just eight days after the attacks, a draft of an anti-terrorism bill was introduced in Congress. After consideration of this and additional drafts by the House and Senate, the final bill passed out of Congress with a Senate vote on 25 October. Only one senator voted nay, Russell Feingold. Bush signed it into law the next day. By the time the bill reached his desk it had become the USA PATRIOT Act, an acronym for the cumbersome title "Uniting and Strengthening America by Providing Appropriate Tools Required to Intercept and Obstruct Terrorism Act of 2001."

As already pointed out, this was not the first anti-terrorist legislation signed into law, and it would not be the last; however, it stands out as a critical step in the American response to the terrorist threat. The law is divided into ten major subdivisions, or titles, encompassing over 1,000 sections; in the paper form approved by Congress the bill included 342 pages, although the final official printed version squeezes it all into 131 pages of dense legalese.[11] The text of sections often simply says that the act changes such and such wording in an existing law. To know what that means requires a reading and interpretation of both the original language and of the change. Therefore, an intelligent and careful reading of the Patriot Act would amount to a nearly impossible task in the time allowed the congressmen and senators before the vote. Put succinctly, in the words of Representative Bobby Scott: "No one has really had an opportunity to look at the bill to see what is in it."[12] There was so much in it and it appeared so quickly after 9/11 that it seems apparent the bill included items that had already been on the wish-list of government departments and agencies.

Aspects of the Patriot Act are unquestionably important and valuable. The 9/11 Commission (2002–2004) concluded that while there were bits of information that, in retrospect, gave warning of a major al-Qaeda operation involving airplanes, this information was not sufficiently shared between government agencies. Such compartmentalization limited the ability to "connect the dots." The Patriot Act addressed this problem immediately after the attacks. Todd Hinnen, acting assistant attorney general for national security, testified: "Provisions in the Patriot Act helped us tear down the so-called FISA 'wall' between law enforcement and intelligence. . . . The wall had two aspects: there were limits on intelligence agents' ability to share information they collected using intelligence tools with criminal investigators; and there were limits on the ability of criminal investigators to share information they collected using criminal tools with their colleagues on the intelligence side."[13]

But more controversial provisions of the Patriot Act include the following: changes in the FISA Act (Section 218), roving wire taps (Section 206), delayed notice warrants (Section 213), access to personal and business records (Section 215), widening the application of National Security Letters (Section 505), and extending the definition of what constitutes criminal "material support" (Section 805).

In studying the Patriot Act, the devil is in the details. Changes that come down to a few words of arcane legalese can make a big difference. This means that we will have to get a bit into the legal weeds to understand what the act does. Yet this is an important exercise in civic education: how minutiae can matter, how the fabric of liberty can depend on the threads.

The changes mandated to the FISA Act by Section 218 seem almost trivial: "Sections 104(a)(7)(B) and section 303(a)(7)(B) (50 U.S.C. 1804(a)(7)(B) and 1823(a)(7)(B)) of the Foreign Intelligence Surveillance Act of 1978 are each amended by striking 'the purpose' and inserting 'a significant purpose.'" However, this wording expands the use of FISA warrants from being solely "to obtain foreign intelligence information" and allowed warrants that only involve "a significant purpose" to obtain such information. This meant they could be used to combat domestic crimes committed by U.S. citizens if the government could argue there was some suspicion of a foreign factor. The key point is that FISA warrants were much easier to obtain than were domestic warrants, because FISA warrants did not require probable cause. One victim of a FISA wiretap, Brandon Mayfield, was unjustly charged with being involved with the terrorists who bombed the Madrid subway in 2004. His phone was tapped, his records seized, and he was arrested and held as a material witness. When the mistake was discovered, he sued the government and eventually received a formal apology and $2 million in damages. The law itself was challenged in court, but the challenge was ultimately unsuccessful in 2009, owing to a legal technicality.

FISA wiretaps, an issue with Section 218, were also addressed in Section 206. Before the Patriot Act, a wiretap would be issued to tap a specific phone number; should the person targeted by surveillance employ a different phone line, there would have to be another warrant for that other number. Section 206 changes the language of the 1978 FISA law to allow the FISA court to authorize tapping whatever phone the targeted person employs. In essence the *person* becomes liable to a wiretap, not the *specific phone*. These "roving wiretaps" allow a much broader invasion of privacy.

Americans were reminded of the importance of FISA warrants by the 2018 controversy over FISA wiretaps of Carter Page as part of inquiries into Russian involvement in the 2016 election and possible obstruction of justice by the Trump administration.

Section 213 of the Patriot Act, entitled "Authority for Delaying Notice of the Execution of a Warrant," allows the government to secure a search warrant, carry out the search, and only inform the suspect of the search "within a reasonable period." Such searches, which soon earned the name "sneak and peek," could, in fact, continue as long as thirty to ninety days. The advantage of such sneak-and-peak searches is that one can gain evidence and gather information without alerting the suspect, who, if alerted, could cover his or her trail, protect confederates, or flee. This "Enhanced Surveillance Procedure," instituted in the name of fighting the war on terrorism, has, in fact, been far more utilized in the war on drugs, as is also the case for roving wiretaps. Susan Herman of the

Table 14.1.
Warrants for "Sneak-and-Peak" Searches, 2007–2016

YEAR	WARRANTS REQUESTED	WARRANTS GRANTED+ GRANTED AS MODIFIED	WARRANTS DENIED	WARRANTS FOR DRUG OFFENSES*	WARRANTS FOR TERRORISM*
2007	419	404+15	0	300 (71.6%)	6 (1.4%)
2008	763	737+23	3	474 (62.1%)	3 (0.4%)
2009	1,150	1,124+21	5	844 (73.4%)	6 (0.5%)
2010	2,395	2,356+23	16	1,764 (73.7%)	21 (0.9%)
2011	3,743	3,698+35	10	2,693 (71.9%)	11 (0.3%)
2012	5,606	5,559+42	5	4,321 (77.1%)	34 (0.6%)
2013	6,480	6,428+43	9	5,191 (80.1%)	39 (0.6%)
2014	7,627	7,563+38	26	5,982 (78.4%)	28 (0.4%)
2015	9,256	9,191+43	22	7,173 (77.5%)	76 (0.8%)
2016	9,191	9140+33	18	7,059 (76.8%)	66 (0.7%)

*Percentages given as percentage of warrants requested.

ACLU terms it "mission creep," but one can only wonder if it is also "bait and switch."[14] A *Washington Post* story published in October 2014 revealed that sneak and peak became not a weapon of counterterrorism, but "an everyday investigative tool."[15]

Table 14.1, based on U.S. government reports, tells the story.[16] First, note the tremendous—twenty-two-fold—increase in such warrants between 2007 and 2016. Second, look at how few requests for warrants have been denied, only 0.2 percent in 2016. Third, see the preponderant use of these warrants to prosecute drug offences (78.8 percent), rather than combating terrorism (0.6 percent).

Section 215 of the Patriot Act granting access to personal and business records is another modification of the FISA Act. This section allows FBI agents to apply for warrants "requiring the production of any tangible things (including books, records, papers, documents, and other items) for an investigation to protect against international terrorism or clandestine intelligence activities." The FISA Court is instructed by law to grant a warrant on the simple assertion by the government that the information sought is "relevant" to a terrorism investigation. Among the various documents that can be demanded are library records of books checked out. This maddened the American Library Association (ALA) and turned staid librarians into civil rights activists. But the authority to subpoena library records did not ultimately draw the greatest criticism of Section 215.

The government interpreted Section 215 as also allowing the collection of metadata on phone and computer communications, such as numbers called, when and where calls were made, and length of conversations. This began as early as 2001. The National Security Agency (NSA) was deeply involved in compiling communications metadata at home and abroad, where it also tapped into actual conversations. Edward Snowden made public many documents that testify to this mass phone surveillance at home and abroad. Overseas surveillance listened into calls of foreign leaders, including German chancellor Angela Merkel. Snowden turned the information over to selected reporters, most notably Glenn Greenwald of the *Guardian*, which first published the revelations on 5 June 2013. This set off a firestorm that damaged the image of the United States abroad.

In June 2013, the ACLU filed a lawsuit on the matter of domestic collection of metadata by the NSA. A court initially decided against the ACLU, but the organization appealed the decision to the United States Court of Appeals for the Second Circuit. In May 2015, the court reversed the decision and upheld the ACLU's case, ruling that Section 215 did *not* authorize the collection of metadata. A reauthorization of the Patriot Act, the USA Freedom Act of 2 June 2015, included revision of Section 215. Phone providers would keep the data, and the government could obtain information on specific individuals with the approval of a federal court.

National Security Letters (NSL) predated the Patriot Act by over two decades, but Section 505 of the act allowed for a much more aggressive use of them. A NSL is a federal subpoena issued to collect information for national security purposes. It does not require a judge's approval, so it can be issued directly by an official of the FBI. It bypasses the requirements of even FISA. In its original legal formulation, the official issuing a NSL had to be high up in the FBI administration, but Section 505 authorized the heads of the fifty-six local field offices to draft their own NSLs. By the time of the Patriot Act, NSLs could be used to get a variety of financial records and phone-communications information. With the greater ease and convenience for the FBI, the number of NSLs served multiplied. The total of NSL requests in 2000, thus pre–Patriot Act, was about 8,500. Then the tally of requests soared, peaking at 48,642 in 2015. It stood at 41,574 for 2017.[17] The NSL listed are more focused on terrorism; from 2003 to 2005, 26 percent of the NSLs concerned terrorism, while 73.6 percent dealt with other counterintelligence matters.[18]

The ease of obtaining a subpoena is only one of the civil rights issues raised by NSLs. Another is that they include a nondisclosure requirement, or, in common language, a "gag order." This means that the person served with the NSL cannot discuss it with anyone except those with a need to know because they would be involved in the process of turning over the information. The gag order is intended to protect the secrecy of the surveillance. But it also forbids a person served with a NSL to discuss it with his or her family members or with colleagues who do not have a need to know. Moreover, if the person served wants to challenge the order in court, he or she cannot even be present in the courtroom, because that would reveal his or her identity. This increases the difficulty of resisting the subpoena. More than one person has seen something Kafkaesque about dealing with a NSL.

The USA PATRIOT Improvement and Reauthorization Act of 2005 modified some provisions of the NSL; it allowed judicial review of NSLs that were challenged and made the gag order somewhat less oppressive. However, this obviously did not deter the employment of NSLs. Further modifications of the provisions for gag orders in 2016 seemed to allow NSLs to pass the constitutional test.[19]

Broadened legal categories of "material support" and "material witness" have proved to be particularly fraught with the dangers of abuse, as was the case for Sami Omar al-Hussayen, Abdullah al-Kidd, and Brandon Mayfield. The Patriot Act extended the definition of "material support" in Section 805, which altered two sections of the United States Code, Title 18, defining federal crimes and federal procedures. The earlier USC 18 Sections 2339A and 2339B criminalized as material support such aid as providing property, money, safe houses, and training. But Section 805 added "expert advice or assistance," which could be interpreted to include any kind of technical information perceived by prosecutors as useful to terrorists. Legal scholar Norman Abrams charges the redefinitions in Section 805 with being "innovative federal crimes" that "have been frequently charged in prosecutions since September 11, 2001, becoming key elements in the government's anti-terrorism efforts."[20] The penalties for material support are severe: a maximum of fifteen years in prison, or life in prison if the death of a person is involved.

The definition of the term *material witness* and the treatment accorded material witnesses is not explicitly addressed in the Patriot Act, but the war on terrorism has entailed a much-increased reliance upon material witness statutes. These allow the arrest and incarceration of individuals believed to have information important in the prosecution of someone else. A material witness need not be charged with having committed any criminal offense, but simply suspected of having information useful in prosecuting someone else charged with a criminal offense. Allowing material witnesses to be held in conjunction with questionable accusations, such as offering material support, greatly increases the potential of abuse.

The potential problems implicit in U.S. material witness statues as applied in criminal cases not involving terrorism drew fire long before 9/11.[21] But material witness arrests have been more widespread in the war on terrorism. In 2011, the ACLU accused the U.S. government of the "systematic misuse of the material witness statute" in terrorist-related prosecutions.[22] One critical article in the *North Carolina Law Review* states that under material witness statutes "the government can now hold people anonymously and indefinitely without filing criminal charges."[23]

In passing the Patriot Act in a hurried manner, Congress added sunset provisions requiring that the act be periodically reviewed and, if need be, modified. After consideration by Congress, a bill that reauthorized the Patriot Act with few revisions was signed by President Bush in March 2006. This bill altered the sunset date for Sections 206, roving wiretaps, and 215, access to records, to 2009 and allowed some additional oversight and some modification of the gag rule involving NSLs. Both roving wiretaps and record collection as to Section 215 were reauthorized in February 2010. The next year, Congress passed and President Obama signed both the FISA Sunsets Extension Act of 2011 and the PATRIOT Sunsets Extension Act of 2011. These again extended Sections 206 and 215, as well as the provisions for surveillance of individuals suspected of terrorist activities but not part of a terrorist group, such as "lone wolves." In June 2015 the USA FREEDOM Act, signed by Obama, reauthorized sections of the Patriot Act that had just expired. The new law imposed limits on the bulk collection of telecommunication metadata, thus the act's acronym for "Uniting and Strengthening America by Fulfilling Rights and Ending Eavesdropping, Dragnet-collection and Online Monitoring Act."

COUNTERTERRORISM BEYOND THE PATRIOT ACT

A detailed account of the meteoric expansion of the counterterrorism regime in the United States is beyond the limits of this chapter. It will have to suffice to note the broad outlines of that expansion after the passage of the Patriot Act.

The Homeland Security Act of 25 November 2002 set up the Department of Homeland Security, established the cabinet-level post of secretary of homeland security, and stipulated which agencies and individuals reported to the new department. It is now the third largest department in the U.S. government, with about 240,000 employees; it is surpassed only by the Department of Defense and the Department of Veterans Affairs. The twenty-two agencies grouped under the aegis of Homeland Security at the start ranged from U.S. Customs and Border Protection to the Secret Service to the Coast Guard.

On 27 December 2004, President Bush signed the Intelligence Reform and Terrorism Prevention Act of 2004 (IRTPA), which, among other things, established the office of Director of National Intelligence, the National Counterterrorism Center, the National Counter Proliferation Center, and the National Intelligence Center. IRTPA addresses issues of collecting and coordinating intelligence gathered by different agencies and departments: connecting the dots. It fashioned the Information Sharing Environment (ISE), which is defined as "the people, projects, systems, and agencies that enable responsible information sharing across the national security enterprise."[24] This was intended to foster a new "whole of government" approach to intelligence in place of separation and competition between rival agencies.

The flow of legislation continued into the decade. As already mentioned, laws reauthorizing the Patriot Act, and in some case modifying its provisions, were passed in 2005, 2006, 2010, 2011, and 2015. There was other basic legislation as well, including the Implementing Recommendations of the 9/11 Commission Act of 2007, which among other things mandated the inspection of all cargo coming into the United States by air or sea. That same year saw the adoption of the Protect America Act of 2007, a controversial act that amended the FISA Act of 1978 to allow warrantless surveillance of individuals "reasonably believed to be located outside of the United States," in order to gain foreign intelligence.[25] The ACLU condemned that law as the "Police America Act," but a FISA Foreign Intelligence Surveillance Court of Review held the provision for this warrantless surveillance to be legal in 2009. Beyond such specific acts, general financial appropriation laws have included changes and additions to existing counterterrorism standards and practices. Such has been the case with Homeland Security Appropriations Acts in 2007, 2008, and 2010. Counterterrorism and homeland security remain works in progress.

In 2010, the *Washington Post* described, with alarm, the growth of the counterterrorism regime in the United States. Its series "Top Secret America" declared: "The top-secret world the government created in response to the terrorist attacks of Sept. 11, 2001, has become so large, so unwieldy and so secretive that no one knows how much money it costs, how many people it employs, how many programs exist within it or exactly how many agencies do the same work."[26] The authors of the series, Dana Priest and William M. Arkin, calculated that "some 1,271 government organizations and 1,931 private companies work on programs related to counterterrorism, homeland security and intelligence in about 10,000 locations across the United States." The total number of people holding top-secret security clearances at that point, 854,000, is also shocking. At that point, the annual appropriation for the civilian National Intelligence Program amounted to $53.1 billion.[27] By June 2011 the total cost of counterterrorism efforts since 9/11 had reached $3.7 trillion.[28]

EXPANDING PRESIDENTIAL PREROGATIVES IN THE GLOBAL WAR ON TERROR

Our consideration of the threats to personal privacy, due process, and constitutional protections in the Patriot Act and other anti-terrorism laws and practices is *not* an argument for dismantling the counterterrorist regime. Rather, we need to understand that the war on terror poses a threat to some basic liberties, and that these sacrifices must not be allowed to exceed what is required by the real threat. And we must be wary of giving up what might in time be hard to regain.

Moreover, these changes have had the effect of shifting the balance of powers in our system of government, granting more leeway and authority to the executive branch. The sacrifices and shifts that have affected our lives at home have also been affected by the way the United States has conducted its war on terror beyond our borders.

War Powers

Since World War II, the authority of presidents to commit the United States to war has increased beyond the principle laid out in the Constitution; but this phenomenon predated the "war on terror" by fifty years. In Article 1, Section 8, Clause 11, the Constitution accords Congress the power to declare war; however, the United States has not formally declared war since World War II. In 1950, President Truman committed American troops to war in Korea without going to Congress. And Congress has accepted that presidents may initiate military actions they deem necessary. The most important piece of legislation on this question came as the United States withdrew its troops from Vietnam. The War Powers Act of 7 November 1973 requires that the president receive congressional approval within sixty days of having engaged U.S. armed forces in a conflict. In fact, even before the War Powers Act, Congress either quickly supported major presidential actions, as in Korea, or authorized them in advance, without a formal declaration of war, as in Vietnam in 1964. Also, mindful of the value of rallying the nation, presidents have sought advance approval for military action, even after the passage of the War Powers Act. Congress authorized the resort to military force in advance of the First Gulf War in 1991, the American intervention in Afghanistan in 2001, and the Second Gulf War in 2003. The most serious charge that a president overstepped the limits of the War Powers Act was levied against Barack Obama for U.S. military intervention in the Libyan civil war in 2011.

The Wars against Terrorism in Afghanistan and Iraq

As an immediate response to 9/11, the United States attacked the Taliban in Afghanistan. This action was in accord with Congress's Authorization for the Use of Military Force, passed on 14 September 2001. It declared:

"The President is authorized to use all necessary and appropriate force against those nations, organizations, or persons he determines planned, authorized, committed, or aided the terrorist attacks that occurred on September 11, 2001, or harbored such organizations or persons, in order to prevent any future acts of international terrorism against the United States by such nations, organizations or persons."[29] Initially, the United States intervened to support the Northern Alliance against the Taliban, but soon U.S. troops and those of our allies, most notably the British, took the lead in the fight. Considering that the Taliban granted al-Qaeda sanctuary in Afghanistan and refused to turn bin Laden and other al-Qaeda leaders over to the United States, war was virtually inevitable. The Taliban were defeated, but, as described in Chapter 13, they reestablished themselves and regained control over much of the country. As of August 2017, the war had cost U.S. taxpayers $1.07 trillion.[30] By February 2018, U.S. troops had suffered 2,400 killed and 20,300 wounded.[31] The number of Afghan civilians killed by August 2016 topped 31,000.[32] And, as noted in Chapter 13, a *New York Times* article published in February 2018 described the war as "unwinnable."[33]

Unlike the war in Afghanistan, the invasion of Iraq in 2003 was not inevitable; it was entirely a war of choice. The George W. Bush administration sold the war by presenting flawed, possibly manufactured, evidence. On 16 October 2002, Bush signed into law the Authorization for the Use of Military Force against Iraq Resolution that had been passed by Congress. Saddam Hussein was quickly toppled when the war began in March 2003, but long-term victory proved elusive as an insurgency and a sectarian civil war followed on the heels of U.S. "victory." The Surge of 2007 and 2008 gave some reason for hope, but it was more respite than rescue. The last U.S. combat troops withdrew from Iraq at the end of 2011, and soon policies of the Iraqi government led by Nuri al-Maliki revived the sectarian struggle and radical Islamist terrorism. U.S. Department of Defense figures list 4,500 U.S. fatalities from the onset of Operation Iraqi Freedom to the official withdrawal of U.S. forces, and another 32,250 wounded in action.[34] A Brown University study estimates that the total monetary cost of American wars since 9/11 will stand at $5.6 trillion by October 2018, when veterans' benefits over time are factored in.[35]

Frustration in Afghanistan and Iraq has revealed the United States to be less than invincible, even with our impressive conventional military. But beyond issues of victory and defeat and beyond the human and monetary costs of war, the conduct of these conflicts has added more weight and momentum to the troubling impetus toward greater executive power generated by the war on terror. Not only domestic legal protections but international law as well have been challenged and, at times, transgressed.

Unlawful Combatants, Military Commissions, and Torture
As a product of armed conflict in Afghanistan and Iraq, and captures made elsewhere in the war on terror, the United States found itself in charge of prisoners unlike those it had held in past wars. In January 2002, President Bush announced that the United States would not abide by the Geneva Conventions when dealing with these new captives. Bush and his advisors took it upon themselves to define the prisoners as "unlawful combatants" or "illegal combatants," a category that denied them the legal status of prisoners of war. Critics of the Bush administration argued that even those not accorded prisoner of war status were guaranteed humane treatment by the Geneva Conventions. Most specifically, Article 75 of the first additional protocol adopted in June 1977 forbade signatories to murder, torture, or commit "outrages upon personal dignity" of all persons in territory occupied by the signatory.[36]

The Bush administration also resurrected the institution of military commissions as the courts in which to try captured unlawful combatants, if they were to be accorded a trial at all. Military commissions had last been employed by the United States during World War II, but these commissions did not become part of the Uniform Code of Military Justice (1951). Investigative journalist Jane Mayer castigates the military commission as "a crude relic of the past."[37] However, resort to such commissions appealed to the president because they bypassed Congress and the Department of Justice. Instead, they were directly administered by the Department of Defense and its neoconservative secretary, Donald Rumsfeld.

Rendition and torture of prisoners have already been mentioned at the start of this chapter. What concerns us here is the view of torture espoused by the Bush administration in the era of the Patriot Act. Those immediately around Bush, particularly Vice President Dick Cheney, David Addington, who served as assistant to the president and chief legal counsel to the vice president, and John Yoo, deputy assistant attorney general in the Justice Department's Office of Legal Counsel, believed that the president could exercise greatly increased executive authority in time of war. This notion of nearly unfettered executive power has been referred to as the "New Paradigm."

In February 2002 Bush backtracked a bit. He held firm that the Geneva Conventions did not apply to the war on terror; however, "as a matter of policy the United States Armed Forces shall continue to treat detainees humanely."[38] This was cleverly worded to apply to the armed forces, but not to the CIA, which continued to employ torture. The administration also declared that torture was not torture. A memo of 1 August 2002, written principally by Yoo, stipulated that an act was torture only if it caused pain "equivalent in intensity to the pain accompanying serious physical injury, such as organ failure, impairment of bodily function, or even death" or psychological suffering that would "result in significant psychological harm" and "be of significant duration, e.g., lasting for months or years."[39] Mayer condemns the memo as having "redefined the crime of torture to make it all but impossible to commit."[40] Notoriously, this reduced waterboarding, long considered torture, to the more pleasant category of "enhanced interrogation techniques." More boldly, Yoo defended the memo in 2004, insisting that Congress cannot "tie the president's hands in regard to torture as an interrogation technique. . . . It's the core of the commander in chief function. They can't prevent the president from ordering torture."[41]

Republican Senator John McCain, himself a victim of torture when held by the North Vietnamese, strongly condemned the use of waterboarding by the CIA as "a mock execution and an exquisite form of torture. Its use was shameful and unnecessary."[42] He argued that torture essentially does not work because "it produced little useful intelligence." He went on to insist: "But, in the end, torture's failure to serve its intended purpose isn't the main reason to oppose its use. I have often said, and will always maintain, that this question isn't about our enemies; it's about us. It's about who we were, who we are and who we aspire to be. It's about how we represent ourselves to the world." For McCain, torture in the name of increased security not only does not work, it corrupts us. It also pulls us down from the moral high ground, weakening our ability to influence international standards for the better.

Two days after his inauguration in 2009, President Obama issued Executive Order 13491 banning the torture of detainees by the CIA and mandating the closing of its detention camps "as expeditiously as possible."[43] In his campaign rhetoric of 2016, Donald Trump advocated a return to torture: "Would I approve waterboarding? You bet your ass I would—in a heartbeat. And I would approve more than that. Don't kid yourself, folks. It works, okay? It works. Only a stupid person would say it doesn't work."[44] Once in the White House, his new secretary of defense, James Mattis, disabused the new president of his faith in torture, and Trump deferred to Mattis.

Drone Strikes

U.S. reliance on unpiloted Unarmed Aerial Vehicles (UAVs), more commonly referred to as drones, has attracted global attention and criticism. Obama is so associated with the use of drones for surveillance and targeted killings that some have called his years in office the "Drone Presidency." The use of drones to attack chosen targets, rather than simply engage in surveillance, has multiplied exponentially. Bush authorized only fifty drone strikes that killed 296 terrorists and 195 civilians, but Obama authorized 506 strikes that killed over 3,000 terrorists and about 400 civilians.[45] Trump has expanded the use of drones since taking office by stripping away Obama-era restrictions on using them in noncombat theaters. But, uncharacteristically, Trump has not trumpeted this change of policy.[46]

Drones have become the go-to weapon for targeted killings, a euphemism for assassinations. In general, U.S. public opinion supports the use of drone strikes against suspected foreign terrorists in foreign countries. A 2013 Gallup poll showed 65 percent of Americans approved of such strikes; however, only 41 percent approved of attacks on U.S. citizens abroad, and only 25 percent supported the idea of attacks on U.S. citizens suspected of terrorism and living in the United States.[47]

However, as measured in 2014 by the Pew Research Center, world opinion sharply condemns U.S. drone strikes.[48] Disapproval ratings are high even among U.S. allies in Europe and Asia: France (72 percent), Germany (67 percent), the United Kingdom (59 percent), South Korea (75 percent), and Japan (82 percent). Muslim countries, in which populations may see drone strikes as directed specifically against Islam, have understandably high disapproval ratings: Jordan (90 percent), Egypt (87 percent), and Turkey (83 percent). Predictably, drone strikes can make for compelling propaganda for radical Islamists. Such attacks are reviled as causing the deaths of innocent Muslims and as being a tactic of cowards, since the operators take no personal risk while raining death on others. They are seen as further justification for the narrative that the West is at war with Islam.

Some critics in the United States charge that the president has taken unto himself the right to order the deaths of whomever he chooses: the power of life or death in the hands of an increasingly powerful and capricious executive. On 8 March 2016, reporter Glenn Greenwald, best known for his association with Edward Snowden, wrote a scathing criticism of Obama's decision to attack what the president identified as al-Shabab terrorists in Somalia, an attack that killed 150. Greenwald doubts that U.S. decisionmakers really knew who the victims were. He insists that drone strikes should be seen as bizarre international behavior: "But for Americans, this is now all perfectly normalized. We just view our president as vested with the intrinsic, divine right, grounded in American exceptionalism, to deem whomever he wants 'Bad Guys' and then—with no trial, no process, no accountability—order them killed."[49]

On the other side of the issue, David Cole defended Obama in 2016, insisting that the president had adopted policies and procedures that limited the use of drones for deadly attacks.[50] He targeted only those fighting as our enemies in war zones, in operations authorized by Congress against al-Qaeda and its allies. Those attacked posed an imminent danger and could not be arrested by local authorities. Moreover, according to Cole, Obama's decisions were not capricious; he employed an elaborate process of identification and review. But we now know that Trump has stripped away some of Obama's restrictions, so that criticisms that were perhaps overstated when directed against Obama would seem to be justified against Trump.

AMERICAN MILITARISM?

It is understandable that, faced with the emergency of war, peoples tend to set aside some of their legal rights and protections in the name of bolstering their safety. Certainly, Americans have done this in the past. When wars are of short duration and a people's sense of its rights in civil society strong, what is temporarily sacrificed need not be permanently lost. However, if wars are long, and people come to regard infringements on their liberties as the new normal, then there is danger. And we face that danger now.

It is often pointed out that the United States has been constantly at war since the fall of 2001. Yet, it can be argued that this unbroken era of warfare really has lasted a decade longer, if we count the First Iraq War and the use of combat air patrols to enforce no-fly zones in Iraq from 1991 to 2003, as well as U.S. military operations in Somalia, Bosnia-Herzegovina, Kosovo, and Yugoslavia. Andrew Bacevich would even go further, speaking of "America's war for the greater Middle East," 1980 to the present.

For a long time, the United States could resist the demands of military necessity that drove European nations to construct huge conscript military establishments. After all, the United States could count on two oceans to guarantee its security east and west, and our neighbors north and south posed no real threat. In 1939 the U.S. Army, with only about 190,000 full-time troops, ranked seventeenth in the world in size, smaller even than Portugal's forces. The United States demobilized immediately after World War II, but with the onset of the Cold War, it had to approach a war footing even in peacetime, and this remained true until the dissolution of the Soviet Union in 1991.

To maintain this hard edge, the United States had to mobilize its population and its economy. No less an authority than Dwight David Eisenhower, American commander in the European theater of World War II and president of the United States from 1953 to 1961, warned his fellow citizens of the challenges posed by what he termed the "military-industrial complex." His farewell address as president on 17 January 1961 is so important to an understanding of the potential conflict between security and liberty that it deserves to be quoted at length:

> Until the latest of our world conflicts, the United States had no armaments industry. American makers of plowshares could, with time and as required, make swords as well. But now we can no longer risk emergency improvisation of national defense; we have been compelled to create a permanent armaments industry of vast proportions. Added to this, three and a half million men and women are directly engaged in the

defense establishment. We annually spend on military security more than the net income of all United States corporations. . . .

In the councils of government, we must guard against the acquisition of unwarranted influence, whether sought or unsought, by the military-industrial complex. The potential for the disastrous rise of misplaced power exists and will persist.

We must never let the weight of this combination endanger our liberties or democratic processes.[51]

Eisenhower spoke as a Cold War–era leader, before terrorism rose to be considered as a primary threat to global security, but he sounded an alarm that we must heed today.

We can frame Eisenhower's prescient remarks in terms of a valid concern with the militarization of the United States and the threat posed by militarism within our cultural and political lives. "Militarization" and "militarism" lend themselves to several meanings; they refer more to tendencies than to categories.[52] For our purposes, militarization refers to the character of institutions, practices, and policies. So, in response to the threats and pressures of the Cold War, the American economy became significantly militarized. Eisenhower witnessed this and worried about its impact. We must also worry about militarism. For our purposes, "militarism" is not a matter of structures and actions, but a cultural shift in values that overemphasizes or exaggerates security, the military, and military values. Militarization and militarism overlap when the latter comes to drive the former.

In his thought-provoking article "The Danger of Militarization in an Endless 'War' on Terrorism," the historian of warfare and civil-military relations Richard Kohn points out that the United States has been militarized since World War II, but he fears that an endless war on terror, with its heightened sense of insecurity among the American citizenry, will engender militarism: "The larger question is whether the war on terrorism will blur militarization into militarism, in which American institutions, practices, values, thinking, and behaviors assume the ideals and ethos of the military in response to the challenge—whether the very character of the American people changes, with the emphasis on freedom and individualism displaced by obedience, discipline, hierarchy, collectivism, authoritarianism, pessimism, and cynicism."[53]

Fear plays a key role here, inspiring the sacrifice of liberty in the name of security. The outspoken Dennis Kucinich, a member of the House of Representatives from 1997 to 2013, put it caustically: "We've come to love our fears more than our freedoms."[54]

In the preceding chapters we have seen how radical terrorists engage in psychological warfare to affect a target audience through fear and outrage. I have argued that the most effective way for that audience to keep the terrorists from achieving their goals is by understanding the terrorists' strategies and stratagems. In coping with terrorism, knowledge is power.

However, in this chapter we have taken a different tack by focusing on the need to ask whether we as a people and a government are responding in ways appropriate to the threat while remaining mindful of our own rights, liberties, and protections. In attempting to maximize our ability to identify terrorists among us and to forestall their attacks, we may endanger our own privacy and weaken guarantees that guard us against unwarranted search and seizure. In addition, given the ease of mounting a terrorist attack, whether perpetrated by a small clandestine cell or an "inspired" individual, absolute security is an illusion. How much are we willing to pay for what we probably cannot achieve?

But Chapter 14 implies something beyond this. The dangers of terrorism are real, but so too are the potential dangers posed by ill-considered counterterrorism. It is possible for those within our own political and security establishments to use the fear of terrorism as leverage to increase their own power. Autocrats can raise the banner of counterterrorism to justify their autocracy and repression; they can play the terrorism card. We could look to Egypt, Uzbekistan, and China as regimes justifying authoritarian means in the name of counterterrorism. But democracy can also be subverted in the name of counterterrorism. In Chapter 8 we noted the authoritarian turn of the democratic government in Uruguay in its struggle against the Tupamaros and the military coup there in 1973. In this chapter we have seen how the powers of the executive and law enforcement have increased in the United States since 9/11. Presidents Bush and Obama both assumed powers in the name of combating terrorism. Donald Trump, as both candidate and president, has spoken of radical Islamist terrorism within the United States in terms that exaggerate its actual violence and threat to American society. There is a saying in American politics, "Eternal vigilance is the price of liberty." While this is incorrectly attributed to Thomas Jefferson, it is nonetheless true, especially when countering terrorism. But our vigilance must be in two directions, toward terrorism and toward the means proposed to fight it.

CHAPTER FIFTEEN

Confronting Terrorism

FIGURE 15.1. The specter of terrorism. jpa1999/iStock.

WE ARE CONFRONTED by the specter of terrorism (Fig. 15.1); that specter is likely to menace and maim throughout the foreseeable future. Radical terrorism looms as a threat to us. It beckons those who are strong in commitment and, while weak in numbers, utterly convinced that violence alone will serve their purposes. It is their vision of warfare, empowering their extremism with the prospect of victory. Terrorists lurk in the shadows, yet emerge to commit acts that command a public spotlight. Theirs is ultimately psychological warfare, potentially allowing them to exert an influence far beyond their physical power. They hope to inflict fear and incite outrage, provoking ill-considered reprisals that ultimately advance the terrorists' cause and increase their strength. Terrorists succeed by transforming their intended victims into unwitting allies. However, if we refuse to be so subverted, we can reduce the specter to futility.

This volume is intended as an introduction to the history of terrorism—an early step in a process. The information and analysis presented in each of the preceding fourteen chapters are offered in the belief that the best way we as citizens can defend against terrorism is by understanding it through learning the record of the past. Only a few of us will be engaged in a face-to-face fight with terrorists, but we all constitute the terrorists' primary target audience.

This chapter surveys what we have said in the fourteen previous chapters and extends it by urging us to approach this threat with intelligence and wisdom. Learn to assess the threat; put that threat in perspective and proportion; and understand what the terrorists want us to do. Defeat them by *not* playing the part that they have scripted for us in their performance of violent political theater.

SURVEYING WHAT WE HAVE LEARNED

We begin by surveying some of the major points made in the book. This is all the more necessary because they will serve as the basis for our counsels on how to confront radical terrorism. As we consider our conclusions, bear in mind that the devil is in the details—in this case the historical details—so it is not enough to reach conclusions; we must know how we arrived at them.

Levels, Waves, and Strategies

We can usefully apply the term *terrorism* to violence along a considerable spectrum. In Chapter 1 we introduced the idea of six levels of terrorism: state, military, social, criminal, radical by groups, and radical by individuals. We will elaborate on these levels a bit more in this conclusion, but we still accept our original list of six. A critical gradient in this differentiation is capacity, from strong to weak; the terrorism at the weak end, radical terrorism, is that which most concerns the news cycle today. Confusing the levels of terrorism leads to misconceptions and miscalculations.

It is accurate and fair to argue that terrorism is as old as civilization itself when focusing on state, military, and social terrorism. However, we have argued here that radical terrorism is essentially modern, coming only after the failure of the Revolutions of 1848. Some terrorist experts would refute this approach; that is understood. Some point to single events or particular groups that one could describe as "terrorist." However, I have insisted that an isolated act does not in itself constitute radical terrorism, which is part of an established and widely shared repertoire of violent political resistance. It is an "ism" with its own recognized practices, doctrine, and literature. As such, radical terrorism did not materialize until the second half of the nineteenth century. Fixing the origins of radical terrorism as sometime after the Revolutions of 1848, we have organized our historical examination of this level of terrorism into three waves, post-1848 to 1920, 1945 to about 1980, and 1980 to the present. Again, these are not hermetically sealed compartments and should be treated flexibly. You need not accept my dating of those waves to recognize that radical terrorism has changed over time, that it has known its own periods.

And our examination has identified four strategies of terrorism: intimidation, initiation, attrition, and evolution. Again, these should not be seen as absolute, but as broad and sometimes blurred analytical categories. So, if readers would rather interpret my four strategies as four "strategic tendencies" or other softer terms, that is fine. In any case, while intimidation is definably the strategy of strong-capacity terrorists, it is a significant factor at all levels of terrorism. But when focusing on radical terrorism, we must also consider the relative roles of initiation, attrition, and evolution.

So, there is our basic framework of levels, waves, and strategies. Consider these not as rules but as analytical categories, aids in posing the right questions and interpreting the answers. And there are exceptions. We have examined U.S. radical right-wing violence and narco-terrorism as forms of terrorism that have their distinct characteristics. Some scholars want to treat every manifestation of terrorism as utterly unique. However, I side with Audrey Kurth Cronin, who condemns as a myth the belief that "terrorism is situation-dependent and can only be understood in the narrow and specific context of a particular group or cause."[1]

We can see commonalities within our matrix of levels, waves, and strategies. For example, we can observe a common fate for weak radical terrorist groups during the second wave that pursued strategies of initiation: they failed in attaining their goals for similar reasons, as explained in Chapter 8. At the other extreme, some sub-state terrorist groups of the second and third waves have recognized that their success required a strategy of evolution; the IS provides the most pressing, but not the only, example of this.

Radical Terrorism Is Entry-Level Warfare
Radical terrorism is by nature weak relative to the adversaries it seeks to overthrow. Yet as violence intended to bring political results, it can be considered as a form of warfare by Clausewitzian standards. A campaign of terrorist violence requires only meager resources. Once a group of radicalized individuals are convinced that violence is the only effective means open to them, they can immediately take up arms. Radical terrorism becomes entry-level warfare. If their strategy is initiation, the terrorist group can dream of great impact without great numbers. Attrition historically requires greater resources, but these can be gradually accrued by a small group. Evolution, of course, is by definition a process of growth from small group to conventional forces and state organization—it assumes conflict begins small but can advance to a higher level.

Because carrying out a terrorist attack requires so little manpower and so few resources, terrorism as a form of warfare is unlikely to disappear. No matter how weak the group, the hope remains powerful. And since terrorism is a form of political violence that can serve different masters, from the Red Brigades, to the Silent Brotherhood, to al-Qaeda, the passing of one "cause" does not imply an end to terrorism. This is all the more reason to try to understand it as a general phenomenon.

Terrorism Is Psychological Warfare
Terrorism, strong or weak, employs physical violence, or the threat of it, to achieve a psychological impact. Actually, it is really about the threat; the physical violence is simply a way for terrorists to convince you that the danger they pose is omnipresent. Radical terrorists kill a few to spread moral shock and a sense of vulnerability among the many. We have been saying this from the opening pages of this book. It is the promise of great impact through relatively small acts of violence against soft targets unable or unprepared to defend themselves that makes terrorism attractive

to extremists. To quote Raymond Aron once more: "An action of violence is labeled 'terrorist' when its psychological effects are out of proportion to its purely physical result."

As psychological war, terrorism is a chain from a *physical act*, or the threat of such an act, to a *psychological impact* that brings about a *political effect* desired by the terrorists. It is to be hoped that our intelligence services, law enforcement, and military can hunt down terrorists and forestall the violence they intend to perpetrate abroad and at home. However, our challenge as citizens is to rob the terrorists of their victory by denying them the psychological impact they require. This should not be accomplished by becoming callous to the suffering of those attacked but by seeking to understand the motives and the intentions of the attackers. In psychological warfare, knowledge and judgment become powerful defenses.

Terrorists Are Rational Actors
As a rule, terrorists are not crazy, not demented psychopaths. Yes, there are some sociopaths among them, like the Shankill Butchers in Northern Ireland. However, the most important commentators on radical terrorism concur that terrorists are "normal," no more likely to be aberrant than are members of the general population. However, they do inhabit a different moral universe. They judge by different moral standards, usually convinced that they can achieve goals they regard as righteous *only* through violence. Even secular terrorists demonstrate religiouslike mindsets that embrace totalist dichotomies between good and evil and espouse apocalyptic obsessions that demand destruction as a prerequisite for creating a better world. Chapters 5, 8, and 9 are particularly strong in making this case.

To say that radical terrorists inhabit another moral universe is to describe not simply their state of mind, but their closed and exclusive communities. Dedicated terrorists characteristically populate a world of likeminded extremists who share the same values and visions. Living in such a community can be one of the keys to radicalization. Opinions stated by terrorists to their comrades tend to be repeated back to them. I have called this a terrorist echo chamber. Repetition reinforces conviction.

Radical Terrorists Make Moral Calculations
Should radical terrorists choose to commit ostentatious atrocities to generate fear and/or outrage among the target community, the choice of victims and violence involves a kind of moral calculation. The terrorist act should be shocking to those targeted but not be so extreme as to alienate the population to which the terrorists look for support. Perhaps it is reasonable to expect that the more radical the narrative and the more it is accepted by the support community, the more that community will tolerate ostentatious atrocities. Still, there are limits to what may be regarded as justified. Recall how bin Laden and al-Zawahiri protested against al-Zarqawi's practices of publicizing gruesome executions and attacking Shia Muslims. It is also important to note that the Tupamaros lost support when they increased the level of their violence, and the Weathermen consciously decided to forgo attacks on people altogether, because they feared that it would undermine their cause. They chose to target property in ways that would seize the public attention but minimize the chances that people would be injured. One way to undermine terrorists' support may be to explain and condemn acts of the terrorists that would horrify and alienate precisely the population being courted by the terrorists. Of course, the IS seems to have gained by advertising its barbarity, but it has publicized its savagery as a way to attract precisely the small number of recruits that share the values of the IS, and to screen out those with less dedication and a weaker stomach for ultraviolence.

Terrorists Learn and Emulate
Terrorists study the means and methods of other terrorists, even those whose goals are radically different from their own. So, for example, the terrorist campaigns of the FLN and of the Tupamaros were praised and studied by the likes of the Red Brigades and the Weathermen, as pointed out in Chapter 8. Radical Islamist theorists of war and terrorism have looked to the secular military classics of conventional warfare and major works of revolutionary warfare, as demonstrated in Chapter 11. Terrorists have produced manifestos on terrorist rationales and practices since 1849, documents noted or quoted in nearly every chapter.

Do not underestimate the intelligence or knowledge of radical terrorists. Their form of warfare has developed doctrines of its own. Among these doctrines are self-conscious Maolike theories of evolving from one form or stage of warfare to another higher form or stage.

Radical Terrorists Are by Definition Criminals
According to our list of traits, terrorist violence is committed for political reasons, including social, economic, and religious rationales. Violence committed only for personal and material gain is simply criminal and not terrorist. In the case of narcoterrorism, this obviously leads to complexities and confusions, discussed in Chapter 13. But as pointed out in that chapter, all radical terrorism can also be considered criminal in that it involves practices, organizations, and, sometimes, ideologies that are declared illegal. Also, radical terrorists turn to thievery and kidnapping, or worse, as ways to raise funds for their political endeavors.

However, to define terrorists as criminals broaches a subject debated within the counterterrorist community. Should terrorists be treated simply as criminals, prosecuted specifically for their criminal acts, or as political or military agents—"unlawful combatants," as President George W. Bush termed them? Concentrating on the act may lead authorities to be reactive, when a more proactive way to stop terrorists may be to prosecute them for their political affiliations. But the latter approach may endanger rights and protections of the law, as discussed in Chapter 14.

IN PRAISE OF CALCULATION
Throughout this volume I have insisted on defining the psychological impact of radical terrorism in terms of both fear and outrage. Fear can be characterized as more passive, the apprehension and anxiety that the kind of misfortune and mistreatment that has afflicted others can afflict *you*. So, fear motivates people to monitor and alter their behavior so as to avoid the fate that has befallen others. Fear is not simply generated by perceptions of a dangerous reality; it is stoked by the imagination that magnifies and multiplies the actual threat. Fear promotes compliance and discourages resistance. It imposes silence, rather than exciting outcry. It is the mainspring of intimidation. Thus, strong-capacity terrorism relies on fear above all.

Outrage clamors for striking out against abuse; it drives reprisal and revenge. It is active, not passive. In retaliating, the outraged target audience replaces the powerlessness of the victim with the power of the avenger. Reprisal is perceived as righteous retribution for injury or punitive pay back for insult. However, outrage provides the terrorist with a second kind of leverage, besides fear, to induce the target audience to do what benefits the terrorists. So the massacre of European colons at Philippeville by the FLN fomented such outrage among the French that they went on a rampage, convincing the Muslim population to support the terrorists. So the PIRA goaded the British troops into a deadly overreaction on Bloody Sunday that won the PIRA a great flood of recruits. Both are described in Chapter 6. Terrorists commit outrages with the aim of inciting their enemies to reveal themselves as being as malicious as the terrorist narrative claims they are.

As much as possible, we must avoid feeding the narrative by our deeds or our words. We have borrowed Daniel Fromkin's language to describe the stratagem of provocation: "Its ingenuity lay in using an opponent's own strength against him. It was a sort of jujitsu."[2] And the art of terrorist jujitsu is not just about violent actions; words matter as well because psychological warfare is a matter of perception *and* imagining. Ill-considered declarations emanating from the target community can aid terrorists to make their case. So, for example, when Western political leaders broadly condemn Islam and Muslims or when public demonstrations defile Muhammad and the Quran, radical Islamists can point to this as further proof that there truly is a Western war against Islam.

The popular sense that we have overcome and bested the terrorists if we simply refuse to be paralyzed by fear contains the serious danger of playing into the terrorists' hands. If we are so determined to demonstrate we are not afraid that we strike out before considering carefully what we are doing, we may fulfill the designs of the terrorists. I am not arguing that we do not need to act forcefully against terrorism and terrorists, but we need to do so out of cold calculation, not heated emotion. There is an old saying, of uncertain origin but of certain value: "Revenge is a dish best served cold."

We have already stressed that radical terrorism is psychological warfare. Terrorists seek to inflict fear and incite outrage. Fear and outrage are emotions, so, in an important sense, terrorism weaponizes emotions. It is worth noting that Aristotle wrote in his *Rhetoric*: "The emotions are all those feelings that so change men as to affect their judgments."[3] Terrorism attempts to affect our judgment, to manipulate us through our emotions. Resist that.

Terrorists are not the only ones who may hope to exploit our fear and outrage. Those among us, even our leaders, may want to use our alarm to their advantage, to "play the terrorism card" to increase their power. Such provocateurs may have every reason to exaggerate the real threat in order to manipulate the population.

ASSESSING THE THREAT: THE ACTORS AND CAPABILITIES
Incorrectly assessing the real danger posed by terrorism can lead to responses that are out of proportion to the threat. Certainly, failure to recognize when we face a great danger can leave us vulnerable, as we were on 9/11. But outsized responses to lesser threats can strengthen the terrorists through terrorist jujitsu, on the one hand, and lead to unwarranted sacrifices of our rights and protections as citizens, on the other. It is critical to maintain senses of proportion and perspective. The study of history and a rational analysis of the present can both help.

Different terrorist actors pose different degrees of threats to different target audiences. We have discussed forms of terrorism by states and militaries at war that have strong capacities to commit violent acts because they command considerable resources. And we have contrasted this with the means and methods employed by radical terrorists who have inherently weak capacity in relation to the adversaries they attack.

In order to make my point better here, I need to make a more nuanced differentiation between the actors in radical terrorism. We have learned enough in the preceding chapters to introduce this now without overcomplicating the discussion. This more nuanced formulation of radical terrorism includes the following actors:

- central terrorist organizations: comparatively large and better resourced groups, such al-Qaeda Central
- terrorist networks: interlocking networks of cells and/or individuals, such as the IS networks in France and Belgium involved in the attacks in Paris and Brussels in 2015 and 2016
- terrorist cells: handfuls of terrorists working together, such as the Leeds-based cell that perpetrated the London bombing on 7 July 2005
- terrorist individuals: individuals inspired by a radical group but acting on their own initiative, as did Omar Mateen, who shot and killed forty-nine at an Orlando nightclub on 12 June 2016

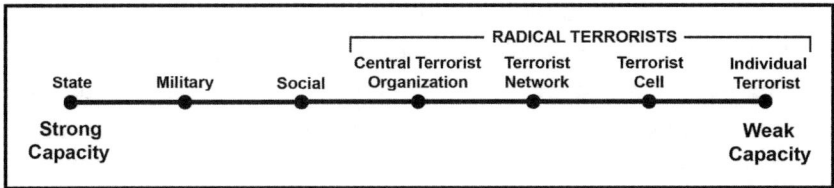

FIGURE 15.2. Scale of Terrorist Actors. This graphic stresses the need to maintain a sense of proportion that recognizes the contrasts between the threats posed by different levels of terrorism. A sense of alarm that may be appropriate concerning strong-capacity groups is hardly ever justified in dealing with small terrorist cells.

These are put on a continuum with other levels of terrorism—state, military, and social—in Figure 15.2.

As an example of how placing terrorist actors and threats along this continuum can aid in maintaining a sense of proportion, consider the remarks made by President Donald Trump at MacDill Air Force Base on 6 February 2017. The president stressed the immediate danger posed by the Islamic State to America: "We're up against an enemy that celebrates death and totally worships destruction. . . . ISIS is on a campaign of genocide, committing atrocities across the world. Radical Islamic terrorists are determined to strike our homeland, as they did on 9/11, as they did from Boston to Orlando to San Bernardino and across Europe. You've seen what happened in Paris and Nice. All over Europe it's happening. It's gotten to a point where it's not even being reported. And in many cases, the very, very dishonest press doesn't want to report it."[4] The IS he justifiably condemned had demonstrated a very strong capacity to commit terrorist acts in Syria and Iraq. As a state, IS enforced its control through brutal punishments and public executions. As an army, the IS was guilty of mass killings of prisoners of war and of civilians. It employed its military forces to carry out social terrorism, as in the genocide against the Yazidis. But such actions on a large scale are only possible where the IS or its *wilayahs* have considerable power. This is certainly not the case in the United States. Islamic terrorists may dream of striking the United States "as they did on 9/11," but that was a one-of-a kind cataclysm. It was perpetrated by al-Qaeda Central, but radical Islamists have not been able to replicate its deadly result anywhere else in the world. To compare genocide or 9/11 with Boston, San Bernardino, or Orlando is a mismatch. It may simply be a product of Trump's penchant for rhetorical fireworks, but whatever its source, such language runs the risk of inciting panic, particularly when the president announces that terrorist attacks are so numerous that the news media does not even report them.

Even to compare what is going on "all across Europe" with the American condition warps reality. The most notable attacks in Europe have been the work of networks or cells. Yes, radicalized lone wolves have also committed terrorist attacks in Europe, but networks have been much more important. These networks are explained by the existence of large alienated support communities of immigrants, the participation of many extremists from these communities in the IS, and the relative ease of access to and from Syria. It is important to note that by mid-2016, about 4,100 individuals from Western Europe had gone to fight in Iraq and Syria, while only 250 Americans had even tried to do so, and many did not make it.[5] The fact is that al-Qaeda and IS attacks on American soil since 9/11 have been the work of lone wolves or pairs of coconspirators, not of large and well-resourced networks or even cells: Nidal Hasan at Fort Hood in November 2009, the Tsarnaev bothers in Boston in April 2013, Syed Farook and Tashfeen Malik at San Bernardino in December 2013, Omar Mateen at Orlando in June 2016, and Sayfullo Saipov in New York on 31 October 2017.

On 6 December 2016, two months to the day before Trump's address at MacDill Air Force Base, President Obama offered a more careful and accurate assessment at the same venue. He pointed out that the Islamist terrorist attacks in the United States at Fort Hood, Boston, San Bernardino, and Orlando were the work of "homegrown and largely isolated individuals who were radicalized online."[6] He switched the emphasis from Trump's specter of mass "genocide" by the IS to the opposite end of the scale of terrorist capacity. The lone wolves "can kill innocent people, but *they don't pose an existential threat* to our nation, and we must not make the mistake of elevating them as if they do." Moreover, he made it clear why declaring them a great threat is counterproductive. "That does their job for them. It makes them more important and helps them with recruitment."

Identifying the actors goes a long way to judging the scale of the threat. Al-Qaeda Central could muster the considerable resources necessary to exploit airliners as cruise missiles on 9/11. Hassan, Farook and Malik, and Mateen carried out their attacks with readily available semi-automatic pistols and rifles. The Tsarnaev brothers had a single pistol, pipe bombs, and crude pressure-cooker bombs easily made following instructions found on the web. Saipov drove down his victims in a rented pickup truck. Certainly, we need to be alert to the dangers of lone wolves. They are hard to locate and neutralize, but they do not "pose an existential threat." Concern should not morph into hysteria that demands unwarranted investments or great constitutional sacrifices.

ASSESSING THE THREAT: LONGEVITY AND FAILURE AMONG TERRORIST GROUPS

Researchers concerned with how terrorism ends offer us some findings on the survival and success or failure of sub-state terrorist groups. Basing her findings on the data set collected by the Memorial Institute for the Prevention of Terrorism (MIPT), Audrey Kurth Cronin concludes that the average life expectancy of a terrorist group is eight years, and about one third of the MIPT sample survived five years or less.[7] David Rapoport estimates an even briefer life span, arguing that 90 percent of terrorist groups operating in the late twentieth century survived less than a year. And of the surviving 10 percent, less than half lasted longer than a decade.[8] A RAND corporation study revealed that of their sample of 268 terrorist groups, 47 percent were eliminated by police and military force and 43 percent entered the political process—in other words, ceased being terrorists and, instead, normalized. Only 10 percent achieved victory in their terms.[9]

There is need for some caution in using past records of terrorist groups as rules for the present. The RAND survey concludes, "The most salient fact about religious terrorist groups is how hard they are to eliminate."[10] While 62 percent of the RAND sample of all terrorist groups had ended, only 32 percent of religious terrorist groups had, meaning 68 percent had not. Since the current third wave is characterized by radical Islamist terrorism, the tenacity of religious terrorist groups is extremely troubling. This does not change the fact that since 9/11 the United States, within its own borders, has only faced terrorism by small cells or individuals, but it does suggest that the threat will continue because the groups that inspire lone wolves are not likely to disappear, although the Islamic State certainly has been defeated as a territorial power in Iraq and Syria.

Small-scale terrorist attacks similar to those of the past decade may remain a threat, but their effect can be blunted by maintaining a sense of proportion and putting things in perspective.

A SENSE OF PROPORTION THROUGH STATISTICS

Statistics on the deadly consequences of terrorism within the borders of the United States provide one way to put the threat in perspective. To be sure, statistical comparison can seem hard and heartless when we are talking about human tragedy. But the appeal to statistics here is a way of putting the threat in proportion while not dismissing the seriousness of the danger.

Let us begin by remembering that on 9/11, nearly 3,000 victims died. This is a horrifying tally, but it is also absolutely unique. No other single attack by radical terrorists at any place or any time had exacted such a huge toll before, and none has since. To frame 9/11 as the characteristic or typical radical terrorist attack of the twenty-first century distorts the reality of the threat we face at present. In fact, from the day following that disaster through July 2018, radical Islamists killed 104 people in the United States. During the same period, far right-wing violence caused the deaths of seventy-three victims.[11] The dead should be remembered and mourned, and their families, friends, and communities deserve our support and our empathy. But grief should not be the basis for our calculations.

Let us also note something from the following statistics. First, until the terrorist attack on an Orlando nightclub on 12 June 2016, more people had died from radical right-wing violence in the United States than from jihadis. In addition, of the seventeen radical Islamists who committed fatal attacks in the United States since 9/11, ten were American-born, two were naturalized U.S. citizens, and the other five held green cards as permanent residents. These last were born in Egypt, Russia, and Pakistan, and Uzbekistan; they were not immigrant refugees from IS-ravaged areas.

In relation to all violent deaths in the United States, those caused by terrorism after 9/11 are a very, very small percentage. During 2015 alone, 33,092 people died in vehicle accidents on American roads.[12] It can be said that such a comparison is a complete mismatch, but it is an astounding tally of violent death, and yet it has not resulted in major political action. And we still crowd the roads with our cars. Gun deaths might be considered a better comparison. The Brady Campaign reports an annual average of 33,880 *gun homicides* during the period 2011–2015.[13] This figure is surprisingly close to the number for traffic fatalities. Of these deaths, the annual average for *gun murders* is 11,564 per year. In Chicago, 447 victims were killed by gun violence in 2015, 720 in 2016, and 635 in 2017.[14]. These figures on gun deaths have not really changed our interpretations of the Second Amendment. For something even more comparable to those killed by radical Islamists, consider the statistics on gang homicides. The figure for 2012, the most recent year reported online by the National Gang Center, stood at 2,363.[15] During 2012 six victims were killed by right-wing terrorists in the United States, while none died at the hands of radical Islamists on American soil.[16]

If we measure the danger posed by radical Islamist terrorism within the United States by the casualties it has inflicted, that danger seems real, but not great, and hardly "existential." In fact, we face a much higher risk of being killed by lightning than of being killed by a radical Islamist terrorist in the Unites States. The number of people killed in the United States by lightning strikes from 2002 to 2017 stands at 531 according to the National Oceanic and Atmospheric Administration—over five times the death toll inflicted by radical Islamist terrorism within American borders during those years.[17]

But is not the cost of terrorism worldwide clearly skyrocketing? Not really. There has been a great deal of flux, but no clear crescendo. In 2007, 22,720 died from terrorist attacks around the globe; this declined steadily until 2012, when only 11,098 were killed, but climbed again to its highest point, 32,727 in 2014, owing in large part to increased casualties in Iraq and Nigeria.[18] In 2015, the number of those killed decreased to 28,328. Not surprisingly, the great majority, 70 percent, of those killed by terrorism in 2015 fell in four countries: Iraq (6,932), Afghanistan (5,292), Nigeria (4,886), and Syria (2,748).[19] The danger is greatest in the homelands of major terrorist organizations.

The annual toll from terrorism in Western Europe has declined. Between 1970 and 1994, the average annual number of fatalities caused by terrorism was roughly a bit over 200, with four years having death totals over 400. From 2002 to 2016, the annual number of fatalities averaged about 50, a number that includes three years with death tolls between 140 and 200: 2004, 2015, and 2016.[20]

WHAT WE CAN EXPECT?

But a sense of proportion about the threat posed by terrorists within the United States at this moment should not lead to complacency. Just to point out the obvious, radical Islamists have been and continue to be a very clear and present danger in other parts of the world, particularly the Middle East and parts of Africa. The level of response to radical Islamist terrorism elsewhere needs to be on an entirely different, more intense and forceful level than what is required to deal with violent Islamists on American soil.

Viewed in a global perspective, I expect that the characteristics of the third wave will remain relevant in the immediate future. Radical terrorism is likely to continue to be dominated by extremist Islamist groups. Unlike the radical terrorists before them, Islamist terrorists can draw upon a large global body of support. It is not that all 1.6 billion Muslims regard radical Islamist terrorists as champions; it is that even if a very tiny minority do, that is still enough to feed recruits and resources to the extremist groups. And the pressures and problems that alienate the Islamist minority are not likely to disappear soon. Also, the more evolutionary character of the third wave is likely to raise the expectations of radical terrorists. Even now, when the Islamic State has been torn down in Iraq and Syria, it will continue to provide a successful example of evolving from a terrorist group to a state, or caliphate, at a rapid pace. As we have seen again and again in this volume, terrorists learn, emulate, and aspire. And as the IS subsides, perhaps al-Qaeda will surge to fill the vacuum.

It is also important to recognize that radical terrorists are not just "them"; they have also been and are "us" as well. Radical terrorism of the extreme left and the far right, secular and religious, is part of our history and a continuing threat. I fear that the radical right will experience a surge in membership, public displays, and violence. Their increasing public presence and influence were already apparent in the 2016 electoral campaign, but the events of 11–12 August 2017 in Charlottesville—the torchlit procession and chants, the clashes of the next day, and the murder of Heather Heyer by a neo-Nazi—shocked the nation. President Trump's astounding response of 15 August—equating the KKK, neo-Nazis, and the violent alt-right with those who protested against them—seemed to legitimize right-wing hatred. The Tweet by KKK icon David Duke thanking the president for his remarks signified a perception of rising status among the radical right. Concentrating only on Islamist extremists may blind us to the very real dangers posed by home-grown American radicals.

But take care when predicting the future. It is humbling to recall that as late as the winter of 2014, few would have predicted the dramatic expansion of the Islamic State in June of 2014. Certainly, President Obama did not; nor did a legion of pundits.

NEW PARAMETERS OF VIOLENCE?
We can wonder about who will be the most dangerous terrorist actors, but we need to consider not just the terrorists, but their weapons. One of the hallmarks of radical terrorism has been the simplicity and availability of those weapons. Sneering at what he called "individual terrorism" back in 1911, Leon Trotsky wrote: "The recipe for explosives is accessible to all, and a Browning [semiautomatic pistol] can be obtained anywhere."[21] That is still true and still basic to radical terrorism. Technology has provided new menacing means, but they have tended to be variations on a theme, the wagon bomb on Wall Street in 1920 and the car bomb in Belfast in 1972. The hard part of transforming an airliner into a bomb was learning how to pilot the plane once it was aloft; otherwise it was just a matter of buying plane tickets and carrying simple weapons.

Changes in the weaponry threaten to change the parameters of terrorism. We need to consider the seeming inevitability of cyber terrorism and the unthinkable, but possible, advent of nuclear terrorism. We have already seen IS exploit the most modern information technologies for recruitment and provocation. The cyber world opens up even more menacing possibilities. Dependence on computer control and coordination of communications, public utilities, industry, and so forth has created new and very serious vulnerabilities that states such as America, Israel, and Russia have already exploited. There is good reason to expect terrorists to take advantage of whatever weaknesses they can exploit. In the past, using different weapons, terrorists have attacked public utilities such as power lines and water supplies that are now vulnerable via computers. Cyber technology is relatively low-cost. A good laptop costs little more than a good pistol. And the internet is essentially everywhere, if you know where to look. Terrorists could engage in cyber terrorism in the relative safety of their own enclaves, far removed from surveillance and attack from their enemies. The essential factor is the ability of a cyber-savvy terrorist, a Ramzi Yousef of the keyboard. Cyber terrorism is not an "if" but a "when."

Nuclear terrorism is potentially more disastrous. In the earliest terrorist manifesto we read in this volume, Karl Heinzen's "Murder," the author proclaimed that the "greatest benefactor of mankind will be he who makes it possible for a few men to wipe out thousands."[22] What would Henizen have thought of a "benefactor" who could wipe out millions with a single blast? And now that can happen. Though it is less likely than cyber terrorism, we must take whatever steps are necessary to keep this Armageddon from looming over us. A dirty bomb employing conventional explosives to spread radioactive waste would be the simplest way for terrorists to take advantage of nuclear technology. We need to be on guard here, because like other traditional means of terrorism, this would be a comparatively easy project. Radioactive byproducts of nuclear medicine and nuclear power are plentiful. On the next level, the catastrophic events at Chernobyl (1986) and Fukashima (2011) demonstrate the consequences of meltdowns at nuclear power plants. Such installations may be tough nuts to crack, but they could be turned into terrorist megaweapons.

However, the apocalyptic destructive power of nuclear bombs looms as the ultimate danger. Radical terrorist groups are by nature small and weak, so the chances of them developing a bomb of their own seem remote. But one could imagine scenarios in which the arsenals of Pakistan or North Korea might become the sources of nuclear weaponry for the worst of extremists. Should the Middle East witness a nuclear arms race, the possible sources of such destructive power could multiply. Once a bomb is obtained, the delivery system could be as simple as a seemingly innocuous shipboard cargo container on a vessel entering an American port. It is no accident that the U.S. Coast Guard is now part of the Department of Homeland Security.

This pressing potential of nuclear destruction would change many of the givens typical of radical terrorism in the past. Faced by the radical terrorists on our shores today and the limited deadly means at their disposal, my counsels of intelligent and proportional response to terrorism are entirely warranted. But different groups and different weapons could require much greater efforts and many more sacrifices.

Let us realize that we have not come to this yet, and hope that we do not in the future. At this time, wisdom is strength.

APPENDIX

A Descriptive Model of Four Strategies of Terrorism

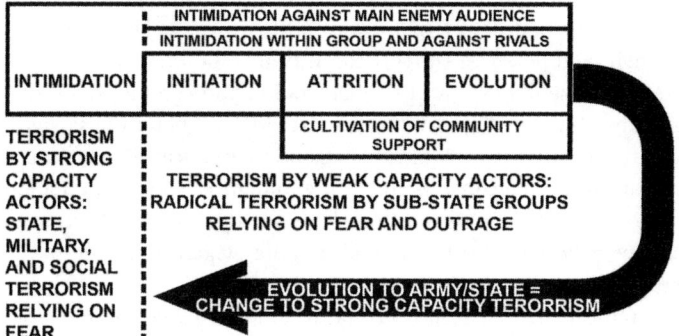

FIGURE A.1. Four Strategies of Terrorism. This graphic combines much of what has been discussed in this volume about terrorist capacities and strategies. It notes constants, such as intimidation, but distinguishes between strategic choices and goals as well, including evolution to other intensities of terrorism and warfare.

Figure A.1 is a model, or graphic representation, of four strategies of terrorism. It may appear overly complicated to some—more an obstacle than an enlightenment—so it is presented separate from the text. But for those of us who like to see a great amount of detail compressed into one model, I believe it to be valuable, at least as a teaching device. When I have presented this figure to different audiences, I have assured them that if they understand all that is in the figure, they have mastered much of what I have to say. However, to comprehend this model, the reader needs to have read the book, at least through Chapter 10, since only then do we discuss the "cultivation of community support" by radical terrorists, in particular Islamist extremists.

Most basically, the model distinguishes among the four strategies of terrorism identified in this volume: intimidation, initiation, attrition, and evolution. Intimidation is the dominant strategy followed by strong-capacity (that is, state, military, and social) terrorism. It is also fundamental to criminal terrorism, as dealt with in Chapter 13. Inflicting fear is the essence of intimidation meant to cow a target audience into compliance and submission. In the model, the recognition of intimidation as the primary strategy of strong-capacity terrorism is indicated by the dotted line separating strong-capacity from weak-capacity terrorism. Throughout this volume I have stressed that radical terrorism seeks to incite outrage as well as to inflict fear, but provoking outrage among a community targeted for submission has little use for strong-capacity terrorism. Passivity, not overassertive reaction, is its ultimate goal.

In contrast, provocation is highly useful to weak-capacity terrorists who employ terrorist jujitsu to achieve their goals of policy and of growth. Nonetheless, intimidation also serves radical sub-state terrorists. On the one hand, it can wear down adversaries or impose chaos among them. On the other hand, radical terrorists rely on intimidation to impose discipline within their own ranks and to overawe rivals within their own potential support community. The FLN, for example, punished slackers and dissenters within the organization and conducted a brutal campaign against other Muslim Algerians in the rival MNA. Therefore, as signified in Figure A.1, intimidation is recognized as useful to weak-capacity terrorists in two manners: "Intimidation against Main Enemy Audience" and "Intimidation within Group and against Rivals." Martha Crenshaw, an expert on the FLN, used the term "compliance terrorism" for the second, a more elegant term but to my mind less precise.

Weak-capacity radical terrorist groups primarily adopt strategies of initiation, attrition, and evolution, as explained and exemplified in this volume. Roughly speaking, initiation requires fewer numbers and fewer resources than attrition and evolution, but it also has the poorest record of success—witness the urban guerrillas of Chapter 8. Attrition, as employed by the PIRA, requires more strength than initiation, but less than evolution. Of course, evolution is the very essence of growing over time, so groups with a strategy of evolution expect to begin small but increase in numbers and resources until they achieve their goals. For me, the strategy of evolution demonstrates the necessity of seeing terrorism as an entry level of warfare—a stage of a conflict that can lead to much more. Radical Islamists have been the most successful at evolutionary strategies.

When a radical terrorist group has risen to the level of a state or protostate, the violence it commits within its own territory and against the population inhabiting it really becomes state or military terrorism. The arrow of evolution turns back on itself. This does make a difference, or ought to make a difference, if the newly evolved state expects to establish security, win acceptance, and achieve stability.

Yet a terrorist group that has risen to a higher level of political organization and warfare may still operate as a radical terrorist group outside its zone of political and military control. Thus at its height, the Islamic State applied intimidation to control the population in its domain and military terrorism on the battlefront, but operated as a radical terrorist network in Europe and through inspired lone wolves in the United States. Yet it would seem that transitioning from terrorist behavior to more recognizable and respectable state behavior is no easy task, particularly in the midst of an ongoing war. IS never lost its emphasis on the ostentatious atrocities that so defined it.

The last factor in terrorist strategy highlighted in Figure A.1 is "cultivation of community support." Mao Zedong spoke of preparing the general population to serve as the "sea" for insurgent guerrillas before beginning the armed struggle. For him "cultivation" meant political education and avoiding abuses that might alienate the population. The focoism of the Cuban revolutionaries and the urban guerrillas argued for entering the armed struggle with minimal delay, without preparing the "sea" to any great extent. This aligned with the hopes and expectations of weak radical terrorist groups pursuing a strategy of initiation. All this was discussed in Chapter 8. But the attention shown by radical Islamist terrorist groups to cultivating community support through providing services to that community reasserts the notion that terrorists gain by courting a support audience beyond simply preaching their ideology and narrative. As demonstrated in Chapters 9–11, terrorist groups can influence populations to look on them favorably by providing social services. This can be an ongoing, not simply preparatory, campaign of meeting the people's needs. Commentators sometimes refer to this kind of mundane cultivation as a "hearts and minds" approach. To provide services and support generally implies greater resources than those available to small groups, and the larger terrorist organizations that do have the resources are likely to be invested in strategies of attrition and evolution. This is shown on Figure A.1.

As is true of other graphics and lists presented in this book, this model is meant as a guide, not a formula. It should be referenced as a helpful, or provocative, proposal, something that reflects reality but should not be imposed on reality.

NOTES

Notice to readers: The URLs cited in these notes are listed as they were in January 2019. However, because URLs change, or even disappear, over time, I intend to update web addresses periodically as necessary and to list these updated URLs on the book's website, www.yalebooks.com/lynn.

CHAPTER 1. ON TERRORISM

1. "New Al-Jazeera Videos: London Suicide Bomber Before 'Entering Gardens of Paradise,' and Ayman Al-Zawahiri's Threats of More Bombings in the West," Middle East Media Research Institute, Special Dispatch No. 979, available on the web at https://www.memri.org/reports/new-al-jazeera-videos-london-suicide-bomber-entering-gardens-paradise-and-ayman-al-zawahiris.
2. John Horgan, *The Psychology of Terrorism* (London: Routledge, 2014), 11. Horgan is referring to Louise Richardson, "Terrorists as Transnational Actors," in Max Taylor and John. Horgan (eds.), *The Future of Terrorism* (London: Frank Cass, 2000), pp. 209–19.
3. Walter Laqueur, *History of Terrorism* (Piscataway, NJ: Transaction, 2001), 79.
4. Jessica Stern, *Terror in the Name of God* (New York: Ecco, 2004), intro., loc. 181 of 7593, Kindle.
5. Caleb Carr, *The Lessons of Terror: A History of Warfare against Civilians* (New York: Random House, 2003) is perhaps the most obvious case of defining terrorism as war against civilians, since the claim is in the title. Not all experts agree. Ami Pedahzur and Arie Perliger, *Jewish Terrorism in Israel* (New York: Columbia University Press, 2009), preface, loc. 233 of 6843, Kindle, include security forces "not on duty or engaged in formal operational activity" as targets of terrorism.
6. James M. Poland, *Understanding Terrorism: Groups, Strategies, and Responses* (Englewood Cliffs, NJ: Prentice Hall, 1988), 11.
7. U.S. Joint Chiefs of Staff, *Department of Defense Dictionary of Military and Associated Terms*, Joint Publication 1–02 (Washington, DC: U.S. Joint Chiefs of Staff, November 8, 2010 (as amended through 15 February 2012), 332.

8. "Democracy Now! Debate with Finkelstein and Shlomo Ben-Ami," 14 February 2006, transcript on the web at http://normanfinkelstein.com/2006/02/14/democracy-now-debate-with-finkelstein-shlomo-ben-ami/.
9. Randall D. Law, *Terrorism: A History* (Cambridge: Polity Press, 2009) declares that assassination is part of the terrorists' "tool box" and devotes entire chapters to tyrannicide.
10. Bruce Hoffman, *Inside Terrorism*, rev. ed. (New York: Columbia University Press, 2006), 40.
11. Walter Laqueur, *The New Terrorism: Fanaticism and the Arms of Mass Destruction* (New York: Oxford University Press, 1999), 46.
12. Raymond Aron, *Peace & War: A Theory of International Relations* (New Brunswick, NJ: Transaction, 2003), 170.
13. David C. Rapoport, "The Four Waves of Modern Terrorism," in Audrey K. Cronin and James M. Ludes, eds., *Attacking Terrorism: Elements of a Grand Strategy* (Washington, DC: Georgetown University Press, 2004), 47.
14. Marc Sageman, *Turning to Political Violence: The Emergence of Terrorism* (Philadelphia: University of Pennsylvania Press, 2017).
15. Ariel Merari, "Terrorism as a Strategy of Insurgency," in Gérard Chaliand and Arnaud Blin, *The History of Terrorism from Antiquity to al-Qaeda*, trans. Edward Schneider, Kathryn Pulver, and Jesse Browner (Berkeley, CA: University of California Press, 2007), 12.
16. Hoffman, *Inside Terrorism*, 26.
17. Merari, "Terrorism as a Strategy of Insurgency," 45.
18. Karl Heinzen, "Murder and Liberty," published in its entirety by Daniel Bessner and Michael Stauch as the centerpiece of their article "Karl Heinzen and the Intellectual Origins of Modern Terror," *Terrorism and Political Violence* 22, no. 2 (2010), 164.
19. Usama Hamdan interview by the authors in Beverley Milton-Edwards and Stephen Farrell, *Hamas: The Islamic Resistance Movement* (Cambridge: Polity, 2010), 148.
20. Carl von Clausewitz, *On War*, trans. and ed. Michael Howard and Peter Paret (Princeton, NJ: Princeton University Press, 1984), 186.
21. Clausewitz, *On War*, 338.
22. Clausewitz, *On War*, 75.
23. Sergey Nechayev, "The Revolutionary Catechism," on the site of the Marxist Internet Archive at https://www.marxists.org/subject/anarchism/nechayev/catechism.htm.
24. Benjamin Netanyahu, *International Terrorism: Challenge and Response* (Piscataway, NJ: Transaction, 1989), 15.
25. Bush quoted in Amy E. Black, "With God on Our Side: Religion in George W. Bush's Foreign Policy Speeches," paper presented at the annual meeting of the American Political Science Association; Chicago, Illinois, 2–5 September 2004, 11.
26. Horgan, *The Psychology of Terrorism*, 13. Horgan is referring to Alex P.

Schmid, "Defining Terrorism: The Response Problem as a Definition Problem," in Ronald D. Crelinsten and Alex P. Schmid, *Western Responses to Terrorism* (London: Frank Cass, 1993), 11.
27. Michael Burleigh, *Blood and Rage: A Cultural History of Terrorism* (New York: HarperCollins, 2009), preface, loc. 55 of 12609, Kindle.
28. Martha Crenshaw, "The Causes of Terrorism," *Comparative Politics* 13, no. 4 (1981), 390.
29. Horgan, *The Psychology of Terrorism*, 51.
30. This manual, entitled "Military Studies in the Jihad against the Tyrants," was discovered on the computer in the home of an al-Qaeda member in Manchester, England. A copy of the manual is available on the web at http://www.justice.gov/sites/default/files/ag/legacy/2002/10/08/manualpart1_1.pdf.
31. Jerrold M. Post, *The Mind of the Terrorist: The Psychology of Terrorism from the IRA to al-Qaeda* (New York: Palgrave MacMillan, 2007), 4.
32. Pedahzur and Perliger, *Jewish Terrorism in Israel*, preface, loc. 177 of 6843, Kindle.
33. For his complete list, see Alessandro Orsini, *Anatomy of the Red Brigades: The Religious Mind-Set of Modern Terrorists*, trans. Sarah J. Nodes (Ithaca, NY: Cornell University Press, 2011), 3–4 and 7.
34. Faranda, in Richard Drake, *The Aldo Moro Murder Case* (Cambridge, MA: Harvard University Press, 1995), 125.
35. This quotation appears in several forms, the most pithy being "The real hell of life is everyone has his reasons." However, the original French, from the dialogue of Renoir's 1939 film *La règle du jeu*, is "Ce que est terrible sur cette terre, c'est que tout le monde a ses raisons."
36. Clausewitz, *On War*, 89.
37. Definition from the Dictionary website at http://www.dictionary.com/browse/stratagem.
38. Martha Crenshaw, *Revolutionary Terrorism: The FLN in Algeria, 1954–1962* (Stanford, CA: Hoover Institution Press, 1978), 43–45.
39. Don DeLillo, *Mao II* (London: Penguin Books, 1992), 158.
40. Mark Juergensmeyer, *Terror in the Mind of God: The Global Rise of Religious Violence*, 3rd ed. (Berkeley, CA: University of California Press, 2003), chap. 7, loc. 2395 of 6988, Kindle.
41. Clausewitz, *On War*, 75.

CHAPTER 2. RULE BY FEAR

1. Sima Qian, trans. Burton Watson, in Carrie Gracie, "Qin Shi Huang: The Ruthless Emperor Who Burned Books," *BBC News Magazine*, 14 October 2012, available on the web at http://www.bbc.co.uk/news/magazine-19922863.
2. Sima Qian, *The First Emperor: Selections from the Historical Records*, ed. and trans. Raymond Dawson, reissue of 1994 edition (Oxford: Oxford University Press, 2007), 74.

3. Sima Qian, *The First Emperor*, 78.
4. Mao Zedong, first speech to the Eighth Party Congress, 8 May 1958, available on the web at http://www.marxists.org/reference/archive/mao/selected-works/volume-8/mswv8_10.htm.
5. Niccolò Machiavelli, *The Prince*, chapter XVII, available on the web at http://www.constitution.org/mac/prince17.htm.
6. Proclamation in David Andress, *The Terror: The Merciless War for Freedom in Revolutionary France* (New York: Farrar, Straus and Giroux, 2005), 178–79.
7. This address can be found on the web at http://www.indiana.edu/~b356/texts/polit-moral.html.
8. Convention decree in Reynald Secher, *A French Genocide: The Vendée* (Notre Dame, IN: University of Notre Dame Press, 2003), 250.
9. Lenin, "Can 'Jacobinism' Frighten the Working Class?," *Pravda* 90, 7 July (24 June) 1917, in *Lenin: Collected Works*, vol. 25 (Moscow: Progress Publishers, 1977) 121–22, available on the Marxist Internet Archive at http://www.marxists.org/archive/lenin/works/1917/jul/07a.htm.
10. Lenin, "A Militant Agreement for the Uprising," *Vperyod* 7, 21 February 1905, from *Lenin: Collected Works*, vol. 8 (Moscow: Foreign Languages Publishing House, 1962), 158–66, available on the web at http://www.marxists.org/archive/lenin/works/1905/feb/21.htm.
11. Leon Trotsky, *Terrorism and Communism (Dictatorship vs. Democracy): A Reply to Karl Kautsky*, English translation (New York: Workers Party of America, 1922) available on the Trotsky Internet Archives at http://www.marxists.org/archive/trotsky/1920/terrcomm/index.htm.
12. Director Felix Dzerzhinsky interviewed in Novaia Zhizn, *New Life*, 14 July 1918. Available on a number of websites, including http://www.uk250.co.uk/frame/440/the-spartacus-internet-encyclopaedia.html.
13. Daniel Johnson, *White King and Red Queen: How the Cold War Was Fought on the Chessboard* (New York: Houghton Mifflin Harcourt, 2008), 30.
14. Joseph Stalin, "Concerning the Policy of Eliminating the Kulaks as a Class," available on the Marxist Internet Archive at http://www.marxists.org/reference/archive/stalin/works/1930/01/21.htm.
15. Alexander Barmine, *One Who Survived* (New York: G. P. Putnam, 1945), 249.
16. See full text of the order in Russian at https://ru.wikisource.org/wiki/%D0%9F%D1%80%D0%B8%D0%BA%D0%B0%D0%B7_%D0%9D%D0%9A%D0%92%D0%94_%D0%BE%D1%82_15.08.1937_%E2%84%96_00486. Many thanks to my colleague Mark Steinberg for translating part of this document for me.
17. Sheila Fitzpatrick, *Everyday Stalinism: Ordinary Lives in Extraordinary Times: Soviet Russia in the 1930s* (Oxford: Oxford University Press, 2000), 190.
18. Nicolas Werth, in Stéphane Courtois, Nicolas Werth, Jean-Louis Panné, Andrzej Paczkowski, Karel Brtosek, and Jean-Louis Margolin, *The Black Book of Communism: Crimes, Terror, Repression*, trans. Jonathan Murphy and Mark

Kramer (Cambridge, MA: Harvard University Press, 1999), 198, available on the web at http://archive.org/details/TheBlackBookofCommunism10.
19. Full text available in Russian at https://ru.wikisource.org/wiki/%D0%9F%D1%80%D0%B8%D0%BA%D0%B0%D0%B7_%D0%9D%D0%9A%D0%92%D0%94_%D0%BE%D1%82_30.07.1937_%E2%84%96_00447.
20. Werth, in Courtois et al., *The Black Book*, 190.
21. Robert Conquest, *The Great Terror: A Reassessment* (Oxford: Oxford University Press, 2008), xvi.
22. Khrushchev speech available on the Nikita Khrushchev Reference Archive at http://www.marxists.org/archive/khrushchev/1956/02/24.htm.
23. Li Zhiwui, *The Private Life of Chairman Mao: The Memoirs of Mao's Personal Physician*, trans. Tai Hung-Chao (New York: Random House, 1994), 200.
24. Frank Dikötter, *Mao's Great Famine: The History of China's Most Devastating Catastrophe, 1958–1962* (New York: Walker & Company, 2011), chap. 37, loc. 6110 of 10798, Kindle.
25. Dikötter, *Mao's Great Famine*, chap. 33, loc. 5226 of 10798, Kindle. Dikötter claims the 4,500 was, indeed, a quota set by the minister of public security, and that this fell to 4,000 in 1960.
26. Roderick MacFarquhar and Michael Schoenhals, *Mao's Last Revolution* (Cambridge, MA: Harvard University Press, 2008), 9.
27. "Circular of the Central Committee of the Communist Party of China on the Great Proletarian Cultural Revolution," 16 May 1966, available on the web at http://www.marxists.org/subject/china/documents/cpc/cc_gpcr.htm.
28. Poster from Schoenhals collection, in MacFarquhar and Schoenhals, *Mao's Last Revolution*, 104.
29. MacFarquhar and Schoenhals, *Mao's Last Revolution*, 60, 62.
30. MacFarquhar and Schoenhals, *Mao's Last Revolution*, 84.
31. MacFarquhar and Schoenhals, *Mao's Last Revolution*, 109.
32. MacFarquhar and Schoenhals, *Mao's Last Revolution*, 107.
33. "Circular of the Central Committee," 16 May 1966, Point 6.
34. Figures and facts in this paragraph from MacFarquhar and Schoenhals, *Mao's Last Revolution*, 123–26.
35. MacFarquhar and Schoenhals, *Mao's Last Revolution*, 119.
36. MacFarquhar and Schoenhals, *Mao's Last Revolution*, 118.
37. Rae Yang, *Spider Eaters: A Memoir*, 15th ed. (Berkeley, CA: University of California Press, 2013), 130–31.
38. MacFarquhar and Schoenhals, *Mao's Last Revolution*, 155.
39. MacFarquhar and Schoenhals, *Mao's Last Revolution*, 245.
40. Song Yongyi, "Chronology of Mass Killings during the Chinese Cultural Revolution (1966–1976)," https://www.sciencespo.fr/mass-violence-war-massacre-resistance/en/document/chronology-mass-killings-during-chinese-cultural-revolution-1966-1976, presents estimates and suggests their mean of 2.95 million. Song Yongyi is author of *Les massacres de la Révolution culturelle* (Paris: Gallimard, 2009).

41. Machiavelli, *The Prince*, chapter XVII, available on the web at http://www.constitution.org/mac/prince17.htm.
42. "Resolution on Certain Questions in the History of our Party since the Founding of the People's Republic of China," available on the web at http://www.marxists.org/subject/china/documents/cpc/history/01.htm.

CHAPTER 3. WAR ON CIVILIANS

1. Metzger's 1999 memory of that night can be found in full on the web at http://timewitnesses.org/english/~lothar.html.
2. Churchill memo in Frederick Taylor, *Dresden* (New York: Harper, 2004), chap. 27, loc. 6693 of 10857, Kindle.
3. See Harlan Ullman and James Wade, Jr., *Shock & Awe: Achieving Rapid Dominance* (Washington, DC: Center for Advanced Concepts and Technology, 1996), 53, available on the web at http://www.dodccrp.org/files/Ullman_Shock.pdf.
4. Jawad Asgar Khan, *Probing War and Warfare* (New Delhi: APH, 2005), 38.
5. Josephus, *The Works of Flavius Josephus*, trans. William Whiston (Philadelphia: Grigg, 1835), vol. 2, 439.
6. William Shakespeare, *Henry V*, Act 3, Scene 3.
7. See Geoffrey Parker, "Early Modern Europe," chap. 4 of Michael Howard, George J. Andreopoulos, and Mark R. Shulman, eds., *The Laws of War: Constraints on Warfare in the Western World* (New Haven, CT: Yale University Press, 1994), 40–58.
8. Parker interpretation of Vitoria, *De Indis et de Ivre Belli Relectiones*, in Parker, "Early Modern Europe," 49.
9. Wayne E. Lee, *Barbarians and Brothers: Atrocity and Restraint in Anglo-American Warfare, 1500–1865* (Oxford: Oxford University Press, 2011), 2.
10. "Discours du maréchal Bugeaud à la Chambre des Députés, le 24 janvier 1845," in Jennifer Sessions, "'Unfortunate Necessities': Violence and Civilization in the Conquest of Algeria," in Patricia M. E. Lorcin and Daniel Brewer, eds., *France and Its Spaces of War: Experience, Memory, Image* (Basingstoke, Hampshire: Palgrave Macmillan, 2009), 31.
11. Alexis de Tocqueville, "Essay on Algeria," in *Writings on Empire and Slavery*, ed. and trans. Jennifer Pitts (Baltimore: Johns Hopkins University Press, 2001), 70–71.
12. Letter of 19 December 1841–2 February 1842, in Sessions, "Unfortunate Necessities," 31.
13. Letter from Saint-Arnaud to his brother, 8 February 1843, in *Lettres du maréchal de Saint-Arnaud, 1832–1854*, ed. M. Sainte-Beuve, 2nd ed., vol. 1 (Paris: Michel Lévy Frères, 1858), 474.
14. "Discours à la Chambre des Députés," 15 January 1840, in Sessions, "Unfortunate Necessities," 33.
15. *La France algérienne*, 26 July 1845, in Sessions, "Unfortunate Necessities," 36.
16. Letter from Sherman to Halleck, 24 December 1864, in *The War of the Rebel-*

lion: A Compilation of the Official Records of the Union and Confederate Armies, ser. 1, vol. 44, pt. 1, 799.

17. Sherman, in Larry J. Daniel, *Days of Glory: The Army of the Cumberland, 1861–1865* (Baton Rouge, LA: Louisiana State University Press, 2004), 386.
18. Available on the web at http://www.dannen.com/decision/int-law.html#C.
19. Available on the website of the International Red Cross, International Humanitarian Law—Treaties and Documents, at http://www.icrc.org/ihl.nsf/FULL/345?OpenDocument.
20. Available on the web at http://www.dannen.com/decision/int-law.html#D.
21. Giulio Douhet, *The Command of the Air*, trans. Dino Ferrari (New York: Coward-McCann, 1942), 58. The full text is available on the web through the Internet Archive at https://archive.org/stream/dominiodellariaeoounse/dominiodellariaeoounse_djvu.txt.
22. Douhet, *The Command of the Air*, 309.
23. Conrad C. Crane, *Bombs, Cities, & Civilians* (Lawrence, KS: University Press of Kansas, 1993), 18.
24. Air Marshal Arthur Harris, commander in chief, Bomber Commander, British Royal Air Force, 25 October 1943, quoted in Tami Biddle, *Rhetoric and Reality in Air Warfare: The Evolution of British and American Ideas about Strategic Bombing, 1914–1945* (Princeton, NJ: Princeton University Press, 2002), 220.
25. Freeman Dyson, *Disturbing the Universe* (New York: Harper & Row, 1979), 30–31.
26. Cabell to Richard Hughes, 8 September 1944, in Crane, *Bombs, Cities, & Civilians*, 106.
27. Eaker to Spaatz, 1 January 1945, in Crane, *Bombs, Cities, & Civilians*, 105.
28. Doolittle to Spaatz, 30 January 1945, in Crane, *Bombs, Cities, & Civilians*, 105.
29. Arnold, in Tami Davis Biddle, "Dresden 1945: Reality, History, and Memory," *Journal of Military History* 72, no. 2 (2008), 441.
30. Marshall, in Michael S. Sherry, *The Rise of American Air Power* (New Haven, CT: Yale University Press, 1987), 109.
31. Transcript from the film *The Fog of War: Eleven Lessons from the Life of Robert S. McNamara*, available on the web at http://www.errolmorris.com/film/fow_transcript.html.
32. Minutes of the 31 May meeting in Richard B. Frank, *Downfall: The End of the Imperial Japanese Empire* (New York: Random House, 1999), 257.
33. The full text of the Geneva Conventions is available as The Geneva Conventions of 12 August 1949, published by the International Red Cross and available on the web at https://www.icrc.org/eng/assets/files/publications/icrc-002-0173.pdf.
34. Final Report of the Commission of Experts Established Pursuant to Security Council Resolution 780 (1992), available on the web at http://www.un.org/ga/search/view_doc.asp?symbol=S/1994/674.
35. ICC website at https://www.icc-cpi.int/Pages/Main.aspx#.

36. George Packer, "Dark Hours: Violence in the Age of the War on Terror," *New Yorker*, 20 July 2015, 74.
37. Keven Buckley, "Pacification's Deadly Price," *Newsweek*, 19 June 1972, 42–43.
38. Alexandra Stiglmayer, "The Rapes in Bosnia-Herzegovina," in *Mass Rape: The War against Women in Bosnia-Herzegovina*, ed. Alexandra Stiglmayer, trans. Marian Faber (Lincoln, NE: University of Nebraska Press, 1994), 82–169.
39. UN Commission in Stiglmayer, "Rapes in Bosnia-Herzegovina," 85.
40. Stiglmayer, "Rapes in Bosnia-Herzegovina," 85.
41. The testimony of "Hatiza" (all names were changed in the article to protect the witnesses) can be found in Stiglmayer, "Rapes in Bosnia-Herzegovina," 91–93.
42. Peter Landesman, "A Woman's Work," *New York Times Magazine*, 15 September 2002, available on the web at http://www.nytimes.com/2002/09/15/magazine/a-woman-s-work.html.

CHAPTER 4. WHITE KNIGHTS

1. *Report of Evidence Taken before the Military Committee in Relation to Outrages Committed by the Ku Klux Klan in Middle and West Tennessee Submitted to the Extra Session of the Thirty-Fifth General Assembly of the State of Tennessee, September 2d, 1868* (Nashville, TN: S. C. Mercer, 1868), 37.
2. Audrey Kurth Cronin, *How Terrorism Ends: Understanding the Decline and Demise of Terrorism Campaigns* (Princeton, NJ: Princeton University Press, 2009), 8.
3. *Chicago Tribune*, in Patrick Riddenberger, *1866: The Critical Year Revisited* (Carbondale, IL: Southern Illinois University Press, 1979), 181.
4. *Daily Avalanche*, in Riddenberger, *1866: The Critical Year Revisited*, 180.
5. Sheridan, in Riddenberger, *1866: The Critical Year Revisited*, 199.
6. *Prescript* in J. C. Lester and D. L. Wilson, *Ku Klux Klan: Its Origin, Growth and Disbandment* (New York: Neale, 1905), 155.
7. Eddy W. Davidson and Daniel Foxx, *Nathan Bedford Forrest: In Search of the Enigma* (Gretna, LA: Pelican, 2007), 432.
8. Powell testimony, *Report of Evidence*, 45–46.
9. For the full text of General Order No. 1, see Susan Lawrence Davis, *Authentic History: Ku Klux Klan, 1865–77* (New York: American Library Service, 1924), 125–28.
10. *Testimony Taken by the Joint Select Committee to Inquire into the Condition of Affairs in the Late Insurrectionary States: Georgia*, vol. 1 (Washington: Government Printing Office, 1872), 67, available on the web at http://onlinebooks.library.upenn.edu/webbin/metabook?id=insurrection1872.
11. The Enforcement Act is available on several websites, including https://loc.gov/law/help/statutes-at-large/42nd-congress/session-1/c42s1ch22.pdf.
12. This account of the fighting at Colfax and other events in Louisiana owes much to the work of James K. Hogue, *Uncivil War: Five New Orleans Street*

Battles and the Rise and Fall of Radical Reconstruction (Baton Rouge, LA: Louisiana State University Press, 2006).
13. Foster, in Vernon O. Burton, *The Age of Lincoln* (New York: Hill and Wang, 2007), 316.
14. Transcript of the Alabama Convention of May 1901, p. 9, available on the web through the Internet Archive at http://www.archive.org/stream/journalofproceed00alabrich/journalofproceed00alabrich_djvu.txt.
15. *Slate*, the Vault, on the web at http://www.slate.com/blogs/the_vault/2013/01/08/lynching_map_tuskegee_institute_s_data_on_lynching_from_1900_1931.html.
16. Stewart E. Tolnay and E. M. Beck, *Festival of Violence: An Analysis of Southern Lynchings, 1882–1930* (Champaign, IL: University of Illinois Press, 1995), 48 and 97.
17. For the lyrics, the reader may consult http://www.lyricsfreak.com/b/billie+holiday/strange+fruit_20017859.html.
18. An AP report by Dennis Cook in June 2005 stated, "Nearly 200 anti-lynching bills were introduced in Congress, and three passed the House. Seven presidents between 1890 and 1952 petitioned Congress to pass a federal law." Available on the web at http://www.nbcnews.com/id/8206697/ns/us_news-life/t/senate-apologizes-inaction-lynchings/#.UaOo4ZxioSk.
19. Thomas Dixon, Jr., *The Clansman: An Historical Romance of the Ku Klux Klan* (New York: Doubleday, 1905), 290.
20. *The Birth of a Nation*, intertitle at 2:44:22. *The Birth of a Nation* can be viewed in its entirely on YouTube at several sites.
21. The clipping of the *Atlanta Constitution*, 28 November 1915, can be found on the web at http://en.wikipedia.org/wiki/File:19151128AC_Klan_re-established.jpg.
22. Henry P. Fry, *The Modern Ku Klux Klan* (Boston: Small, Maynard, 1922), 29.
23. *Ideals of the Ku Klux Klan*, 3–4, available on the web at http://archive.lib.msu.edu/DMC/AmRad/idealskkk.pdf.
24. This cover can be seen on the web at http://content.time.com/time/covers/0,16641,19240623,00.html.
25. *Washington Post*, in Wyn Craig Wade, *The Fiery Cross: The Ku Klux Klan in America* (New York: Simon and Schuster, 1987), 253.
26. Wade, *The Fiery Cross*, 276.
27. King's "I Have a Dream" speech can be found on the website of Stanford University's Martin Luther King, Jr. Research and Education Institute at https://kinginstitute.stanford.edu/king-papers/documents/i-have-dream-address-delivered-march-washington-jobs-and-freedom.
28. King's impressive "Letter from Birmingham Jail" can be found on the web from the Stanford King Institute at https://kinginstitute.stanford.edu/king-papers/documents/letter-birmingham-jail.
29. This interesting point is made by George Packer, "Dark Hours: Violence in the Age of the War on Terror," *New Yorker*, 20 July 2015, 73.

30. Kennedy, in Robert D. Loevy, *On the Forward Edge: American Government and the Civil Rights Act of 1964* (Lanham, MD: University Press of America, 2005), 53.
31. Cronkite, in the 1997 documentary *4 Little Girls*, by Spike Lee.
32. Bob Ingram, "Loyalist Faction Wins; 'White Supremacy' Goes," *Birmingham News*, 21 January 1966, available on the web at http://archive.org/details/RacistDemocraticPartyLogo.
33. Shelton obituary, *New York Times*, 20 March 2003.

CHAPTER 5. PROPAGANDA OF THE DEED

1. Testimony of Mikhail Frolenko, a member of the executive committee of the Narodnaya Volya Party, in his memoirs, quoted in Ze'ev Iviansky, "Individual Terror: Concept and Typology," *Journal of Contemporary History* 12, no. 1 (1977), 47.
2. Edvard Radzinsky, *Alexander II: The Last Great Czar*, trans. Antonina W. Bouis (New York: Free Press, 2005), 406–07.
3. Vera Figner, *Memoirs of a Revolutionist* (DeKalb, IL: Northern Illinois University Press, 1991), 99.
4. Randall D. Law, *Terrorism: A History*, 2nd ed. (Cambridge: Polity, 2016).
5. Samuel K. Cohn, Jr., *Lust for Liberty: The Politics of Social Revolt in Medieval Europe, 1200–1425* (Cambridge, MA: Harvard University Press, 2008), chap. 2, loc. 391 of 5497, Kindle.
6. Yves Marie Bercé, *The Social Origins of Rebellion in Early Modern France* (Ithaca, NY: Cornell University Press, 1990), 327.
7. Cohn, *Lust for Liberty*, chap. 1, loc 331 of 5497, Kindle, and chap. 3, loc. 759 of 5497, Kindle.
8. The discussion of barricades here is based primarily on Mark Traugott, *The Insurgent Barricade* (Berkeley, CA: University of California Press, 2010). I have also made use of Jonathan M. House, *Controlling Paris: Armed Forces and Counter-Revolution, 1789–1848* (New York: New York University Press, 2014).
9. On the Flour War see Charles Tilly, *The Contentious French* (Cambridge, MA: Belknap Press, 1986), 222–24, and especially the works of Cynthia A. Bouton: "Gendered Behavior in Subsistence Riots: The French Flour War of 1775," *Journal of Social History* 23, no. 4 (Summer 1990), 735–54, and her volume *The Flour War: Gender, Class, and Community in Late Ancien Régime French Society* (University Park, PA: Pennsylvania State University Press, 1993).
10. Bakunin, in Paul Avrich, *Anarchist Portraits* (Princeton, NJ: Princeton University Press, 1990), 46.
11. Traugott, *The Insurgent Barricade*, chap. 7, loc. 5127–5262 of 13132, Kindle.
12. From "Du régicide", *Le moniteur républicain* 6 (16 Floréal, an 46), in Jean-Noël Tardy, "Tuer le tyran ou la tyrannie? Attentat et conspiration politique: Distinctions et affinités en France de 1830 à 1870," *La Révolution française:*

Cahiers de l'Institut d'histoire de la Révolution française 1 (2012), available on the web at http://journals.openedition.org/lrf/438. Marc Sageman, *Turning to Political Violence: The Emergence of Terrorism* (Philadelphia: University of Pennsylvania Press, 2017), 122, refers to this revealing quotation, which brought it to my attention.

13. William Dwight Porter Bliss, ed., *The Encyclopedia of Social Reform* (New York: Funk & Wagnalls, 1897), 98.
14. Karl Marx, "The Victory of the Counter-Revolution in Vienna," *Neue Rheinische Zeitung* 136 (6 November 1848), trans. Marx-Engels Institute, 1994, available on the Marxist Internet Archive at https://www.marxists.org/archive/marx/works/1848/11/06.htm.
15. Auguste Blanqui, *Instruction pour une prise d'armes* (1866), trans. Andy Blunden, available on the Marxist Internet Archive at https://www.marxists.org/reference/archive/blanqui/1866/instructions1.htm.
16. Blanqui, *Instructions*.
17. Friedrich Engels, Introduction to the 1895 edition of Karl Marx, *The Class Struggles in France 1848 to 1850*, available on the web at https://www.marxists.org/archive/marx/works/1850/class-struggles-france/intro.htm.
18. Walter Laqueur, ed., *Voices of Terrorism: Manifestos, Writings and Manuals of Al Qaeda, Hamas, and other Terrorists from around the World and throughout the Ages* (New York: Reed Press, 2004), 50.
19. Friedrich Engels, "The Communists and Karl Heinzen," in *Deutsche-Brüsseler-Zeitung* 79 and 80 (3 and 7 October 1847), available on the Marxist Internet Archive at http://www.marxistsfr.org/archive//marx/works/1847/09/26.htm.
20. Heinzen's "Murder and Liberty" in Bessner and Stauch, "Karl Heinzen and the Intellectual Origins of Modern Terror," 143-76, is the edition of "Murder and Liberty" that will be used in this chapter.
21. Karl Heinzen, "Murder," in Laqueur, *Voices of Terrorism*, 57. "Der Mord" is available in translation in its entirely in *Voices of Terrorism*, 57–67. My thanks to Daniel Bessner, who supplied me with photocopies of the original issues of *Die Evolution*.
22. Heinzen, "Murder," 58.
23. Heinzen, "Murder," 60–61.
24. Heinzen, "Murder and Liberty," 163.
25. Heinzen, "Murder," 66–67.
26. Heinzen, "Murder and Liberty," 166.
27. Heinzen, "Murder," 65.
28. Heinzen, "Murder," 62.
29. Heinzen, "Murder and Liberty," 164.
30. Heinzen, "Murder and Liberty," 163.
31. Heinzen, "Murder and Liberty," 163.
32. Heinzen, "Murder and Liberty," 161.
33. Hans Kohn, *The Idea of Nationalism: A Study in Its Origins and Background* (Piscataway, NJ: Transaction, 2005), 9.

34. Benedict Anderson, *Imagined Communities: Reflections on the Origin and Spread of Nationalism*, rev. ed. (London: Verso, 2006), 6.
35. Proudhon, *Qu'est-ce-que la propriété? Ou recherches sur le principe du droit et du gouvernement*, 237, available on the Internet Archive at https://archive.org/details/questcequelapro02prougoog/page/n9.
36. Kropotkin in the *Encyclopedia Britannica* (1910), available on the Marxist Internet Archive at http://www.marxists.org/reference/archive/kropotkin-peter/1910/britannica.htm.
37. Max Nettlau, "An Anarchist Manifesto" (1 May 1895), available on the web at http://theanarchistlibrary.org/library/max-nettlau-an-anarchist-manifesto.
38. *The Alarm*, 18 October 1884, in Paul Avrich, *The Haymarket Tragedy* (Princeton, NJ: Princeton University Press, 1986), 166.
39. Michael Burleigh, *Blood and Rage: A Cultural History of Terrorism* (New York: HarperCollins, 2009), 74.
40. Leon Trotsky, "Why Marxists Oppose Individual Terrorism" (originally published in German in *Der Kampf*, November 1911), available on the web at http://www.marxists.org/archive/trotsky/1911/11/tia09.htm.
41. Carlo Pisacane, "Political Testament" (1857), available on the web at http://robertgraham.wordpress.com/2011/09/22/carlo-pisacane-propaganda-by-the-deed-1857/.
42. Mikhail Bakunin, "Letters to a Frenchman on the Present Crisis" (1970), available on the web at http://marxists.org/reference/archive/bakunin/works/1870/letter-frenchman.htm. The italics are in the original.
43. G. M. Stekloff, *History of the First International*, trans. E. and C. Paul (London: Lawrence, 1928), 359, available on the web at https://www.marxists.org/archive/steklov/history-first-international/ch32.htm.
44. Kropotkin in *La révolte* 32 (18–24 March 1894), in Martin A. Miller, *Kropotkin* (Chicago: University of Chicago Press, 1976), 174.
45. Nechayev's "Revolutionary Catechism" is available on the Marxist Internet Archive at http://www.marxists.org/subject/anarchism/nechayev/catechism.htm.
46. S. Stepniak, *Underground Russia: Revolutionary Profiles and Sketches from Life* (New York: Scribners, 1883), 39–42.
47. Turgenev, "The Threshold," from the web at http://novaonline.nvcc.edu/eli/evans/his241/Notes/Turgenev_Threshold.html. One website that provides the text for "The Threshold" (http://usefulbowl.tumblr.com) claims the poem was inspired by the execution of Sophia Peroveskaya for her part in the assassination of Alexander II. However, since the poem was written in 1878, that would have been impossible. The poem was inspired by the acts and life of Vera Zasulich.
48. Mazzini, in Sageman, *Turning to Political Violence*, 135.
49. James H. Billington, *Fire in the Minds of Men: Origins of the Revolutionary Faith* (New York: Basic Books, 1980), 405.

50. Mathew Carr, *The Infernal Machine: A History of Terrorism* (New York: New Press, 2007), 14.
51. The letter is available in its entirety as an appendix to Figner, *Memoirs of a Revolutionist*, 307–12.
52. Anna Geifman, *Thou Shalt Kill: Revolutionary Terrorism in Russia, 1894–1917* (Princeton, NJ: Princeton University Press, 1995), 20–25.
53. Geifman, *Thou Shalt Kill*, 21–22.
54. Louise Michel before the revolutionary group of the 19th Arrondissement, quoted in Louis Andrieux, *Souvenirs d'un préfet de police*, vol. 1 (Paris: Jules Rouff, 1885), 346–47.
55. John Merriman, *The Dynamite Club: How a Bombing in Fin-de-Siècle Paris Ignited the Age of Modern Terror* (New York: Houghton Mifflin Harcourt, 2009), 51.
56. Ernest Alfred Vizetelly, *The Anarchists* (London: John Lane, 1911), 153.
57. Henry's statement in Merriman, *The Dynamite Club*, 157.
58. Henry's defense statement in Merriman, *The Dynamite Club*, 187.
59. Henry's defense in George Woodcock, ed., *The Anarchist Reader* (Hassocks, Sussex: Harvester Press, 1977), 195.
60. Merriman, *The Dynamite Club*, 87 and 206.
61. Merriman, *The Dynamite Club*, 76.
62. Vizetelly, *The Anarchists*, 163–64.
63. Pelloutier, "Anarchism and the Workers Unions," published in *Les temps nouveaux* of 2–8 November 1895, available on the web at http://libcom.org/library/anarchism-workers-unions-fernand-pelloutier.
64. *New York Times*, 12 September 1898, available on the web at https://timesmachine.nytimes.com/timesmachine/1898/09/12/102527052.html?pageNumber=1.
65. Richard Bach Jensen, *The Battle against Anarchist Terrorism* (Cambridge: Cambridge University Press, 2014), 135.
66. Diena, in 1898 article, in Jensen, *The Battle against Anarchist Terrorism*, 133.
67. Jensen, *The Battle against Anarchist Terrorism*, 136.
68. Jensen, *The Battle against Anarchist Terrorism*, 137.
69. A full text of the protocol drafted at the Rome Conference can be found in Jensen, *The Battle against Anarchist Terrorism*, 366–71.
70. Roosevelt in in Jensen, *The Battle against Anarchist Terrorism*, 259.
71. Wilhelm, in Jensen, *The Battle against Anarchist Terrorism*, 326.
72. Carlos Marighella, *Minimanual of the Urban Guerrilla* (1969), "Armed Propaganda," available on the Marxist Internet Archive at https://www.marxists.org/archive/marighella-carlos/1969/06/minimanual-urban-guerrilla/.

CHAPTER 6. SECOND-WAVE ETHNO-NATIONALIST TERRORISM

1. Drif, in Alistair Horne, *A Savage War of Peace: Algeria, 1954–1962* (New York: New York Review Books, 2011), chap. 9, loc. 4020–4023 of 15322, Kindle.
2. Drif, in Martin Evans, *Algeria: France's Undeclared War* (Oxford: Oxford University Press, 2013), chap. 7, loc. 3852–3854 of 10145, Kindle.

3. Guirard, in Evans, *Algeria*, chap. 8, loc. 4714 of 10145, Kindle.
4. Both quoted in Claudia Feldman, "French Author and 'Hustonphile' Speaks Up for Innocents Caught in Crossfires of War," *Houston Chronicle*, 22 February 2013, available on the web at https://www.houstonchronicle.com/life/article/French-author-and-Houstonphile-speaks-up-for-4301198.php.
5. Abane, in Horne, *Savage War of Peace*, chap. 9, loc. 4052–4054 of 15322, Kindle. This would seem to be the source of the lines put in the mouth of Larbi M'Hidi in Pontecorvo's film: "And doesn't it seem to you even more cowardly to drop napalm bombs on defenseless villages, so that there are a thousand times more innocent victims? Of course, if we had your airplanes it would be a lot easier for us. Give us your bombers, and you can have our baskets."
6. The Brazzaville Declaration included the following points:
   1. The French Empire would remain united.
   2. Semiautonomous assemblies would be established in each colony.
   3. Citizens of France's colonies would share equal rights with French citizens.
   4. Citizens of French colonies would have the right to vote for the French parliament.
   5. The native population would be employed in public service positions within the colonies.
   6. Economic reforms would be made to diminish the exploitative nature of the relationship between France and its colonies.
7. Evans, *Algeria*, chap. 8, loc. 4281–4284 of 10145, Kindle.
8. De Gaulle address in Horne, *Savage War of Peace*, chap. 16, loc. 7590–7591 of 15322, Kindle.
9. Tillon account in Horne, *Savage War of Peace*, chap. 10, loc. 4705–4706 of 15322, Kindle.
10. Mauriac, in Evans, *Algeria*, chap. 7, loc. 4103–4106 of 10145, Kindle.
11. Horne, *A Savage War of Peace*, chap. 16, loc. 7458–7460 of 15322, Kindle.
12. Joly, in Douglas Porch, *Counterinsurgency: Exposing the Myths of the New Way of War* (Cambridge: Cambridge University Press, 2013), 188.
13. Paul Aussaresses, *The Battle of the Casbah: Terrorism and Counterterrorism in Algeria, 1955–1957*, trans. Robert L. Miller (New York: Enigma Books, 2002), chap. 14, loc. 2032–2036 of 3006, Kindle.
14. O'Hara, in Rogelio Alonso, *The IRA and Armed Struggle* (London: Routledge, 2007), 76.
15. Patrick Magee, in Richard English, *Armed Struggle: The History of the IRA* (Oxford: Oxford University Press, 2003), chap. 4, loc. 3240 of 12348, Kindle.
16. Joe Cahill quoted in an interview with O'Connell's grandson in the BBC Northern Ireland documentary on Bloody Friday, produced and directed by Lena Ferguson.
17. Price, in English, *Armed Struggle*, chap. 4, loc. 3474–3476 of 12348, Kindle.
18. IRA, *Green Book*, 8, in the electronic edition of volumes 1 and 2, available

on the web at http://tensmiths.files.wordpress.com/2012/08/15914572-ira-green-book-volumes-1-and-2.pdf.
19. IRA, *Green Book*, 2.
20. Archbishop Ó Fiaich in Peter Taylor, *Provos: The IRA & Sinn Féin* (London: Bloomsbury, 1997), chap. 15, loc. 4451 of 8209, Kindle.
21. Morrison, in English, *Armed Struggle*, chap. 5, loc. 4598 of 12348, Kindle.
22. Price, in English, *Armed Struggle*, chap. 8, loc. 6341 of 12348, Kindle.
23. Weir interview with John Hume in Bonnie Weir, "From Bullets to Ballots: The Political Transformation of Violent Opposition Movements" (Ph.D. diss., University of Chicago, 2012), 46.
24. Weir, "From Bullets to Ballots," 29.

CHAPTER 7. TALES OF TWO TRAGEDIES
1. Beverley Milton-Edwards and Stephen Farrell, *Hamas: The Islamic Resistance Movement* (Cambridge: Polity, 2010), 9.
2. Alexander Scholch, "The Demographic Development of Palestine, 1850–1882," *International Journal of Middle East Studies* 17, no. 4 (November 1985), 503.
3. Benny Morris, *Righteous Victims: A History of the Zionist–Arab Conflict, 1881–1998* (New York: Vintage, 2001), chap. 2, loc. 1103 of 20176, Kindle.
4. Morris, *Righteous Victims*, chap. 2, loc. 1338–1340 of 20176, Kindle.
5. The Balfour Declaration is available on the web on the site of the Avalon Project, Yale Law School, at http://avalon.law.yale.edu/20th_century/balfour.asp.
6. Eban quoted on *BBC News*, 18 November 2002, available on the web at http://news.bbc.co.uk/2/hi/middle_east/2486473.stm.
7. Morris, *Righteous Victims*, chap. 1, loc. 599–603 of 20176, Kindle.
8. Menachem Ussishkin, in Morris, *Righteous Victims*, chap. 4, loc. 3518–3521 of 20176, Kindle.
9. Ben-Gurion, in Morris, *Righteous Victims*, chap. 4, loc. 3540–3544 of 20176, Kindle.
10. Ben-Gurion, in Morris, *Righteous Victims*, chap. 5, loc. 4186–4189 of 20176, Kindle.
11. Ben-Gurion, in Ilan Pappe, *The Ethnic Cleansing of Palestine* (Oxford: Oneworld, 2007), chap. 3, loc. 1017 of 7469, Kindle.
12. For percentages, see "Demographics of Israel" in the Jewish Virtual Library at http://www.jewishvirtuallibrary.org/jewish-and-non-jewish-population-of-israel-palestine-1517-present.
13. Pappe, *The Ethnic Cleansing of Palestine*, preface, loc. 211 of 7469, Kindle.
14. Arie Perliger, "Israel's Response to the Crisis in Syria," *CTC Sentinel* 6, no. 8 (August 2013), 9.
15. The text of Resolution 242 can be found on the web at http://www.un.org/en/ga/search/view_doc.asp?symbol=S/RES/242(1967).
16. The Palestinian National Charter can be found on the web on the site of Yale

University's Avalon Project at http://avalon.law.yale.edu/20th_century/plocov.asp.

17. Abu Iyad, with Eric Rouleau, *My Home, My Land: A Narrative of the Palestinian Struggle*, trans. Linda Butler Koseoglu (New York: Times Books, 1981), 51.
18. This is a common phrase in the literature on terrorism. See, for example, Michael Scott Duran, "Somebody Else's Civil War," *Foreign Affairs*, January/February 2002, 22–42.
19. Sharon, in Morris, *Righteous Victims*, chap. 11, loc. 12019–12021 of 20176, Kindle.
20. Milton-Edwards and Farrell, *Hamas*, 185.
21. See for example, Bernard Gwertzman, "Haig Contends U.S. Failed in Lebanon," *New York Times*, 1 April 1984, available on the web at http://www.nytimes.com/1984/04/01/world/haig-contends-us-failed-in-lebanon.html.
22. Begin, in Morris, *Righteous Victims*, chap. 11, loc. 12398 of 20176, Kindle.
23. Morris, *Righteous Victims*, chap. 11, loc. 12997 of 20176, Kindle.
24. Dan Williams, "Israeli Minister Sees 50 Percent More Settlers in West Bank by 2019," Reuters, 16 May 2014, available on the web at http://www.reuters.com/article/2014/05/16/us-palestinian-israel-idUSBREA4F0AD20140516. Construction and Housing Minister Uri Ariel foresees 850,000–950,000 Israelis in the West Bank and East Jerusalem by 2019.
25. Letter in William B. Quandt, *Peace Process: American Diplomacy and the Arab–Israeli Conflict since 1967* (Berkeley, CA: University of California Press, 2001), 252.
26. Reagan, in Geraint Hughes, *My Enemy's Enemy: Proxy Warfare in International Politics* (Eastbourne, Sussex: Sussex Academic Press, 2012), 104.
27. The full Kahan Commission Report can be found on the web on the Jewish Virtual Library at https://www.jewishvirtuallibrary.org/jsource/History/kahan.html.
28. Ze'ev Schiff and Ehud Ya'ari, *Israel's Lebanon War*, trans. and ed. Ina Friedman (New York: Simon and Schuster, 1984), 301.
29. Text of a videotaped speech by bin Laden in October 2004, printed in the *Guardian* on 29 October 2004, available on the web at http://www.theguardian.com/world/2004/oct/30/alqaida.september11.
30. Begin, in Harry Zvi Hurwitz, *Begin: His Life, Words and Deeds* (Jerusalem: Gefen, 2004), 229.

CHAPTER 8. URBAN GUERRILLAS

1. The Holger Meins poster can be found on the website that accompanies this book. It can also be found on the Palestinian Poster Project Archives at https://www.palestineposterproject.org/poster/freiheit-fur-alle-gefangenen.
2. Guevara's classic *Guerrilla Warfare* is available on the web at several sites, including http://www3.uakron.edu/worldciv/pascher/che.html.

3. Marysa Gerassi, "Uruguay's Urban Guerrillas," *New Left Review* 62 (July–August 1970), 23, states that "at least 70 per cent of its 2,560,000 inhabitants live in cities and almost half in Montevideo alone."
4. Gatto, in Pablo Brum, *The Robin Hood Guerrillas: The Epic Journey of Uruguay's Tupamaros* (CreateSpace Independent Publishing Platform, 2014), 16.
5. Che Guevara speech in Brum, *The Robin Hood Guerrillas*, 20–21.
6. Lindsey Churchill, *Becoming the Tupamaros: Solidarity and Transnational Revolutionaries in Uruguay and the United States* (Nashville, TN: Vanderbilt University Press, 2014), 10.
7. Gerassi, "Uruguay's Urban Guerrillas," 24–25.
8. Gerassi, "Uruguay's Urban Guerrillas," 25.
9. Marighella, *Minimanual of the Urban Guerrilla*, "The Logistics of the Urban Guerrilla," available on the Marxist Internet Archive at https://www.marxists.org/archive/marighella-carlos/1969/06/minimanual-urban-guerrilla/.
10. Leaflet, in Churchill, *Becoming the Tupamaros*, 17.
11. Martínez, in Brum, *Robin Hood Guerrillas*, 59.
12. Hal Brands, *Latin America's Cold War* (Cambridge, MA: Harvard University Press, 2010), 102.
13. From *Guerrilla* 19 (March 1971) in the Marshall Bloom Alternative Press Collection, 1967–2002, Archives and Special Collections, Amherst College Library, Amherst, MA, cited in Churchill, *Becoming the Tupamaros*, 66.
14. Churchill, *Becoming the Tupamaros*, 18.
15. Che Guevara, *Guerrilla Warfare* (Lanham, MD: Scholarly Resources, 2004), 121.
16. "The Robin Hood Guerrillas," *Time* 93, no. 20 (16 May 1969), 70.
17. Concerning Plan Satán, see Brum, *Robin Hood Guerrillas*, 139–71.
18. Brum, *Robin Hood Guerrillas*, 163.
19. Frank Roberts, "The Tupamaros: Rise and Fall," originally published in *International Socialism* 66 (February 1974), available on the Marxist Internet Archive at https://www.marxists.org/history/etol/newspape/isj/1974/no066/roberts.htm.
20. "Weatherman War Council: The Year of the Fork?," *Fifth Estate* 4, no. 19 (20 January–4 February 1970), 13.
21. Cathy Wilkerson, *Flying Close to the Sun: My Life and Times as a Weatherman* (New York: Seven Stories Press, 2007), 1.
22. Ayers in the film *The Weather Underground*, produced by Carrie Lozano, directed by Bill Siegel and Sam Green, New Video Group, 2003.
23. Klehr, the Andrew W. Mellon professor of politics and history at Emory University in Atlanta, quoted in Daniel J. Wakin, "Quieter Lives for 60's Militants, but Intensity of Beliefs Hasn't Faded," *New York Times*, 24 August 2013, available on the web at http://www.nytimes.com/2003/08/24/nyregion/quieter-lives-for-60-s-militants-but-intensity-of-beliefs-hasn-t-faded.html.
24. This 21 May 1970 declaration of war can be found on the web at http://

genius.com/Weather-underground-a-declaration-of-a-state-of-war-communique-1-annotated.
25. WUO, *Prairie Fire: The Politics of Revolutionary Anti-Imperialism—the Political Statement of the Weather Underground* (Communications Co., 1974), foreword and 20. *Prairie Fire* can be found on the web at http://www.sds-1960s.org/PrairieFire-reprint.pdf.
26. Jeremy Varon, *Bringing the War Home: The Weather Underground, the Red Army Faction, and Revolutionary Violence in the Sixties and Seventies* (Berkeley, CA: University of California Press, 2004), 298.
27. "Weatherman War Council: The Year of the Fork?," 12.
28. Meinhof, in Varon, *Bringing the War Home*, 205.
29. Interview with Bernardine Dohrn in Varon, *Bringing the War Home*, 59.
30. Susan Stern, *With the Weathermen: The Personal Journal of a Revolutionary Woman* (New Brunswick, NJ: Rutgers University Press, 2007), 176–77.
31. Point 6 in Nechayev's "Revolutionary Catechism," which is available on the Marxist Internet Archive at http://www.marxists.org/subject/anarchism/nechayev/catechism.htm.
32. 21 May 1970 declaration of war.
33. Jeff Jones, in Varon, *Bringing the War Home*, 57.
34. "Weatherman War Council: The Year of the Fork?," 12 (italics mine).
35. Jane Albert, *Growing Up Underground* (New York: Citadel Press, 1990), 12.
36. Paul Ginsborg, *A History of Contemporary Italy, 1943–1988* (New York: St. Martin's Press, 2003), 362.
37. Resolution of the BR's strategic management document of April 1975, in Alessandro Orsini, *Anatomy of the Red Brigades: The Religious Mind-Set of Modern Terrorists*, trans. Sarah J. Nodes (Ithaca, NY: Cornell University Press, 2011), 11.
38. Moretti, in Orsini, *Anatomy of the Red Brigades*, 14.
39. Donatella della Porta, "Left-Wing Terrorism in Italy," in Martha Crenshaw, ed., *Terrorism in Context* (University Park, PA: Pennsylvania State University Press, 1995), 130, Table 4.1: "Functions of Terrorist Actions."
40. David Moss, *The Politics of Left-Wing Violence in Italy, 1969–85* (New York: St. Martin's Press, 1989), 66, Table 2.7: "Red Brigades' Members and Actions, 1970–1982."
41. The brigadist "Claudio," in Orsini, *Anatomy of the Red Brigades*, 48.
42. Faranda, in Richard Drake, *The Aldo Moro Murder Case* (Cambridge, MA: Harvard University Press 1995), 126.
43. Faranda, in Orsini, *Anatomy of the Red Brigades*, 57.
44. Court of Turin, Public Prosecutor's Charge, in Della Porta, "Left-Wing Terrorism in Italy," 140.
45. Orsini, *Anatomy of the Red Brigades*, 79, Table 1: "Red Brigades Membership by Profession," and Table 2: "Red Brigades Membership by Gender."
46. Della Porta, "Left-Wing Terrorism in Italy," 134.
47. For Orsini's list of the "gnostic mentality" of terrorists, see Orsini, *Anatomy of the Red Brigades*, 3–4 and 7.

48. Interview with the BR cadre Ferrandi, "Una pistola per riconquistare il paradiso," 7 March 1984, in Orsini, *Anatomy of the Red Brigades*, 8.
49. Morucci, in Orsini, *Anatomy of the Red Brigades*, 9.
50. Morucci, in Orsini, *Anatomy of the Red Brigades*, 18.
51. Meins, in Varon, *Bringing the War Home*, 230.
52. Morucci, in Orsini, *Anatomy of the Red Brigades*, 43.
53. Faranda, in Orsini, *Anatomy of the Red Brigades*, 17.
54. Peci, in Orsini, *Anatomy of the Red Brigades*, 11.
55. Mellen, in Varon, *Bringing the War Home*, 172.
56. Moretti Orsini, *Anatomy of the Red Brigades*, 106.
57. Peci, in Orsini, *Anatomy of the Red Brigades*, 50.
58. Fiore, in Orsini, *Anatomy of the Red Brigades*, 48.
59. Thomas Gilovich, Dacher Keltner, Serena Chen, and Richard E. Nisbett, *Social Psychology*, 3rd ed. (New York: W. W. Norton, 2012), 472.
60. Festinger, in Gilovich et al., *Social Psychology*, 472–473.
61. Wilkerson, *Flying Close to the Sun*, 293.
62. Wilkerson, *Flying Close to the Sun*, 318.
63. Mair-Witt, in Varon, *Bringing the War Home*, 253.
64. Heinrich Böll, in J. Smith and André Moncourt, *The Red Army Faction: A Documentary History*, vol. 1: *Projectiles for the People* (Oakland, CA: PM Press, 2009), chap. 4, loc. 2519 of 14667, Kindle.

CHAPTER 9. ISLAMIST TERRORISM

1. Emily Greenhouse, "The Charlie Hebdo Affair: Laughing at Blasphemy," *New Yorker*, 28 September 2012, available on the web at http://www.newyorker.com/news/news-desk/the-charlie-hebdo-affair-laughing-at-blasphemy.
2. Charb, in Eric Wahlberg, "Hebdo vs, Al Jazeera: A Tale of Two Journalisms," 11 January 2015, available on the web at http://ericwalberg.com and http://www.intrepidreport.com/archives/14919.
3. Dan Bilefsky and Maïa de la Baumejan, "Terrorists Strike Hebdo Newspaper in Paris, Leaving 12 Dead," *New York Times*, 7 January 2015, available on the web at https://www.nytimes.com/2015/01/08/world/europe/charlie-hebdo-paris-shooting.html.
4. See transcript of the broadcast at http://edition.cnn.com/TRANSCRIPTS/1501/19/ebo.01.html.
5. Jeff Victoroff, "The Mind of the Terrorist: A Review and Critique of Psychological Approaches," *Journal of Conflict Resolution* 49, no. 1 (2005), 35.
6. John Horgan, *The Psychology of Terrorism* (London: Routledge, 2014), 43.
7. Victoroff, "The Mind of the Terrorist," 3.
8. Marc Sageman, *Leaderless Jihad: Terror Networks in the Twenty-First Century* (Philadelphia: University of Pennsylvania Press, 2008), Chapter 3, "The Jihadist's Profile."
9. Merari, in Jessica Stern, *Terror in the Name of God: Why Religious Militants Kill* (New York: HarperCollins, 2009), 51.

10. Stern, *Terror in the Name of God*, 284.
11. Stern, *Terror in the Name of God*, 231.
12. Fair, in Sebastian Rotella, "Terror Group Recruits from Pakistan's 'Best and Brightest,'" *ProPublica*, April 4, 2013, available on the web at http://www.propublica.org/article/terror-group-recruits-from-pakistans-best-and-brightest.
13. Alexis Akwagyiram, "Islamist Radicalism: Why Does It Lure Some Africans?," *BBC News*, 30 May 2013, available on the web at http://www.bbc.com/news/world-africa-22688781.
14. Terrorist, in Stern, *Terror in the Name of God*, 136.
15. Stern, *Terror in the Name of God*, 283.
16. Stern, *Terror in the Name of God*, 285.
17. Audrey Kurth Cronin, "How Fighting Ends: Asymmetric Wars, Terrorism, and Suicide Bombing," in Hew Strachan and Holger Aflerbach, eds., *How Fighting Ends: A History of Surrender* (Oxford: Oxford University Press, 2012), 420.
18. All quotations from the Quran here are from *The Koran*, trans. N. J. Dawood, rev. ed. (London: Penguin Books, 2003).
19. Taimiyya, in Mary Habeck, *Knowing the Enemy: Jihadist Ideology and the War on Terror* (New Haven, CT: Yale University Press, 2006), chap. 2, loc. 170 of 2066, Kindle.
20. Excerpt from http://www.bidah.com/articles/rwmef-explanation-of-the-shariah-definition-of-bidah-and-its-proofs.cfm. The Arabic term translated as innovation is *bi'dah*, which carries a negative connotation. See as well in http://www.islamicacademy.org/html/Articles/English/BID%27AH%20-%20Innovation%20in%20Islam.htm: "Every innovation is a misguidance and every misguidance goes to Hell fire."
21. Rida, in Daniel Benjamin and Steven Simon, *The Age of Sacred Terror* (New York: Random House, 2002), chap. 2, loc. 1062 of 9279, Kindle.
22. Habeck, *Knowing the Enemy*, chap. 2, loc. 285 of 2066, Kindle.
23. John L. Esposito, *Unholy War: Terror in the Name of Islam* (Oxford: Oxford University Press, 2002), 26.
24. Qutb, in Esposito, *Unholy War*, 55.
25. Qutb, in Benjamin and Simon, *The Age of Sacred Terror*, chap. 2, loc. 1219 of 9279, Kindle.
26. Qutb, in Esposito, *Unholy War*, 56.
27. Qutb, in Habeck, *Knowing the Enemy*, chap. 6, 1094 of 2066, Kindle.
28. Qutb, in Benjamin and Simon, *The Age of Sacred Terror*, chap. 2, loc. 1230 of 9279, Kindle.
29. Sayyid Qutb, *In the Shade of the Qur'an*, trans. Adil Salahi, web edition, vol. 4, 185, available at https://www.kalamullah.com/Books/InTheShadeOfTheQuranSayyidQutb/volume_4_surah_5.pdf.
30. Andrew McGregor, "'Jihad and the Rifle Alone:' Abdullah Azzam and the Islamist Revolution," *Journal of Conflict Studies* 23, no. 2 (2003), 92–113.
31. Shayke Abdullah Azzam, *Join the Caravan*, 23, available on the web at http://archive.org/stream/JoinTheCaravan/JoinTheCaravan_djvu.txt.

32. Azzam, *Join the Caravan*, 27.
33. Hadith, in Azzam, *Join the Caravan*, 4.
34. Azzam, *Join the Caravan*, 7.
35. Azzam, *Join the Caravan*, 9.
36. Samuel Huntington, *The Clash of Civilizations and the Remaking of World Order* (New York: Simon and Schuster, 2011), chap. 1, loc. 243 of 9316, Kindle.
37. Eduardo Aninat, "China, Globalization, and the IMF," 14 January 2001, available on the web at http://www.imf.org/external/np/speeches/2001/011401.htm.
38. Ismail Abu Shanab, in Stern, *Terror in the Name of God*, 41.
39. Ajmal Qadri, in Stern, *Terror in the Name of God*, 227.
40. Bernard Lewis, "The Roots of Muslim Rage," *Atlantic*, September 1990, available on the web at https://www.theatlantic.com/magazine/archive/1990/09/the-roots-of-muslim-rage/304643/.
41. Tom Pyszczynski, "What Are We So Afraid Of? A Terror Management Theory Perspective on the Politics of Fear," *Social Research* 71, no. 4 (2004), 832 (italics mine).
42. Thomas A. Pyszczynski, Sheldon Solomon, and Jeff Greenberg, *In the Wake of 9/11: The Psychology of Terror* (Washington, DC: American Psychological Association, 2003), 100.
43. John L. Esposito and Dalia Mogahed, *Who Speaks for Islam?: What a Billion Muslims Really Think* (New York: Gallup Press, 2007).
44. Pew Research Center, The Pew Forum on Religion & Public Life, *The World's Muslims: Unity and Diversity* (9 August 2012), available on the web at http://www.pewforum.org/2012/08/09/the-worlds-muslims-unity-and-diversity-executive-summary/; and *The World's Muslims: Religion, Politics and Society* (2013), available at http://www.pewforum.org/2013/04/30/the-worlds-muslims-religion-politics-society-overview/.
45. Esposito and Mogahed, *Who Speaks for Islam?*, 5.
46. Pew, *The World's Muslims: Religion, Politics and Society*, 134.
47. Pew, *The World's Muslims: Religion, Politics and Society*, 136.
48. Pew, *The World's Muslims: Religion, Politics and Society*, 34.
49. Pew, *The World's Muslims: Religion, Politics and Society*, 15.
50. Al Jazeera, in Esposito and Mogahed, *Who Speaks for Islam?*, 36.
51. Pew, *The World's Muslims: Religion, Politics and Society*, 52 and 54.
52. Esposito and Mogahed, *Who Speaks for Islam?*, 80.
53. Esposito and Mogahed, *Who Speaks for Islam?*, 108.
54. Pew, *The World's Muslims: Religion, Politics and Society*, 93.
55. Esposito and Mogahed, *Who Speaks for Islam?*, 51–52.
56. Esposito and Mogahed, *Who Speaks for Islam?*, 80.
57. Esposito and Mogahed, *Who Speaks for Islam?*, 88.
58. Esposito and Mogahed, *Who Speaks for Islam?*, 87.
59. Esposito and Mogahed, *Who Speaks for Islam?*, 125.

60. Sageman, *Leaderless Jihad*, viii.
61. Sageman, *Leaderless Jihad*, viii.
62. Horgan, *The Psychology of Terrorism*, 93.
63. Faranda, in Horgan, *The Psychology of Terrorism*, 96.
64. Taylor and Quayle, *Terrorist Lives*, in Horgan, *The Psychology of Terrorism*, 89 (italics are Horgan's).
65. Elliot, in Horgan, *The Psychology of Terrorism*, 80.
66. Mark Juergensmeyer, *Terror in the Mind of God: The Global Rise of Religious Violence*, 3rd ed. (Berkeley, CA: University of California Press, 2003), chap. 4, loc. 1633 of 6988, Kindle.
67. Stern, *Terror in the Name of God*, 185.
68. Sageman, *Leaderless Jihad*, 107.
69. Sageman, *Leaderless Jihad*, 156–57.
70. Stern, *Terror in the Name of God*, 4.
71. Mia Bloom, "Female Suicide Bombers: A Global Trend," *Dædalus* 136, no. 1 (Winter 2007), 96.
72. Mia Bloom, *Bombshell: Women and Terrorism* (Philadelphia: University of Pennsylvania Press, 2011), chap. 8, "The Four Rs Plus One," 233–50.
73. Berko, in Bloom, *Bombshell*, 245–46.
74. Bloom, *Bombshell*, 245.
75. Bloom, *Bombshell*, 245.
76. Stern, *Terror in the Name of God*, intro., loc. 341 of 7593, Kindle.
77. Juergensmeyer, *Terror in the Mind of God*, chap. 8, loc. 2976 of 6988, Kindle.
78. Juergensmeyer, *Terror in the Mind of God*, chap. 8, loc. 3283–3296 of 6988, Kindle.
79. Rapoport, in Juergensmeyer, *Terror in the Mind of God*, chap. 7, loc. 2514 of 6988, Kindle.
80. Pew, *The World's Muslims: Unity and Diversity*, 65.
81. There are many sources for this well-known quotation. See, for example, Bob Fredericks, "Slain Charlie Hebdo Editor: 'I Prefer to Die Standing,'" *New York Post*, 8 January 2015, available on the web at https://nypost.com/2015/01/08/slain-charlie-hebdo-editor-i-prefer-to-die-standing-than-live-on-my-knees/.
82. From Justice Murphy's statement of the 9–0 opinion of the U.S. Supreme Court in *Chaplinsky v. New Hampshire*, 1942. This can be found on the Cornell Law School website at https://www.law.cornell.edu/supremecourt/text/315/568.
83. Lester Pearson, *Democracy in World Politics* (Princeton, NJ: Princeton University Press, 1955), 83–84, in Huntington, *The Clash of Civilizations*, chap. 12, loc. 6511 of 9316, Kindle.
84. Esposito and Mogahed, *Who Speaks for Islam?*, 87.
85. Rebecca Hawkes, "Hayao Miyazaki: *Charlie Hebdo* Mohammed Cartoons Were 'A Mistake,'" *Telegraph*, 17 February 2015, available on the web at http://

www.telegraph.co.uk/culture/film/film-news/11417395/Hayao-Miyazaki-Charlie-Hebdo-Mohammed-cartoons-were-a-mistake.html.

CHAPTER 10. REGIONAL JIHAD

1. Dates of casualties in the report are from 1 March to 7 May 2002. "Report of Secretary-General on Recent Events in Jenin, Other Palestinian Cities," 1 August 2002, available on the web at https://www.un.org/press/en/2002/SG2077.doc.htm.
2. Asef Bayat, *Life as Politics: How Ordinary People Change the Middle East*, 2nd ed. (Stanford, CA: Stanford University Press, 2013), 227.
3. Augustus Richard Norton, *Hezbollah: A Short History* (Princeton, NJ: Princeton University Press, 2014), 34.
4. Robert Pape, *Dying to Win: The Strategic Logic of Suicide Terrorism* (New York: Random House, 2005), chap. 8, loc. 2070 of 5263, Kindle.
5. Hezbollah manifesto, in Augustus Richard Norton, *Amal and the Shi'a: Struggle for the Soul of Lebanon* (Austin, TX: University of Texas Press, 1987), 171.
6. Hezbollah manifesto, in Norton, *Amal and the Shi'a*, 170.
7. Norton, *Amal and the Shi'a*, 173.
8. For examples, see Robin Wright, *Sacred Rage: The Wrath of Militant Islam*, rev. ed. (New York: Simon and Schuster, 2001), 95.
9. Nicholas Blanford, "Hizbullah Chief Offers Carrot, Stick," *Christian Science Monitor*, 31 July 2003.
10. Norton, *Hezbollah*, 41.
11. Norton, *Hezbollah*, 85.
12. Council on Foreign Relations Backgrounders, "Hezbollah," at http://www.cfr.org/lebanon/hezbollah-k-hizbollah-hizbullah/p9155.
13. Interview with Daniel Byman, May 2008, available on the website of the Council of Foreign Relations at http://www.cfr.org/lebanon/hezbollah-most-powerful-political-movement-lebanon/p16378?breadcrumb=%2F.
14. Zur, in Yaakov Katz, "Israeli Military Studies Hezbollah's Resilience," *USA Today*, 14 September 2006, available on the web at http://usatoday30.usatoday.com/news/world/2006-09-13-israel-army_x.htm.
15. These excerpts of the Winograd Commission Report are taken from Steven Erlanger, "Israeli Inquiry Finds 'Grave Failings' in '06 War," *New York Times*, January 31, 2008, available on the web at http://www.nytimes.com/2008/01/31/world/middleeast/31mideast.html?pagewanted=print&_r=0.
16. Human Rights Watch, vol. 19, no. 5(E), "Why They Died: Civilian Casualties in Lebanon during the 2006 War," 4, available on the web at http://www.hrw.org/reports/2007/lebanon0907/index.htm.
17. Norton, *Hezbollah*, xi.
18. Ideological declaration of 30 November 2009, in Norton, *Hezbollah*, 175.
19. Dr. Haider Abdel Shafi, in Beverley Milton-Edwards and Stephen Farrell,

Hamas: The Islamic Resistance Movement (Cambridge: Polity Press, 2010), 44 (italics mine).
20. Report from author interview with Avner Cohen, at the time an advisor to the Israeli military authorities, in Milton-Edwards and Farrell, *Hamas*, 54.
21. For the Hamas Covenant, see Yale Law School, Avalon Project, Documents in Law, History, and Diplomacy, at http://avalon.law.yale.edu/20th_century/hamas.asp.
22. See the letters on the web at http://unispal.un.org/UNISPAL.NSF/0/369174 73237100E285257028006C0BC5.
23. On casualties, see Rami Nasrallah, "The First and Second Palestinian *Intifadas*," in Joel Peters and David Newman, eds., *The Routledge Handbook on the Israeli–Palestinian Conflict* (Abingdon, Oxon: Routledge, 2013), 60–61.
24. Dr. Mahmoud Zahar, 29 May 1995, in Milton-Edwards and Farrell, *Hamas*, 67.
25. See Ami Pedahzur and Arie Perliger, *Jewish Terrorism in Israel* (New York: Columbia University Press, 2009), chapter 2, concerning Goldstein and the Kach Movement.
26. Clyde Haberman, "West Bank Massacre; Israel Orders Tough Measures against Militant Settlers," *New York Times*, 28 February 1994, available on the web at http://www.nytimes.com/1994/02/28/world/west-bank-massacre-israel-orders-tough-measures-against-militant-settlers.html.
27. "Fmr. Israeli Foreign Minister Shlomo Ben Ami Debates Outspoken Professor Norman Finkelstein on Israel, the Palestinians, and the Peace Process," 14 February 2006, available on the web at http://www.democracynow.org/2006/2/14/fmr_israeli_foreign_minister_shlomo_ben.
28. "Suha Arafat Admits Husband Premeditated Intifada," *Jerusalem Post*, 29 December 2012, available on the web at http://www.jpost.com/Middle-East/Suha-Arafat-admits-husband-premeditated-Intifada.
29. The Mitchell Report, available on the website of the Jewish Virtual Library at http://www.jewishvirtuallibrary.org/the-mitchell-report-may-2001.
30. Efraim Benmelech and Claude Berrebi, "Human Capital and the Productivity of Suicide Bombers," *Journal of Economic Perspectives* 21, no. 3 (2007), 225–27. The authors limited their sample to bombings by Palestinians about whom they knew the age and education of the bombers. They found only eight attacks carried out by female bombers.
31. "Report of Secretary-General on Recent Events in Jenin, Other Palestinian Cities," 2 August 2002, Press Release at http://www.un.org/press/en/2002/SG2077.doc.htm.
32. David Pratt, *Intifada: The Long Day of Rage* (Philadelphia: Casemate, 2007), 235.
33. B'Tselem Press Release, "Disproportionate Force Suspected in Northern Gaza Strip," 18 October 2004, available on the web at http://www.btselem.org/press_releases/20041018.
34. "10 Years to [since] the Second Intifada—Summary of Data," Press Release,

B'Tselem, available on the web at http://www.btselem.org/press_releases/20100927.
35. "Intifada Toll 2000–2005," *BBC News*, 8 February 2005, available on the web at http://news.bbc.co.uk/2/hi/middle_east/3694350.stm.
36. "House Demolitions as Punishment: Statistics on Punitive House Demolitions," B'Tselem, originally published 1 January 2011, updated 19 November 2014, available on the web at http://www.btselem.org/punitive_demolitions/statistics.
37. Fares Mohammed, author interview, Ramallah, 12 July 2003, in Milton-Edwards and Farrell, *Hamas*, 238.
38. Al-Shanti, in Milton-Edwards and Farrell, *Hamas*, 233.
39. See B'Tselem, "Statistics: Fatalities during Operation Cast Lead," available on the web at http://www.btselem.org/statistics/fatalities/during-cast-lead/by-date-of-event.
40. The "Report of the United Nations Fact Finding Mission on the Gaza Conflict" can be found on the web at http://image.guardian.co.uk/sys-files/Guardian/documents/2009/09/15/UNFFMGCReport.pdf.
41. These numbers are from B'Tselem, "Attacks on Israeli Civilians by Palestinians: Rocket and Mortar Fire into Israel," updated to 24 July 2014, available on the web at http://www.btselem.org/israeli_civilians/qassam_missiles.
42. "B'Tselem's Findings: Harm to Civilians Significantly Higher in Second Half of Operation Pillar of Defense," B'Tselem, Press Release, 8 May 2013, available on the web at http://www.btselem.org/press_releases/20130509_pillar_of_defense_report.
43. United Nations Office for the Coordination of Humanitarian Affairs (OCHA), "Fragmented Lives: An Overview 2014" (March 2015), 4, available on the web at http://reliefweb.int/sites/reliefweb.int/files/resources/annual_humanitarian_overview_2014_english_final.pdf.
44. Milton-Edwards and Farrell, *Hamas*, 286.
45. Mohammed Omer, "Hamas Growing in Military Stature, Say Analysts," *Middle East Eye*, available on the web at http://www.middleeasteye.net/news/hamas-gains-credibility-fighting-force-analysts-say-371780262.
46. Amos Harel and Gili Cohen, "Hezbollah: From Terrorist Group to Army," *Haaretz*, 12 July 2016, available on the web at http://www.haaretz.com/st/c/prod/eng/2016/07/lebanon2/.

CHAPTER 11. GLOBAL JIHAD

1. This video in its entirety was available on the web at http://leaksource.info/2014/08/19/graphic-video-islamic-state-beheads-american-journalist-james-foley/. It now seems to have been removed from the web.
2. The 1996 *fatwa* is available on several websites, including that of the Combating Terrorism Center at https://ctc.usma.edu/app/uploads/2013/10/Declaration-of-Jihad-against-the-Americans-Occupying-the-Land-of-the-Two-Holiest-Sites-Translation.pdf.

3. This 1998 fatwa is available on several websites, including https://fas.org/irp/world/para/docs/980223-fatwa.htm.
4. Zawahiri, *Knights*, in Laura Mansfield, ed. and trans., *His Own Words: Translation and Analysis of the Writings of Dr. Ayman Al Zawahiri* (Old Tappan, NJ: TLG, 2006), 21.
5. See the al-Qaeda document "Azzam on the Achievements of the Services Office," in J. M. Berger, ed., *Beatings and Bureaucracy: The Founding Memos of Al-qaeda* (N.p.: Intelwire Press, 2012), Azzam document, loc. 886 of 932, Kindle.
6. Zawahiri letter quoted by Lawrence Wright, "The Master Plan: For the New Theorists of Jihad, Al-Qaeda Is Just the Beginning," *New Yorker*, 11 September 2006, available on the web at http://www.newyorker.com/magazine/2006/09/11/the-master-plan.
7. Details of Hussein's book and English passages are taken from Wright, "The Master Plan."
8. Abu Bakr Naji, *The Management of Savagery: The Most Critical Stage through Which the Ummah Will Pass*, trans. William McCants, funding for translation provided by the John M. Olin Institute for Strategic Studies at Harvard University, 23 May 2006, available on the web on the Internet Archive at https://archive.org/stream/TheManagementOfBarbarismAbuBakrNaji/The+Management+of+Barbarism+-+Abu+Bakr+Naji_djvu.txt.
9. Naji, *The Management of Savagery*, 7.
10. Michael W. S. Ryan, *Decoding Al-Qaeda's Strategy: The Deep Battle Against America* (New York: Columbia University Press, 2013) discusses the work of several important Islamist military authors, with an emphasis on Qurashi, two of whose works are translated and presented as appendixes to the book.
11. William R. Polk, "Sayyid Qutub's Fundamentalism and Abu Bakr Naji's Jihadism," posted December 3, 2013, available on the web at http://www.mepc.org/articles-commentary/commentary/sayyid-qutubs-fundamentalism-and-abu-bakr-najis-jihadism.
12. Problems of Strategy in China's Revolutionary War can be found in the Marxist Internet Archive at https://www.marxists.org/reference/archive/mao/selected-works/volume-1/mswv1_12.htm.
13. Abd al-Aziz al-Muqrin, *A Practical Course for Guerrilla War*, translated in its entirety in Norman Cigar, *Al-Qa'ida's Doctrine for Insurgency: Abd al-Aziz al-Muqrin's "A Practical Course for Guerrilla War"* (Washington, DC: Potomac Books, 2009), 94.
14. Naji, *The Management of Savagery*, 9, 50, and others.
15. Lawrence Wright, *The Looming Tower: Al-Qaeda and the Road to 9/11* (New York: Knopf, 2006), chap. 6, loc. 2361 of 9375, Kindle.
16. Aryn Baker, "A Nightmare Returns: Emboldened by Success in Syria, al-Qaeda Occupies Its Old Haunts," *Time*, 20 January 20, 2014, 32.
17. *The 9/11 Commission Report* (New York: W. W. Norton, 2004), 489, n. 10.

18. Richard Clarke, *Against All Enemies: Inside America's War on Terror* (New York: Free Press, 2004), 145–47.
19. *9/11 Commission Report*, 265.
20. Wright, *The Looming Tower*, chap. 16, loc. 5025 of 9375, Kindle.
21. Abdul Bari Atwan, *The Secret History of al-Qaeda*, rev. ed. (Berkeley, CA: University of California Press, 2008), 179.
22. Ahmed Zaidan, Pakistani correspondent for Al Jazeera, in William Cran's PBS documentary *Jihad: The Men and Ideas Behind al-Qaeda*, broadcast April 2007.
23. For a condemning but convincing analysis of the Bush administration's true rationale for fighting the 2003 Iraq War, see Andrew Bacevich, *America's War for the Greater Middle East: A Military History* (New York: Random House, 2017), Chapter 13, "Kicking Down the Door." Note particularly his summary loc. 4489–95, Kindle. The Bacevich book only came to my attention when this volume was well into the publication process, so I have not been able to integrate it into the text. Yet, while he centers on the period 1980 to the present, an era coincident with the rise of third wave radical Islamist terrorism, he does not focus primarily on terrorism or counterterrorism. He directs his attention to American military policy and actions.
24. Dana Milbank and Claudia Deane, "Hussein Link to 9/11 Lingers in Many Minds," *Washington Post*, 6 September 2011.
25. Milbank and Deane, "Hussein Link to 9/11."
26. I first broached this argument in John A. Lynn II, "Fear and Outrage as Terrorists' Goals," *Parameters* 42, no. 1 (Spring 2012), 51–62.
27. Patrick Cockburn, *The Rise of Islamic State: ISIS and the New Sunni Revolution*, rev. ed. (London: Verso, 2015), chap. 7, loc. 1012 of 2112, Kindle.
28. Carlotta Gall, "Bombing at Hotel in Pakistan Kills at Least 53," *New York Times*, 21 September 2008, available on the web at http://www.nytimes.com/2008/09/22/world/asia/22islamabad.html?_r=0. "Pakistan al-Qaeda leaders 'Dead,'" *BBC News*, posted 9 January 2009, available on the web at http://news.bbc.co.uk/2/hi/south_asia/7819305.stm.
29. Abu Musab Al-Suri, *The Global Islamic Resistance Call*, available on the Internet Archive at https://archive.org/stream/TheGlobalIslamicResistanceCall/The_Global_Islamic_Resistance_Call_-_Chapter_8_sections_5_to_7_LIST_OF_TARGETS_djvu.txt.
30. Scott Shane, "Times Square Suspect Drew Inspiration from Militant Cleric," *New York Times*, 7 May 2010, available on the web at http://www.nytimes.com/2010/05/07/world/middleeast/07awlaki-.html.
31. Sageman, *Leaderless Jihad*, 146.
32. Asef Bayat, *Life as Politics: How Ordinary People Change the Middle East*, 2nd ed. (Stanford, CA: Stanford University Press, 2013), preface, loc. 78 of 8186, Kindle.
33. Bayat, *Life as Politics*, chap. 15, loc. 6142 of 8186, Kindle.
34. Hashem Ahelbarra, "Tunisia: The End of an Era," *Al Jazeera*, 14 January

2011, available on the web at http://www.mwcnews.net/focus/analysis/7969-tunisia-the-end-of-an-era.html.
35. Fawaz A. Gerges, *The Rise and Fall of Al-Qaeda* (Oxford: Oxford University Press, 2011), 3.
36. Richard Wike, "Widespread Concerns about Extremism in Muslim Nations, and Little Support for It," Pew Research Center, 5 February 2015, available on the web at http://www.pewresearch.org/fact-tank/2015/02/05/extremism-in-muslim-nations/.
37. Audrey Kurth Cronin, "ISIS Is Not a Terrorist Group: Why Counterterrorism Won't Stop the Latest Jihadist Threat," *Foreign Affairs*, March/April 2015, available on the web at https://www.foreignaffairs.com/articles/middle-east/isis-not-terrorist-group.
38. See, for examples, "Obama Has Touted Al-Qaeda's Demise 32 Times since Benghazi Attack," *CNS News*, 1 November 2012, available on the web at http://cnsnews.com/news/article/obama-touts-al-Qaeda-s-demise-32-times-benghazi-attack-0.
39. Fareed Zakaria, "End the War on Terror and Save Billions," *Washington Post*, 6 December 2012, available on the web at https://www.washingtonpost.com/opinions/fareed-zakaria-end-the-war-on-terror-and-save-billions/2012/12/06/a468db2a-3fc4-11e2-ae43-cf491b837f7b_story.html?utm_term=.64fc955dc82c.
40. For the full text of the Jeh Johnson speech, "The Conflict against Al-Qaeda and Its Affiliates: How Will It End?," delivered on 30 November 2012 before the Oxford Union, see https://www.lawfareblog.com/jeh-johnson-speech-oxford-union.
41. David Remnick, "Going the Distance: On and Off the Road with Barack Obama," *New Yorker*, 27 January 2014, available on the web at http://www.newyorker.com/magazine/2014/01/27/going-the-distance-david-remnick.
42. Secretary of State Colin L. Powell, "Remarks to the United Nations Security Council," New York City, 5 February 2003, available on the website of the Department of State at https://2001-2009.state.gov/secretary/former/powell/remarks/2003/17300.htm.
43. Excerpts from his talk can be found in "New Al-Jazeera Videos: London Suicide Bomber before 'Entering Gardens of Paradise,' and Ayman Al-Zawahiri's Threats of More Bombings in the West," Middle East Media Research Institute, Special Dispatch No. 979, available on the web at http://www.memri.org/report/en/print1465.htm.
44. Nance estimate and quotation from Andrew Tilghman, "The Myth of AQI," *Washington Monthly*, October 2007, available on the web at https://washingtonmonthly.com/2007/09/06/the-myth-of-aqi/.
45. Cronin, "ISIS Is not a Terrorist Group." In this quote, she says "AQI"; however, by this point the organization was ISI, and so I use that label. Available on the web at https://www.foreignaffairs.com/articles/middle-east/isis-not-terrorist-group.

46. Peter R. Mansoor, *Surge: My Journey with General David Petraeus and the Remaking of the Iraq War* (New Haven, CT: Yale University Press, 2013), 260–61.
47. Martin Chulov, "ISIS: The Inside Story," *Guardian*, 11 December 2014, available on the web at http://www.theguardian.com/world/2014/dec/11/-sp-isis-the-inside-story.
48. "Strategic Plan," in Willam McCants, *The ISIS Apocalypse: The History, Strategy, and Doomsday Vision of the Islamic State* (New York: St. Martin's Press, 2015), 80.
49. Stern and Berger, *ISIS*, 60.
50. Theo Padnos, "Theo Padnos, American Journalist, on Being Kidnapped, Tortured and Released in Syria," *New York Times Magazine*, 29 October 2014, available on the web at http://www.nytimes.com/2014/10/28/magazine/theo-padnos-american-journalist-on-being-kidnapped-tortured-and-released-in-syria.html?_r=2.
51. Figures in this paragraph from Baker, "A Nightmare Returns," 32.
52. CIA estimate 20,000–31,500 reported by CNN 12 September 2014, available on the web at http://edition.cnn.com/2014/09/11/world/meast/isis-syria-iraq/.
53. Stern and Berger, *ISIS*, 46.
54. Patrick Cockburn, "Isis Consolidates," *London Review of Books* 36, no. 16, 21 August 2014, 3–5, available on the web at http://www.lrb.co.uk/v36/n16/patrick-cockburn/isis-consolidates.
55. Hassan Hassan, "Insurgents Again: The Islamic State's Calculated Reversion to Attrition in the Syria-Iraq Border and Beyond," *CTC Sentinel* 10, no. 11, 1–8, Combating Terrorism Center, U.S. Military Academy, West Point, NY, available on the site of the CTC at https://ctc.usma.edu/ctc-sentinel/.
56. Eric Schmitt, "Thousands of ISIS Fighters Flee in Syria, Many to Fight Another Day," *New York Times*, 5 February 2018, available on the web at https://www.nytimes.com/2018/02/04/world/middleeast/isis-syria-al-qaeda.html.
57. Adnani, "Indeed Your Lord Is Ever Watchful," 11, available on the web at https://scholarship.tricolib.brynmawr.edu/bitstream/handle/10066/16495/ADN20140922.pdf?sequence=1.
58. Adnani, "That They Live by Proof," translated and published by Al Hayat Media Center (2016), 12. Available on the web at https://aussiemadness.files.wordpress.com/2016/06/al-hayat-that-they-live-by-proof.pdf.
59. Michael Weiss and Hassan Hassan, *ISIS: Inside the Army of Terror*, rev. ed. (New York: Regan Arts, 2016), 30.
60. Cockburn, *The Rise of Islamic State*, chap. 8, loc. 1274–1276 of 2112, Kindle.
61. J. M. Berger, "For Global Jihadist Supporters, Islamic State's Massacre Wipes Out Any Sympathy over U.S. Strikes," *Intelwire*, 18 August 2014, available on the web at http://news.intelwire.com/2014/08/for-global-jihadist-supporters-islamic.html.
62. Official quoted in Ahmad al-Bahri, "In Raqqa, an All-Female ISIS Brigade Cracks Down on Local Women," *Syria Deeply*, 15 July 2014, available on the

web at https://www.newsdeeply.com/syria/articles/2014/07/15/in-raqqa-an-all-female-isis-brigade-cracks-down-on-local-women.
63. Stern and Berger, *ISIS*, 209.
64. Gyorgy Busztin, the deputy special representative in Iraq of the UN secretary general, in Jane Arraf, "Islamic State Persecution of Yazidi Minority Amounts to Genocide, UN Says," *Christian Science Monitor*, 7 August 2014, available on the web at https://www.csmonitor.com/World/Middle-East/2014/0807/Islamic-State-persecution-of-Yazidi-minority-amounts-to-genocide-UN-says.
65. Rukmini Callimachi, "ISIS Enshrines a Theology of Rape," *New York Times*, 13 August 2015, available on the web at http://www.nytimes.com/2015/08/14/world/middleeast/isis-enshrines-a-theology-of-rape.html?emc=eta1&_r=0.
66. The text of *Questions and Answers on Taking Captives and Slaves* is available on the web at http://www.memrijttm.org/islamic-state-isis-releases-pamphlet-on-female-slaves.html.
67. Letter of 21 May 2012 from Abu Basir, head of AQAP, to Abu Musab Abdul Wadud, emir of AQIM, available on the web at https://assets.documentcloud.org/documents/1236725/abubasirletter.pdf.
68. Letter quoted in Stern and Berger, *ISIS*, 114.
69. McCants, *The ISIS Apocalypse*, 59.
70. Zawahiri letter, in Mansfield, *His Own Words*, 268.
71. Zawahiri letter, in Mansfield, *His Own Words*, 271.
72. Jacob Poushter, "In Nations with Significant Muslim Populations, Much Disdain for ISIS," Pew Research Center, 17 November 2015, available on the web at http://www.pewresearch.org/fact-tank/2015/11/17/in-nations-with-significant-muslim-populations-much-disdain-for-isis/. See as well Mohammed Hafez, "The Curse of Cain: Why Fratricidal Jihadis Fail to Learn from Their Mistakes," *CTC Sentinel*, December 2017, 1–7, which identifies indiscriminate and savage violence as an explanation for the failure of IS.
73. McCants, *The ISIS Apocalypse*, 7.
74. Filiu, in McCants, *The ISIS Apocalypse*, 145.
75. Abu Musab al-Suri, *A Terrorist's Call to Global Jihad: Deciphering Abu Musab al-Suri's Islamic Jihad Manifesto*, ed. Jim Lacey (Annapolis, MD: Naval Institute Press, 2008), 25.
76. Zarqawi, in McCants, *The ISIS Apocalypse*, 12.
77. Mariam Karouny, "Apocalyptic Prophecies Drive Both Sides in Syrian Battle for the End of Time," Reuters, 1 April 2014, available on the web at http://www.reuters.com/article/us-syria-crisis-prophecy-insight-idUSBREA3013420140401.
78. See their commentary on the ISIS video series *Clanging of the Swords*" in Stern and Berger, *ISIS*, 106–12.
79. Stern and Berger, *ISIS*, 244.
80. Naji, *The Management of Savagery*, 41.

81. Issues of *Dabiq* can be found on the site of the Clarion Project at http://www.clarionproject.org/news/islamic-state-isis-isil-propaganda-magazine-dabiq#.
82. Stern and Berger, *ISIS*, 7.
83. Usama Hamdan interview by the authors in Beverley Milton-Edwards and Stephen Farrell, *Hamas: The Islamic Resistance Movement* (Cambridge: Polity, 2010), 148.
84. The Soufan Group, "Foreign Fighters: An Updated Assessment of the Flow of Foreign Fighters into Syria and Iraq," 4–5, available on the web at http://soufangroup.com/wp-content/uploads/2015/12/TSG_ForeignFightersUpdate3.pdf.
85. The text of this segment of the video can be found at http://www.juliagorin.com/wordpress/?p=3121.
86. McCants, *The ISIS Apocalypse*, 148.
87. Carter interview statements in Robin Wright, "After the Islamic State," *New Yorker*, 12 December 2016, available on the web at https://www.newyorker.com/magazine/2016/12/12/after-the-islamic-state.
88. Adnani, "That They Live by Proof," 5.
89. Adnani, "That They Live by Proof," 11.
90. Wright, "After the Islamic State."

CHAPTER 12. RADICAL RIGHT-WING VIOLENCE IN THE UNITED STATES

1. Andrew MacDonald, *The Turner Diaries*, 2nd ed. (Fort Lee, NJ: Barricade Books, 1996; first published 1978), 62. The text of *The Turner Diaries* can be found on the web, but respecting copyright is an issue, thus I do not list any site.
2. "McVeigh: Sorry for Deaths, but Defiant," *ABC News*, 9 June 2001, available on the web at http://abcnews.go.com/US/story?id=93140&page=1.
3. Donatella della Porta, Manuela Caiani, and Claudius Wagermann, *Mobilizing on the Extreme Right: Germany, Italy, and the United States* (Oxford: Oxford University Press, 2012), 71.
4. James Ridgeway, *Blood in the Face: The Ku Klux Klan, Aryan Nations, Nazi Skinheads, and the Rise of a New White Culture*, 2nd ed. (New York: Thunder's Mouth Press, 1995), 32–33, "Web of Racism" chart.
5. Arie Perliger, *Challengers from the Sidelines: Understanding America's Violent Far-Right* (West Point, NY: Combating Terrorism Center, 2012), 14–15, available on the web at https://ctc.usma.edu/app/uploads/2013/01/ChallengersFromtheSidelines.pdf.
6. Lou Michel and Dan Herbeck, *American Terrorist: Timothy McVeigh and the Oklahoma City Bombing* (New York: HarperCollins, 2001), chap. 4, loc. 1881–1889 of 8546, Kindle.
7. Michel and Herbeck, *American Terrorist*, chap. 6, loc. 2830 of 8546, Kindle.
8. Figure, "Deadly Attacks by Ideology and Year," *Terrorism in America after 9/11*, available on the New America website at https://www.newamerica.org/in-depth/terrorism-in-america/what-threat-united-states-today/.

9. Perliger, *Challengers from the Sidelines*, 22, Figures 4 and 4A.
10. Perliger, *Challengers from the Sidelines*, 31 and 34.
11. Dennis Tourish and Tim Wohlforth, *On the Edge: Political Cults Right and Left* (Abington, Oxon: Routledge, 2015; first published 2000), 57.
12. See Mark Potok, "The Year in Hate and Extremism," *Intelligence Report*, 2017 Spring Issue, 41, available on the SPLC website at https://www.splcenter.org/fighting-hate/intelligence-report/2016/year-hate-and-extremism. See as well https://www.splcenter.org/sites/default/files/intelligence_report_162.pdf and the newest hate group figures at https://www.splcenter.org/hate-map.
13. Potok, "The Year in Hate and Extremism."
14. Kevin Flynn and Gary Gerhardt, *The Silent Brotherhood* (New York: Signet, 1990), Prologue, loc. 182 of 1022, Kindle.
15. Jessie Daniels, "Race, Civil Rights, and Hate Speech in the Digital Age," in Anna Everett, ed., *Learning Race and Ethnicity: Youth and Digital Media* (Cambridge, MA: MIT Press, 2008), 132 and 134; and Daryl Johnson and Mark Potok, *Right-Wing Resurgence: How a Domestic Terrorist Threat Is Being Ignored* (Lanham, MD: Rowman & Littlefield, 2012), 207.
16. Robert L. Snow, *Terrorists among Us: The Militia Threat* (Cambridge, MA: Perseus, 1999), 109. Reuther estimate in Tourish and Wohlforth, *On the Edge*, 57.
17. North, in Mark Juergensmeyer, *Terror in the Mind of God: The Global Rise of Religious Violence*, 3rd ed. (Berkeley, CA: University of California Press, 2003), chap. 2, loc. 650 of 6988, Kindle.
18. Ellison in Jessica Stern, *Terror in the Name of God: Why Religious Militants Kill* (New York: HarperCollins, 2009), Jessica Stern, *Terror in the Name of God: Why Religious Militants Kill* (New York: HarperCollins, 2009), 18.
19. Aryan Nations, Church of Jesus Chris Christian, Declaration of Independence, 12 March 1996, available on the web at https://archive.org/details/AryanNationsDeclaration.
20. Peter Applebome, "Terror in Oklahoma: The Background, a Bombing Foretold, in Extreme-Right 'Bible,'" *New York Times*, 26 April 1995, available on the web at http://www.nytimes.com/1995/04/26/us/terror-in-oklahoma-the-background-a-bombing-foretold-in-extreme-right-bible.html.
21. "Gun control is also an important issue to Christian Identity supporters, since they believe that this is how the 'Jewish-UN-liberal conspirators,' as they call them, intend to eliminate the last possibilities of rebellion against centralized power." Jeurgensmeyer, *Terror in the Mind of God*, chap. 2, loc. 783 of 6988, Kindle.
22. MacDonald, *The Turner Diaries*, 160–61.
23. MacDonald, *The Turner Diaries*, 210.
24. See Jeurgensmeyer, *Terror in the Mind of God*, chap. 8, loc. 2957 of 6988, Kindle.
25. Jeurgensmeyer, *Terror in the Mind of God*, chap. 8, loc. 2963 of 6988, Kindle.
26. This definition adapts the FBI definition of hate crime as a "criminal offense

against a person or property motivated in whole or in part by an offender's bias against a race, religion, disability, sexual orientation, ethnicity, gender, or gender identity." See the FBI page on Hate Crimes at https://www.fbi.gov/about-us/investigate/civilrights/hate_crimes/overview.

27. On recent the ebb and flow of Klan membership, see Casey Williams, "How Anonymous Is Fighting White Supremacy Online?," *Huffington Post*, 27 April 2016, available on the web at https://www.huffingtonpost.com/entry/anonymous-shut-down-kkk-website_us_5720c204e4b0b49df6a9b333; and Mark Potok, "The Year in Hate and Extremism," Southern Poverty Law Center, 17 February 2016, available at https://www.splcenter.org/fighting-hate/intelligence-report/2016/year-hate-and-extremism.
28. Jesse McKinley, "Neo-Nazi Father Is Killed; Son, 10, Steeped in Beliefs, Is Accused," *New York Times*, 10 May 2011, available on the web at https://www.nytimes.com/2011/05/11/us/11nazi.html.
29. SPLC page on the National Socialist Movement at https://www.splcenter.org/fighting-hate/extremist-files/group/national-socialist-movement.
30. Flynn and Zwicker, *Silent Brotherhood*, Prologue, loc. 190 of 7022, Kindle.
31. See "Computer Millionaires Fund Hate: Carl Story, Vincent Bertollini and the 11th Hour Remnant Messenger" ADL story at https://web.archive.org/web/20121011200704/http://www.adl.org/tycoons/The_Ideology.asp.
32. Henry Schuster, "An Unholy Alliance," *CNN*, 29 March 2005, available on the web at http://www.cnn.com/2005/US/03/29/schuster.column/.
33. On their Aryan ties, see Jennifer Petersen, *Murder, the Media, and the Politics of Public Feelings: Remembering Matthew Shepard and James Byrd Jr.* (Bloomington, IN: Indiana University Press, 2011), chap. 3, loc. 1613–1631 of 3240, Kindle.
34. Noble, in Stern, *Terror in the Name of God*, Introduction, loc. 78 of 7593, Kindle.
35. Katherine Bishop, "Neo-Nazi Activity Is Arising among U.S. Youth," *New York Times*, 13 June 1988, available on the web at http://partners.nytimes.com/library/national/race/061388race-ra.html.
36. See Hammerskin Nation website at http://www.hammerskins.net/.
37. SPLC, "Tom Metzger," available on the SPLC website at https://www.splcenter.org/fighting-hate/extremist-files/individual/tom-metzger.
38. WAR Hotline, 27 June 1988, in Steven E. Atkins, *Encyclopedia of Right-Wing Extremism in Modern American History* (Santa Barbara, CA: ABC-CLIO, 2011), 55.
39. Declaration, in Tourish and Wohlforth, *On the Edge*, 63.
40. Perliger, *Challengers from the Sidelines*, 68.
41. Chip Berlet and Matthew N. Lyons, *Right Wing Populism in America: Too Close for Comfort* (New York: Guilford Press, 2000), chapter 14, available on the web at http://www.researchforprogress.us/rwpop/nwo.html.
42. Thompson, in Perliger, *Challengers from the Sidelines*, 29.
43. SPLC report of 4 January 2016, available on the web at https://www.spl

center.org/news/2016/01/04/antigovernment-militia-groups-grew-more-one-third-last-year.
44. Statistics for anti-abortion violence, threats of violence, and disruptions are taken from the National Abortion Federation, "NAF Violence and Disruption Statistics," 1977–2015, available on the web at http://5aa1b2xfmfh2e2mko3kk8rsx.wpengine.netdna-cdn.com/wp-content/uploads/2015-NAF-Violence-Disruption-Stats.pdf.
45. Juergensmeyer, *Terror in the Mind of God*, chap. 2, loc. 636 of 6988, Kindle.
46. Copies of the Army of God Manual, without the explicit bombing and arson instructions, can be found on the web on extreme pro-life sites.
47. "'White Rose' Activists Preach Violence against Abortion Clinics, Gays," *Church & State* (April 2001), available on the web at https://www.au.org/church-state/april-2001-church-state/people-events/april-2001-people-events.
48. Hill, in Stern, *Terror in the Name of God*, 167.
49. Alan Cooperman, "Is Terrorism Tied to Christian Sect?," *Washington Post*, 2 June 2003, available on the web at https://www.washingtonpost.com/archive/politics/2003/06/02/is-terrorism-tied-to-christian-sect/7510f762-4ac6-43b5-9b15-479a8cef16d4/?noredirect=on&utm_term=.8c251d428e63.
50. Michael Reynolds, "Homegrown Terror," *Bulletin of the Atomic Scientists* (November/December 2004), 48–57.
51. The full text of this letter is available on the web at http://www.foxnews.com/story/2001/04/26/mcveigh-apr-26-letter-to-fox-news.html.
52. Roof letter in Alan Blinder and Kevin Sack, "Dylann Roof, Addressing Court, Offers No Apology or Explanation for Massacre," *New York Times*, 4 January 2017, available on the web at https://www.nytimes.com/2017/01/04/us/dylann-roof-sentencing.html.
53. Elisagetta Povledo, "'Racial Hatred' Cited after African Immigrants Are Shot in Italy," *New York Times*, 3 February 2018, available on the web at https://www.nytimes.com/2018/02/03/world/europe/macerata-italy-shooting.html.
54. Katrin Bennhold, "Workers of Germany, Unite: The New Siren Call of the Far Right," *New York Times*, 5 February, 2018, available on the web at https://www.nytimes.com/2018/02/05/world/europe/afd-unions-social-democrats.html.
55. Dan Bilefsky and Steven Castle, "British Far-Right Group Exults over Attention from Trump," *New York Times*, 30 November 2017, available on the web at https://www.nytimes.com/2017/11/29/world/europe/britain-first-trump.html.

CHAPTER 13. NARCOTERRORISM

1. Jon Lee Anderson, "The Afterlife of Pablo Escobar: In Colombia, a Drug Lord's Posthumous Celebrity Brings Profits and Controversy, *New Yorker*, 5 March 2018, 50–59. On the web at https://www.newyorker.com/magazine/2018/03/05/the-afterlife-of-pablo-escobar.

2. Marighella, Minimanual of the Urban Guerrilla, on web at https://www.marxists.org/archive/marighella-carlos/1969/06/minimanual-urban-guerrilla/.
3. Mujib Mashal, "Afghan Taliban Awash in Heroin Cash, a Troubling Turn for War," *New York Times*, 29 October 2017, available on the web at https://www.nytimes.com/2017/10/29/world/asia/opium-heroin-afghanistan-taliban.html.
4. This figure is a reinterpretation of the one presented in Tamara Makarenko, "The Crime—Terror Continuum: Tracing the Interplay between Transnational Organized Crime and Terrorism," *Global Crime* 6, no. 1 (2004), 131. Thanks to my student Logan Nagel for introducing me on to the Makarenko continuum.
5. Makarenko, "The Crime—Terror Continuum," 131.
6. Makarenko, "The Crime—Terror Continuum," 138.
7. Power Point presentation, "The Nexus between Drugs and Terrorism," by Brian Dodd, chief, Counter-Narcoterrorism Operations Center Special Operations Division, DEA, available on the web at https://ndiastorage.blob.core.usgovcloudapi.net/ndia/2010/homeland/Dodd.pdf.
8. Mark Bowden, *Killing Pablo: The Hunt for the World's Greatest Outlaw* (New York: Atlantic Monthly Press, 2011), 11.
9. Bowden, *Killing Pablo*, 14.
10. Patrick Cockburn, "Farmer's Son Who Bribed and Murdered His Way into Drugs: Neither Government Forces nor Other Drug Traffickers Were Interested in Taking Pablo Escobar Alive," *Independent*, 2 December 1993, available on the web at http://www.independent.co.uk/news/world/farmers-son-who-bribed-and-murdered-his-way-into-drugs-neither-government-forces-nor-other-drug-1465001.html.
11. Letter, in Bowden, *Killing Pablo*, 52.
12. Anderson, "The Afterlife of Pablo Escobar."
13. Human Rights Watch, *World Report 1995*, available on the web at https://www.hrw.org/reports/1995/WR95/AMERICAS-03.htm#P157_60227.
14. Human Rights Watch, *World Report 2010*, 212, available on the web at https://www.hrw.org/sites/default/files/reports/wr2010.pdf.
15. Simón Trinidad interview with Leech, 14 June 2000, in Garry Leech, *The FARC: The Longest Insurgency* (London: Zed Books, 2012), 45.
16. Jorrit Kamminga, "Peace with the FARC: Integrating Drug-Fueled Guerrillas into Alternative Development Programs?," *CTC Sentinel* 6, no. 6 (June 2013), 27.
17. Quoted in Leech, *The FARC*, 2.
18. Villegas quoted in Steven Gill, "300 Guerrillas Deserted FARC since Institutional Peace Deal Was Rejected," Colombia Reports, 15 December 2016, available on the web at https://colombiareports.com/300-guerrillas-deserted-farc-since-initial-peace-deal-rejected-report/6/.
19. Max Fisher, "In Afghanistan Unwinnable War, What's the Best Loss to Hope For?," *New York Times*, 1 February 2018, available on the web at https://www.nytimes.com/2018/02/01/world/asia/afghanistan-war.html. Fisher regards

"the war as failed, American aims as largely unachievable and Afghanistan's future as only partly salvageable."

20. From interview project by the Toronto *Globe and Mail*, in Gretchen Peters, *Seeds of Terror: How Drugs, Thugs, and Crime Are Reshaping the Afghan War*, 2nd ed. (New York: Picador, 2010), chap. 4, loc. 1885 of 6579, Kindle.
21. Peters, *Seeds of Terror*, chap. 1, loc. 222–25 of 6579, Kindle.
22. Edward Follis and Douglas Century, *The Dark Art: My Undercover Life in Global Narco-Terrorism* (New York: Berkley/Penguin, 2014), 187–88.
23. Official, in Peters, *Seeds of Terror*, chap. 6, loc. 2529 of 6579, Kindle.
24. UN Assistance Mission in Afghanistan (UNAMA) reports on "Protection of Civilians in Armed Conflict," 2009–2015, can be found on the UN website at http://www.ohchr.org/EN/Countries/AsiaRegion/Pages/HRReports.aspx.
25. Sebastian Junger, "America's Forgotten War," *Vanity Fair*, April 2006, available on the web at http://www.vanityfair.com/news/2006/04/junger200604.
26. Human Rights Watch, *World Report 2008: Events of 2007*, 238, available on the web at https://www.hrw.org/legacy/wr2k8/pdfs/wr2k8_web.pdf.
27. "Afghanistan: Harrowing Accounts Emerge of the Taliban's Reign of Terror in Kunduz," 1 October 2015, available on the Amnesty International website at https://www.amnesty.org/en/latest/news/2015/10/afghanistan-harrowing-accounts-emerge-of-the-talibans-reign-of-terror-in-kunduz/.
28. Frank G. Hoffman, "Hybrid vs. Compound War," *Armed Forces Journal*, 1 October 2009, available on the web at http://armedforcesjournal.com/hybrid-vs-compound-war/.
29. Wankal, in Peters, *Seeds of Terror*, chap. 1, loc. 356 of 6579, Kindle.
30. Sylvia Longmire, *Cartel: The Coming Invasion of Mexico's Drug Wars* (New York: St. Martin's Press, 2011), 122.
31. George W. Grayson, *The Evolution of Los Zetas in Mexico and Central America: Sadism as an Instrument of Cartel Warfare* (Carlisle, PA: Strategic Studies Institute and U.S. Army War College Press, 2014), 37, Figure 3, available on the web at http://ssi.armywarcollege.edu/pdffiles/pub1195.pdf.
32. U.S. Department of Justice, National Drug Intelligence Center, *National Drug Threat Assessment 2008* (October 2007), available on the web at https://www.justice.gov/archive/ndic/pubs25/25921/25921p.pdf.
33. For some *narcocorrido* lyrics, see "The 10 Best Narcocorrido Songs," Complex, available on the web at http://www.complex.com/music/2012/05/the-10-best-narcocorrido-songs/.
34. Ioan Grillo, "Behind Mexico's Wave of Beheadings," *Time*, 8 September 2008, available on the web at http://content.time.com/time/world/article/0,8599,1839576,00.html.
35. Tim Johnson, "Why Are Beheadings So Popular with Mexico's Drug Gangs?," McClatchy News Service, Washington, DC, 1 April 2010, available on the web at http://www.mcclatchydc.com/news/nation-world/world/article24578650.html#storylink=cpy.
36. Hal Brands, *Mexico's Narco-Insurgency and U.S. Counterdrug Policy*, U.S.

Army, Strategy Studies Institute (May 2009), 5, available on the web at https://ssi.armywarcollege.edu/pubs/display.cfm?pubID=918.
37. Tracy Wilkinson, "Calderón Delivers Blunt View of Drug Cartels' Sway in Mexico," *Los Angeles Times*, 4 August 2010, available on the web at http://articles.latimes.com/2010/aug/04/world/la-fg-mexico-Calderón-20100805.

CHAPTER 14. HOMELAND SECURITY

1. Juror John Steger, in AP, "No Conviction for Student in Terror Case," *New York Times*, 11 June 2004, available on the web at http://www.nytimes.com/2004/06/11/us/no-conviction-for-student-in-terror-case.html?src=pm.
2. Al-Kidd, in Adam Liptak, "Threats and Responses: The Detainees: For Post-9/11 Material Witness, It Is a Terror of a Different Kind," *New York Times*, 19 August 2004, available on the web at http://www.nytimes.com/2004/08/19/us/threats-responses-detainees-for-post-9-11-material-witness-it-terror-different.html.
3. Geoffrey R. Stone, *Perilous Times: Free Speech in Wartime from the Sedition Act of 1798 to the War on Terrorism* (New York: W. W. Norton, 2004), 5.
4. A complete transcript of Executive Order 9066 can be found on the web at https://www.ourdocuments.gov/doc.php?doc=74&page=transcript.
5. DeWitt, in T. A. Frail, "The Injustice of Japanese-American Internment Camps Resonates Strongly to This Day," *Smithsonian Magazine*, January/February 2017, available on the web at http://www.smithsonianmag.com/history/injustice-japanese-americans-internment-camps-resonates-strongly-180961422/.
6. Truman, in David McCullough, *Truman* (New York: Simon and Schuster, 1992), 553.
7. The text of Executive Order 12947 can be found on the Treasury Department website at https://www.treasury.gov/resource-center/sanctions/Documents/12947.pdf.
8. The text of AEDPA can be found on the congressional website at https://www.congress.gov/bill/104th-congress/senate-bill/735/text/enr.
9. Hertz and Liebman, in Anthony Gregory, *The Power of Habeas Corpus in America* (Cambridge: Cambridge University Press, 2013), 177.
10. Lincoln Caplan, "The Destruction of Defendants' Rights," *New Yorker*, 21 June 2015, available on the web at http://www.newyorker.com/news/news-desk/the-destruction-of-defendants-rights.
11. The USA Patriot Act can be found in its entirely on the website of the Government Printing Office at https://www.gpo.gov/fdsys/pkg/BILLS-107hr3162enr/pdf/BILLS-107hr3162enr.pdf.
12. Scott quote at "OnTheIssues: Bobby Scott on Homeland Security," available on the web at http://www.ontheissues.org/VA/Bobby_Scott_Homeland_Security.htm.
13. Todd Hinnen, acting assistant attorney general for national security, statement to the House Judiciary Subcommittee on Crime, 30 March 2011,

available on the web at http://www.justice.gov/nsd/opa/pr/testimony/2011/nsd-testimony-110330.html.
14. Susan N. Herman, *Taking Liberties: The War on Terror and the Erosion of American Democracy* (New York: Oxford University Press, 2011), 113.
15. Radley Balko, "Surprise! Controversial Patriot Act Power Now Overwhelmingly Used in Drug Investigations," *Washington Post*, 29 October 2014, available on the web at https://www.washingtonpost.com/news/the-watch/wp/2014/10/29/surprise-controversial-patriot-act-power-now-overwhelmingly-used-in-drug-investigations/?utm_term=.619a1a012dfe.
16. Warrants for "sneak-and-peek" searches from the annual *Report of the Director of the Administrative Office of the United States Courts on Applications for Delayed-Notice Search Warrants and Extensions*, 2007–2016. These reports can be accessed on the U.S. government website at http://www.uscourts.gov/statistics-reports/analysis-reports/delayed-notice-search-warrant-report.
17. The figure for 2000 is taken from the website of the Electronic Privacy Information Center (EPIC) at https://epic.org/privacy/nsl/. The figures for 2003–2011 come from U. S. Department of Justice, Office of the Inspector General, *A Review of the Federal Bureau of Investigation's Use of National Security Letters: Assessment of Progress in Implementing Recommendations and Examination of Use in 2007 through 2009*, August 2014, 65, available on the web at https://oig.justice.gov/reports/2014/s1408.pdf. Figures for 2015 and 2017 come from Office of the Director of National Intelligence, *Statistical Transparency Report Regarding Use of National Security Authorities, Calendar Year 2017*, 38, available on the web at https://www.dni.gov/files/documents/icotr/2018-ASTR——CY2017——FINAL-for-Release-5.4.18.pdf.
18. From U. S. Department of Justice, Office of the Inspector General, *A Review of the Federal Bureau of Investigation's Use of National Security Letters* (March 2007), 39. On the web at https://oig.justice.gov/reports/2016/o1601b.pdf.
19. Judge Susan Illston declared the NSLs unconstitutional in a 2013 ruling, but declared in April 2016 that amendment of the law "cures the deficiencies previously identified by this court." Elizabeth Warmerdam, "Clinton-Appointed Judge Supports Gag Orders on FBI National Security Letter Recipients," AllGov, 23 April 2016, available on the web at http://www.allgov.com/news/controversies/clinton-appointed-judge-supports-gag-orders-on-fbi-national-security-letter-recipients-160423?news=858702.
20. Norman Abrams, "The Material Support Terrorism Offenses: Perspectives Derived from the (Early) Model Penal Code," *Journal of National Security Law & Policy* 1, no. 1 (2005), 5–6.
21. See, for example, Ronald L. Carson and Mark S. Voelpel, "Material Witness and Material Injustice," *Washington University Law Quarterly* 58, no. 1 (1980), available on the web at http://openscholarship.wustl.edu/cgi/viewcontent.cgi?article=2401&context=law_lawreview.
22. ACLU, "US: Misuse of the Material Witness Statute," Amicus Curiae brief

filed with the Supreme Court, 28 January 2011 posting, available on the web at https://www.hrw.org/news/2011/01/28/us-misuse-material-witness-statute.
23. Rachel Stevens, "Center for National Security Studies v. United States Department of Justice: Keeping the USA Patriot Act in Check One Material Witness at a Time," *North Carolina Law Review* 81, no. 5 (June 2003), 2175, available on the web at https://scholarship.law.unc.edu/nclr/vol81/iss5/.
24. ISE website at https://www.ise.gov/about-ise.
25. The text of this law can be found on the web at https://www.gpo.gov/fdsys/pkg/PLAW-110publ55/html/PLAW-110publ55.htm.
26. Dana Priest and William Arkin, "Top Secret America: A Washington Post Investigation," *Washington Post*, 19 July 2010 and 3 October 2010, available on the web at http://www.pulitzer.org/cms/sites/default/files/content/washpost_tsa_item1.pdf.
27. Michael B. Kraft and Edward Marks, *U.S. Government Counterterrorism: A Guide to Who Does What* (Boca Raton, FL: CRC Press, 2012), 12.
28. Kraft and Marks, *U.S. Government Counterterrorism*, xxviii.
29. This act can be found on the web at https://www.congress.gov/107/plaws/publ40/PLAW-107publ40.pdf.
30. Cost figures from Neil McCarthy, "The Financial Cost of U.S. Involvement in Afghanistan," *Forbes*, 24 August 2017, available on the web at https://www.forbes.com/sites/niallmccarthy/2017/08/24/the-financial-cost-of-u-s-involvement-in-afghanistan-infographic/#45f700f51ee3.
31. Department of Defense casualty figures on the web at http://www.defense.gov/casualty.pdf. These Afghan war totals figures combine those for Operation Enduring Freedom and Operation Freedom's Sentinel.
32. Watson Institute on International and Public Affairs, Brown University, "Costs of War, Afghan Civilians," available on the web at http://watson.brown.edu/costsofwar/costs/human/civilians/afghan.
33. Max Fisher, "In Afghanistan's Unwinnable War, What's the Best Loss to Hope For?," *New York Times*, 1 February 2018, available on the web at https://www.nytimes.com/2018/02/01/world/asia/afghanistan-war.html.
34. Department of Defense casualty figures available on the web at http://www.defense.gov/casualty.pdf. The figures here are those for Operation Iraqi Freedom and Operation New Dawn.
35. Neta C. Crawford, "A Summary of the $5.6 Trillion in Costs for the US Wars in Iraq, Syria, Afghanistan and Pakistan, and Post-9/11 Veterans Care and Homeland Security," Watson Institute, International & Public Affairs, Costs of War, November 1917, 1, available on the web at https://watson.brown.edu/costsofwar/files/cow/imce/papers/2017/Costs%20of%20U.S.%20Post-9_11%20NC%20Crawford%20FINAL%20.pdf.
36. For Article 75, see *Protocols Additional to the Geneva Conventions of 12 August 1949* (Geneva: International Red Cross, 2010), 53–54, available on the web at https://www.icrc.org/eng/assets/files/other/icrc_002_0321.pdf.
37. Jane Mayer, *The Dark Side: The Inside Story of How the War on Terror Turned*

into a War on American Ideals (New York: Doubleday, 2009), chap. 5, loc. 1567 of 7740, Kindle.
38. Text of 7 February 2002 order in Mayer, The Dark Side, chap. 6, loc. 2436 of 7740, Kindle.
39. Text of the memo in Mayer, The Dark Side, chap. 7, loc. 2969–2971 of 7740, Kindle.
40. Mayer, The Dark Side, chap. 7, loc. 2968 of 7740, Kindle.
41. Yoo, in Mayer, The Dark Side, chap. 7, loc. 3002 of 7740, Kindle.
42. To view the very impressive floor statement by Senator John McCain on Senate Intelligence Committee Report on CIA Interrogating Methods, 9 December 2014, see the video that is available on the web at https://www.nbcnews.com/politics/politics-news/john-mccain-cia-report-proves-what-i-know-experience-n264806.
43. Executive Order 13491, 22 January 2009, can be found on the web at https://www.govinfo.gov/content/pkg/CFR-2010-title3-vol1/pdf/CFR-2010-title3-vol1-eo13491.pdf.
44. Jenna Johnson, "Donald Trump on Waterboarding: 'If It Doesn't Work, They Deserve It Anyway,'" Washington Post, 23 November 2015, available on the web at https://www.washingtonpost.com/news/post-politics/wp/2015/11/23/donald-trump-on-waterboarding-if-it-doesnt-work-they-deserve-it-anyway/.
45. Figures taken from Micah Zenko, "Obama's Embrace of Drone Strikes Will Be a Lasting Legacy," New York Times, 12 January 2016, available on the web at http://www.nytimes.com/roomfordebate/2016/01/12/reflecting-on-obamas-presidency/obamas-embrace-of-drone-strikes-will-be-a-lasting-legacy.
46. Daniel J. Rosenthalloren and Loren de Jonge Schulman, "Trump's Secret War on Terror: Drone Strikes Continue to Spread–Away from Public Scrutiny or Congressional Oversight," Atlantic, 10 August 2018, available on the web at https://www.theatlantic.com/international/archive/2018/08/trump-war-terror-drones/567218/.
47. See Gallup, "In U.S., 65% Support Drone Attacks on Terrorists Abroad," 25 March 2013, available on the web at http://www.gallup.com/poll/161474/support-drone-attacks-terrorists-abroad.aspx.
48. Pew Research Center, Global Opposition to U.S. Surveillance and Drones, but Limited Harm to America's Image, July 2104, available on the web at http://www.pewglobal.org/2014/07/14/global-opposition-to-u-s-surveillance-and-drones-but-limited-harm-to-americas-image/.
49. Glenn Greenwald, "Nobody Knows the Identities of the 150 People Killed by U.S. in Somalia, but Most Are Certain They Deserved It," Intercept, 8 March 2016, available on the web at https://theintercept.com/2016/03/08/nobody-knows-the-identity-of-the-150-people-killed-by-u-s-in-somalia-but-most-are-certain-they-deserved-it/.
50. Statements here about Obama's policies and procedures are drawn from David Cole, "The Drone Presidency," New York Review of Books, 18 August

2016, available on the web at http://www.nybooks.com/articles/2016/08/18/the-drone-presidency/.

51. The full text of Eisenhower's military-industrial complex speech is available on the website of the Avalon Project, Yale Law School, at http://avalon.law.yale.edu/20th_century/eisenhower001.asp.

52. The contrast between the militarization and militarism stressed here was inspired by Richard Kohn's thought-provoking article "The Danger of Militarization in an Endless 'War' on Terrorism," *Journal of Military History* 73, no. 1 (January 2009), 177–208.

53. Kohn, "The Danger of Militarization in an Endless 'War' on Terrorism," 180–81.

54. Kucinich, in Herman, *Taking Liberties*, 39.

CHAPTER 15. CONFRONTING TERRORISM

1. Audrey Kurth Cronin, "How Fighting Ends: Asymmetric Wars, Terrorism, and Suicide Bombing," in Hew Strachan and Holger Aflerbach, eds., *How Fighting Ends: A History of Surrender* (Oxford: Oxford University Press, 2012), 421.

2. Daniel Fromkin, "The Strategy of Terrorism," *Foreign Affairs* 53, no. 4 (July 1975), 688.

3. Aristotle, *Rhetoric*, trans. W. Rhys Roberts, available on the web at http://classics.mit.edu/Aristotle/rhetoric.mb.txt.

4. Quoted in Aric Jenkins, "Read President Trump's Speech Claiming the Press Doesn't Report Terror Attacks," *Time*, 6 February 2017, available on the web at http://time.com/4661658/donald-trump-terror-attacks-speech-macdill-air-force-base/.

5. It is estimated that in late 2016 around 4,100 Europeans from France, Germany, the United Kingdom, Belgium, Sweden, Austria, the Netherlands, Spain, Denmark, and Italy were foreign fighters in Syria and Iraq. At this time, about 250 had left the U.S. to become foreign fighters, but not all had arrived. Also, many of these Americans went to fight against IS. See http://www.pbs.org/wgbh/frontline/article/how-europe-left-itself-open-to-terrorism/ for figures on Europeans, and http://www.npr.org/2015/09/29/444398846/report-250-americans-have-gone-to-syria-and-iraq-to-fight on the American count.

6. Barack Obama, "Remarks by the President on the Administration's Approach to Counterterrorism," 6 December 2016, full text available on the web at https://obamawhitehouse.archives.gov/the-press-office/2016/12/06/remarks-president-administrations-approach-counterterrorism (italics mine).

7. Cronin, *How Terrorism Ends*, 75 and 213, Figure A.1.

8. Cronin, *How Terrorism Ends*, 244.

9. Seth G. Jones and Martin C. Libicki, *How Terrorist Groups End: Lessons for Countering al Qa'ida* (Santa Monica, CA: RAND Corporation, 2008), 19,

Figure 2.1, available on the web at https://www.rand.org/pubs/monographs/MG741-1.html.
10. Jones and Libicki, *How Terrorist Groups End*, 138.
11. The figures on Islamist and far-right terrorism, from a study by New America, are available on the web at https://www.newamerica.org/in-depth/terrorism-in-america/what-threat-united-states-today/.
12. Figures from the National Highway and Traffic Safety Administration at https://www-fars.nhtsa.dot.gov/Main/index.aspx.
13. Figures from the Brady Campaign at http://www.bradycampaign.org/key-gun-violence-statistics.
14. A good source for figures on Chicago gun deaths is HeyJackass at http://heyjackass.com/.
15. For figures on gang deaths, see the calculations of the National Gang Center at https://www.nationalgangcenter.gov/survey-analysis/measuring-the-extent-of-gang-problems.
16. See the study by New America: https://www.newamerica.org/in-depth/terrorism-in-america/what-threat-united-states-today/.
17. For weather death statistics, see the National Weather Service site at https://www.weather.gov/safety/lightning-victims.
18. The Jewish Virtual Library has compiled figures at http://www.jewishvirtuallibrary.org/statistics-on-incidents-of-terrorism-worldwide.
19. "National Consortium for the Study of Terrorism and Responses to Terrorism: Annex of Statistical Information, 2015," U.S. Department of State, available on the web at https://www.state.gov/j/ct/rls/crt/2015/257526.htm.
20. Figures extrapolated from data set provided at http://www.datagraver.com/case/people-killed-by-terrorism-per-year-in-western-europe-1970–2015. This graph is based on numbers from the START Global Terrorism Database, home page at https://www.start.umd.edu/gtd/.
21. Leon Trotsky, "Why Marxists Oppose Individual Terrorism," available on the Marxist Internet Archive at https://www.marxists.org/archive/trotsky/1911/11/tia09.htm.
22. Karl Heinzen, "Murder," in Walter Laqueur, ed., *Voices of Terrorism: Manifestos, Writings and Manuals of Al Qaeda, Hamas, and other Terrorists from around the World and throughout the Ages* (New York: Reed Press, 2004), 62.

SUGGESTED FURTHER READING

CHAPTER 1: ON TERRORISM

A must-read study on terrorism is Bruce Hoffman, *Inside Terrorism*, 3rd ed. (Columbia University Press, 2017). Good treatments of the history of terrorism include Gérard Chaliand and Arnaud Blin, eds., *The History of Terrorism: From Antiquity to ISIS*, rev. ed. (University of California Press, 2016); Walter Laqueur, *A History of Terrorism*, expanded ed. (Columbia University Press, 2016); and Randal Law, *Terrorism: A History*, 2nd ed. (Polity, 2016). I have one trouble with the Law book: I believe he overemphasizes assassination as terrorism per se. For a work on assassination, see Franklin L. Ford, *Political Murder: From Tyrannicide to Terrorism* (Harvard University Press, 1987). Works on the psychology of terrorism are of extreme interest and can be contentious. See Walter Reich, ed., *Origins of Terrorism: Psychologies, Ideologies, Theologies, States of Mind* (Woodrow Wilson Center Press, 1998), and Jerrold M. Post, *The Mind of the Terrorist: The Psychology of Terrorism from the IRA to al-Qaeda* (St. Martin's Press, 2007). John Horgan, *The Psychology of Terrorism* (Routledge, 2014), provides the most sophisticated discussion. Audrey Kurth Cronin, *How Terrorism Ends: Understanding the Decline and Demise of Terrorism Campaigns* (Princeton University Press, 2009), stands as the benchmark for the subject she addresses.

CHAPTER 2: RULE BY FEAR

We addressed three examples of state regime terrorism that dovetail into one another. For the Reign of Terror, see Peter McPhee, *Liberty or Death: The French Revolution* (Yale University Press, 2016), and David Andress, *The Terror: The Merciless War for Freedom in Revolutionary France* (Farrar, Straus and Giroux, 2006). David P. Jordan, *The Revolutionary Career of Maximilien Robespierre* (University of Chicago

Press, 1989), deals with the signature proponent of the terror, Robespierre. For insight on the Stalinist purges, see Robert Conquest, *The Great Terror: A Reassessment* (Oxford University Press, 2008), and Sheila Fitzpatrick, *Everyday Stalinism: Ordinary Life in Extraordinary Times* (Oxford University Press, 1999). Oleg K. Khlevniuk, *Stalin: New Biography of a Dictator* (Yale University Press, 2015), offers an authoritative, and recent, biography of Stalin. Moving to the Chinese Cultural Revolution, see Frank Dikötter, *The Cultural Revolution: A People's History, 1962–1976* (Bloomsbury Press, 2016), and Roderick MacFarquhar and Michael Schoenhals, *Mao's Last Revolution* (Belknap Press, 2008). Mao makes repeated appearances in this book; get to know him in Maurice Meisner, *Mao Zedong: A Political and Intellectual Portrait* (Polity, 2006).

CHAPTER 3: WAR ON CIVILIANS

The humanitarian law of war is fundamental to this entire volume, and certainly to this chapter. On this important subject see Michael Howard and George Andreopoulos, *The Laws of War: Constraints on Warfare in the Western World* (Yale University Press, 1997); Stephen C. Neff, *War and the Law of Nations: A General History* (Cambridge University Press, 2005); and Christine Chinkin and Mary Kaldor, *International Law and New Wars* (Cambridge University Press, 2017). Wayne E. Lee has written a fascinating study of the culture values that underwrite restraint or license excess in his *Barbarians and Brothers: Atrocity and Restraint in Anglo-American Warfare, 1500–1865* (Oxford University Press, 2011). On the French conquest of Algeria, see Jennifer E. Sessions, *By Sword and Plow: France and the Conquest of Algeria* (Cornell University Press, 2014). On the way the North made war on civilian resources during the Civil War, including Sherman's March to the Sea, consult Mark Grimsley, *The Hard Hand of War* (Cambridge University Press, 2005). Concerning the bombing of civilians by the Allies during World War II, see Richard Overy, *The Bombing War: Europe, 1939–1945* (Allen Lane, 2013), and Conrad C. Crane, *American Airpower Strategy in World War II: Bombs, Cities, Civilians, and Oil* (University Press of Kansas, 2016). The return of organized rape as a weapon of military terrorism is a sad commentary on the "progress" of civilization; read, with a mixture of compassion and outrage, Alexandra Stiglmayer, ed., *Mass Rape: The War against Women in Bosnia-Herzegovina*, trans. Marion Faber (University of Nebraska Press, 1994).

CHAPTER 4: WHITE KNIGHTS

In Chapter 4 we focus on White supremacy and the oppression of African-Americans from Reconstruction to 1965. However, Native Americans were also the targets of social terrorism in the United States; see Gary Clayton Anderson, *Ethnic Cleansing and the Indians: The Crime that Should Haunt America* (University of Oklahoma Press, 2014), and Jeffrey Ostler, *Surviving Genocide: Native Nations and the United States from the American Revolution to Bleeding Kansas* (Yale University Press, 2019). Concerning the Ku Klux Klan, see Wyn Craig Wade, *The Fiery Cross: The Ku Klux Klan in America* (Simon and Schuster, 1987), for the basics. For the origins of the Klan, see Elaine Frantz Parsons, *Ku-Klux: The Birth of the Klan during Reconstruction* (University of North Carolina Press, 2016). James Hogue traces the use of violence by Whites in Louisiana to repress the Black population and take over the state government in *Uncivil War: Five New Orleans Street Battles and the Rise and Fall of Radical Reconstruction* (Louisiana State University Press, 2006). For the rise and fall of the second Klan, see Linda Gordon, *The Second Coming of the KKK* (Liveright, 2017). On the third, anti-civil-rights Klan and the triumph of the civil rights movement, see Juan Williams, *Eyes on the Prize: America's Civil Rights Years, 1954–1965* (Penguin, repr. 2013). For a more close-up view of critical events, see Derek Charles Catsam, *Freedom's Main Line: The Journey of Reconciliation and the Freedom Rides* (University Press of Kentucky, 2008), and Bruce Hartford, *The Selma Voting Rights Struggle and the March to Montgomery* (Westwind Writers, 2014). David J. Garrow highlights Martin Luther King, Jr., in *Bearing the Cross: Martin Luther King, Jr., and the Southern Christian Leadership Conference* (Open Road Media, repr. 2015).

CHAPTER 5: PROPAGANDA OF THE DEED

First-wave radical terrorism takes center stage in Chapter 5. My particular approach to the onset of first-wave terrorism owes much to two enlightening books: Charles Tilly, *The Contentious French: Four Centuries of Popular Struggle* (Belknap Press, 1989), on repertoires of violence; and Mark Traugott, *The Insurgent Barricade* (University of California Press, 2010), on the role of mass crowds and the barricades. The major scholar in terrorist studies, Marc Sageman, argues for pushing the origins of the first wave back to the French Revolution in his *Turning to Political Violence: The Emergence of Terrorism* (University of Pennsylvania Press, 2017). Martin Miller, *The Foundations of Modern Terrorism* (Cambridge University Press, rev. ed. 2012), also traces it back to the French Revolution. Much, but by no means all, radical terrorism during the first wave can be ascribed to anarchists; see Richard Bach Jensen, *The Battle against Anarchist Terrorism: An International History, 1878–1934* (Cambridge University Press, 2013). For more information on first-wave Russian terrorism, see Ana Siljak, *Angel of Vengeance: The Girl Who Shot the Governor of St. Petersburg and Sparked the Age of Assassination* (St. Martin's Press, 2008), and Anna Geifman, *Thou Shalt Kill: Revolutionary Terrorism in Russia, 1894–1917* (Princeton University Press, 1995). On aspects of the terrorism that afflicted France, see Constance Bantman, *The French Anarchists in London, 1880–1914: Exile and Transnationalism in the First Globalisation* (Liverpool University Press, 2013), and John Merriman, *The Dynamite Club: How a Bombing in Fin-de-Siècle Paris Ignited the Age of Modern Terror* (Yale University Press, 2009). To learn about the deadliest act of anarchist terrorism in the United States during the first wave, see Beverly Gage, *The Day Wall Street Exploded: A Story of America in Its First Age of Terror* (Oxford University Press, 2009). On the assassination of Archduke Franz-Ferdinand, an attack of the greatest possible importance, see David James Smith, *One Morning in Sarajevo: 28 June 1914* (Orion, 2009).

CHAPTER 6: SECOND-WAVE ETHNO-NATIONALIST TERRORISM

Our treatment of the second wave begins with ethno-nationalist terrorism, and we center on the FLN and the PIRA. For an overview of the Algerian War of Independence, see Alistair Horne's classic *A Savage War of Peace: Algeria, 1954–1962*

(New York Review Books, repr. 2011; originally published 1977), and Martin Evans's excellent *Algeria: France's Undeclared War* (Oxford University Press, 2013). An American pioneer of terrorist studies, Martha Crenshaw Hutchinson first turned her attention to the FLN in her *Revolutionary Terrorism: The FLN in Algeria* (Hoover Institution Press, 1978). For two very different perspectives on the struggle, see Zohra Drif, *Inside the Battle of Algiers: Memoir of a Woman Freedom Fighter*, trans. Andrew Farrand (Just World Books, 2017), and Paul Aussaresses, *The Battle of the Casbah: Terrorism and Counterterrorism in Algeria, 1955–1957*, trans. Robert L. Miller (Enigma Books, 2002), the story told by a French intelligence officer who carried out torture against Muslim Algerians. On the Troubles in Northern Ireland and the part the PIRA played in those decades of violence, see Tim Pat Coogan, *The Troubles: Ireland's Ordeal and the Search for Peace* (Arrow Books, 2002), and Richard English, *Armed Struggle: The History of the IRA* (Oxford University Press, 2003). The Protestant UVF paramilitary is the subject of Aaron Edwards, *UVF: Behind the Mask* (Merrion Press, 2017). More specific takes on the Troubles come out of Peter Pringle and Philip Jacobsen, *Those Are Real Bullets: Bloody Sunday, Derry, 1972* (Grove Press, 2002), and David Beresford, *Ten Men Dead: The Story of the 1981 Irish Hunger Strike* (Atlantic Monthly Press, repr. 1997).

CHAPTER 7: TALES OF TWO TRAGEDIES

The Israeli-Palestinian conflict has produced acts of terrorism on both sides. For an overview of this complicated and controversial subject, with all its trials and tragedies, see Benny Morris, *Righteous Victims: A History of the Zionist-Arab Conflict, 1881–2001* (Knopf, repr. 1999); Shlomo Ben-Ami, *Scars of War, Wounds of Peace: The Israeli-Arab Tragedy* (Oxford University Press, 2006); and Ari Shavit, *My Promised Land: The Triumph and Tragedy of Israel* (Spiegel & Grau, 2013). Twenty years after Israel became an independent state, the PLO embarked on its campaigns of radical terrorism; for some of the basics, see Barry Rubin, *Revolution Until Victory?: The Politics and History of the PLO*, rev. ed. (Harvard University Press, 1996), and for a discussion of its leader see Bassam Abu Sharif, *Arafat and the Dream of Palestine: An Insider's Account* (St. Martin's Press, 2009). Ami Pedahzur and Arie Perliger, *Jewish Terrorism in Israel* (Columbia University Press, 2009), provides a unique survey of terrorism by Jewish actors. Nur Masalha, *The Palestinian Nakba: Decolonising History, Narrating the Subaltern, Reclaiming Memory* (Zed Books, 2012), offers a Palestinian's view of the fate of his people at the hands of Israel. Steve Reeve recounts the Munich Massacre of 1972 and the Israeli response in *One Day in September: The Full Story of the 1972 Munich Olympics Massacre and the Israeli Revenge Operation "Wrath of God"* (Arcade, 2000). Ze'ev Schiff and Ehud Ya'ari, *Israel's Lebanon War*, trans. and ed. Ina Friedman (Simon and Schuster, 1984), recounts the history of Israel's ill-fated invasion of Lebanon in 1982, the event that ends Chapter 7.

CHAPTER 8: URBAN GUERRILLAS

Two authors have written recent works that trace the rise and fall of the Tupamaros, the Marxist terrorist group that defined the urban guerrilla: Pablo Brum,

The Robin Hood Guerrillas: The Epic Journey of Uruguay's Tupamaros (CreateSpace Independent Publishing Platform, 2014), and Lindsey Churchill, *Becoming the Tupamaros: Solidarity and Transnational Revolutionaries in Uruguay and the United States* (Vanderbilt University Press, 2014). The United States had its own would-be urban guerrillas, the Weather Underground. Bryan Burrough takes on the entire phenomenon of New Left radical groups in *Days of Rage: America's Radical Underground, the FBI, and the Forgotten Age of Revolutionary Violence* (Penguin, 2015). Jeremy Peter Varon explores both the Weathermen and the German Red Army Faction (RAF) in *Bringing the War Home: The Weather Underground, the Red Army Faction, and Revolutionary Violence in the Sixties* (University of California Press, 2004). For an authoritative account of the RAF, see Stefan Aust, *Baader-Meinhof: The Inside Story of the R.A.F.*, trans. Anthea Bell, rev. ed. (Oxford University Press, 2009). The Italian Red Brigades command much attention; for works with a broad focus, see Robert Meade, Jr., *Red Brigades: The Story of Italian Terrorism* (Palgrave, 1990), and David Moss, *The Politics of Left-Wing Violence in Italy, 1969–85* (St. Martin's Press, 1989). Richard Drake describes the trials of those accused of the kidnapping and murder of Aldo Moro in *The Aldo Moro Murder Case* (Harvard University Press, 1995). Another work advances a convincing argument that the mind-set of Red Brigades terrorists included important tenets that mirror religious attitudes and doctrine: Alessandro Orsini, *Anatomy of the Red Brigades: The Religious Mind-Set of Modern Terrorists*, trans. Sarah J. Nodes (Cornell University Press, 2011).

CHAPTER 9: ISLAMIST TERRORISM

The noted, and controversial, historian and military commentator Andrew Bacevich recently published *America's War for the Greater Middle East: A Military History* (Random House, 2017). This volume covers American military involvement in what he calls the Greater Middle East—North Africa to Afghanistan—from 1980 to 2017, the period we identify as the age of third-wave Islamist terrorism. Whether you agree with it all or not, it is an important book. Islamism combines a fundamentalist form of Islam with an insistence that government promote and enforce that fundamentalism on its population; radical Islamists are willing to use violence to bring about this vision of religion and politics. For a general overview, see Tarek Osman, *Islamism: A History of Political Islam from the Fall of the Ottoman Empire to the Rise of ISIS* (Yale University Press, 2017). Two books put radical Islamism in the context of other forms of religious violence: Mark Juergensmeyer, *Terror in the Mind of God: The Global Rise of Religious Violence*, 4th ed. (University of California Press, 2017), and Jessica Stern, *Terror in the Name of God: Why Religious Militants Kill* (Ecco, 2004). On the nature and history of Islamist theology and ideology, see Mary Habeck, *Knowing the Enemy: Jihadist Ideology and the War on Terror* (Yale University Press, 2006). John L. Esposito and Dalia Mogahed, *Who Speaks for Islam?: What a Billion Muslims Really Think* (Gallup Press, 2007), employs polling data to reveal religious, political, and social opinion among the *ummah* around the globe. One element of Islamist ideology, representing a disturbingly high percentage of Muslim opinion, is the idea that the Christian West is inherently hostile to Islam.

For a classic study of the clash of civilizations, see Samuel Huntington, *The Clash of Civilizations and the Remaking of World Order* (Simon and Schuster, 2011). Bernard Lewis offers another view of such cultural difference and the tensions it creates in *What Went Wrong?: The Clash between Islam and Modernity in the Middle East* (Harper, 2003). Terror management theory (TMT), while it may seem extreme to some, offers another explanation of the way in which shared cultural values explain identity and solidarity within one culture and its hostility toward those outside that culture. For this view used to explain the American reaction to 9/11, see Tom Pyszczynski, Sheldon Solomon, and Jeff Greenberg, *In the Wake of 9/11: The Psychology of Terror* (American Psychological Association, 2003). We describe the process by which average individuals become violent extremists as "radicalization." This is a major subject in the study of radical Islamists. Horgan's *The Psychology of Terrorism*, mentioned already, deals with the state of our knowledge on radicalization. See as well Farad Khosrokhaver, *Radicalization: Why Some People Choose the Path of Violence*, trans. Jane Marie Todd (New Press, 2017), and Marc Sageman, *The Leaderless Jihad: Terror Networks in the Twenty-First Century* (University of Pennsylvania Press, 2008). The most enlightening book on the deradicalization of extremists is Daniel Koehler, *Understanding Deradicalization: Methods, Tools and Programs for Countering Violent Extremism* (Routledge, 2017).

CHAPTER 10: REGIONAL JIHAD

Joshua L. Gleis and Benedetta Berti, *Hezbollah and Hamas: A Comparative Study* (Johns Hopkins University Press, 2012), deals with both the focuses of this chapter. For more on Hezbollah, see Augustus Richard Norton, *Hezbollah: A Short History* (Princeton University Press, 2009), and Eitan Azani, *Hezbollah: The Story of the Party of God: From Revolution to Institutionalization* (Palgrave, 2011). For some of the actions of Hezbollah outside Lebanon, see Matthew Levitt, *Hezbollah: The Global Footprint of Lebanon's Party of God* (Georgetown University Press, 2013). Valuable studies of Hamas include the following: Zaki Chehab, *Inside Hamas: The Untold Story of the Militant Islamic Movement* (Nation Books, 2007); Beverley Milton-Edwards and Stephen Farrell, *Hamas: The Islamic Resistance Movement* (Polity, 2010); and Paola Caridi, *Hamas: From Resistance to Government*, trans. Andrea Teti (Seven Stories Press, 2012). Consider as well David Pratt, *Intifada: The Long Day of Rage* (Casemate, 2007), a discussion of the First and Second Intifadas; and Jonathan Schanzer, *Hamas vs. Fatah: The Struggle for Palestine* (St. Martin's Press, 2008).

CHAPTER 11: GLOBAL JIHAD

Chapter 11 changes focus to al-Qaeda and ISIS, or the Islamic State. Two recent volumes that study both are Daniel Byman, *Al-Qaeda, the Islamic State, and the Global Jihadist Movement: What Everyone Needs to Know* (Oxford University Press, 2015), and Lawrence Wright, *The Terror Years: From al-Qaeda to the Islamic State* (Knopf, 2016). On al-Qaeda consider Michael W. S. Ryan, *Decoding al-Qaeda's Strategy: The Deep Battle against America* (Columbia University Press, 2003). Ali Soufan, *The Black Banners: The Inside Story of 9/11 and the War against al-Qaeda* (W. W. Norton, 2011), discusses 9/11 and the counterterrorism effort that followed. Along the same path, see Seth Jones, *Hunting in the Shadows: The Pursuit of al Qa'ida since 9/11* (W. W. Norton, 2013). See as well, Bacevich, *America's War for the Greater Middle East*, already cited. Four works that detail the nature and history of ISIS on the rise are: Jessica Stern and J. M. Berger, *ISIS: The State of Terror* (Ecco, 2015); Patrick Cockburn, *The Rise of Islamic State: ISIS and the New Sunni Revolution*, rev. ed. (Verso, 2015); William McCants, *The ISIS Apocalypse: The History, Strategy, and Doomsday Vision of the Islamic State* (St. Martin's Press, 2015); and Michael Weiss and Hassan Hassan, *ISIS: Inside the Army of Terror*, rev. ed. (Regan Arts, 2016). We await a book that offers a full treatment of the dissolution of the Islamic State from 2016 to 2018.

CHAPTER 12: RADICAL RIGHT-WING VIOLENCE IN THE UNITED STATES
With all the attention given to third-wave Islamist terrorism, we run the risk of not recognizing the threat from the radical right in the United States. To understand the variety of goals and groups on the radical right, see Arie Perliger, *Challengers from the Sidelines: Understanding America's Violent Far-Right* (2012). It is available for free on the website of the Combating Terrorism Center at https://ctc.usma.edu/posts/challengers-from-the-sidelines-understanding-americas-violent-far-right. To grasp the ties between this kind of terrorism and religion, read Michael Barkun, *Religion and the Racist Right: The Origins of the Christian Identity Movement* (University of North Carolina Press, 1996), and Chris Hedges, *American Fascists: The Christian Right and the War on America* (Free Press, 2007). On the White supremacist movement's organizations and practices, see Pete Simi, *American Swastika: Inside the White Power Movement's Hidden Spaces of Hate* (Rowman and Littlefield, 2010). The "patriot" militia movement is covered in Daniel Levitas, *The Terrorist Next Door: The Militia Movement and the Radical Right* (Thomas Dunne Books, 2002) and Darren J. Mulloy, *American Extremism: History, Politics and the Militia Movement* (Routledge, 2008). Eleanor J. Bader and Patricia Baird-Windle, *Targets of Hatred: Anti-Abortion Terrorism* (Praeger, 2015), recounts the history of the violent anti-abortion movement in America. Jennifer Jefferis discusses the most dangerous anti-abortion group in *Armed for Life: The Army of God and Anti-Abortion Terror in the United States* (Praeger, 2011). The best book on the life and mind of Timothy McVeigh remains Lou Michel and Dan Herbeck, *American Terrorist: Timothy McVeigh and the Tragedy at Oklahoma City* (Harper, 2002). The political far right is making a resurgence in America and Europe; two books dealing with this are Nancy MacLean, *Democracy in Chains: The Deep History of the Radical Right's Stealth Plan for America* (Viking, 2017), and Tjitske Akkerman, Sarah L. de Lange, and Matthijs Rooduijn, *Radical Right-Wing Populist Parties in Western Europe* (Routledge, 2016).

CHAPTER 13: NARCOTERRORISM
The phenomenon of narcoterrorism constitutes a deadly convergence of terrorism with crime. This makes it difficult to describe narcoterrorism simply in terms of

political terrorism. On this convergence see Jennifer L. Hesterman, *The Terrorist-Criminal Nexus: An Alliance of International Drug Cartels, Organized Crime, and Terror Groups* (CRC Press, 2013). Chapter 13 emphasizes the FARC, the Taliban, the Colombian Medellín cartel, and Mexican drug cartels. On the FARC, see Garry Leech, *The FARC: The Longest Insurgency* (Zed Books, 2011). The Shining Path in Peru parallels the FARC in important ways, except for its longevity; see Gustavo Gorriti, *The Shining Path: A History of the Millenarian War in Peru*, trans. Robin Kirk (University of North Carolina Press, 2000). On the intertwining of the opium trade and civil war in Afghanistan, see Gretchen Peters, *Seeds of Terror: How Drugs, Thugs, and Crime Are Reshaping the Afghan War* (Thomas Dunne Books, 2009). Edward Follis and Douglas Century, *The Dark Art: My Undercover Life in Global Narcoterrorism* (Avery, 2014), is a fascinating story of a DEA agent active in Afghanistan and elsewhere. On the Medellín cartel, read Guy Gugliotta and Jeff Leen, *Kings of Coca: Inside the Medellín Cartel* (Simon and Schuster, 1989). Mark Bowden, *Killing Pablo: The Hunt for the World's Greatest Outlaw* (Atlantic Monthly Press, 2001), traces the efforts to find and eliminate the most notorious drug lord in Colombia. William C. Rempel, *At the Devil's Table: The Untold Story of the Insider Who Brought Down the Cali Cartel* (Random House, 2011), tells how Escobar's major rival, the Cali cartel, was undone. On the Mexican drug wars, see Paul Rexton Kan, *Cartels at War: Mexico's Drug-Fueled Violence and the Threat to U.S. Security* (Potomac Books, 2012). The cartels also involve themselves in other money-making criminal ventures; for an example see Guadalupe Correa-Cabrera, *Los Zetas Inc.: Criminal Corporations, Energy, and Civil War in Mexico* (University of Texas Press, 2017).

CHAPTER 14: HOMELAND SECURITY

Our efforts to craft a counterterrorism regime of laws and organization prove a threat to our constitutional liberties and protections. The president of the American Civil Liberties Union, Susan N. Herman, sounds the warning in *Taking Liberties: The War on Terror and the Erosion of American Democracy* (Oxford University Press, 2011). The investigative journalist Jane Mayer discusses gross abuses in *The Dark Side: The Inside Story of How the War on Terror Turned into a War on American Ideals* (Doubleday, 2008). On the historical American willingness to sacrifice rights to increase security, see Geoffrey R. Stone, *Perilous Times: Free Speech in Wartime from the Sedition Act of 1798 to the War on Terrorism* (W. W. Norton, 2004), and Anthony Gregory, *The Power of Habeas Corpus in America: From the King's Prerogative to the War on Terror* (Cambridge University Press, 2013). A detailed listing and description of the offices and agencies involved in counter-terrorism can be found in Michael B. Kraft and Edward Marks, *U.S. Government Counterterrorism: A Guide to Who Does What* (CRC Press, 2012). The power of the U.S. presidency to initiate and conduct warfare increased greatly after World War II, and the war on terrorism has accelerated that trend; see Louis Fisher, *Presidential War Power*, 3rd ed. (University Press of Kansas, 2013). On the new phenomenon of drone warfare as exercised by the executive and the military, see Chris Woods, *Sudden Justice: America's Secret Drone Wars* (Oxford University Press, 2015).

CHAPTER 15: CONFRONTING TERRORISM

Above all, the American population must understand the nature and magnitude of the terrorist threat and act intelligently to avoid disproportionate responses generated by fear and outrage. On this subject see Marc Sageman, *Misunderstanding Terrorism* (University of Pennsylvania Press, 2016). Raymond B. Flannery, *Coping with Anxiety in an Age of Terrorism* (Lantern Books, 2017), addresses the increased stress generated by the fear of terrorism. Concerning the potential future of terrorism, consider Walter Laqueur and Christopher Wall, *The Future of Terrorism: ISIS, Al-Qaeda, and the Alt-Right* (Thomas Dunne Books, 2018). Fred Kaplan, *Dark Territory: The Secret History of Cyber War* (Simon and Schuster, 2016), and P. W. Singer and Allan Friedman, *Cybersecurity and Cyberwar: What Everyone Needs to Know* (Oxford University Press, 2014), deal with cyber warfare, a likely direction of web-savvy terrorists. And there looms the potential of weapons of mass destruction, a danger we must make every effort to forestall. On the ultimate nightmare, see Graham Allison, *Nuclear Terrorism: The Ultimate Preventable Catastrophe* (Times Books, 2004), and Michael Levi, *On Nuclear Terrorism* (Harvard University Press, 2009).

INDEX

Page numbers in *italics* refer to illustrations.

Abane, Ramdane, 153
Abbas, Mahmoud, 284
Abdulmutallab, Umar Farouk, 307
Abrams, Norman, 402–3
Abu Ghraib, 391
ACLU. *See* American Civil Liberties Union
Adams, Gerry, 167, 177
Addington, David, 408–9
al-Adnani, Abu Muhammad, 317–18, 330–31
Afghanistan, 237–38, 250–51, 297–301, 303–4, 406–8. *See also* Taliban
African-Americans, 9–10, 77–80, 82–90, 97–101
Ahmed, Abu, 313
aircraft hijacking, 195, 198, 207, 302–3
Alabama, 87, 98–103, 168
Alexander II, czar, *105*, 105–6, 108, 133, 136–38, 141, 187
Alexander III, czar, 139
Algeria, 26–28, 59–61, 152–62. *See also* National Liberation Front (FLN)
Algerian Muslims, 152, 154–59, 161

Algerian War of Independence, 28, 154–64, 181
Algiers Milk Bar, *151*, 151–53
ALN. *See* Armée de Libération Nationale
alt-right movement, 356–57
American Civil Liberties Union (ACLU), *389*, 390, 399–401, 403, 405
American Nazi Party, 342
Amir, Yigal, 281
AN. *See* Aryan Nations
anarchism, 127–30, 132, 141–44, 146–50
Anderson, Terry, 273
anti-abortion violence, 338, 351–55
anti-apartheid campaign, in South Africa, 167
anti-federalist militias, 347–51
anti-Semitism, 91, 186–87, 338–40
anti-war activism, 209–10, 218–19
AOG. *See* Army of God
apocalypse, 325–26, 337–41, 432
Appomattox, 81–82
AQI. *See* al-Qaeda in Iraq
Arab League, 193
Arab Revolt, 189–90

Arabs, 184–86, 188–93, 195
Arab Spring, 308–9, 314
Arafat, Yasser, 193, 197–99, 201, 280–81, 283–84
Areco, Pacheco, 213
Argov, Shlomo, 199
Arkin, William M., 405
armed propaganda, 214–15
Armée de Libération Nationale (ALN), 156–61
Army of God (AOG), 352–53
Aron, Raymond, 10–11, 27, 420
Aryan Nations (AN), 335, 342–44
Ashurnasirpal II, 56
al-Assad, Bashar, 314
al-Assad, Hafez, 201
assassination, 7, 100–101, 114; of Alexander II, 105, 105–6, 108, 133, 136–38, 141, 187; of Berg, A., 343; by BR, 205, 206, 208, 227–28; of Carnot, 144–45; of civil rights activists, 97–98, 103; of Elizabeth, 146–47; by Fawkes, 109; of Ferdinand, 127, 131, 153; by Hashashins, 109–10; Heinzen on, 124; of King, Jr., 103; by KKK, 97–98, 103–4; of Lara, 368; Marighella on, 150; of McKinley, 146, 149; of Moro, 205, 205–6, 227; of Mountbatten, 175; of Nuqrashi Pasha, 247; of Rossa, 227; by SR, 139–40; of Stolypin, 140; by Tupamaros, 208
assassination attempt: on Argov, 199; on Gaviria, 360; on Napoleon III, 135–36; on Nasser, 248; on Philippe, 117–18; by Zasulich, 136–38
Ataturk, Kemal, 293
Atef, Mohammed, 302, 304
atomic weapons, 68–69
attentats, 117–18, 134–35, 141–43
attrition, terrorist strategy of, 23–26, 29, 107, 150, 160–61, 174, 179–81, 296, 316, 355, 364, 418–19, 433–35
Aussaresses, Paul, 163
al-Awlaki, Anwar, 307, 309
Ayers, Bill, 220–22

Azzam, Abdullah Yusuf, 249–51, 279, 292–93, 297–98

Babeuf, Gracchus, 115
Bacevich, Andrew, 412
Baer, Robert, 272
al-Baghdadi, Abu Bakr, 293–94, 310, 313–17, 326
Bakunin, Mikhail, 115, 132–33
Balfour Declaration, 188
al-Banna, Hassan, 247, 279
barricades, 116–22, 141
Barricades Week, 159
Basir, Abu, 323
Bastille, storming of, 112, 114
Batista, Fulgencio, 211
Battle of Algiers, 152, 157, 160. *See also* Algerian War of Independence
The Battle of Algiers (1966), 163, 217, 220, 450n5
Battle of Colfax, 85–86
Battle of the Bogside, 168
Baxley, William, 101
Bayat, Asef, 268, 308
Beck, E. M., 89
Beckwith, Byron De La, 100–101
Begin, Menachim, 183, 184–85, 197, 199–201, 204
beheadings, 289, 289–90, 312, 319, 386–87
Beirut, 6, 201–3, 272
Belfast, 167–68, 171–73
Ben Ali, Zine El Abidine, 308
Ben-Ami, Shlomo, 7, 281
Ben-Gurion, David, 189–91
Beni-Naâseur, 60
Bercé, Yves Marie, 111
Berg, Alan, 343
Berg, Nick, 312, 319, 386
Bergen, Peter, 304
Bergen-op-Zoom, 58–59
Berger, J. M., 315, 321, 326
Berko, Anat, 262
bin Abdullaah, Jabir, 246
bin Laden, Osama, 2, 12–13, 19, 203, 249, 294, 377; in Afghanistan, 300–301, 303–4; *fatwa* of, 250, 291–92, 306;

on global conflict, 291–93; al-Qaeda and, 297–300; on U.S., 291–92, 325; al-Zarqawi and, 311–12, 323–24; al-Zawahiri and, 299, 312, 323–25, 330
Birmingham, Alabama, 98–101
The Birth of a Nation (1915), 91
Black Liberation Army, 222
Black Panther Party, 219–20
Blacks. *See* African-Americans
Black September, 196
Blanqui, Auguste, 115–16, 118, 121
Bloody Friday, 172–73
Bloody Sunday, 102, 171–72
Bloom, Mia, 262
Bojinka Plot, 300
Böll, Heinrich, 234
Bologna Massacre, 226
Bolsheviks, 37–38, 48–49, 251–52
bombing, 65–69, 97–98, 130, 297, 307; of Algiers Milk Bar, *151*, 151–53; by anti-abortion extremists, 351–53; Bloody Friday, 172–73; of Café Terminus, 143–44; by Fatah, 195; by FLN, *151*, 151–53; by French anarchists, 141, 143–44; by the Irgun, *183*, 184, 190; of King David Hotel, *183*, 190; by Melville, 219; by Narodnaya Volya, *105*, 105–6; by Orsini, F., 135–36; by PIRA, 172–75, 177–78; by al-Qaeda, 300–302; by RIRA, 180; truck, 202–3, *332*, 332–33, 345, 357; by UKA, 101; of U.S. embassies, 202–3, 301, 396–97; by UVF, 171, 174; by the Weathermen, 220–21. *See also* Murrah Office building
bombs, 130–31, 135, 144, 172–74
Bordaberry, Juan, 217
Bosnia-Herzegovina, 70, 72–74, 79
Boston Marathon bombing, 307
Boumedienne, Houari, 158, 161
Bouton, Cynthia, 112
Bowden, Mark, 366
BR. *See* Red Brigades
Branch Davidians, 332–33, 348–50
Brands, Hal, 387
Bray, Michael, 352–54

Brazzaville Declaration, 155, 450n6
Breivik, Anders Behring, 357–58
Bresci, Gaetano, 146
Brigate Rosse. *See* Red Brigades
British Army, 171–73
Browning, John, 131
Brownmiller, Susan, 224
Brum, Pablo, 216
B Specials, 170–71
B-29 bombers, 67–68
Bugeaud, Thomas Robert, 59–61
Buonarroti, Philippe, 115
Burleigh, Michael, 20, 230
Burnett, George, 84
Bush, George H. W., 339
Bush, George W., 12–13, 19, 244, 297, 336, 391, 404, 407–9
Butler, Richard Girnt, 338, 342, 344
Byman, Daniel, 275

Cabu, Jean, 236
Café Terminus, 143–44
Café Wars, 159
Calderón, Felipe, 387
caliphate, 249, 291–94, 310, 315–17, 324–26, 331
Camp David Summit, 185, 197, 281–82
Caplan, Lincoln, 396
car bombs, 172–74
the Carbonari, 115, 135
Carnot, Sadi, 144–45
Carr, Michael, 138
Casalegno, Carlo, 227
Caserio, Santo Jeronimo, 144
Catholics, 90, 109, 164, 166–70, 174
Cavaignac, Louis-Eugène, 120
Cave of the Patriarchs massacre, 280–81
Chabat, Jorge, 386
Challe, Maurice, 159
Chaney, James Earl, 101
Charbonnier, Stéphane, 235, 236–37, 265
Charlie Hebdo, 235, 235–37, 254, 261, 265–66
Cheney, Dick, 408–9
Chicago, Democratic National Convention, of 1968 in, 209, 219

Chinese Communist Party, 42, 44–45, 47–48, 50
Chinese Cultural Revolution, 9, *31*, 33–34, 41–48, 210–11
Christian Democracy Party, *205*, 206
Christian Identity, 337–43
Christianity, 242–45, 335
civilians, 7, 64–66, 153, 157, 160–61, 191–92
civilizations, clash of, 251–58, 266
civil liberties and protections, 392–95
civil rights movement, 9–10, 79, 95, 97–104, 167–68
Civil War, Lebanese, 270–71
Civil War, U.S., 62, 77–78, 80–83, 392. *See also* Reconstruction
Clarke, Edward Young, 92
Clarke, Richard, 301, 396
clash of civilizations, 251–58, 266
Clausewitz, Carl von, 15, 18, 22, 28, 295
Clichy martyrs, 142
Clinton, Bill, 178, 280, 301, 396
Coastal Road Massacre, *183*, 184–85, 198
Cockburn, Patrick, 315–16
Coco, Francesco, 227
Cohn, Samuel, 111
Cold War, 394, 412, 414
Cole, David, 411
Colfax, massacre at, 85
Colombia, 10, 359–60, 365–69, 383–84, 388. *See also* Fuerzas Armadas Revolucionarias de Colombia
colonialism, 153–55, 163–64, 188
colons, Algeria, 155–57, 159–62
Colorado Klan, 93–94
Combat Organization, of SR, 139–40
the Commune, barricades of, 120–21
communism, 127–29, 251–52
Communist Party, 38, 40–42, 44–45, 47–48, 50
compliance terrorism, 24
concealed handguns, 130–31
Confederacy, 81–83, 87, 103
Congress of Racial Equality (CORE), 97, 99, 101–2
Connor, Bull, 99–100

Conquest, Robert, 39–40
conspiracies, anti-Semitic, 338–40
Constitution, U.S., 392–93
Corday, Charlotte, 114–15
CORE. *See* Congress of Racial Equality
Coulibaly, Amedy, 236, 317
counterterrorism, 145–50, 391–92, 395–97, 404–5, 414–15
Courts, Gus, 97–98
Covenant, the Sword, and the Arm of the Lord (CSA), 344–45
Crane, Conrad C., 66
Crenshaw, Martha, 20, 24
crime, and terrorism, 7, 133, 147–49, 175, 259, 292, 334, 343, 356, 361–63, 379, 385, 388, 399, 422
crime-terrorism continuum, in narco-terrorism, 362–65, *363*, 375, 382
Cronin, Audrey Kurth, 79–80, 90, 94, 104, 181, 217, 241, 313
the Crusades, 249
CSA. *See* Covenant, the Sword, and the Arm of the Lord
Cuban Revolution, 211
cult character, of terrorist mindset, 230–33
Cultural Revolution. *See* Chinese Cultural Revolution
Cultural Worldview (CWV), 253–55, 264
cyber terrorism, 431–32
Czolgosz, Leon, 146

DAS. *See* Departmento Administrativo de Seguridad
Day of the Barricades, 112
Days of Rage, 219–20
D-Company, 379–80
DEA. *See* Drug Enforcement Administration
Dear, Robert, 352
Debray, Regis, 211–12, 223
Decembrist Revolt, 136
Declaration of Independence, 81
Dees, Morris, 344
Democratic Front for the Liberation of Palestine, 198

Democratic National Convention, 1968, 209, 219
Deng Xiaoping, 44, 47–48
Departmento Administrativo de Seguridad (DAS), 359–60
Derry, 167–68
desegregation, 95–99
Deuteronomy, 56, 58
DeWitt, John L., 394
the Diaspora, Jews of, 186–87
digital age, terrorism in, 326–30
Dikötter, Frank, 44
Dixon, Thomas, 91
Doherty, Kieran, 177
Dohrn, Bernadette, 220–23
Dole, Robert, 396
Donald, Michael, 104
Doolittle, James, 67
Douhet, Giulio, 65–66
Downing Street Declaration, 178
Dozier, James Lee, 227
Dresden, fire-bombing of, 51, 52–53, 67, 74
Drif, Zohra, 151, 151–52
drone strikes, 410–11
drug cartels, 374–75, 382–88
Drug Enforcement Administration (DEA), 363–64, 382
dynamite, 130, 132, 144
Dyson, Freeman, 66

Eaker, Ira, 67
Easter Rebellion, 165
Easter Rising, 170
Egypt, 192–94, 196–97, 247–48, 308
Eisenhower, Dwight D., 96, 412–13
Elizabeth, empress, 146–47
Elliott, Andrea, 259–60
Ellison, James, 339, 345
Emelyanov, Ivan, 106
Emmanuel, Victor, 136
Enforcement Act, of 1871, 84–85
Engels, Friedrich, 122–23, 129
England, 2–3, 27, 164–65, 171–75, 177, 188–90
Escobar, Pablo, 10, 359, 359–60, 365–70
Espionage Act of 1917, 393

Esposito, John L., 248, 256–59, 266
ethnic cleansing, 10, 70, 73–75, 78, 192
ethno-nationalism, 126, 153, 181, 207
Europe, 109, 124–25, 251, 357–58, 426
European radicals, 113, 120, 122, 125
Evans, Hiram Wesley, 92–93
Evans, Martin, 156
Evers, Medgar, 100–101
evolution, terrorist strategy of, 23–26, 198, 211–12, 238, 269, 274, 276, 278, 288, 294–97, 310, 323, 326, 334, 355, 364, 370, 418–19, 430, 433–35
explosives, 130, 138–39, 148. *See also* bombing
expulsion and extradition, of anarchists, 148–49

Fair, C. Christine, 240
La Familia Michoacana, 386
Faraj, Muhammad abd-al-Salam, 249, 291
Faranda, Adriana, 21, 228, 231, 259
FARC. *See* Fuerzas Armadas Revolucionarias de Colombia
Farrell, Stephen, 186
fascism, 63–64, 225–26, 251–52
Fatah, 184, 193, 195–96, 198, 284–85
fatwa, 250, 291–92, 306
Faubus, Orval, 96
Fawkes, Guy, 109
fear, 6, 17–18, 33–34, 422–24
February Revolution, of 1848, 118–22
Feltrinelli, Giangiacomo, 225
female terrorists, 203, 262
Ferrandi, Mario, 230
Festinger, Leon, 233
Fifteenth Amendment, 86, 103
Figner, Vera, 106
Fiore, Raffaele, 232
First Five-Year Plan, 39
First Intifada, 268, 278–80, 282
First Jewish-Roman War, 57, 109
first-wave radical terrorism, 7, 110, 118, 125, 129–50
FISA. *See* Foreign Intelligence Surveillance Act of 1978

fitna, between al-Qaeda and IS, 323–26
FLN. *See* National Liberation Front
Florion, Émile, 141
Flour War of 1775, 112
Foca, 73
focoism, 210–12, 223, 274
Foley, James, 289, 289–90, 389
Follis, Edward, 379
Foreign Intelligence Surveillance Act of 1978 (FISA), 395, 398–401, 400, 405
Forrest, Nathan Bedford, 83–84, 92
Foster, Murphy, 87
four strategies, of terrorism, 23–26, 149–50, 364, 418, 433, 433–35
Fourteenth Amendment, 86
France, 35, 59–61, 64, 127, 144, 187; *attentats* in, 141–43; barricades, 116–22, 141; Évian Accords, with FLN, 159–60; February Revolution, 118–22; Flour War of 1775, 112; gendarmes of, 155–56; torture, by soldiers of, 157, 162–63. *See also* Algerian War of Independence; Paris
Franco-Prussian War, 120, 132
Frank, Leo, 91–92
Franz Ferdinand, 127, 131, 153
freedom of speech, 265–66
Freedom Riders, 97, 99–101
Freedom Summer, 101–3
French Reign of Terror, 34–37, 48, 123
French Revolution, 9, 13–14, 34–38, 41, 48–49, 111–14, 126
Frieschi, Giuseppe, 117
Fromkin, Daniel, 26–27, 100, 161, 423
Fuerzas Armadas Revolucionarias de Colombia (FARC), 364–65, 370–77, 382
Furrow, Buford, 343

Gacha, José, 359–60
Gale, William Potter, 347
Gallardo, Félix, 384
Galleani, Luigi, 146
Gambetta, Léon, 141
Gantz, Benny, 276
Gatto, Herbert, 212

de Gaulle, Charles, 155, 158–59
Gaviria, César, 360
Gaza Strip, 191, 194, 267, 278, 283–88
Geifman, Anna, 139–40
Gemayel, Bashir, 199–201
gendarmes, 155–56
Genesis, Book of, 337–38
Geneva Conventions, 17, 69–70, 409
genocide, 70–71, 74, 78–79
Gerges, Fawaz, 300–301, 309
Germany, 63–67, 72–73, 123, 127. *See also* Red Army Faction
Giles, Jackson, 87–88
Ginsborg, Paul, 225
global Islamist struggle, caliphate and, 291–94
globalization, 252, 254
global *ummah*, 249–50, 258
global war on terror, 405–11
Glorious Revolution, of 1688, 164
the Golan, 197
Goldstein, Baruch, 280–81
Good Friday Agreement, 154, 164, 177, 179–80
Goulding, Cathal, 167–69
Grant, Ulysses S., 81, 84, 86
Great Britain, 166, 170, 179
the Great Leap Forward, 43–44, 46
the Great Proletarian Cultural Revolution, 33, 44–45
the Great Purge, 34, 37–41, 48
the Great Revolt, 57
Greenberg, Jeff, 253
Green Book, of PIRA, 174, 232
Greenwald, Glenn, 401, 411
Grillo, Ioan, 386
Grinevitsky, Ignati, 105–6, 133
group polarization, 232–33
Guatemalan Civil War, 74
Guevara, Che, 197, 211–13, 225
Guillén, Abraham, 212
Guiraud, Nicole, 151, 152
gunpowder, 130–31

Habash, George, 193
habeas corpus, 392–93, 396

Habeck, Mary, 246
hadith, 242, 244–45, 250, 256
Haganah, 189–91
Hamas, 186, 238, 252, 260, 267, 267–69, 277–88
Hammerskin Nation, 346
Harkis, 156, 158
Harris, Arthur "Bomber," 66
Harris, Kevin, 349
Hashashins, 109–10
HaShomer, 188–89
Hassan, Hassan, 319
Hassan, Nidal, 261, 307
hate crimes, 334, 341, 344, 346
hate groups, 341–47
Hayes, Rutherford B., 86
Haymarket Riot, 146
Heinzen, Karl, 15, 17, 121–24, 127, 130–32, 432
Henry, Émile, 134, 143–44
Herman, Susan, 399–400
Hertz, Randy, 396
Hertzl, Theodor, 187, 189
Hezbollah, 199, 202, 238, 270–77, 287–88
hijacking, 195, 198, 207, 215, 302–3
hijira, 243
Hill, Paul Jennings, 353
Hiroshima, 68–69
Hitler, Adolf, 63, 342
Hoffman, Bruce, 8, 15, 17
Hoffman, Frank G., 381–82, 387
Holmes, Oliver Wendell, 88
the Holocaust, 79, 187
Homeland Security Act, 404
home rule bills, 165
Hoover, J. Edgar, 103
Horgan, John, 3, 20, 238–39, 251, 259–61
House Un-American Activities Committee (HUAC), 394–95
HRW. *See* Human Rights Watch
HUAC. *See* House Un-American Activities Committee
hudud, 320–21
Human Rights Watch (HRW), 373–74, 381
Hume, John, 169, 179

Hundred Flowers Campaign, 43
Hundred Years' War, 57
Hunt, Leamon, 228
Huntington, Samuel P., 251–53, 266
al-Hussayen, Sami Omar, 390–91, 402
Hussein, Fouad, 294
Hussein, king, 195–96
Hussein, Saddam, 12–13, 305
hybrid warfare, 160–61, 381–82, 387

IAF. *See* Israeli Air Force
Ibrahim, Dawood, 379–80
ICC. *See* International Criminal Court
IDF. *See* Israeli Defense Force
imagined community, 126–27
Imperialist Multinational State, 225
Indiana Klan, 92–93
Indian Removal Act, 78
individuals, 11–12, 89, 238, 240
Indochina, 156
industrial proletariat, 210–11
initiation, terrorist strategy of, 23–24, 107, 150, 172, 212, 223, 233, 355–56, 364, 418–19, 433–35
INLA. *See* Irish National Liberation Army
Intelligence Reform and Terrorism Prevention Act of 2004 (IRTPA), 404
International Anarchist Congress, 132
International Criminal Court (ICC), 70–71
internet, 260–61, 327
intimidation, terrorist strategy of, 5, 23–24, 25, 26, 33, 63, 98, 159, 161, 321, 354–56, 358, 364, 365, 374, 383, 418, 422, 433–35
IRA. *See* Irish Republican Army
Iran, 272, 277
Iranian Revolution of 1979, 202, 237, 241–42, 308
Iraq, 310, 314–15. *See also* Islamic State of Iraq; al-Qaeda in Iraq
Iraq War, 54, 297, 305–6, 309, 313, 406–8
IRB. *See* Irish Republican Brotherhood
Ireland, 153–54, 164–67, 169. *See also* Northern Ireland; Provisional Irish Republican Army

the Irgun, *183*, 184, 190–91
Irish Free State, 166
Irish National Invincibles, 165
Irish National Liberation Army (INLA), 169, 176
Irish Rebellion, of 1798, 164
Irish Republican Army (IRA), 166–67, 169. *See also* Provisional Irish Republican Army
Irish Republican Brotherhood (IRB), 165
Irish Republican Socialist Party, 169
Irish Volunteers, 165–66
IRTPA. *See* Intelligence Reform and Terrorism Prevention Act of 2004
IS. *See* Islamic State
ISI. *See* Islamic State of Iraq
Islam, 237–38, 242–49, 257, 264–65, 337, 378
Islamic fundamentalism, 241–42, 244
Islamic Jihad Organization, 272
Islamic Resistance Movement, 279
Islamic State (IS), 13, 16, 25, 29, 234; on apocalypse, 325–26; al-Baghdadi in, 293–94, 310, 313–17, 326; on caliphate, 293, 310, 315–17, 324–26, 331; Foley beheading by, 289, 289–90; *hudud* and, 320–21; JTJ and, 311–17; lone wolves of, 317–18, 330; in media, 326–28; Obama on, 310–11, 314; propaganda of, 327–29; al-Qaeda and, 290–91, 293–95, 314–15, 323–31; Trump on, 425–26; ultraviolence, 327–30; Zarqawism and, 318–23
Islamic State of Iraq (ISI), 312–14
Islamism, 2, 186, 192, 241–43, 246, 277–78. *See also* radical Islamists
Islamiyah, Jemaah, 305
Ismay, Hastings, 53
Israel, 185–86, 199–203, 237–38, 267, 267–69, 279; Gaza Strip and, 191, 194, 278, 283–87; Hamas and, 283–87; Hezbollah at war with, 273–76; Palestinian prisoners of, 196; Second Intifada and, 283–84; in Six-Day War, 193–94; War of Independence, 186, 191, 277

Israeli Air Force (IAF), 194
Israeli Defense Force (IDF), 191, 193–95, 198–203, 268, 283, 286–87
Israeli-Palestinian conflict, 185, 203–4, 269
Israeli Plan D, 192
Italian Communist Party (PCI), 206
Italy, 63–64, 115, 131–32, 134–36, 224–26, 229
Iyad, Abu, 195
Izz al-Din al-Qassam Brigades, 279, 281, 288

Jackson, Andrew, 78
Jackson, Edward L., 93
Jackson, Jimmie Lee, 102
the Jacobins, 36–38
Jacobs, John, 219
Jama'at al-Tawid wal-Jihad (JTJ), 311–17, 319
Japan, 67–69
Japanese internment, 393–94
Jefferson, Thomas, 415
Jerusalem, 57, 109
Jesus, 243–44
the Jewish Agency, 190
Jewish National Fund (JNF), 187–89
Jewish state, 184, 189–90, 192. *See also* Israel
Jews, 57, 79, 90, 109, 335; anti-Semitism toward, 91, 186–87, 338–40; Arab Revolt and, 189–90; of the Diaspora, 186–87; in Palestine, 184–89; the Yishuv, 187–92; Zionists, 184, 187–88, 191, 249. *See also* Israel
Jiang Qing, 47
jihad, 2, 239–40, 245–51, 265, 291–94, 307–8, 312
Jihadi John, 289–90
Jim Crow, 79–80, 86–88, 94, 97
JNF. *See* Jewish National Fund
Johnson, Lyndon, 101, 103, 168
Jordan, 189, 191, 193–96
JTJ. *See* Jama'at al-Tawid wal-Jihad
Juergensmeyer, Mark, 28, 260, 263

jujitsu, terrorist, provocation, 23, 27, 100, 154, 161, 172, 255, 328–30, 423–24, 431, 434
June Days, of 1848, 119–22
Junger, Sebastien, 381

Kahalid Sheikh Mohammed (KSM), 300, 302, 319
Kahan, Yitzhak, 201–2
Kahl, Gordon, 348
Kane, Joseph and Jerry, 348
Kennedy, John F., 96, 100–101
Kennedy, Paul, 295
Khan, Haji Juma, 379
Khan, Mohammad Sidique, 312
Khobar Towers bombing, 300
Khrushchev, Nikita, 41–45, 48
al-Kidd, Abdullah, 390–91, 402
Killen, Edgar Ray, 102
King, Jr., Martin Luther, 95, 98, 100, 102–4
King David Hotel, 183, 190
Kirov, Sergei, 39
KKK. *See* Ku Klux Klan
Klassen, Ben, 341
Klehr, Harvey, 220
The Knights of Mary Phagan, 91–92
Koenigstein, François, 142–43
Kohn, Hans, 126
Kohn, Richard, 413
Koresh, David, 350
Kouachi, Chérif and Said, 235, 235–37, 265
Krar, William J., 354
Kropotkin, Peter, 128, 132, 145
Krylenko, N. V., 38
KSM. *See* Kahalid Sheikh Mohammed
Ku Klux Klan (KKK), 7, 77, 79–85, 90–104, 342

Lah, Kyung, 237
Lahouaiej-Bouhlel, Mohamed, 318
Laqueur, Walter, 4, 8, 122–23
Lara, Rodrigo, 368
Lashkar-e-Taiba (LeT), 240, 380
Law, Randall, 7, 108

law of war, 17–18, 53–54, 61–63, 65, 68–75, 284
Lazcano, Heriberto, 385
Leaderless Jihad (Sageman), 292, 307–8
Léauthier, Léon-Jules, 142–43
Lebanese Civil War, 197–98
Lebanon, 6, 196, 199–203, 269–76
Lebanon War, 199–203, 237, 275–76
Lee, George W., 97–98
Lee, Herbert, 100
Lee, Robert E., 81
Lee, Wayne, 8–10, 59
leftists. *See* Marxists; New Left
Lehder, Carlos, 368
LeMay, Curtis, 67–68
Lenin, Vladimir Ilyich, 37–39, 42, 129, 210
LeT. *See* Lashkar-e-Taiba
Lewis, Bernard, 253
liberalism, 126–27
Liberation Tigers of Tamil Elam (LTTE), 16, 181, 207
Libya, 196
Lieber, Francis, 62
Lieber Code, 61–63, 69
Liebman, James S., 396
Lin Biao, 47
Lincoln, Abraham, 392–93
Lin Piao, 44
Li Si, 32
Liuzzo, Viola, 103
Locke, John Galen, 94
lois scélérates, 145
London terrorist attacks, of 2005, 2–3, 27
lone wolf, 11–12, 144, 306–7, 317–18, 330, 354
Longmire, Sylvia, 382–83
Louisiana, 85–87
LTTE. *See* Liberation Tigers of Tamil Elam
Lucheni, Luigi, 146–47
lynchings, 7, 88–90, 94

MacDonald, Andrew. *See* Pierce, William
MacFarquhar, Roderick, 44
Machiavelli, Niccolò, 33–34, 49

madrassas, 239–40
Madrid terrorist attacks, 2–3
Magdeburg, 58
Mair-Witt, Silke, 233
MAK. *See* Maktab al-Khidamat
Makarenko, Tamara, 362–64, *363*
Maktab al-Khidamat (MAK), 298
al-Maliki, Nuri, 309
The Management of Savagery (Naji), 29, 296, 326–27
Mansoor, Peter, 313
Maoism, 222–23
Mao Zedong, 25, 32, 50, 274, 294–96.
    See also Chinese Cultural Revolution
Marat, Jean-Paul, 114–15
Marcuse, Herbert, 210
Marighella, Carlos, 150, 212, 218, 361
Marshall, George C., 68
Martínez, Efraín, 214
martyrdom, 132–34, 142, 150
Marx, Karl, 38, 121–22, 129, 210
Marxism, 153, 168–69, 210–11, 225
Marxists, 21, 49, 131, 139, 141, 143, 206–7, 213
al-Masri, Abu Ayyub, 312–13
mass crowd action, 107–8, 112, 116–17, 121–22
Massu, Jacques, 157, 162
Mateen, Omar, 261, 317–18
material witness, 403
Mathews, Robert, 343
Mattis, James, 410
Mauriac, François, 161
May Day, 1891, 142
Mayer, Jane, 408–9
Mayfield, Brandon, 399, 402
Mazzini, Giuseppe, 135, 138
McCain, John, 409
McCants, William, 324
McCarthy, Joseph, 394–95
McGuinness, Martin, 180–81
McKinley, William, 146, 149
McNamara, Robert, 68
McVeigh, Timothy, 146, 303, 332, 332–36, 339–40, 345, 354–56, 395–96
Medellín cartel, 359, 365–67

media, 5, *289*, 289–90, 326–28
Mehaidli, Sana'a, 202–3
Meinhof, Ulrike, 223
Meins, Holger, 207, 231
Mellen, Jim, 232
Melville, Sam, 219
The Memphis Massacre, 82
Merari, Ariel, 15, 239, 260
Meredith, James, 96
Merriman, John, 143–44
Metzger, Lothar, 52–53
Metzger, Thomas, 346
Mexico, 382–88, *387*
Mezentsov, Nikolai, 138
Michel, Louise, 141
Michel-Chich, Danielle, *151*, 152
Michigan Militia, 350–51
militarism, American, 411–14
military-industrial complex, 412–13
military terrorism, 54–69, 74–75
Militia of Montana (MOM), 350–51
militias, anti-federalist, 347–51
Millennium Plot, 301, 311
Mills, C. Wright, 210
Milton-Edwards, Beverley, 186
mindset, of terrorists, 10–11, 21, 132–34, 230–33, 238–39
Mississippi, 96–101
Mitchell, George, 178, 282
Mitrione, Dan, 216
MNA. *See* Mouvement National Algérienne
MNF. *See* Multi-National Force
Mogahed, Dalia, 256–59, 266
Mohammed Omar, mullah, 299
MOM. *See* Militia of Montana
Mongol empire, 246
Montgomery, Alabama, 102–3, 168
Montgomery Bus Boycott, 98–99
Moore, Harriette, 97–98
morality, 18–20, 233, 421
moral shock, 19–20, 254
Moretti, Mario, 206, 226–27, 229
Morice Line, 161
Morley, Clarence F., 93–94
Moro, Aldo, 205, 205–6, 227

Morris, Benny, 188, 191–92, 200
Morrison, Danny, 177
Morsi, Mohamed, 308
mortality salience, 254–55
Mortier, Édouard, 117
Morucci, Valerio, 231
Moss, David, 226
Mosul, 310, 315
motivations, of terrorists, 238–39
Mountbatten, Louis, 175
Mouvement National Algérienne (MNA), 156, 159, 162
Muawiyah, 243
Mughrabi, Dalal, *183*, 185
Muhammad, 236–37, 242–46, 250, 265–66
Muhammadism, 241
ibn Muhieddine, Abdelkader, 59–60
al-Mujamma' al-Islami, 277–78, 284
Mujica, José, 214, 218
Multi-National Force (MNF), 202
Munich Olympics, 1972, 196
al-Muqrin, Abd al-Aziz, 296
murder, technology of, 130–31
Murrah Office Building, *332*, 332–33, 336, 355–56, 395–96
Muslim Brotherhood, 247–48, 277, 308
Muslims, 2, 73, 109, 242, 258, 292–93; Algerian, 152, 154–59, 161; American, 260–62; on *Charlie Hebdo*, 236–37, 254. *See also* Islam
Mussolini, Benito, 63–64
My Lai massacre, 71–72
mystique, in terrorist mindset, 132–34

NAACP. *See* National Association for the Advancement of Colored People
Nagasaki, 68–69
Naji, Abu Bakr, 29, 295–96, 326–27
Nakba, 186, 191–92, 195
Nance, Malcolm, 312
Napoleonic Wars, 15
Napoleon I, 114–15
Napoleon III, emperor, 127, 135–36
NAR. *See* Nuclei Armati Rivoluzionari

narcoterrorism, 359, 361–70, *363*, 379, 382–88. *See also* Escobar, Pablo; Fuerzas Armadas Revolucionarias de Colombia; Taliban
Narodnaya Volya, 24, *105*, 105–7, 128, 137–40
Nasser, Gamel Abdel, 192–94, 248
Nassrallah, Hassan, 271
Nast, Thomas, *76*, 77
National Abortion Federation, 351–52
National Army, of Irish Free State, 166
National Association for the Advancement of Colored People (NAACP), 97–98, 100
nationalism, 123, 134–36, 155, 169, 251, 335. *See also* ethno-nationalism
National Liberation Front (FLN), 24, 26–28, *151*, 151–63, 181
National Security Letters (NSL), 401–2
National Socialist Movement, 342
Nazism, 63–64, 79, 97, 187, 342–47
Nechayev, Sergey, 15, 18–19, 132–33, 150, 174, 223
neo-Nazis, 342–47
Netanyahu, Benjamin, 19, 288
Netanyahu, Yonatan, 198
Nettlau, Max, 128–29
Neuva Helvecia, 213
New Left, 153, 206–7, 210, 233–34
New World Order (NWO), 339
Nicholls, Francis, 86
Nichols, Terry, 333
Nidal, Abu, 199
Nie Yuanzi, 45
nihilism, 127–29
9/11. *See* September 11, 2001
9/11 Commission, 302, 398, 404–5
nitroglycerine, 130
Nixon, Richard, 221, 396
Nobel, Albert, 130
Noble, Kerry, 345
noncombatants, 4, 6, 54
nonviolence, 97–100, 170
North, Gary, 338
North Carolina, 87, 99

Northern Ireland, 24, 153–54, 166–68, 170–73, 178–79. *See also* the Troubles
Northern Ireland Assembly, 170, 179–80
North Vietnamese Army (NVA), 71–72
Norton, Augustus, 271–73, 276
NSL. *See* National Security Letters
nuclear terrorism, 432
Nuclei Armati Rivoluzionari (NAR), 225–26
al-Nusra Front, 314
NVA. *See* North Vietnamese Army
NWO. *See* New World Order
Nyiramashuko, Pauline, 74

OAS. *See* Organisation de l'Armée Secrète
Obama, Barack, 289–90, 309–11, 314, 336, 403–4, 410–11, 426
Oberholtzer, Madge, 93
Ochoa, Jorge Luis, 368
October Revolution, 37, 39
Official IRA (OIRA), 169, 172
Ó Fiaich, Tomás, 176
O'Hara, Sean, 172
OIRA. *See* Official IRA
Oklahoma City bombing, 16, 146, 303. *See also* McVeigh, Timothy; Murrah Office Building
Oklahoma Constitutional Militia, 351
Old and New Testaments, 243–44
Omar, Abu, 326
On War (Clausewitz), 15, 18, 295
OPEC. *See* Organization of Petroleum Exporting Countries
Operation Banner, 171
Operation Cast Lead, 285–86
Operation Days of Penitence, 283
Operation Defensive Shield, 268
Operation Demetrius, 171
Operation Gladio, 224
Operation Grapes of Wrath, 273
Operation Litani, 185, 198–99
Operation Motorman, 173
Operation Peace for Galilee, 199
Operation Pillar of Defense, 286–87
Operation Protective Edge, 286–87
Operation Speedy Express, 72
Operation Thunderclap, 67
Operation Wrath of God, 196
opium trade, 378–79
Orange Order, 164
Organisation de l'Armée Secrète (OAS), 156, 159–60
Organization of Petroleum Exporting Countries (OPEC), 198
Orsini, Alessandro, 21, 230–31
Orsini, Felice, 127, 135–36, 144
Oslo Accords, 197, 280–81
Ottoman Empire, 59, 187–88, 270
Ouled Riah tribe, 61
outrage, 6, 17–18, 422–24

PA. *See* Palestinian Authority
Page, Wade Michael, 347
Paisley, Ian, 170, 180
Pakistan, 239–40, 249–50, 379–80
Palestine, 184–92. *See also* Israeli-Palestinian conflict
Palestine Liberation Organization (PLO), 7, 16, 26, 181–82, 199; under Arafat, 197–98; Coastal Road Massacre, 183, 184–85; expulsion from Jordan, 195–96; Fatah in, 184, 193; Hamas and, 186, 269, 279–80, 285; on Israel, 194; in Lebanon, 196, 201; al-Mujamma' al-Islami and, 277–78; Palestinian National Charter of, 194; PIRA, RAF and, 207
Palestinian Authority (PA), 280, 284
Palestinians, 186, 189–91, 192–99, 268, 278–79, 281–86
pan-Arabism, 192–93
Pape, Robert, 202, 271
Pappe, Ilan, 192
paramilitaries, 85–86, 165–66, 189–90, 348–51
Paris, 37, 115–17, 119–20, 122, 130, 135
the Paris Commune, 120–21, 141
Parker, Theodore, 104
Parks, Rosa, 98
Parsons, Albert, 130
Pasha, Nuqrashi, 247

Passover Massacre, 267, 267–68, 283
Patriot Act of 2001, 389, 392, 397–405
Patriot Groups, 336
PCI. *See* Italian Communist Party
Pearson, Lester, 266
Peci, Patrizio, 231–32
Peck, James, 99–100
Pedahzur, Ami, 21, 280–81
Peel Commission, 189
Pélissier, Aimable, 61
Pelloutier, Fernand, 145
Peng Dehuai, 46–47
People's Liberation Army (PLA), 47
Peres, Shimon, 280
Perliger, Arie, 21, 280–81, 334–36, 352
Perovskaya, Sophia, 106
Peters, Gretchen, 378–79
Petraeus, David, 313
PFLP. *See* Popular Front for the Liberation of Palestine
Phalangist militia, 201–3
Philippe, Louis, Duke of Orléans, 116–19, 121–22
Pianori, Giovani, 135
Pierce, William, 333–34, 339–43
PIRA. *See* Provisional Irish Republican Army
Pisacane, Carlo, 131–32
pistols, 131
PL. *See* Prima Linea
PLA. *See* People's Liberation Army
Planned Parenthood, 352
Plekhanov, Georgi, 38, 129
PLO. *See* Palestine Liberation Organization
Poland, James M., 6
political violence, 13–14, 34, 107–8, 112–13, 117–18, 238
Polk, William R., 295
Pontecorvo, Gillo, 163, 450n5
Popular Front for the Liberation of Palestine (PFLP), 193, 195, 198, 207
populism, 127–29, 137
Porta, Della, 226, 229–30
Posse Comitatus, 347–48
Post, Jerrold M., 20–21
poverty, 239–41

Powell, Lewis, 83–84
Prague Spring, 209
Pratt, David, 283
presidential prerogatives, expanding, in global war on terror, 405–11
Price, Marian, 173, 179
Priest, Dana, 405
Prima Linea (PL), 226, 229
propaganda, 7, 214–15, 327–29
Propaganda Due (P2), 224
propaganda of the deed, 131–32, 141, 145, 150
property, 5, 62, 128
protected persons, 70
Protestants, 90, 164–65, 167–68, 170–71
The Protocols of the Elders of Zion, 187, 338–39
Proudhon, Pierre-Joseph, 128
Provisional Irish Republican Army (PIRA), 24, 164–67, 179–82, 207; in Bloody Sunday, 171–72; bombings by, 172–75, 177–78; FLN and, 153–54, 163; Good Friday Agreement, 154; *Green Book* of, 174, 232; in H-Blocks, 176; Provisional Sinn Féin in, 169; RIRA and, 179; SDLP versus, 169–70; Special Category Status for, 175, 177. *See also* the Troubles
Provisional Sinn Féin, 169
provocation. *See* jujitsu
psychological impact, of radical terrorism, 10–12, 28–29, 108, 419–20
psychology, 20–22, 232–33, 238, 253
P2. *See* Propaganda Due
Pyszczynski, Tom, 253–54

Qadri, Ajmal, 252
al-Qaeda, 1–3, 6, 20, 239, 292, 308–10; Atef in, 302, 304; bin Laden and, 297–300; bombings by, 301–2, 396–97; IS and, 290–91, 293–95, 314–15, 323–31; KSM, 300, 302; lone wolves, 306–7; Millennium Plot, 301; 9/11 and, 297, 302–6, 397–98; Taliban and, 407

al-Qaeda in Iraq (AQI), 293–94, 306, 309, 312–13
Qin Shi Huang, 31–33, 49–50
Quran, 2, 242, 244–45, 248
al-Qurashi, Abu Ubayd, 295
Qutb, Sayyid, 248–49

Rabin, Gail, 185
Rabin, Yitzhak, 279–81
Racial Holy War, 341
racism, 78, 95, 335, 356. *See also* Ku Klux Klan; White supremacy
racist skinheads, 345–47
radical Islamists, 2–3, 192, 267–69, 337, 429–31; Azzam and, 249–50; on clash of civilizations, 252; emergence of, 237–38; Faraj and, 249; global struggle, 291–94; Ibn Taymiyyah and, 246–47; ideology of resistance and jihad, 245–51; on Islam, 241–45; against Israel, 237–38; material incentives for, 239–41; Qutb and, 248–49; radicalization of, 258–62; recruitment, 260–61; social networking, 259–61; theory of evolving stages in warfare, 294–97; women as, 262; against Zionism, 249. *See also* Hamas; Hezbollah; Islamic State; al-Qaeda
radicalism, 113, 120, 122–29
radical right-wing extremists: alt-right movement, 356–57; anti-abortion violence, 351–54; anti-federalist militias, 347–51; anti-Semitic conspiracies and, 338–40; apocalypse and, 337–41; Christian Identity and, 337–43; in Europe, 357–58; hate groups of, 341–47; lone wolves of, 354; magnitude, of threat of, 335–37; McVeigh and, 332, 332–33, 335–36; neo-Nazis, 342–47; Patriot Groups, 336; recruitment by, 346; strategy of intimidation, 354–56; Trump and, 356–57; *The Turner Diaries* for, 333–34, 339–41
radical terrorism, 28, 34, 78, 110–14, 123, 149, 422; emerging, context of, 124–29; as entry-level war, 15–18, 419; for ethno-nationalist goals, 153, 181; failure of revolutionary methods and, 118; against international law of war, 71; morality in, 18–20, 421; psychological impact of, 10–12, 28–29, 108, 419–20; by sub-state groups, 10–11, 13–15, 89, 107; violent political resistance and, 107–8; as warfare, 22–23, 54–55. *See also* first-wave radical terrorism; second-wave radical terrorism; third-wave radical terrorism
Radio Saraní, 215
RAF. *See* Red Army Faction
rape, 62, 70, 72–74, 262, 321–22
Rapoport, David C., 13–14, 138, 153, 207, 263
rational actors, terrorists as, 22, 29, 420
Ravachol, 142–43
Ray, James Earl, 103
razzias, 60, 62
Reagan, Ronald, 200–201
Real IRA (RIRA), 179–80
Reconstruction, 79–86
recruitment, 228–29, 260–61, 328–30, 346
Red Army Faction (RAF), 196–97, 206–7, 231, 233–34
Red Brigades (BR), 21, 205, 205–6, 208, 224–31
Red Guard, 31, 33–34, 44–47, 49
Reid, Richard, 307
Reign of Terror, French, 34–37, 48, 123
religion, 245, 254, 335. *See also* Christianity; Islam
religious terrorism, 262–65
repertoires of violent resistance, 107–21, 129, 418, 481
republicanism, 126–27, 165–67, 169–72
resistance, jihad and, 245–51
revolution, 38, 50, 112–13, 124–25, 131, 209. *See also* Chinese Cultural Revolution; Cuban Revolution; French Revolution; Iranian Revolution of 1979; October Revolution

revolutionaries, 12–13, 18–19, 117–18, 212–14, 221
Revolutions of 1848, 13–15, 107, 110–14, 118–22, 134–35, 165
Rey, Corinne, 235–36
Reynolds, Albert, 178
Richardson, Louise, 3
Rida, Rashid, 247
Ridgeway, James, 335
right-wing. *See* radical right-wing extremists
RIRA. *See* Real IRA
Robbins, Terry, 220
Robespierre, Maximilien, 35–37, 44, 49
Robin Hood guerrillas, 215–16
Rockwell, George Lincoln, 342
Rogan, Chanah, 268
Roman law, 245
Rome, 57, 134–35, 147–49
Roof, Dylann, 356
Roosevelt, Franklin D., 394
Roosevelt, Theodore, 149
Rossa, Guido, 227
Rousseff, Dilma, 218
Royal Air Force, 52–53, 66
Royal Ulster Constabulary (RUC), 166–68, 170–71
Ruby Ridge, 348–49
RUC. *See* Royal Ulster Constabulary
Rudolf, Eric, 353–54
Russia, 128, 132–33, 136–40, 147, 149, 187. *See also* Soviet Union
Russian Revolutions, 38, 140
Russo-Afghan War, 237–38, 293
Rwanda, 70, 74
Rysakov, Nikolai, 106

Sabbah, Hassan-i, 109
sacking, of besieged cities, 55–59
Sadat, Anwar, 184, 196–97, 249
Sageman, Marc, 13–14, 34, 112–13, 239, 255, 258–61, 292, 307–8
Saint-Arnaud, Armand-Jacques Leroy de, 60
Saipov, Sayfullo, 318
Salafist Islam, 243, 246, 248

Salvador, Santiago, 144
Salvi, John, 353
Sands, Bobby, 177
Santos Gorrostieta, Maria, 383
Saudi Arabia, 247, 291, 298, 300, 390
Scarlet Guards, 47
Schiff, Ze'ev, 203
Schmid, Alex P., 20
Schoenhals, Michael, 44
schools, desegregation of, 95–97
Schwerner, Michael, 101
SCLC. *See* Southern Christian Leadership Conference
Scott, Bobby, 397–98
SDLP. *See* Social Democratic and Labor Party
SDS. *See* Students for a Democratic Society
Second Amendment, 332, 340
Second Intifada, 267, 267–68, 282–84
second-wave radical terrorism, 153, 207, 233–34. *See also* National Liberation Front; Provisional Irish Republican Army
Sedition Act of 1918, 393
segregation, 87, 95–96, 99–100
self-esteem, 253–54
self-radicalized individuals, 89
Selma, Alabama, 102–3
Sendic, Raul, 214–15
September 11, 2001 (9/11), 1, 1–3, 19, 22, 29–30, 255; 9/11 Commission, 302, 398, 404–5; Patriot Act after, 397–98, 402–3; al-Qaeda and, 297, 302–6, 397–98
Seraw, Mulugetta, 346
Serbian soldiers, in Bosnian War, 72–74, 79
Shahzad, Faisal, 307
Shamir, Yitzhak, 204
Shankill Butchers, 174
Shannon, Rachelle, 353
sharia law, 245, 256–57, 322
Sharon, Ariel, 197, 199–200, 202, 282
Shelton, Robert Marvin, 100, 104
Sheridan, Philip, 82

Sherman's march, 62
Shias, 109, 243, 276, 313–14
Shipp, Thomas, 89
Shlaim, Avi, 191–92
Shuttlesworth, Fred, 98, 100
Sicariis, 109–10
Silent Brotherhood, 343
Sima Qian, 31–32
Simmons, William Joseph, 92
Sinai War, 192–93
Sinaloa cartel, 385
Sinn Féin, 165–66, 169, 177
SIP. *See* Social Identity Perspective
Six-Day War, 193–94, 200
16th Street Baptist Church bombing, 101
slavery, 76, 77, 81, 322
Smith, Abram, 89
Smith, Lamar, 98
SNCC. *See* Student Nonviolent Coordinating Committee
"Sneak-and-Peek" searches, warrants for, 399–400, 400
Snell, Richard, 347
Snowden, Edward, 401, 411
Social Democratic and Labor Party (SDLP), 169–70, 179
Social Identity Perspective (SIP), 255
socialism, 127–29, 141
Socialist Education Movement, 44
Socialist Revolutionary Party (SR), 139–40
social media, 327–28
social networking, 259–61
social psychology, 232–33, 253
social terrorism, 9–10, 77–81, 88–90
Society of the Seasons, 118
Solomon, Sheldon, 253
Sossi, Mario, 227
Soummam Conference, 157
South Africa, 167
South Carolina, 88
Southern Christian Leadership Conference (SCLC), 98, 102
Southern Poverty Law Center (SPLC), 104, 336, 342, 344, 346, 351
sovereign citizen movement, 348

Soviet Union, 9, 12, 38–41, 72–73, 251–52, 297–99, 394, 412
Special Category Status, for PIRA prisoners, 175, 177
Specially Designated Nationals List, 396
Spencer, Richard B., 356
Spitz, Donald, 353
SPLC. *See* Southern Poverty Law Center
SR. *See* Socialist Revolutionary Party
Stalin, Joseph, 9, 12, 38–39, 41–42, 48–49. *See also* the Great Purge
Stapleton, Benjamin F., 93–94
state-regime terrorism, 9, 33–41, 48–49. *See also* Chinese Cultural Revolution
Stephenson, David Curtiss, 93
Stepnyak-Kravchinsky, Sergey, 133
Stern, Jessica, 4, 239–40, 252, 260–61, 263, 315, 321, 326
Stern, Susan, 223
Stern Gang, 190–91
Stethem, Robert, 272
Stimson, Henry, 68
Stolypin, Peter, 140
Stone, Geoffrey, 392
Stormfront, 336–37
storming of the Bastille, 112, 114
stratagem, of terrorism, 26, 29, 184, 281, 414, 423
Student Nonviolent Coordinating Committee (SNCC), 99–101
Students for a Democratic Society (SDS), 218, 220
sub-state groups, 7–8, 10–15, 89, 107, 114, 355
Sudan, 298–99, 301
Suez Canal, 192, 194, 197
suicide bombers, 17, 27–28, 202–3, 267, 281–83, 301–2
Sunni Awakening, 309, 313
Sunningdale Agreement, 173, 179
Sunnis, 109, 243, 313–14
al-Suri, Abu Musab, 325
Swift, Wesley, 338
Syria, 193–94, 197, 200, 314
Syrian Social Nationalist Party, 203

Tabor, Robert, 295
tactics, 23, 54–55, 72, 160, 208
Taliban, 299, 303–4, 371, 376–82, 406–7
Tamil Tigers. *See* Liberation Tigers of Tamil Elam
Tanzim al-Jihad, 249
Tennessee, 82–83
terror, 36, 38, 53–55, 67, 72
terrorism, 416; defining, traits of, 4–8, 10–12; entry level war, 15–18, 55, 210, 297, 419; four strategies of, *433*, 433–35; psychological warfare, 6, 27, 29, 321, 380, 414, 416, 419–20, 423; six levels of, 7–13, *11*, 22, 417–19; statistics on, sense of proportion through, 428–29; tactics and strategy, 54–55; three waves of, 13–15, 417–18. *See also specific topics*
Terrorist Brigade, of SR, 139–40
terrorists, 8–9, 22–23, 175, 421–22, 429–31; actors, assessing threat of, 424–27, *425*; female, 203, 262; groups, assessing threat of, 427; mindset of, 10–11, 21, 132–34, 230–33, 238–39; as psychologically "normal," 20–22; as rational actors, 22, 29, 420. *See also specific topics*
Terror Management Theory (TMT), 253–55, 264
Tet Offensive, 209
Texas Klan, 92
Thatcher, Margaret, 177–78
third-wave radical terrorism, 203, 237. *See also* Islamic State; al-Qaeda
Thompson, Linda, 351
Three Bitter Years, 44
Tikrit, 310
Tillion, Germaine, 160
Tilly, Charles, 107
TMT. *See* Terror Management Theory
Tocqueville, Alexis de, 60
Tokyo, fire-bombing of, 68
Tolnay, Stewart E., 89
Topolansky, Lucía, 218
torture, 42, 157, 162–63, 216, 408–10
trafficking, 362, 368, 379, 383–84

Trail of Tears, 78
transfer, of population, in Israel, 70, 189–91, 194
Traugott, Mark, 117–18
Treviño, Miguel, 385
Trial of the Thirty, 145
Trochmann, John and David, 350
Les trois glorieuses, 116–17
Trotsky, Leon, 38–39, 131, 431
the Troubles, 153, 182; Algerian War for Independence and, 163–64; Battle of the Bogside, 168; Bloody Friday, 172–73; Bloody Sunday, 171–72; Catholics in, 169–70, 174; government, of Northern Ireland in, 170, 172; loyalists in, 170–72, 174; OIRA in, 172; onset of, 167–69; Operation Demetrius, 171; peace process and, 177–81; PIRA and, 163, 169, 172–77; prison protests, 175–77; Protestants in, 170–71; republicans in, 169–72; Shankill Butchers in, 174; UVF bombing, 171, 174
truck bombing, 202–3, *332*, 332–33, 345, 357
Truman, Harry S., 95, 394
Trump, Donald, 356–57, 399, 410–11, 414–15, 425–26
Tsarnaev brothers, 307
Tuchachevsky, Mikhail, 40
Tunisia, 160–61, 308
Túpac Amaru II, 212
Tupamaros, 206–8, 212–18, 225
Turgenev, Ivan, 133
The Turner Diaries (Pierce), 333–34, 339–41, 343
Tuskegee Institute, 88–89, 94

UAR. *See* United Arab Republic
UAVs. *See* Unarmed Aerial Vehicles
UCDC. *See* Ulster Constitution Defence Committee
UDA. *See* Ulster Defence Association
UDR. *See* Ulster Defense Regiment
UFF. *See* Ulster Freedom Fighters
UKA. *See* United Klans of America

Ulster Constitution Defence Committee (UCDC), 170
Ulster Defence Association (UDA), 170, 177
Ulster Defense Regiment (UDR), 170–71
Ulster Freedom Fighters (UFF), 170
Ulster Protestant Volunteers (UPV), 170
Ulster Volunteer Force (UVF), 170–71, 174
Ulster Volunteers, 165
ultraviolence, 319–20, 322–24, 327–30, 383, 386–88
ummah, 249–50, 258–59, 264, 309, 329
UNAMA. *See* United Nations Assistance Mission in Afghanistan
Unarmed Aerial Vehicles (UAVs), 410
United Arab Republic (UAR), 193
United Klans of America (UKA), 100–101, 104
United Nations, 69–70, 184, 190
United Nations Assistance Mission in Afghanistan (UNAMA), 380
United Nations Special Committee on Palestine (UNSCOP), 190
United States (U.S.), 81–82, 123, 145–46, 148–49; bin Laden on, 291–92, 325; civil liberties and protections in, 392–95; Constitution, 392–93; domestic counterterrorism in, 391–92; embassies, al-Qaeda bombing, 301, 396–97; expanding presidential prerogatives, in global war on terror, 405–11; incineration of Japanese cities, 67–69; Iraq War, 305–6, 309, 406–8; in Middle East, 193; militarism, 411–14; Muslims in, 260–62; Native Americans, 78; neo-Nazis of, 342–47; patriotism, after 9/11, 255; as target, of al-Qaeda, 297; in Vietnam War, 71–72; war in Afghanistan, 304, 406–8. *See also* African-Americans; Civil War, U.S.; radical right-wing extremists; White supremacy; *specific states*
unlawful combatants, 408
UNSCOP. *See* United Nations Special Committee on Palestine

UPV. *See* Ulster Protestant Volunteers
urban guerrillas, 206–10, 212, 215–16, 221, 224–25
urban race riots, of 1866, 82
urban rebellions, 111–12
Uruguay, 212–13, 216–17
U.S. *See* United States
UVF. *See* Ulster Volunteer Force

Vaillant, Auguste, 143
Varon, Jeremy, 221
Vattel, Emer de, 58
the Vendée, 37
Victoroff, Jeff, 238–39
video, as medium, 327–29
Viet Cong, 71–72, 209
Vietnam, 156, 211
Vietnam War, 71–72, 208, 218, 221, 225–26
violence, 5–8, 127, 131, 174; anti-abortion, 338, 351–55; political, 13–14, 34, 112–13, 117–18, 238; revolutionary, 212–14, 221; ultraviolence, 319–20, 322–24, 327–30, 383, 386–88; White supremacist repression by, 97–99, 101. *See also specific topics*
La Violencia, 365–67, 388
Vitoria, Francisco de, 58
Vizetelly, Henry, 144
Voltaire, 241
voter registration, 101–2
voting rights, for African-Americans, 84, 86–88
Voting Rights Act (1965), 103

Waco, 332–33, 348–50
al-Wahhab, Muhammad ibn Abd, 243, 246–47
Wallace, George, 96
Wankal, Doug, 382
war, 15–18, 28, 153, 263, 419. *See also* law of war; *specific wars*
WAR. *See* White Aryan Resistance
war crimes, crimes against humanity, 17, 53–54, 62, 63, 69–74, 268, 284, 287, 322, 376, 391

warfare, 16, 65, 250–52; hybrid, 160–61, 381–82, 387; psychological, 419–20; radical terrorism as, 22–23, 54–55; revolutionary, 295–96; theory of evolving stages in, 294–97
War of Independence, Israeli, 186, 191, 277
war on terror, 297, 397, 405–11
War Powers Act of 1973, 406
warrants, FISA, 398–401, 400
waves of terrorism, 13–15, 417–18
Weathermen. *See* Weather Underground Organization (WUO)
Weather Underground Organization (WUO), 5, 49, 206–8, 218–24, 232
Weaver, Randy, 348–49
Weir, Bonnie, 179–81
Weiss, Michael, 319
Werth, Nicolas, 40
West Bank, 191, 194, 200, 267–68
Westergaard, Kurt, 236
White Aryan Resistance (WAR), 346
White Leagues paramilitary, 85–86
White supremacy, 9–10, 76, 341; Christian Identity and, 337–39; Jim Crow, 79–80, 86–88; lynchings and, 88–90; paramilitaries, 85–86; segregation and, 87, 95–96, 99–100; social terrorism of, 77–81; victory of, during Reconstruction, 81–86; violent repression by, 97–99, 101. *See also* Ku Klux Klan; radical right-wing extremists
Wilkerson, Cathy, 220, 233
Wolfe Tone Society, 167
World Trade Center, 1, 203, 297, 300, 303, 395–96. *See also* September 11, 2001

World War I, 65, 69, 165, 188, 393
World War II, 63–75, 79, 97, 190, 209, 393–94, 412
Wright, Lawrence, 299–301, 304
Wright, Robin, 272, 331
WUO. *See* Weather Underground Organization

Ya'ari, Ehud, 203
Yacef, Saadi, 152, 157, 160
Yagoda, Genrikh, 41
Yassin, Ahmed, 277–78, 280, 283
Yazidis, 321–22
Years of Lead, 224, 226–27
Yezhov, Nikolai, 41
the Yishuv, 187–92
Yom Kippur War, 197
Yoo, John, 408–9
Young Irelander Rebellion, 165
Yousafzai, Malala, 381
Yousef, Ramzi, 300

Zahar, Mahmoud, 280
al-Zarqawi, Abu Musab, 293–94, 311–13, 318–26, 330
Zasulich, Vera, 136–38
al-Zawahiri, Ayman, 292–94, 299, 306, 312, 314, 323–25, 330
Zemlya i Volya, 137–38
Los Zetas, 365, 383–87
Zidan, Tarak, 268
Zionism, 184, 187–88, 191, 249
Zionist Occupation Government (ZOG), 338–39, 343
Zola, Émile, 133–34, 144
Zur, Guy, 275